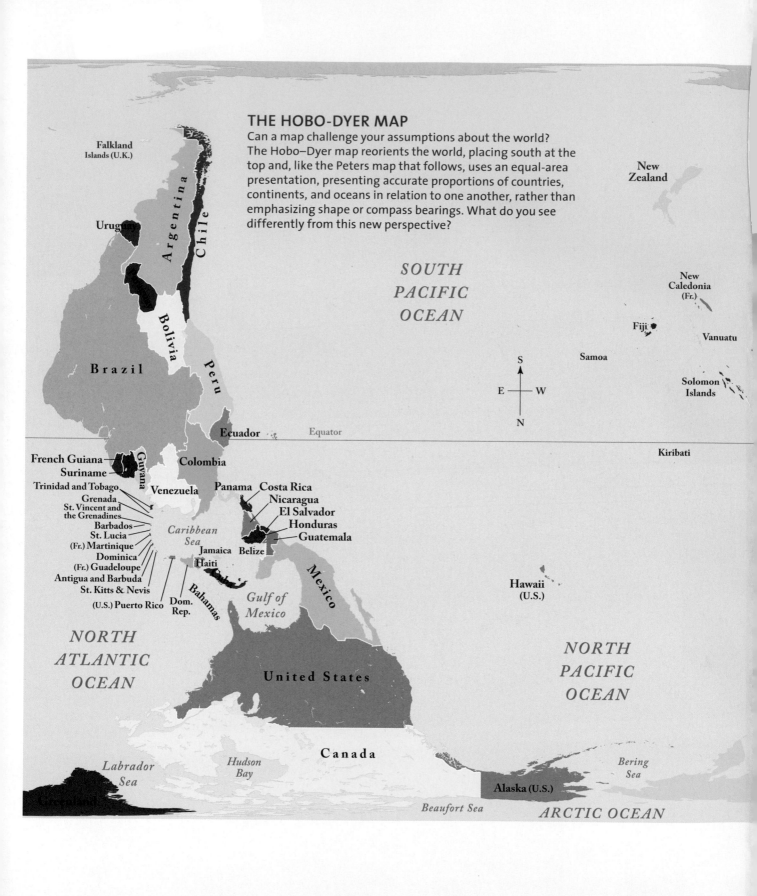

THE HOBO-DYER MAP

Can a map challenge your assumptions about the world? The Hobo–Dyer map reorients the world, placing south at the top and, like the Peters map that follows, uses an equal-area presentation, presenting accurate proportions of countries, continents, and oceans in relation to one another, rather than emphasizing shape or compass bearings. What do you see differently from this new perspective?

Falkland
Islands (U.K.)

New Zealand

SOUTH PACIFIC OCEAN

New Caledonia (Fr.)

Uruguay

Argentina

Chile

Fiji

Vanuatu

Bolivia

Peru

Samoa

B r a z i l

Solomon Islands

Ecuador · · · Equator

Kiribati

French Guiana — Guyana
Suriname
Colombia
Trinidad and Tobago
Grenada
St. Vincent and the Grenadines
Barbados
St. Lucia
(Fr.) Martinique
Dominica
(Fr.) Guadeloupe
Antigua and Barbuda
St. Kitts & Nevis
(U.S.) Puerto Rico
Dom. Rep.

Venezuela
Panama   Costa Rica
Nicaragua
El Salvador
Honduras
Guatemala
Caribbean Sea
Jamaica   Belize
Haiti
Cuba
Bahamas

Hawaii (U.S.)

Mexico

Gulf of Mexico

NORTH ATLANTIC OCEAN

NORTH PACIFIC OCEAN

United States

C a n a d a

Labrador Sea

Hudson Bay

Bering Sea

Greenland

Alaska (U.S.)

Beaufort Sea   *ARCTIC OCEAN*

Antarctica

Australia

(Fr.) Réunion
Mauritius

INDIAN
OCEAN

Madagascar

Comoros

SOUTH
ATLANTIC
OCEAN

South
Africa

Lesotho
Swaziland

Mozambique

Botswana

Zimbabwe

Malawi

Zambia

Namibia

Angola

East Timor

Papua
New
Guinea

I n d o n e s i a

Singapore

Malaysia

Brunei

Palau

Micronesia

Philippines

Cambodia

Thailand

Vietnam

Myanmar

Taiwan

Japan

South Korea

North Korea

Sea of
Japan

East
China
Sea

South
China
Sea

Sri
Lanka

Maldives

Bay of
Bengal

India

Bangladesh

Bhutan

China

Pakistan

Afghanistan

Tajikistan

Kyrgyzstan

Uzbekistan

Turkmenistan

Mongolia

Kazakhstan

Aral Sea

Caspian
Sea

Arabian Sea

Seychelles

Equator

Somalia

Djibouti

Yemen

Oman

U.A.E.

Qatar

Bahrain

Persian
Gulf

Kuwait

Jordan

Iraq

Iran

Azerbaijan

Armenia

Georgia

Saudi
Arabia

Egypt

Libya

Tanzania

Burundi
Rwanda

Kenya

Uganda

Democratic
Republic
of the
Congo

South
Sudan

Sudan

Eritrea

Red
Sea

Chad

Niger

Congo

Gabon

Cameroon

Sao Tome
and Principe

Equatorial
Guinea

Nigeria

Benin

Togo

Ghana

Burkina
Faso

Mali

Côte d'Ivoire

Liberia

Sierra Leone

Guinea

Guinea-
Bissau

Gambia

Senegal

Cape
Verde

Mauritania

Western
Sahara

Algeria

Morocco

Tunisia

Mediterranean Sea

Israel
Lebanon
Cyprus

Syria

Turkey

Greece

Mac.
Alb.
Kos.
Mont.
B.H.
Serb.
Cro.
Slo.

Italy

Rom.

Moldova

Ukraine

Black Sea

Spain

Portugal

France

Switz.

Lux.

Belgium

Neth.

U.K.

Ireland

Svk.

Cz. Rep.

Hung.

Ger.

Poland

Belarus

Lith.

Latvia

Estonia

Finland

Sweden

Norway

Iceland

North
Sea

Russia

Lake
Baikal

Sea of
Okhotsk

Laptev Sea

Kara Sea

Barents Sea

OCEAN

Barents Sea Kara Sea Laptev Sea

orway
Finland
Estonia
Latvia
Lith.
Poland Belarus
Rep.
Ukraine
Moldova
Rom.
Georgia
Black Sea
Armenia
Kos.
Greece Turkey
Mac.
Alb.
Cyprus
Mediterranean Sea
Israel
Iraq Iran
Lebanon
Jordan
bya Egypt
Saudi
Arabia
Red Sea
Oman

Russia

Lake
Baikal

Sea of
Okhotsk

Kazakhstan
Aral Sea
Caspian
Sea
Uzbekistan
Kyrgyzstan
Turkm.
Tajikistan
Azerbaijan
Afghanistan
Pakistan

Mongolia

China

North
Korea
South
Korea

Sea of
Japan

Japan

Bhutan

East
China
Sea

Taiwan

NORTH
PACIFIC
OCEAN

Kuwait
Bahrain
Qatar
U.A.E.

India

Bangladesh

Myanmar

Arabian
Sea

Laos
Thailand
Vietnam

South
China
Sea

Micronesia

Sudan
Eritrea
Yemen
Djibouti

South
Sudan
epublic

Dem.
Rep.
of the
Congo

Uganda
Rwanda
Burundi

Kenya

Bay of
Bengal

Cambodia

Philippines

Palau

Sri
Lanka

Brunei

Malaysia

Maldives

Singapore

Equator

Kiribati

Tanzania

INDIAN

OCEAN

I n d o n e s i a

Papua
New
Guinea

Solomon
Islands

Seychelles
Comoros

East Timor

Angola

Malawi

Zimb.

Mozambique

Madagascar

Mauritius

Réunion (Fr.)

N

W   E

S

Samoa

Vanuatu

Fiji

New
Caledonia
(Fr.)

Namibia

Swaziland

Australia

South
Africa

Lesotho

THE PETERS WORLD MAP

How do maps shape the way you think about the world and its
people? The Earth is round. So every flat, rectangular map involves
distortions. But which distortions? The Peters world map is an
equal-area map, showing countries and continents in accurate
proportion with one another and reducing the visual dominance of
the Northern Hemisphere by shifting the equator to the middle of the
map, both in sharp contrast to the more familiar Mercator projection.

New
Zealand

A n t a r c t i c a

WORLD · POLITICAL

NATIONAL BOUNDARIES

While man's impact is quite evident, and even striking, on many remotely sensed scenes, sometimes, as in the case with most political boundaries, it is invisible. State, provincial, and national boundaries can follow natural features, such as mountain ridges, rivers, or coastlines. Artificial constructs that possess no physical reality—for example, lines of latitude and longitude—can also determine political borders. The world political map (right) represents man's imaginary lines as they slice and divide Earth.

The National Geographic Society recognizes 192 independent states in the world as represented here. Of those nations, 185 are members of the United Nations.

Winkel Tripel Projection

Cultural Anthropology

Anthropologists look beyond surface images to examine the complexities of human life in local and global context. Here, a young Tamil woman migrant worker picks tea leaves in Kerala, south India. What more might the tools of anthropology reveal?

Cultural Anthropology

A TOOLKIT FOR A GLOBAL AGE

KENNETH J. GUEST
BARUCH COLLEGE
THE CITY UNIVERSITY OF NEW YORK

W. W. NORTON & COMPANY
NEW YORK   LONDON

W. W. Norton & Company has been independent since its founding in 1923, when William Warder Norton and Mary D. Herter Norton first published lectures delivered at the People's Institute, the adult education division of New York City's Cooper Union. The firm soon expanded its program beyond the Institute, publishing books by celebrated academics from America and abroad. By mid-century, the two major pillars of Norton's publishing program—trade books and college texts— were firmly established. In the 1950s, the Norton family transferred control of the company to its employees, and today—with a staff of four hundred and a comparable number of trade, college, and professional titles published each year—W. W. Norton & Company stands as the largest and oldest publishing house owned wholly by its employees.

Editor: Karl Bakeman
Developmental Editor: Alice Vigliani
Manuscript Editor: JoAnn Simony
Managing Editor, College: Marian Johnson
Electronic Media Editor: Eileen Connell
Associate Editors: Kate Feighery, Nicole Sawa
Associate Editor, Media: Laura Musich
Marketing Manager: Julia Hall
Production Manager: Ashley Horna
Photo Editor: Trish Marx
Photo Researchers: Julie Tesser, Ted Szczepanski, Rona Tuccillo
Art Director: Hope Miller Goodell
Book Design: Binocular, New York
Permissions Manager: Megan Jackson
Editorial Assistant: Lindsey Thomas
Editorial Assistant, Media: Cara Folkman
Composition: Jouve North America
Manufacturing: TransContinental

Library of Congress Cataloging-in-Publication Data has been applied for.

ISBN: 978-0-393-92957-7

W. W. Norton & Company, Inc., 500 Fifth Avenue, New York, NY 10110-0017
wwnorton.com

W. W. Norton & Company Ltd., Castle House, 75/76 Wells Street, London W1T 3QT

1 2 3 4 5 6 7 8 9 0

About the Author

Kenneth J. Guest is Associate Professor of Anthropology at Baruch College, CUNY, and author of *God in Chinatown: Religion and Survival in New York's Evolving Immigrant Community* (2003). His research focuses on immigration, religion, globalization, ethnicity and entrepreneurialism.

Professor Guest's ethnographic research in China and the United States traces the immigration journey of recent Chinese immigrants from Fuzhou, southeast China, who, drawn by restaurant, garment shop, and construction jobs and facilitated by a vast human smuggling network, have revitalized New York's Chinatown. His writing explores the role of Fuzhounese religious communities in China and the United States; the religious revival sweeping coastal China; the Fuzhounese role in the rapidly expanding U.S. network of all-you-can-eat buffets and take-out restaurants; and the higher education experiences of the Fuzhounese second generation.

A native of Florida, Professor Guest studied Chinese at Beijing University and Middlebury College. He received his B.A. from Columbia University (East Asian Languages and Cultures), an M.A. from Union Theological Seminary (Religious Studies), and the M.A., M.Phil., and Ph.D. from The City University of New York Graduate Center (Anthropology).

Brief Contents

Contents

PART 1   Anthropology for the 21st Century

Chapter 4   Language   113

PART 2 Unmasking the Structures of Power

Chapter 6 Race and Racism 195

PART 3   Change in the Modern World

Preface

Anthropology may be the most important course you take in college. That may seem like a bold statement. But here's what I mean.

Cultural Anthropology: A Toolkit

The world in the twenty-first century is changing at a remarkable pace. We are experiencing an interaction with people, ideas, and systems that is intensifying at breathtaking speed. Communication technologies link people instantaneously across the globe. Economic activities challenge national boundaries. People are on the move within countries and between them. As a result, today we increasingly encounter the diversity of humanity, not on the other side of the world but in our schools, workplaces, neighborhoods, religious communities, and families. How will we develop the skills and strategies for engaging and navigating the complex, multicultural, global, and rapidly changing reality of the world around us?

Anthropology is the toolkit you are looking for. Cultural anthropology is the study of humans, particularly the many ways people around the world today and throughout human history have organized themselves to live together: to get along, to survive, to thrive, and to have meaningful lives. *Cultural Anthropology: A Toolkit for a Global Age* will introduce you to the fascinating work of anthropologists and the research strategies and analytical perspectives that anthropologists have developed—our tools of the trade—that can help you better understand and engage today's world as you move through it.

I teach Introduction to Cultural Anthropology to hundreds of students every year at Baruch College, a senior college of The City University of New York. Baruch has an incredibly diverse student body, with immigrants from over a hundred countries, speaking dozens of languages and thinking about culture, race, gender, and family in as many different ways. Some of my students will become anthropology majors. More will become anthropology minors. But at Baruch, in fact, most students will become business majors.

This book emerges from my efforts to make anthropology relevant to all of my students as they navigate their everyday lives, think about the world as it is and as it is becoming, and consider tackling the crucial issues of our times. On a practical level, we all employ the skills of anthropology on a daily basis. Every time you walk into a room and try to figure out how to fit into a new group of people—in your classroom, in a student club, at the office, at a party, in your religious community, when your new love interest takes you home to meet the family—how in the world do you deduce what the rules are? Where you fit in? What you're supposed to do? What the power dynamics are? What you can contribute to the group? *Cultural Anthropology: A Toolkit for a Global Age* is designed to help you develop those skills—to think more deeply and analyze more carefully—and to prepare you to use them in a diversity of settings at home or around the world.

Why a New Textbook?

The world has changed dramatically in the past forty years and so has the field of anthropology. *Cultural Anthropology: A Toolkit for a Global Age* presents the theoretical, methodological, and pedagogical innovations that are transforming anthropology and highlights both historical and contemporary research that can provide students with insights about how anthropologists are approaching the crucial challenges and questions of our times.

Globalization

As the world is changing, so too are the people anthropologists study. Even the way anthropologists conduct research is changing. In the contemporary period of rapid globalization, the movement, connection, and interrelatedness that have always been a part of human reality have intensified and become more explicit, reminding us that our actions have consequences for the whole world, not just for our own lives and those of our families and friends. This book integrates globalization into every chapter, analyzing its effects throughout the text rather than in a series of boxes, icons, or the occasional extra chapter so commonly seen in contemporary textbooks. The introductory chapter, "Anthropology in a Global Age," establishes an analytical framework of globalization that is developed in every succeeding chapter—whether the topic is fieldwork, language, ethnicity, economics, kinship, or art—and gives students the tools to understand its impact on people's lives as they encounter them in ethnographic examples throughout the book.

Reframing the Culture Concept

The concept of culture has been central to anthropological analysis since the beginning of our field. But anthropologists have significantly reframed our thinking about culture over the past forty years. In the 1960s, Clifford Geertz synthesized anthropological thinking about culture as a system of meaning—shared norms, values, symbols, and categories. In the ensuing years, anthropologists have paid increasing attention to the relationship of power to culture, building on the work of Antonio Gramsci, Michel Foucault, and Eric Wolf to examine the ways cultural meanings are created, learned, taught, enforced, negotiated, and contested. *Cultural Anthropology: A Toolkit for a Global Age* integrates this holistic and complex concept of culture into every chapter, exploring both meaning and power in human culture. Chapter 6, for example, is entitled "Race and Racism," acknowledging that not only is race a social construction of ideas but also that ideas of race

can be expressed and made real through cultural processes, institutions, and systems of power—racism—in ways that create patterns of stratification and inequality in U.S. culture and in cultures around the world.

Anthropology for the Twenty-First Century

Cultural Anthropology: A Toolkit for a Global Age reflects the field of anthropology as it is developing in the twenty-first century. While carefully covering the foundational work of early anthropologists, every chapter has been designed to introduce the cutting-edge research and theory that make anthropology relevant to today's world. Chapters on classic anthropological topics such as language, religion, kinship, and art incorporate contemporary research and help students understand why anthropological thinking matters in day-to-day life. A chapter on human origins presents the current scholarship in physical anthropology and creates opportunities for engaging the current U.S. evolution debates. Chapters on sexuality, the global economy, class and inequality, migration, and health and illness give students a sense of historical and contemporary research in the field and bring the presentation of anthropology fully into the twenty-first century.

Ethnography

Anthropologists conduct fascinating research about the lives of people all over the world. In many ways ethnography is at the heart of anthropology, reflecting our unique research strategies, our analytical methodologies, and our deep commitment to the project of cross-cultural understanding and engagement in our attempts to make the world a better place. But ethnographies often get lost in introductory textbooks. *Cultural Anthropology: A Toolkit for a Global Age* introduces over ninety separate ethnographic studies set in dozens of different countries, presenting both new research and classic studies in ways that are accessible to undergraduates so that the rich work of anthropologists comes alive over the course of the semester.

Relevance

Cultural Anthropology responds to my students' request for relevance in a textbook. Each chapter opens with a recent event that raises central questions about the workings of human culture. Key questions throughout the chapter guide students through an introduction to the anthropological strategies and analytical frameworks that can enable them to think more deeply about the chapter-opening event and the underlying issues they may confront in their own lives. A student exercise in each chapter, "Your Turn: Fieldwork," provides students—either individually or in groups—with an opportunity to try out the ideas and strategies introduced in the chapter. "Thinking Like an Anthropologist" sections wrap up each chapter and challenge students to apply what they have learned.

Anthropologists Engage the World

Whether anthropologists teach in a university or work as applied anthropologists, they use the practical tools and analytical insights of anthropology to actively engage crucial issues facing our world. In the "Anthropologists Engage the World" feature, this book introduces some of the field's leading personalities and practitioners discussing why they have chosen to be anthropologists, what tools they think anthropology brings to understanding and addressing global challenges, and why they think anthropology can help students understand how the world really works. This feature offers students insights into what it can mean to be an anthropologist and how the skills of anthropology can be invaluable for living in a global age.

Additional Resources

Learn more at **wwnorton.com/instructors**

The media package for *Cultural Anthropology: A Toolkit for a Global Age* provides additional pedagogical tools that inspire students to DO anthropology and apply it to their own lives. Instructors have everything they need to make traditional and online classes easier to manage: a DVD of clips that will enliven lectures and spark discussion; an Instructor Resource Disc with illustrated PowerPoints that include instructor-view lecture notes; and a fully customizable coursepack for Blackboard and other course-management systems.

Ebook
Available at **nortonebooks.com**

Cultural Anthropology is also available as an ebook. An affordable and convenient alternative, the ebook retains the content of the print book and allows students to highlight and take notes with ease.

Instructor Resource Disc
David Anderson, Radford University/Roanoke College

This helpful classroom presentation tool features:

- **Lecture PowerPoints**. These visually dynamic lecture PowerPoint slides include a suggested classroom lecture outline in the notes field that will be particularly helpful to first-time teachers.
- **Art PowerPoints and JPEGs**. All of the art from the book sized for classroom display.

Instructor DVD
Russell Sharman

The Instructor DVD features documentary and ethnographic film clips for initiating classroom discussion and showing students how anthropology is relevant to their lives. Filmmaker and anthropologist Russell Sharman has selected clips that are both engaging and pedagogically useful. The clips are also offered in streaming versions in the coursepack. Each streamed clip is accompanied by a quiz, exercise, or activity.

Coursepack
David Anderson, Radford University/Roanoke College, and Chad T. Morris, Roanoke College

Cultural Anthropology's coursepack offers assessment and review materials for instructors who use Blackboard, Moodle, Canvas, and other learning-management systems. In addition to chapter-based assignments, test banks and quizzes, and an optional ebook, the coursepack includes interactive learning tools that will enliven hybrid, online, or traditional classrooms.

Test Bank
Jennifer Cardinal, University of New Mexico; Andrew Carey, University of New Mexico; Shirley Heying, University of New Mexico; Jayne Howell, California State University, Long Beach; Michelle Raisor, Blinn College; Nicholas Rattray, Butler University

The test bank for *Cultural Anthropology* is designed to help instructors prepare exams. Devised according to Bloom's taxonomy, the test bank includes 75 questions per chapter. In addition to Bloom's, each question is tagged with metadata that place it in the context of the chapter, as well as difficulty level, making it easy to construct tests that are meaningful and diagnostic.

Interactive Instructor's Guide
The Interactive Instructor's Guide makes lecture development easy with an array of teaching resources that can be searched and browsed according to a number of criteria. Resources include chapter outlines and summaries; lecture ideas; discussion questions, recommended readings, videos, and websites; video exercises with streaming video; and activities with downloadable handouts. Instructors can subscribe to a mailing list to be notified of periodic updates and new content.

Acknowledgments

Writing a book of this scope is a humbling experience. I have been awed by the remarkable work of the anthropologists I have encountered, whether through written texts, films, or one-on-one conversations. And I have been inspired by the commitment of my fellow anthropologists to deep understanding of people and cultures, to the search for insights into how the world really works, and to engagement with the world and its people in ways that may help make the world a better place. I have learned a great deal, personally and professionally, on this journey. Along the way it has been my privilege to have the support and encouragement of a remarkable array of people.

First, I would like to thank all of the reviewers who shared comments on different stages of the manuscript and suggested ways to improve the book. I have adopted many of the recommendations that they made.

Tracy J. Andrews, Central Washington University
James D. Armstrong, College at Plattsburgh, State University of New York
Elizabeth Arnold, Grand Valley State University
Christine B. Avenarius, East Carolina University
Diane Baxter, University of Oregon
O. Hugo Benavides, Fordham University
Deborah A. Boehm, University of Nevada, Reno
Susan Brownell, University of Missouri, St. Louis
Ronda Brulotte, University of New Mexico
Jan Brunson, University of Hawaii at Manoa
Jennifer Chase, University of North Texas
Paula Clarke, Columbia College
Kimberley Coles, University of Redlands
Elizabeth E. Cooper, University of Alabama
Joanna Davidson, Boston University
Dona Davis, University of South Dakota
Haley Duschinski, Ohio University
Terilee Edwards-Hewitt, Montgomery College
Todd French, Depauw University
John Fritz, Salt Lake Community College
Sue-Je Gage, Ithaca College
Ismael García Colón, College of Staten Island
Peter M. Gardner, University of Missouri
Henri Gooren, Oakland University
Peter B. Gray, University of Nevada, Las Vegas
Thomas Gregor, Vanderbilt University

Joyce D. Hammond, Western Washington University
Melissa D. Hargrove, University of North Florida
Tina Harris, University of Amsterdam
Jude Higgins, Salt Lake Community College
Dorothy L. Hodgson, Rutgers University
Derek Honeyman, University of Arizona
Kendall House, Boise State University
Jayne Howell, California State University, Long Beach
Arianne Ishaya, De Anza College
Alice James, Shippensburg University
Alana Jolley, Saddleback College
Jessica Jones-Coggins, Madison Area Technical College
Hannah Jopling, Fordham University
Ingrid Jordt, University of Wisconsin, Milwaukee
Peta Katz, University of North Carolina at Charlotte
Neal B. Keating, College at Brockport, State University of New York
Ashley Kistler, Rollins College
Kathryn Kozaitis, Georgia State University
David M. Lipset, University of Minnesota
Michael Mauer, College of the Canyons
Seth Messinger, University of Maryland, Baltimore County

Ryan Moore, Florida Atlantic University
Jeremy Nienow, Inver Hills Community College
Craig Palmer, University of Missouri
Crystal Patil, University of Illinois at Chicago
Ramona Pérez, San Diego State University
Dana Pertermann, Blinn College
Holly Peters-Golden, University of Michigan
Erica Prussing, University of Iowa
Michelle Raisor, Blinn College
Richard Sattler, University of Montana
Scott Schnell, University of Iowa
Suzanne Simon, University of North Florida
Brian Spooner, University of Pennsylvania

Chelsea Starr, University of Phoenix
Erin E. Stiles, University of Nevada, Reno
Michelle Stokely, Indiana University Northwest
Noelle Sullivan, Northwestern University
Patricia Tovar, John Jay College of Criminal Justice
Deana Weibel, Grand Valley State University
Cassandra White, Georgia State University
Jennifer Wies, Eastern Kentucky University
Benjamin Wilreker, College of Southern Nevada
Scott Wilson, California State University, Long Beach
Paul C. Winther, Eastern Kentucky University

I would also like to thank the editors and staff at W. W. Norton who took a chance on this project to rethink the way anthropology is learned and taught. Julia Reidhead years ago encouraged me to keep my lecture notes in case I might write a textbook someday. Pete Lesser, my first editor, embraced the vision of this book, signed me, and brought me into the Norton fold. Developmental editor Alice Vigliani pushed me to greater clarity of thinking and writing, and JoAnn Simony was an excellent copyeditor. Trish Marx and her staff of photo researchers, Julie Tesser, Ted Szczepanski and Rona Tuccillo, insightfully identified photo options that challenge the reader to think. Marian Johnson masterfully stitched the many pieces of this project—words, photos, graphs, maps, captions, and more—into whole cloth. Associate editors Kate Feighery and Nicole Sawa helped with many parts of the process. Editorial assistant Lindsey Thomas and production manager Ashley Horna handled every part of the manuscript and managed to keep the countless pieces of the book moving through production. Norton's cultural anthropology marketing and sales team, Julia Hall, Natasha Zabohonski, Julie Sindel, and Jonathan Mason, have advocated for the book with enthusiasm and boundless energy. Eileen Connell, Laura Musich, Cara Folkman, Kathryn Young, and Alice Garrard put together all of the media resources that accompany the textbook. When it comes to creating new digital resources to help anthropologists teach in the classroom or teach online, I couldn't ask for a better team of people. Karl Bakeman, my editor, has sagely shepherded and advised this project—and its author—through the many adventures of textbook writing and has been the guiding force behind making this a book worthy of my colleagues and students. Thanks to you all.

Heartfelt thanks to my many colleagues who have helped me think more deeply about anthropology, including members of the Sociology and Anthropology Department at Baruch College, especially Glenn Petersen, Robin Root, Carla Bellamy, Barbara Katz-Rothman, Angie Beeman, Myrna Chase, and Shelley Watson, as well as Jane Schneider, Louise Lennihan, Ida Susser, Peter Kwong, Michael Blim, Jonathan Shannon, Christa Salamandra, Russell Sharman, Dana Davis, Jeff Maskovsky, Rudi Gaudio, Charlene Floyd, and Zöe Sheehan Saldana. Colleagues featured in "Anthropologists Engage the World" inspired me with their stories and their work. Members of the New York Academy of Sciences Anthropology Section helped me think more deeply about the relationship of culture and power. Leslie Aiello and the staff of the Wenner-Gren Foundation provided a vibrant venue to engage the cutting edges of anthropological research. The board of the American Ethnological Society allowed me to explore the theme of anthropologists engaging the world through their spring 2012 conference. My research assistants Alessandro Angelini, Andrew Hernann, Chris Grove, Suzanna Goldblatt, Lynn Horridge and Chris Baum continually introduced me to the richness of contemporary scholarship and creative strategies for teaching and learning. Thanks also to a wonderful group of friends and family who have supported and encouraged me during this fascinating and challenging journey: K and Charlene, Zöe, Sally and Steve, Asher, Douglas, Marty and Linda, the guys at the Metro Diner—Nick, Marco, Antonio, and Mario—the SPSA community, the Ajax soccer family, Shari, Vicki, Frances Helen, and Thomas Luke.

Finally, I would like to thank my students at Baruch College who every class ask to be introduced to an anthropology that is relevant to their daily lives, that tackles significant contemporary issues, and that provides them the tools of analysis and empowerment to live awake, conscious, and engaged. This book is dedicated to you and your potential to make the world a better place.

Perhaps the quintessential human task is to pass to the next generation the accumulated insights, understandings, and knowledge that will empower them to live life fully and meaningfully and to meet the challenges confronting humanity and the planet. I hope this book might contribute to that existential endeavor.

Cultural Anthropology

Anthropologists in the twenty-first century engage a world that is experiencing an unprecedented **interaction of people, ideas, images, and** things that continues to **intensify.** Communication **technologies** link people instantaneously across **the globe.** Economic **activities challenge** national **boundaries.** People are on the move between countries and within them. Here, young **Afghan** women **work** at the **first** women-only **Internet** café **in Kabul, 2012.** How can *you* use the tools of **anthropology to engage** this world on **the move?**

Coca Cola
Go Back
Go Back
NAPM

Indian village women protest the Coca Cola company's exploitation of underground water supplies.

p. 9

p. 9

p. 11

p. 12

p. 15

p. 29

CHAPTER 1
Anthropology in a Global Age

Every morning the women of Plachimada, a rural area in southern India, begin a five-kilometer (three-mile) trek in search of fresh water. The morning journey for water is a common task for many women across the world, for one-third of the planet's population lives with water scarcity. But such scarcity is new for the people of Plachimada, an area of typically rich agricultural harvests.

Local residents trace the changes to March 2000, when the Coca-Cola Company opened a bottling plant in the village. The plant is capable of producing 1.2 million bottles of Coke, Sprite, and Fanta every day. Nine liters of fresh water are needed to make one liter of Coke, so Plachimada's large underground aquifer was an attractive resource for the company. But according to local officials, when the company began to drill more wells and install high-powered pumps to extract groundwater for the factory, the local water table fell dramatically—from 45 meters (147.5 feet) below the surface to 150 meters (492 feet), far more than could be explained by periods of limited rainfall. Hundreds of local non-Coca-Cola wells ran dry, and harvests became much less productive. Local residents also claimed that Coca-Cola workers were dumping chemical wastes on land near the factory and that the runoff was polluting the groundwater. Local women organized protests and a sit-in at the factory gates.

With the assistance of local media and international human rights networks, the protestors' activism drew national and international attention. It even spurred solidarity actions, including support from university students in the United States, Canada, the United Kingdom, and Norway. As a result, the local village council withdrew the Coca-Cola factory's

MAP 1.1
Plachimada

license. But the state government maintained its support. The case finally reached the highest state court, which ruled that Coca-Cola must cease illegal extraction of groundwater in Plachimada (Shiva 2006; Aiyer 2007).

For those of us who often enjoy a Coke with lunch or dinner—or breakfast—the story of the women of Plachimada offers a challenge to consider how our lives connect to theirs. It is a challenge to explore how a simple soft drink, made by a U.S. corporation with global operations, may link people halfway around the world in ways both simple and profound. This is also the challenge of anthropology today: to understand the rich diversity of human life and to see how our particular life experiences connect to those of others. By bringing these perspectives together, we can grasp more fully the totality and potential of human life.

At the same time, the world is changing before our eyes. Whether we call it a global village or a world without borders, we in the twenty-first century are experiencing a level of interaction among people, ideas, and systems that is intensifying at a breathtaking pace. Communication technologies link people instantaneously across the globe. Economic activities challenge national boundaries. People are on the move within countries and among them. Violence and terrorism disrupt lives. Humans have had remarkable success at feeding a growing world population, yet income inequality continues to increase—among nations and also within them. And increasing human diversity on our doorstep opens possibilities, both for deeper understanding and for greater misunderstanding. Clearly, the human community in the twenty-first century is being drawn further into a global web of interaction.

For today's college student, every day can be a cross-cultural experience. This may manifest itself in the most familiar places: the news you see on television, the music you listen to, the foods and beverages you consume, the women or men you date, the classmates you study with, the religious communities you attend. Today you can realistically imagine contacting any of our seven billion co-inhabitants on the planet. You can read their posts on Facebook and watch their videos on YouTube. You can visit them. You wear clothes that they make. You make movies that they view. You can learn from them. You can affect their lives. How do you meet this challenge of deepening interaction and interdependence?

Anthropology provides a unique set of tools, including strategies and perspectives, for understanding our rapidly changing, globalizing world. Most of you are already budding cultural anthropologists without realizing it. Wherever you may live or go to school, you are probably experiencing a deepening encounter with the world's diversity. This phenomenon leads to broad questions such as, How do we approach human diversity in our universities, businesses, families, and religious communities? How do we understand the impact of global transformations on our lives?

FIGURE 1.1 In the twenty-first century, people are experiencing unprecedented levels of interaction, encounter, movement, and exchange. Here, passengers board an overcrowded train in Dhaka, Bangladesh, returning home to celebrate the Muslim holy day of Eid al-Fitr.

Whether our field is business or education, medicine or politics, we all need a skill set for analyzing and engaging a multicultural and increasingly interconnected world and workplace. *Cultural Anthropology: A Toolkit for a Global Age* introduces the anthropologist's tools of the trade to help you to better understand and engage the world as you move through it, and if you so choose, to apply those strategies to the challenges confronting us and our neighbors around the world. To begin our exploration of anthropology, we'll consider four key questions:

- What is anthropology?
- Through what lenses do anthropologists gain a comprehensive view of human cultures?
- What is globalization, and why is it important for anthropology?
- How is globalization transforming anthropology?

What Is Anthropology?

Anthropology is the study of the full scope of human diversity and the application of that knowledge to help people of different backgrounds better understand one another. The word *anthropology* derives from the Greek words *anthropos* ("human") and *logos* ("thought," "reason," or "study"). The roots of anthropology lie in the eighteenth and nineteenth centuries, as Europeans' economic and colonial expansion increased that continent's contact with people worldwide.

anthropology: The study of the full scope of human diversity, past and present, and the application of that knowledge to help people of different backgrounds better understand one another.

Brief Background

Technological breakthroughs in transportation and communication during the eighteenth and nineteenth centuries—shipbuilding, the steam engine, railroads, the telegraph—rapidly transformed the long-distance movement of people, goods, and information, in terms of both speed and quantity. As colonization, communication, trade, and travel expanded, groups of merchants, missionaries, and government officials traveled the world and returned to Europe with reports and artifacts of what seemed to them to be "exotic" people and practices. More than ever before, Europeans encountered the incredible diversity of human cultures and appearances. *Who are these people?* they asked themselves. *Where did they come from? Why do they appear so different from us?*

From the field's inception in the mid-1800s, anthropologists have conducted research to answer specific questions confronting humanity. And they have applied their knowledge and insights to practical problems facing the world.

Franz Boas (1858–1942), one of the founders of American anthropology, became deeply involved in early twentieth-century debates on immigration, serving for a term on a presidential commission examining U.S. immigration policies. In an era when many scholars and government officials considered the different people of Europe to be of distinct biological races, U.S. immigration policies privileged immigrants from northern and western Europe over those from southern and eastern Europe. Boas worked to undermine these racialized views of immigrants. He conducted studies that showed the wide variation of physical forms within groups of the same national origin, as well as the marked physical changes in the children and grandchildren of immigrants as they adapted to the environmental conditions in their new country (Baker 2004; Boas 1912).

Audrey Richards (1899–1984), studying the Bemba people in what is now Zambia in the 1930s, focused on issues of health and nutrition among women and children, bringing concerns for nutrition to the forefront of anthropology. Her ethnography, *Chisungu* (1956), featured a rigorous and detailed study of the coming-of-age rituals of young Bemba women and established new standards for the conduct of anthropological research. Richards's research is often credited with opening a pathway for the study of nutritional issues and women's and children's health in anthropology.

Today anthropologists apply their knowledge and research strategies to a wide range of social issues. For example, they study HIV/AIDS in Africa, immigrant farm workers in the United States, ethnic conflict in the former Yugoslavia, street children in Brazil, and Muslim judicial courts in Egypt. Anthropologists trace the spread of disease, promote economic development in underdeveloped countries, conduct market research, and lead diversity-training programs in schools, corporations, and community organizations. Anthropologists also study our human origins, excavating and analyzing the bones, artifacts, and DNA of our ancestors from millions of years ago to gain an understanding of who we are and where we've come from.

Sixty percent of anthropologists today work in *applied anthropology*—that is, they work outside of academic settings to apply the strategies and insights of anthropology directly to current world problems. Even many of us who work full time in a college or university are deeply involved in public applied anthropology.

Anthropology's Unique Approach

Anthropology today retains its core commitment to understanding the richness of human diversity. Specifically, anthropology challenges us to move beyond **ethnocentrism**—the strong human tendency to believe that one's own culture or way of life is normal, natural, and superior to the beliefs and practices of others. Instead, as we will explore throughout this book, the anthropologist's toolkit of research strategies and analytical concepts enables us to appreciate, understand, and engage the diversity of human cultures in an increasingly global age. To that end, anthropology has built upon the key concerns of early generations to develop a set of characteristics unique among the social sciences.

FIGURE 1.2 Anthropology's scope is global. Anthropologists' research spans issues as diverse as (*top left*) the needs of pregnant women in Guinea, West Africa; *right*, the plight of Brazilian street children; *bottom left*, the struggles of migrant farm-workers in central Florida.

ethnocentrism: The belief that one's own culture or way of life is normal and natural; using one's own culture to evaluate and judge the practices and ideals of others.

Anthropology Is Global in Scope Our work covers the whole world and is not constrained by geographic boundaries. Anthropology was once noted for the study of faraway, seemingly exotic villages in developing countries. But from the beginning, anthropologists have been studying not only in the islands of the South Pacific, in the rural villages of Africa, and among indigenous peoples in Australia and North America, but also (though to a lesser degree) among factory workers in Britain and France, among immigrants in New York, and in other communities in the industrializing world. Over the last thirty years, anthropology has turned significant attention to urban communities in industrialized nations. With the increase of studies in North America and Europe, it is fair to say that anthropologists now embrace the full scope of humanity—across geography and through time.

Anthropologists Start with People and Their Local Communities Although the whole world is our field, anthropologists are committed to understanding the local, everyday lives of the people we study. Our unique perspective focuses on the details and patterns of human life in the local community and then examines how particular cultures connect with the rest of humanity. Sociologists, economists, and political scientists primarily analyze broad trends, official organizations, and national policies, but anthropologists—particularly cultural anthropologists—adopt **ethnographic fieldwork** as their primary research strategy (see Chapter 3). They live with a community of people over an extended period to understand their lives by "walking in their shoes."

ethnographic fieldwork: A primary research strategy in cultural anthropology involving living with a community of people over an extended period to better understand their lives.

Anthropologists have constantly worked to bring often-ignored voices into the global conversation. As a result, the field has a history of focusing on the cultures and struggles of non-Western and nonelite people. In recent years, some anthropologists have conducted research on elites—"studying up," as some have called it—by examining financial institutions, aid and development agencies, medical laboratories, and doctors. But the vast majority of our work has addressed the marginalized segments of society.

Anthropologists Study Both People and the Structures of Power Human communities are full of people, the institutions they have created for managing life in organized groups, and the systems of meaning they have built to make sense of it all. Anthropology maintains a commitment to studying both the people and the larger structures of power around them. These include families, governments, economic systems, educational institutions, militaries, the media, and religions, as well as ideas of race, ethnicity, gender, class, and sexuality.

To comprehensively examine people's lives, anthropologists consider the structures that empower and constrain those people, both locally and globally. At the same time, anthropologists seek to understand the "agency" of local

FIGURE 1.3 Once noted for the study of seemingly far away and "exotic" people and places, anthropologists today increasingly study the complex interaction of diverse communities in global cities like London.

people—in other words, the central role of individuals and groups in determining their own lives, even in the face of overwhelming structures of power.

Anthropologists Believe That All Humans Are Connected Anthropologists believe that all humans share connections that are biological, cultural, economic, and ecological. Despite fanciful stories about the "discovery" of isolated, seemingly lost tribes of "stone-age" people, anthropologists suggest that there are no truly isolated people in the world today and that there rarely, if ever, were any in the past. Clearly, some groups of people are less integrated than others into the global system under construction today. But none are completely isolated. And for some, their seeming isolation may be of recent historical origins. In fact, when we look more closely at the history of so-called primitive tribes in Africa and the Americas (more recently called *indigenous*), we find that many were complex state societies before colonialism and the slave trade led to their collapse.

Although some anthropology textbooks show "tribal"-looking people in brightly colored, seemingly exotic clothing holding cell phones, which suggests the rapid integration of isolated people into a high-tech, global world, anthropological research indicates that this imagined isolation never really existed. Despite the world's incredible cultural diversity, human history is the story of movement and interaction, not of isolation and disconnection. Yes, today's period of rapid globalization is intensifying the interactions among people and the flow of goods, technology, money, and ideas within and across national

FIGURE 1.4 This map shows the King of Mali, west Africa, in 1375, seated at the center of his vast kingdom—a key point along trade routes stretching across Africa and into the Middle East and beyond.

boundaries, but interaction and connection are not new inventions. They have been central to human history. Our increasing connection today reminds us that our actions have consequences for the whole world, not just for our own lives and those of our families and friends.

Through What Lenses Do Anthropologists Gain a Comprehensive View of Human Cultures?

One of the unique characteristics of anthropology in the United States is that it has developed four "lenses" for examining humanity. Constituting the **four-field approach**, these interrelated fields are physical anthropology, archaeology, linguistic anthropology, and cultural anthropology. In Europe, the four fields are quite separate, but the history of anthropology in the United States (see Chapter 3) has fostered a holistic approach for examining the complexity of human origins and human culture, past and present.

Holism refers to anthropology's commitment to look at the whole picture of human life—culture, biology, history, and language—across space and time. The field's cross-cultural and comparative approach considers the life experiences of people in every part of the world, comparing and contrasting cultural beliefs and practices to understand human similarities and differences on a global scale. Anthropologists conduct research on the contemporary world and also look deep into human history.

four-field approach: The use of four interrelated disciplines to study humanity: physical anthropology, archaeology, linguistic anthropology, and cultural anthropology.

holism: The anthropological commitment to consider the full scope of human life, including culture, biology, history, and language, across space and time.

Because we analyze both human culture and biology, anthropologists are in a unique position to offer insights into debates about the role of "nature" versus "nurture." How do biology, culture, and the environment interact to shape who we are as humans, individually and as groups? The four-field approach is key to implementing this holistic perspective within anthropology.

Physical Anthropology

Physical anthropology, sometimes called *biological anthropology*, is the study of humans from a biological perspective—in particular, how they have evolved over time and have adapted to their environments. Most scholars agree that modern humans share a common ancestor with other primates such as chimpanzees, apes, and monkeys. In fact, genetic studies reveal that humans share 97.7 percent of DNA with gorillas and 98.7 percent with chimpanzees. Both the fossil record and the genetic evidence suggest that the evolutionary line leading to modern humans split from the one leading to modern African apes between five and six million years ago. Through a complex evolutionary process that we are learning more about every day, *Homo sapiens* (the group of modern humans to which you and I belong) evolved in Africa fairly recently in the grand scheme of things—probably less than 200,000 years ago—and gradually spread across the planet (Larsen 2011).

physical anthropology: The study of humans from a biological perspective, particularly focused on human evolution.

FIGURE 1.5 Paleoanthropologists trace the history of human evolution by reconstructing the human fossil record. Here, Ketut Wiradyana unearths a fossilized human skeleton buried in a cave in Indonesia's Aceh province.

Physical anthropology has several areas of specialization. **Paleoanthropology** traces the history of human evolution by reconstructing the human fossil record. Thus, paleoanthropologists excavate the teeth, skulls, and other bones of our human ancestors and analyze them to track changes in human physical form over time. From these fossils they map changes in key categories such as overall body size, cranial capacity, hand structure, head shape, and pelvic position. Such changes reveal developments in walking, diet, intelligence, and capacity for cultural adaptation. Since the late 1970s, paleoanthropologists have also used molecular genetics to trace changes in human ancestors over time. The sequencing of DNA allows us to measure how closely humans are related to other primates and even to follow the movement of groups of people through the flow of genes. For instance, mitochondrial DNA (passed on from mother to daughter) indicates that modern *Homo sapiens* first appeared in Africa around 150,000 years ago and migrated out of Africa 100,000 years ago. This DNA evidence generally matches the findings of the archaeological record.

Primatology is another specialization within physical anthropology. Primatologists study living, nonhuman primates and primate fossils—including monkeys, apes, chimpanzees, and gorillas—to see what clues their biology, evolution, behavior, and social life might provide about our own, particularly our early human behavior. Careful observation of primates in their natural habitats and in captivity has offered significant insights into sexuality, parenting, male/female differences, cooperation, intergroup conflict, aggression, and problem solving.

Physical anthropologists also study the diversity of human physical forms that have evolved over time. Humans come in all shapes and sizes. Our differences range from body size and facial shape to skin color, height, blood chemistry, and susceptibility to certain diseases. Physical anthropologists attribute general patterns of human physical variation to adaptation to different physical environments as humans spread from Africa across the other continents. Variations in skin color, for instance, can be traced to the need to adapt to different levels of ultraviolet light as humans migrated away from the equator (see Chapter 5).

However, studies of human biology show that the physical similarities among the world's people far outweigh the differences. In fact, there is more variation *within* what are assumed to be "groups" than *between* groups. This is clearly evident in terms of the thorny concept of race (see Chapter 6). A biologically distinct race would include people in a group who share a greater statistical frequency of genes and physical traits than do people outside the group. Physical anthropologists find no evidence of distinct, fixed, biological races. Rather, there is only one human race. Attempts to identify distinct biological races are flawed and arbitrary, as no clear biological lines exist to define different races. Racial categories, which vary significantly from culture to culture, are loosely

FIGURE 1.6 Primatologist Jane Goodall studies chimpanzee behavior in an African nature preserve.

based on a few visible physical characteristics such as skin color, but they have no firm basis in genetics (Larsen 2011; Mukhopadhyay, Henze, and Moses 2007). We will return to this discussion of the biological and social dimensions of race in Chapters 5 and 6.

Archaeology

Archaeology involves the investigation of the human past by means of excavating and analyzing material remains (artifacts). The goal is not to recover buried treasure, but to understand past human life. Some archaeologists study the emergence of early states in places such as Egypt, India, China, and Mexico. They have unearthed grand sites such as the pyramids of Egypt and Mexico and the terra-cotta warriors guarding the tomb of China's Qin Dynasty emperor. Others focus on the histories of less spectacular sites that shed light on the everyday lives of people in local villages and households.

Archaeology is our only source of information about human societies before writing began (around 5,500 years ago). Because we are unable to travel back through time to observe human behavior, **prehistoric archaeology** seeks to reconstruct human behavior from artifacts that give significant clues about our ancestors' lives. Campsites, hunting grounds, buildings, burials, and especially garbage dumps are rich sources of material. There archaeologists find tools, weapons, pottery, human and animal bones, jewelry, seeds, charcoal, ritual items, building foundations, and even coprolites (fossilized fecal matter). Through excavation and analysis of these material remains, archaeologists

archaeology: The investigation of the human past by means of excavating and analyzing artifacts.

prehistoric archaeology: The reconstruction of human behavior in the distant past (before written records) through the examination of artifacts.

reconstruct family and work life. What animals did the people eat? What seeds did they plant? What tools and crafts did they make? Coprolites reveal a great deal about the local diet. Burial sites provide significant data about how people treated their elders and their dead, what rituals they may have practiced, and their ideas about the afterlife. Archaeological evidence can suggest trade patterns, consumption habits, gender roles, and power stratification.

Historic archaeology explores the more recent past and often combines the examination of physical remains and artifacts with that of written or oral records. Historic archaeologists excavate houses, stores, factories, sunken slave ships, even polar ice caps to better understand recent human history and the impact of humans on the environment. For example, recent excavations of former slave plantations in the southern United States, combined with historical records such as deeds, census forms, personal letters, and diaries, have provided rich insight into the lives of African slaves in the seventeenth and eighteenth centuries. Students in the North Atlantic Biocultural Organisation international field school conduct excavations in Iceland that reveal not only historical information about the settling of the North Atlantic but also data on major changes in the contemporary global climate. Core samples from borings drilled through the glaciers reveal sediments deposited from the air over thousands of years as the glaciers formed; such samples allow archaeologists to track global warming and the impact of greenhouse gases on climate change.

In a very contemporary example of applied archaeology, since 1973 archaeologist William Rathje, a "garbologist" at the University of Arizona, has been learning about contemporary culture by examining what people throw away. Although many studies of consumption, waste disposal, and eating and drinking habits focus on surveys and interviews, Rathje's Garbage Project has involved analyzing huge quantities of garbage in Tucson (by hand). He has found that what people actually do and what they say they do can be completely different. In this case, only 15 percent of households responding to a survey reported drinking some beer and none reported drinking more than eight cans a week, but analysis of the garbage from the same neighborhood showed that 80 percent drank some beer and 50 percent drank more than eight cans a week.

In 1987 the Garbage Project began investigating landfills across the United States and Canada to uncover what is thrown away and what happens to it once it reaches the landfills. Like the earlier project in Tucson, expectations did not match reality. Landfills were not overwhelmed by dirty diapers and fast food containers but by paper that could have been easily recycled, including newspapers that, when buried deep within the landfills, took far longer to biodegrade than anticipated. The surprising data developed from the Garbage

historic archaeology: The exploration of the more recent past through an examination of physical remains and artifacts as well as written or oral records.

FIGURE 1.7 Prehistoric garbage dumps provide rich sources of material for understanding cultural practices of human ancestors. Today, "garbologists" also learn about contemporary culture by examining what people throw away, including in large trash landfills like the one pictured here.

Project excavations has helped shape waste disposal practices and landfill management and has provided further impetus to the movement for comprehensive recycling programs that are now commonplace in many parts of the country (Rathje and Murphy 2001).

Linguistic Anthropology

Linguistic anthropology involves the study of human language in the past and the present. Languages are complex, vibrant, and constantly changing systems of symbols through which people communicate with one another. (Think about how hard it is to get your ideas across in your college papers, in text messages, or even in conversation with your parents.) Languages are very flexible and inventive. (Consider how English has adapted to the rise of the Internet to include such new words and concepts as spam, instant messages, Googling, and Skyping.) A language clearly reflects a people's ideas of and experiences with the world. But linguistic anthropologists suggest that language may also limit and constrain a people's views of the world. In other words, can we think clearly about something if we don't have an adequately sophisticated language?

Language is perhaps the most distinctive feature of being human. It is the key to our ability to learn and share culture from generation to generation, to cooperate in groups, and to adapt to our environment. While some animals—including dolphins and whales, bees, and ravens—have a limited range of communication, human language is more complex, creative, and extensively used.

Linguistic anthropology includes three main areas of specialization. **Descriptive linguists** work to carefully describe spoken languages and preserve

linguistic anthropology: The study of human language in the past and present.

descriptive linguists: Those who analyze languages and their component parts.

THROUGH WHAT LENSES DO ANTHROPOLOGISTS GAIN A COMPREHENSIVE VIEW OF HUMAN CULTURES?   17

historic linguists: Those who study how language changes over time within a culture and how languages travel across cultures.

sociolinguists: Those who study language in its social and cultural contexts.

cultural anthropology: The study of people's communities, behaviors, beliefs, and institutions, including how people make meaning as they live, work, and play together.

participant observation: A key anthropological research strategy involving both participation in and observation of the daily life of the people being studied.

ethnology: The analysis and comparison of ethnographic data across cultures.

them as written languages. For example, some descriptive linguists spend years in rural areas helping local people construct a written language from their spoken language. **Historic linguists** study how language changes over time within a culture and as it moves across cultures. **Sociolinguists** study language in its social and cultural contexts. They examine how different speakers use language in different situations or with different people. They explore how language is affected by factors such as race, gender, age, and class. Consider the so-called "N-word"—a very controversial word in the United States today. Sociolinguists would explore the word's usage in American English: Where did it come from? Who uses it, and in what situations? How does its meaning change according to the speaker and the context? When is it a term of racial hatred? When is it a term of camaraderie? We will explore these issues further in Chapter 4.

Cultural Anthropology

Cultural anthropology is the study of people's everyday lives and their communities—their behaviors, beliefs, and institutions. Cultural anthropologists explore all aspects of human culture, such as war and violence, love and sexuality, child rearing and death. They examine what people do and how they live and work together. But they also search for patterns of meaning embedded within each culture, and they develop theories about how cultures work. Cultural anthropologists examine the ways in which local communities interact with global forces.

Ethnographic fieldwork is at the heart of cultural anthropology. Through **participant observation**—living and working with people on a daily basis, often for a year or more—the cultural anthropologist strives to see the world through the eyes of others. Intensive fieldwork has the power to educate the anthropologist by (1) making what may at first seem very unfamiliar into something that ultimately seems quite familiar, and (2) taking what has seemed very familiar and making it seem very strange. Through fieldwork, anthropologists look beyond the taken-for-granted, everyday experience of life to discover the complex systems of power and meaning that all people construct. These include the many systems we will cover throughout this book: gender, sexuality, race, ethnicity, religion, kinship, and economic and political systems.

Cultural anthropologists analyze and compare ethnographic data across cultures in a process called **ethnology**. This process looks beyond specific local realities to see more general patterns of human behavior and to explore how local experiences intersect with global dynamics. Ultimately, through intensive ethnographic fieldwork and cross-cultural comparison, cultural anthropologists seek to help people better understand one another and the way the world works.

What Is Globalization, and Why Is It Important for Anthropology?

The term **globalization** refers to the worldwide intensification of interactions and the increased movement of money, people, goods, and ideas within and across national borders. Growing integration of the global economy has driven the intense globalization of the past forty years. Corporations are relocating factories halfway around the world. People are crossing borders legally and illegally in search of work. Goods, services, and ideas are flowing along high-speed transportation and communication networks. People, organizations, and nations are being drawn into closer connection.

Globalization is not an entirely new phenomenon. Intensification of global interaction occurred in earlier eras as breakthroughs in communication and transportation brought the world's people into closer contact. The present period of globalization, however, has reached a level of intensity previously unknown.

Although globalization is often portrayed in a positive light in the media and popular discourse, the realities are much more complicated. The new technologies associated with globalization may indeed allow more and more people to interact and communicate, but billions of other people are being left out of these advances. Moreover, along with the economic expansion and growth associated with globalization, there are equally significant global economic inequalities.

globalization: The worldwide intensification of interactions and increased movement of money, people, goods, and ideas within and across national borders.

FIGURE 1.8 Increasing movement of people within and between countries, often under precarious circumstances, is one key characteristic of globalization. Here, Italian Coast Guard divers rescue African immigrants whose boat has run aground off the Italian coast.

Globalization and Anthropology

Globalization and anthropology are intricately intertwined, both in history and in the contemporary world. As we have noted, the field of anthropology emerged in the mid-nineteenth century during a time of intense globalization. At that time, technological inventions in transportation and communication were consolidating a period of colonial encounter, the slave trade, and the emerging capitalist economic system and were enabling deeper interactions of people across cultures. Early anthropologists sought to organize the vast quantity of information that was emerging about people across the globe, though, unlike most contemporary anthropologists, who conduct research in the field, they did so primarily from the comfort of their own homes and meeting halls.

Today another era of even more intense globalization is transforming the lives of the people whom anthropologists study in every part of the world. And, as we will see throughout this book, it is also transforming the ways anthropologists conduct research and communicate their findings. To understand these sweeping changes, we must understand the key dynamics of globalization at play in the world today (Inda and Rosaldo 2002; Lewellen 2002).

Globalization: Key Dynamics

Globalization today is characterized by several key dynamics. These are time-space compression, flexible accumulation, increasing migration, uneven development, and rapid change. These dynamics are reshaping the ways humans adapt to the natural world, and the ways the natural world is adapting to us.

time-space compression: The rapid innovation of communication and transportation technologies associated with globalization that transforms the way people think about space and time.

Time-Space Compression According to the theory of **time-space compression**, the rapid innovation of communication and transportation technologies has transformed the way we think about space (distances) and time. Jet travel, supertankers, superhighways, high-speed railways, telephones, fax machines, computers, the Internet, digital cameras, and cell phones have compressed time and space, changing our sense of how long it takes to do something and how far away someplace or someone is. The world is no longer as big as it used to be.

Consider these examples of a changing sense of time. Today we can fly from New York to Paris in eight hours or from Los Angeles to Hong Kong in twelve. A letter that once took ten days to send from Texas to Kenya now can be attached as a PDF and e-mailed with a few clicks of a mouse. We instant message, text message, Skype, and videoconference. The order placed at a McDonald's drive-through may be taken by a phone operator in California, entered in a computer, and come out as a Quarter Pounder with Cheese at the pickup window in Hawaii (Richtel 2006). These kinds of changes have transformed not only how long it takes us to do something, but also how quickly we expect other people to do things. For example, how much time do you have to respond to an e-mail or text message before someone thinks you are rude or irresponsible?

Flexible Accumulation A second characteristic of today's globalization, **flexible accumulation**, reflects the fact that advances in transportation and communication have enabled companies to move their production facilities around the world in search of cheaper labor, lower taxes, and fewer environmental regulations—in other words, to be completely flexible about the way they accumulate profits (see Chapter 12). Companies in developed countries move their factories to export-processing zones in the developing world, a process called offshoring. Other corporations shift part of their work to employees in other parts of the world, a process called outsourcing. For example, General Motors used to make all of its automobiles in Flint, Michigan. But now the company has factories in Mexico, Brazil, China, and Thailand. Walmart, once known for its advertising campaign "Made in America," now has five thousand factories in China.

Other examples span the globe as well: Phone and computer companies hire English-speaking operators and technicians in Bangalore, India, to answer customers' questions called in on 800 numbers. A company based in Sierre Leone, West Africa, processes traffic tickets issued in New York City. X-rays, CAT scans, and MRIs taken in Colorado may be read and interpreted by doctors in Manila, the Philippines. Clearly, flexible accumulation allows corporations to maximize profits, while time-space compression enables the efficient management of global networks and distribution systems (Harvey 1990).

Increasing Migration A third characteristic of globalization is **increasing migration**, in terms of the movement of people both within countries and between countries. In fact, recent globalization has spurred the international migration of nearly 200 million people, 38 million of them to the United States alone (see Chapter 13). Perhaps 400 million more are internal migrants within their own countries, usually moving from rural to urban areas in search of work. The Chinese government counts nearly 230 million internal migrants floating in China's cities, drawn by construction projects, service jobs, and export-oriented factories.

In countries from Pakistan to Kenya to Peru, rural workers migrate to urban areas seeking to improve their lives and the lives of their families back home. This movement of people within and across national borders is stretching out human relationships and interactions across space and time. Immigrants send money home, call and e-mail friends and family, and sometimes even travel back and forth. Migration is building connections between distant parts of the world, replacing face-to-face interactions with more remote encounters and potentially reducing the hold of the local environment over people's lives and imaginations.

flexible accumulation: The increasingly flexible strategies that corporations use to accumulate profits in an era of globalization, enabled by innovative communication and transportation technologies.

increasing migration: The accelerated movement of people within and between countries.

Uneven Development Globalization is also characterized by **uneven development**. Although many people associate globalization with rapid economic development and progress, globalization has not brought equal benefits to the world's people. Some travel the globe for business or pleasure; others have absolutely no access to any form of transportation. Although 50 percent of the world's people now have cell phones, the distribution is uneven. Europe, North America, and Asia account for well more than 50 percent of such high-tech consumption, while areas of Africa are marginalized and excluded from the globalization process. Such uneven development and uneven access to the benefits of globalization reflect the negative side of changes in the world today.

Although the global economy is creating extreme wealth, it is also creating extreme poverty. Excluding China (which has experienced rapid economic growth), global poverty has increased over the past twenty years. Fully 40 percent of the world's population lives in poverty, defined as income of less than $2 per day. And nearly 1 billion people live in extreme poverty, surviving on less than $1.00 each day (United Nations 2012). Even in the United States, the wealthiest country in the world, some full-time workers who earn the minimum wage make so little money that they must rely on state welfare programs for food stamps and medical care for themselves and their children. In Chapter 12, we will explore the possibility that the rapid growth seen in globalization actually *depends on* uneven development—extracting the resources of some to fuel the success of others.

Rapid Change Globalization is driving **rapid change** in human activities and in the physical world. Although change has been a constant in human history, the pace of change in the modern era—particularly the rate of technological innovation and development—is unlike anything humans experienced in the past. Our economic, social, and political institutions and practices would be nearly unrecognizable to people living even two to three hundred years ago.

Adapting to the Natural World Of course, modern humans and our ancestors have been adapting to changes for millions of years. In fact, perhaps our most unique characteristic is our ability to adapt—to figure out how to survive and thrive in a world that is rapidly changing. Although change has been a constant, so has human adaptation, both biological and cultural.

Our species has successfully adapted genetically to changes in the natural environment over millions of years. We walk upright on two legs. We have binocular vision and see in color. We have opposable thumbs for grasping. Our bodies also adapt temporarily to changes in the environment on a daily basis. We sweat to keep cool in the heat, tan to block out the sun's ultraviolet rays, shiver to generate warmth in the cold, and breathe rapidly to take in more oxygen at high altitudes.

As our ancestors evolved and developed greater brain capacity, they invented cultural adaptations to navigate the natural environment—tools, the controlled use of fire, and weapons. Today our use of culture to adapt to the world around us is incredibly sophisticated. In the United States, we like our air conditioners on a hot July afternoon and our radiators in the winter. Oxygen masks deploy for us in sky-high airplanes, and sunscreen protects us against sunburn and skin cancer. These are just a few familiar examples of adaptations our culture has made. Looking more broadly, the worldwide diversity of human culture itself is a testimony to human flexibility and adaptability to particular environments.

Shaping the Natural World But to say that humans adapt to the natural world is only part of the story, for humans actively shape the natural world as well. Humans have planted, grazed, paved, excavated, and built on at least 40 percent of Earth's surface. Our activities over several million years have caused profound changes in the atmosphere, soil, and oceans. Whereas our ancestors struggled to adapt to the uncertainties of heat, cold, solar radiation, disease, natural disasters, famines, and droughts, today we confront changes and social forces that we ourselves have set in motion. These changes include climate change, water scarcity, overpopulation, extreme poverty, biological weapons, and nuclear missiles. As globalization intensifies, it escalates the human impact on the planet and on other humans, further accelerating the pace of change.

Human activity already threatens the world's ecological balance. We do not need to wait to see the effects. For instance, population growth and consumption patterns have placed incredible stress on Earth's water resources, both freshwater

FIGURE 1.9 Actual stomach contents of a baby albatross on the remote north Pacific Midway Atoll, two thousand miles from the nearest continent. Thousands die as their parents feed them lethal quantities of floating plastic trash that they mistake for food as they forage over the polluted Pacific Ocean. © Chris Jordan, courtesy of Kopeikin Gallery, Los Angeles.

Holly Barker

"While islands may be distant in our psyches we need to remember that our planet is also a remote island in the universe and its future, like that of the Marshall Islands, is ultimately one and the same" (Barker 2008).

Anthropologist Holly Barker focuses her work on the Marshall Islands, a group of coral atolls spread over a seventy-square-mile area in the northern Pacific Ocean. Although Pacific islands may conjure images of warm water, white sandy beaches, and blissful vacation escapes, Barker's work focuses on much less idyllic matters, such as the impact of twelve years of atmospheric nuclear testing conducted by the United States in the Marshalls after World War II and the current impact of climate change on the islands' people. Though some in developed nations may debate the effects of climate change, small island nations around the world are on the front lines of climate change today.

Barker first arrived in the Marshall Islands in 1988 as a volunteer with the U.S. Peace Corps to teach English on a remote island of fisherfolk and subsistence farmers. After four hundred years of colonization by various countries, the Marshall Islands had finally achieved independence from the United States two years earlier, and its people were trying to figure out how to self-govern for the first time in four centuries.

Upon returning to the United States, Barker worked for Rhode Island Senator Claiborne Pell in Washington, D.C., but nobody on Capitol Hill had time to hear about the Marshall Islands. "So one day I just called up the Marshall Island embassy and encouraged them to make an appointment with the senator. But they had never had any luck with that and simply replied, 'Why don't you come and work for us?' So I did—for seventeen years. It was a phenomenal experience. My role as the anthropologist was to show the Marshallese government leaders how the U.S. government works and then get out of the way and let them speak for themselves. They certainly

know what to say and what they want to ask for. That's not the role of an outsider. My role was to help them make connections and show them how to be effective in the U.S. cultural context."

When Barker began her graduate studies in anthropology, she was still employed by the embassy. "I was learning all the ideas of anthropology and applying them immediately to my job, thinking about anthropological theories and then connecting them back to the Marshall Islands. I wasn't just studying academic ideas in isolation. I was coming to work every day and putting them to use. That brought anthropology alive for me. I remember learning about the concept of structural violence, looking at how institutions do harm to people. There I was in D.C. looking at the political system's failure to recognize health care needs of the Marshallese and trying to push

Anthropologist Holly Barker

the U.S. political institutions to change policies that were leaving people dying without access to health care. Then I began to see concepts like structural violence with shocking clarity."

Today the Marshall Islands confront the rising impact of climate change: "For the older generation of the Marshallese, the life-defining issue was certainly nuclear testing. They're a culture and nation with amazing resilience, to constantly work through those kinds of issues and still have their culture intact, adapting to change and still maintaining a sense of humor. But for the next generation or two generations removed from the testing, their life-threatening issue is climate change. On the islands there's no buffer. The effects are profound. The current generation will see the tombs of ancestors fall into the sea and watch their inheritance be swept away by the encroaching waters. They can see the change. It's rapid. Globalization makes everything seem to happen faster. But the wholesale relocation of communities is something we're not prepared for yet. That's the challenge I think with globalization. We're used to seeing rural people slowly shifting to urban environments, new uses of technology, or gradual cultural changes. But with climate change on islands, we're talking about rapidly making environmental refugees of gigantic proportions.

"We don't have the luxury to only think about our own lives anymore. Our atmospheres are connected. Our seas are connected. Everything is. Today we need to rethink our notions of scale and proportion, to step back and see the Earth through a wider lens. The same holds for the islands. We imagine the islands as these little beautiful paradises that exist in tourist brochures without the human beings that populate these places. We think of them as oases, retreats that await us anytime we want happiness. But we don't think of them as places that we take our own irresponsibilities to. That would mean thinking about the islands and their history as test sites for our nuclear bombs and their experience of climate change—places colonial powers take activities that they don't want in their own nations.

MAP 1.2
Marshall Islands

Despite the fact that small island nations are responsible for only three-hundredths of 1 percent of the global carbon emissions from burning fossil fuels that drive global warming, they are the ones confronting the most devastating impacts of climate change so far. If we can't deal with the Marshallese, who are U.S. allies and formerly colonized by the United States—if we can't take care of people with whom we have a unique history and entangled close relationships, how are we going to be able to deal with the multitude elsewhere? So it calls for us to do a better job. To be clearer about how we are all connected."

Barker teaches the Introduction to Cultural Anthropology course at the University of Washington and tries to get across this basic idea to her students: "We need you! We as a society cannot afford for you not to become engaged. Each generation gets passed the inheritance, the legacy, to carry on human beings into the next generation. To be adequately equipped for that, you have to be able to see the potential of human beings around you. You have to be able to communicate across boundaries. I feel that in every generation we are compelled to get the next generation ready to deal with the challenges that are undoubtedly coming their way. Anthropology is a discipline that provides the skills and theories but also the hope, the sense of our human potential and the possibilities of doing better. Anthropology is about being the best human beings we can be. Sometimes we screw up and screw up massively. But we have the potential to do better. Anthropology asks that of us and gives us the tools to make it possible."

and saltwater. As the opening story of Plachimada, India, reveals, the struggle to gain access to the freshwater in lakes, rivers, and aquifers can be a source of conflict. Private companies are buying up rights to water in many countries, and bottled water sales have grown to a $50 billion global business today. The seemingly vast oceans are also experiencing significant distress. In the middle of the Pacific Ocean sits a floating island of plastic the size of Texas, caught in an intersection of ocean currents. The plastic originates mainly from consumers in Asia and North America. Pollution from garbage, sewage, and agricultural fertilizer runoff, combined with overfishing and spills from offshore oil drilling, may kill off edible sea life completely by 2048. These sobering realities are characteristic of today's global age and the impacts of increasing globalization.

Humans and Climate Change Human activity is also producing rapid **climate change**. Driven by the increase of greenhouse gases in the atmosphere, largely from the burning of fossil fuels, global warming is already reshaping the physical world and threatening to radically change much of modern human civilization. Scientists predict a rise in global temperatures of between 2.5 and 10 degrees Fahrenheit by 2100. Changing weather patterns have already begun to alter agricultural patterns and crop yields. Global warming has spurred rapid melting of polar ice and glaciers, well before most scientists had predicted, and the pace is increasing.

Melting glaciers mean rising sea levels. Given the current speed of melting, a one- to two-foot sea-level rise in the coming decades is entirely possible. Half of the world's population lives within fifty miles of the coast, so the implications are enormous—especially in low-lying delta regions. Bangladesh, home to more than 150 million people, will be largely underwater. Miami will have an ocean on both sides. Should all the glacier ice on Greenland melt, sea levels would rise an estimated twenty-three feet.

How will the planet cope with the growth of the human population from seven billion in 2012 to more than nine billion in 2050? Our ancestors have successfully adapted to the natural world around us for millions years, but human activity and technological innovation now threaten to overwhelm the natural world beyond its ability to adapt to us.

climate change: Changes to Earth's climate, including global warming produced primarily by increasing concentrations of greenhouse gases created by human activity such as burning fossil fuels and deforestation.

How Is Globalization Transforming Anthropology?

The field of anthropology has changed significantly in the past thirty years as the world has been transformed by globalization. Just as the local cultures and communities we study are changing in response to these forces, our focus and strategies must also change.

Making a Can of Coke Unfamiliar

Throughout this book we will be exploring how anthropology's holistic, cross-cultural, and comparative approach can help us think more deeply about other people and cultures and live more consciously in our global world. As humans we take for granted many things about our lives and how the world works, whether it is our notions of race or the cheap cost of a bar of chocolate or a can of Coke. But anthropologists often describe how doing fieldwork can make the familiar strange and the strange familiar.

Take a can of Coke, for instance. After rereading the opening story of the Coca-Cola factory in Plachimada, India, go buy a can of Coke and put it on your desk. Can you make this most familiar cultural object unfamiliar? What would an anthropologist want to know about that can of Coke? What can you learn about yourself, your culture, or globalization in general from that can of Coke? How does the social life of a can of Coke intersect with the lives of people in each stage of its production, distribution, and consumption?

- What's in it? Where did the ingredients come from?
- Who made it? What is their life like?
- What is the impact of Coke on the local community where it is produced? Where it is consumed?
- What is the relationship of the people in Plachimada to a can of Coke? Do they drink it? Do they work in the factory that makes it? How much do they earn? How much has the Coca-Cola factory changed their lives? Has it affected people in the community differently based on age, gender, or class?
- What do you pay for a twelve-ounce can? What are the real social costs of producing a can of Coke—in terms of water, power systems, sewage treatment, pollution, garbage disposal, and roads for transportation? Who pays for them?
- What is the environmental impact of making a can of Coke, considering what it takes to grow and process ingredients such as high-fructose corn syrup and the quantity of water required to produce the finished product?

By exploring the complex social life of a can of Coke, you are applying a set of analytical tools that may help you look more carefully and consciously at other familiar elements of culture.

What can you learn about yourself, your culture, or globalization from a can of Coke?

Changing Communities

As time and space compress, the world gets smaller. Migration, economic activity, and flows of money, ideas, media images, and the elements of popular culture such as music, movies, and television have created a new diversity of experiences that reach every corner of the world. As they do so, they mingle with and influence local cultures and challenge traditions and customs. As a result, many local cultural patterns are being forced to shift and adapt.

Debates over the effects of globalization on local cultures and communities are intense. Vulnerable people and cultures are encountering powerful economic forces. Many communities are seeing the redefinition of aspects of personal lives and cultural beliefs—in terms of family, gender roles, ethnicity, sexuality, love, and work patterns. Critics of globalization warn of the dangers of homogenization and the loss of traditional local cultures as products marketed by global companies flood into local communities. (Many of these brands originate in Western countries: for example, Coca-Cola, Microsoft, McDonald's, Levi's, Disney, Walmart, CNN, and Hollywood.) Yet proponents note the new exposure to diversity that is now available to people worldwide, opening possibilities for personal choice that were previously unimaginable. As in the case of Plachimada, India, although global forces are increasingly affecting local communities, local communities are also actively resisting these forces, fighting detrimental changes, negotiating better terms of engagement, and embracing new opportunities.

Changing Research Strategies

Globalization is transforming not only the communities that we study, but also the strategies we use to study them (see Chapter 3). Today it is impossible to study a local community without considering the global forces that affect it. Thus, anthropologists are engaging in more multi-sited ethnographies, comparing communities linked, for instance, by migration, production, or communication. My own research is a case in point.

Multi-sited Ethnography: China and New York When I began my fieldwork in New York City's Chinatown in 1997, I anticipated conducting a year-long study of Chinese immigrant religious communities—Christian, Buddhist, and Daoist—and their role in the lives of new immigrants. I soon realized, however, that I did not understand why tens of thousands of immigrants from Fuzhou, China, were taking such great risks—some hiring human smugglers at enormous cost—to come and work in low-paying jobs in restaurants, garment shops, construction trades, and nail salons. To figure out why so many were leaving China, one summer I followed their immigrant journey back home.

I boarded a plane from New York to Hong Kong and on to Fuzhou, the capital of Fujian Province on China's southeast coast. From Fuzhou, I took a

MAP 1.3
Fuzhou / New York

FIGURE 1.10 Rural Fuzhou villagers worship at a Chinese temple constructed with funds sent home by members working in the United States.

local bus to a small town at the end of the line. A ferry carried me across a river to a three-wheeled motor taxi that transported me across dirt roads to the main square of a rural fishing village at the foot of a small mountain. I began to hike up the slope and finally caught a ride on a motorcycle to my destination.

Back in New York, I had met the master of a temple, an immigrant from Fuzhou who was raising money from other immigrant workers to rebuild their temple in China. He had invited me to visit their hometown and participate in a temple festival. Now, finally arriving at the temple after a transcontinental journey, I was greeted by hundreds of pilgrims from neighboring towns and villages. "What are you doing here?" one asked. When I told them that I was an anthropologist from the United States, that I had met some of their fellow villagers in New York, and that I had come to learn about their village, they began to laugh. "Go back to New York!" they said. "Most of our village is there already, not here in this little place." Then we all laughed together, acknowledging the irony of my traveling to China when they wanted to go to New York—but also marveling at the remarkable connection built across the ten thousand miles between this little village and one of the most urban metropolises in the world.

Over the years I have made many trips back to the villages around Fuzhou. My research experiences have brought alive the ways in which globalization is transforming the world and the practice of anthropology. Today 70 percent of the village population resides in the United States, but the villagers live out time-space compression as they continue to build strong ties between New York and China. They travel back and forth. They build temples, roads, and schools back home. They transfer money by wire. They call, text, Skype, and post videos online. They send children back to China to be raised by grandparents in the village. Parents in New York watch their children play in the village using webcams and the Internet.

Back home, local factories built by global corporations produce toys for Disney and McDonald's and Mardi Gras beads for the city of New Orleans. The local jobs provide employment alternatives, but they have not replaced migration out of China as the best option for improving local lives.

These changes are happening incredibly rapidly, transforming people's lives and communities on opposite sides of the world. But globalization brings

TOOLKIT

Thinking Like an Anthropologist: Getting Started

As you begin your exploration of anthropology, the women of Plachimada discussed in the chapter opening may provide you with a powerful image to keep in mind and challenge you to think more anthropologically about the world and its people. *Cultural Anthropology: A Toolkit for a Global Age* is designed to help you explore the richness of human diversity, uncover your conscious and subconscious ideas of how the world works (or should work), and develop some strategies for living, working, and learning in an environment where diversity is a part of daily life.

Solving the challenges that face the human race in your lifetime will require greater engagement, interaction, and cooperation—not more isolation and ignorance. The future of the planet requires everyone to develop the skills of an anthropologist if our species is to thrive and, perhaps, even to survive. These skills include cross-cultural knowledge and sensitivity; perceptiveness of other people; understanding of systems of meaning and systems of power; and consciousness of one's own culture, assumptions, beliefs, and power. By the end of this book, you will have many of the skills needed to think carefully about these questions.

You also will discover that the study of anthropology helps you rethink many of your assumptions about the world and how it works. For the magic of anthropology lies in unmasking the underlying structures of life, in spurring the analytical imagination, and in providing the skills to be alert, aware, sensitive, and successful in a rapidly changing—and often confusing—multicultural and global world.

Key Terms

anthropology (p. 7)

ethnocentrism (p. 9)

ethnographic fieldwork (p. 10)

four-field approach (p. 12)

holism (p. 12)

physical anthropology (p. 13)

paleoanthropology (p. 14)

primatology (p. 14)

archaeology (p. 15)

prehistoric archaeology (p. 15)

historic archaeology (p. 16)

linguistic anthropology (p. 17)

descriptive linguists (p. 17)

historic linguists (p. 18)

sociolinguists (p. 18)

cultural anthropology (p. 18)

participant observation (p. 18)

uneven benefits that break down along lines of ethnicity, gender, age, language, legal status, kinship, and class. These disparities give rise to issues that we will address in depth throughout this book. Such changes mean that I as an anthropologist have to adjust my own fieldwork to span my subjects' entire reality, a reality that now encompasses a village in China, the metropolis of New York City, and many people and places in between (Guest 2003). And as you will discover throughout this book, other anthropologists are likewise adapting their strategies to meet the challenges of globalization. Learning to think like an anthropologist will enable you to better navigate our increasingly interconnected world.

ethnology (p. 18)
globalization (p. 19)
time-space compression (p. 20)
flexible accumulation (p. 21)
increasing migration (p. 21)
uneven development (p. 22)
rapid change (p. 22)
climate change (p. 26)

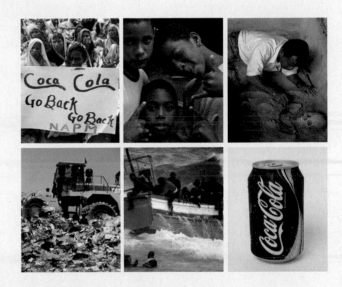

For Further Exploration

Do the Math. 2012. 350.org. Documentary film about global climate change. http://act.350.org/signup/math-movie.

Guest, Kenneth J. 2003. *God in Chinatown: Religion and Survival in New York's Evolving Immigrant Community*. New York: NYU Press.

Mardi Gras: Made in China. 2005. Directed by David Redmon. Carnivalesque Films. Ethnographic film showing factory in China making Mardi Gras beads, and their use in the New Orleans festival.

United Nations. "Millennium Development Goals: End Poverty 2015." www.un.org/millenniumgoals /poverty.shtml.

U.S. Census Bureau. "U.S. and World Population Clocks." www.census.gov/main/www/popclock.html.

When is a kiss more than a kiss? Richard Gere kisses Shilpa Shetty during an AIDS awareness program for truck drivers in New Delhi, India.

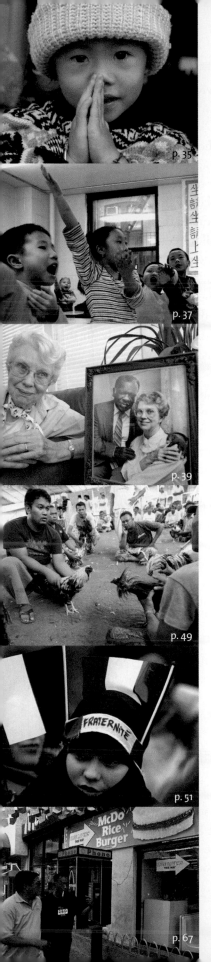

p. 35

p. 37

p. 39

p. 49

p. 51

p. 67

CHAPTER 2
Culture

In April 2007, U.S. movie star Richard Gere stood on a stage near Delhi, India, and led thousands of truck drivers in a Hindi-language chant of "No condoms, no sex! No condoms, no sex!" HIV / AIDS has become an epidemic among Indian truck drivers, who transport millions of tons of goods and produce around the country as India's economy grows. Gere and other movie stars have lent their celebrity to raise awareness about the need for HIV / AIDS prevention in the Indian trucking community. At the end of the chant, Gere reached across the stage to Indian movie star Shilpa Shetty, dipped her backward, and kissed her on both cheeks as the crowd roared.

Video images of this kiss spread like wildfire across India, replayed on television and published on the front pages of newspapers. Although many Indians ignored it, the kiss drew violent protests from others—particularly religious fundamentalists and Hindu nationalists. A spokesperson for the Hindu nationalist Bharatiya Janata Party condemned the kiss, saying, "Such a public display is not part of Indian tradition." Demonstrators in Mumbai (Bombay) burned images of Gere and Shetty in effigy and set fire to glamour shots of Shetty. They deplored the public display of sexuality, especially because the pair is not married and Gere is a foreigner. In the northern city of Meerut, crowds of hundreds of thousands chanted, "Down with Shilpa Shetty!" A court in Rajasthan issued warrants for the arrest of Gere and Shetty. Said Shetty, "I understand this [kissing] is his [Gere's] culture, not ours. But this was not such a big thing or so obscene for people to overreact in such a manner."

Have you kissed someone lately? Perhaps your kiss didn't inspire nationwide protests. But kissing can be tricky, even in your own culture. Whom can you kiss? How should you kiss them? How do you know? What if

33

you read the signals wrong? What if you kiss the wrong person? What if you do it in the wrong place?

Although Americans may consider kissing as "doing what comes naturally," as an instinctive or biological impulse to show affection or sexuality, the world's cultures have remarkably different ideas about kissing and touching, about love and sex. Ten percent of the people in the world don't kiss at all. In Tahiti, kissing was unknown until European colonialists introduced the practice. Brazilians kiss and hug with gusto. Faithful Catholics may kiss the Pope's ring to show reverence. Parents kiss their children's foreheads as a sign of blessing. In much of Europe, where kissing is the primary greeting, practices vary by country and even within countries. In Paris, four kisses is standard, starting with the left cheek, while in most of the rest of France two kisses suffice. In the Netherlands, kisses begin and end on the right cheek, with three at least, and more to show affection to a close relative or the elderly. In the United Kingdom, there is very little kissing. Handshakes and nods are the normal greetings there.

Kissing is a powerful symbolic action that arouses intense personal feelings and expresses complicated social meanings. It might be easier if someone handed us a kissing manual. Instead we have culture. Culture is our manual for understanding and interacting with the people and the world around us. It includes shared meanings, belief systems, and cultural knowledge—in other words, shared ways of seeing and understanding the world. It shapes every aspect of our human experience. But culture is not fixed in stone or accepted by everyone, even those living in a particular place or time. So culture also provides the arena where our ideas about how to behave—even what we ought to say and think—are debated, challenged, and enforced.

In this chapter, we will apply an anthropologist's viewpoint to culture and consider its crucial role in shaping how we behave and what we think. In particular, we will consider:

- What is culture?
- How has the culture concept developed in anthropology?
- How are culture and power related?
- How much of who you are is determined by biology and how much by culture?
- How is culture created?
- How is globalization transforming culture?

By the end of the chapter you should have a clear sense of how anthropologists think about culture and use culture to analyze human life. By exploring this seemingly familiar concept, you can become conscious of the many unconscious patterns of belief and action that you accept as normal and natural. You can also begin to see how such patterns shape your everyday choices and even your basic conceptions of what is real and what isn't.

What Is Culture?

When people hear the word *culture,* they often think about the material goods or artistic forms produced by distinct groups of people—Chinese food, Middle Eastern music, Indian clothing, Greek architecture, African dances. Sometimes people assume that culture means elite art forms such as those displayed in museums, operas, or ballets. But for anthropologists, culture is much more: it encompasses people's entire way of life.

Culture is a system of knowledge, beliefs, patterns of behavior, artifacts, and institutions that are created, learned, and shared by a group of people. Culture includes shared norms, values, symbols, mental maps of reality, and

culture: A system of knowledge, beliefs, patterns of behavior, artifacts, and institutions that are created, learned, and shared by a group of people.

material objects as well as structures of power—including the media, education, religion, and politics—in which our understanding of the world is shaped, reinforced, and challenged. Ultimately, the culture that we learn shapes our ideas of what is normal and natural, what we can say and do, and even what we can think.

Culture Is Learned and Taught

Humans do not genetically inherit culture. We learn culture throughout our lives from the people and cultural institutions that surround us. Anthropologists call the process of learning culture **enculturation**. Some aspects of culture we learn through formal instruction: English classes in school, religious instruction, visits to the doctor, history lessons, dance classes. Other processes of enculturation are informal and even unconscious as we absorb culture from family, friends, and the media. All humans are equally capable of learning culture and of learning any culture they are exposed to.

The process of enculturation, passing cultural information within populations and across generations, is not unique to humans. Many animals learn social behavior from their immediate group: Wolves learn hunting strategies from the wolf pack. Whales learn to produce and distinguish the unique calls of their pod. Among monkeys and apes, our closest biological relatives, learned behaviors are even more common. Chimpanzees have been observed teaching their young to create rudimentary tools, stripping bark from a twig that they then insert into an anthill to extract a tasty and nutritious treat. But the human capacity to learn culture is unparalleled.

Culture is taught as well as learned. Humans establish cultural institutions as mechanisms for enculturating their members. Schools, medical systems, media, and religious institutions promote the ideas and concepts that are considered central to the culture. Rules, regulations, laws, teachers, doctors, religious leaders, police officers, and sometimes militaries promote and enforce what is considered appropriate behavior and thinking.

Culture Is Shared Yet Contested

Enculturation occurs as part of a group. No individual has his or her own culture. Culture is a shared experience developed as a result of living as a member of a group. Through enculturation, humans learn how to communicate and establish patterns of behavior that allow life in community, often in close proximity and sometimes with limited resources. Cultures may be shared by groups, large and small. For example, anthropologists may speak of Indian culture (1 billion people) as well as the culture of the Yanomami tribe (several thousand people) living in the Amazonian rainforest. Your college classroom has a culture, one that you must learn in order to succeed academically. A classroom

enculturation: The process of learning culture.

FIGURE 2.2 How is culture learned and taught? Here, kindergartners learn Mandarin Chinese at the New York Chinese School.

culture includes shared understandings of what to wear, how to sit, when to arrive or leave, how to communicate with classmates and the instructor, and how to challenge authority, as well as formal and informal processes of enculturation.

Although culture is shared by members of groups, it is also constantly contested, negotiated, and changing. Culture is never static. Just as cultural institutions serve as structures for promoting enculturation, they also serve as arenas for challenging, debating, and changing core cultural beliefs and behaviors. Intense debates erupt over school curriculums, medical practices, media content, religious practices, and government policies as members of a culture engage in sometimes dramatic confrontations about their collective purpose and direction.

Culture Is Symbolic and Material

Through enculturation, over time the members of a culture develop a shared body of cultural knowledge and patterns of behavior. Though anthropologists no longer think of culture as a completely separate, unique possession of a specific group of people, most argue that a common cultural core exists, at least among the dominant segments of the culture. Norms, values, symbols, and mental maps of reality are four elements that an anthropologist may consider in attempting to understand the complex workings of a culture. These are not universal; they vary from culture to culture. Even within a culture not everyone shares equally in that cultural knowledge, nor does everyone agree completely on it. But the elements of a culture powerfully frame what its participants can say, what they can do, and even what they think is possible and impossible, real or unreal.

Norms Norms are ideas or rules about how people should behave in particular situations or toward certain other people—what is considered "normal" and appropriate behavior. Norms may include what to wear on certain occasions such as weddings, funerals, work, and school; what you can say in polite company; how younger people should treat older people; and who you can date or, as the opening anecdote demonstrated, who you can kiss. Many norms are assumed, not written down. We learn them over time—consciously and unconsciously—and incorporate them into our patterns of daily living. Other norms are formalized in writing and made publicly available, such as a country's laws, a system of medical or business ethics, or the code of academic integrity in your college or university. Norms may vary for segments of the population, imposing different expectations on men and women, for instance, or children and adults. Cultural norms may be widely accepted, but they also may be debated, challenged, and changed.

Consider the question of who you can marry. You may consider the decision to be a matter of personal choice, but in many cultures the decision is not left to the whims of young people. The results are too important. Often it is two families who arrange the marriage, not two individuals, although these patterns are under pressure from the globalization of Western cultural practices.

Cultures have clear norms, based on ideas of age, kinship, sexuality, race, religion, class, and legal status, that specify what is normal and what is not. Let's consider some extreme cases. In Nazi Germany, the Nuremburg Laws passed in 1935 banned marriage between whites and nonwhites, particularly Jews. From 1949 to 1985, South Africa's apartheid government, dominated by white lawmakers, declared marriage and sex between whites and "coloreds" (people of mixed race), Asians, and blacks to be a crime under the Prohibition of Mixed Marriages Act and the Immorality Act. In the history of the United States, as many as forty states passed antimiscegenation laws—that is, laws barring interracial marriage and sex. Such laws targeted marriages between whites and nonwhites—primarily blacks, but also Asians and Native Americans. Only in 1967 did the U.S. Supreme Court unanimously rule (in *Loving v. Virginia*) that these laws were unconstitutional, thereby striking down statutes still on the books in sixteen states (all the former slave states plus Oklahoma).

In this landmark legal case, Mildred and Richard Loving were arrested in their bedroom in 1958 for breaking Virginia's Racial Integrity Act, which barred interracial marriage. They had been married in Washington, D.C., earlier that year, but returned to live in their small hometown, Central Pointe, Virginia. In 1959 the couple pled guilty to the charge. The Virginia judge sentenced them to one year in prison, with the sentence suspended if they agreed to leave Virginia

norms: Ideas or rules about how people should behave in particular situations or toward certain other people.

for twenty-five years. Supported by the NAACP (National Association for the Advancement of Colored People) Legal Defense Fund, the Japanese American Citizens League, and a coalition of Catholic bishops, the Lovings won their appeal to the U.S. Supreme Court. The Court's ruling invalidated the remaining state antimiscegenation laws. Those defunct laws were formally removed by the states over the years—although notably in South Carolina only in 1998 (by 62 percent of the vote), and in Alabama only in 2000 (by 59 percent of the vote), showing a strong residue of resistance to interracial marriages.

Cultural norms may discourage *exogamy* (marriage outside one's "group") and encourage *endogamy* (marriage within one's "group"). Think about your own family. Who could you bring home to your parents? Could you cross boundaries of race, ethnicity, nationality, religion, class, or gender? Although U.S. culture has very few formal rules about who one can marry—with some exclusions around age, sexuality, and certain kinship relations—cultural norms still powerfully inform and enforce our behavior.

Most people, though not all, accept and follow a culture's norms. If they choose to challenge the norms, other members of the culture have means for enforcing its standards, whether through shunning, institutionalized punishment such as fines or imprisonment, or in more extreme cases, violence and threats of violence. Protestors in India certainly took steps to enforce perceived cultural norms about public sexuality and nationalism in the case of Richard Gere and Shilpa Shetty.

Values Cultures promote and cultivate a core set of **values**—fundamental beliefs about what is important, what makes a good life, and what is true, right, and beautiful. Values reflect shared ultimate standards that should guide people's

values: Fundamental beliefs about what is important, true, or beautiful, and what makes a good life.

behavior, as well as goals that people feel are important for themselves, their families, and their community. What would you identify as the core values of U.S. culture? Individualism? Independence? Care for the most vulnerable? Freedom of speech, press, and religion? Equal access to social mobility?

As with all elements of culture, cultural values are not fixed. They can be debated and contested. And they may have varying degrees of influence. For example, if you pick up a newspaper in any country you will find a deep debate about cultural values. Perhaps the debate focuses on modesty versus public displays of affection in India, economic growth versus environmental pollution in China, or land settlement versus peace in the Middle East. A hot global topic is the proper balance of security and privacy. Stand in line to board an airplane anywhere in the world, and you will experience the changing landscape in this debate. In the United States after the attacks of September 11, 2001, on the World Trade Center in New York and the Pentagon in Washington, D.C., the country has hotly debated these competing values. In 2002 and 2007, the U.S. Congress passed the USA PATRIOT Acts to reduce the danger of terrorism by easing restrictions on government eavesdropping on telephone calls and e-mails, surveillance of noncitizens, and indefinite detention of suspected terrorists. Civil rights groups have protested the unchecked invasion of privacy, warning that the legislation undermines the most highly valued aspects of our culture. This debate continues today.

Ultimately, values are not simply platitudes about people's ideals about the good life. Values are powerful cultural tools for clarifying cultural goals and motivating people to action. Values can be so potent that some people are willing to kill or die for them.

Symbols Cultures include complex systems of symbols and symbolic actions—in realms such as language, art, religion, politics, and economics—that convey meaning to other participants. In essence, a **symbol** is something that stands for something else. For example, language enables humans to communicate abstract ideas through symbols—written and spoken words, as well as unspoken sounds and gestures (see Chapter 4). People shake hands, wave, whistle, nod, smile, give two thumbs up, give thumbs down, give someone the middle finger. These symbols are not universal, but within their particular cultural context they convey certain meanings.

Much symbolic communication is nonverbal, action-based, and unconscious. Religions include powerful systems of symbols that represent deeper meanings to their adherents. Consider mandalas, the Koran, the Torah, the Christian cross, holy water, statues of the Buddha—all carry greater meanings and value than the physical material they are constructed of. National flags, which are mere pieces of colored cloth, are symbols that stir deep political emotions. Even

symbol: Anything that signifies something else.

money is simply a symbolic representation of value guaranteed by the sponsoring government. It has no value, except in its symbolism. Estimates suggest that only about 10 percent of money today exists in physical form. The rest moves electronically through banks, stock markets, and credit accounts (Graeber 2011).

Symbols change in meaning over time and from culture to culture. Not understanding another culture's collective understandings—sets of symbolic actions—can lead to embarrassing misunderstandings and cross-cultural miscues. As an undergraduate student in Beijing, I was approached on a public bus by a Chinese man who wanted to practice his English. Standing within a foot of me, he began to pepper me with questions. I backed away, uncomfortable with how close he was. He simply continued to move toward me, closing any gap I attempted to open and being clearly puzzled by my attempts to move away. From my cultural perspective, he was rudely invading "my space." From his perspective, he was moving into appropriate conversational distance and I was acting strangely by repeatedly backing up.

I was comforted later to find that studies reveal four spatial comfort zones specific to U.S. culture that differ from those in other cultures. For example, our *public zone* of 12 feet or more is the comfortable amount of space in a public forum between a speaker and an audience, such as a classroom or lecture hall. The *social zone* of 4 to 12 feet is appropriate for people who do not know each

FIGURE 2.4 How close is too close? Passengers crowd onto a long-distance bus in Chengdu in Southwest China's Sichuan province. Collective understandings about personal space vary across cultures.

other well but need to communicate directly, as in an interview or professional meeting. The *personal zone*, from 1.5 to 4 feet, is appropriate for casual friends sitting together or chatting. Finally, the *intimate zone*, from 1.5 feet to contact, you can imagine for yourself (Hall 1966). In some instances, we cannot maintain these distances and so adjust our behavior to compensate for awkwardness and discomfort. In a crowded elevator everyone stops talking, balances out the space between them, and stares at the moving floor number lights. On a crowded bus, train, or subway, people avoid eye contact, limit physical contact even with people inches away, and stop talking. Men look up at the ceiling when standing at urinals in crowded bathrooms. Our collective understandings of space are largely unconscious but very powerful. Compliance or noncompliance with these notions symbolically communicates significant information.

mental maps of reality: Cultural classifications of what kinds of people and things exist, and the assignment of meaning to those classifications.

Mental Maps of Reality Along with norms, values and symbols, another key component of culture is **mental maps of reality**. These are "maps" that humans construct of what kinds of people and what kinds of things exist. Because the world presents overwhelming quantities of data to our senses, our brains create shortcuts—maps—to navigate our experience and organize all the data that comes our way. A roadmap condenses a large world into a manageable format (one that you can hold in your hands or view on your portable GPS system) and helps us navigate the territory. Likewise, our mental maps organize the world into categories that help us sort out our experiences and what they mean. We do not want all the details all the time. We could not handle them anyway. From our general mental maps we can then dig deeper as required.

Our mental maps are shaped through enculturation, but they are not fixed. Like other elements of culture, they can be challenged and redrawn. Today globalization continues to put pressure on mental maps of reality as people on the planet are drawn into closer contact with the world's diversity. We will examine these transformations throughout this book, especially in chapters on language, race, ethnicity, gender, sexuality, and kinship.

Mental maps have two important functions. *First, mental maps classify reality*. Starting in the eighteenth century, European naturalists such as Carolus Linnaeus (1707–1778) began creating systems of classification for the natural world. These systems included five kingdoms subdivided into phylum, class, order, family, genus, and species. Through observation (this was before genetics), these naturalists sought to organize a logical framework to divide up the world into kinds of things and kinds of people. In a similar way, our cultures' mental maps seek to classify reality—though often a culture's mental maps are drawn from the distinct vantage point of those in power.

A culture creates a concept such as time. Then we arbitrarily divide it into millennia, centuries, decades, years, seasons, months, weeks, hours, morning, afternoon, evening, minutes, seconds. Categories of time are assumed to be scientific, universal, and "natural." But mostly they are cultural constructs. The current Gregorian calendar, which is used in much of the world, was introduced in 1582 by the Catholic Church, but its adoption occurred gradually; it was accepted in the United States two hundred years later in 1756, and in China in 1949. Until 1949 and still today, much of China relies on a lunar calendar in which months and days align with the waxing and waning of the moon. New Year's Day shifts each year. So do Chinese holidays and festivals. Even in the Gregorian calendar, the length of the year is modified to fit into a neat mental map of reality. A year (how long it takes Earth to orbit the sun) is approximately 365.2425 days long, so every four years the Gregorian calendar must add a day, creating a leap year of 366 days rather than 365.

Now check your watch. Even the question of what time it is depends on accepting a global system of time zones centered at the Greenwich meridian in England. But countries regularly modify the system according to their needs. The mainland United States has four time zones. China, approximately the same physical size, uses only one time zone. Russia has eleven. There is a time change of three and a half hours when you cross the border between China and Afghanistan. As these examples demonstrate, categories that seem completely fixed and "natural" are in reality flexible and variable, showing the potential role of culture in defining our fundamental notions of reality.

Mental maps of reality become problematic when people treat cultural notions of difference as being scientifically or biologically "natural." Race is a key example. As we will see in Chapter 6, the notion of race is assumed in popular culture and conversation to have a biological basis. There is, however, no scientific basis for this assumption. The particular racial categories in any given culture do not correlate directly to any biological differences. Although most people in the United States would name whites, blacks, Hispanics, Asians, and perhaps Native Americans as distinct races, no genetic line marks clear differences among these categories. The classifications are created by our culture and are specific to our culture. Other cultures draw different mental maps of the reality of human physical variation. The Japanese use different racial categories than the United States. Brazilians have more than five hundred racial classifications.

Second, mental maps assign meaning to what has been classified. Not only do people in a culture develop mental maps of things and people, but they also place values and meanings upon those maps. For example, we divide the life span into categories—infants, children, adolescents, teenagers, young adults, adults, and seniors, for example—but then we give different values to different ages. Some carry more respect, more protection, and more rights, privileges, and responsibilities. In the United States, these categories determine at what age you can marry, have sex, drink alcohol, drive, vote, go to war, stand trial, retire, or collect Social Security and Medicare benefits.

In considering the earlier discussion of time, we can see how these classifications gain value and meaning. U.S. culture puts a premium on time, discourages idle leisure, and encourages people to work hard and stay busy. "Time is money!" we often hear, and so it should not be wasted. Assuming that our mental maps of reality are natural can cause us to disregard the cultural values of others. For instance, we may see as lazy those whose cultures value a midday nap. This effect of our mental maps is important for anthropologists to understand (Wolf-Meyer 2012).

Ethnocentrism, Cultural Relativism, and Human Rights

Anthropology challenges the strong human tendency toward ethnocentrism, the belief that one's own culture or way of life is normal, natural, or even superior, and the tendency to use one's own culture to evaluate and judge the cultural ideas and practices of others. With intensifying globalization, the world's people are increasingly confronting the diversity of global cultures. Multicultural encounters happen closer and closer to home. Anthropology seeks to broaden our worldview, to enable people to see their own culture as one expression within the context of global cultural diversity, and to recognize that what may seem unusual or unnatural from one cultural perspective may be normal and commonplace from another.

For generations, anthropologists have adopted an approach to cross-cultural research known as **cultural relativism** to counteract the effects of ethnocentrism on our work. Cultural relativism calls for the suspension of

cultural relativism: Understanding a group's beliefs and practices within their own cultural context, without making judgments.

judgment while attempting to understand a group's beliefs and practices within their own cultural context. Anthropologists begin with the assumption that shared norms, values, beliefs, and practices make sense to the participants in a culture. The anthropologist's task is first to understand a culture's internal logic and system of meaning. Thus, anthropologists seek to objectively, accurately, and sensitively represent the diversity of human life and culture.

Anthropologists may at times struggle with situations in which the cultural practices they are studying do not match their own ideas of fairness and justice. The commitment to a research strategy of cultural relativism does not, however, require anthropologists to ignore their own sense of right and wrong, disregard international standards of human rights, or defend the cultural practices of a particular group. In fact, anthropologists frequently raise challenging questions on matters of human rights. Are there international human rights standards that should be available to all humans regardless of their particular culture or religion? What is a particular culture's ability to meet the basic human needs of its people, or of certain segments of a population that may be marginalized—needs for food, shelter, health, education, safety, and equal treatment under the law?

The American Anthropological Association's (AAA) Declaration on Anthropology and Human Rights draws heavily on international principles as articulated in three United Nations documents: the Universal Declaration of Human Rights, the International Covenant on Civil and Political Rights, and the International Covenant on Social, Economic, and Cultural Rights. Reflecting a commitment to cross-cultural research, the AAA's statement also warns against an overreliance on the abstract legal uniformity of Western traditions. Ultimately, each anthropologist must choose how to apply international standards of human rights to cultural practices considered in his or her research.

As our opening story illustrated, the study of culture can be extremely complicated. Richard Gere's kiss of Shilpa Shetty was a symbolic act that communicated certain information to people across India—most likely, information that Gere, as a foreigner, had not intended. The kiss and its interpretation represent one prominent concept of culture as a system of meaning: a shared set of ideas, norms, and values learned over time and embodied in objects and behavior that become symbolic—something that stands for or means something else. Gere's kiss also sparked an intense debate over cultural ideas and patterns of behavior, including ideas about sexuality, religion, nationalism, and even globalization. This reaction reveals that culture is also an arena where relationships of power among people are worked out and worked on. To fully grasp the anthropological understanding of culture, we will examine the historical development of the culture concept before turning our attention to more recent notions of culture as a system of meaning and as a system of power.

How Has the Culture Concept Developed in Anthropology?

The concept of culture has been central to anthropology ever since the English anthropologist Edward Burnett Tylor (1832–1917) crafted his definition in the opening paragraph of his book *Primitive Culture* in 1871: "Culture or Civilization, taken in its wide ethnographic sense, is that complex whole which includes knowledge, belief, art, morals, law, custom and any other capabilities and habits acquired by man as a member of society."

Tylor understood culture to be a unified and complex system of ideas and behavior learned over time, passed down from generation to generation, and shared by members of a particular group. Over the past century and a half, culture has become more than a definition; it is a key theoretical framework for anthropologists attempting to understand humans and their interactions.

Early Evolutionary Frameworks

Edward Burnett Tylor and James Frazer (1854–1941) of England and Lewis Henry Morgan (1818–1881) of the United States were among the leading early anthropologists. They sought to organize the vast quantities of data about the diversity of cultures worldwide that were being accumulated through colonial and missionary enterprises during the nineteenth century. These anthropologists were influenced by Charles Darwin's theory of biological evolution, which maintains that the diversity of biological species resulted from gradual change over time in response to environmental pressures. Thus they suggested that the vast diversity of cultures represented different stages in the evolution of human culture.

The early anthropologists suggested that all cultures would naturally evolve through the same sequence of stages, a concept known as **unilineal cultural evolution**. They set about plotting the world's cultures along a continuum from most simple to most complex, using the terms *savage—barbarian—civilized*. Western cultures were, perhaps too predictably, considered the most evolved or civilized. By arranging all of the world cultures along this continuum, the early anthropologists believed that they could trace the path of human cultural evolution, understand where some cultures had come from, and predict where other cultures were headed.

Succeeding generations of anthropologists rejected unilineal cultural evolution as being too Eurocentric, too hierarchical, and lacking adequate data to support its grand claims. Franz Boas, the founder of American anthropology, and Bronislaw Malinowski, a Polish anthropologist who spent most of his life in teaching in England, represent two main schools of anthropology that moved beyond the evolutionary framework for viewing cultural differences.

FIGURE 2.6 British anthropologist Edward Burnett Tylor.

unilineal cultural evolution: The theory proposed by nineteenth-century anthropologists that all cultures naturally evolve through the same sequence of stages from simple to complex.

American Historical Particularism

Franz Boas (1858–1942) conducted fieldwork among the Kwakiutl indigenous people of the Pacific Northwest of the United States and Canada before becoming a professor of anthropology at Columbia University in New York and a curator of the American Museum of Natural History. Boas rejected unilineal cultural evolution, its generalizations, and its comparative method. Instead he advocated for an approach called **historical particularism**. He claimed that cultures arise from different causes, not uniform processes. According to Boas, anthropologists could not rely on an evolutionary formula to explain differences among cultures but must study the particular history of each culture to see how it developed. Evolutionists such as Tylor, Frazer, and Morgan argued that similarities among cultures emerged through independent invention as different cultures independently arrived at similar solutions to similar problems. Boas, in contrast, while not ruling out some independent invention, turned to the idea of *diffusion*—the borrowing of cultural traits and patterns from other cultures—to explain apparent similarities.

historical particularism: The idea, attributed to Franz Boas, that cultures develop in specific ways because of their unique histories.

Boas's belief in the powerful role of culture in shaping human life exhibited itself in his early twentieth-century studies of immigrants. His research with the children of immigrants from Europe revealed the remarkable effects of culture and environment on their physical forms, challenging the role of biology as a tool for discrimination. As a Jewish immigrant himself, Boas was particularly sensitive to the dangers of racial stereotyping, and his work throughout his career served to challenge white supremacy, the inferior ranking of non-European people, and other expressions of racism.

Boas's students Ruth Benedict (1887–1948) and Margaret Mead (1901–1979) continued his emphasis on the powerful role of culture in shaping human life and the need to explore the unique development of each culture. Benedict's popular studies, *Patterns of Culture* (1934) and *The Chrysanthemum and the Sword* (1946), explored the ways in which cultural traits and entire cultures are uniquely patterned and integrated. Mead conducted research in Samoa, Bali, and Papua New Guinea and became perhaps the most famous anthropologist of the twentieth century, promoting her findings and the unique tools of anthropology to the general American public.

Mead turned her attention particularly to enculturation and its powerful effects on cultural patterns and personality types. In her book *Coming of Age in Samoa* (1928), she explored the seeming sexual freedom and experimentation of young Samoan women and compared it with the repressed sexuality of young women in the United States, suggesting the powerful role of enculturation in shaping behavior—even behavior that is imagined to have powerful biological origins. Mead's controversial research and findings over her career challenged biological assumptions about women and contributed to heated debates about the role of women in U.S. culture in the twentieth century.

FIGURE 2.7 American anthropologist Ruth Benedict.

British Structural Functionalism

Between the 1920s and 1960s, in a rejection of unilineal cultural evolution, many British social anthropologists viewed anthropology more as a science and field-work more as a science experiment that could focus on the specific details of a local society. These anthropologists viewed human societies as living organisms, and through fieldwork they sought to analyze each part of the "body." Each part of society—including the kinship, religious, political, and economic structures—fit together and had its unique function within the larger structure. Like a living organism, a society worked to maintain an internal balance, or equilibrium, that kept the system working. Under this conceptual framework, called **structural functionalism**, British social anthropologists employed a synchronic approach to control their science experiments—analyzing contemporary societies at a fixed point in time without regard to historical context. By isolating as many variables as possible, especially by excluding history and outside influences such as neighboring groups or larger national or global dynamics, these anthropologists sought to focus narrowly on the culture at hand.

Early practitioners of this approach included Bronislaw Malinowski (1884–1942), who employed an early form of functionalism in his ethnography of the Trobriand Islands, *Argonauts of the Western Pacific* (1922), discussed in more detail in Chapter 3; and E. E. Evans-Pritchard (1902–1973) in his classic ethnography of the Sudan, *The Nuer* (1940), which we will consider further in Chapters 3 and 10. Later, British anthropologists, including Max Gluckman (1911–1975), in his work on rituals of rebellion, and Victor Turner (1920–1983), in his work on religious symbols and rituals, critiqued earlier structural functionalists for ignoring the dynamics of conflict, tension, and change within the cultures they studied. Their intervention marked a significant turn in the study of culture by British anthropologists.

Culture and Meaning

One predominant view within anthropology in recent decades sees culture primarily as a set of ideas or knowledge shared by a group of people that provides a common body of information about how to behave, why to behave that way, and what that behavior means. The anthropologist Clifford Geertz (1926–2006), a key figure in this **interpretivist approach**, urged anthropologists to explore culture primarily as a symbolic system in which even simple, seemingly straightforward actions can convey deep meanings.

In a classic example, Geertz examines the difference between a wink and a twitch of the eye. Both involve the same movement of the eye muscles, but the wink carries a meaning, which can change depending on the context in which it occurs. A wink can imply flirting, including a friend in a secret, or slyly signaling agreement. Deciphering the meaning requires a complex, collective

structural functionalism: A conceptual framework positing that each element of society serves a particular function to keep the entire system in equilibrium.

MAP 2.1
Trobriand Islands

interpretivist approach: A conceptual framework that sees culture primarily as a symbolic system of deep meaning.

(shared) understanding of unspoken communication in a specific cultural context. Collective understandings of symbols and symbolic actions enable people to interact with one another in subtle yet complex ways without constantly stopping to explain themselves.

Geertz's essay "Deep Play: Notes on a Balinese Cockfight" (1973) describes in intricate detail a cockfight—a common activity even today in local communities across Bali, a small island in the South Pacific. Geertz describes the elaborate breeding, raising, and training of the roosters; the scene of bedlam at the fight; the careful selection of the birds; the rituals of the knife man, who provides the razors for the birds' feet; the fight itself; the raucous betting before and during the fight; and the aftermath, with the cutting up of the losing cock and the dividing of its parts among participants in the fight.

Geertz argues that such careful description of cultural activity is an essential part of understanding Balinese culture. But it is not enough. He claims that we must look beneath the surface activities to see the layers of deep cultural meaning in which those activities are embedded. The cockfight is not simply a cockfight. It also represents generations of competition among the village families for prestige, power, and resources within the community. It symbolizes the negotiation of those families' prestige status and standing within the larger groups. For Geertz, all activities of the cockfight reflect these deeper webs of meaning, and their analysis requires extensive description that uncovers those deeper meanings. Indeed, according to Geertz, every cultural action is more than the action itself; it is also a symbol of deeper meaning. (Even a simple kiss, as Richard Gere found out, carries a deeper cultural meaning.)

FIGURE 2.8 Preparations for a cockfight outside a Hindu temple in Bali. How do you analyze the deep webs of meaning of play in any cultural event?

MAP 2.2
Bali

How Are Culture and Power Related?

Anthropologists have often separated culture from power. The field has focused primarily on culture as a system of ideas, as represented in the section you have just read. But more recent scholarship has pushed anthropology to consider the deep interconnections between culture and power (Gramsci 1971; Foucault 1977; Wolf 1982), and the chapters of this book take this challenge seriously.

Power is often described as the ability or potential to bring about change through action or influence, either one's own or that of a group or institution. This may include the ability to influence through force or the threat of force. Power is embedded in many kinds of social relations, from interpersonal relations, to institutions, to structural frameworks of whole societies. Throughout this book we will work to unmask the dynamics of power embedded in culture, including systems of power such as race and racism, ethnicity and nationalism, gender, human sexuality, economics, and family.

The anthropologist Eric Wolf (1923–1999) urged anthropologists to see power as an aspect of all human relationships. Consider the relationships in your own life: teacher/student, parent/child, employer/employee, landlord/tenant, lender/borrower, boyfriend/girlfriend. Wolf (1990; 1999) argued that all such human relationships have a power dynamic. Though cultures are often assumed to be composed of groups of similar people who uniformly share norms and values, in reality people in a given culture are usually diverse and their relationships are complicated.

Power in a culture reflects **stratification**—uneven distribution of resources and privileges—among participants. Some people are drawn into the center of the culture. Others are ignored, marginalized, or even annihilated. Power may be stratified along lines of gender, racial or ethnic group, class, age, family, religion, sexuality, or legal status. These structures of power organize relationships among people and create a framework through which access to cultural resources is distributed. As a result, some people are able to participate more fully in the culture than others. This balance of power is not fixed; it fluctuates over time. By examining the way access to the resources, privileges, and opportunities of a culture are shared unevenly and unequally, we can begin to use culture as a conceptual guide to power and its workings.

Power and Cultural Institutions

One key to understanding the relationship between culture and power is to recognize that a culture is more than a set of ideas or patterns of behavior shared among a collection of individuals. A culture also includes the powerful institutions that these people create to promote and maintain their core

power: The ability or potential to bring about change through action or influence.

stratification: The uneven distribution of resources and privileges among participants in a group or culture.

FIGURE 2.9 A young Muslim woman with two French flags pulled over her head-covering marches in Paris against a French ban on religious symbols, including head-coverings, in public schools.

values. Ethnographic research must consider a wide range of institutions that play central roles in the enculturation process. For example, schools teach a shared history, language, patterns of social interaction, notions of health, and scientific ideas of what exists in the world and how the world works. Religious institutions promote moral and ethical codes of behavior. The various media convey images of what is considered normal, natural, and valued. Other prominent cultural institutions that reflect and shape core norms and values include the family, medicine, government, courts, police, and the military.

These cultural institutions are also locations where people can debate and contest cultural norms and values. In 2003, an intense debate erupted in France about Muslim girls wearing headscarves to public schools. Although few girls actually wore headscarves, the controversy took on particular intensity in the aftermath of the events of September 11, 2001, the invasions of Afghanistan and Iraq, and terrorist incidents in Europe. For many people in France, the wearing of head coverings represented a grave danger to French society, particularly its commitment to equality for women, its history of ethnic assimilation, and its tradition of the separation of church and state. Passage of a law banning the headscarf from public schools was intended as a signal (to people both inside and outside France) of the country's commitment to these principles.

Despite legal challenges, strikes by students, and street demonstrations in opposition to the law, in 2004 the French government banned any clothing in public schools that indicates particular religious beliefs. Although the language of the law was broadly stated to include all religions, everyone understood that the headscarves of Muslim girls were the target. France's public schools had become the venue for debating, contesting, and enforcing key French cultural norms and values (Bowen 2006). As we will see, cultural institutions such as schools are not only places where norms are enforced, but also places where powerful ideas of what is normal and natural are shaped.

Hegemony

The Italian political philosopher Antonio Gramsci (1891–1937) described two aspects of power. Material power, the first component, includes political, economic, or military power. It exerts itself through coercion or brute force. The second aspect of power involves the ability to create consent and agreement within a population, a condition that Gramsci called **hegemony** (1971).

Gramsci recognized the tremendous power of culture—particularly the cultural institutions of media, schools, and religion—to shape, often unconsciously, what people think is normal, natural, and possible, and thereby directly influence the scope of human action and interaction. Cultures, which develop slowly over time, include a shared belief system of what is right and what is wrong, and what is normal and appropriate. In this hegemony of ideas, some thoughts and actions become unthinkable, and group members develop a set of "beliefs" about what is normal and appropriate that come to be seen as natural "truths." The French sociologist Michel Foucault (1926–1984), in *Discipline and Punish* (1977), described this hegemonic aspect of power as the ability to make people discipline their own behavior so that they believe and act in certain "normal" ways—often against their own interests, even without a tangible threat of punishment for misbehavior.

Jean and John Comaroff describe the workings of hegemony in their study of colonialism in South Africa, particularly in the interaction between indigenous Tswana-speaking people and British missionaries from 1820 to

FIGURE 2.10 Presbyterians at their main rural mission station in Tembuland, South Africa.

1920. Whereas British colonialists used force to establish military and economic control over South Africa, British missionaries sought to convert Africans to Christianity by convincing them of the supremacy of an alternative set of worldviews. Missionary churches and schools introduced Christian ideas embedded in European images and messages about numerous cultural practices, including education, language, notions of ritual, rainmaking, time, clothing, and architecture, as well as relationships of gender, kinship, and property. The Comaroffs show how, instead of through military conquest, missionaries attempted to change these indigenous people by redefining how they thought about their everyday lives. Though the Tswana often contested the missionaries' worldviews, this new hegemony gradually influenced fundamental notions of what was normal, thinkable, doable, and sayable in South Africa for generations that followed (Comaroff and Comaroff 1991).

MAP 2.3
South Africa

Earlier in this chapter we discussed antimiscegenation laws in the history of the United States. These laws drew upon cultural beliefs in "natural" biological differences among races and the seemingly unnatural, deviant practice of intermarriage. Despite the elimination of these formal laws, a certain hegemony of thought remains: many in U.S. culture still see interracial marriage as unthinkable and undoable. As evidence, consider current intermarriage rates in the United States (Figure 2.11). According to the U.S. Census Bureau (2010), there were 60 million married people in the United States in 2010. Of these, there were only 2,005,000 (3.32 percent) white–Hispanic marriages; 748,000 (1.24 percent) white–Asian marriages; 504,000 (0.83 percent) black–white marriages; 129,000 (0.21 percent) black–Hispanic marriages; and 48,000 (0.08 percent) black–Asian marriages. The 2010 Census also allowed people, for the first time,

FIGURE 2.11 U.S. Interracial Marriage Patterns, 2010

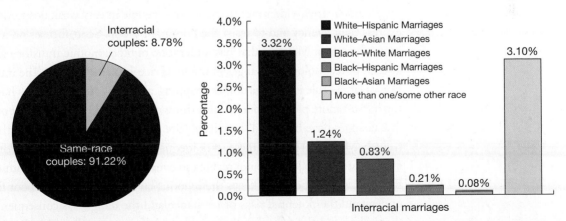

SOURCE: *U.S. Census Bureau. 2010. America's Families and Living Arrangements: 2010, Table FG3. www.census.gov/hhes/families/files/cps2010/tabFG4-all.xls.*

to mark more than one race or ethnicity. There were 1,869,000 (3.10 percent) interracial marriages in which at least one of the respondents had marked more than one race or the "Some other race" category. (The total number of mixed marriages, 5,303,000, represents 8.78 percent of the entire 60 million.)

Clearly, although U.S. culture has very few formal rules about whom one can marry, cultural norms still powerfully inform and enforce our behavior. As this example shows, views against interracial marriage do not require legal sanction to remain dominant, hegemonic norms.

Human Agency

Although hegemony can be very powerful, it does not completely dominate people's thinking. Individuals and groups have the power to contest cultural norms, values, mental maps of reality, symbols, institutions, and structures of power—a potential known as **agency**. Cultural beliefs and practices are not timeless; they change and can be changed. Cultures are not biologically determined; they are created over time by particular groups of people. By examining human agency, we see how culture serves as a realm in which battles over power take place—where people debate, negotiate, contest, and enforce what is considered normal, what people can say, do, and even think.

Although a dominant group may have greater access to power, resources, rights, or privileges, the systems of power they create are never absolute, and their dominance is never complete. Individuals and groups with less power or no power may contest the dominant power relationships and structures, whether through political, economic, religious, or military means. At times these forms of resistance are visible, public, and well organized, including negotiations, protests, strikes, or rebellions. At other times the resistance may be more subtle, discreet, and diffuse.

For example, James Scott's book *Weapons of the Weak: Everyday Forms of Peasant Resistance* (1986) identifies strategies that people in very weak positions use to express their agency and to resist the dominant group. Scott focuses on a village in northwestern Malaysia that has undergone rapid economic transformation as a result of technological changes in the local rice-growing process. The introduction of large-scale irrigation, double cropping, and harvesting machines has made the harvest more plentiful but has also thrown many landless farmers out of work. The changes have benefited the village elite (mostly Chinese) and hurt the poor (mostly Malay). In light of these stark inequalities, Scott asks why the poor farmers who are the majority do not revolt and overturn the social and economic order that makes them poor and keeps them poor. Scott suggests that the poor farmers understand the potential risks of resistance and the dangerous consequences for themselves and their families that could result from a conflict with the rich and powerful minority. So they often avoid obvious, public displays of resistance and

agency: The potential power of individuals and groups to contest cultural norms, values, symbols, mental maps of reality, institutions, and structures of power.

FIGURE 2.12 Resistance to unfair conditions takes many forms. *Top,* Egyptian protestors in Tahrir Square, Cairo, demonstrate against their government. *Bottom,* Malaysian farmers conduct a slowdown to protest working conditions.

choose subtler, nonconfrontational forms of resistance, including foot-dragging, slowdowns, theft, sabotage, trickery, arson, and false compliance with regulations.

Some scholars question whether these are really forms of resistance because they are not aimed at, and do not necessarily achieve, change. But Scott argues that not all resistance is revolutionary and that many acts of everyday resistance can bring change over time. Through these processes of contestation, the norms and values, mental maps of reality, symbols, organizations, and institutions that appear to be timeless and accepted are actually undergoing constant change and renegotiation as people express their human agency even in the face of overwhelming displays of power.

Jena High School: Connecting Meaning and Power

In the central courtyard of Jena High School in Jena, Louisiana, stood a "white tree" where the white students liked to gather during breaks. At a school assembly in September 2006, Kenneth Purvis, a black student, asked the principal if he could sit under the tree and was told that he could sit wherever he wanted. The next day, Purvis and a cousin went to stand under the tree. The following morning, three nooses were found swinging from the tree.

Three white students, members of the rodeo team, were identified as the perpetrators. The principal recommended their expulsion, but the superintendent and the mostly white school board imposed three days of in-school suspension instead. "Adolescents play pranks," the superintendent told the *Chicago Tribune*. "I don't think it was a threat against anyone."

Was this really a harmless, meaningless prank? Why were the nooses hung in *that* tree at *that* time? Having thought about the cultural intersection of meaning and power in this chapter, how do we begin to understand these events from an anthropological perspective?

To someone from another culture, perhaps a noose is simply a piece of rope twisted and threaded into an elaborate knot. But to those who know U.S. cultural history, this manipulated rope holds deep meaning and expresses stark relationships of power. Historically, nooses are closely associated in U.S. culture with the practice of whites lynching blacks that began after the Civil War. Nooses and lynchings were intended to terrorize. They signaled to the

FIGURE 2.13 Marchers gather in Jena, Louisiana, to protest the treatment of black teenagers in the aftermath of a fight sparked by several nooses being hung from a tree in the courtyard of Jena High School.

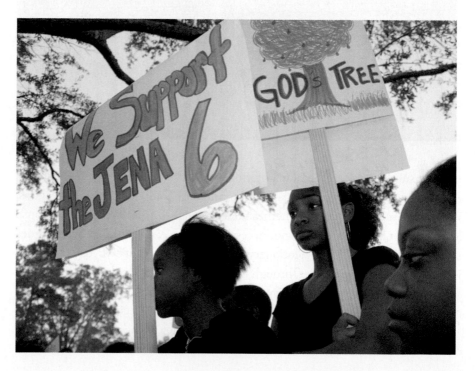

African American population that although they may have won certain legal rights and protections, they should not consider themselves safe: not everyone in the society would obey the law, and some would take violent action outside the law to enforce the cultural norms that they considered appropriate. Although lynchings ended in the United States by the 1940s, the image of the noose is deeply embedded in the culture and its symbolism remains chillingly clear. In this historical context, perhaps we can begin to see that the hanging of three nooses from a tree in the Jena school courtyard was not a random act but one that employed the deep symbolic meaning of the twisted and knotted rope to send a message about what some students thought were the proper relations of power in their school and community. As we consider the intersection of symbols and power in culture, and in this case in a key cultural institution—a school—from an anthropological perspective, how do we understand the role of the actors in the incident, including the students, principal, school board, superintendent, and community?

How Much of Who You Are Is Determined by Biology and How Much by Culture?

Biology is important. We live in our bodies, after all. We feel, smell, taste, hear, and see the world around us through our bodies. We communicate with and through our bodies. And, yes, we have certain biological drives that are essential for survival. All humans must eat, drink, and sleep. But no matter how strong our biological needs or our hormones, odors, and appetites might be, culture exerts an overwhelming influence on what we think, on how we behave, and even on the shape and functions of our bodies.

Biological Needs versus Cultural Patterns

Although popular discourse often assigns biology the primary role in determining who we are and establishing the framework of culture, anthropological research consistently reveals the powerful role culture plays in shaping our lives. Human genetic codes are 99.9 percent identical, so if behavior were entirely biologically driven, we should expect to find very similar behavioral responses to biological influences. Instead, we find remarkable variety across cultures. Even the most basic human activities, such as eating, drinking, sleeping, and defecating, are carried out in remarkably distinct ways. All humans must do these things. But shared biological needs do not ensure shared cultural patterns.

Of course, food and liquid enter the body through the mouth and get digested in the stomach and intestines. But what goes in and how it goes in are other stories. Perhaps you find dog or snake or pony to be inedible, although these are delicacies in other cultures. Many Chinese dislike cheese, a staple of North American and European diets. Even how and where you eat and drink, or how many times a day, varies from culture to culture. You may use forks, knives, spoons, chopsticks, or hands. You may eat once a day, three times a day, or—like many Americans—six times a day (breakfast, "coffee break," lunch, afternoon snack, dinner, midnight snack).

Everyone sleeps each day, but some people sleep six hours a night, others eight. Americans nap, Argentinians take a siesta, and Chinese *xiu-xi*. Many college students average six hours of sleep a night during the week and ten on the weekend. Who you sleep with also varies by culture, with variations including husbands and wives, parents and children, siblings, mothers and children, grandparents and grandchildren. All these patterns vary by culture, and even within a culture they may vary by age, gender, and class.

What about defecation? Surely this is simple enough that we all do it in the same way. But in China, men and women squat to defecate. In North America, they sit on toilets and use toilet paper. In India, instead of toilet paper, many people use water from a brass bowl applied by splashing with their left hand. In cities, this may take place in a bathroom; in rural areas, it takes place in the fields or on the beach.

Nature versus Nurture

Many popular debates claim that basic patterns of human behavior, intellectual capacity, and psychological tendencies are determined by biology. In a speech in the fall of 2005, economist Lawrence Summers, then president of Harvard University, wondered aloud whether one of the reasons his school and others like it had more men than women on the science and math faculties related to different biological endowments—that men's brains were better suited for success in these areas. Summers's comments plunged him into the middle of an intense worldwide debate about what determines humans' fundamental character—our biology or our culture, our nature or our nurture (Pollitt 2005). Whether the debate involves issues of gender difference, racial categories, ethnic divisions, or sexuality, impassioned and often uninformed opinions find voice on all sides.

Assessing Evolutionary Perspectives Evolutionary psychologists believe that fundamental aspects of who we are, how we think and behave, and how we organize our societies are directly related to how we evolved over millions of years and are hardwired in our DNA. They argue that (1) patterns of survival, which developed when humans were primarily hunters and gatherers, selected for different physical and mental abilities among men and women, and (2) these patterns continue to evidence themselves in patterns of life today and in fact drive much of human behavior (Pinker 2002). So, the argument goes, as hunters, men developed better spatial skills and higher levels of aggression. Women, the gatherers, stayed closer to home and became more nurturing and empathetic.

Today, popular psychology commonly suggests that the problems men have with women (and vice versa) can be traced to these evolutionary differences. One popular relationship self-help book even suggests that *Men Are from Mars and Women Are from Venus* (Gray 2004). The title implies that men and women are so fundamentally different that they might as well be different species from different planets.

This belief in the biological and evolutionary basis for human behavior and cultural ideas is inadequate in a number of key areas. Anthropological studies of hunter-gatherer societies have shown that the division of roles imagined by evolutionary psychologists was never so distinct (Fedigan 1986; Stange 1997). Men also gathered, women also hunted, and there were many other shared social tasks as well. Although contemporary genetic discoveries are opening new realms of understanding about human biology, we are not close to linking certain genes or groups of genes with particular behaviors. At best, we can imagine these connections based on perceived patterns of behavior.

FIGURE 2.14 Would you agree that *Men Are from Mars, Women Are from Venus*—as if from two different planets? How much of who we are as individuals has been shaped by the process of human evolution, and how much is shaped by the culture we grow up in?

Connecting Culture and Behavior We do have, however, much clearer indications of the ways cultural patterns and beliefs shape human behavior. In the debate over the origins of gender inequality in the upper echelons of math and science careers, we might look instead to gender stereotyping in the classroom, enculturation of girls, and conscious and unconscious gender bias in hiring and promotion practices. It may feel more comfortable to trace inequality to innate biological differences; a link might enable us to dismiss or excuse the inequality as "natural." But there is no biological evidence of this link. The current evidence is that these patterns of inequality and stratification are culturally constructed and completely changeable (Hopkins 1999; Pollitt 2005).

Culture is learned from the people around us. It is not written into our DNA. Instead, we are born with the ability to learn any culture that we might be born into or move into. We have the ability to learn any language and master any set of beliefs, practices, norms, or values. This may seem obvious, but it is a crucial principle to understand as we examine the many cultural patterns in our own experience that we regard as normal, even natural. Such cultural practices are not universal to all humans. Rather, they are uniquely created in each culture. Recognition of this fact allows us to consider how learned patterns of belief and practice have been created and how they might be changed.

Questioning the Biological Basis of Behavior Anthropologists' comparisons of diverse cultures allow us to question the biological basis for most if not all of human behavior. As you saw in the opening anecdote about the kiss, what may seem natural, biological, or universal is actually deeply embedded in the particular

William Ury

Anthropologist William Ury specializes as a mediator and negotiation advisor in conflicts from workplace disputes to labor strikes to ethnic wars in the Middle East, the Balkans, and the former Soviet Union. More recently he has been involved in helping to end a civil war in Indonesia and helping to prevent one in Venezuela. An author of numerous books, including *Getting to Yes* (Fisher, Ury, and Patton 2012) and *The Power of a Positive No* (Ury 2007), Ury was the co-founder of Harvard University's Program on Negotiation and is currently a Distinguished Senior Fellow of the Harvard Negotiation Project.

In his work of conflict resolution, Ury sees a deep connection between anthropology and mediation and negotiation. "At the heart of anthropology is the ability to put yourself in the shoes of someone whose culture on the surface seems quite different from your own. That is the essential competence of mediation as well. Mediators need the ability to put themselves in the shoes of both parties, or all parties, to try to understand how they see the world and what their interests and needs are. We need to try to understand "the other" from within their frame of reference, and then try to understand the rules of the game as they see them."

Central to Ury's conflict-resolution strategy is the concept of the third side. Although many conflicts involve two opposing sides, Ury works to resolve conflicts by mobilizing the surrounding community—the third side—around the conflict. The third side plays a constructive role in the negotiations by reminding the arguing parties what is really at stake, thus helping to restore a sense of perspective to an often emotionally charged situation.

"Yes, we're capable of violence. We're also capable of cooperating and resolving our differences. Each of us has the ability to exert peer pressure and use the power of community to prevent conflicts, to resolve conflicts that arise, and to contain those conflicts that might escalate.

"That to me is the essential challenge today in this world: How do we mobilize a third side powerful enough to become a container for the conflicts that exist in today's world? How do we transform those conflicts from destructive forms such as violence to constructive forms such as cooperation? But the third side is not new. It is actually an articulation of patterns that humans have developed over our evolutionary trajectory to survive, function, and thrive—patterns that our cultures have forgotten or moved away from. We're having to rediscover the third side. That's what's interesting. We're having to reinvent what is actually our most ancient of human heritages for dealing with conflict. The challenge

Anthropologist William Ury

before us is to translate the third side into forms that work in today's system.

"I've had the privilege over the last thirty-five years of having a front-seat view of a revolution taking place around the planet—a revolution in the way that human beings make decisions. I think of it as the negotiation revolution. A generation or two ago, the principal method for making decisions in most areas in life was pretty much top-down. The people on the top of the pyramid gave the orders, and the people on the bottom followed them. But there's been a process, a trend, that goes back several centuries in some cases, but is most evident in the past thirty years, toward a flattening of those pyramids of power into organizational forms that resemble networks. As this happens, decision-making changes gradually from vertical to horizontal, from top-down orders to joint problem-solving. Today, in order to get something done, we are more and more reliant on people over whom we exercise no direct control. This is increasingly true in politics in democracies, in work, and at home. So, effectively, what we're doing is negotiating all the time—restoring negotiation as one of the preeminent forms of making decisions. And because there's often no clear authority that enforces what to do, it means we need to turn to the third side, with the use of mediation and community councils, for example, to help resolve issues that can't be resolved by both sides alone.

"Amazingly, this heritage comes from our hunter-gatherer ancestors. Hunting and gathering was the dominant form of human subsistence for ninety-nine percent of our history. Today this way of life is disappearing from the face of the planet. I find it fascinating that we are experiencing at just this time a phenomenon I like to think of as 'the great recurrence.' There's a way in which many of the older patterns and organizational forms, particularly of cooperation, are reemerging in a new way. Acknowledging the huge difference in conditions today, there are some striking similarities between the world we are now entering and the world that our hunter-gatherer ancestors faced. Today you see humans roaming around the globe again, increasingly nomadic, and also being dependent upon resources that aren't concentrated as land and crops are. Today our principal resource appears to be information, which is also scattered and requires a lot of cooperation to produce. The basic organizational form that increasingly seems to work in today's information society is more horizontal and less hierarchical. In this time of horizontal relationships, we need to reinvent the third side, which is our oldest human heritage for transforming conflict."

In thinking about the significance of anthropology, Ury offers this insight: "In a macro sense, right now we are living in an era in which, for the first time in the human story, thanks to the communications revolution, thanks to the Internet, thanks to other processes of globalization, all the human tribes on the planet are in touch with each other. Thousands of language groups—call them tribes if you like—are all in touch. Future anthropologists may look back one day and call it the era of the 'human family reunion.' Like many family reunions, this one is not all peace and light. There are a lot of injustices and resentments. So the question is: How are we going to get along? How are we going to understand each other? Anthropology is a key discipline to understand what's going on at this macro level.

"Then at a micro level, because the classroom is becoming more and more multicultural, students are going to see evidence of the human family reunion right there in the classroom. How do you understand 'the other'? How do you understand other cultures, other ways of seeing the world? This ability to understand the other is actually critical to success at work, whether you work in the nonprofit sector, in business, or in government. It's the essential perspective you need to be able to negotiate for what you want and need, because you're likely going to be dealing with people who come from very different backgrounds. The ability to understand others and to negotiate in this diverse world depends crucially on the basic competencies that you learn in anthropology."

culture around us. Consider the smile. Evidence suggests that most people worldwide agree on the meaning of certain facial expressions. But even a smile can be complicated to interpret when combined with certain subtle physical or facial gestures—especially for people not born into that culture. Although there may be general agreement about the core role of the smile, its complex meanings are not fixed in the body or brain. Instead, culture gives meaning to the biology of the smile (Lancaster 2003). Later in this book, in the chapters on race, ethnicity, gender, family, and human sexuality, we will explore the nature versus nurture debates in further detail.

It is impossible to separate human nature from human culture. As popular as it may be to think that nature has driven our development as humans, even our long evolutionary process has been deeply influenced by culture. Ultimately, it is culture that has made us human, enabling us to evolve physically and in our patterns of relationship with others. When we examine our human origins in Chapter 5, we will begin to see, for example, that with the development of simple stone tools as early as 2.5 million years ago, culture allowed our ancestors to adapt to the world around them. Stone tools (in particular, hand axes and choppers) enabled our ancestors to butcher meat more quickly and efficiently, thereby providing higher quantities of protein for the developing brain and influencing the direction of our physical adaptation. In cases such as these, the power of culture to direct and modify biological instincts is indisputable. Over time, cultural adaptations—from the control of fire, to the development of language, to the invention of condoms and birth control pills—have replaced genetic adaptations as the primary way humans adapt to and manipulate their physical and social environments.

How Is Culture Created?

Culture does not emerge out of the blue. It is created over time, shaped by people and the institutions they establish. Culture is not fixed. It is changed, contested, and negotiated. Just as we have examined the relationship between culture and power, we can analyze the processes through which culture is created by considering the creation of a consumer culture as part of twentieth-century capitalism.

Culture and economics are closely linked. The German political philosopher Max Weber (1864–1920), in his book *The Protestant Ethic and the Spirit of Capitalism* (1905), linked the emergence of capitalism in Europe directly to the cultural ideas of Protestant Christianity that developed in the seventeenth century. Weber suggests that although the material conditions for the emergence of capitalism were present in other cultures, those cultures lacked the necessary values to allow capitalism to take hold. In contrast, thrift, modesty, moderation, frugality, and self-denial—what Weber called the "Protestant ethic"—formed the core culture of Western civilization and enabled early capitalism to flourish.

As capitalism has grown and shifted over the centuries into its present global form, so has the culture that supports and shapes it.

Manufacturing the Desire to Consume

Twentieth- and early twenty-first-century global capitalism is deeply tied to a culture of consumerism that has emerged with the support and promotion of corporations, governments, and financial institutions. The culture of consumerism includes norms, values, beliefs, practices, and institutions that have become commonplace and accepted as normal, and that cultivate the desire to acquire consumer goods to enhance one's lifestyle (McCracken 1991; 2005).

Advertising, marketing, and financial services industries work to transform the cultural values of frugality, modesty, and self-denial of the old Protestant ethic into patterns of spending and consumption associated with acquiring the material goods of a middle-class lifestyle. The culture of consumerism promotes spending and consumption even when people don't have money. Today, through global marketing and media advertising campaigns, increased trade, and rising migration, the desire for this lifestyle is being promoted around the world. Over the last few decades, following economic and political reforms in India, China, Russia, and the Middle East, hundreds of millions more people are now seeking that middle-class lifestyle seen on television and advertised on the Internet. This trend is placing incredible stress on the planet's natural resources and environment.

In many parts of the world, consumerism has become more than an economic activity. It is a way of life, a way of looking at the world—a culture. In fact, many key cultural rituals now focus on consumption. In the United States, holidays such as Valentine's Day, Mother's Day, and Father's Day all promote the purchase of gifts, as do birthdays, weddings, and anniversaries. Christmas, which in early U.S. history featured public drinking, lewd behavior, and aggressive begging, by the nineteenth century was being transformed into a family-centered ritual of gift giving by parents to children. Moreover, the invented character of Santa Claus was promoted as the mythical mediator of gift exchange and the symbol of Christmas consumer marketing (Nissenbaum 1996).

Consumerism also shapes our calendar. For example, the U.S. Congress shifted Thanksgiving to fall earlier in November to add another week to the Christmas shopping season, and candy company lobbyists succeeded in having daylight saving time start a week earlier so children would have an extra hour of daylight to collect candy on Halloween.

And consumption metaphors infiltrate our daily speech: "Let's have a beer" means "perhaps we can be better friends." "Let's have lunch" means "let's get to know each other better." "Can I buy you a drink?" means "I find you attractive." Even romance has become associated with conspicuous consumption. How else to show love and affection than by splurging on a fancy dinner and buying expensive gifts of flowers and jewelry?

College Students and Consumer Culture

College students are not immune to efforts to create a consumer culture. In fact, you are deeply immersed in it. With your classmates, try this collective project. Ask yourself what you need to have to feel like an average college student? Think about all the things you own. List your electronics (computer, cell phone, iPod, television, sound system) and your school supplies (books, notebooks, pens, calculator, backpack). Mentally go through your closets and dressers to list your clothing, then note the differences in items identified by your male and female classmates. Don't forget your clothes for different seasons and special occasions, as well as accessories (bags, hats, belts, and shoes) and grooming items and cosmetics. Include your mode of transportation, household furnishings, appliances, and so on. Once you have created your own list or a collective list with your classmates, try to assess what all of these things cost. Now ask yourself whether each of these are things that you *need* or things that you *want*. For all of those items you identify as things you want more than you absolutely need, ask yourself how the desire to acquire them—to consume them—was aroused and cultivated. Take into account our discussion about how culture is created, and consider how those insights can be applied to this exercise.

Advertising

The advertising industry is key in arousing our desires for goods and services. Consider that children in the United States watch up to 40,000 television commercials a year (American Academy of Pediatrics 2006). Many children's television programs are themselves thinly disguised advertisements for products featuring their characters, from lunch boxes to clothing to action figures. Advertising appears before and during movies in the theater, at sporting events, in department stores and shopping malls, on billboards, and in store windows. Your favorite websites and social media are covered with advertisements. So are your clothes. Even your classroom is full of advertisements that you most likely do not notice: all the labels and tags on computers, pens, notebooks, backpacks, food packaging, and soda cans.

Advertising is a powerful tool of enculturation, teaching us how to be "successful" in consumer culture, how to be cool and normal. Commercials promise that clothes, perfume, deodorant, haircuts, and expensive gifts will bring us love. Having our teeth straightened and whitened will help us network. A large, expensive car and proper insurance will protect our families and make us responsible and mature men and women. Magazines, television shows, and films promote stars who we are encouraged to emulate. If only we could dress like them and imitate their lifestyles, then we would be more desirable. The culture of consumerism tells us that having these things will bring us better friends, better sex, stronger families, higher-paying jobs, fancier houses, faster

FIGURE 2.15 What stirs your desire to consume? Shopping on Black Friday in the Lenox Square Mall in Atlanta, Georgia. Black Friday, the day after Thanksgiving, marks the start of the U.S. holiday shopping season.

cars, sharper picture definition, and truer sound quality. Do you find yourself believing this is true?

Financial Services and Credit Cards

The financial services industry makes sure that once our desires are aroused, we have access to money to make our dreams a reality—at a small price. With the advent of computers and the deregulation of banking in the 1970s, credit cards burst on the scene, transforming the financial environment. Banks, chain stores, and financial services corporations carry out intensive marketing to promote their cards. In 2012, the average American carried ten credit cards, and U.S. credit card debt was $793 billion, an average of $15,799 per household (StatisticBrain.com 2013).

College students are a key target of the credit industry, which promotes credit cards on campus and through the mail regardless of students' ability to repay. Credit cards grease the wheels of consumer culture. To pay them off, we need to intensify our participation: Work harder. Make more money. Then we can shop more. Underlying these shifts is the fundamental drive of contemporary capitalism for perpetual growth. People need to buy, make, invest, and profit more and more each year if the economy is to keep growing. And so contemporary capitalism invests heavily to arouse our desire and promote the expansion of the culture of consumerism.

As credit card limits maxed out in the 1990s, banks and mortgage companies encouraged homeowners to refinance their homes, taking out second mortgages to pay for day-to-day expenses and speculating that housing prices would remain high and continue to increase. Unfortunately, in the latter part of the 2000s, housing prices collapsed, homeowners owed more in mortgages than the remaining value of their homes, loan payments were missed, and banks and financial service companies placed millions of homes into foreclosure. These outcomes are indicative of the pitfalls of the twentieth- and early twenty-first centuries' emphasis on a capitalistic consumer culture.

How Is Globalization Transforming Culture?

Cultures have never been completely isolated or bounded groups of people located in a particular place. As we discussed in Chapter 1, anthropologists resist the myths of isolated and "primitive" groups who have lived on their own without contact. Encounter, interaction, movement, and exchange have been much more fundamental aspects of humanity. Cultures have always been influenced by the flow of people, ideas, and goods, whether through migration, trade, or invasion. Today's flows of globalization are intensifying the exchange and diffusion of people, ideas, and goods, creating more interaction and engagement among cultures. Let's consider three key interrelated effects of globalization on local cultures: homogenization, a two-way transference of culture through migration, and increased cosmopolitanism.

A Homogenizing Effect

The development of global corporations, products, and markets has produced what some anthropologists consider a homogenized, global culture of McDonald's, Levi's, Coca-Cola, CNN, Hollywood, and U.S. cultural values. Anthropologists and other cultural activists worry that the spread of this culture — fueled by goods, images, and ideas from Western cultures — is creating a homogenizing process that will diminish the diversity of the world's cultures as foreign influences inundate local practices, products, and ways of thinking.

At the same time, the elements of global culture symbolically represent to many people in developing countries the opportunity for economic advancement and participation in the idealized middle-class lifestyle of consumption associated with these consumer products. In *Golden Arches East: McDonald's in East Asia* (1998), James Watson suggests that East Asians in Tokyo, Japan; Seoul, Korea; Hong Kong; Beijing, China; and Taipei, Taiwan, go to McDonald's not so much for the food but to participate in what they view as a middle-class activity. By eating out and eating Western fast food, they hope to align themselves with the Western middle-class norms and values to which they aspire.

Migration and the Two-Way Transference of Culture

The movement of people in large numbers within and across national boundaries associated with contemporary globalization reveals that cultures are not necessarily bound to a particular geographic location. People migrate with their cultural

FIGURE 2.16 A McDonald's restaurant in downtown Manila, capital of the Philippines, advertises the McDo Rice Burger, a local product added to McDonald's standard global menu.

beliefs and practices. They incorporate the cultural practices of their homelands into their new communities. They build links to their homelands through which culture continues to be exchanged.

Robert Smith's book *Mexican New York* (2006) reveals the deep transnational connections—links across national borders—that have become increasingly common in today's globalizing world. Direct flights physically link immigrants living in the suburbs of New York City to their hometowns in Mexico in five hours. Telephone calls, e-mails, and videoconferences connect families and communities. The Mexican town of Tihuateca relies heavily on money sent back from villagers in New York City to build roads, water systems, and schools. Community leaders travel between countries to strengthen relationships, promote projects, and raise funds. In Boston, meanwhile, immigrants from India, Pakistan, Ireland, and Brazil maintain intense connections with their home communities, particularly through transnational religious practices. And a charismatic preacher from Brazil can lead thousands of Brazilians gathered in a Boston auditorium in worship by satellite hookup (Levitt 2007). These stories and many others reveal how global flows of people are transforming local cultures in both the sending and receiving countries (see Chapter 13).

Increasing Cosmopolitanism

A third significant effect of globalization on culture is that the increasing flow of people, ideas, and products has allowed worldwide access to cultural patterns that are new, innovative, and stimulating. Local cultures are exposed to a greater range of cultural ideas and products—such as agricultural strategies and medicines, to name just two. Globalization means that communities in the most remote parts of the world increasingly participate in experiences that bridge and link cultural practices, norms, and values across great distances, leading to what some scholars have called a new cosmopolitanism.

Cosmopolitanism is a very broad, sometimes global, outlook, rather than a limited, local one—an outlook that combines both universality and difference (Appiah 2006). The term is usually used to describe sophisticated urban professionals who travel and feel at home in different parts of the world. But anthropologist Lila Abu-Lughod's study *Dramas of Nationhood: The Politics of Television in Egypt* (2005) explores the emergence of cosmopolitanism even among Egypt's rural poor. Her book explores the role of television dramas—much like American soap operas, but more in tune with political and social issues—in creating ideas of a national culture, even among rural Egyptians, and crafting the identity of the new Egyptian citizen.

Abu-Lughod's ethnography of television pushes us to move beyond notions of single cultures sharing a set of ideas and meanings distinct from other cultures

cosmopolitanism: A global outlook emerging in response to increasing globalization.

MAP 2.4
Egypt

FIGURE 2.17 In a globalizing age, local cultures are increasingly exposed to a vast array of people, ideas, and products. Here, a montage of images from a day on Egyptian television, with channels from Egypt and across the Middle East, including comedy and music from Lebanon, old Egyptian films, American entertainment, and news and religious discussion programs.

in an era of mass media, migration, and globalization. Television, she argues, "is an extraordinary technology for breaking the boundaries and intensifying and multiplying encounters among life-worlds, sensibilities and ideas" (2005, 45). By the 1990s, there were six million television sets in Egypt, and more than 90 percent of the population had access. In this reality, television provides material—produced somewhere else—that is consumed locally; it is inserted into, mixed up with, and interpreted by local knowledge and systems of meaning.

> Thinking about Zaynab [Abu-Lughod's key informant] watching Egyptian dramatic serials and films, interviews with criminals, broadcasts of Parliament in session, American soap operas, imported nature programs that take her to the Caribbean or the Serengeti Plain, and advertisements for candy, ceramic toilets, chicken stock cubes and Coca-Cola leads me to begin thinking about her and others in this village not as members of some kind of unified Egyptian or Upper Egyptian peasant culture—one in which it is improper for women over thirty to marry or older women to be out and about going to school—but in terms of the cosmopolitanism they might represent. (2005, 46)

Even though poverty prevents the people in Abu-Lughod's study from fully participating in the consumer culture of commodities promoted by television programming and commercials, they are not untouched by these features of cosmopolitanism.

The influences of globalization ensure that even in rural Egyptian peasant culture, the knowledge of other worlds comes not only from television but also from foreign friends, tourists, visiting scholars / anthropologists, relatives

TOOLKIT

Thinking Like an Anthropologist: The Kiss as a Cultural Act

Every day, culture is all around us. It informs our thoughts and actions; guides us through complex interactions in our families, schools, jobs, and other personal relationships; and even shapes the way we perceive reality. Thinking like an anthropologist can help you to better understand yourself and those around you, and to analyze your own culture and other cultures you encounter in this globalizing world.

In thinking about the kiss between Richard Gere and Shilpa Shetty, consider the questions we have raised about culture.

- What is culture?
- How has the culture concept developed in anthropology?
- How are culture and power related?
- How much of who you are is determined by biology and how much by culture?
- How is culture created?
- How is globalization transforming culture?

After putting these questions into anthropological perspective, think about how your culture's norms, values, symbols, and mental maps of reality affect your understanding of Gere's kiss of Shetty.

We see the kisses of others symbolically—as deeply entwined in webs of meaning. We "read" differences in how they kiss—on the cheek, forehead, or lips; short or long; lips puckered or deeply enmeshed. We differentiate kisses of affection, social greeting, ceremony, and eroticism.

We see kisses between lovers of opposite genders, between lovers of the same gender, between parents and children, between young and old, and we "understand" each one differently through the lens of culture. Perhaps you believe that much is revealed through a first kiss. Is the person strong, sensitive, hot, reserved, passionate, a good lover, a good mother for your children, a frog or a prince? This chapter has demonstrated how all these "instincts" are filtered through and constructed by our enculturation—what we have been taught through agents such as family, school, friends, religion, and the media.

Beyond symbolism, we see how culture and power are connected. We know there may be physical consequences if we break the norms. We know that kisses can be expressions of physical dominance and aggression, expressions of the power of one person over another. Being kissed against one's will is associated with rape or adult/child incest and sexual abuse in which cultural notions of sexuality intersect with notions of gender, age, and kinship. Erotic kissing between relatives is shunned. And public kissing between same-sex couples may put them in physical danger. A kiss, Gere's kiss of Shetty, may also be an opportunity to explore relationships of power—perhaps in terms of gender, sexuality, nationalism, or religion. Gere did not think carefully about what his kiss would mean. But now that you are thinking like an anthropologist, you can.

Key Terms

culture (p. 35)
enculturation (p. 36)

migrating to find work in cities, imported movies and electronics, and even teachers trained by the Egyptian state and their approved textbooks. This is just one example of the powerful effects of the intersection of culture and globalization. No matter where you look in the twenty-first century, you are sure to find some elements of this intersection.

For Further Exploration

American Anthropological Association. "Declaration on Anthropology and Human Rights." www.aaanet .org/about/Policies/statements/Declaration-on -Anthropology-and-Human-Rights.cfm.

Guess Who's Coming to Dinner. 1967. Directed by Stanley Kramer. Sony Pictures. Classic film starring Sidney Poitier, Spencer Tracy, and Katharine Hepburn that addresses interracial marriage. U.S. antimiscegenation laws were struck down by the U.S. Supreme Court during the year of the film's release.

Hopkins, Nancy. 1999. "A Study on the Status of Women Faculty in Science at MIT." *MIT Faculty Newsletter 11 (4): 1–15. http://web.mit.edu/fnl /women/fnl114x.pdf.*

The Nuer. 1971. By Robert Gardner and Hilary Harris for the Film Study Center at Harvard University. Documentary film about the lives of the Sudanese Nuer group.

Ury, William. 2002. *Must We Fight? From the Battlefield to the Schoolyard — A New Perspective on Violent Conflict and Its Prevention.* San Francisco: Jossey-Bass.

Ury, William. 2010. "The Walk from 'No' to 'Yes.'" www.ted .com/talks/william_ury.html. TED Conference talk by anthropologist William Ury about creative cross-cultural strategies for conflict resolution.

Mother and child in a Rio de Janeiro favela, Brazil.

p. 75

p. 86

p. 88

CHAPTER 3
Fieldwork and Ethnography

I have seen death without weeping,
The destiny of the Northeast is death,
Cattle they kill,
To the people they do
Something worse

—Anonymous Brazilian singer (1965)

Over many years, Nancy Scheper-Hughes, now a professor of cultural anthropology at the University of California, Berkeley, invested herself in trying to understand the lives of the women and children of one particular shantytown in Brazil. Her research resulted in numerous articles and an award-winning ethnography, *Death without Weeping: The Violence of Everyday Life in Brazil* (1992). Scheper-Hughes's efforts reflect the deep commitment of anthropologists to ***ethnographic fieldwork***—a research strategy for understanding the world through intense interaction with a local community of people over an extended period. Take a few moments to read this excerpt drawn from her fieldwork experience:

p. 94

p. 106

p. 108

"Why do the church bells ring so often?" I asked Nailza de Arruda soon after I moved into a corner of her tiny mud-walled hut near the top of the shantytown called the Alto do Cruzeiro (Crucifix Hill). I was then a Peace Corps volunteer and community development / health worker. It was the dry and blazing hot summer of 1965, the months following the military coup in Brazil, and save for the rusty, clanging bells of N. S. das Dores

73

ethnographic fieldwork: A primary research strategy in cultural anthropology involving living with a community of people over an extended period to better understand their lives.

church, an eerie quiet had settled over the market town that I call Bom Jesus da Mata. Beneath the quiet, however, there was chaos and panic. "It's nothing," replied Nailza, "just another little angel gone to heaven."

Nailza had sent more than her share of little angels to heaven, and sometimes at night I could hear her engaged in a muffled but passionate discourse with one of them, two-year-old Joana. Joana's photograph, taken as she lay propped up in her tiny cardboard coffin, her eyes open, hung on a wall next to one of Nailza and Ze Antonio taken on the day they eloped.

Nailza could barely remember the other infants and babies who came and went in close succession. Most had died unnamed and were hastily baptized in their coffins. Few lived more than a month or two. Only Joana, properly baptized in church at the close of her first year and placed under the protection of a powerful saint, Joan of Arc, had been expected to live. And Nailza had dangerously allowed herself to love the little girl.

In addressing the dead child, Nailza's voice would range from tearful imploring to angry recrimination: "Why did you leave me? Was your patron saint so greedy that she could not allow me one child on this earth?" Ze Antonio advised me to ignore Nailza's odd behavior which he understood as a kind of madness that, like the birth and death of children, came and went. Indeed the premature birth of a stillborn son some months later "cured" Nailza of her "inappropriate" grief, and the day came when she removed Joana's photo and carefully packed it away.

More than fifteen years elapsed before I returned to the Alto do Cruzeiro, and it was anthropology that provided the vehicle of my return. Since 1982 I have returned several times in order to pursue a problem that first attracted my attention in the 1960s. My involvement with the people of the Alto do Cruzeiro now spans a quarter of a century and three generations of parenting in a community where mothers and daughters are often simultaneously pregnant.

The Alto do Cruzeiro is one of three shantytowns surrounding the large market town of Bom Jesus in the sugar plantation zone of Pernambuco in Northeast Brazil, one of the many zones of neglect that have emerged in the shadow of the now tarnished economic miracle of Brazil. For the women and children of the Alto do Cruzeiro the only miracle is that some of them have managed to stay alive at all. . . .

MAP 3.1
Brazil

My research agenda never wavered. The questions I addressed first crystallized during a veritable "die-off" of Alto babies during a severe drought in 1965. The food and water shortages and the political and economic chaos occasioned by the military coup were reflected in the handwritten entries of births and deaths in the dusty, yellowed pages of the ledger books kept at the public registry office in Bom Jesus. More than 350 babies died in the Alto during 1965 alone—this from a shantytown population of little more than 5,000. But that wasn't what surprised me. There were reasons enough for the deaths in the miserable conditions of shantytown life. What puzzled me was the seeming indifference of Alto women to the death of their infants and their willingness to attribute to their own tiny offspring an aversion to life that made their death seem wholly natural, indeed all but anticipated.

Although I found that it was possible, and hardly difficult, to rescue infants and toddlers from death by diarrhea and dehydration with a simple sugar, salt and water solution (even bottled Coca-Cola worked fine), it was more difficult to enlist a mother herself in the rescue of a child she perceived as ill-fated for life or better off dead, or to convince her to take back into her threatened and besieged home a baby she had already come to think of as an angel rather than as a son or daughter.

I learned that the high expectancy of death, and the ability to face child death with stoicism and equanimity, produced patterns of nurturing that differentiated between those infants thought of as thrivers and survivors and those thought of as born already "wanting to die." The survivors were nurtured, while stigmatized, doomed infants were left to die, as mothers say, *a mingua*, "of neglect." Mothers stepped back and allowed nature to take its course. This pattern, which I call mortal selective neglect, is called passive infanticide by anthropologist Marvin Harris. The Alto situation, although culturally specific in the form that it takes, is not unique to Third World shantytown communities and may have its correlates in our own impoverished urban communities in some cases of "failure to thrive" infants. . . .

Part of learning how to mother in the Alto do Cruzeiro is learning when to let go of a child who shows that it "wants" to die or that it has no "knack" or no "taste" for life. Another part is learning when it is safe to let oneself love a child. Frequent child death remains a powerful shaper of maternal thinking and practice. In the absence of firm expectation that a child

FIGURE 3.1 Burial of an infant in the Alto do Cruzeiro favela in northeast Brazil. How did anthropologist Nancy Scheper-Hughes make sense of the "death without weeping" that she found in this poor community?

will survive, mother love as we conceptualize it (whether in popular terms or in the psychobiological notion of maternal bonding) is attenuated and delayed with consequences for infant survival. In an environment already precarious to young life, the emotional detachment of mothers toward some of their babies contributes even further to the spiral of high mortality—high fertility in a kind of macabre lock-step dance of death. . . .

What, then, can be said of these women? What emotions, what sentiments motivate them? How are they able to do what, in fact, must be done? What does mother love mean in this inhospitable context? Are grief, mourning, and melancholia present, although deeply repressed? If so, where shall we look for them? And if not, how are we to understand the moral visions and moral sensibilities that guide their actions?

I have been criticized more than once for presenting an unflattering portrait of poor Brazilian women, women who are, after all, themselves the victims of severe social and institutional neglect. I have described these women as allowing some of their children to die, as if this were an unnatural and inhuman action rather than, as I would assert, the way any one of us might act, reasonably and rationally, under similarly desperate conditions. Perhaps I have not emphasized enough the real pathogens in this environment of high risk: poverty, deprivation, sexism, chronic hunger, and economic exploitation. If mother love is, as many psychologists and some feminists believe, a seemingly natural and universal maternal script, what does it mean to women for whom scarcity, loss, sickness and deprivation have made that love frantic and robbed them of their grief, seeming to turn hearts to stone? . . .

Life in the Alto do Cruzeiro resembles nothing so much a battlefield or an emergency room in an overcrowded inner-city public hospital. Consequently, mortality is guided by a kind of "life-boat ethics," the morality of triage. The seemingly studied indifference toward the suffering of some of their infants, conveyed in such sayings as "little critters have no feelings," is understandable in light of these women's obligation to carry on with their reproductive and nurturing lives.

In their slowness to anthropomorphize and personalize their infants, everything is mobilized so as to prevent maternal over-attachment and, therefore, grief at death. The bereaved mother is told not to cry, that her tears will dampen the wings of her little angel so that she cannot fly up to her heavenly home. Grief at the death of an angel is not only inappropriate, it is a symptom of madness and of a profound lack of faith. (Scheper-Hughes 1989, 8ff)

What did you learn about fieldwork by reading this story? Nancy Scheper-Hughes, a middle-class woman from the United States, traveled to one of the poorest places in the world, learned the language, lived in the community, built relationships of trust, accompanied local people through the births and deaths of their children, and searched for meaning in the midst of the pain. As you might imagine from the reading, the fieldwork experience can become more than a strategy for understanding human culture. Fieldwork has the potential to radically transform the anthropologist. Can you imagine making the same commitment Scheper-Hughes did?

The term *fieldwork* implies going out to "the field" to do extensive research. Although in the history of anthropology this may have meant going a long way from home, as Scheper-Hughes did, contemporary anthropologists also study human culture and activities in their own countries and communities. By exploring the practice of fieldwork, you will gain a deeper understanding of how anthropologists go about their work. In particular, in this chapter we will consider:

- What is unique about ethnographic fieldwork, and why do anthropologists conduct this kind of research?
- How did the idea of fieldwork develop?
- How do anthropologists get started conducting fieldwork?
- How do anthropologists write ethnography?
- What moral and ethical concerns guide anthropologists in their research and writing?
- How are fieldwork strategies changing in response to globalization?

By the end of the chapter you will see both how professional anthropologists employ fieldwork strategies and how fieldwork can provide a valuable toolkit for gathering information to make decisions in your own life. Fieldwork skills and strategies can help you navigate the many unfamiliar or cross-cultural experiences you will encounter at work or school, in your community, or in your family. And hopefully you will see how key fieldwork strategies can help you become a more engaged and responsible citizen of the world.

What Is Unique about Ethnographic Fieldwork, and Why Do Anthropologists Conduct This Kind of Research?

Ethnographic fieldwork is the unique strategy that anthropologists—particularly cultural anthropologists—have developed to put people first as we analyze how human societies work. Chemists conduct experiments in laboratories. Economists analyze financial trends. Demographers crunch census data. Historians pore over records and library archives. Sociologists, economists, and political scientists analyze trends, quantifiable data, official organizations, and national policies. But anthropologists start with people and their local communities. Even though the whole world is our field, our unique perspective first focuses on the details and patterns of human life in the local setting.

Fieldwork Begins with People

Through fieldwork, we try to understand people's everyday lives, to see what they do and to understand why. By living with others over an extended period, we seek to understand their experience through their eyes. We participate in their activities, take careful notes, conduct interviews, take photographs, and record music. We make maps of communities, both of the physical environment and of family and social relationships. Although careful observation of the details of daily life is the first step, through intensive fieldwork anthropologists look beyond the taken-for-granted, everyday experience of life to discover the complex systems of power and meaning that people construct to shape their existence. These include the many systems discussed throughout this book: gender, sexuality, race, ethnicity, religion, kinship, and economic and political systems. As we extend our analysis as anthropologists, we try to see how local lives compare to others and fit into larger human patterns and global contexts.

Fieldwork Shapes the Anthropologist

Fieldwork experience is considered an essential part of an anthropologist's training. It is the activity through which we learn the basic tools of our trade, earn credibility as effective observers of culture, and establish our reputation as full members of the discipline. Through the process, we learn the basic research strategies of our discipline and hone those skills—careful listening and observation, engagement with strangers, cross-cultural interaction, and deep analysis of human interactions and systems of power and privilege. Through fieldwork we learn empathy for those around us, develop a more global consciousness, and uncover our own ethnocentrism. Indeed, fieldwork is a rite of passage, an initiation into our discipline, and a common bond among anthropologists who have been through the experience.

Fieldwork transforms us. In fact, it is quite common for anthropologists entering the field to experience culture shock—a sense of disorientation caused by the overwhelmingly new and unfamiliar people and experiences encountered every day. Over time, the disorientation may fade as the unfamiliar becomes familiar. But then, many anthropologists feel culture shock again when returning home, where their new perspective causes previously familiar people and customs to seem very strange.

The Nacirema In a now-famous article, "Body Ritual among the Nacirema" (1956), anthropologist Horace Miner helps readers understand the dichotomy between familiar and strange that anthropologists face when studying other cultures. Miner's article examines the cultural beliefs and practices of a group in North America who he finds have developed elaborate and unique practices focusing on care of the human body. He labels this group the Nacirema.

Miner hypothesizes that underlying the extensive rituals he has documented lies a belief that the human body is essentially ugly, is constantly endangered by forces of disease and decay, and must be treated with great care. Thus, the Nacirema have established extensive daily rituals and ceremonies, rigorously taught to their children, to avoid these dangers. For example, Miner describes the typical household shrine—the primary venue for Nacirema body rituals:

> While each family has at least one shrine, the rituals associated with it are not family ceremonies but are private and secret. . . . The focal point of the shrine is a box or chest which is built into the wall. In this chest are kept the many charms and magical potions without which no native believes he could live. . . . Beneath the charm-box is a small font. Each day every member of the family, in succession, enters the shrine room, bows his head before the charm-box, mingles different sorts of holy water in the font, and proceeds with a brief rite of ablution. (Miner 1956)

In addition, the Nacirema regularly visit medicine men and "holy-mouth men." These individuals are specialists who provide ritual advice and magical potions.

> The Nacirema have an almost pathological horror of and fascination with the mouth, the condition of which is believed to have a supernatural influence on all social relationships. Were it not for the rituals of the mouth, they believe that their teeth would fall out, their gums bleed, their jaws shrink, their friends desert them and their lovers reject them. The daily body ritual performed by

FIGURE 3.2 A healing specialist conducts an elaborate ceremony, the facial treatment, a key body ritual among the Nacirema.

everyone includes a mouth-rite. It was reported to me that the ritual consists of inserting a small bundle of hog hairs into the mouth, along with certain magical powders, and then moving the bundle in a highly formalized series of gestures.

Do these exotic rituals of a seemingly distant tribe sound completely strange to you, or are they vaguely familiar? Miner's descriptions of the Nacirema are intended to make the strange seem familiar and the familiar strange. "Nacirema" is actually "American" spelled backward. Miner's passages describe the typical American bathroom and personal hygiene habits: "Holy water" pours into the sink. The "charm-box" is a medicine cabinet. The Nacirema medicine men are doctors, and the "holy-mouth men" are dentists. The "mouth-rite" is tooth brushing.

Development of the anthropological perspective through fieldwork, in which we investigate the beliefs and practices of other cultures, enables us to perceive our own cultural activities in a new light. Even the most familiar aspects of our lives may then appear exotic, bizarre, or strange when viewed through the lens of anthropology. Through this cross-cultural training, anthropology offers the opportunity to unlock our ability to imagine, see, and analyze the incredible diversity of human cultures. It also enables us to avoid the tendencies of ethnocentrism, in which we often view our own cultural practices as "normal" and against which we are inclined to judge the cultural beliefs and practices of others.

Fieldwork as Social Science and as Art

Fieldwork is simultaneously a social scientific method and an art form. It is a strategy for gathering data about the human condition, particularly through the life experiences of local people in local situations. Fieldwork is an experiment for testing hypotheses and building theories about the diversity of human behavior and the interaction of people with systems of power—a scientific method for examining how the social world really works. As such, anthropologists have developed techniques such as participant observation, field notes, interviews, kinship and social network analysis, life histories, and mapping—all of which we will discuss in this chapter.

But fieldwork is also an art. Its success depends on the anthropologist's more intuitive ability to negotiate complex interactions, usually in an unfamiliar cultural environment, to build relationships of trust, to make sense of patterns of behavior, to be conscious of one's own biases and particular vantage point. Ethnographic fieldwork depends on the ability of an outsider—the anthropologist—to develop close personal relationships over time in a local community and to understand the everyday experiences of often-unfamiliar people. It requires the anthropologist to risk being changed in the process—the risk of mutual transformation. Successful ethnographic fieldwork also depends on the anthropologist's ability to tell the subjects' stories to an audience that has no knowledge of them and in ways that accurately reflect the subjects' lives and shed light on the general human condition. This is also an art.

Fieldwork Informs Daily Life

Anthropologist Brackette Williams suggests that fieldwork can even be a kind of "homework"—a strategy for gathering information that will help the anthropologist to make informed decisions in order to act morally and to weigh in advance the likely consequences of her or his actions. Williams studied homelessness and begging in New York City and Tucson, Arizona, over a period of several years. She began with some very practical questions about whether to give money to homeless people begging on the subway she took to work in New York City every day.

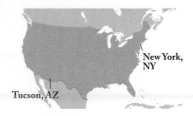

MAP 3.2
Tucson/New York

In her article "The Public I / Eye: Conducting Fieldwork to Do Homework on Homelessness and Begging in Two U.S. Cities," she writes:

> My goal in the investigation was not to write an ethnography of homelessness, begging, charity, work, and their interconnections but simply to try to understand whether or to whom I might or ought to give charity. As I do in making decisions about what I take to be politically proper conduct in most social interaction, I tried to become as conscious as possible of the character and process of the acts that constitute the social interaction. Like everyone else, I was daily confronted with a multitude of decision points at which I had to figure out why I did one thing and not another. (Williams 1995, 25)

Williams began with careful observation of all the people involved, including homeless individuals and all the others on the subway. She continued with informal and formal interviews, careful note taking, and background reading. In the process she began to identify a clear set of stories and begging styles, and to examine the complicated set of responses made by people on the subway who were being asked for money.

Williams suggests that this approach to her daily dilemma was not only an interesting use of her ethnographic fieldwork skills and training, but also "socially required homework" for anyone who confronts complex problems in daily life, whether with family, friends, school, work, or politics. Can you imagine using this strategy to explore a problem, puzzle, or question in your life?

How Did the Idea of Fieldwork Develop?

Early Accounts of Encounters with Others

Descriptive accounts of other cultures existed long before anthropologists came on the scene. For centuries, explorers, missionaries, traders, government bureaucrats, and travelers recorded descriptions of the people they encountered. For example, nearly 2,500 years ago, the Greek historian Herodotus wrote about his travels in Egypt, Persia, and the area now known as Ukraine. In the thirteenth century, the Venetian explorer Marco Polo chronicled his travels from Italy across the silk route to China. And the Chinese admiral Zheng He reported on his extended voyages to India, the Middle East, and East Africa in the fifteenth century, seventy years before Columbus arrived in the Americas. These are just a few of the many early accounts of encounters with other peoples across the globe.

Nineteenth-Century Anthropology and the Colonial Encounter

The roots of anthropology and of fieldwork lie in the intense globalization of the late nineteenth century. At that time, the increased international movement of Europeans — particularly merchants, colonial administrators, and missionaries — generated a broad set of data that stimulated scientists and philosophers of the day to make sense of the emerging picture of humanity's incredible diversity (Stocking 1983). They asked questions like these: Who are these other people? Why are their foods, clothing, architecture, rituals, family structures, and political and economic systems so different from ours and from one another's? Are they related to us biologically and culturally? If so, how?

Fieldwork was not a common practice at the beginning of our discipline. In fact, many early anthropologists, such as Edward Burnett Tylor (1832–1917), are now considered "armchair anthropologists" because they did not conduct their own research; instead, they worked at home in their armchairs analyzing the reports of others. One early exception was Louis Henry Morgan (1818–1881), who conducted fieldwork among Native Americans in the United States. As we discussed in Chapter 2, Tylor and Morgan were leading figures in attempts to organize the data that was accumulating, to catalogue human diversity, and to make sense of the many questions it stimulated. These men applied the theory of unilineal cultural evolution — the idea that all cultures would naturally evolve through the same sequence of stages from simple to complex, and that the diversity of human cultural expressions represented different stages in the evolution of human culture, which could be classified in comparison to one another.

FIGURE 3.3 Early anthropologists encountered a world of people already in motion. The 1375 Catalan Atlas shows the world as it was then known. It depicts the location of continents and islands as well as information on ancient and medieval tales, regional politics, astronomy, and astrology.

The Professionalization of Social Scientific Data-Gathering and Analysis

Succeeding generations of anthropologists in Europe and North America rejected unilineal cultural evolution as being too Eurocentric, too ethnocentric, too hierarchical, and lacking adequate data to support its grand claims. Anthropologists in the early twentieth century developed more sophisticated research methods—particularly ethnographic fieldwork—to professionalize social scientific data-gathering.

Franz Boas: Fieldwork and the Four-Field Approach In the United States, Franz Boas (1858–1942) and his students focused on developing a four-field approach to anthropological research, which included gathering cultural, linguistic, archaeological, and biological data. Boas's early work among the indigenous Kwakiutl people of the Pacific Northwest of the United States and Canada firmly grounded him in the fieldwork process, as he learned about others' culture through extensive participation in their daily lives, religious rituals, and economic activities. After settling in New York City in the early twentieth century as a professor of anthropology at Columbia University and curator of the American Museum of Natural History, Boas (and his students) embarked on a massive project to document Native American cultures being devastated by the westward expansion of settlers across the continent.

Often called **salvage ethnography** because of the speed at which it was conducted, Boas's approach required the rapid gathering of all available material, including historical artifacts, photographs, recordings of spoken languages, songs, and detailed information about cultural beliefs and practices—from religious rituals to family patterns, from gender roles to political structures. Pressed for time (because the Native cultures were rapidly disappearing) and having limited financial resources, these ethnographers often met with a small number of elderly informants and focused on conducting oral interviews rather than observing actual behavior. Despite the limitations of this emerging fieldwork, these early projects built upon Boas's commitment to historical particularism when investigating local cultures (see Chapter 2) and defined a continuing characteristic of American anthropology: a combined focus on culture, biology, artifacts, and language that today we call the four-field approach (see Chapter 1).

Another key contribution of Boas and his students was a commitment to the development of cultural relativism as a basic fieldwork perspective: to see each culture on its own merits; to understand it first from the inside, according to its own logic and structure. This rejection of ethnocentrism became a cornerstone of anthropology for generations to come (Stocking 1989).

Bronislaw Malinowski: The Father of Fieldwork Across the Pacific Ocean, Bronislaw Malinowski (1884–1942), considered by many to be the "father of

FIGURE 3.4 American anthropologist Franz Boas in Inuit clothing during fieldwork in the Pacific Northwest of North America, 1883.

salvage ethnography: Fieldwork strategy developed by Franz Boas to rapidly collect cultural, material, linguistic, and biological information about U.S. Native populations being devastated by Western expansion.

fieldwork," went even further than Boas in developing cultural anthropology's research methods. Malinowski, a Polish citizen who later became a leading figure in British anthropology, found himself stuck for a year on the Trobriand Islands as a result of World War I. His classic ethnography, *Argonauts of the Western Pacific* (1922), has become most famous for its examination of the Kula ring, an elaborate system of exchange. The ring involved thousands of individuals across many islands, some of whom traveled hundreds of miles by canoe to exchange Kula valuables (in particular, shell necklaces and armbands).

Argonauts also set new standards for fieldwork. In the opening chapter, Malinowski proposes a set of guidelines for conducting fieldwork based on his own experience. He urges fellow anthropologists to stay for a long period in their field sites, learn the local language, get off the veranda (that is, leave the safety of their front porch to mingle with the local people), engage in participant observation, and explore the "mundane imponderabilia"—the seemingly commonplace, everyday items and activities of local life.

Although some of these suggestions may seem obvious to us nearly a century later, Malinowski's formulation of a comprehensive strategy for understanding local culture was groundbreaking and has withstood the test of time. Of particular importance has been his conceptualization of **participant observation** as the cornerstone of fieldwork. For anthropologists, it is not enough to observe from a distance. We must learn about people by participating in their daily activities, walking in their shoes, seeing through their eyes. Participant observation gives depth to our observations and helps guard against mistaken assumptions based on observation from a distance (Kuper 1983).

participant observation: A key anthropological research strategy involving both participation in and observation of the daily life of the people being studied.

FIGURE 3.5 British anthropologist Bronislaw Malinowski at a bachelor's house in Kasanaj, Trobriand Islands, ca. 1915–18.

E. E. Evans-Pritchard and British Social Anthropology Between the 1920s and 1960s, many British social anthropologists viewed anthropology more as a science designed to discover the component elements and patterns of society (see Chapter 2). Fieldwork was their key methodology for conducting their scientific experiments. Adopting a *synchronic approach*, they sought to control their experiments by limiting consideration of the larger historical and social context in order to isolate as many variables as possible.

E. E. Evans-Pritchard (1902–1973), one of the leading figures during this period, wrote a classic ethnography in this style. In *The Nuer* (1940), based on his research with a Sudanese "tribe" over eleven months between 1930 and 1936, Evans-Pritchard systematically documents the group's social structure—political, economic, and kinship, capturing the intricate details of community life. But later anthropologists have criticized his failure to consider the historical context and larger social world. Indeed, the Nuer in

MAP 3.3
The Nuer Region of East Africa

FIGURE 3.6 British anthropologist E. E. Evans-Pritchard seated among Nuer men and boys in southern Sudan, ca. 1930.

FIGURE 3.7 American anthropologist Margaret Mead with a mother and child in the Admiralty Islands, South Pacific, 1953.

Evans-Pritchard's study lived under British occupation in the Sudan, and many Nuer participated in resistance to British occupation despite an intensive British pacification campaign against the Sudanese during the time of Evans-Pritchard's research. Later anthropologists have questioned how he could have omitted such important details and ignored his status as a British subject when it had such potential for undermining his research success.

Margaret Mead: Fieldwork and Public Anthropology Margaret Mead conducted pioneering fieldwork in the 1920s, famously examining teen sexuality in *Coming of Age in Samoa* (1928) and, later, gender roles in Papua New Guinea. Perhaps most significant, however, Mead mobilized her fieldwork findings to engage in crucial scholarly and public debates at home in the United States. At a time when many in the United States argued that gender roles were biologically determined, Mead's fieldwork testified to the fact that U.S. cultural norms were not found cross-culturally but were culturally specific. Mead's unique blending of fieldwork and dynamic writing provided her with the authority and opportunity to engage a broad public audience and made her a powerful figure in the roiling cultural debates of her generation.

The People of Puerto Rico: **A Turn to the Global** During the 1950s a team of anthropologists headed by Julian Steward, and including Sydney Mintz and Eric Wolf, engaged in a collaborative fieldwork project at multiple sites on the island of Puerto Rico. Steward's resulting ethnography, *The People of Puerto Rico*

MAP 3.4
Samoa

(1956), marked the beginning of a significant anthropological turn away from studies of seemingly isolated, small-scale, nonindustrial societies toward studies that examined the integration of local communities into a modern world system. In particular, the new focus explored the impact of colonialism and the spread of capitalism on local people. Mintz, in *Sweetness and Power* (1985), later expanded his fieldwork interests in Puerto Rican sugar production to consider the intersections of local histories and local production of sugar with global flows of colonialism and capitalism. Wolf, in *Europe and the People without History* (1982), continued a lifetime commitment to reassert forgotten local histories—or the stories of people ignored by history—into the story of the modern world economic system.

Annette Weiner: Feminism and Reflexivity In the 1980s, anthropologist Annette Weiner retraced Malinowski's footsteps to conduct a new study of the Trobriand Islands sixty years later. Weiner quickly noticed aspects of Trobriand culture that had not surfaced in Malinowski's writings. In particular, she took careful note of the substantial role women played in the island economy. Whereas Malinowski had focused attention on the elaborate male-dominated system of economic exchange among islands, Weiner found that women had equally important economic roles and equally valuable accumulations of wealth.

In the course of her fieldwork, Weiner came to believe that Malinowski's conclusions were not necessarily wrong but were incomplete. By the time of Weiner's study (1988), anthropologists were carefully considering the need for **reflexivity** in conducting fieldwork—that is, a critical self-examination of the role of the anthropologist and an awareness that who one is affects what one finds out. Malinowski's age and gender influenced what he saw and what others were comfortable telling him. By the 1980s, feminist anthropologists such as Weiner and Kathleen Gough, who revisited Evans-Pritchard's work with the Nuer (1971), were pushing anthropologists to be more critically aware of how their own position in relationship to those they studied affected their scope of vision.

reflexivity: A critical self-examination of the role the anthropologist plays and an awareness that one's identity affects one's fieldwork and theoretical analyses.

Barbara Myerhoff: A Turn to Home Barbara Myerhoff's first book, *Peyote Hunt* (1974), traces the pilgrimage of the Huichol Indians across the Sierra Madre of Mexico as they retell, reclaim, and reinvigorate their religious myths, rituals, and symbols. In her second book, *Number Our Days* (1978), Myerhoff turns her attention closer to home. Her fieldwork as described in the 1978 book focuses on the struggles of older Jewish immigrants in a southern California community and the Aliyah senior citizens

FIGURE 3.8 Anthropologist Barbara Myerhoff with two members of the Aliyah Senior Center in Southern California, the focus of her book, *Number Our Days*.

center through which they create and remember ritual life and community as a means of keeping control of their daily activities and faculties as they age. Their words pour off the pages of her book as she allows them to tell their life stories. Myerhoff becomes a character in her own book, tracing her interactions and engagements with the members of the center and reflecting poignantly on the process of self-reflection and transformation that she experiences as a younger Jewish woman studying a community of older Jews.

Number Our Days marks a turn in anthropology from the study of the "other" to the study of the self—what Victor Turner calls in his foreword to Myerhoff's book "being thrice-born." The first birth is in our own culture. The second birth immerses the anthropologist in the depths of another culture through fieldwork. Finally, the return home is like a third birth as the anthropologist rediscovers his or her own culture, now strange and unfamiliar in a global context.

How Do Anthropologists Get Started Conducting Fieldwork?

Today cultural anthropologists call on a set of techniques designed to assess the complexity of human interactions and social organizations. You probably use some variation of these techniques as you go about daily life and make decisions for yourself and others. For a moment, imagine yourself doing fieldwork with Nancy Scheper-Hughes in the Brazilian shantytown of Alto do Cruzeiro. How would you prepare yourself? What strategies would you use? How would you analyze your data?

Preparation

Prior to beginning fieldwork, anthropologists go through an intense process of preparation. We start by reading everything we can find about our research site and the particular issues we will be examining. This **literature review** provides a crucial background for the experiences to come. Following Malinowski's recommendation, anthropologists also learn the language of their field site. The ability to speak the local language eliminates the need to work through interpreters and allows us to participate in the community's everyday activities and conversations, which richly reflect local culture.

Before going to the field, anthropologists search out possible contacts: other scholars who have worked there, community leaders, government officials, perhaps even a host family. A specific research question or problem is defined and a research design created. Grant applications are submitted to seek financial support for the research. Permission to conduct the study is sought ahead of time from the local community and, where necessary, from appropriate government agencies. Protocols are developed to protect those who will be the focus of research. Anthropologists attend to many of these logistical matters following a preliminary visit to the intended field site before fully engaging the fieldwork process.

Finally, we assemble the **anthropologist's toolkit**—all the equipment needed to conduct our research. What tools would Nancy Scheper-Hughes have needed to conduct her research on a daily basis in Brazil? Today this toolkit—most likely a backpack—might include a notebook, pens, camera, voice recorder (and batteries!), maps, cell phone, dictionary, watch, and identification.

If you look back at the excerpt from Scheper-Hughes's work on pages 73–77, you can see evidence of some of the preparation strategies discussed here. Here's how she approached her research question:

> The questions I addressed first crystallized during a veritable "die-off" of Alto babies during a severe drought in 1965. . . . But that wasn't what surprised me. . . . What puzzled me was the seeming indifference of Alto women to the death of their infants and their willingness to attribute to their own tiny offspring an aversion to life that made their death seem wholly natural.

Here she refers to work done in terms of a literature review:

> Mothers stepped back and allowed nature to take its course. This pattern, which I call mortal selective neglect, is called passive infanticide by anthropologist Marvin Harris. The Alto situation . . . is

literature review: The process of reading all the available published material about a research site and / or research issues, usually done before fieldwork begins.

anthropologist's toolkit: The tools needed to conduct fieldwork, including a notebook, pen, camera, voice recorder, and dictionary.

not unique to Third World shantytown communities and may have its correlates in our own impoverished urban communities in some cases of "failure to thrive" infants.

Strategies

Once in the field, anthropologists apply a variety of research strategies for gathering quantitative and qualitative data. **Quantitative data** include statistical information about a community—data that can be measured and compared, including details of population demographics and economic activity. **Qualitative data** include information that cannot be counted but may be even more significant for understanding the dynamics of a community. Qualitative data consist of personal stories and interviews, life histories, and general observations about daily life drawn from participant observation. Qualitative data enable the ethnographer to connect the dots and answer the questions of why people behave in certain ways or organize their lives in particular patterns.

Central to a cultural anthropologist's research is participant observation. By participating in our subjects' daily activities, we experience their lives from the perspective of an insider. Through participant observation over time, we establish **rapport**—relationships of trust and familiarity with members of the community we study. The deepening of that rapport through intense engagement enables the anthropologist to move from being an outsider toward being an insider. Over time in a community, anthropologists seek out people who will be our advisors, teachers, and guides—sometimes called **key informants** or cultural consultants. Key informants may suggest issues to explore, introduce community members to interview, provide feedback on research insights, and warn against cultural miscues. (Again, quoting from Scheper-Hughes: "Ze Antonio advised me to ignore Nailza's odd behavior, which he understood as a kind of madness that, like the birth and death of children, came and went.")

Another key research strategy is the **interview**. Anthropologists are constantly conducting interviews while in the field. Some interviews are very informal, essentially involving a form of data gathering through everyday conversation. Other interviews are highly structured, closely following a set of questions. Semi-structured interviews use those questions as a framework but leave room for the interviewee to guide the conversation. One particular form of interview, a **life history**, traces the life story of a key informant as a means of understanding change over time in that person's life and illuminating the interlocking network of relationships in the community. Life histories provide insights into the frameworks of meaning that individuals build around their life experiences. **Surveys** can also be developed and administered to gather quantitative data and reach a broader sample of participants around key issues, but

---

quantitative data: Statistical information about a community that can be measured and compared.

qualitative data: Descriptive data drawn from nonstatistical sources, including participant observation, personal stories, interviews, and life histories.

rapport: The relationships of trust and familiarity developed with members of the community being studied.

key informant: A community member who advises the anthropologist on community issues, provides feedback, and warns against cultural miscues. Also called *cultural consultant*.

interview: A research strategy of gathering data through formal or informal conversation with informants.

life history: A form of interview that traces the biography of a person over time, examining changes and illuminating the interlocking network of relationships in the community.

survey: An information-gathering tool for quantitative data analysis.

---

rarely do they substitute for participant observation and face-to-face interviews as the anthropologist's primary strategy for data collection.

We also map human relations. **Kinship analysis**, a traditional strategy, enables anthropologists to explore the interlocking relationships of power built on family and marriage. In more urban areas where family networks are diffuse, a **social network analysis** may prove illuminating. One of the simplest ways to analyze a social network is to identify who people turn to in times of need.

Central to our data-gathering strategy, anthropologists write detailed **field notes** of our observations and reflections. These field notes take various forms. Some are elaborate descriptions of people, places, events, sounds, and smells. Others are reflections on patterns and themes that emerge, questions to be asked, and issues to be pursued. Some field notes are personal reflections on the experience of doing fieldwork—how it feels physically and emotionally to be engaged in the process. Although the rigorous recording of field notes may sometimes seem tedious, the collection of data over time allows the anthropologist to revisit details of earlier experiences, to compare information and impressions over time, and to analyze changes, trends, patterns, and themes.

Sophisticated computer programs can assist in the organization and categorization of data about people, places, and institutions. But in the final analysis, the ability to recognize key themes and patterns relies on the instincts and insights of the ethnographer. Dedication to rigorous recording of field notes supports the process of thick description as defined by Clifford Geertz (see Chapter 2), in which detailed description affords deeper insights into the underlying meaning of words and actions.

Mapping

Often one of the first steps an anthropologist takes upon entering a new community is to map the surroundings. **Mapping** takes many forms and produces many different products. While walking the streets of the field site, the ethnographer develops a spatial awareness of where people live, work, worship, play, and eat, and of the space through which they move. After all, human culture exists in real physical space. And culture shapes the way space is constructed and used. Likewise, physical surroundings influence human culture, shaping the boundaries of behavior and imagination. Careful observation and description, recorded in maps and field notes, provide the material for deeper analysis of these community dynamics.

Urban ethnographers describe the power of the **built environment** to shape human life. Most humans live in a built environment, not one made up solely or primarily of nature. By focusing on the built environment—what we have built around us—scholars can analyze the intentional development

kinship analysis: A traditional strategy of examining genealogies to uncover the relationships built upon structures such as marriage and family ties.

social network analysis: A method for examining relationships in a community, often conducted by identifying who people turn to in times of need.

field notes: The anthropologist's written observations and reflections on places, practices, events, and interviews.

mapping: The analysis of the physical and / or geographic space where fieldwork is being conducted.

built environment: The intentionally designed features of human settlement, including buildings, transportation and public service infrastructure, and public spaces.

of human settlements, neighborhoods, towns, and cities. Growth of the built environment is rarely random. Rather, it is guided by political and economic choices that determine funding for roads, public transportation, parks, schools, lighting, sewers, water systems, electrical grids, hospitals, police and fire stations, and other public services and infrastructure. Local governments establish and enforce tax and zoning regulations to control the construction of buildings and approved uses. Mapping the components of this built environment may shed light on key dynamics of power and influence in a community.

Anthropologists turn to quantitative data to map who is present in a community, including characteristics such as age, gender, family type, and employment status. This demographic data may be available through the local or national census, or the anthropologist may choose to gather the data directly by surveying the community if the sample size is manageable. To map historical change over time in an area and discern its causes, anthropologists also turn to archives, newspaper databases, minutes and records of local organizations, historical photos, and personal descriptions, in addition to census data.

Mapping today may be aided by the use of online tools such as satellite imagery, geographic information system (GIS) devices and data, online archives, and electronic databases. All can be extremely helpful in establishing location, orientation, and in the case of photo archives, change over time. On their own, however, these tools, do not provide the deep immersion sought by anthropologists conducting fieldwork. Instead, anthropologists place primary emphasis on careful, first-hand observation and documentation of physical space as a valuable strategy for understanding the day-to-day dynamics of cultural life.

Mapping may produce a tremendous variety of products. Hand-drawn maps reveal the intricate character of the built environment and force the ethnographer toward a deeper consciousness of details. Photos present a visual map seen through the camera's lens, a map that may be extremely valuable when writing up an ethnographic report and in leaving a visual record of a particular place viewed at a particular time. Film captures moving images and sounds that may make the fieldwork site come alive for those who are unable to experience it firsthand. Blogs and wikis present opportunities to work collaboratively and publicly in the mapping process, creating open-source documents that can be regularly updated, enhanced, and engaged with by members of a research team or by members of the community under study.

Skills and Perspectives

Successful fieldwork requires a unique set of skills and perspectives that are hard to teach in the classroom. Ethnographers must begin with open-mindedness about the people and places they study. We must be wary of any prejudices we might have formed before our arrival, and we must be reluctant to judge once we are in the field. Boas's notion of cultural relativism is an essential starting point: Can we see the world through the eyes of those we are studying? Can we understand their systems of meaning and internal logic? The tradition of anthropology suggests that cultural relativism must be the starting point if we are to accurately hear and retell the stories of others.

A successful ethnographer must also be a skilled listener. We spend a lot of time in conversation, but much of that time involves listening, not talking. The ability to ask good questions and listen carefully to the responses is essential. A skilled listener hears both what is said and what is not said—something we refer to as zeros. **Zeros** are the elements of a story or a picture that are not told or seen, key details omitted from the conversation. Who or what is missing from it? Zeros offer key insights into issues and topics that may be too sensitive to discuss or display publicly.

zeros: Elements of a story or a picture that are not told or seen and yet offer key insights into issues that might be too sensitive to discuss or display publicly.

A good ethnographer must be patient, flexible, and open to the unexpected. Sometimes sitting still in one place is the best research strategy because it offers opportunities to observe and experience unplanned events and unexpected people. For instance, I have a favorite tea shop in one Chinese village where I like to sit and wait to see what happens. The overscheduled fieldworker can easily miss the "mundane imponderabilia" that constitute the richness of everyday life.

At times the most important, illuminating conversations and interviews are not planned and scheduled ahead of time. On a research trip to China, for example, I had hoped to better understand the Catholic Church in the area where I was doing fieldwork. I visited a number of parishes but realized that I really needed an interview with the bishop—the head of all Catholic churches in the region. Unable to arrange one through official channels, I was about to leave China but made one last visit to a large rural church. As I climbed the hill from the town to the church, I met an old man sitting on the steps reading a book. I greeted him, and as we began to talk his outer cloak fell back to reveal a large cross hanging around his neck. "Are you by any chance the bishop?" I asked. "Yes, my son," he answered. "How may I help you?"

Patience and a commitment to conduct research over an extended period allow the ethnographic experience to come to us on its own terms, not on the schedule we assign to it. This is one of the significant differences between anthropology and journalism. It is also a hard lesson to learn and a hard skill to develop.

A final perspective essential for a successful ethnographer is openness to the possibility of **mutual transformation** in the fieldwork process. This is risky business because it exposes the personal component of anthropological research. It is clear that by participating in fieldwork, anthropologists alter—in ways large and small—the character of the community being studied. But if you ask them

mutual transformation: The potential for both the anthropologist and the members of the community being studied to be transformed by the interactions of fieldwork.

FIGURE 3.9 Student-made maps of blocks along East Broadway, a street on Manhattan's Lower East Side that serves as both a gateway into the country and the economic hub for Chinese immigrants seeking a foothold in the United States today.

about their fieldwork experience, they will acknowledge that in the process they become transformed on a very personal level—their self-understanding, their empathy for others, their worldviews. The practice of participant observation over time entails building deep relationships with people from another culture and directly engages the ethnographer in the life of the community.

Nancy Scheper-Hughes could not have returned unchanged by her research experience. The people of Alto do Cruzeiro would not let her simply observe their lives; they made her work with them to organize a neighborhood organization to address community problems. Indeed, the potential for the fieldworker to affect the local community is very great. So is the potential for the people being studied to transform the fieldworker.

Analysis

As the fieldwork experience proceeds, anthropologists regularly reflect on and analyze the trends, issues, themes, and patterns that emerge from their carefully collected data. One framework for analysis that we will examine in this book

YOUR TURN: FIELDWORK

Mapping a Block

Develop your ethnographic skills of observation and description by drawing a map of a block or public space in your community and writing a narrative description of what you find.

Select an interesting location for your mapping project. You may choose to map a block defined as an area bounded on four sides by streets; as both sides of a single street (include the corners); or as the four corners of an intersection. Alternatively, you may choose to map an outdoor public space such as a park or campus quadrangle, or an indoor space such as a shopping mall or your college's student center. In these cases, focus on what is inside the space or inside the building's four walls.

Bring your anthropologist's toolkit, and spend time in your chosen location. Take careful notes. Pay attention to details. Draw a map of what you see. For an outdoor space, note streets, buildings, businesses, residences, schools, hospitals, and infrastructure such as streetlights, sewers, telephone and electric lines, and satellite dishes, as well as transportation and pedestrian traffic. For an indoor space, note rooms, offices, businesses, hallways, entry and exit locations, public and private areas,

lighting, sounds, smells, and types and flows of people. Notice what is absent that you might have expected to find. Not all information presents itself immediately, so be patient. Consider taking photos or shooting video of your location as part of your data gathering and to supplement your hand-drawn map. To observe changes in your location, visit more than once. Vary the time of day or the day of the week. Write a description of the block, comparing the findings of your multiple visits.

If time permits, continue your mapping project by examining census data for your location. You can access U.S. census data at http://projects.nytimes.com/census/2010/explorer. Also consider searching local archives and databases to collect historical information about how your chosen location has changed over time.

When presenting your mapping project, consider supplementing your hand-drawn map and narrative description with photos, Google Earth images, film clips, and statistical data. If you are working in a team, consider posting your research as a blog or wiki to promote collaboration, integrate multiple media sources, and enhance your presentation.

is power: Who has it? How do they get it and keep it? Who uses it, and why? Where is the money, and who controls it? The anthropologist Eric Wolf thought of culture as a mechanism for facilitating relationships of power—among families, between genders, and among religions, classes, and political entities (1999). Good ethnographers constantly assess the relations of power in the communities they study.

Whereas earlier anthropologists such as Evans-Pritchard focused narrowly on the local culture being studied, today's anthropologists explore and analyze global connections as well—relationships between the local community and the global processes that affect it. For example, in the 2005 film *Mardi Gras: Made*

FIGURE 3.10 What is the global journey of Mardi Gras beads? *Left*, hands of a Chinese woman burned, cracked, and stained from making Mardi Gras beads in sweatshop conditions. The beads are exported for sale in the United States at the annual Mardi Gras festival in New Orleans, Louisiana. *Right*, young American women exchange nudity for the beads in New Orleans's French Quarter during Mardi Gras.

in China, the ethnographic filmmakers David Redmon and Ashley Sabin trace the connection between (1) the beads used in New Orleans Mardi Gras festivities to entice women to bare their breasts, and (2) the sweatshop factories in China where the beads are made by young teenage girls who work twelve-hour days, six days a week. As globalization intensifies in the twenty-first century, anthropologists who conduct fieldwork in local communities are paying increasing attention to these kinds of local–global links.

Ethnographers also submit their local data and analysis to cross-cultural comparisons. We endeavor to begin from an **emic** perspective—that is, understanding the local community on its own terms. But the anthropological commitment to understanding human diversity and the complexity of human cultures also requires taking an **etic** perspective—viewing the local community from the anthropologist's perspective as an outsider. This provides a foundation for comparison with other relevant case studies. The overarching process of comparison and assessment, called **ethnology**, utilizes the wealth of anthropological studies to compare the activities, trends, and patterns of power across cultures. The process enables us to better see what is unique in a particular community and how it contributes to identifying larger patterns of cultural beliefs and practices. Perhaps the largest effort to facilitate worldwide comparative studies is the Human Relations Area Files at Yale University (www.yale.edu.hraf), which has been building a database of ethnographic material since 1949 to encourage cross-cultural analysis.

emic: An approach to gathering data that investigates how local people think and how they understand the world.

etic: Description of local behavior and beliefs from the anthropologist's perspective in ways that can be compared across cultures.

ethnology: The analysis and comparison of ethnographic data across cultures.

How Do Anthropologists Write Ethnography?

After gathering data through fieldwork, anthropologists must decide how to tell the stories of the people they study. Although ethnographic films are a vibrant part of our field, most anthropologists make their contributions through ethnographic writing—either articles or books. The art of ethnographic writing has been a particularly hot topic within anthropology for the past twenty-five years, and both style and content have changed dramatically since Malinowski and Evans-Pritchard published their books in the early twentieth century.

Ethnography has changed as anthropology has changed. More women and people of color are writing, bringing their unique perspectives into the anthropological discourse. More people from non-Western countries are writing, challenging the position of Western writers as unquestioned authorities on other cultures. And with better communication systems, people are reading what we write about them, even when we write it halfway around the world. This has had a profound effect on the conversations between author and subject and on the ethnographer's final product.

It is unavoidable that what we write will in some way provide only a limited view of the lives of those we study. The process of collecting, organizing, and analyzing our data presumes not only that we present facts, but also that we choose which facts to present, which people to highlight, and which stories to tell. As authors, we have the power to interpret the people and their experiences to our audience. This is an awesome and sometimes overwhelming responsibility, which often leaves the ethnographer at a loss for how to proceed. In researching my book, *God in Chinatown*, for instance, I conducted more than one hundred interviews, each lasting one hour or more. The process of selecting certain stories and specific quotes was arduous.

Polyvocality

Changes in ethnographic fieldwork and writing over recent decades have sought to make the process more participatory and transparent. Today most ethnographic projects involve people from the community in the research process and include their voices more directly in the written product. Nancy Scheper-Hughes, for example, strives to include both her own voice and those of the people of Alto do Cruzeiro in her writing. In this chapter's opening excerpt, through direct quotes we hear the bereaved mother Nailza trying to make sense of the death of her daughter Joana ("Why did you leave me? Was your patron saint so greedy that she could not allow me one child on this earth?").

polyvocality: The practice of using many different voices in ethnographic writing and research question development, allowing the reader to hear more directly from the people in the study.

Polyvocality—the use of many voices in ethnographic writing—allows the reader to hear directly from the people in the study and, by bringing their stories to life, makes them more vibrant and available to the reader. Anthropologists also increase polyvocality in their research by inviting key informants to help design the research, including interview and survey questions. Others may be invited to read sections of the manuscript as it is being drafted. In contemporary ethnographic writing, the author's voice also comes out more clearly as ethnographies have moved from the style of Evans-Pritchard (1940) toward that of Geertz (1973)—from being a scientific report toward being thick description and an interpretation of what is observed.

Reflexivity

In this chapter's opening story, Nancy Scheper-Hughes's feelings about her experiences come through in the text, making the ethnographer herself come alive as well. This practice of reflexivity—self-reflection on the experience of doing fieldwork—has become more prevalent in written ethnographies. Contemporary writers make an effort to reveal their own position in relationship to their study so that readers can assess what biases, strengths, or handicaps the author may have. The ethnographer's age, gender, race/ethnicity, nationality, sexuality, and religious background may have a direct impact on (1) the ease with which he or she establishes rapport or gains access to the research community, and (2) the successful analysis of his or her findings. A careful ethnographer must address these issues in the research design and implementation and may choose to reflect on them in the written report.

Tone and Style

Anthropologists today write for a wide variety of audiences, and the tone and style of our writing shift accordingly. We write for students, both undergraduate and graduate, in the hopes of inspiring an interest in a particular topic or in fieldwork itself. We write for colleagues or other specialists in the field with whom we engage in debates and discussions. A recent emphasis on creating a public anthropology, one that more directly explores contemporary issues and problems, has led some anthropologists to write for the general public and even for government agencies and nongovernmental organizations that might address problems in the community by using the information presented in the anthropologists' reports.

We also write for the people we study. In today's world of linked communications, the people we are writing about often read our work, even if they live on the other side of the globe. People expect to see their lives accurately portrayed and their community's concerns appropriately expressed. Balancing the expectations and needs of these at times contradictory audiences makes the ethnographer's task quite complicated.

Ethnographic Authority

Ultimately, the ethnographer must wrestle with the question of ethnographic authority: What right does he or she have to present certain material, make certain claims, and draw certain conclusions? That authority is not automatically given, so authors make efforts, often early on in the ethnography, to establish their credentials and identify the grounds on which readers should trust them and the decisions they made during fieldwork and writing. These attempts to establish ethnographic authority include discussions of the length of time engaged in the study, language skills, special training and preparation, research design and implementation, and the quality of the relationship with subjects in the study. The quality and persuasiveness of the writing can also be significant in establishing the ethnographer's credibility. The inclusion of direct quotes can confirm the author's conclusions, provide more direct access to the fieldworker's data, and enable the reader to better assess the author's conclusions.

Experiments in Ethnographic Writing

Ethnographic writing can take many different literary forms. Contemporary ethnographers explore the full range. James Clifford suggests that in the ever-changing world of those being studied, an anthropologist can really only know some of the truth. Ethnographic writing should reflect this self-acknowledged limit on the experience of reality. Once acknowledged and presented in this way, the "cultural" text—a ritual, an institution, a life history—can come alive, set free from the ethnographer's limited gaze to become "a speaking object, who sees as well as is seen, who evades, argues, probes back" (Clifford and Marcus 1986, 14; Crapanzano 1980).

In *A Thrice-Told Tale* (1992), Margery Wolf presents three perspectives on one set of events that occurred during her fieldwork in Taiwan in the 1960s. In a village where Wolf was studying, a young mother began to act very strangely, at times suicidal. The villagers could not agree on what ailed her. Some said that a god possessed her, others that she was becoming a shaman. A number of villagers felt she had a terrible mental illness that required medication, physical restraint, or institutionalization. The most skeptical said that her husband was manipulating her, attempting to get money and sympathy from neighbors and fellow villagers. Eventually, the woman was sent away from the village to live with her mother. But this did not end the debate for many of the villagers.

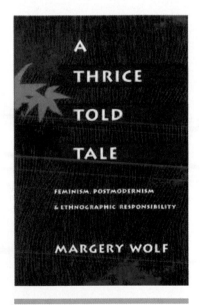

FIGURE 3.11 In *A Thrice Told Tale*, anthropologist Margery Wolf tells the story of a woman in a Taiwanese village from three distinct perspectives, revealing the multiple ways that the same events can be represented, even by the same anthropologist.

MAP 3.5
Taiwan

Drawing on her field notes of the time, Wolf created three different texts. First, she presents a fictional short story written soon after the events occurred. Second, she presents her actual field notes as a kind of text—raw and unedited, available for the reader to analyze and assess. Finally, thirty years later, Wolf produced an anthropological article published in *American Ethnologist*, one of the field's leading academic journals. By presenting these three texts side by side, three different representations of the same event, Wolf explores the many uses of field notes and the experimental ethnography they can inform.

What Moral and Ethical Concerns Guide Anthropologists in Their Research and Writing?

Anthropologists often face moral and ethical dilemmas while conducting fieldwork. These dilemmas require us to make choices that may affect the quality of our research and the people we study. Indeed, the moral and ethical implications of anthropological research and writing are of deep concern within the discipline and have been particularly hot topics at various times in its history. As a result, the American Anthropological Association (AAA) has developed an extensive set of ethical guidelines, which you can view at www.aaanet.org.

Do No Harm

At the core of our ethics code is the mandate to do no harm. Even though as anthropologists we seek to contribute to general human knowledge, and perhaps shed light on a specific cultural, economic, or political problem, we must not do so at the expense of the people we study. In fact, this issue spurred the creation of the AAA's code of ethics. The organization's website presents a great variety of advice about the anthropologist's responsibility to the people being studied.

Several key examples in the history of anthropology demonstrate the importance of the "Do no harm" mandate. In the 1960s and 1970s, anthropologists came under heavy criticism for their role in colonialism, particularly for intentionally and unintentionally providing information on local cultures to colonial administrators and military agents. After World War II, anthropology as a discipline was criticized for aiding the European colonial encounter, assisting colonial administrators by providing detailed descriptions and analysis of local populations, many of which were actively engaged in struggles against colonial rule. Anthropology was criticized for helping to create an image of colonial subjects as unable to govern themselves and in need of Western guidance and rule (Asad 1973). During the Vietnam War in the 1960s, some anthropologists were criticized for collaborating with the U.S. military occupation and counterinsurgency efforts. In the 1970s, the AAA experienced internal political turmoil as it addressed accusations of covert research conducted in Southeast Asia by anthropologists (Wakin 1992).

More recently, the ethical practices of two American researchers, anthropologist Napolean Chagnon and geneticist-physician James Neel, who worked among Brazil's indigenous Yanomami people (1968) in the 1960s and following, have come under question. In his book *Darkness in El Dorado* (2000), journalist Patrick Tierney has claimed, among other things, that Chagnon and Neel compromised their subjects' health to see how unprotected indigenous populations would respond to the introduction of infectious disease. Later investigations did not support Tierney's most serious charges, and the original findings of the AAA against Chagnon and Neel were rescinded. The controversy, however, stimulated a significant debate within anthropology about the code of ethics expected of all members.

Recently the U.S. military has actively recruited anthropologists for service as cross-cultural experts in Iraq and Afghanistan, renewing impassioned debates within the discipline about the proper role of anthropologists in military and covert operations. Through the Human Terrain Systems program, the U.S. military recruits, trains, and deploys anthropologists to be embedded with combat units and to advise military commanders on building local community relationships. The role of anthropologists in military-sponsored "nation-building" projects has been supported by some (McFate 2005) but criticized by many others who have warned of the "weaponizing of anthropology"—turning anthropological research strategies and knowledge into a tool of war (Price 2011).

FIGURE 3.12 *Left,* an American soldier in rural Vietnam, 1967. *Right,* U.S. Marines in Marjah, Afghanistan, 2012. The relationship of anthropology to colonialism and war has been complicated. During the Vietnam War, for instance, some anthropologists were criticized for collaborating with the U.S. military occupation and counterinsurgency efforts. Today the controversy continues as the U.S. military's Human Terrain Systems program recruits anthropologists to help troops understand local culture and make better decisions in the field.

Obtain Informed Consent

One of the key principles for protecting research subjects involves obtaining **informed consent**. It is imperative that those who we study agree to participate in the project. To do so, they must understand clearly what the project involves and the fact that they have the right to refuse to participate. After all, anthropological research is not undercover investigation using covert means and deception. The anthropologist's hallmark research strategy is participant observation, which requires establishing rapport—that is, building relationships of trust over time. To develop rapport, the subjects of our studies must be clearly informed about the goals and scope of our projects and must willingly consent to being a part of them.

U.S. federal regulations protect human subjects involved in any research, and proposals to conduct research on humans, including anthropological research, must be reviewed by the sponsoring organization. Such regulations were originally designed to cover medical research, but anthropologists—whether students or professionals—now participate in these institutional reviews before conducting research.

Ensure Anonymity

Anthropologists take precautions to ensure the privacy and safety of the people they study by providing anonymity in research notes and in publications. We frequently change the names and disguise the identities of individuals or, at times, whole communities. For example, Nancy Scheper-Hughes disguises the identities of people and places in Brazil to protect the community and individuals she worked with (for example, "the market town that I call Bom Jesus da Mata"). **Anonymity** provides protection for the people in our studies who may be quite vulnerable and whose lives we describe in intimate detail. This consideration becomes particularly important and sometimes controversial in situations in which research involves illegal activities—for instance, Claire Sterk's ethnography about prostitution (2000) or Philippe Bourgois's work with drug dealers in New York City (2003).

How Are Fieldwork Strategies Changing in Response to Globalization?

The increased movement of people, information, money, and goods associated with globalization has transformed ethnographic fieldwork in terms of both its process and its content.

Changes in Process

Changes in communication and transportation have altered the ongoing relationship between the anthropologist and the community being studied. Global communication allows the fieldworker and the community to maintain contact long after the anthropologist has left the field, facilitating a flow of data, discussions, and interpretation that in the past would have been very difficult to continue. The expansion of global transportation networks means that an anthropologist may find someone from the researched community showing up on his or her doorstep from another part of the world.

Changes in Content

Globalization has also deeply affected fieldwork content. No longer can an anthropologist study a local community in isolation from global processes. As even the most remote areas are affected by intensifying globalization—whether through media, tourism, investment, migration, or global warming—ethnographers are increasingly integrating the local with the global in their studies. In some cases, particularly in studies of migration, ethnographic fieldwork is now multi-sited, encompassing research in two or more locations to represent more fully the scope of the issue under study.

Nancy Scheper-Hughes's career reflects many recent changes in ethnographic fieldwork. Her earliest research, introduced in the chapter opener, focused on local life in the Brazilian shantytown Alto do Cruzerio. She has carefully monitored changes in the community in the ensuing years, including dramatic recent improvements in infant mortality rates stemming from Brazilian economic growth combined with direct government promotion of local health care services (Scheper-Hughes 2013), and is reporting these changes in a revised and updated version of her classic ethnography, *Death without Weeping*.

Scheper-Hughes's most recent work places Alto do Cruzeiro in the middle of an illicit global trade in harvested human organs. While Scheper-Hughes continues to explore the richness of local life in Brazil, she has expanded her research scope to examine how the experiences of the poor in one community are mirrored in the lives of poor people in many other countries and are linked by a gruesome global trade driven by demand from the world's economic elite.

> For many years I have been documenting the violence of everyday life—the many small wars and invisible genocides—resulting from the structural violence of poverty and the increasing public hostility to the bodies, minds, children, and reproductive capacities of the urban poor. Here I will be addressing an uncanny dimension of the usual story of race and class hatred to which we have become so accustomed. This is the covert violence

occurring in the context of a new and thriving global trade in human organs and other body parts for transplant surgery. It is a business that is justified by many—including doctors and bio-ethicists—as serving "altruistic" ends. But for the poorest and most marginalized populations living on the fringes of the new global dis-order, the scramble for fresh organs for transplant surgery increases the already profound sense of ontological insecurity in a world that values their bodies more dead—as a reservoir of spare parts—than alive.

Descend with me for a few moments into that murky realm of the surreal and the magical, into the maelstrom of bizarre stories, fantastic allegations and a hideous class of rumors that circulate in the world's shantytowns and squatter camps, where this collaborative research project had its origins. The rumors were of kidnapping, mutilation, and dismemberment—removal of blood and organs—for commercial sale. I want to convey to you the terror and panic that these rumors induce in the nervous and hungry residents of urban shantytowns, tent cities, squatter camps, and other "informal settlements" in the Third World.

I first heard the rumor in the shantytowns of Northeast Brazil in the mid-1980s, when I was completing research for my book, *Death without Weeping*, on maternal thinking and practice in the context of extremely high infant and child mortality. The rumors told of the abduction and mutilation of poor children who were eyed greedily as fodder for an international traffic in organs for wealthy transplant patients in the first world. Residents of the ramshackle hillside favela of Alto do Cruzeiro, the primary site of my research, reported multiple sightings of large blue and yellow combi-vans [the so-called "gypsy taxis" used by the poor the world over] driven by American or Japanese "agents" said to be scouring poor neighborhoods in search of stray youngsters, loose kids and street children, kids that presumably no one would miss. The children would be grabbed and shoved into the van. Later their discarded and eviscerated bodies—minus certain organs—heart, lungs, liver, kidneys, and eyes—would turn up on roadsides, between rows of sugarcane, or in hospital dumpsters. "They are looking for donor organs. You may think this is just nonsense," said my friend and research assistant, "Little Irente" in 1987. "*But we have seen things with our own eyes in the hospitals and the morgues and we know better.*" . . .

Soon after I began writing articles that interpreted the Brazilian organ-stealing rumors in terms of the normal, accepted, everyday violence practiced against the bodies of the poor and the marginal in public medical clinics, in hospitals and in police mortuaries, where their ills and afflictions were often treated with scorn, neglect, and general disrespect, I began to hear other variants of the organ-theft stories from anthropologists working in Argentina, Colombia, Peru, Guatemala, Honduras, Mexico, India and Korea. Though most of the stories came from Central and South America, organ-theft rumors were also surfacing in Poland and Russia, where it was reported that poor children's organs were being sold to rich Arabs for transplant surgery. Luise White recorded blood-sucking/blood-stealing vampire stories from East and Central Africa, and South African anthropologist Isak Niehaus recorded blood- and organ-stealing rumors in the Transvaal collected during fieldwork in 1990–93. The African variants told of "firemen" or paramedics driving red combi-vans looking to capture unsuspecting people to drug and to kill in order to drain their blood or remove their organs and other body parts—genitals and eyes in particular—for magical medicine (*muti*) or for more traditional medical purposes. The Italian variants identified a black ambulance as the kidnap vehicle.

The rumors had powerful effects, resulting in a precipitous decline in voluntary organ donation in some countries, including Brazil and Argentina. What does it mean when a lot of people around the world begin to tell variants of the same bizarre and unlikely story? How does an anthropologist go about interpreting the uncanny and the social imaginary of poor, third-world peoples? To folklorists like Alan Dundes and Veronique Campion-Vincent, and to oral historians like Luise White, the rumors are seen as constituting a genre, an oral literary form, the "urban legend." The stories are circulated and repeated because they are "good to tell," they entertain by fright just like good old-fashioned ghost stories. The French folklorist Campion-Vincent interprets the organ-theft stories as the literary inventions of semiliterate people who lack the skills to sort out the credible and realistic from the incredible and the fantastic. To members of the global transplant community of surgeons and patient activists, the rumors are groundless, pernicious lies that need to be exposed, refuted, and killed.

To the anthropologist, however, working closely with the urban poor, the rumors spoke to the ontological insecurity of people "to whom almost anything could be done." They reflected everyday threats to bodily security, urban violence, police terror, social anarchy, theft, loss and fragmentation. Many of the poor imagined,

Nancy Scheper-Hughes

Nancy Scheper-Hughes's research frames this chapter on anthropological fieldwork. As you consider her writings, what principles and techniques can you identify that link her work among poor mothers in northeastern Brazil to the global trade in human organs? How does anthropology help her to understand and engage our changing and globalizing world?

Today Scheper-Hughes is a professor of medical anthropology at the University of California, Berkeley, and co-founder and director of Organs Watch, a human rights project focusing on the global trade in human organs. But her interest in other cultures and in anthropology began at an early age. Scheper-Hughes recalls two early experiences that drew her to the field. One was visiting the American Museum of Natural History in New York City with her family, a place full of anthropological collections, including displays of cultures from around the world. "As a child growing up in a poor immigrant section of Brooklyn, I would go to free concerts, free activities. It's how we got our education—from public schools and public institutions. At the American Museum of Natural History, I was awed by the collection, even if now I am somewhat critical of how those collections were presented. The enormous storehouses of culture were inspirational to me as an eight-year-old."

In college Scheper-Hughes was inspired to take up anthropology by the teaching of Hortense Powdermaker, who herself was a student of Bronislaw Malinowski, a foundational figure in anthropology introduced in this chapter. Remembering her first anthropology professor's teaching style, Scheper-Hughes recalls, "She did not lecture, but rather engaged her students directly. Her teaching forced you to think, and I came away from her class with an enormous curiosity about the world and its people."

Scheper-Hughes has always sought out experiences that allowed her to engage in acts of solidarity with marginalized people. In Brazil she worked as a Peace Corps volunteer and a local community health activist. Upon returning to the United States, she went to Selma, Alabama, the site of a massive campaign during the civil rights movement, to support the work for equality and justice. "They wanted me to focus on research, but after my work on health and community in the Peace Corps, I wanted to be an activist. So, combining research and activism, we were trying to understand what it meant to be a black tenant farmer or share-cropper in Alabama at that time, and particularly the role of federal agencies like the Department of Agriculture and its policies regarding tenant farmers who were excluded from entitlements that went to the landowners, such as cotton allotment checks and FHA home loans. With a team of volunteers we conducted a survey of over five hundred families. What we found was intense suffering, malnutrition, and morbidity [death]. Our report on the extinction of the black farmer in Selma was published, and the case did go to court and eventually changed legislation."

Anthropologist Nancy Scheper-Hughes with her key informant, Dona Dalina, in Alto do Cruzeiro, northeastern Brazil, ca. 1985.

Scheper-Hughes's career has continued these early themes of deep engagement with struggling local communities, an anthropology "with feet on the ground" as she describes it. Her research has included examining the mental health needs of rural farmers in Ireland, the deinstitutionalization of the mentally ill in Boston, the homeless mentally ill in the Bay Area of California, the prevalence of political and everyday violence in South Africa, and most recently, the global trafficking in human organs.

Anthropology has been central to Scheper-Hughes's current research on the illicit trade in human organs, particularly its methodological flexibility. "If you can't define a theoretical approach or precedent within anthropology, you can invent one. Anthropology may well be the most wide open discipline, a Renaissance profession, if you will. You can be a humanist if you wish, and you can be empirically oriented. For instance, medical anthropology allows you to consider a vast array of issues, really anything that has to do with the body, suffering, illness, health, life and death, life crisis events, the subjectivity of the sufferer, pain, modes of knowledge, and ways of knowing. That is true of all the branches of anthropology; it's a protean [versatile] discipline. If you don't like it, you can remake it."

For students wondering why they should take anthropology, Scheper-Hughes considers it a central part of preparing to be a responsible citizen and member of society. "Anthropology should be required for citizenship for people who are native-born because it helps them to understand the world we live in, the country we live in, the histories we have. People really don't know much about their own culture, their own country. For instance, people really don't know to what extent the United States has mistreated its own native peoples. In my home state of California, we had veritable genocide that lasted from the period of the gold rush to the first decade of the twentieth century. We have never really confronted and acknowledged that. To move forward, we have to face our complicated history with indigenous genocide, slavery,

and eugenics applied to immigrants in the 1920s as well. Our history is not all negative, of course. I love to travel across the country by car every few years to meet with and talk with Americans from different parts of the country. There is also a lot to be proud of in being an American. But we do have to understand how our nation came into its present form. We're no different from any other country. All nations are born in violence. But our role is to make them less violent, make them more viable, make them more equitable. That's where anthropology comes in. I think anthropology helps us to look and question what Virginia Woolf called "unreal loyalties"—loyalties to a particular definition of an ethnic group or an origin story. Instead, anthropology helps us to understand and engage the richness, complexity, and conflict involved in making the United States. In this way anthropology can help us become better Americans."

More broadly, Scheper-Hughes thinks anthropology is unique in providing people a way to see themselves as part of humanity in its widest sense. "Our human default system is to be distrustful of what we don't know, whether it's unfamiliar people, places, or things. Anthropology helps people become more culturally literate, and in the process it helps make the individual a bit more at home in the world. It's not only about making the exotic familiar. It's also about taking our own familiarity—our own unquestioned assumptions about people and cultures—and making them strange. If we can do that, we can begin to think outside the box, begin to approach people differently. You know how you suspend your disbelief about what's happening when you're reading a novel or watching a film? When you are in another culture, you have to do the opposite. You have to suspend your belief that your way of life is the only way to live and be and think about the world. You enter another people's social and cultural world and become familiar with it and sometimes fall in love with another culture. That's anthropology."

FIGURE 3.13 A middleman and two young Filipino men with scars; each of the two men has sold a kidney as part of the global trade in human organs.

with some reason as it turns out, that autopsies were performed to harvest usable tissues and body parts from those whose bodies had reverted to the state: "Little people like ourselves are worth more dead than alive." At the very least the rumors were "like the scriptures" metaphorically true, operating by means of symbolic substitution. The rumors express the existential and ontological insecurities of poor people living on the margins of the postcolonial global economies where their labor, their bodies, and their reproductive capacities are treated as spare parts to be bought, bartered, or stolen. Underlying the rumors was a real concern with a growing commodification of the body and of body parts in these global economic exchanges. (Scheper-Hughes 2002, 33–36)

As an engaged medical anthropologist, Scheper-Hughes has spent countless hours investigating the extensive illegal international trade in smuggled human organs. Contemporary globalization, especially the time-space compression of transportation and communication, enables trafficking networks to spread across national boundaries and around the world. These same cornerstones of globalization have allowed Scheper-Hughes and her organization, Organs Watch, based at the University of California, to develop an extensive global network of anthropologists, human rights activists, transplant surgeons, journalists, and government agencies that have collaborated to address issues of human organ trafficking in India, Pakistan, Israel, South Africa, Turkey, Moldova, Brazil, the Philippines, and the United States.

As a member of two World Health Organization panels on transplant trafficking and transplant safety, Scheper-Hughes has seen firsthand the global search for kidneys: the often-poor kidney sellers; the kidney hunters who track them down; and the kidney buyers willing to cross borders, break laws, and pay as much as $150,000 in advance to the organ brokers for a chance at a new kidney and a new life. In 2009 the U.S. Federal Bureau of Investigation arrested a Brooklyn rabbi who had been arranging kidney sales, highlighting the deep integration of illegal international organ trafficking into developed-country markets where, for example, 80,000 Americans linger on a kidney waiting list, struggling through dialysis to stay alive, and where the wait times for a donor in some parts of the country are as long as nine years.

The trajectory of Scheper-Hughes's career from fieldwork in a small favela in Brazil to fieldwork in international organ-trafficking networks reflects many of the transformations shaping anthropological fieldwork over the last forty years. No local community can be viewed as isolated. Anthropologists must consider each local fieldwork site in light of the myriad ways in which local dynamics link to the world beyond. Today fieldwork includes attention to global flows, networks, and processes, as anthropologists trace patterns across national and cultural boundaries while keeping one foot grounded in the lives of people in local communities.

Thinking Like an Anthropologist: Applying Aspects of Fieldwork to Your Own Life

You don't have to go to Brazil to use the skills of an anthropologist. Maybe you will be inspired by this book to explore a culture in another part of the world, perhaps by a language you study, a professor whose class you take, or a new friend you meet. Or maybe you will apply these skills nearer to home. In Chapter 1 you were asked to begin seeing yourself as a budding anthropologist, one who is already working hard to understand the complicated, globalizing world and how you fit into it. Fieldwork skills are the key to navigating what lies ahead of you.

As you think back to the fieldwork of Nancy Scheper-Hughes, remember the questions we asked at the beginning of the chapter:

- What is unique about ethnographic fieldwork, and why do anthropologists conduct this kind of research?
- How did the idea of fieldwork develop?
- How do anthropologists get started conducting fieldwork?
- How do anthropologists write ethnography?
- What moral and ethical concerns guide anthropologists in their research and writing?
- How are fieldwork strategies changing in response to globalization?

Consider how the concepts we have discussed can be applied not only by a professional anthropologist but also by each one of us in our daily lives.

You already use many of the strategies, skills, and perspectives of ethnographic fieldwork to navigate your daily journey through life. Whether in your family, your workplace, or your school, you have to understand the people with whom you interact. You participate and observe, establish rapport, listen, interview, gather life histories, and map out family and social networks. If you keep a journal or diary, you already have started taking field notes about the people and cultural patterns around you. You are constantly assessing who has power, how they got it, and how they use it. While you may already use many of these tools, the goal of this chapter has been to show the rigor with which they can be applied if you take fieldwork seriously, and to enable you to apply them in a more systematic and self-conscious way in your daily life.

Key Terms

ethnographic fieldwork (p. 74)

salvage ethnography (p. 83)

participant observation (p. 84)

reflexivity (p. 87)

literature review (p. 89)

anthropologist's toolkit (p. 89)

quantitative data (p. 90)

qualitative data (p. 90)

rapport (p. 90)

key informant (p. 90)

interview (p. 90)

life history (p. 90)

survey (p. 90)

kinship analysis (p. 91)

social network analysis (p. 91)

field notes (p. 91)

mapping (p. 91)

built environment (p. 91)

zeros (p. 93)

mutual transformation (p. 93)

emic (p. 96)

etic (p. 96)
ethnology (p. 96)
polyvocality (p. 98)
informed consent (p. 102)
anonymity (p. 102)

For Further Exploration

Borofsky, Robert. 2005. *Yanomami: The Fierce Controversy and What We Can Learn from It*. Berkeley: University of California Press. Examines the ethical dilemmas of the Yanomami controversy as scholars debate the issues and students decide where they stand. Book royalties support improved Yanomami health care.

Dan Rather Reports: Kidney Pirates (Jan. 12, 2010). http://blip.tv/hdnet-news-and-documentaries/dan-rather-reports-kidney-pirates-5455011. Documentary about the global trade in human organs, featuring Nancy Scheper-Hughes.

Evans-Pritchard, Edward E. 1963. "Some Reminiscences and Reflections on Fieldwork." In *Witchcraft, Oracles and Magic among the Azande*, 239–54. Oxford, UK: Clarendon Press. Personal reflections on fieldwork.

Malinowski, Bronislaw. (1922) 2002. "Introduction: The Subject, Method and Scope of This Enquiry." In *Argonauts of the Western Pacific*, 1–25. Reprint, London: Routledge. Personal reflections on fieldwork.

Mead, Margaret. 1972. *Blackberry Winter; My Earlier Years*. New York: Morrow. Personal reflections on fieldwork.

Rabinow, Paul, and Robert Neelly Bellah. 1977. *Reflections on Fieldwork in Morocco*. Berkeley: University of California. Personal reflections on fieldwork.

Scheper-Hughes, Nancy. 1989. "Death without Weeping: Has Poverty Ravaged Mother Love in the Shantytowns of Brazil?" *Natural History* 98 (10): 8–16. Read the full article that was excerpted at the beginning of this chapter.

Scheper-Hughes, Nancy. 2013. "No More Angel Babies on the Alto do Cruziero: A Dispatch from Brazil's Revolution in Child Survival." *Natural History*. www.naturalhistorymag.com/features/282558/no-more-angel-babies-on-the-alto-do-cruzeiro. Report on dramatic recent improvements in child survival in the area of Scheper-Hughes's original fieldwork.

U.S. Census Data by zip code. http://projects.nytimes.com/census/2010/explorer. Explore the demographics of your community by accessing U.S. Census data available through this *New York Times* website.

Wolf, Margery. 1992. *A Thrice-Told Tale*. Stanford, CA: Stanford University Press. One anthropologist's experiment with ethnographic writing, presenting one story from a Taiwanese village in three different ways.

Could language use have marked you with "a reasonable suspicion of being undocumented" under a 2010 Arizona law? A billboard in Phoenix, Arizona, warns of uncertainty ahead.

p. 115

p. 117

p. 125

p. 136

p. 141

p. 144

CHAPTER 4
Language

Everything you and I have worked for is being wiped out before our eyes. Our borders, our language, and our culture are under siege.
— Michael Savage, author and radio talk show host, 2003

In April 2010, the state of Arizona passed a law mandating police to arrest anyone who gives a reasonable suspicion of being an undocumented immigrant. If that person cannot prove his or her legal status, he or she must be detained immediately. The law treats a very contentious issue. Arizona lawmakers argue that the law responds to the federal government's failure to monitor borders and protect U.S. citizens from foreigners who they fear will take their jobs and endanger their neighborhoods. The statement quoted above echoes this sentiment, revealing the way many people closely link language change to social upheaval. Civil rights activists, however, ask how police will determine "a reasonable suspicion of being undocumented." They fear that law enforcement officers will rely on how the person looks (skin color), dresses, or speaks. Will someone who speaks Spanish or who speaks English with a Spanish accent be more likely to be arrested and detained? Is language an effective screen for legal status or citizenship?

Debates about language have been raging in the United States over the past twenty years. Thirty states have passed English-only laws limiting classroom instruction, driver's license exams, road signs, and even health warnings to one language. The U.S. House of Representatives has passed legislation several times declaring English to be the national language of the United States, although these bills have never been signed into law.

113

The United States, historically, has been a country of many languages: Dutch, French, Spanish, German, Italian, Chinese, not to mention hundreds of Native American languages and hundreds of others spoken by contemporary immigrants. Spanish has been spoken in what is now the U.S. South and Southwest since the 1500s, when the Spanish conquistadors Francisco Vásquez de Coronado and Hernando Cortéz explored and colonized the area on behalf of the Spanish Crown. How has language come to be such a hot-button issue in the United States today?

Nearly seven thousand languages are currently in use in the world. Through linguistic anthropology, one of the four fields of anthropology, we explore not only the details of a language's vocabulary and grammar but also the role of language in people's lives—both as individuals and as communities. Languages are not abstract concepts with ideal forms perfectly displayed in a dictionary or a textbook. Languages are dynamic and alive. Communication is a social act. Words are part of actions. We call a friend, text a classmate, tell a story, say a prayer, ask a favor. Human language uses an infinite number of forms to communicate a vast array of information. We communicate through poetry, prose, gestures, signs, touch, text messaging—even anthropology textbooks. Not only can we communicate content in great detail, but we also have the wondrous capacity to share the content of our imaginations, our anger, fear, joy, and the deepest longings of our souls.

Humans are born with the ability to learn language—not a particular language, but whatever one they are exposed to as they grow up. Exactly what we learn and the context in which we learn it vary widely. Languages change and grow, constantly adapting to the needs and circumstances of the people who speak them. Although the number of languages shrinks every year under the pressures of globalization, the remarkable diversity of human language reflects humans' dramatically different ways of perceiving, thinking about, and engaging with the world. Because languages are deeply embedded in culture—languages *are* culture—they also become arenas where norms and values are created, enforced, and contested, where group identity is negotiated, and where systems of power and status are taught and challenged.

In this chapter we will consider how anthropologists study human language and communication. In particular, we will ask:

- What is language and where does it come from?
- Can language shape our ways of thinking?
- How do systems of power intersect with language and communication?
- What are the effects of globalization on language?
- How is the digital age changing the way people communicate?

By the end of the chapter you will have a better understanding of how language works, have the conceptual tools to analyze the role of language in your personal life and within your language community, and comprehend the forces that will shape language and communication in our increasingly global future.

What Is Language and Where Does It Come From?

Language is a system of communication that uses symbols—such as words, sounds, and gestures—organized according to certain rules, to convey any kind of information. All animals communicate in some fashion, often relying on a *call system* of sounds and gestures that are prompted by environmental stimuli. Ants share information through chemical trails and pheromones; bees dance to communicate distance and direction to flower petals and nectar. Dogs growl or bark to express hostility or warning. And a border collie named Betsy, featured on the cover of *National Geographic* magazine, could recognize more than 340 distinct words and commands (Morrell 2008). Dolphins produce complicated vocal signals—clicks, whistles, squeaks, trills. Whales have been found to "sing"—to create a vocalization that appears to have a unique tune or accent for each clan or pod of whales.

Although these are all examples of communication—providing information by a sender to a receiver—they are not symbolic language as humans use it. In comparison, human language is a complex system that involves the combination of many small, meaningful elements into larger syllables, words, and sentences following certain rules but with infinite variations. Human language involves sounds and gestures along with myriad symbols with deep historical and cultural meaning. It is remarkably flexible and creative, rapidly adapting to changes in human life and the environment.

The Origins of Human Language

In searching for the evolutionary origins of human language, anthropologists, particularly primatologists, have investigated language use and communication among our nearest primate relatives—chimpanzees, orangutans, and other great apes—with some surprising results. In their natural habitats, primates produce an astonishing array of vocalizations to communicate information about food, sex, and potential predators. These calls are passed along genetically through the generations. Nonhuman primates lack the physical apparatus to create human sounds and human speech. Specifically, their ability to manipulate their vocal chords, tongue, and lips is far more limited than that of humans. But do they have the mental capacity to create human language? In recent years, a set of studies has explored nonhuman primate language capabilities.

language: A system of communication organized by rules that uses symbols such as words, sounds, and gestures to convey information.

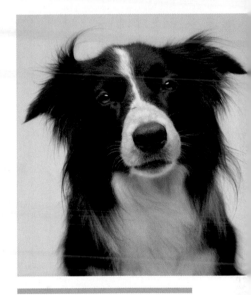

FIGURE 4.1 All animals communicate in some fashion. A border collie named Betsy could recognize more than 340 distinct words and commands.

A chimpanzee named Viki, raised by researchers as a member of a family in the 1950s, was systematically taught human speech but was only able to master four words: *mama, papa, up,* and *cup* (Hayes 1951). But what if Viki's inability to speak arose from her limited physical capacity rather than her cognitive ability? Later studies explored this possibility by teaching American Sign Language rather than spoken English. Because chimps, gorillas, orangutans, and other primates use their hands extensively to express themselves, the theory was that sign language might more accurately reflect their cognitive capacity for language.

A number of primates have been taught, trained, and observed over the last half century in primate research facilities in the United States. A chimpanzee named Washoe, who died in 2007 at age forty-two, was the first to use sign language, mastering more than 130 different signs (Gardner, Gardner, and Van Cantfort 1989). Koko, a gorilla, mastered more than 400 signs (Patterson 1978). Chantek, an orangutan born at a primate research center in Georgia in 1977, was raised much like a human child from nine months of age by anthropologist Lyn Miles at the University of Tennessee at Chattanooga. Now living at Zoo Atlanta in a special habitat, Chantek has mastered several hundred signs and can also understand some spoken English. Reports on the language development of Washoe, Koko, and Chantek suggest that they have the ability to move beyond rote memorization of certain signs, and indicate a more humanlike capacity to lie, swear, tell jokes, invent new words by combining signs, and even the desire to try to teach language to others (Fouts 1997; Miles 1993).

Scholars disagree about the final implications of research on nonhuman primate language capacity. Some have suggested that although this capacity is not as complex as human language, these nonhuman primates can develop language skills at the level of a two- or three-year-old human child (Miles 1993). Others argue that their behavior is mostly imitative—imitating their caregivers rather than using language creatively (Sebeok and Umiker-Sebeok 1980; Terrace et al. 1979). Certainly chimpanzees, gorillas, and orangutans can master rudimentary language signs and can even, at times, exhibit key aspects of human language skills. Their language use reflects **productivity**, meaning that they can use known words to invent new word combinations. Their language can also exhibit **displacement**—that is, the ability to use words to refer to objects or events not immediately present or events happening in the past or future. But, fundamentally, these primates do not use language in the human sense. They do not create and use basic language elements in their natural habitats. They cannot achieve the extremely complex human language system that is perhaps the most distinct aspect of human culture and that enables us to store and pass on huge quantities of information not embedded in our genes.

If our most immediate primate relatives do not approach the physical or mental language capacity of humans, then how did human language capacity

productivity: The linguistic ability to use known words to invent new word combinations.

displacement: The ability to use words to refer to objects not immediately present or events occurring in the past or future.

evolve? Recent genetic information and archeological evidence provide strong clues. Let's consider the genetic information first. Around 1990, a family in Britain (now known only as KE to protect their privacy) was discovered to have a rare mutation of the *FOXP2* gene. The same variant of *FOXP2* is found in chimpanzees. More than half of the members of the KE family inherited severe speech problems that made them unintelligible even to their own relatives (Trivedi 2001). Not only were affected family members unable to physically form words because of a limited ability to make fine lip and tongue movements, but cognitive differences also led them to have difficulty in recognizing and using grammar. As children, these family members were taught to use certain hand gestures to compensate. Genetic analysis indicates that the presence of the particular *FOXP2* gene variant may be crucial for activating and inactivating key human speech capacities, an evolutionary development that appears to be essential to human speech. Such analysis also traces the emergence of human language to within the past 150,000 years.

Archeological evidence provides further clues to the origins of human language. Fossilized brain casts from archaic *Homo sapiens* known as Neandertals (who lived from about 120,000 to about 35,000 years ago) and even earlier *Homo* species reveal the neurological and anatomical features necessary for speech. Our early human ancestors' capacity to cooperate in hunting and tool making also suggests that some language ability existed before the evolution of *Homo sapiens*. Cultural evidence supporting extensive language use appears around 50,000 years ago, including art, tool making, and other technologies that required language to facilitate their transmission from generation to generation. Language as it has developed among modern humans would have enhanced the capacity for group cooperation and the transmission of cultural knowledge; in this way, it conveyed a significant advantage in adapting to less hospitable natural environments and increasing the potential for survival.

Descriptive Linguistics

Language is a system of symbols. It is a system of otherwise meaningless sounds, marks (writing), and gestures that are made meaningful by a group of people through the collective history and tradition of their culture. Think of the English word *pig*. Say it out loud. Now create a mental image of a pig. Why do those three letters and that particular sound represent a pig? They don't look like a pig or sound like any of the noises that a pig makes. But when you say the word, an image is transferred from your brain into sound, which travels through the air into another person's ears and to that person's brain, where an image appears that is similar to yours—if not precisely the same. **Descriptive linguistics** is the study of the construction of those sounds, their meanings, and their combination into forms that communicate meaning.

Through descriptive linguistics, anthropologists work to describe the elements and rules of a particular language. Imagine that you went to do ethnographic fieldwork in a village in the mountains of the Philippines where the residents had no writing system for their local language. Your task would be to learn that language and to create a system for writing it down, perhaps using the English alphabet. Where would you begin? After identifying a person or a few people from the village who would be your teachers, perhaps you would work your way from the most simple aspects of the language to the most complex. A language has a limited number of **phonemes**—the smallest units of sound that can make a difference in meaning. For instance, the English letters *b* and *p* sound very similar, but they make a significant difference in meaning. If you failed to carefully distinguish the different phoneme use in the village where you were working, you might mistakenly switch one for the other in a word followed by the sound *ig* when describing your host's home. In that case, you would end up with *pig* instead of *big*. The study of what sounds exist and which ones are important in a particular language is called **phonology**.

descriptive linguistics: The study of the sounds, symbols, and gestures of a language, and their combination into forms that communicate meaning.

phonemes: The smallest units of sound that can make a difference in meaning.

phonology: The study of what sounds exist and which ones are important for a particular language.

FIGURE 4.3 Humans have been communicating in writing for thousands of years. *Left,* ancient Egyptian stele with hieroglyphics, ca. 27th to 25th century B.C.E. *Right,* rune stone on Adelso Island near Stockholm, Sweden, 11th century C.E.

Extending your linguistic analysis, you would know that **morphemes** are the smallest units of sound that carry meaning on their own. (Phonemes, in contrast, have no meaning of their own.) So, for instance, the morphemes *cow* or *horse* can convey meaning without needing additional sounds. The study of the patterns and rules of how sounds combine to make morphemes is called **morphology**. In human languages, we combine morphemes to form phrases and sentences, relying on specific patterns and rules called **syntax**. So, following Standard American English syntax, we would place a possessive pronoun before the noun, not afterward. We would say or write *my pig,* not *pig my*—although the latter pattern might be linguistically appropriate in another language. **Grammar** encompasses the combined set of observations about the rules governing the formation of morphemes and syntax that guide language use.

Kinesics and Paralanguage

To fully describe and understand another language, the linguist must master more than its spoken and written elements. Human language is accompanied by and embedded in a gesture–call system—made up of body movements, noises, and tone of voice—that also conveys significant amounts of information. **Kinesics**, the study of the relationship between body movements and communication, explores all the facial expressions, gestures, and postures that convey messages with or without words. For example, nods, handshakes, bows, and arms folded tightly across the chest all communicate information, although their meanings are not universal; they vary from culture to culture. The thumbs-up

morphemes: The smallest units of sound that carry meaning on their own.

morphology: The study of patterns and rules of how sounds combine to make morphemes.

syntax: The specific patterns and rules for constructing phrases and sentences.

grammar: The combined set of observations about the rules governing the formation of morphemes and syntax that guide language use.

kinesics: The study of the relationship between body movements and communication.

paralanguage: An extensive set of noises (such as cries) and tones of voice that convey significant information about the speaker.

:-)	=	Smile
:-(	=	Frown
;-)	=	Wink
:-P	=	Tongue Out
:-D	=	Laughing
:-[	=	Embarrassed
:-\	=	Undecided
=-O	=	Surprise
:-*	=	Kiss
>:o	=	Yell
8-}	=	Cool
:-$	=	Money Mouth
:-!	=	Foot in mouth
O:-)	=	Innocent
:'(	=	Cry
:-X	=	Lips are Sealed

FIGURE 4.4 Did you ever wonder why emoticons developed in emails and text messages?

and the "okay" hand signals used in North America are considered rude gestures in certain other cultures. North Americans point with their fingers, but Filipinos point with their lips. Have you ever had the experience of making a motion or gesture that someone else misunderstood? If so, what was the cultural context?

Human language is also accompanied by **paralanguage**—an extensive set of noises (such as laughs, cries, sighs, yells) and tones of voice that convey significant information about the speaker. Paralanguage indicates whether the speaker is (for example) happy, sad, angry, tired, scared, disgusted, or enthusiastic. Try saying the sentence *The exam is on Thursday* using each of these tones of voice. The effect on communication is really quite stunning.

As much as 90 percent of emotional information is communicated through body movements and paralanguage. No wonder that e-mail and text messaging have developed an extensive set of "emoticons"—symbols that indicate the emotional content intended by the sender. E-mails and text messaging are beneficial developments in that they allow rapid response over distances great and small in our globalizing world, and they are increasingly used in the business world and personal life. But because they are devoid of the kinesics and paralanguage that play such key roles in face-to-face human communication, they significantly increase the potential for misunderstandings. Do you trust e-mail or text messaging to communicate your most intimate thoughts?

Can Language Shape Our Ways of Thinking?

The power of language to shape human thought and culture has been a hot topic in linguistic anthropology for many generations. Linguistic anthropologists have considered questions such as Is there an underlying, genetically structured grammar to all languages? Do languages evolve in response to local environments? Do vocabularies and classifications of reality embedded in a language affect the way its speakers think and see the world? In this section we will look at research on the relationships among language, thought, and culture, as well as a culturally specific phenomenon known as *focal vocabulary*.

Language, Thought, and Culture

In the nineteenth and twentieth centuries, a number of linguists, including Ferdinand de Saussure and Claude Levi-Strauss, proposed theories of language that assumed an underlying structure to all the world's languages. In the 1950s Noam Chomsky, a linguist and philosopher, suggested that the human brain is hardwired with a basic framework for organizing language that creates a universal grammar—a similar structure in all languages (1957). In Chomsky's view, all humans share a similar language ability and ways of thinking. He felt that this proposition explains our ability to learn other languages and to translate fluidly from one language to another.

The work of Edward Sapir and his student Benjamin Lee Whorf—later given the name **Sapir-Whorf hypothesis**—took a different direction, suggesting that different languages create different ways of thinking (Sapir and Swadesh 1946). Their hypothesis proposed that languages establish certain mental categories, or classifications of reality, almost like a grammar for organizing the worldview that shapes peoples' ways of perceiving the world. Whorf's linguistic research with the Hopi, a Native American group in the southwestern United States, suggested that the Hopi language differs from English both in vocabulary and in basic grammatical categories that are key to conceptualizing how the world works. For instance, rather than using separate verb tenses expressing past, present, and future, the Hopi language combines past and present into one. Whorf suggested that this pattern reflects a different conceptualization of time and a unique worldview in which past and present reflect lived reality whereas the future is hypothetical or potential (Carroll 1956).

Sapir-Whorf hypothesis: The idea that different languages create different ways of thinking.

"Shakespeare in the Bush": A Nigerian (Mis)interpretation of *Hamlet*

Laura Bohannan explores the challenges that different vocabulary and conceptualizations of the world pose for translation between languages and cultures. She relates her discoveries in the article "Shakespeare in the Bush: An American Anthropologist Set Out to Study the Tiv of West Africa and Was Taught the True Meaning of *Hamlet*" (1966). While Bohannan was conducting fieldwork in a small village in Nigeria, Tiv elders asked her to tell them a story from her own culture. She attempted to explain *Hamlet*, one of the classic stories of English literature, but time and again was unable to translate directly from English to Tiv. Words such as *chief* and *leader* hold distinctly different meanings and roles in the two cultures; they do not translate. The "dead" in Hamlet do not translate because the Tiv have no concept of ghosts. Instead, they imagined Shakespeare's characters as beset by witchcraft.

As Bohannan attempted to use Tiv words to tell Shakespeare's story, the original meanings of the English words became blurred, and the standard message of *Hamlet* was lost in translation. Bohannan's insights as related in "Shakespeare in the Bush" reveal both the power of our environment to shape our language and the power of our language to shape the way we see the world.

MAP 4.1
Nigeria

"Wisdom Sits in Places": The Western Apache Worldview

Keith Basso's beautifully written ethnography *Wisdom Sits in Places* (1996) explores the connections among language, thought, and culture for the Western Apache. His exploration focuses on the unique names that these people give to places in the surrounding natural landscape and the stories and cultural values that they connect to those places.

Over thirty years of living and working on the Fort Apache Reservation of Arizona, Basso mapped the Apache names and stories for 296 locations spread over forty-five square miles. Each place on the landscape had become part of Apache folklore and a key touchstone in instilling the community's values. Through the use of place names in storytelling, these places—with their deep sense of meaning—had become detached from the physical landscape and integrated into the people's daily thought and behavior. Places in the landscape were intimately linked to stories of the Apache ancestors' struggles and wisdom, and then were reinterpreted for the living generation.

Basso recalls watching stories being shot like arrows at people in conversations, usually by elders telling a story to make a point. Consider the following example. A teenage girl, recently returned from a boarding school in Utah, attended a coming-of-age ritual for another girl in the community. Despite the well-known tradition that participants wear their hair down as a sign of respect for the ritual and its sponsors, this young girl wore her hair up in pink curlers. Although people were uniformly unhappy with her behavior, no one spoke to her about it. Several weeks later, the girl attended a birthday party given by her grandmother for a grandson. After dinner, as the company gathered in conversation, Basso recalls how the grandmother began to tell the well-known historical tale of the "forgetful Apache policeman who behaved too much like a white man"—a story associated with a particular place in the local landscape named Men Stand Above Here and There. When the story was finished, the granddaughter quietly stood up and walked back to her home. When Basso asked the grandmother what had happened, she replied, "I shot her with an arrow" (Basso 1996: 56–57).

Two years later, Basso met the young woman again and asked if she remembered the evening at her grandmother's home. "I think maybe my grandmother was getting after me, but then I think maybe not, maybe she's working on somebody else. Then I think back on that dance and I know it's me for sure. I sure don't like how she's talking about me, so I quit looking like that. I threw those curlers away." As Basso and the girl passed near the rock outcropping called Men Stand Above Here and There—the place associated with the grandmother's story—the girl said, "I know that place. It stalks me every day."

This young woman had been the target of an Apache historical tale told by her grandmother and reinforced by a physical landmark she knew well. The landmark would always remind her—and other tribal members—of the tension between retaining traditional Apache values and adopting aspects of white culture. In this way, Basso's ethnography illustrates the deep connection among stories, the individual, and the landscape; among language, thought, and culture.

MAP 4.2
Fort Apache Reservation

FIGURE 4.5 The North Fork of the White River flows through a canyon on the Fort Apache Indian Reservation, Whiteriver, Arizona.

The Role of Focal Vocabulary

Contemporary studies in linguistic anthropology suggest that although the vocabulary and grammar of the language we learn may influence the way we see the world, language does not control or restrict our thinking. Languages are dynamic. They change and adapt as the natural and cultural worlds shift. Humans creatively invent new words and concepts to describe and discuss the changing world as they experience it. Evidence of this adaptability can be found in a language's **lexicon**—all the words for names, ideas, and events that make up a language's dictionary.

Of particular interest to linguistic anthropologists is a language's **focal vocabulary**—that is, words and terminology that develop particular sophistication to describe the unique cultural realities experienced by a group of people. Thus the Bolivian Aymar Indians have two hundred names for potatoes, reflecting the potato's role as a major source of food in their diet. The Nuer of Sudan, studied by E. E. Evans-Pritchard (1940), relied on cattle in their economy, political system, and kinship structures; thus they developed more than four hundred words to distinguish different types of cattle. In today's globalizing world, a focal vocabulary has emerged to describe and engage in digital communication. Words such as *mouse, modem, download*, and *attachment*—even *e-mail, text*, and *tweet*—are very recent creations designed to facilitate communication among those working in the digital communication age.

Even the human description and perception of the color spectrum varies across and within cultures, seemingly according to need. Anthropologist Robin Lakoff (2004) examined how color terms in American English have expanded over the last fifty years, being promoted by the fashion and cosmetics industries.

lexicon: All the words for names, ideas, and events that make up a language's dictionary.

focal vocabulary: The words and terminology that develop with particular sophistication to describe the unique cultural realities experienced by a group of people.

An extensive color vocabulary is not uniform among Americans; it varies primarily by gender. Women are far more likely than men, for instance, to be able to distinguish between salmon and peach, teal and mauve, or cranberry and dusky orange. A similar gender-based focal vocabulary exists in American sports language. This highly specialized set of terms and distinctions, used primarily by men, allows complex communication about complicated human activity but is applicable in extremely limited scenarios.

Clearly, language, including vocabulary, provides categories for recognizing and organizing the world; but language also reflects reality. Language is not rigidly structured or controlling. It is remarkably flexible and fluid, responding to changes in the surrounding culture and enabling us to describe and analyze our world with remarkable specificity.

How Do Systems of Power Intersect with Language and Communication?

Language comes alive when people communicate with one another. But languages are deeply embedded in the patterns of particular cultures. What people actually say and how they say it are intricately connected to the cultural context, to the speakers' social position, and to the larger systems of power within which the language operates. Linguistic anthropologists, especially sociolinguists, study these connections. **Sociolinguistics**, which we will consider in this section, is the study of the ways in which culture shapes language and language shapes culture—particularly the intersection of language with cultural categories and systems of power such as age, race, ethnicity, sexuality, gender, and class (Wardhaugh 2009).

sociolinguistics: The study of the ways culture shapes language and language shapes culture, particularly the intersection of language and systems of power such as race, gender, class, and age.

The "N-Word"

Words can be very powerful. They can hurt. They can heal. Some do so more than others. Words also are symbols. They can carry profound meanings based on the history of their use in a culture. As we explore the intersection of language and culture, particularly the intersection of language and systems of power, a consideration of the history and contemporary usage of the "N-word" provides rich insights. In U.S. culture, the "N-word" carries such powerful connotations that many people are reluctant to say it out loud or put it in print. Television stations censor it from their broadcasts. Politicians shy away from controversy over its usage. It is so powerful that most people only refer to it as the "N-word."

Nigger has been used as a derogatory term for African Americans throughout much of U.S. history—as a symbol of white power, slavery, and the threat of violence. In the twentieth century, the use of "*the N-word*" in public discourse was replaced successively by the use of *Negro, colored, black,* and *African American*.

FIGURE 4.6 How would socio-linguists analyze the history and contemporary usage of the "N-word" so commonly deployed by U.S. rappers, including Jay-Z (*left*) and Kanye West (*right*), here performing in concert?

In 1962, the U.S. federal government legally changed the offending name on all public properties under its control, replacing it with *Negro* (Severson 2011). The "N-word", however, has not disappeared. It continues to hold tremendous symbolic power as its use invokes the history of racism, inequality, and the threat to make those dangers real in the present.

Despite its sordid history, today the use of the "N-word" has been revived among African American youth and in hip-hop and rap music. As a result, a debate has raged even within the African American community about its appropriateness. Many older African Americans reject its use because of its long-standing association with U.S. systems of race and racism. In contrast, younger generations often articulate their desire to appropriate the term for their own generation and rob it of its historical power.

My students remind me that some young people today quite commonly use the "N-word" to express friendship and camaraderie, not anger and hostility. At the same time, they recognize distinct rules about this usage — rules that factor in race, gender, age, and status and that attempt to mitigate against the former role of the "N-word" in this country's systems of race and racism. These young people carefully say "niggah," not "nigger," perhaps taking a slight edge off the word's powerful meaning. They only use it among friends. White people rarely address a person of color with the greeting. Boys never call girls "niggah." Girls rarely use it among themselves. Young people never use it in reference to older people. And students never use it in addressing a professor.

Think about how you feel when you hear the "N-word" spoken aloud. Is your reaction affected by your race, gender, age, or status, or by those of the speaker? Do you feel comfortable using the "N-word" in daily speech? If so, where, when, and with whom? If not, what is the source of your discomfort? Sociolinguists study language in this way. They examine the use of language in its specific contexts and the way language shapes and is shaped by other dynamics of power.

Language and Gender

Ethnic and racial dynamics are not the only sources of tension in communication. Have you ever walked away from a conversation with someone of the opposite sex and thought to yourself, s/he has no idea what I'm talking about! You are not alone. Bookstores are full of titles that promise to help you figure it out: *Men Are from Mars, Women Are from Venus* (Gray 2004); *The 5 Love Languages: The Secret to Love That Lasts* (Chapman 2010); *You Just Don't Understand: Women and Men in Conversation* (Tannen 2001). Clearly, women and men are developing different patterns of language use. How and why?

There is no hard evidence that the brains of men and women are wired differently, leading to gender differences in language and other behavior. But linguistic anthropologists have examined the powerful role of culture in shaping language. In this instance, language and gender are intricately intertwined in personal and public conversations, among groups of men or groups of women, and in mixed-sex talk. In particular, linguists use two main theoretical frameworks for analyzing these patterns. The frameworks are sometimes known as the *difference model* and the *dominance model*.

Linguistic anthropologist Deborah Tannen's popular book *You Just Don't Understand: Women and Men in Conversation* (2001) is built on the difference model. Tannen suggests that conversations between men and women are basically a form of cross-cultural communication. Between the ages of five and fifteen, boys and girls grow up in different linguistic worlds. At the time when most children are developing and perfecting their communication skills, boys and girls are operating in largely segregated gender groups. Girls mostly hang out in small groups, indoors in more intimate conversations. Boys tend to play in larger groups, often outdoors, and compete with one another for group status, often through verbal jokes, stories, and challenges. These patterns, according to Tannen, are reinforced in later years through socializing, sports, and work. No wonder that boys and girls have a difficult time communicating with one another when they finally begin to look for relationships. It is as if they have grown up in two different cultures, two different worlds.

But is miscommunication always rooted in misunderstanding? Or are there real, underlying conflicts between the genders that lead to the miscommunication (Cameron 2007)? Other linguistic anthropologists, working from the dominance model, examine how the cultures of communication learned by boys and girls intertwine with gender dynamics throughout the larger culture: at home, school, work, and play, and even through religion. According to these scholars, if gender stratification and hierarchy are prevalent in the larger culture (see Chapter 8), and if men are generally in positions of superiority, then language will reflect men's dominance and may play a key role in enabling it (West 1998; Lakoff 2004).

Research on mixed-sex communication over the past thirty years consistently shows that many men adopt linguistic strategies that allow them to establish and maintain dominance in conversation and in social interaction. Men are more likely to use dominant speech acts such as commands, explanations, contradictions, criticisms, challenges, and accusations. Women are more likely to ask, request, agree, support, accommodate, accept, and apologize. Men are more likely to interrupt other speakers to insert their ideas or concerns, express doubts, or offer advice.

Despite stereotypes to the contrary, men also tend to dominate conversations through the amount of talking they do. Men claim more "air time" than women in meetings, seminars, board rooms, and classrooms—especially in public forums where they see some possibility of maintaining or increasing their power and status. Working from the dominance model of mixed-sex communication, many linguistic anthropologists suggest that language and gender, as reflected in male and female communication patterns, are intricately connected to patterns of stratification in the culture at large (Holmes 2008).

FIGURE 4.7 Did you ever wonder why men and women struggle to communicate? Are their brains wired differently for language, or have they grown up in different social worlds learning different communication skills?

Does "No" Really Mean "No"? Don Kulick's (2003) study of the use of the word *no* in sexual relations considers how words can take on different meanings depending on the gender of the speaker and the listener. What does "no" mean when a woman says it to a man who desires sex? In court cases involving rape or sexual harassment, men regularly state that they have misunderstood a woman's refusal of their sexual advances. They often blame the victim for not being clear enough with her "no." How can this miscommunication be possible? After all, "no" means "no." Or does it?

According to Kulick's findings, some men apparently think a woman's "no" actually means "yes" or "keep trying." Kulick suggests that men don't hear the actual word but instead hear what they think the word is supposed to mean. Specifically, his study suggests that men in a patriarchal (male-dominated) culture may not even hear a woman's "no" because it does not make sense within their cultural expectations of what a woman is supposed to say. Because U.S. culture casts women as sexual objects, "no" does not meet the cultural expectations of what a woman is or how a woman should behave. Within U.S. cultural formations of gender roles and sexuality, women are imagined to say "no," to resist, when they actually mean "yes." Is it possible that based on their gender, the men and women in your class might even react differently to hearing the results of this study?

The power of culture to shape the meaning of language can have implications for men as well. Men in U.S. culture are expected to say "yes" to women's sexual initiatives, never "no." With a "no" the man risks undermining his masculine identity, perhaps raising questions about his sexuality. A simple and straightforward linguistic expression — *No!* — struggles for clarity in the murky cultural context of gender relationships and power (MacKinnon 1993).

Language and Dialect

Politics and power can play key roles in how we evaluate a system of communication. For instance, how do we distinguish between a language and a dialect? Is it purely on a linguistic basis? A language is commonly described as a complete system of communication, while a **dialect** is considered a nonstandard variation of a language. Naming something a dialect generally places it in a subordinate relationship to the language. However, from a linguistic anthropologist's perspective, the distinction is not always simple. Human languages vary widely in spoken and written form and in accent, pronunciation, vocabulary, and grammar. Yet, from a linguistic perspective, all languages serve as effective communication tools for the people who speak them.

The categorization and evaluation of certain ways of speaking as a dialect and others as a language can frequently be traced to the exertion of power — political power of the nation, the state, the media, and even the stratification

dialect: A nonstandard variation of a language.

Language and Gender in the Classroom

The classroom is one of the most important places in which we learn social roles, including gender roles. We learn not only from the materials we read but also, and perhaps more important, from the people and the institution around us. Talk is a key component of education. We learn through talking, thinking out loud, exploring new ideas with a group of people, and making ideas our own.

But studies have consistently shown that boys dominate classroom conversations. Myra Sadker and David Sadker (1985) surveyed one hundred classrooms and found that boys spoke three times as much as girls and called out answers eight times as often. A study in East Midlands, northeast England (Swann 2007), used video recordings of teachers and students to document both verbal and nonverbal patterns of behavior. There, boys contributed more often and used more words than girls. But the differences were not uniform by gender. Some of the boys were quieter than some of the girls. And classroom conditions affected the action. Boys spoke more when open classroom discussion allowed them to just jump in. When teachers called on students by name, girls had a slight advantage. In another classroom, if the teacher called on students in response to raised hands, boys again were favored; the videotapes showed that they raised their hands more quickly and decisively.

Swann suggests that the unequal participation of boys and girls must be viewed in light of a wide variety of linguistic and nonlinguistic features that combine to create an environment where boys feel more comfortable and secure to actively participate in classroom talk. For instance, she notes that students in the classroom do not act alone; rather, they engage with a teacher who mediates and controls the dynamics, who calls on students directly, and whose body language, positioning, and gaze informally promote certain communication patterns. The

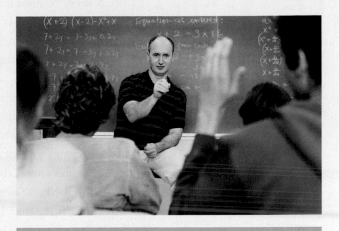

Can you see ways in which gender affects language use in your classrooms?

classroom reflects larger cultural patterns according to which it may seem normal for men to talk more, leading to complicity by boys, girls, and the adults who teach them.

Can you see the dynamics of gender and language at work in your own life? This week, conduct an analysis of gender and language in the classroom. As you attend classes, take careful notes about who speaks. Are they male or female? How long do they speak? Try to be more specific and count the number of words they use. What tendencies do you notice in the speech acts of men and women and the way they present themselves through language? Also, consider that classrooms are mediated and controlled by an instructor. What is the instructor's role in encouraging or discouraging communication by men and women in the classroom, either through words or through body language? How often does he or she call on men and women? Does the instructor's body language or gaze affect participation? Does the instructor's own gender influence the way he or she interacts with members of the class? Analyze your observations to develop a hypothesis about language and gender in the classroom.

among racial and ethnic groups. Yiddish linguist Max Weinreich reputedly once said that a dialect is a language without an army or a navy. In other words, the elevated status associated with a language derives not from its superior linguistic form or communication capacity, but from its ability to establish—perhaps impose—a particular form as the norm by which to judge other ways of speaking. A particular language variation or way of speaking may be elevated in a culture as the **prestige language**, associated with wealth, success, education, and power.

French sociologist Pierre Bourdieu proposes that language skills serve as a type of cultural capital—a resource or asset available to language users that can be converted into financial capital, such as wages and benefits. Mastery over it brings a set of resources that enable the individual to be more successful. Bourdieu notes that linguistic standards are established and reinforced by a culture's educational institutions, government, media, and religious organizations. They may be taught in schools, used in national media broadcasts such as radio and television, or selected as a sign of competence in business hiring practices. Other language variations are then judged against the norm of the prestige language, and their speakers—often said to be speaking a dialect—are associated with inferior positions within the culture (Bourdieu 1982, 1984).

Language Variation in the United States

Although globally the English language varies widely in pronunciation, vocabulary, and grammar, in the United States—through national television, radio, and the educational system—the midwestern accent and grammatical usage have become the prestige language variation. This is sometimes called Standard Spoken American English (SSAE) or simply Standard English, against which all other variations are judged. As we explored in this chapter's opening story, judgments about language can have consequences well beyond the realm of communication. We turn first to consider issues of class and race as they intersect with Standard English.

Language and Class Stratification Speakers of a language are viewed not only as individuals but also as members of a speech community that exists within a complicated and often stratified culture. Language, along with occupation, education, and socioeconomic status, is often used as an indicator of social class. Language variation in the United States that does not conform to the national prestige norm often has a negative implication: it is seen to indicate that the speaker is uneducated or low class, even though these speech variations are not linguistically flawed. This evaluation may have concrete effects on the life chances of speakers.

prestige language: A particular way of speaking, or language variation, that is associated with wealth, success, education, and power.

FIGURE 4.8 Language is often used as an indicator of social class. Do you think employers at the H&M casual clothing store (*top*) or at Hugo Boss (*bottom*), a luxury men's clothing store, hire sales clerks whose language use reflects the relative prestige of their stores?

In examining the intersection of language and class, in 1966 William Labov (1972b) conducted a study of the variation in pronunciation of the letter *r* in words like *car, floor, card,* and *fourth* in New York City. The pronunciation of *r* varies widely across the United States and has changed over the country's history, including both *r* and *r*-less usage. Areas around Boston and the U.S. South originally adopted and continue to retain *r*-less pronunciation modeled after British prestige speech patterns. After an early period of pronouncing the *r*, residents of New York City in the nineteenth century began to go *r*-less. But by the late twentieth century, the *r* was returning to prestige-speak.

Labov surveyed sales clerks in three Manhattan department stores with different clientele: Saks on 50th Street and Fifth Avenue, the most prestigious; Macy's on 34th Street and Herald Square; and Klein's at Union Square and 14th Street, the least prestigious. Labov found that sales clerks' use of *r* increased both with the prestige of the store and within each store according to the escalation of prices on each floor. His study closely linked the increased pronunciation of *r* with increased prestige. Employers, perhaps subconsciously associating *r*-less pronunciation with the lower classes, used speech patterns to evaluate potential sales clerks, matched workers' language to the relative prestige of their stores, and assigned sales tasks according to the employees' perceived class, thereby directly affecting employee wages.

Code Switching in Academia In cultures with distinct language variations, dialects, and accents, individuals may become skilled at **code switching** — that is, switching back and forth between one variation and another according to cultural context. Code switching takes many different forms, as speakers may switch from language to language and from linguistic style to style.

Educational systems tend to resist acknowledging speech variations as equally effective, instead choosing to promote a prestigious version as inherently better. (For instance, think about the linguistic standards your instructor used to grade your last English paper.) In educational environments, as a result, students, teachers, and administrators all learn to switch frequently from informal to formal styles of speaking and writing as required. Talking with friends in the hallway may assume a very different form than responding to a professor's query in class. Writing a text message or a posting on Facebook elicits a distinctly different writing style compared with polishing a research paper for a class assignment.

Recently I received the following e-mail from a student who appears to have struggled to understand when to switch codes:

> *Hi, how r u? this is xxxx from ur class which is on monday n wednesday @ 9:30. i just wanted to ask u that about the book critique. I know what i as suppose to do in terms of writing about the book however i am lost n not sure wht i should do abt the articles and how u want us to relate it to our paper. I mean am i suppose to write abt the book n then relate it to da article n den offer my own opinion on it? plz let me know how i should b doing dis or if this is how i should be doing it. . . . . . Thank you*

While this use of language may serve perfectly well in a text or e-mail with a friend or peer, the failure to code switch in a communication with a professor runs the risk of sending the wrong signals. What evaluations might a professor make of a communication like this one written by a student in text-speak?

Black English: "Spoken Soul" Linguistic anthropologists and other scholars of language have extensively studied one particular form of English that is spoken by millions of African Americans in the United States. At times, this variation has been referred to as Black English, Black English Vernacular, or African American Vernacular English.

Black English is perhaps the most stigmatized variation of American English, mistakenly criticized as broken or flawed English and associated with urban African American youth. But from a linguistic perspective, Black English is a complete, consistent, and logical variation of the English language with a unique history and a distinct and coherent pronunciation, vocabulary, and grammar. Studies by Labov (1972a) and other scholars have carefully demonstrated that Black English is not an ungrammatical jumble but a sophisticated linguistic system with clear rules and patterns (Table 4.1).

Scholars disagree about the exact origins of Black English. Some trace its vocabulary and grammar to the West African linguistic roots of slaves who were forcibly brought to work in the American colonies. Others trace its heritage to nonstandard English used by poor English immigrants who interacted with African slave workers in the plantation system of the American South. The creole languages—blends between the indigenous language and the colonial language—found in Jamaica, Trinidad, Barbados, and Guyana that developed during and after the slave trade may also have been potential sources for the unique forms that Black English has taken (Rickford and Rickford 2000).

Despite its stigmatization within certain parts of American society and the intense cultural pressure to assimilate to Standard English, Black English not only has survived and developed but has become a symbol of identity and solidarity for many within the African American community. Rickford and Rickford (2000) document how this "Spoken Soul"—spoken by African Americans of all ages across the United States and closely associated with African American identity and culture—comes alive in the African American community. Indeed, it is vibrant in homes, schools, streets, and churches and on the airwaves. It is representative of a culture, history, and worldview that are distinct from white culture and ways of speaking.

TABLE 4.1 Contrasts between Standard English Vernacular and Black English

Standard English	Standard English Contraction	Black English Vernacular
You are ready	You're ready	You ready
He is ready	He's ready	He ready
We are ready	We're ready	We ready
They are ready	They're ready	They ready

SOURCE: *William Labov. 1972a. Language in the Inner City: Studies in the Black English Vernacular. Philadelphia: University of Pennsylvania Press.*

FIGURE 4.9 Here, the Oakland, California, Task Force on the Education of African American Students presents a resolution on Ebonics in public education, on January 12, 1997.

The linguistic status of Black English entered prominently into the U.S. national debate in 1996. At that time, the Oakland Unified School District in California recommended recognizing it, under the name Ebonics—from *ebony* ("black") + *phonics* ("sounds")—as a distinct language and supporting student speakers of Black English as if they were learning Standard English as a second language in school. The ensuing controversy obscured the Oakland school district's efforts to address a local problem with national implications—the struggles of African American children to succeed in school. Critics warned that the "teaching of Ebonics" in U.S. public schools (which was never the stated goal of the Oakland school district) would undermine the use of Standard English, which they considered central to U.S. national identity, unity, and progress.

Although the school district revised its plan and the controversy subsided, traces of the resistance to recognizing Black English have lingered. They have created negative stereotypes for efforts to understand the unique linguistic character of Black English and the struggles that young Black English speakers may have in educational settings dominated by Standard English. In fact, the debate about English language diversity and the place of Standard English in U.S. culture continues through efforts at the local, state, and national levels.

Mock Spanish Despite efforts by linguistic anthropologists to educate the public that all languages are linguistically equal, as we have seen in this chapter's opening story, language is often used as an indicator of social position and status. The hierarchical relationship between Spanish and English in the United States offers insights into the process of creating and maintaining hierarchies of power—including hierarchies of race—that stigmatize and marginalize speakers of nonprestige languages.

Bonnie Urciuoli's (1996) study of bilingual Puerto Ricans in New York City found that speakers experience language in two distinct spheres. In an inner sphere of communication with family, friends, and neighbors, both English and Spanish are used freely. Linguistic boundaries are blurred as speakers create fluent and elaborate patterns of communication drawing from both languages. In contrast, in the outer sphere, speakers encounter strangers and gatekeepers: government officials, schoolteachers, hospital staff, and employers. In the outer sphere, bilinguals experience powerful expectations that English and Spanish will be kept separate. Linguistic boundaries are expected to remain sharp and language use neatly ordered. Even the Spanish accents of fluent English-speaking Puerto Ricans are met with resistance and marked as signs of racial difference and otherness. The shift between inner and outer spheres creates intense stress for speakers who are fluently bilingual in the inner sphere but confront intolerance for mixing and "disorder" in the outer sphere. Puerto Rican use of English is frequently found wanting in the outer sphere when compared with the dominant expectations of mono-linguistic orderliness.

Jane Hill (2008) suggests that an opposite dynamic exists for whites who use Spanish in the United States. Whereas Puerto Ricans are disciplined at the boundary of English and Spanish, whites are allowed to cross the boundary without repercussions. Whites use heavily accented Spanish, broken Spanish grammar, and colloquial Spanish terms, mixing English and Spanish without criticism. The language mixture includes terms such as *macho, adios, hasta la vista,* and *cojones* in a kind of Mock Spanish that makes fun of Spanish speakers while enhancing the status of English speakers as cosmopolitan, authentic, or humorous. Written use of Spanish by whites on street signs, public health announcements, T-shirts, and greeting cards is often ungrammatical. Elements of Spanish and English morphology are mixed, adding the suffix *-o* and modifiers such as *mucho* or *el* to create terms such as *el-cheap-o* or *mucho-trouble-o*.

Hill says these practices are allowed and sometimes celebrated because language use in the United States occurs in a "white public space." In this space, white language use is considered normal, objective, and standard, unnoticed and almost invisible even when mixing Spanish and English; in contrast, language used by Spanish speakers is visibly marginalized. Hill warns that the use of Mock Spanish and the marginalization of Spanish speakers within the white public sphere borders on a "racist discourse" that elevates whiteness and English while denigrating other ethnic groups and Spanish-speaking populations. Such a discourse, warns Hill, creates opportunities for racist political campaigns and moral panics about the future of the nation.

As the examples discussed above indicate, language and power intersect in many arenas. Socioeconomic class, educational environments, and racial/ethnic group status are just some of these. In addition, the histories of languages themselves can reflect the effects of systems of power. The study of historical linguistics, discussed below, explores how languages evolve in relation to factors such as geography, migration, and political control.

Historical Linguistics

historical linguistics: The study of the development of language over time, including its changes and variations.

Historical linguistics is the study of the development of language over time, including its changes and variations. By analyzing vocabulary and linguistic patterns, historical linguists trace the connections between languages and identify their origins. For example, through comparative analysis of vocabulary, syntax, and grammar, we know that Spanish and French historically developed from their parent language, Latin. English, German, Dutch, and other Scandinavian languages evolved from an earlier proto-Germanic language. Both Latin and proto-Germanic branched out from an even earlier language called Proto-Indo-European; it was spoken more than six thousand years ago and also gave birth to the languages spoken today in Greece, India, Iran, and Eastern Europe (Mallory and Adams 2006; McWhorter 2001).

language continuum: The idea that variation in languages appears gradually over distance so that groups of people who live near one another speak in a way that is mutually intelligible.

Over thousands of years of adaptation, growth, and change, human language developed more along the lines of a **language continuum** rather than into distinct languages. In a language continuum, people who live near one another speak in a way that is mutually intelligible. The farther one travels, the more the language varies, but it tends to be at least partially mutually intelligible to those living nearby—if not 100 percent, then substantially. Although

FIGURE 4.11 Street signs in Nice, southern France, include both standard French, based on the French spoken in Paris, and below it the local language, called Niçard.

disrupted to some extent over centuries by migration and the strengthening of nation-states, language continuums still exist in many parts of the world. For instance, a strong language continuum has existed between Italy and France. If you were to walk from village to village beginning at the southern tip of Italy, travel northward, and then head northwest into France, you would find that people at either end of the journey would not be able to communicate with one another—their languages would be mutually unintelligible. But along the journey, the local residents of each village you pass through would be able to understand their neighbors in the nearby villages. Changes would be evident from location to location, but communication would be mutually intelligible.

Today we are taught to think that all people in France speak French and that those in Italy speak Italian. This is a definition of language based more on power—the establishment of a national border—than linguistics. In this case, the border between languages is established not by mutual intelligibility but by politics. It is just as likely, because of the language continuum, that when crossing the border from Italy to France, you would find that the people in the villages on either side of the border can understand one another. Of course, the people on the French side may be considered to be speaking a "dialect" of French, whereas "standard French" (based on the French spoken in Paris) is promoted through the government, the schools, and the national media. In effect, "standard French" has an army and a navy. The local language spoken in the village on the French/Italian border does not. This language continuum has been disrupted in recent years by the efforts of the French government to impose a standard dialect across the country. But new laws passed by the European Union have guaranteed that national governments recognize minority languages within their borders and have given new standing to local languages.

An extensive language continuum exists in China as well. Though written Chinese is essentially the same throughout the country, there are thousands of local variations of spoken Chinese, most of which are mutually unintelligible. For example, speakers of Mandarin, Cantonese, Shanghainese, Fuzhounese, and Sichuanese cannot understand one another. Linguistically none is considered superior or inferior to another, but they do vary in prestige. Mandarin is the most widely spoken Chinese language variation. Called *Putonghua* ("the common language") or *Guoyu* ("the national language"), Mandarin is based on the local version of Chinese spoken in and around the national capital, Beijing. For centuries, imperial administrators who governed areas across China on behalf of the emperor in Beijing adopted Mandarin, so it became the norm associated with China's economic and political elite. After the Chinese civil war in 1949, the new government established *Putonghua* as the national standard for all media broadcasts as well as for instruction in all schools. As a result, regardless of the local variations of the Chinese language, today everyone learns *Putonghua* as a second language. But this is a political decision, not a statement of its linguistic superiority.

Clearly, languages evolve as human groups use them, adapt them, or surrender them to more prevalent forms. The current age of globalization will provide even more opportunities for languages to meet and either mix or remain largely unchanged. This means that the field of historical linguistics will continue to trace dynamic aspects of language variation and change well into the future.

What Are the Effects of Globalization on Language?

The movement of people throughout human history has played a role in the way that languages change and develop. As people move, elements of vocabulary and grammar are loaned to and imposed on populations that come into contact. Languages are full of loanwords that have been adopted from others. The encounter of linguistic communities occurs with increasing rapidity in the contemporary era of globalization. Still, approximately seven thousand languages resound around the world today. A few have hundreds of millions of speakers. Most have a few thousand. However, globalization is consolidating language use among a small group of languages while threatening the extinction of thousands of others (Table 4.2).

Diminishing Language Diversity
The current pattern of increasing global interconnection threatens to diminish language diversity worldwide. In an earlier era of globalization, colonialism spread English, Spanish, Portuguese, French, Dutch, German, and Russian

TABLE 4.2 Top Twenty World Languages, 2010

Language	Number of Native Speakers
1. Chinese	1,213 million
2. Spanish	329 million
3. English	328 million
4. Arabic	221 million
5. Hindi	182 million
6. Bengali	181 million
7. Portuguese	178 million
8. Russian	144 million
9. Japanese	122 million
10. German	90.3 million
11. Javanese	84.6 million
12. Lahnda	78.3 million
13. Telugu	69.8 million
14. Vietnamese	68.6 million
15. Marathi	68.1 million
16. French	67.8 million
17. Korean	66.3 million
18. Tamil	65.7 million
19. Italian	61.7 million
20. Urdu	60.6 million

SOURCE: *M. Paul Lewis, ed. 2009.* Ethnologue: Languages of the World, *16th ed. Dallas: SIL International. www.ethnologue.org / ethno_docs / distribution.asp?by=size.*

beyond Europe to people around the globe. Because these former colonial languages provide points of access to the current global economic and political system, many of them continue to expand today. In addition, increasing migration to urban centers often leads speakers of less widely used languages to assimilate and adopt the more widely used language. The more prominent languages—including the former colonial languages and other regional or national languages—dominate global media, including television, radio, print, and digital media. Through this dominance they are crowding out the less widely used languages and their speakers.

As a result of these dynamics, today the ten most prominent languages are spoken by more than 50 percent of the world's population. The top eighty-three languages account for 80 percent of humanity. The 3,500 least widely used languages, in total, account for only 0.2 percent of the world's language users (Harrison 2007). English has a unique position in the world at the moment, with as many as two billion speakers. Many of these are nonnative speakers who learn English as a second language because of its central role in universities, medicine, computing, entertainment, and intergovernmental relationships. English is currently a prestige language that provides effective access to international economic activity and political engagement.

Hastening Language Loss

Linguistic anthropologists warn that as many as half of the seven thousand languages in the world today could be lost by the end of the twenty-first century. In 2005, 204 languages had fewer than ten speakers. Another 344 had fewer than one hundred speakers. Together, these 548 languages represent almost 10 percent of the world's languages. They have very little chance of survival and face almost certain language death. This is the outcome of **language loss**. On average, one language is lost every ten days (Harrison 2007). The most rapid disappearances are in northern Australia, central South America, the Pacific Northwest of North America, and eastern Siberia; this group also includes the Native American languages spoken in Oklahoma and the southwestern United States.

Languages develop over time to enable human groups to adapt to a particular environment and to share with one another information that is essential to their local culture. When a language is lost, when it is crowded out by more widely used languages, we lose all of the bodies of information and local knowledge that had been developed—perhaps over thousands of years—by that community. Within a language is embedded rich knowledge about plants, animals, and medicines. Within a language is embedded a particular group's unique way of knowing the world and thinking and talking about human experience.

Language Revitalization Most languages have never been written down. Does this surprise you? If you are a speaker of one of the more prominent languages, such as English, perhaps it does. As many of the less widely used languages face extinction, some groups are undertaking efforts to preserve them in written form.

Documenting a local language may involve years of work in a detailed and painstaking process that draws on all the basic skills of fieldwork and descriptive linguistics. One of the most extensive efforts to create written records

language loss: The extinction of languages that have very few speakers.

FIGURE 4.12 Globalization threatens the loss of many smaller local languages, and with them their local knowledge and ways of understanding the world. *Left*, a Seri herbalist carries home lavender from the desert. The Seri are an indigenous people in Mexico. *Right*, Ramona Dick is an elder in the Washoe tribe, which is based mainly in California and Oregon. As a child, she refused to be sent to a school where students were required to speak only English.

of small languages is the work of a group called the Summer Institute of Linguistics (SIL). Formerly known as the Wycliff Bible Translators, SIL sends missionaries to the field, often to remote areas, to live with a community and create a written language in order to translate the Christian Bible into the local language.

Some linguistic anthropologists consider SIL's work to be controversial. They are concerned that the Christian nature of the project means that certain aspects of local culture—including indigenous religious beliefs, ritual language, songs, and art connected to local religion—are at risk of being ignored and extinguished. Other scholars acknowledge the significant data that would be lost if SIL translators were not doing the detailed work of documenting hundreds of local languages that are threatened with extinction in small communities worldwide. Despite this controversy, SIL has succeeded in producing a widely used compendium of all the world's languages called *Ethnologue*. Although it started with only forty entries in 1951 as a language guide for Christian missionaries, in 2009 *Ethnologue*'s 1,200-page sixteenth edition catalogued 6,909 languages (Lewis 2009).

Preserving Endangered Languages Information technology is beginning to transform the ways in which linguistic anthropologists document and preserve endangered languages, creating new opportunities for revitalization. Consider the Native American Lakota language. Its approximately fifty thousand speakers live primarily in tribal areas scattered across North and South Dakota, as well as in cities, towns, and rural areas across the United States. Their tribally owned lands are in some of the poorest U.S. counties. Few children learn Lakota today, threatening the language with eventual extinction. So the Lakota have placed a high priority on preserving their language and culture and increasing Lakota language use among young people. Linguists have been working to document the Lakota language by collecting and preserving language samples, cultural knowledge, and artifacts. Some have even done intensive immersion in the Lakota language. But limited resources, combined with the geographic dispersion of Lakota speakers, have inhibited these efforts.

Recently, a small local company, LiveAndTell, has been building an online digital platform for Lakota language preservation and instruction. Using participatory social media technology similar to that of YouTube and Flickr, LiveAndTell has been creating opportunities for Lakota speakers to collaborate, create, and share digital artifacts. Families are writing family stories and posting photos, audio recordings, videos, and online annotations. School research projects are being uploaded to community sites. In these ways, the dispersed Lakota language community is creating an online archive of the living language. For instance, one contributor posted a picture of a car and then tagged each part — steering wheel, mirror, tire, and so on — with the Lakota name and an audio file of its pronunciation. Entries like these provide detailed linguistic information that is not available in standard dictionaries and may never come to light in formal oral interviews with professional linguists (Arobba et al. 2010).

As the Lakota example shows, innovative use of information technology has the potential to transform the study of endangered languages. For a discussion of additional efforts to preserve small languages, see "Anthropologists Engage the World," pages 144–45.

How Is the Digital Age Changing the Way People Communicate?

Human communication has experienced periods of rapid and dramatic transformation. The invention of the printing press, as well as the printing of the Gutenberg Bible in Germany in the 1400s, transformed human communication through the mass production of books, newspapers, and pamphlets. These printed materials facilitated the widespread exchange of ideas and information across vast distances. Today the transformation of communication proceeds at a spectacular pace and on a global scale, having rapidly integrated more than a billion people into a new world of connection in just three decades. Technological

FIGURE 4.13 World Languages by Country, 2005 The languages of the world are spread across countries in ways that may surprise you. Take a moment to identify the ten countries with the most and least language diversity.

SOURCE: *data from Ethnologue.com*

developments in communication are collapsing our basic notions of time and space and driving today's globalization process.

In their book *Born Digital*, John Palfrey and Urs Gasser (2008) discuss the emergence of what they call **digital natives**, a generation of people—including many of you reading this book—born after 1980 who have been raised in the digital age and have spent their entire lives thinking digitally. Think about your own communication equipment. It fits comfortably in your hands: laptops, smartphones, tablets, digital video cameras and readers. High-speed cable and wireless Internet enable you to travel swiftly and easily in a digital world of texts, tweets, posts, instant messages, file sharing, Googling, Skype, and You-Tube. You use social networking sites like Facebook to enhance interactions with "friends." You navigate around websites, wikis, blogs, and online gaming. All of this is new in the last thirty years, most of it in the last twenty (Table 4.3).

digital natives: A generation of people born after 1980 who have been raised in a digital age.

David Harrison

David Harrison became interested in endangered and little-documented languages almost by accident. "I was in a summer language program in Lithuania. We visited a small town, Trakai, and our guide told us that a minority people called the Karaim lived in this town. And I just happened to have my little tape recorder with me.

"So I went off and I knocked on a few doors and asked around. And I found a gentleman who turned out to be the spiritual leader of the Karaim community. He sat down with me for an interview and explained that their language was going extinct, that there were only a couple hundred speakers left. They were all elderly, and the younger generation had switched over to speaking Lithuanian and Russian, the more dominant languages. So I was completely fascinated by this idea that languages could go extinct."

As a field researcher, Harrison focused his investigations on Turkic languages in central Asia, including Tuvan, Tsengel Tuvan, Tofa, Ös (Middle Chulym), and Monchak. More recently he has studied languages of northeast India, as well as Siletz Dee-ni in Oregon and Kallawaya in Bolivia. His ethnographic research examines indigenous knowledge, folklore, oral epics, conceptual systems, and naming practices.

"My research focus and my specialty involves thinking about language extinction not only as a very personal, lived experience in the lives of people, but also as a global trend that has social and real-life consequences for all of us. So, I've devoted the last decade or more to traveling around the world, taking the pulse of some of the world's smallest languages, and meeting with the last speakers of these languages.

"We are in the middle of a language extinction crisis. It can be a bit depressing because languages don't voluntarily go extinct. Languages go extinct because of political and social oppression and coercion, and in some cases even genocide, where the policies of nation-states force the language assimilation of a whole people. As horrible as that sounds, that was historically the practice and the policy of the U.S. government as well as the Canadian government. Many modern nation-states have engaged in this project, to forcibly unite indigenous peoples. We're still living in the aftermath of genocide-inflicted assimilation. Talk to any person in the Native American community involved in language, especially the elders, and you will hear horror stories about being sent off to boarding schools where they were punished for speaking their languages, made to feel ashamed of doing it."

On his visits to indigenous communities, Harrison finds that people are responding to the disappearance of their languages. Youth especially are developing ways to use cultural activism and new technologies to revitalize endangered languages. "I don't want to paint it only as a grim scenario. There's also a very exciting, global grassroots movement to sustain small languages. I encounter a younger generation that I like to refer to as 'language

Linguistic anthropologist David Harrison

warriors'—people who have made a distinctive choice to not let their language go extinct. They're doing very exciting things, like performing hip-hop in the language, or text messaging in the language, using social media in their language. They're doing creative things with it. They're telling their stories. They're making films, creating Facebook pages."

Globalization has both negative and positive impacts on language diversity, says Harrison. "Globalization allows a small number of very large languages to spread and dominate and impose themselves. And so you can think of this as creating the conditions under which smaller languages are forced into extinction. On the other hand, I see that through social media and community collaboration, small languages can achieve a global voice, many times more than their number of speakers."

Why does the diversity of languages matter to everyone, including those of us who speak globalized languages like English? Harrison believes that each language frames our conception of the world differently, a notion called *linguistic relativity*. Languages employ metaphors in different ways, for example. "If you are helplessly in love with someone in Tuvan, you say, 'My liver aches.' Because to them, the liver is the seat of emotion. Now, we know that's not true, of course. The brain is the seat of emotion, but that doesn't stop us from using the heart as the seat of emotion in American culture. So, two very different cultural choices about where we think emotion resides. But a metaphor is very powerful when it's used by your culture."

Language shapes our idea of time, as well. "In English, we think of the future of being in front of us, being in front of us physically, being in front of us in space. We say things like, 'I'm looking forward to next week,' or 'Christmas is coming up soon.' And we think of the past as being behind us. But in Tuva, they reverse the space-time mapping. They talk about the future as being behind them, unseen, invisible, as if it were sneaking up from behind. And the past is what's out in front of you because you can see it. So, when you find a very different metaphor, or a different way of seeing the world in another language, it forces you to circle back and realize that your own cultural assumptions are not about the world per se, but rather just one of many ways to frame and understand the world. And I think this is one of the virtues of anthropology, to question your own cultural views and values, and realize that they are just that. They are relative."

Harrison was raised monolingual, but he stresses the deep importance of learning other languages. "As soon as you study another language, even a little tiny bit, you immediately begin to see how differently it views the world, in terms of everything from numbers, to the names we give our relatives, to concepts like love. You stop being a prisoner of your own cultural point of view. You're suddenly able to leverage these very different understandings of the world. That expands your ability to think, as well as to solve problems. No culture has a monopoly on human genius. We never know where the next great idea is going to come from. Different languages and cultures produce different patterns of thinking and different ways of solving problems. So, linguistic diversity is intellectual diversity; it's the foundation for intellectual diversity, and that's the foundation for how we're going to survive on this planet."

TABLE 4.3 The Digital Revolution, in Historical Perspective

1840	Camera / photography
1843	Electric telegraph
1870s	Telephone
1893	Wireless telegraph
1895	Portable moving picture camera
1900s	Radio
1920s	Black-and-white television
1940s	First computers
1950	Color television
Early 1970s	Handheld mobile phones
Late 1970s	First online bulletin board system
Early 1980s	Usenet groups
1981	First laptop computer
Late 1980s	E-mail
1991	World Wide Web becomes widely accessible
1992	First text message
Early 1990s	Browsers simplify Web searches
Late 1990s	Search engines, portals, e-commerce
2000	Social networks
2001	Polaroid declares bankruptcy; digital cameras begin domination of market
2003	Launch of MySpace
2004	Launch of Facebook
2005	Creation of YouTube
2006	Tower Records is liquidated
2007	First iPhone
2008	iTunes becomes largest music distributor
2010	Twitter, launched in 2006, reaches 4 billion tweets in first quarter of the year

SOURCE: *Adapted from John Palfrey and Urs Gasser. 2008.* Born Digital: Understanding the First Generation of Digital Natives. *New York: Basic Books.*

Palfrey and Gasser refer to a slightly older generation as *digital immigrants*. Members of this generation (including the author of this book) use the technology and platforms of the digital age but have had to learn them as if immigrating into a new culture or learning a second language. Digital technology is never as comfortable and easy for us as it is for digital natives.

Clearly, the digital age is transforming the way a huge segment of the world's population communicates, studies, gathers information, gets their news, writes, and works. Across the globe, businesses, politicians, religious groups, social service agencies, human rights groups, factory workers, other laborers, and students are exploring new ways of communicating, publicizing their work, and building networks of support.

Digital Activism

The digital age—especially the development of cell phones, the Internet, search engines, Facebook, YouTube, and Twitter—has transformed political activism. In fact, a growing phenomenon of today's global age is digital activism, as evidenced by recent events of the 2011 Arab Spring throughout North Africa; political movements in Iran, Syria, and Myanmar; and the Occupy Wall Street protests in the United States and beyond (see Chapter 14).

At least 400 million of China's 1.3 billion people participate in the digital age thanks to massive investments by the Chinese government to keep cell phone and Internet service costs low. This infrastructure now provides the framework for China's digital activists, including tens of thousands of migrant workers who are organizing for their rights in a country that has adamantly resisted independent labor unions and popular democracy movements (Yang 2009; Barboza and Bradsher 2010). As China's experience illustrates, even governments that devote extensive resources to monitoring and censoring digital communication struggle to keep up with highly decentralized sources of information available in the digital age and made possible by the very technologies required for economic modernization.

During the spring and summer of 2010, a wave of worker strikes hit foreign companies operating in China. Over the previous twenty years, abundant and inexpensive Chinese labor, low taxes, and lax environmental laws had drawn companies to relocate their production sites to China. But in recent years thousands of isolated strikes and uprisings have spread across the vast nation to protest environmental degradation, local government corruption, and oppressive working conditions. The successful strikes in 2010 against Honda and other foreign companies drew particular attention because of the strikers' extensive use of digital technology to mobilize workers, coordinate strikes among factories in different parts of the country, standardize wage demands, and communicate their situation to the Chinese public and the international press. Striking women workers shot photos and video of violence by factory security guards and uploaded them to Chinese sites such as Youku.com and 56.com. Text messages kept fellow workers apprised of quick changes in strategy.

As we will examine further in Chapter 14, students, democracy advocates, human rights organizations, and other digital activists in countries from South Korea to Burma, Ukraine, and Iran have utilized cell phones, digital cameras, Internet cafés, Twitter, and Facebook to amplify ideas, coordinate activities, broadcast developments, and ask for donations. Activities such as these are unique to the digital age and will surely continue as individuals and groups use social media and other electronic networks to communicate their shared experiences and objectives.

"Digital Natives" Go to College

Technological advances of the digital age are also transforming education. Consider the following facts: Class Facebook pages, blogs, websites, and discussion boards facilitate communication outside the classroom. Cell phone cameras capture whiteboard images. Laptops and smartphones enable students to explore lecture details during class. Students submit papers online. Professors use online programs to check for plagiarism. And RateMyProfessor.com provides student evaluations of instructors' classroom performance. As you well know, these are the facts of life in today's academic classrooms.

In a YouTube video posted in 2007 called *A Vision of Students Today*, students in anthropologist Michael Wesch's Introduction to Cultural Anthropology class at Kansas State University explored the tension between "digital native" students and the often antiquated facilities and communication strategies employed in U.S. universities (Wesch 2008). Two hundred students collaborated in a class project to tell their own education stories. They read a lot, but they read texts, e-mails, Web pages, and Facebook profiles—not books. They write thousands of pages a year, but in tweets, texts, posts, and e-mails—not college research papers. How does your own educational experience compare to those at Kansas State? Watch the video (see For Further Exploration at the end of this chapter). Then consider surveying your classmates about the way their digital lives intersect with the educational practices of your college or university.

Wesch suggests that there is a tension between the traditional practices of educational institutions and the emerging patterns of the digital age. The tension arises because educational institutions have traditionally operated on the assumption that information is scarce (and available only through them); but in a digital age, students can find information everywhere through the click of a mouse, the keys on a laptop, or the screen of a smartphone. These transformations are shaking most U.S. institutions of higher education as students (mostly digital natives) work with faculty and administrators (mostly digital immigrants) to move education into the digital age.

The Digital Divide

Despite the rapid expansion of digital communication to include one billion people over the last several decades, a vast digital divide separates the world into digital haves and have-nots. Five and a half billion people, representing 85 percent of the world's population, are still left out. This division reflects the tendency of globalization to increase uneven development (see Chapter 1).

Participation in the digital age requires computers, cell phones, Internet access, education systems that emphasize critical thinking, and even more fundamentally, electricity—a commodity that is not available to many people in the world on a consistent basis. A laptop that is so common in U.S. colleges and universities, for instance, costs more than many of the world's people earn in a year. Access to these resources is stratified on a global level, often along lines of race, class, and nationality. Even in a country such as China, where national investments have narrowed the digital divide to the extent that 400 million people now have access to cell phones and the Internet, 900 million Chinese still find themselves shut out of the digital age.

Thinking Like an Anthropologist: Language, Immigration, and U.S. Culture

As you encounter the complexities of language in daily life—communicating with a boyfriend or girlfriend, collaborating with classmates from other places, studying abroad, working with people in multinational corporations, debating immigration policy, or understanding gender in classroom dynamics—thinking like an anthropologist can help you better understand your own experiences and those of others. First, take a moment to review the questions we asked at the beginning of this chapter:

- What is language and where does it come from?
- Can language shape our ways of thinking?
- How do systems of power intersect with language and communication?
- What are the effects of globalization on language?
- How is the digital age changing the way people communicate?

In our opening story, we considered how language has entered the immigration debates in Arizona. Now that you have been studying anthropology—and in this chapter, linguistic anthropology—how would you analyze the underlying issues at play in this debate? Why has language become such a hot-button issue in U.S. politics? How is English intertwined with notions of American identity, class, and belonging? As we will see in Chapter 13, the long-held model of incorporating new immigrants into U.S. culture—the melting pot that blends everyone's diversity into one big stew—now competes with a salad bowl metaphor in which immigrants don't blend in completely but contribute their unique diversity to a multicultural salad. This new model has encountered resistance, particularly from people who fear a fragmentation of U.S. culture.

Language use has become symbolic of these larger debates. Studies consistently show that the children of immigrants grow up speaking English as their first language, not the language of their parents' country of origin (Portes, Fernandez-Kelly, and Haller 2009). Yet the debate over language instruction in education continues. Along with Arizona's new immigration law, the Arizona Department of Education has instituted new policies for bilingual education programs. In 2010, fully 150,000 of the state's 1.2 million public school students were categorized as English Language Learners—a long-term pattern. How to best educate those students has been a topic of heated debate for years. In the 1990s, Arizona recruited thousands of bilingual teachers to lead bilingual classes for students who may have grown up speaking Spanish at home. Many of the new teachers were recruited from Latin America, and their first language was Spanish. Then, in 2000, Arizona voters passed a referendum mandating that instruction of nonnative English speakers be in English only. The 2010 policy changes adopted new fluency standards for teachers, focusing on pronunciation and writing. Teachers who were unable to meet the new standards were removed from the classrooms of nonnative English speakers (Jordan 2010).

The Arizona education debates reveal the way that language functions as more than a system of symbols that enable people to communicate. Language is also a key cultural arena in which norms are established, values are promoted, and relationships of power are negotiated.

Key Terms

language (p. 115)
productivity (p. 116)
displacement (p. 116)
descriptive linguistics (p. 118)

For Further Exploration

Basso, Keith. 1996. *Wisdom Sits in Places: Landscape and Language among the Western Apache.* Albuquerque: University of New Mexico Press.

Berkman Center for Internet & Society at Harvard University. http://cyber.law.harvard.edu. Website dedicated to exploring the development of cyberspace, particularly related to legal issues and censorship. Hosts online lectures and discussions.

The Linguists. 2008. Produced and directed by Seth Kramer, Daniel A. Miller, and Jeremy Newberger. Ironbound Films. www.thelinguists.com. A documentary film following the work of David Harrison and Greg Anderson as they track and record dying languages around the world.

National Geographic. *Disappearing Languages.* www.languagehotspots.org. An interactive website on languages nearing extinction.

N-Word: Divided We Stand. 2007. Produced by Helena Echegoyen. A Post Consumer Media Production, distributed by MediaLink Entertainment. A video exploring the history and current usage of the "N-word" in American culture.

Tannen, Deborah. 2001. *You Just Don't Understand: Women and Men in Conversation,* 2nd ed. New York: Ballantine Books.

Wesch, Michael. 2008. *An Anthropological Introduction to YouTube.* www.youtube.com/watch?v=TPAO-lZ4_hU&feature=channel.

Wesch, Michael. 2007. *A Vision of Students Today.* www.youtube.com/watch?v=dGCJ46vyR9o&feature=channel.

Laetoli footprints, Tanzania, left by two human ancestors, one tall, one small, hiking together across the plain 3.6 million years ago.

p. 154

p. 155

p. 165

p. 180

p. 184

p. 189

CHAPTER 5

Human Origins

Who are we? Where do we come from? What does it really mean to be human? Theologians, philosophers, and historians in every culture have asked these questions. Each of us individually, at one time or another, has also likely wondered about the meaning of life. This chapter examines the unique perspectives of physical anthropologists on the origins of the human species, and it explores amazing discoveries that are opening windows onto our past and, perhaps, our future. Let's begin with a few stories about discoveries relating to these topics.

- In 1923, scientists began to unearth hundreds of fossils in caves overlooking a river valley at Zhoukoudian, outside Beijing (then called Peking), China. The fossils of what came to be known as Peking Man, dating to approximately 700,000 years before the present (yBP), were found along with fossils from more than fifty other individuals, some seventeen thousand stone artifacts, and clear evidence that these human ancestors had controlled fire and used it to cook and keep warm. Peking Man—who walked upright and stood 57 to 70 inches tall—had the same physical characteristics as fossils of *Homo erectus* found earlier in Africa and Indonesia. Such similarities revealed the early and unexpected spread of this species as far as East Asia.
- In 1924, Australian anthropologist Raymond Dart, working in South Africa, received a box of curious rocks and fossils from a local quarry in the nearby town of Taung. Intrigued by one in particular, he spent months painstakingly chipping away at the fossilized rock until the encased fossil emerged—a childlike skull. What came to be known as Dart's Taung child—about age four when it died—was the first fossil evidence of a group of prehuman ancestors, Australopithecines.

These individuals were smaller in stature than modern humans and lived in Africa between 4 million and 1 million years ago (mya).

- In 1940, four teenagers hiking with their dog in southwestern France stumbled upon a complex of caves filled with more than two thousand spectacular wall paintings and carvings. Lascaux Cave's depictions of large animals, humans, and abstract forms dating to 16,000 yBP revealed the complex artistry and symbolism fashioned by so-called modern humans, who were still hunting and gathering as their main means of survival.

- One sunny morning in 1959, anthropologist Mary Leakey (who, along with her husband, Louis, had been searching the dusty and swelteringly hot Olduvai Gorge in East Africa's Rift Valley for nearly thirty years) happened upon a bone with human teeth attached that was sticking out of the ground. The Leakeys' long-sought discovery, named *Australopithecus boisei*, dated from between 2.3 and 1.2 mya. Added to Dart's Taung child, the Leakeys' discovery expanded researchers' picture of the Australopithecines' physical variation and range of habitat.

- One November morning in 1974, northeast of the Olduvai Gorge in a similarly arid region of Hadar, Ethiopia, archaeologist Donald Johanson and his graduate student, Tom Gray, turned their Land Rover aside on a hunch. On the slope of a gully that their team had examined unsuccessfully on previous occasions, Johanson spied a protruding arm bone and near it the back of a skull, a piece of a femur, and many more pieces of a skeleton exposed by recent wind and rain. Eventually more than 40 percent of a 3.2 million-year-old *Australopithecus afarensis* was excavated. "Lucy"—who was 44 inches tall, weighed approximately 65 pounds, and looked like a chimpanzee but walked erect like modern humans—was named as the team celebrated while listening to the Beatles' song "Lucy in the Sky with Diamonds."

• In 1976, in nearby Laetoli, Tanzania, two paleoanthropologists in a group headed by Mary Leakey were playfully tossing elephant dung at one another. When one stumbled to the ground, the loose soil parted to reveal a trail of footprints fossilized just below the surface. Apparently 3.6 million years before, as rain fell on ground recently covered by ash from a volcanic explosion, two human ancestors, one tall and one small, had hiked together across the plain. Their footsteps, preserved in the ash when it dried like cement (along with the imprints of many other animals present in the area at the time), provide evidence of exactly how early our ancestors were walking in ways hardly different from our own.

• In 1996, two young men headed out to see a hydroplane boat race on the Columbia River near Kennewick in Washington State. While wading along the riverbank, they stumbled upon a skull and other bones. Eager to make the race on time, they hid their discovery in nearby bushes. Returning later, they put the skull in a bucket and carried it back to their truck before eventually handing it to a passing off-duty police officer. Eventually a full skeleton was recovered from the riverbank and shallows. What has come to be known as Kennewick Man dates to 9,200 yBP, making it one of the earliest descendants of the first immigrants to the Americas and an ancestor of today's Native Americans. Additional evidence from the site has offered insights into the culture and lifestyle of humans nearly ten thousand years ago, including clear indications that members of the forty-six-year-old man's group had buried him themselves.

These stories represent just a few of the thousands of discoveries that illuminate our human origins. This chapter considers what we know about where we have come from, how we know it, and what we may be able to learn about where our species is heading. In particular, the chapter considers the following questions:

- Where do humans fit in the story of life on Earth?
- How do scientists learn about prehistoric life?
- How does the theory of evolution explain the diversity of life?
- How does evolution work?
- What do we know about our human ancestors?
- What has made modern humans so successful at survival?
- Where did variations in human skin color come from?
- Are we still evolving?

By the end of the chapter you will have caught a glimpse of the story of human evolution over time, our unparalleled ability to combine biology and culture to survive and thrive, and the deep connection of humans with all life around us.

Where Do Humans Fit in the Story of Life on Earth?

The story of humans makes a very short chapter in the overall narrative of Earth's natural history and of the universe as a whole. The story of fully modern humans, those *Homo sapiens* anatomically like those of us living today, is even more limited. How do we begin to see ourselves in this larger story, when today we often regard history as only that which has been recorded since the invention of writing, while everything else is relegated to prehistory? Archaeologists and physical anthropologists offer us some insights.

Deep Time

To understand where humans have come from, we need a sense of the natural history of our planet and universe. Scholars call this **deep time** (Gould 1987). The universe is calculated to be 14 billion years old and planet Earth only 4.5 billion. Life on Earth emerged 3.5 billion years ago in the form of single-celled organisms; more complicated multicelled organisms appeared a billion years later. The dinosaurs lived between 230 and 65 mya. Primates—a group that now includes humans, chimpanzees, monkeys, gorillas, orangutans, lemurs, tarsiers, and others—emerged between 65 and 55 mya. Contemporary humans and great apes, including orangutans, gorillas, and chimpanzees, shared a common ancestor as recently as between 15 and 12 mya. The ancestors of modern orangutans branched off from the common line at this point. Then, between 7 and 6 mya, our ancestors branched off from the line that eventually led to chimpanzees.

How can you conceptualize this deep time? Perhaps you might start with your own family—your direct ancestors. Many of us have met our grandparents. A few may have met a great-grandparent. But beyond two or three generations, our recollections get fuzzy. Can you imagine ten generations back to the founding of the United States in 1776? Or twenty-five generations back to the sailing of Christopher Columbus in 1492? How about five hundred generations back to the first use of agriculture by humans ten thousand years ago? Now can you imagine eight thousand generations back to the first modern human who looked like us about 170,000 years ago? You still haven't begun to scratch the surface of deep time. To understand the process through which life on Earth has emerged and evolved requires stretching your imagination even farther.

We calculate 60 seconds in every minute; 3,600 seconds in an hour; 86,400 in a day; 604,800 in a week; and 31,536,000 in a year. If we start counting seconds, and if we say that every second equals one year, then we would reach back to the origins of the first modern humans in just over two days of counting. To reach the time when dinosaurs became extinct (65 mya), we would have to count continuously each second for two years. To reach one billion seconds, we would have to count for thirty-one years and eight months, night and day. To mark 4.5 billion years in seconds—the beginning of planet Earth—would require counting for more than 139 years nonstop, night and day, every second. From this perspective, the modern human chapter in the story of Earth's natural history is indeed remarkably brief. Humans do not take up much space on the deep time calendar.

deep time: A framework for considering the span of human history within the much larger age of the universe and planet Earth.

How Do Scientists Learn about Prehistoric Life?

Scientists have gathered an immense amount of physical evidence over the past two hundred years about the life of modern humans, our immediate human ancestors, and all living beings on Earth. Living organisms provide a vivid record of how evolution has worked, but we only see the lineages that have survived. Far many more have not. Yet thousands of fossil finds and recent genetic research tell a fascinating story of the many species that came before us and led to life on Earth as we currently know it.

Fossil Evidence

Fossils are the remains of an organism that have been preserved through a natural chemical process that turns them partially or wholly into rock (Figure 5.2). A fossil may also be an impression of those remains left behind, imprinted and preserved in surrounding sediment; these "trace fossils" can include impressions of hair, skin, or other soft tissues, or even leaves, seeds, and feathers. Fossils are like memories of life on Earth in the past. They recall for us moments in our history that have been set aside but not forgotten.

Fossils provide the only direct physical evidence of our past and how various species, including our own, have changed over time. Fossils not only are evidence of past physical forms of living beings but, as with the incredible Laetoli footprints already described, are also evidence of their behavior. As we collect fossils, we use them to reconstruct our past and our evolution through time.

The human fossil record is far from complete, despite the rapidly increasing rate of discoveries in recent years. One difficulty in completing the picture is that very few organisms end up as fossils. In fact, it takes rather unique circumstances to create and preserve a fossil. Today, bones and teeth represent 99 percent of the fossil record. Why? Largely because of their density and hardness. Teeth are the hardest part of the human body. Bones, particularly skulls and leg bones, are dense and large. The larger and harder the physical remains are, the better their chance of becoming fossilized because they take longer to decay. Soft tissues such as skin or internal organs decay too rapidly to be fossilized, so discoveries of that type are rare. Furthermore, to become a fossil, a leg bone or a skull must be protected from scavengers. It must be buried in certain kinds of sediment—oxygen-free, with limited bacterial activity that would promote decomposition, and of the right chemical composition to facilitate its transformation partially or wholly into rock. Moreover, not all areas and periods experience the kind of geologic activity best suited for creating and preserving fossils. Given these challenges, fossilization is an extremely rare event.

Another difficulty in reconstructing the human past is that not all periods of time or species of living organism are equally represented in the fossil record. To become a part of our story, not only do physical remains need to be fossilized, but we must find them thousands and millions of years later. For instance, there are many fossils of early human ancestors in eastern and southern Africa, such as the Taung child or Lucy. But in all likelihood this is not the whole story. Our ancestors may have lived all over the African continent.

A hominid collapses and dies on shore.

After the soft-tissue remains of the hominid decay, only the skeleton is left.

The water level of the lake rises, and the lake sediments settle and cover the hominid's bones and footprints.

The hominid's footprints are left in the mud.

The bones fossilize in the thick layer of sediment at the bottom of the lake, while sediments continue to be deposited as layers. The lake dries, and other geologic processes occur. A volcanic eruption, for example, spews ash over the region, providing more layers. The fossil is now embedded in a geologic stratum.

TIME

Erosion exposes deep strata in a geologic column, revealing the fossil skeleton and footprints.

A physical anthropologist examines the fossilized hominid remains. The bones provide material for study. The ancient soils (paleosols) provide material for environmental reconstruction.

FIGURE 5.2 Fossilization Process

Until recently, the fossil record had not confirmed this. But then came a 2001 discovery in the southern Sahara desert (in Chad, Central Africa): *Sahelanthropus tchadensis*, dating to between 7 and 6 mya, provided the long-sought evidence of a wide-ranging prehuman habitat (Brunet et al. 2002). The discovery, found with animal fossils in the same site—bones and teeth of horses, elephants, crocodiles, fish, rodents, and other primates—showed that this *Sahelanthropus* lived near a lake in a forested area. Such bits of information offer additional insight into the lifestyles and behavior of an ancestor who (counting years in seconds) lived 81 days ago on our clock of deep time.

Our contemporary ability to explore and excavate has been restricted in certain areas. Geologic activity such as volcanic eruptions, earthquakes, and plate shifts (steady but slow movement of the tectonic plates underlying Earth's crust) has transformed the face of the planet over millions of years. So have global warming and cooling cycles. Thus what may have been open savannah grassland may now be dense forest, making it almost impossible to explore. Areas where geologic activity has exposed lower layers are easier to investigate. In East Africa, for instance, the greatest number of discoveries has been in dry, arid regions where geologic activity has exposed the deep strata of sediment and where wind, rain, and natural erosion continue to expose fossils just beneath the surface. Limestone caves have preserved the largest number of fossils in southern Africa. In Europe, many finds have come from public works projects involving road construction and building excavation.

Finding fossils also requires painstaking efforts by paleoanthropologists—scientists who study the fossil remains of our human ancestors. Their work involves extensive searches, intensive time commitments, meticulous research, and a fair amount of luck. Moreover, they must handle recovered fossils with extreme care. To excavate the remains, paleoanthropologists use small brushes and tools as delicate as the ones your dentist might employ. All items are mapped, numbered, and photographed. Careful record is made of the sediment in which each fossil is found and any fossilized plant or animal remains that may be with it. This record-keeping serves not only to establish the context in which the organism lived but also to assist in establishing the time frame during which it lived.

Absolute and Relative Dating

There are two primary means for dating fossils and placing them in chronological relationship to the vast record of natural history and human evolution. We date the fossil itself, a process called *absolute dating*. We also date the context in which the fossil was found, a process called *relative dating*. Relative dating entails comparing the fossil to what is found nearby, including plants, animals, or cultural artifacts such as stone tools whose dates have been previously established.

Most often, relative dating relies on *stratigraphy*—a process that determines the ages of the layers of sediment above and below the fossil. This process reflects the geologic assumptions that what is deeper is older and that layers of sediment have built up over succeeding millennia.

Absolute dating of the fossil itself draws on two primary chemical assessments, radiocarbon (carbon-14) dating for organic material and radiopotassium (potassium-40) dating for nonorganic matter. *Radiocarbon dating* tracks the half-life of carbon as it decays in organic matter. It is most accurate in assessing the age of matter up to between 70,000 and 50,000 yBP. Radiocarbon dating can be used directly on bones and teeth to establish their age within this timeframe.

Radiopotassium dating does not measure the organic material in a fossil, but rather the amount of argon in volcanic rock and ash found on or around a fossil. This dating process is based on the fact that the heat of volcanic eruptions eliminates all argon from ash and rock. The only argon in volcanic rock and ash found today has been created since the eruption by the decay of potassium, which produces new argon at a steady rate. Measuring the new argon enables us to calculate when materials erupted from a volcano and so provides a reliable date for any fossil found in such material. Because volcanic eruptions spread a layer of ash over vast distances, this method has proven extremely valuable in determining the age of many fossil finds (Larsen 2011).

Of course, even these "absolute" dating techniques do not provide a precise year, month, or day of origin. However, they do yield a reliable date range that enables us to see where fossils fit in the vast record of natural history and to further understand the major events in the story of evolution.

DNA Analysis

Over the past twenty years, breakthroughs in our understanding of DNA have provided another tool for dating key events in the evolution of species. **DNA** (deoxyribonucleic acid) provides the genetic code for an organism, essentially giving it a "blueprint" for development and growth. Because DNA mutates (changes spontaneously or in response to the environment) at a steady rate, the number of mutations can serve to date an organism's evolutionary history. Scientists who specialize in this type of analysis are called **paleogeneticists.**

Genetic studies of mitochondrial DNA—passed down from generation to generation through our mothers—on people worldwide reveal that all living modern humans have a matrilineal "most common ancestor." This ancestor lived in Africa approximately 170,000 years ago—that is, eight thousand generations back from the present (Cann, Stoneking, and Wilson 1987). Mitochondrial DNA comparisons reveal more variation in Africa, evidence of an older population there, and less variation the farther away from Africa one goes. These observations support earlier theories based on the fossil record that we are all from Africa originally. DNA studies indicate that humans migrated out of Africa approximately 100,000 years ago, first populating the Middle East and then Europe, Asia, the Pacific, and eventually the Americas (Li et al. 2008).

New technology is also enabling paleogeneticists to extract DNA from the bones and teeth of ancient fossils. The recovered genetic material reveals a great deal about ancient human populations, including the diseases they were exposed to, their population movements, and distinctions among groups. For example, by comparing similarities between DNA in living Native Americans and their ancestors' fossil remains, paleogeneticists have discovered that Native Americans' genetic structure is quite old and thus most likely derives from a single, common group of founding ancestors. DNA patterns among some northeast Asians suggest that this founding group migrated from northeast Asia to the Americas. According to calculations of DNA mutation rates, the migration likely took place around 15,000 yBP, corresponding roughly to the archeological record (Forster et al. 1996).

FIGURE 5.4 A paleogeneticist extracts DNA from a sample of fossilized Neandertal bone.

How Does the Theory of Evolution Explain the Diversity of Life?

Physical anthropologists consider the **theory of evolution** to be the key to understanding the diversity of life on Earth today and how it relates to life in the past. The theory states that biological adaptation to changes in the natural environment occurs over generations. The fundamental concept of evolution is

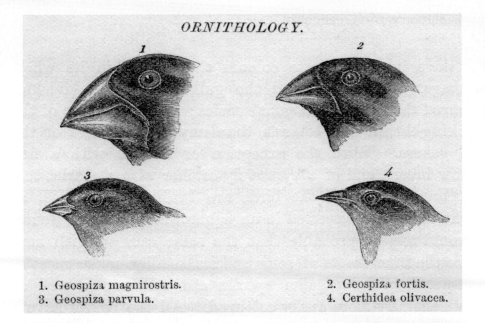

ORNITHOLOGY.

1. Geospiza magnirostris.
3. Geospiza parvula.
2. Geospiza fortis.
4. Certhidea olivacea.

FIGURE 5.5 Charles Darwin's sketches of finches with beaks adapted to different diets, observed in the Galapagos Islands, spurred his thinking about natural selection.

that all living species share a common ancestry from which they have descended. The more closely two organisms are related biologically, the more recent their common ancestor.

Differences between species and within species—called *variation*—come from random genetic changes in individual organisms that have allowed them to better survive and reproduce when shifts in the natural environment or competition for food or mates have made life more difficult. Evolutionary change in the whole population does not occur at once, but over many generations. Sometimes it takes place gradually and sometimes in fits and starts, as the success of the new variation leads to higher rates of survival and reproduction.

By *theory* we do not mean a guess or an untested assumption. Rather, we mean an overarching idea that links and makes sense of many pieces of factual evidence. Theories serve to explain the relationship between facts and to predict the outcome of observed natural processes. Physical anthropologists use the theory of evolution to make sense of how all the fossil finds and DNA discoveries fit together. Evolution explains the relationship of current living things to those that have come before and predicts how biological change will occur in the future. In this way, it creates a scientific framework for the history of life on Earth. Theories can be tested. In fact, the theory of evolution through natural selection has been tested extensively over the 150 years since the English naturalist Charles Darwin (1809–1882) first articulated it in his book *On the Origin of Species by Means of Natural Selection, or the Preservation of Favoured Races in the Struggle for Life* (1859).

Evolution versus Creationism

Evolution is not a controversial subject among scientists. Rather, it is assumed to be a reality in biology, genetics, chemistry, epidemiology, and many other sciences. Evolution is, however, a controversial topic in U.S. culture. For more than a hundred years it has stirred courtroom battles, school board fights, election campaigns, and theological debates.

In 2006, an opinion poll conducted by the Pew Forum on Religion in Public Life found the U.S. population to be divided on the origins of life. Among respondents, 42 percent stated that they believe humans and other living organisms have existed in their present form since the creation of the world; 51 percent believed that life has evolved over time; and 7 percent did not know. Among those who believe life has evolved over time, 21 percent said that a supreme being has guided evolution, 26 percent said that evolution has occurred through natural selection alone (see later discussion), and 4 percent did not know how life has evolved.

Opposition to evolution most often rests on the literal interpretation of biblical texts and the related religious conviction that God created Earth and all the creatures on it. In this view, humans are a special creation, not the result of random adaptations to changes in the natural environment. Young Earth **creationism**, which is popular among many evangelical Protestant Christians, argues that God created Earth between six and ten thousand years ago, based on calculations of the genealogy of biblical ancestors. Young Earth creationists attribute fossil finds to the extinctions that occurred during the worldwide flood described in the biblical book of Genesis, when not all creatures were saved on Noah's ark. Other proponents of creationism accept that Earth is 4.5 billion years old, but they argue that God—not the process of evolution—created the separate species (Scott 2009; Rosenhouse 2012).

A recent version of creationism, called **intelligent design**, proposes an evidence-based rather than religious-based argument to undermine theories of evolution through natural selection. Proponents suggest that life is too complex to be random. Consider the human eye, they argue. How could its complex inner workings have evolved through natural selection? This complexity, according to intelligent design supporters, requires the involvement of an intelligent designer. Though the identity of the intelligent designer is not specified, the promotion of intelligent design theory by particular Christian groups and related think tanks leaves the impression that the designer is the Christian God (Scott 2009).

As we can see in the Pew poll, a firm belief in God's active role in individual lives and human history is common for many Americans, regardless of political persuasion—whether conservative or progressive; left, right, or middle. Religious belief and acceptance of the theory of evolution are not mutually exclusive. In fact, many national religious organizations have taken positions

creationism: A belief that God created Earth and all living creatures in their present form as recently as six thousand years ago.

intelligent design: An updated version of creationism that claims to propose an evidence-based argument to contradict the theory of evolution.

supporting evolution and opposing the teaching of creationism in the science curriculum of public schools. The Catholic Church since 1950 has held evolution to be compatible with Christian teachings, and in the United States the following churches have made similar statements: the United Methodist Church, the Presbyterian Church, the Episcopal Church, the United Church of Christ, and the Central Council of American Rabbis (Lieberman and Kirk 1996). Moreover, surveys of scientists find that most of them are people of faith. In the Pew poll, even the half of the general population who accepted the notion of evolution also indicated that they believe God intervenes in history and creates through evolution.

Battles over the Teaching of Evolution

In the United States, cultural battles over evolution and religion have often taken place in the educational arena. These conflicts reflect some people's strong religious convictions that it is not appropriate for schools to teach a theory of human origins that contradicts their beliefs.

In 1925, high school teacher John Scopes was fined $100 under Tennessee's Butler Act for teaching evolution. The now-famous Scopes Trial became a lightning rod for the battle between science and religion, drawing attention nationwide. After trial and appeal, Tennessee's supreme court upheld the Butler Act but threw out Scopes's fine on a technicality. In 1968, the U.S. Supreme Court overturned state laws banning the teaching of evolution, citing the Constitution's clause against establishing a state religion. The bans, the Court found, were driven by religious beliefs. (Tennessee had repealed the Butler Act in 1967.)

FIGURE 5.6 Schools have often been the arena for cultural battles over evolution. Here, evangelist T. T. Martin's books against the theory of evolution are sold in Dayton, Tennessee, 1925, scene of the Scopes trial. Clarence Darrow (*left*), a lawyer for the American Civil Liberties Union, defended John Scopes, a biology teacher, in his test of Tennessee's law banning the teaching of evolution. William Jennings Bryan (*right*), testified for the prosecution as a Bible expert.

Battles over the teaching of evolution continue. In a landmark 2005 U.S. federal court case, *Tammy Kitzmiller v. Dover Area School District*, eleven parents of children in the Dover, Pennsylvania, school district brought suit to challenge the district's requirement that high school science teachers include intelligent design as an alternative to evolution as an "explanation of the origin of life." After a three-month court battle, including expert witnesses on evolution and intelligent design, the judge (a self-described conservative Republican) ruled that intelligent design had no basis in science and should not be taught in a public high school science curriculum. What was your own high school experience in this regard? If you attended school outside the United States, did you learn anything about evolution, creationism, or other explanations for the origins of human life?

Cultural battles over the origins of human life continue unabated in the United States and are unlikely to subside anytime soon. The scientific community, however, remains unified on the central role of the theory of evolution in explaining both the origins of humanity and the natural processes of change and adaptation in all living organisms.

How Does Evolution Work?

Evolution is happening around us all the time. Modern medicine, biology, chemistry, genetics, and even pest control rely on the principles of evolution. For example, the widespread appearance of drug-resistant bacteria is directly related to their successful evolution in the face of antibiotics. And scientists' inability to develop a cure for HIV/AIDS reflects one particular virus's ability to evolve rapidly. Even the survival of cockroaches despite increasingly stronger pesticides is a testimony to ongoing evolutionary success.

Evolution is harder to study in humans because of the relatively long time between generations, as well as people's general reluctance to be studied. But the unified study of evolution that brings together biology, taxonomy, genetics, morphology, comparative anatomy, paleontology, and physical anthropology provides clear evidence of evolution in our human past and the continuing activity of evolutionary forces in the human present. Four key evolutionary forces are mutation, natural selection, gene migration, and genetic drift.

Mutation

Research in molecular biology during the twentieth century produced significant discoveries that shed light on the role of mutation as a crucial evolutionary force. We now know that DNA (deoxyribonucleic acid) provides the genetic code for an organism's cells, giving them a blueprint for development and growth. As a result, the organism is said to develop according to its particular genotype—that is, the hereditary factors that provide a framework for the organism's physical form. DNA almost always replicates itself exactly, but sometimes an error or collection of errors spontaneously occurs in the copying process. If uncorrected by enzymes that monitor the DNA, a mutation results. A **mutation** is a deviation from the standard DNA code.

Mutations may occur spontaneously in the copying process, or they may result from environmental agents called *mutagens* (which are usually of human origin). A **mutagen** is any agent that increases the frequency or extent of mutation. Mutagens increasingly are being identified in the human environment and include X-rays and toxic chemicals. Although rare, considering the large number of copies made in a lifetime, spontaneous mutations do occur; in humans, one new potentially significant mutation occurs in every other person born (Larsen 2011).

The impact of mutations is highly variable and depends on the location of the mutation within an individual's DNA sequence and chromosomes. Most mutations are harmless and have no impact on an individual's health, well-being, or survival, although the most extreme mutations may result in debilitating conditions such as Down syndrome or Klinefelter syndrome. On a population level, mutations make no difference unless they provide an advantage for survival and reproduction that can be extended to the group. In the process of evolution, mutations are particularly notable because they are the only source of new genetic material in a population.

Natural Selection

Natural selection is another force of evolution. It is often directly associated with Darwin's theory and the catchphrase "survival of the fittest." **Natural selection** occurs when individuals within a population have certain characteristics that provide an advantage that enables them to survive and reproduce at a higher rate than others in the population. This reproductive success shows their "fitness" to survive in a particular environment. If they survive and reproduce more successfully, their unique genetic advantage has been "selected" by the natural environment and will become increasingly prevalent in the population.

The peppered moth, *Biston betularia*, provides an example of natural selection in the animal world. Common today in Great Britain, until the mid-1800s the peppered moth population was primarily white with black specks. This coloration provided important camouflage in the light-colored moss and lichen growing on tree trunks and was an effective protection against the moths' primary predators—birds. However, from the late nineteenth century to the mid-twentieth century, the peppered moth population's coloration gradually shifted so that 90 percent of the moths were black, not white. How did this happen?

During the Industrial Revolution, pollution—particularly from coal-burning factories—blanketed surrounding trees with a layer of black soot,

mutation: A deviation from the standard DNA code.

mutagen: Any agent that increases the frequency or extent of mutations.

natural selection: The evolutionary process by which some organisms, with features that enable them to adapt to the environment, preferentially survive and reproduce, thereby increasing the frequency of those features in the population.

covering the lichen and changing the peppered moths' natural environment. The mainly white moths were now much more visible and vulnerable to predators, but the few moths born black were likely to avoid detection, survive, and reproduce. The coloration of the population gradually shifted to primarily black through the process of natural selection. When environmental protections implemented in the late twentieth century reduced pollution and soot levels, trees returned to their earlier lighter coloration. When we consider the powerful process of natural selection in evolution, perhaps it is not surprising that in response, white peppered moths again increased in the population, rising from 10 percent in 1983 to more than 90 percent in the late 1990s (Larsen 2011).

Sickle-cell anemia provides an example of natural selection at work in the human population. Sickle-cell anemia is a genetically inherited blood disease with no known cure. The disease gives red blood cells a sickle shape, not a round shape, thus limiting their ability to carry oxygen through narrow capillaries and resulting in anemia and death. In general, the sickle-cell gene does not provide an advantage for survival and reproduction. Thus, we might expect the sickle-cell gene to be selected out in the evolutionary process. Surprisingly, though, in the mid-twentieth century, medical research in certain African countries—mainly along the equator—found that 20 to 30 percent of the populations carried the sickle-cell gene. If sickle-cell anemia is generally associated with such high rates of disease, why would these populations carry it at such unusually high rates?

Researchers, including Anthony Allison (2004) working in Kenya and Frank B. Livingstone (1958) working in West Africa, uncovered a fascinating connection. They found that high rates of the sickle-cell gene appeared in areas with widespread incidence of malaria, a deadly parasitic infection spread by mosquitoes. Furthermore, they found that groups in regions of endemic malaria had higher survival rates for malaria infection if they carried the sickle-cell gene. Apparently the gene, although not advantageous in areas without malaria, actually provided a selective advantage in areas with widespread malaria. People with the sickle-cell gene were more likely to survive and reproduce in this environment than those without it. As a result, the rate of sickle-cell anemia increased in the population, in response to the process of natural selection.

The geographic distribution of sickle-cell anemia extends beyond Africa, occurring also in the Mediterranean region, parts of the Arabian peninsula, and parts of Southeast Asia. In these areas it provides human populations with protection against the widespread risk of malaria infection.

Gene Migration

Today most human populations are not small and isolated, but large and interconnected. They interact and interbreed relatively freely. In fact, as globalization and access to international travel accelerate, this pattern introduces

FIGURE 5.7 Two peppered moths. One, white with black spots, is well camouflaged against the tree's moss and lichen. The other, primarily black, stands exposed. Which do you think is more vulnerable to predators? Which is more likely to survive to reproduce the species?

ample opportunity for another evolutionary force to show its impact—gene migration.

Gene migration is the swapping of genetic material within a population and among diverse populations. As genes travel from one population to another in a species, they increase the diversity of the gene pool in a particular population and decrease the genetic diversity among groups. Gene migration explains the deep genetic similarities within the human population (which is 99.9 percent identical genetically) and the deep interconnections of the human gene pool.

Genes flow as people migrate. For instance, Christopher Columbus's voyage to the Americas marked the beginning of an extensive gene migration from Europe to the Americas. Marriage patterns and kinship structures within populations also play a role in facilitating or restricting gene migration. Consider Australian aborigines, who are highly endogamous (they marry primarily within their group). As a result, they experience very limited gene flow with other groups and have limited genetic diversity within their group. Other marriage patterns of exogamy (marrying outside the group) promote gene flow among populations related by marriage. Gene flow among and between populations continues to increase today as time-space compression and global migration are increasing the levels of interaction and interbreeding, not only with nearby but also with distant populations.

gene migration: The movement of genetic material within a population and among diverse populations.

Genetic Drift

Genetic drift, the fourth force of evolution, occurs when the gene pool of one population or one part of a population "drifts away" from another related

genetic drift: The process whereby one segment of a population is removed from the larger pool, thereby limiting the flow of genetic material between the two groups.

part, cutting off or limiting the flow of genetic material between them. When this occurs, a small number of successful mutations can more easily influence the smaller populations. Migration almost always plays a causative role in this phenomenon. And the phenomenon is usually observable in changes in phenotype—that is, physical characteristics expressed in the form of detectible, biological traits that result from the interaction of the organism's genotype with the environment.

Founder effect is one example of genetic drift. When a small part of a population—perhaps several hundred members with some unique phenotypical characteristics—breaks off from the larger group, migrates to a new location, and begins to reproduce separately from the original population, it effectively "founds," or establishes, a new and distinct group. Scholars often cite founder effect to explain the origins of Native Americans and, in particular, their distinctive genetic characteristics. Some genetic evidence suggests that a small group of Asians with unique phenotypical characteristics broke off and migrated into the Americas likely about 15,000 yBP and perhaps earlier. There they began to reproduce separately from the larger Asian population, founding a new population that eventually settled throughout the Americas (Larsen 2011).

Perhaps you can imagine the four forces of evolution at work (admittedly in an oversimplified example) on the student body in your college. Start with your current classroom, which may represent a gene pool of twenty to three hundred students. Imagine that your class formed a distinct group. Over several generations of swapping genetic material among your classmates and their offspring, the genetic makeup of the individuals would become more similar. Of course, spontaneous mutations would continue to occur to add diversity to the population; but unless the natural environment changed dramatically and selected some particular mutation for enhanced survival, these mutations would have little or no effect on the population.

Now imagine that after several generations some of your classmates or their offspring were to migrate across the hall to a nearby class and swap some genetic material with that group of students. This would be an example of gene migration. It would increase the genetic diversity within the classroom and decrease the diversity that may have emerged between the two populations in your college species. Then imagine further that several students with a similar phenotype—perhaps red hair—get angry for some reason, break away from the others, and establish their own population in another unoccupied classroom, swapping genetic material exclusively among themselves over generations and producing offspring primarily with red hair (unlike the original population). This would be an example of founder effect and genetic drift. These concepts are useful in considering the story of our human ancestors, to which we now turn.

What Do We Know about Our Human Ancestors?

Human evolution took a dramatic turn between six and seven million years ago. At that time, the ancestral line leading to modern humans split from the line leading to today's chimpanzees. Seven million years is a fleeting moment in deep time and in the evolution of living organisms on the planet. But in these seven million years the key characteristics of being human have emerged. They include bipedalism (walking on two feet instead of four), expanded brain capacity and complex mental functions, creation and use of tools and other forms of culture (including language), and global migration.

The Awash River Valley: "Where It All Began"

The fossil and DNA evidence of human evolution over the past six to seven million years continues to emerge from sites and artifacts worldwide. Recent discoveries shed even more light on the movement of our human ancestors toward the physical form, mental capacity, and cultural capabilities of modern *Homo sapiens*. One site in particular, the Middle Awash River Valley in northeastern Ethiopia, has provided many of the most remarkable finds of the past twenty-five years.

Ethiopians call the area of the Middle Awash River Valley the place "where it all began." The arid territory, populated by herders, their cows, and small villages of simple mud and brick homes, rests on the fault line of three tectonic plates that are slowly pulling apart at a rate of one centimeter per year. Regular earthquakes, flooding, and geologic shifts of Earth's crust have created a landscape of ridges and ravines with geologic strata exposed to wind and water erosion—perfect for revealing fossils to paleoanthropologists. The Middle Awash site has become one of the richest troves of discoveries in the world, not only in the number of finds but also in the representation of almost every major grouping of human ancestor over the last six million years. This remarkable record of many species in one location enables scholars to identify patterns of continuity and change that fill in the historical record of evolutionary change in our immediate human ancestors (White et al. 2009).

Paleoanthropologists group our immediate ancestors into five primary categories. Pre-Australopithecines, an intermediate form between apes and humans, lived between 7 and 4 mya. Australopithecines, including the Taung Child and Lucy discussed above, lived between 4 and 1 mya. The genus *Homo* emerged from the Australopithecines: first with the species *Homo habilis* between 2.5 and 1.8 mya; then with the species *Homo erectus* between 1.8 million and 300,000 yBP; and finally with the species *Homo sapiens*. Early archaic *Homo sapiens* emerged as early as 350,000 yBP, and fully modern *Homo sapiens* with modern people's anatomical characteristics emerged as early as 200,000 yBP

MAP 5.1
Middle Awash River Valley

FIGURE 5.8 *Left*, the Awash River Valley, northeastern Ethiopia, and its landscape of ridges and ravines, has provided many of the most remarkable fossil finds of the past twenty-five years. *Right*, fossil hunters in the Awash River Valley excavate a lower jaw of *Ardipithecus ramidus*, 4.4 million years old.

species: A group of related organisms that can interbreed and produce fertile, viable offspring.

(Larsen 2011). By **species** we refer to a group of related organisms that can interbreed and produce fertile, viable offspring. Discoveries in the Middle Awash area have provided insights into almost all of these species.

Pre-*Australopithecus*

Two species of pre-*Australopithecus*, the 5.8 mya *Ardipithecus kadabba* and the 4.4 mya *Ardipithecus ramidus*, were discovered in the Middle Awash region in the 1990s. These species provided the first evidence of a transitional figure between the primate line and Australopithecines and later humans. The 2001 find of another pre-Australopithecine in Chad—*Sahelanthropus tchadensis*, dating to between 7 and 6 mya—confirmed the hypothesis that our pre-Australopithecine ancestors lived throughout Africa (Brunet et al. 2002).

Together, the *Ardipithecus* and *Sahelanthropus* fossils—including a partial skeleton, skull, bones, and teeth—showed two key signs of the evolutionary transition toward humans. Despite being extraordinarily primitive and about one meter tall, all showed signs of bipedalism (walking on two feet rather than all four limbs) and a clear change in dental patterns toward canine teeth adapted for chewing (rather than cutting and slicing, which is characteristic of earlier ancestral primates). The discovery of fossilized seed and wood in the surrounding sediment, along with the teeth and bones of forest-dwelling monkeys, suggest that these early ancestors lived in wooded settings. The shape of particular foot bones, the femur, and the pelvis suggests that these individuals spent a great deal of time on the ground, but still some time in the trees.

The shift to **bipedalism** is one of the key distinguishing characteristics of humans and our immediate ancestors. It is usually attributed to the evolutionary advantages of moving from trees to the ground as the pre-Australopithecines adapted to a cooling environment that had less forest and more savannah grassland. Bipedalism offered numerous benefits. It provided a significant advantage over walking on all four limbs when gathering and carrying food, and allowed our ancestors to see greater distances over open spaces, reach food higher up on trees and bushes, stay cooler with less body mass exposed to direct sunlight, carry infants more efficiently, and move quickly over long, open distances. Imagine all the activities made possible today—millions of years later—by the shift to bipedalism, especially the use of modern technology from automobiles and laptop computers to cell phones and digital cameras!

The new evidence from the Awash River Valley and other sites that pre-*Australopithecus* lived in wooded environments along the lake edge rather than primarily on the savannah seems to establish a slightly different environment for the evolution of bipedalism. But it does not contradict the narrative completely. Scholars' understanding of this geologic and environmental period is still in formation. We may find that the pre-Australopithecines' habitat of intermittent woodlands, open grasslands, and lakes was also conducive to the evolutionary shift to bipedalism (White et al. 2009).

Australopithecus

The genus *Australopithecus*, dating from 4 to 1 mya, is the second major grouping of human ancestors after the split seven million years ago. Researchers have collected hundreds of fossils from at least seven species of Australopithecines, including the following: *Australopithecus (A.) anamensis* (4 mya); *A. afarensis* (3.6 to 3 mya, including Lucy); *A. africanus* (3 to 2 mya); *A. robustus*; *A. aethiopicus*; *A. boisei*; and *A. garhi*. Rather than a direct line of descent from one species to the next, the Australopithecine lineage looks more like the branches of a tree (Figure 5.9). Some Australopithecine species appear to have ended, either dying out or assimilating into other groups. A few, such as *A. afarensis* and *A. garhi*, are clearly part of the lineage that eventually led to modern humans. Scholars are still sorting out where some others fit in.

A. garhi, found at the Middle Awash River Valley site in 1999, dates to around 2.5 mya and is most likely the immediate ancestor of the *Homo* genus to which we belong. *A. garhi* is considered the first human ancestor to have made and used stone tools. Although no tools were found at its excavation site, recovered animal bones show cut marks where stone tools were used to remove flesh from the bone. At a contemporary site on the nearby Gona River, stone tools have been recovered. These **Oldowan tools**, named by Mary and Louis Leakey after the Olduvai Gorge where the style was first discovered, include a variety of stones shaped into chopping and cutting edges by striking one stone surface against another to break flakes away from a core.

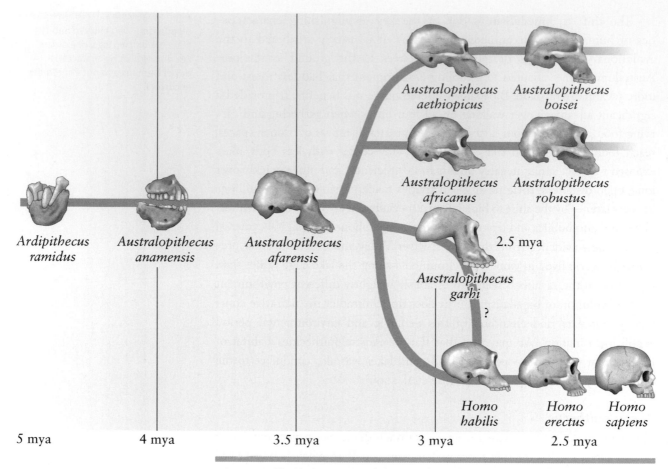

Ardipithecus
ramidus

Australopithecus
anamensis

Australopithecus
afarensis

Australopithecus
aethiopicus

Australopithecus
boisei

Australopithecus
africanus

Australopithecus
robustus

2.5 mya

Australopithecus
garhi

?

Homo
habilis

Homo
erectus

Homo
sapiens

5 mya   4 mya   3.5 mya   3 mya   2.5 mya

FIGURE 5.9 The Human Ancestral Lineage The evolutionary relationships among the various *Australopithecus* species suggest two main lineages: one leading to modern *Homo sapiens* and the other leading to a number of australopithecines.

Evidence of bone tools used for digging has also been found. All indications are that by 2.5 mya our Australopithecine ancestors were creating tools and using these early cultural forms to manipulate and adapt to the natural world around them. They may have made and used tools before this period; but if the tools were constructed of wood, grass, or other soft material, they would have been less likely to be preserved.

Australopithecines became extinct by 1 mya. The reasons for their disappearance are unclear. Paleoanthropologists have noted, however, that over a period of three million years, the Australopithecines' brain size and body size remained consistent. Eventually the evolutionary advantages that earlier made them more successful than the pre-Australopithecines may not have been sufficient to adjust to new environmental changes or competition for resources with *Homo habilis* or *Homo erectus* (Larsen 2011).

FIGURE 5.10 By 2.5 million years ago, our ancestors were making tools to manipulate and shape the natural world around them. These Oldowan stone tools, dating to around 1.85 million years ago, were shaped by striking one stone surface against another.

Homo habilis

When *Homo habilis* emerged around 2.5 mya and then *Homo erectus* around 1.8 mya, both were for a time contemporary with Australopithecines. However, with these two new groups our ancestors experienced a dramatic increase in intelligence and the use of material culture. And this increase accelerated with the appearance of *Homo sapiens* around 350,000 yBP.

Homo habilis lived in southern and eastern Africa, showing roughly the same geographic distribution as the Australopithecines. Distinguishing characteristics of *Homo habilis* compared to Australopithecines include increased cranial capacity, presumably greater mental capacity, and increased use of tools. Stone tools are more common at *Homo habilis* sites. At a key moment in human evolutionary history, it appears that the introduction of culture—in this case, stone tools—may have had a powerful effect on biological evolution. Better tools allowed more efficient processing of meat and higher protein intake. Increased levels of protein, in turn, supported an increase in cranial capacity, brain size, and—most likely—mental functions.

Although *Homo habilis* differed from Australopithecines in intelligence and tool use, the two groups, contemporaries for a time, were quite similar in other areas. Excavations in Tanzania's Olduvai Gorge in 1980 uncovered a partial skeleton of a *Homo habilis*—an individual only 3.5 feet tall, about the same size as an Australopithecine. Like Australopithecines, the *Homo habilis* skeleton also had short legs relative to its arms. This observation suggests that although fully bipedal, *Homo habilis* did not share the efficient walking stride of later *Homo erectus* and *Homo sapiens*. This factor may have contributed to the later *Homo erectus* being the first of these immediate ancestors to migrate out of Africa (Johanson et al. 1987).

Homo erectus

Homo erectus lived between 1.8 mya and 300,000 yBP, overlapping with Australopithecines, *Homo habilis*, and even our own species, *Homo sapiens*. Fossils of *Homo erectus* have been found in Africa, Asia, and Europe. The earliest and most spectacular fossil is an 80 percent complete skeleton of an eleven-year-old boy found in 1984 on the shore of Lake Turkana in Nariokotome, Kenya. Nariokotome Boy, sometimes called Turkana Boy, looked much more like modern humans than *Homo habilis*, standing 66 inches tall. His shorter arms and longer legs indicate a fully modern stride that shows fully developed bipedalism and adaptation to live on the ground, not in the trees. *Homo erectus* was significantly larger than *Australopithecus* and 35 percent larger than *Homo habilis*, including a significantly larger cranial capacity (McHenry and Coffing 2000).

FIGURE 5.11 An 80 percent complete skeleton of an eleven-year-old boy *Homo erectus*, sometimes called Turkana Boy, Nariokotome, Kenya.

Acheulian stone tools: Stone tools associated with *Homo erectus*, including specialized hand axes for cutting, pounding, and scraping.

Homo erectus was the first of our direct ancestors to migrate out of Africa. Indeed, migration is a pattern of movement that has come to characterize human life. Fossil evidence indicates that *Homo erectus* rapidly spread eastward, arriving in the area of modern-day Georgia (in southwest Asia) as early as 1.7 mya, and in the area of modern-day Indonesia between 1.8 and 1.6 mya. *Homo erectus* increasingly turned to cultural innovations to build adaptive strategies as they moved out of Africa. Remnants of game found at *Homo erectus* sites, including bones of hippos, baboons, and elephants, indicates enhanced use of tools for throwing and thrusting (such as spears) as well as chopping, cutting, and scraping. The **Acheulian stone tools** associated with *Homo erectus*, including specialized hand axes for cutting, pounding, and scraping, are more varied and served for many more tasks than the tools of the Australopithecines or *Homo habilis*.

Hunting game would have required complex social structures as groups cooperated to track and kill large, fast, or dangerous animals. Although scholars are not sure exactly when speech developed among our human ancestors, the more complex social interactions required for big game hunting indicate that some rudimentary capacity to communicate may have been present. Speech developed certainly within the past two million years, although perhaps quite late in that period.

The *Homo erectus* site at Zhoukoudian outside Beijing, China, dated to between 600,000 and 400,000 yBP, reveals the controlled use of fire. Burned remnants of bones, stone tools, plants, charcoal, and ash indicate that *Homo erectus* individuals at this time (and perhaps earlier) were manipulating and controlling their environment with fire. This cultural development provided light, warmth, and the ability to cook food—making it easier to chew, digest, and process nutrients (Shapiro 1974).

Homo erectus successfully colonized Africa, Asia, and finally Europe, with sites in Spain and Italy dating between 800,000 and 400,000 yBP. Their migration relied on the unique ability to use biology and culture—including hunting, migration, tools, fire, and forms of communication—to adapt to and control their surroundings, even extreme environments of hot and cold (Anton and Swisher 2004). The increasing role of culture, in turn, continued to influence biology. Brain size and complex mental activities increased with access to protein. Increased tool use for food processing and preparation, from cutting to cooking, led to a reduction in the size of teeth, jaws, and face, eventually drawing the physical proportions of these ancestors closer to our own (Anton 2003).

Homo sapiens

Homo sapiens, dating from 350,000 yBP to the present, constitute the fifth major group in our evolutionary chain. They include both archaic *Homo sapiens*, who lived between 350,000 and 28,000 yBP, and modern *Homo sapiens*, who appeared as early as 200,000 yBP in Africa and eventually replaced archaic *Homo sapiens*.

Archaic *Homo sapiens*, including one late variety prevalent in Europe—**Neandertals**—have often been depicted as slow, unintelligent, and inarticulate cave dwellers who were far removed physically and mentally from modern humans. But these views are inaccurate. The Neandertal brain had achieved modern size. These individuals were physically active and able to survive and settle in the most extreme of natural environments. They made elaborate tools. They hunted big game with sophistication and success, revealing strength, intelligence, culture, and social organization. Neandertals buried their dead. Carefully laid out skeletons have been recovered from burial pits, showing a distinct level of care and intention between the living and the dead. Neandertal anatomy would have enabled them to speak.

Neandertal: A late variety of archaic *Homo sapien* prevalent in Europe.

Like those of *Homo erectus*, archaic *Homo sapiens* fossils can be found in Africa, Asia, and Europe. Excavations throughout these regions have uncovered quite a few nearly complete skeletons and accompanying artifacts. Neandertals provide some of the most well known and most studied fossils of our human ancestors (Trinkaus and Shipman 1994).

Modern *Homo sapiens* emerged in Africa as early as 200,000 yBP. One of the earliest modern *Homo sapiens* finds, discovered in the Middle Awash River Valley, dates to 160,000 to 154,000 yBP. Its physical characteristics suggest a body and a mental capacity much like our own. By 100,000 yBP, modern *Homo sapiens* were migrating out of Africa into Europe and Asia. The exact reasons for their migration may never be known, but they likely include effects of climate change on the natural habitat, stress on food resources because of increasing population, and competition for scarce resources (Larsen 2011).

Fossil records show at least a four-thousand year period, between 32,000 and 28,000 yBP, when archaic and modern *Homo sapiens* coexisted in Europe. By the time modern *Homo sapiens* first encountered Neandertals, the Neandertal culture would have been technically and behaviorally quite advanced. But the

Human Origins in the Museum

After reading this chapter, visit your local natural history museum. You many find one on campus or in the nearest town; or you may need to travel some distance. Museums are designed to teach the public about art and history through personal interactions with artifacts and displays. At the museum, take some time to walk through displays, focusing on the exhibits that teach about human origins. How are the exhibits presented? How do they compare to the presentation of material in this textbook? Do the exhibits help you think about human evolution from a new angle?

Ask the museum staff if it is possible to interview the curator of the human origins section. A curator is the professional, often an anthropologist, who designs a museum exhibit and works to acquire the materials for display. You may want to call ahead to set up an appointment. Ask where the staff gathered material for the display and how they developed the key concepts that serve to frame the material. Consider asking the curator how he or she became interested in the subject and whether his or her particular interests are reflected in the exhibition. Ask about the history of the exhibit: Is it new or old? How and why did the museum decide to mount this exhibit? Ask whether the exhibit has been controversial.

If you are unable to visit a museum in person, spend time investigating the online exhibit of the American Museum of Natural History's Hall of Human Origins (www.amnh.org/exhibitions/permanent/humanorigins/). This is an extensive site with rich text and excellent photos and graphics. Then read "Anthropologists Engage the World" on pages 180–81. It introduces you to paleoanthropologist Ian Tattersall, curator of the Hall of Human Origins exhibit.

---

multiregional continuity thesis: The theory that modern *Homo sapiens* evolved directly from archaic *Homo sapiens* living in regions across the world.

"out of Africa" theory: The theory that modern *Homo sapiens* evolved first in Africa, migrated outward, and eventually replaced the archaic *Homo sapiens*. Also called *replacement theory*.

exact interaction between the two groups, as well as the ultimate fate of the Neandertals, is still under debate. Some scholars argue that modern *Homo sapiens* evolved directly from archaic *Homo sapiens* living in regions across the world—the **multiregional continuity thesis**. Others argue that modern *Homo sapiens* evolved first in Africa, migrated outward, and eventually replaced the archaic *Homo sapiens* (Larsen 2011). In this **"out of Africa"** (or **replacement**) **theory**, archaic *Homo sapiens* may have been wiped out—perhaps losing a resource war to their more modern successors. Or, as some genetic studies hint, Neandertals may have interbred and been gradually assimilated into the modern human population. In this case, Neandertal genes may have survived in the modern *Homo sapiens* gene pool—our very own (Stringer and McKie 1998).

Archaeological evidence shows that many modern *Homo sapiens* advances in behavior and culture occurred first in Africa—not in Europe, as scholars had earlier thought. The first ornamentation of shell beads was widespread in the area of modern-day Congo, Central Africa, by 80,000 yBP. The first evidence of fishing was also found in Congo, dating to 75,000 yBP. Painting, abstract art, and the use of symbolism also appear to have originated in Africa,

FIGURE 5.12 Emerging evidence continues to debunk stereotypes of Neandertals as far removed physically and mentally from modern humans. For instance, the careful burial of this Neandertal, discovered at La Chapelle-aux-Saints, France, reveals a distinct level of intentionality between the living and the dead.

Ian Tattersall

Paleoanthropologist Ian Tattersall didn't originally plan to work in a museum. But he has spent his entire career as a curator at the American Museum of Natural History in New York City, where he conducts research on human origins, manages the biological anthropology collection, designs exhibits, and engages in public education. Tattersall, who has conducted fieldwork in Madagascar, Vietnam, Surinam, Yemen, and Mauritius, is one of the foremost scholars of human evolution, particularly the recognition and analysis of the human fossil record, and a prolific author dedicated to interpreting human origins for the general public.

Tattersall curated the recently renovated Hall of Human Origins at the museum, his third such exhibition over the course of his career. "Permanent exhibits are the main fabric, the main exhibits that people walk through. But creating exhibitions is very expensive, time consuming, and resource consuming, so the permanent exhibits that we do have to last a long time.

"It's a very visual thing, paleontology. It deals in three-dimensional information, and this is what museums can uniquely do: show you three-dimensional things in the round, in the original size, and in the original detail. There's no other media that can actually do that currently.

"In a museum we can provide tangible evidence. And one of the things we wanted to do in this hall was to show just how much of it there is. Although it's true that the fossil record will never be complete and we're always just going to be seeing a tiny corner of what existed, it's also true that we have collected a fossil record for humankind that's really quite extraordinary. It's a very good fossil record by the standards of most mammalian families. In the exhibition, we wanted to show the richness of this record. Today we aren't basing our theories about human evolution on a few fossils discovered here and there. We

have a substantial record at the beginning of the twenty-first century.

"There is an astonishing amount that is already known and is already demonstrable. I think the basic outlines of the human evolutionary story are pretty clear. At this point it's unlikely that any individual discovery is going to cause anybody to rewrite the textbook, which at one time was happening. The press would like you to

Paleoanthropologist Ian Tattersall

believe that today every time a new fossil is found, we have to rush off and revise the textbooks. Actually, no. We might have to add a detail or two here or there. But it's not going to change the big picture.

"We can't show real human fossils in the Hall of Human Origins, but what we can do is show them exactly as they look and give people the experience of seeing the real thing. That's what's great about a museum and the opportunity to create an exhibition. People can come and see for themselves and hopefully think about it a little bit and arrive at their own conclusions. You can't do that in any other medium. People do start thinking. They do start talking. When you go into the hall and eavesdrop on conversations, you find that people really are talking to each other and comparing notes."

Tattersall's most recent book, *The Masters of the Planet* (2012), strives to make paleoanthropology and the story of human origins approachable and applicable to the nonspecialist.

"Over my career, the Museum has given me the opportunity to write a lot of books. And this one is sort of a summary of where I am in terms of understanding how human beings became the extraordinary creatures that we are. It's a very good thing to step back once in a while from one's research—in my case it's the details of systematics and how we recognize species in the fossil record—to see how the smaller issues that one deals with on a daily basis fit into the bigger picture.

"I begin the story seven million years ago, and I want people to understand that humans didn't come out of nowhere. There is a long, long history behind us. If anything that had happened in vertebrate history going back four hundred million years had not happened, then we wouldn't have been able to have had the outcome that we have today. All of those steps along the way are essential to what we are. But I think the thing that makes us so uniquely different from anything else is the way we process information in our minds. That's the thing that really

distinguishes us from our closest relatives. And that was very recent. In fact, it's so recent that the first *Homo sapiens* didn't do it. I'm trying to understand how that might have emerged.

"A framework is developing within which we can begin to appreciate that we are totally continuous with the rest of nature, but at the same time there is something advantageous about us that is totally unique. Or 'dangerously unique,' one might say. By dangerously unique, I mean our ability as humans to ruin the environment and ignore the fact that we're doing it. Those are two different aspects of the same basic ability that we have. It's a kind of cognitive dissonance. Maybe we can have cognitive dissonance because we have the kind of cognition that can be dissonant. But anyway, that is our big uniting feature."

In thinking about how to explain the importance of paleoanthropology, Tattersall reflects, "I've often thought that because humans are such a new thing, there is nothing that we can't understand about ourselves on a functional day-to-day basis simply by looking around us at the way we behave today. It sounds like a fairly disloyal statement to paleoanthropology because we always rationalize the study of our evolution in terms of understanding how we came to be who we are today. I think you can understand who we are today without necessarily understanding the evolutionary background. But a key part of what we are is insatiably curious about ourselves, about our origins, and about where we fit into the rest of nature. And you cannot approach that without understanding human evolution. We can't really understand where we fit into nature. And that is perhaps the most profound question that we can ask about ourselves because we are these insatiable, curious, intellectual entities. That is what we are doing when we study evolution. We are answering this need to know that we have—that is so much a part of ourselves. And, in a sense, if we're not asking these questions, we're not complete. And if we're not answering them, we're not complete either."

although the stunning imagery of artwork found in French and Spanish caves has garnered much of the media and scientific attention (Powell, Shennan, and Thomas 2009).

By 40,000 yBP, intrepid modern *Homo sapiens* immigrants had settled in Australia and the Pacific Islands. In a cooling climate, water was drawn toward the polar caps, with the effect of lowering sea levels, exposing more land and creating more avenues for human migration.

Until recently, all human remains discovered in East Asia dating to 40,000 yBP or later appeared to be fully modern *Homo sapiens*. Recent research, however, challenges the impression of successive, discreet steps in human evolution in this region and globally. Fossil remains from Denisova Cave in north-central Asia suggest that the species of human ancestor living there around 30,000 yBP was genetically distinct from Neandertals but was not *Homo sapiens*. What appears to be a new species may instead possibly be an isolated *Homo sapiens* descendant of *Homo erectus*, complicating the picture of human evolution in the region (Krause et al. 2010).

In 2003, the skeletal remains of a very short, primitive species was discovered on the island of Flores in Indonesia and quickly dubbed the "Hobbit" in the popular press. The skeleton, dated to 18,000 yBP, revealed a very tiny brain similar in size to the brains of earlier Australopithecines and only a quarter of the size of a living human's brain. Primitive wrist bones appear to be like those found in apes. Some scholars argue that, especially with no evidence of ancestors, the find may simply be a modern human suffering from a genetic abnormality such as microcephaly. Many scholars, however, suggest this skeleton may be evidence of a group of primitive humans (named *Homo floresiensis* by Peter Brown and colleagues [2004]) that became isolated in early human evolution. The primitive wrist bones and general characteristics of the fossil have led many to think that this may be a new species that originated in Africa well before *Homo sapiens*.

With these two finds, the picture of our human ancestors as late as 30,000 yBP becomes unexpectedly complicated (Larsen 2011). In addition, continuing work on Neandertal DNA confirms their presence in multiple sites globally, though by 30,000 yBP they appear to have been barely holding on in the Iberian peninsula of western Europe before their ultimate demise (Krause et al. 2007). Modern humans, originating in Africa, were spreading everywhere by 30,000 yBP. Taken together, these four species present an emerging picture of dynamic human evolution that reveals surprising diversity in our immediate past, really just a blink of an eye before the present in the scope of deep time (Larsen 2011).

By around 15,000 yBP, a founding population of modern *Homo sapiens* had left northeastern Asia and traveled across the newly exposed Bering land bridge between Siberia and Alaska. Subsequently they populated North and South

FIGURE 5.13 *Homo floresiensis* (*left*), dubbed the "Hobbit," compared to the cranium of a modern human (*right*). *Homo floresiensis*, discovered in Indonesia, dates to 18,000 yBP.

America and completed our species' colonization of the entire planet (Steele and Powell 1993).

What Has Made Modern Humans So Successful at Survival?

One of the key characteristics of humans is our ability to adapt to a changing world. Human adaptation takes four primary forms: genetic adaptation through evolution; developmental adaptation during the individual life cycle; acclimatization to immediate environmental changes; and cultural adaptation using tools to moderate or control the effects of the natural environment. Together, these four types of adaptation provide humans with a remarkable set of tools to survive, thrive, and pass our genetic inheritance on to future generations.

Genetic Adaptation

Genetic adaptation occurs at the population level as a result of natural selection. We have already discussed human genetic adaptations to malaria through the sickle-cell mutation. Later in the chapter we will examine human genetic adaptation to ultraviolet (UV) light. In examining genetic adaptation, anthropologists focus not on changes to an individual's genotype but on cumulative changes that occur as a population evolves over many generations. Genetic adaptations are inherited from one generation to another, and they are not reversible in an individual's lifetime.

genetic adaptation: Changes in genetics that occur at a population level in response to certain features of the environment.

Developmental Adaptation

Although DNA provides a blueprint for an individual's growth, one's actual development is strongly influenced by the environment and the events one experiences. **Developmental adaptations** can begin in the womb and continue through the human growth cycle, being influenced by nutrition, disease, and other environmental factors. Height, for instance, is influenced not only by DNA but also by the quality and quantity of food eaten and the diseases experienced. Did you have enough protein, calcium, and vitamins during your growth spurts? Were you immunized against polio, measles, mumps, and rubella? If so, you were able to maximize the growth potential in your DNA blueprint.

developmental adaptation: The way in which human growth and development can be influenced by factors other than genetics, such as nutrition, disease, and stress.

Research has confirmed that nutrition and stress during prenatal development have a dramatic impact on our physical and mental abilities. Inadequate nutrition or a mother's smoking, drinking, or drug intake can create powerful stresses on the fetus. David Barker's *fetal origins hypothesis*, now commonly referred to as the developmental origins of health and disease, suggests that individuals who experienced these stresses in the womb or during the first

FIGURE 5.14 The Aymaran people, who dwell in the Andes region of highland Bolivia, develop larger lung capacity as a result of living at such a high altitude. This allows them to process more oxygen in a low-oxygen environment, an example of developmental adaptation.

two years of childhood tend to be smaller, more prone to disease, and likely to have shorter lives than those who did not. Barker, a nutrition scientist, studied sixteen thousand people in Hertfordshire, England, and found "a direct and strong correlation between low birth weight and death from coronary disease." Specifically, individuals born weighing less than 5.5 pounds were twice as likely to die of coronary heart disease at some point over their lifetime than individuals weighing 7.5 pounds or more at birth (Barker 1998).

Another study of developmental adaptation has focused on children who grow up at high altitudes in the highlands of South America. These individuals develop larger lung capacity, an adaptation that enables them to process more oxygen in a low-oxygen environment. This is a permanent developmental adaptation that does not reverse if the individuals move to a lower altitude later in life. But like all developmental adaptations, the development of larger lungs only affects the individual's body; it does not affect the underlying genetic code in the individual's DNA and so is not passed down to the next generation. What is inherited is the ability to make this developmental adaptation in the next generation, if necessary (Beall 2001, 2006).

Acclimatization

acclimatization: The process of the body temporarily adjusting to the environment.

Beginning in the womb and continuing through old age, humans also experience temporary physiological adaptations, sometimes called **acclimatization**. These occur every day as our bodies make temporary adjustments to changes in the environment. When your body is hot, it perspires to cool down. When it is cold outside, you may start to shiver—an attempt to stay warm by moving. When it is dark outside, your pupils dilate to allow in more natural light; in bright sun, they narrow to protect your eyes. If you travel to high altitudes where the air has less oxygen, your heart rate speeds up and your breathing becomes shallower to extract more oxygen from the air. All of these are temporary, usually short-term, adaptations to changes in the immediate environment.

Cultural Adaptation

Humans' innovative, complex, and widespread **cultural adaptations** to the natural environment set us apart from other animal species. When it is cold outside, we light a fire, put on a coat, build a shelter, or turn up the furnace. When it is hot outside, we turn on the fan or the air conditioner. When it is dark, we turn on the lights; when it is too bright, we pull down the shades. When professional basketball and football teams travel to play games in high-altitude cities such as Denver, they keep an oxygen tank next to the bench to make it easier for the players to breathe. Airplanes are equipped with oxygen masks to help passengers deal with the low oxygen levels at high altitudes in the event of a "sudden drop in cabin pressure" during the flight.

Cultural adaptations have even affected our biological evolution. The cultural invention of stone tools as early as 2.5 mya enabled our human ancestors to butcher and process meat more efficiently and provided the increased protein needed for the development of larger brains. Today, culture is the primary way we adapt to the natural environment.

Where Did Variations in Human Skin Color Come From?

Skin color comes in infinite variations, and it, too, reflects adaptation to the environment through natural selection. Physical anthropologists suggest that such variations are a direct result of genetic adaptations to varying levels of UV light (Jablonski and Chaplin 2000). Where UV light is strongest—for instance, near the equator or at higher altitudes—skin color is darkest. Where UV light is weakest—closer to the poles—skin color is lightest. But how do these variations actually happen?

The Role of Ultraviolet Light

Jablonski and Chaplin (2000) argue that variation in skin color is the result of a genetic balancing act between getting too much UV light and too little. Too much UV light can destroy folic acid in the body, a vitamin that is essential to healthy fetal development. In fact, extremely low levels of folic acid can lead to birth defects. (Although too much UV light can also lead to skin cancers, these develop later in life and do not affect reproduction and evolution of the species.)

Too little UV light can also be a problem. It is essential to the process of synthesizing vitamin D, which in turn is necessary for absorbing calcium. We

cultural adaptation: A complex innovation, such as fans, furnaces, and lights, that allows humans to cope with their environment.

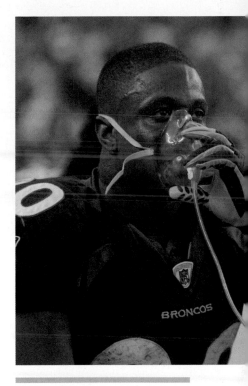

FIGURE 5.15 A member of the Denver Broncos football team receives oxygen to combat the effects of the high altitude in Denver, Colorado, an example of cultural adaptation to the natural environment.

need calcium to build and preserve strong bones. A lack of vitamin D may lead to bone-softening diseases such as rickets in children and osteomalacia in adults. The latter is particularly devastating for women whose weakened pelvic bones may be unable to support the stress of giving birth. The nutrients needed for the body to synthesize vitamin D are also found in a few fatty fish such as salmon, tuna, mackerel, sardines, and catfish — foods not commonly associated with the early human diet. UV light is the primary and most readily available source (Jablonski 2006).

Melanin and Melanocytes

Melanin, the pigment that gives our skin color, is produced by melanocytes in the skin. All humans have a similar number of these pigment-producing cells, but not all of them are genetically programmed to create the same amount. Melanin is a natural sunscreen. Because we know that our ancestors all originated in Africa, which is close to the equator, we can assume that they had more active melanocytes, more melanin, and darker skin as an adaptation to a high UV light environment.

When humans began to migrate out of Africa, away from the equator and into areas with less UV light, the role of melanin-rich dark skin as a powerful sunscreen likely became less positive, as it blocked too much of the UV light needed to synthesize vitamin D. American physiologist William Loomis (1967) suggests that because of these conditions, as groups of humans migrated out of Africa away from the equator, natural mutations that created lighter skin color would have been more successful and helped those individuals survive and reproduce more effectively. Gradually, over hundreds or thousands of generations and many miles of migration, changes in the natural environment interacted with variations in skin color to select the color variation most effective for survival. As levels of UV light change gradually with increasing distance from the equator, so did skin color shift gradually as the human population migrated, adapting genetically to changes in the natural environment. Individuals with appropriate levels of melanin to absorb the UV light in a region would be more likely to survive and reproduce, gradually expanding their representation in the population's gene pool. The maps in Figure 5.16 show the corresponding clinal variations (reflecting gradual change over space and time) of UV light and skin color.

Skin color varies so gradually that there are no clear boundaries between one population and another, nor color groupings that distinguish one population from another. Nevertheless, imaginations of distinct populations — sometimes called races — identifiable by skin color or other physical features have been prominent in cultures worldwide with powerful effect. In Chapter 6 we explore the implications of these ideas for the cultural construction of race and racism.

melanin: The pigment that gives human skin its color.

(a)

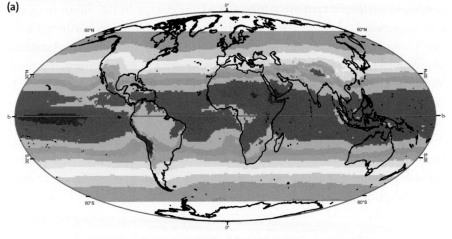

FIGURE 5.16 Skin Color Variation
(a) Clinal distribution of ultraviolet (UV) light intensity with highest intensity near the equator and lowest near the poles. **(b)** Clinal distribution of skin color, closely tracking the intensity of ultraviolet light.

MODIFIED FROM NINA G. JABLONSKI. 2006. *SKIN: A NATURAL HISTORY*. *Berkeley: University of California Press. Images by George Chaplin.*

(b)

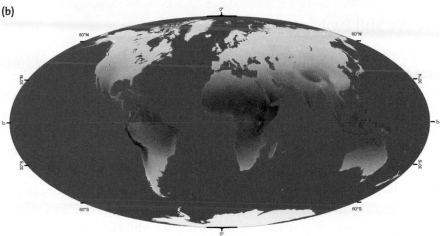

Physiological and Cultural Adaptations to Ultraviolet Light

Humans adapt to UV light in other ways, both physical and cultural. Tanning, for instance, is an adaptation of our bodies to UV light; but it is a temporary acclimatization, not a permanent change. Tanning does not affect the genes and is not passed along through the gene pool to the next generation. If I were to move from New York to Miami, my "white" skin's melanocytes would become more active, making more pigmentation—a tan—for protection. But even if I lived in Miami for thirty years, working and playing every day in the sun, my tan would never become permanent. If I later moved back to New York, my tan would gradually fade and my melanin production and skin color would return to their pre-Miami pink. Modern-day human cultural adaptations to UV light include sunscreen, hats, sunglasses, long-sleeve shirts, and umbrellas to protect lighter-colored skin from damage.

Another cultural adaptation to UV light is announced on the front of every milk carton: "vitamin D fortified." Why is vitamin D added to milk? In the early twentieth century, the rise of industrial jobs in northern U.S. cities combined with increased mechanization of agriculture in the South to spur a vast migration of African Americans from southern farms to northern factories. Cases of rickets and osteomalacia became rampant in African American populations that were no longer exposed to enough UV light in northern states. With the discovery of dietary vitamin D, a public health campaign led the U.S. government to initiate a program of fortifying milk and milk-based infant formulas in the 1930s. This cultural response to low levels of UV light led to a near disappearance of rickets in the United States by the 1960s. However, rickets has reemerged as a health concern in recent years as cultural practices have limited people's exposure to sunlight without regard to the dangers of vitamin D deficiency (Rajakumar and Thomas 2005).

Are We Still Evolving?

Today, living organisms—including humans—continue to adapt to changes in the natural environment. Indeed, evolution is happening all around us. Bacteria are evolving in response to antibiotics. Hospitals in the United States are reporting an alarming rise in drug-resistant infections, and healthcare workers worldwide are finding strains of tuberculosis that are resistant to many common antibiotic treatments. Insects are evolving in response to pesticides, with the emergence of DDT-resistant mosquitoes ending twentieth-century hopes of eliminating malaria. Studies of fish are revealing the emergence of smaller bodies and faster reproduction to compensate for overfishing. Clearly, species are continuing to adapt as their diversity and mutations interact with changes in the natural environment that alter the conditions for survival and reproduction (Larsen 2011).

Physiological Adaptation

Humans, too, continue to adapt and evolve. Changes in the human face and dentition over the last ten thousand years provide evidence of how the human form continues to be shaped in response to the environment. A look at the mouths of most teenagers in the United States gives a clear indication that our jaws are no longer large enough to accommodate the number and size of teeth inherited from our recent ancestors. Today's braces, tooth extractions, and retainers all work as cultural tools to help human bodies adapt to overcrowded mouths. Fossils from ten thousand years ago show no such overcrowding. Bones grow in size in direct relationship to the stress and pressure placed on them. With the rise of agriculture ten thousand years ago, the introduction of domesticated plants such as grains into the human diet gradually reduced the stresses on the human jaw and the stimulation needed to produce large jaws.

Tooth size, however, is not susceptible to the same environmental pressures. Reduction in jaw size without a change in the size and number of teeth has led to a lot of overcrowded mouths in the twenty-first century. Although changes in jaw size and face shape may relate more directly to individuals' physiological adaptation to diet rather than genetic changes in the population, these shifts in dentition do reveal evolution and adaptation at work in the human population today (Larsen 2010).

Genetic Adaptation

Current genetic evolution in the human species is harder to see. The long human life cycle and our general reluctance to be subjects of laboratory experiments make the task of observing change over time difficult. The conditions for evolution, however, are very clearly present. Spontaneous mutations continue to occur in every species, including humans. And the natural environment of human life—of all life—is changing dramatically. Global warming is altering weather patterns and causing sea levels to rise. Ozone depletion is allowing more exposure to solar radiation. Pollution is adding carcinogenic mutagens to the air, water, and soil. The environment, a key element in shaping genetic adaptations, is undergoing significant changes. Environmental conditions exist today that could put pressure on the human physical form and create an environment suitable to genetic adaptation.

As the environment changes, it will affect the biology and evolution of all living organisms. Other animal species—from corals to birds to polar bears to orangutans—are already facing massive extinctions. As the world changes around us, our generation and future generations will change as well. There are good reasons to believe that current trends in energy consumption, population growth, and economic globalization will continue. As a result, we can expect intense and perhaps cataclysmic pressures on the human species that will force us to adapt. What specific form those adaptations might take we cannot predict.

FIGURE 5.17 *Left,* straightening teeth has become so common that in the United States orthodontics is a multibillion-dollar industry. *Right,* crowding of the teeth appears in some archaeological skeletal remains, but it became common only after humans adopted agriculture around ten thousand years ago.

Cultural Adaptation

Culture is now the primary tool that humans use to adapt to changes in the environment. As humans face increasing levels of UV light, our first adaptive line of defense is to use sunscreens, sun-protective clothing, and sunglasses. As sea levels rise or warming waters stimulate stronger hurricanes and tropical storms, we build seawalls and levees to protect our homes and communities. As diseases such as tuberculosis, malaria, and HIV/AIDS mutate and develop more virulent strains, humans turn to more intense pharmaceutical research and expensive antivirals, pesticides, and antibiotics. But will these cultural

TOOLKIT

Thinking Like an Anthropologist: Looking Ahead, Looking Behind

Where did we come from? Where are we going? What does it mean to be human? Throughout this chapter we have explored our human origins and pondered these questions, as well as the others listed below. The chapter's opening stories provide windows into the evidence that physical anthropologists are uncovering about the human story in the perspective of deep time.

- Where do humans fit in the story of life on Earth?
- How do scientists learn about prehistoric life?
- How does the theory of evolution explain the diversity of life?
- How does evolution work?
- What do we know about our human ancestors?
- What has made modern humans so successful at survival?
- Where did variations in human skin color come from?
- Are we still evolving?

Everything we do today is contingent on the evolutionary developments discussed in this chapter, including opposable thumbs, bipedalism, an enlarged pelvis, and an enlarged brain. Which one of our Australopithecine ancestors could have imagined humans today walking and texting? Or speaking into cell phones and communicating

with others on the opposite side of the world? Or the elaborate forms of symbolic and abstract art, media, and language that our brains have enabled us to create? Today we integrate these evolutionary developments into the most contemporary context, and they have repercussions that we ourselves have difficulty imagining.

Where does the explosion of technology fit in our process of adaptation? Will this change our notion of what it means to be human? How will digital technology influence our cognitive development? What is the cumulative impact of television, videos, cell phones, the computer, and the Internet? Is it possible to imagine that the way we have evolved may actually limit our capacity to see the world and understand it? As we have seen, the human chapter in the story of life on Earth is just a few brief pages in the encyclopedic narrative of deep time. But the pace of change in contemporary human culture is extraordinarily rapid, and we must carefully consider the developments of the present, seen in the context of our evolutionary past, to catch a glimpse of where we are going.

Key Terms
deep time (p. 157)
fossil (p. 158)
DNA (p. 162)
paleogeneticist (p. 162)

adaptations be enough to protect us as a species if the changes to the natural environment are extreme?

Perhaps just as important, who will have access to these cultural tools? When drought caused by changes in climate patterns disrupts clean water supplies, not everyone will have the resources to dig deeper wells, build water filtration plants, or construct aqueducts to move water across parched lands. When hurricanes increase in strength or frequency, not everyone will have seawalls and levees high enough or strong enough to guarantee protection. Not all humans will have an equal chance at survival.

theory of evolution (p. 162)

creationism (p. 164)

intelligent design (p. 164)

mutation (p. 167)

mutagen (p. 167)

natural selection (p. 167)

gene migration (p. 169)

genetic drift (p. 169)

species (p. 172)

bipedalism (p. 173)

Oldowan tools (p. 173)

Acheulian stone tools (p. 176)

Neandertal (p. 177)

multiregional continuity thesis (p. 178)

"out of Africa" (replacement) theory (p. 178)

genetic adaptation (p. 183)

developmental adaptation (p. 183)

acclimatization (p. 184)

cultural adaptation (p. 185)

melanin (p. 186)

For Further Exploration

Cave of Forgotten Dreams. 2010. Directed by Werner Herzog. IFC Films. Documentary film explores the cave art in Chauvet Cave in southern France.

Jablonski, Nina G. 2006. *Skin: A Natural History.* Berkeley: University of California Press.

Pew Forum on Religion & Public Life. www.pewforum.org. This website explores American attitudes toward religion and politics.

National Center for Science Education. www.ncse.com. Resources to further explore the processes of evolution and the debates between evolution and creationism.

Tattersall, Ian. 2012. *Masters of the Planet: The Search for Our Human Origins.* New York: Palgrave Macmillan. An accessible presentation of human evolutionary development.

What lies beneath the surface of any beautiful scene? The project of anthropology includes unmasking the structures of power—the deep complexities of how humans organize themselves in groups. In Part 2 we will explore structures of race, ethnicity, gender, sexuality, kinship, and class in order to help you develop the analytical tools to see more deeply, navigate more carefully, and engage more fully the world around you. Here, children play soccer in the street at La Boca, Buenos Aires, Argentina.

Is there really any such thing as a "natural disaster"? New Orleans neighborhood devastated by flooding after Hurricane Katrina.

p. 198

p. 199

p. 202

p. 205

p. 225

p. 233

CHAPTER 6

Race and Racism

On August 29, 2005, Hurricane Katrina slammed into the Louisiana coast. The U.S. population watched their television sets in horror as the storm surge breached the New Orleans levee system and water flooded into the city's urban center, engulfing homes, businesses, and churches. Following the storm, news broadcasts showed residents wading through fetid water to find food, Coast Guard helicopters rescuing stranded residents from rooftops, and tens of thousands of desperate people—including children, the elderly, and the disabled—begging to be rescued from the Superdome and Convention Center, which had been designated the shelter of last resort but lacked food, water, and working bathrooms. The U.S. government, apparently crippled in its disaster response, took days to deliver emergency aid. More than one hundred countries offered assistance as the world watched, stunned by scenes more commonly associated with a developing country in Africa or Asia.

When Katrina struck the coast, the storm center actually missed New Orleans. Yet, heavy rain and storm surge overwhelmed the city's aged pumping system, and 80 percent of the city flooded when the levees broke. The city's poor—overwhelmingly African American—were the most severely affected and largely had to fend for themselves. Because the government was unprepared and slow to respond, more than half the population was displaced from New Orleans. The city's population of 454,000 in 2005 plummeted to 210,000 a year later (Elliot 2009), and the proportion of African American residents, 68 percent before Katrina, only rebounded to 60 percent by 2010. By mid-2011 the total population had only recovered to 360,740 (U.S. Census Bureau 2013).

Anthropologist and geographer Neil Smith makes the point that "there is no such thing as a natural disaster." Hurricanes, tsunamis, earthquakes, droughts, and volcanic eruptions are all natural events. Whether they become a disaster, however, depends on social factors: location, vulnerability of the population, government preparedness, effectiveness of the response, and sustained reconstruction efforts. The difference between who lives and who dies in a natural event is largely determined by social inequality. For instance, rising sea levels related to climate change are making cities such as Venice, Dacca (Bangladesh), and New Orleans especially vulnerable to floods; but the impact on certain people in those places will be determined by racial hierarchies and income stratification (Smith 2006).

Is it possible to view the events around Hurricane Katrina and New Orleans through the lens of race? Race and racism are incredibly difficult topics of conversation in U.S. culture, whether we are in a classroom, a religious community, a hospital, or the halls of Congress. How do we create opportunities to explore ideas of race and the way those ideas shape our lives and culture? In a country that likes to think of itself as color-blind, how do we as anthropologists make sense of the continuing inequality in income, wealth, education, access to health care, and incarceration rates that breaks so clearly along color lines (Shanklin 1998)?

Anthropologists view race as a framework of categories created to divide the human population. Western Europeans originally developed this framework as part of their global expansion beginning in the 1400s (Sanjek 1994a). As they encountered, mapped, and colonized people in Africa, Asia, the Pacific, and the Americas, Europeans placed them into an "international hierarchy of races, colors, religions and cultures" (Trouillot 1994, 146). The exact labels and expressions have varied over time and place as colonial powers engaged with local cultures and confronted local resistance. But the underlying project— to stratify people into groups based on assumptions of natural differences in intelligence, attractiveness, capacity for civilization, and fundamental worth in relation to people of European descent—has been remarkably consistent (Mullings 2005).

As we will explore in this chapter, today anthropologists find no scientific basis for classifications of race. Genetically there is only one race—the human race, with all its apparent diversity. Yet despite consistent efforts over the last century by anthropologists and others to counter the inaccurate belief that races are biologically real, race has remained a powerful framework through which many people see human diversity and through which those in power organize the distribution of privileges and resources. Race—which is scientifically not real—has become culturally real in the pervasive racism found in many parts of the globe, including the United States.

Over the past five hundred years, race as a way of organizing the world has been put to destructive use, wreaking an enormous toll on both its victims and its proponents. Race and racism have justified the conquest, enslavement, forced transportation, and economic and political domination of some humans by others for more than five centuries. Today race and racism have become so integral to patterns of human relations in many parts of the world that inherited racial categories may seem to be natural and the inequality built on racism may seem to represent "real" differences among "real" races.

In this chapter, we will critique arguments for the existence of discrete biological human groups called races. We will consider the roots of race and racism in the European colonial past and their expression in various places today. We will examine the construction of race in the United States over the past four hundred years and the way race and racism continue to shape U.S. culture. In particular, we will consider the following questions:

- Do biologically separate races exist?
- How is race constructed around the world?
- How is race constructed in the United States?
- What is racism?

We will examine **race** as a flawed system of classification, created and re-created over time, that uses certain physical characteristics (such as skin color, hair texture, eye shape, and eye color) to divide the human population into a few supposedly discrete biological groups and attribute to them unique combinations of physical ability, mental capacity, personality traits, cultural patterns, and capacity for civilization. Drawing on anthropological research, we will see, however, that racial categories have no biological basis. We might even say that races, as a biological concept, do not exist. The danger in this statement about biological race is that it may lead us to the mistaken conclusion that race does not exist. On the contrary, race has very real consequences.

race: A flawed system of classification, with no biological basis, that uses certain physical characteristics to divide the human population into supposedly discrete groups.

Race is a deeply influential system of thinking that affects people and institutions. Over time, imagined categories of race have shaped our cultural institutions—schools, places of worship, media, political parties, economic practices—and have organized the allocation of wealth, power, and privilege at all levels of society. Race has served to create and justify patterns of power and inequality within cultures worldwide, and many people have learned to see those patterns as normal and reasonable. So in this chapter we will also examine **racism**: individuals' thoughts and actions, as well as institutional patterns and policies, that create or reproduce unequal access to power, privilege, resources, and opportunities based on imagined differences among groups (Omi and Winant 1994).

racism: Individual thoughts and actions and institutional patterns and policies that create unequal access to power, resources, and opportunities based on imagined differences among groups.

By the end of the chapter, you will have the anthropological tools to understand not only the flaws in arguments for biologically discrete races, but also the history and current expressions of race and racism globally and in the United States. You will be prepared to apply those tools, if you so choose, to engaging in efforts against racism on your college campus, in your community, and throughout the world.

Do Biologically Separate Races Exist?

Many of us were enculturated to believe that "race" refers to distinct physical characteristics that mark individuals as clearly belonging in one group and not in another. However, anthropologists see race very differently. Contemporary studies of human genetics reveal no biologically distinct human groups. We can state this with certainty despite centuries of scientific effort to prove the existence of distinct biological races, and despite widespread popular belief that different races exist. In fact, humans are almost identical, sharing more than 99.9 percent of our DNA. The small differences that do exist are not distributed in any way that would correspond with popular or scientific notions of separate races. Race is not fixed in nature but, as we will explore later in this chapter, is created, perpetuated, and changed by people through individual and collective action.

First, however, let's explore some of the science behind race.

Fuzzy Boundaries in a Well-Integrated Gene Pool

Some physical anthropologists have compared modern humans to a little village that has grown very quickly. Throughout the short 200,000-year history of modern humans, we have basically been functioning as one enormous, interconnected gene pool, swapping genetic material back and forth (by interbreeding) quite freely within the village. Over the years, our family trees have intersected again and again.

If you trace your own family back for thirty generations—parents to grandparents to great-grandparents, and so on—you will find that in just over a thousand years you have accumulated one billion relatives. So it is not hard to imagine the myriad and unpredictable exchanges of genetic material among that large a group. Now extend your family tree back 100,000 years—the time it has taken for a few small groups of humans to migrate out of Africa and populate the entire planet. It is easy to imagine the billions of times this growing population has exchanged genetic material. Such deep integration of the human gene pool means that no clear and absolute genetic lines can be drawn to separate people into distinct, biologically discrete, "racial" populations.

As a result of this gene flow, human variation changes gradually over geographic space in a continuum (what physical anthropologists refer to as a cline), not by abrupt shifts or clearly marked groups. If you flew from western Africa to Russia, you would notice distinct variations in physical human form between the population where you boarded the plane and the population where you disembarked. But if you walked from western Africa to Russia, there would never

FIGURE 6.1 What can you know about a person's genetic makeup based on their outward appearance? Variations of skin color or other visible characteristics often associated with race are shaped by less than 0.1 percent of our genetic code. Contrary to certain stereotypes, they do not predict anything else about a person's genetic makeup, physical or mental capabilities, culture, or personality.

be a point along the way where you would be able to stop and say that the people on one side of the road are of one race and the people on the other side are of a different race.

Perhaps more surprising, a person who starts walking in western Africa may have more in common genetically with someone at the end of her trek in Russia than she does with a neighbor at home. This seems hard to imagine because we have been enculturated to believe that a very small number of traits—including skin color, hair texture, and eye color and shape—can serve to categorize people into distinct groups and predict larger genetic patterns. This is a flawed assumption. The human gene pool continues to be highly integrated. Genetic variations such as skin color, expressed in an individual's external appearance, are only 0.1 percent of that person's genetic code; they do not predict anything else about his or her genetic makeup. People in a particular region of the world whose ancestors inhabited that area for an extended period may have some increased probability of genetic similarity because of the greater probability of swapping genetic material with those geographically closer. But group boundaries are fuzzy and porous. People move and genes flow. Ultimately, group genetic probabilities cannot predict any one individual's reality.

Think about human physical variation as you would the grades you earn in school. Teachers often assign grades on a continuum from 0 to 100. Some teachers use letter grades instead. We may choose to call a 79 a C and an 80 a B. These are decisions based on convenience or the need to differentiate student success. Likewise, dividing people into separate races along the continuum of human genetic diversity is not based in nature but in human choices.

The Wild Goose Chase: Linking Phenotype to Genotype

In considering human physical diversity, physical anthropologists distinguish between genotype and phenotype. **Genotype** refers to the inherited genetic factors that provide a framework for an organism's physical form; these factors constitute the total genetic endowment that the organism, in turn, can pass down to its descendants. In contrast, **phenotype** refers to the way genes are expressed in an organism's physical form (both visible and invisible) as a result of the interaction of genotype with environmental factors, such as nutrition, disease, and stress.

The widespread belief that certain phenotypes such as skin color are linked to physical and mental capabilities, personality types, or cultural patterns is incorrect but deeply ingrained and difficult to reimagine.

As individuals, we may make snap judgments based on phenotypical traits that we erroneously assume indicate a person's "race"; with a quick glance we may think we know something significant about that individual. On the basis of phenotype alone, we may consider someone to be smarter, faster, stronger,

genotype: The inherited genetic factors that provide the framework for an organism's physical form.

phenotype: The way genes are expressed in an organism's physical form as a result of genotype interaction with environmental factors.

safe or dangerous, better at business, better at math, a better dancer or singer, more prone to alcoholism, more artistic, more susceptible to certain diseases, a better lover. You might call this the "White Men Can't Jump" or "Asians Are Better at Math" way of thinking about race and genes. We assume that we can know something significant about a person's genetic makeup just by looking at her phenotype. But can we really tell anything about someone from the way he or she looks?

A relatively small number of genes control the traits frequently used today to distinguish one "race" from another—skin color, eye shape, or hair texture. As a result, in the short history of modern humans these genes have been able to change rapidly in response to the environment. For example, as humans moved out of Africa and across the globe into a wide variety of physical environments, traits such as skin color, shaped by a relatively small cluster of genes, were more susceptible to environmental pressures and adapted more quickly. In contrast, traits such as intelligence, athletic or artistic ability, and social skills appear to be shaped by complex combinations of thousands or tens of thousands of genes, so they have been much less susceptible to environmental pressures. Adaptations in skin color were not accompanied by adaptations in, say, intelligence, musical ability, or physical ability. It is important to note that genetic research consistently shows that the genes that influence skin color, eye shape, or hair texture are not linked to any other genes and cannot predict anything about the rest of a person's underlying genotype (Mukhopadhyay, Henze, and Moses 2007).

Jonathan Marks, a leading physical anthropologist, compares the problem of sorting people into races with the problem children might have in sorting blocks into categories. Imagine that you start with a pile of blocks and ask a group of children to sort them into "large" and "small." They might agree on some—the largest and the smallest. But others in between might be harder to classify. "The fact that the blocks can be sorted into the categories given, however, does not imply that there are two kinds of blocks in the universe, large and small—and that the child has uncovered a transcendent pattern in the sizing of the blocks. It simply means that if categories are given, they can be imposed upon the blocks" (Marks 1995, 159).

What if you asked the children to sort instead by color or to distinguish among wooden, metal, and plastic blocks? What about blocks with smooth sides or grooved sides? The children could sort the blocks into any of these categories. But if you didn't link the multiple characteristics of the blocks—all the red blocks wooden, or all the plastic blocks grooved—then the children would end up with a completely different arrangement of blocks depending on whatever categories they arbitrarily decided to sort for.

The same is true for humans and the concept of race. If you give people a limited range of categories for skin color groups, they will be able to place

FIGURE 6.2 Looks can be deceiving. Which group is more genetically diverse?

many people into these categories. Some individuals who lie in the boundaries may be more difficult to categorize. But would this exercise uncover some deep, intrinsic pattern about humans? No, because traits like skin color are not linked to any other particular set of genes and cannot serve to predict anything else about the underlying genotype.

Why Not Construct Race on the Basis of Earwax?

From a genetic viewpoint, the use of skin color as the primary variable in constructing a person's "race" appears to be quite arbitrary. A number of other genes or gene combinations create phenotypic differences that could serve the same purpose. Why not choose eye color, hairiness (amount and location), earlobe shape, fingerprints, nose shape, tongue rolling, tooth shape and size, double-jointed fingers, height, or weight? Another possibility could be earwax.

There are two primary types of earwax (Jurmain and Nelson 1994). One is dry, gray, and crumbly. The other is wet, yellow, and sticky. Fully 90 percent of Europeans and only 4 percent of people in northern China have the second variety. Imagine dividing up your classmates into races based on one of these earwax characteristics, rather than skin color. How would you configure the group? Do you think that one subgroup/race would have any natural advantages over the others?

Can you imagine hierarchical systems of race that affect distribution of power and resources and that are based on differences in earwax? What if students in your college were guaranteed individual tutoring by the instructor if they had wet earwax? What if students were required to sit in the back of the room, where it is harder to hear the lecture, if they had dry earwax? Surely, such distinctions will strike you as absurd. Why not, then, regard distinctions made on the basis of skin color as equally absurd?

Would you be surprised to learn that there is more genetic difference between two penguins than between two humans? Penguins appear identical to the human eye and are found in a small range of habitats (unlike humans, who range over the entire globe). But penguins have been around a lot longer than modern humans, so they have had more time to evolve and develop greater genetic variation within their species. Does knowing this challenge you to be more skeptical of assumed links between outward appearances and underlying genotype?

How Is Race Constructed around the World?

Racial categories are human constructs; they are not found in nature. Yet they have become so deeply internalized that they feel natural and provide one of the most powerful frameworks through which we experience the world (Mukhopadhyay, Henze, and Moses 2007, 113). Anthropologists examine race and racism on a global scale and thus from different angles, identifying their similarities and variations and, in the process, revealing the ways those concepts have evolved and might be changed through individual and collective action.

Race and the Legacy of Colonialism

Contemporary global expressions of race and racism are deeply rooted in the systems of classification that western Europeans created as they expanded their colonial empires into Africa, Asia, the Pacific, and the Americas beginning in the 1400s. **Colonialism** became the centerpiece of European global economic activity, combining economic, military, and political control of people and places to fuel Europe's economic expansion and enhance the European position in the emerging global economy (see Chapter 12). The classification of people based on phenotype, particularly skin color, became the key framework for creating a hierarchy of races—with Europeans at the top—that linked people's looks with assumptions about their intelligence, physical abilities, capacity for culture, and basic worth. Eventually this framework served to justify colonial conquests, the trans-Atlantic slave trade, and the eradication of much of the indigenous population of the Americas (Gregory and Sanjek 1994).

Taking a global perspective, anthropologists often refer to "racisms" in the plural, reflecting the varieties of ways race has been constructed among people in different places. Locally, racisms and systems of racial classification are complex frameworks built out of the encounter of colonialism with local cultural patterns, global migration, and specific movements of resistance.

FIGURE 6.3 Diagram of a slave ship from the Atlantic slave trade.

colonialism: The practice by which a nation-state extends political, economic, and military power beyond its own borders over an extended period of time to secure access to raw materials, cheap labor, and markets in other countries or regions.

Racial frameworks and systems of racism have changed significantly over the last century. After World War II, colonial-era racisms shifted as national liberation movements struggled to end occupations by foreign powers. In addition, in this postcolonial period, key internal struggles challenged long-term patterns of race and racial discrimination. Notably, the antiapartheid movement in South Africa resisted dominant white rule, eventually reversing decades of legal structural discrimination and violence. The civil rights movement challenged more than three hundred years of race-based inequality in the United States. Today globalization has brought about new experiences of race and racism (as we will see in the case studies that follow).

Indeed, in today's global world, flexible accumulation produces new relationships between corporations and workers; the migration of workers within countries and across national borders yields new racial formations; and time-space compression enhances communication tools that can be employed to resist old hierarchies while also perpetuating old racial frameworks on a global scale. Racisms today, though rooted in similar historic realities, are shifting as they intersect with other systems of power, whether those are ethnicity, gender, sexuality, kinship, or class (Mullings 2005). The exact expression of these constructs varies from culture to culture and place to place.

Race, Skin Color, and Class in the Dominican Republic When Christopher Columbus landed on the island of Hispaniola (now comprising the Dominican Republic and Haiti) in 1492, he launched the complicated story of race, colonization, and globalization for the people who would inherit the land over the next four hundred years. Within fifty years of Columbus's arrival, perhaps

MAP 6.1
Haiti / Dominican Republic

hundreds of thousands of the indigenous inhabitants had been killed through
brutal forced labor, new diseases introduced from Europe, and suicide. The
Spanish imported the first African slaves in 1520 to work the sugar plantations
that were feeding Europeans' growing sugar addiction (Mintz 1985). Subsequently, the French took possession of the western third of the island and continued the slaving practice until they were overthrown by a slave rebellion in the
Haitian Revolution of 1804 (Trouillot 1994).

Drawing on ideas of liberty, fraternity, and equality that were central to
the French Revolution (1789–99), after the Haitian Revolution the island's residents established an independent nation of former African slaves—the first
in the world—and changed the dynamic of the growing global economy and
slave trade (see Chapter 12).

On the eastern two-thirds of the island, Dominican nationalists declared
independence from Spain in 1821 and moved to shape a distinct national identity in opposition to Haiti. Within this process they emphasized the connection
to their former colonial ruler, Spain, not to Africa. The Dominican Republic thus became integrated into the economic system dominated by Europe
and the United States, where racial thinking was stratified around whiteness.
Dominicans' early identification as Hispanics, not as blacks, is a dynamic that
still pervades the population's racial thinking today.

The Dominican Republic is an active participant in the current global
economic system. Sugar, coffee, cacao, and tobacco production for export still
play a significant role in the national economy. More recently, tourism, export-
processing factories, and money sent home from Dominican migrants have
expanded Dominican integration into the global economy, an integration that

reaches to the island's most rural levels. The republic's agriculture, tourism, and construction trades draw a steady stream of Haitian migrants across the border, both legally and illegally. Haitian migrants do back-breaking labor for meager wages and also endure constant discrimination by Dominicans (Gregory 2006).

Race, with a significant overlay of class, has become a powerful framework for organizing difference in the Dominican Republic. This framework stratifies people along a continuum from dark skin to light skin. In a small country of ten million people where linguistic (Spanish) and religious (Catholic) differences are limited, skin color serves as the key signifier—although higher-class status can "lighten" Dominicans, a dynamic we will also explore below in the case of Brazil. Unlike the United States, where conceptions of race are usually limited to four or five skin-color classifications, Dominicans use a wide range of variable and often inconsistent color terms, including *coffee, chocolate, cinnamon, wheat, indio, rosy, faded, blond, fair, dark,* and *ashen.*

None of the Dominican racial identifiers denote "black." A cornerstone of this framework is the rejection of African ancestry and of blackness more generally. Haitians, who are generally darker skinned than many Dominicans, mostly speak Creole, not Spanish; and they practice Catholicism intertwined with African religious beliefs. These factors mark Haitians as racially "other" in the Dominican Republic. Anti-Haitian sentiment is widespread, and false stereotypes repeated in popular conversation and in the press warn of the "Haitian threat" to the economy and national stability (Gregory 2006; Howard 2001; Martinez 1996).

However, in a sign of how complicated the constructs of race and racism are, anti-black and anti-Haitian sentiments are not uniform across the Dominican Republic. In both urban and rural settings, individual encounters within a local community context often overcome the stereotypes. Samuel Martinez (2003, 89) points out that "even as a numerically sizable minority of Dominicans voice blatantly racist sentiments, it is common for people of lower-income groups to identify themselves and their loved ones as 'black' in song and folklore." Deborah Pacini-Hernandez (1995) has documented the song-dance genre *bachata* that is prevalent in poor urban neighborhoods and rural work sites. *Bachata* commonly uses *negro, prieto,* and *morena,* terms for black or dark men and women, to refer to the singers, their lovers, and their audience. These uses reflect a more sympathetic engagement with blackness and race at the local level, among the rural and urban working classes who have dark skin and lower social status.

The work of Martinez and Pacini-Hernandez challenges us to acknowledge the complexity of analyzing race in the Dominican Republic. In fact, their work underscores the importance of examining local expressions of race and

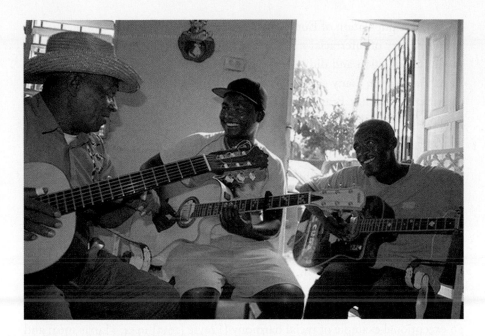

FIGURE 6.5 *Bachata* music portrays the complex understanding of race in the Dominican Republic.

racism and the ways in which communities continue to reimagine the racial categories imposed by colonial powers and contemporary Western media.

Race, Class, and Gender, and Hundreds of Races in Brazil Brazil provides another location to explore the cultural construction of race and the application of ideas of race to the creation of stratification. The United States and Brazil are today the two largest multiracial countries in the Western Hemisphere, although they have traveled two very different paths in framing racial identities and hierarchies. By the time Brazil outlawed slavery in 1888, the country had the largest African population in the New World. This situation reflected the grim fact that during and after Brazil's time as a colony of Portugal (1500–1815), 40 percent of all Africans in the Atlantic slave trade were brought to Brazil to work on Portuguese plantations and mines. Brazil was the last country in the Americas to outlaw slavery—a full generation after the U.S. Emancipation Proclamation in 1863.

Today Brazilians describe the human physical diversity called race in great detail. Although Brazil's system of racial classification is color-coded, its color terminology is far more expansive, encompassing hundreds of categories (Freyre 1933; Harris 1964, 1970). Terms include *alva* (pure white), *alva-escuro* (off-white), *alva-rosada* (pinkish white), *branca* (white), *clara* (light), *branca morena* (darkish white), *branca suja* (dirty white), *café* (coffee colored), *café com leite* (coffee with milk), *canela* (cinnamon), *preta* (black), and *pretinha* (lighter black) (Fluehr-Lobban 2006). Race categories follow along a nuanced continuum of appearance rather than a few rigid categories such as those used in the United States.

MAP 6.2
Brazil

miscegenation: A demeaning historical term for interracial marriage.

Brazil's population of Europeans, Africans, and indigenous people has had a long history of interracial mixing. The Portuguese colonial government promoted assimilation and did not bar **miscegenation**—that is, interracial marriage. As a result, many single Portuguese men who settled in Brazil chose to intermarry. Nor has Brazil applied the rule of hypodescent—the "one drop of blood" rule—that in the United States meant that having even one black ancestor out of many could mark an individual as black (see "The Rule of Hypodescent" below). As a result, a family may include children who are categorized as various shades of white, brown, and black.

Race in Brazil is not solely a function of skin color. In fact, race intersects closely with class—including land ownership, wealth, and education—in determining social status. Because of the power of class, a Brazilian's racial position can be modified by his or her level of affluence. Affluence can shift a Brazilian's racial identity in spite of skin color and other supposedly "racial" markers (Walker 2002).

Some scholars refer to Brazil as a "racial democracy" and extol the nation as an exceptional example of racial harmony (Freyre [1933] 1944; Harris 1964; and Kottak 2006). Brazil's government abolished the use of racial categories in the 1930s and constitutionally banned racism in 1951. The complex and fluid color classifications—the absence of a clear color line between black and white—are seen as a sign of tolerance. In addition, the incorporation of key African cultural practices (including carnival, samba, Candomblé religious practices, capoeira, and specific cuisine) as symbols of the Brazilian nation is often cited as supporting evidence for the racial democracy thesis (Downey 2005).

Other scholars have noted that despite the appearance of racial democracy, inequality exists in almost every area of Brazilian life and is directly linked to color. Darker-skinned Brazilians face higher levels of exclusion and injustice, including a systemic correlation between color and economics. Most of the poor are Afro-Brazilians. Most of the rich are white. Racial democracy may instead be simply a myth that serves as a cornerstone of Brazil's national denial of the existence of racism (Harrison 2002b, 160).

In *Laughter Out of Place* (2003), anthropologist Donna Goldstein writes about working poor women from the bleak favela (shantytown), ironically named Felicidade Eterna ("eternal happiness"), who support their families as domestic workers in the homes of middle-class Brazilian families in the affluent sections of Rio de Janeiro. Gloria, poor and dark skinned, raising fourteen children, including nine of her own, works as a domestic servant, shopping, cooking, and cleaning. She earns five dollars a day—just enough to feed herself and her family. The pay is off the books, so she has no legal labor protections, no insurance, and no pension. Goldstein links the contemporary culture of domestic work, particularly the employer–domestic servant relationships, to the historic institution of slavery in Brazil. Middle-class families enjoy a kind of learned helplessness similar to that of the slave owner—allowing their workers to do the dirty, manual chores. The employer–domestic servant relationship, like the owner–slave relationship, is characterized by domination, strict rules, and social separation.

How do Brazil's marginalized and oppressed people make sense of their lives—lives overburdened with poverty, violence, and work at the bottom of a global hierarchy of race, class, and gender; yet lives that also display dignity and resilience? Goldstein explores the role of laughter and humor as means to cope with persistent brutality. She particularly notes a humor that recognizes life's absurdities and ironies and provides perspective to a sense of injustice. She recalls, for instance, the awkwardness of "laughter out of place," as domestic workers and employers laugh at different times and for different reasons when they watch the local soap operas that dramatize middle-class Brazilian life. The distinctive life experiences of worker and employer create vastly different viewing experiences, casting the televised dramas and traumas of the Brazilian middle class in sharp contrast to the survival needs of the domestic workers living in the favela—a contrast so absurd as to evoke laughter out of place.

Race, Gender, and Globalization in Malaysia The development of the idea of race in Malaysia, mixed with notions of ethnicity and religion, reveals how "race" is not a fixed category. A hierarchy of race was originally introduced while Malaysia was a colony of the Dutch, Portuguese, and British, and it continues to change in today's postcolonial era in response to the globalization of media, finance, labor, and diseases (including HIV/AIDS), which cross national boundaries.

When Portuguese and Dutch colonial powers led western Europe's expansion into Malaysia in the sixteenth and early seventeenth centuries, social relations in the country were primarily organized around land. Local and regional chiefs dominated economic and political life and provided protection in return for village loyalty. Geography, cultural practices, and economic strategies were the main differences among people, not assumptions about biology, phenotype, or the idea of race. The local land-oriented groups initially resisted colonial attempts to exploit Malaysia's (originally called Malaya) mineral resources. Beginning in 1786, however, overwhelming British military power and persistent colonial administration began a three-hundred-year process that dismantled Malaysian social patterns and replaced them with a European-style, race-based structure with three distinct categories: Indian, Chinese, and Malay.

Differing treatment of the three groups reinforced the race-based system. British colonial authorities recruited immigrant laborers from India to work

MAP 6.3
Malaysia

on coffee, sugar, and rubber plantations, and they brought in Chinese laborers to mine tin. They also trained some Indians for mid-level, colonial civil service jobs and encouraged Chinese immigrant entrepreneurs in the main port cities to establish the urban small-business core of the national economy. The British left the majority, largely rural, and uneducated Malay population working in the rice paddies, although a few local Malay elite were co-opted into the colonial administration.

Even though the country's economic activities have shifted over the centuries, particularly after Malaysian independence in 1957, the racial categories that the British established are still in use today. They are no longer legally enforced, but the patterns of economic and political interaction organized along racial lines continue. Deep dissatisfaction over the constructed racial identities, and particularly the vast economic inequities that operate along racial lines, have led to social unrest and political struggle, including massive rioting in 1969. Again in 2005, Malays, who constitute 60 percent of the population, took to the streets to protest what they considered to be an unequal distribution of wealth among the main social groups in the country, which also include Chinese (25 percent), Indians (8 percent), and the indigenous Orang Asli.

In an attempt to minimize racial disparities, Malaysia opened its doors in the 1970s to the forces of globalization by establishing one of the first export-processing zones in Southeast Asia. These low-tax, low-wage zones attracted multinational corporations in search of cheap labor to supply products for a global assembly line, especially in the electronics industry. Over the past thirty-five years, factories in Malaysia's export-processing zones have attracted hundreds of thousands of young migrant women workers, popularly known as Minah Karan (Ong 1987).

Minah, a common Malay woman's name, reflects the mass migration of rural workers to the factories. However, *Karan* carries two meanings. The first ("electric current") situates these women in the electronics factories. But the second meaning implies sexual electricity. These young women—predominantly rural, unmarried, and Malay—have driven the expansion of electronics-exporting factories, a key factor in the growth of the national, regional, and global economies. Their work has provided financial resources for their rural families back home during times of agricultural distress, and by giving these women access to wages it has transformed gender relationships at many levels.

Minah Karan have also reframed the racial order that British colonial administrators established centuries ago. Although export-processing zones were established as geographically bounded areas where manufacturing could take place, they have also served as places where many different people interact with a frequency and diversity not seen before in Malaysia. As a result, factories, and the export-processing zones in general, have become places of multiracial encounter in a nation with clear racial boundaries. As factories have drawn workers from across Malaysia and from neighboring countries, unusual and countercultural "mixing" has been taking place. In this context, mixing may simply mean enjoying social interactions or may also refer to sexual relations among individuals of different social groups. Malay, Chinese, Indian, and other immigrant women mix on the factory floor. Rural, young, and unmarried women workers interact with male, married, Chinese and Indian managers and engineers.

The name Minah Karan suggests the complicated interaction of ideas of race with ideas of gender, foreignness, sexuality, modernity, moral deterioration, and sexually transmitted diseases such as HIV/AIDS. Women factory workers, many of them teenagers, have broken the gender–racial boundaries of Malaysian culture by working in the multiracial, multigendered, foreign-owned factories. Though imagined as "electric" by some, this racial mixing appears to others as morally questionable. By working away from their villages, earning their own income as young women, laboring on night shifts, and generally operating outside the disciplinary oversight of family members and community elders, these women have gained a reputation as undisciplined, "loose," and

FIGURE 6.6 The racial framework established by British colonialists, while no longer legally enforced, still shapes Malaysian culture today. *Clockwise from left*: A Minah Karan assembling electronic components in a Malaysian export processing factory. Malaysian Chinese entrepreneurs open a coffee shop. A diverse group of students crossing the street in Penang, Malaysia.

"easy." Early on, observers considered their mixing with men and people of other classes, kinship networks, and social groups as risky, even dangerous, behavior that might lead to moral contamination, impurity, and disease.

Anthropologist Robin Root has conducted research on HIV/AIDS inside the electronics factories. In particular, she has examined the intersection of globalization, Malaysian ideas of race and sexuality, and the real and imagined risks of disease for the women factory workers. The Malaysian government has long promoted export processing as key to the country's economic development and as a route to improving centuries of economic disparity built around imported conceptions of race. Multiracial, multigendered factories have drawn young women workers into a space of mixed and transgressed boundaries. Although the risks for HIV/AIDS are elevated in the export-processing zones, Root also finds that many Malaysians assume these risks are elevated because of the racial and sexual mixing. This attitude exposes a moral imagination that is rooted in long-established cultural norms, values, and power structures as well as in the imported three-race racial hierarchy. Those who express this perspective have resisted change brought by globalization, including the possibility of change in racial and gender boundaries, by discouraging women from working in these factories and by stigmatizing those who do so (Root 2006).

How Is Race Constructed in the United States?

Race is perhaps the most significant means used to mark difference in U.S. culture. References to it can be found on census forms, school applications, and birth certificates, as well as in the media and casual conversation. Race is also a key framework that shapes the allocation of power, privilege, rewards, and status, and infuses all of our political, economic, religious, recreational, educational, and cultural institutions (Smedley 1993). Yet it is one of the least discussed topics in U.S. culture and one of most difficult to explore, even in anthropology. How do we begin to engage this difficult dialogue?

At the beginning of every semester I ask my students to start the process by naming the different races. This seems like an easy task at first. Then students begin to struggle with the categories that U.S. culture has handed them. We quickly see that ideas of race are complicated by geography, language, skin color, and even religion. "Who is Asian?" I ask. "Are Filipinos Asian? Or are they Pacific Islanders? Are the people who live in the eastern two-thirds of Russia Asians? After all, they do live on the continent of Asia. Are Pakistanis Asian?"

"They were before Pakistan was partitioned from India. Now they're Middle Easterners," says a student.

"Middle Eastern is not one of the racial categories usually on the list," I reply. "And by the way, can race shift along political lines?"

"Middle Easterners are white," says another student.

"But what countries are in the Middle East?" asks another. "Professor, my mom is from China and my dad is from Bolivia. What race am I?"

How can anthropology help make sense of race as you experience it in the classroom, your workplace, your family, and today's rapidly globalizing world? Because race is not biologically fixed, we must instead examine the process through which race has been—and still is being—constructed in the United States.

Race and the U.S. Census

The U.S. Census, taken every ten years since 1790, provides a fascinating window into the changing conception of "race." The 1850 census had three categories: White, Black, and Mulatto. Mulatto referred to people of mixed race. The 1870 census expanded to five categories to incorporate new immigrants from China and to count the Native American population: White, Black, Mulatto, Chinese, and Indian (Native American). Respondents did not identify their own race; instead, census workers assigned them to a racial category based on their appearance.

By 1940, the census form had eight categories, eliminating the option for mixed race and adding more categories from Asia, including Hindu, a religion: White, Negro, Indian, Chinese, Japanese, Filipino, Hindu, and Korean (Figure 6.8a). The 2010 census form included fourteen separate "race" boxes (Figure 6.8b). Respondents could check one, many, or all of them.

This brief look at changes in the census form provides clear indications that race has been and still is an evolving human construction. The changing race categories do not reflect a change in human genotype or phenotype, but in how the government organizes the diversity of people within its borders. The census construction of race reflects the U.S. government's power to establish certain categories and apply those categories to make decisions about government resources.

Borderlands where racial categories are under debate provide a glimpse of the nation's changing racial past and future. For instance, increased immigration

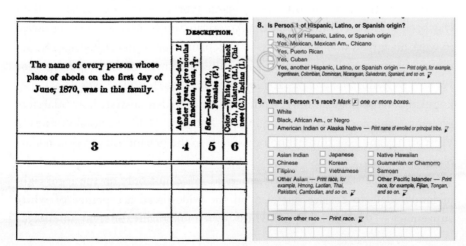

FIGURE **6.7** What can changes in the U.S. census form tell us about shifting concepts of race? Here, comparable parts of the United States Census Questionnaire, 1870, and the United States Census Questionnaire, 2010.

from Latin America, Asia, the Pacific Islands, and the Middle East has complicated the census form and discussions about race in the United States. Note the rapid expansion of options in the census for people from Asia.

The position of Hispanics is also in flux. Beginning with the 2000 census, for instance, "Hispanic" was removed from the race question. In effect, Spanish/Hispanic/Latino became a unique ethnic group with its own separate question. Unlike others—for example, Irish, Welsh, Italians, or Greeks—the census form now suggests that Hispanics are the only U.S. ethnic group that could be of any race. It remains to be determined whether U.S. culture will move beyond the underlying black/white dichotomy, or whether the current flux is simply a reorganizing of new immigrants into that dichotomy (Rodriguez 2000).

History of U.S. Racial Categories: Constructing Whiteness

The U.S. racial system developed in the vortex of slavery and the European conquest of indigenous people of the North American continent. From its origins, American colonial life was built on the importation of indentured workers from Europe and slaves from Africa, along with the expropriation of land from Native Americans. Intensive agricultural work, particularly in the U.S. South, required a reliable and plentiful labor supply. Native Americans suffered quick and brutal extermination in other parts of the Americas through forced labor, violence, and disease, but they largely resisted forced labor in the North American colonies. European indentured laborers were in short supply. So imported African slaves became the preferred workforce. Over three hundred years, millions were forcibly transported to the Americas through the trans-Atlantic slave trade.

The economics of slavery benefited all the American colonies. In Dutch New Amsterdam (now New York City), people of African descent made up 25 percent of the population as early as 1640. New York served as a hub for the slave trade. Slave ships delivered Africans for resale across the colonies as well as to plantations in Latin America and the Caribbean. Cargo ships brought the products of slave labor—cotton, sugarcane, tobacco—to New York on their way back to Europe. Throughout the American South, Africans were enslaved to work on agricultural plantations. In fact, plantation owners often sought out those Africans who had specialized agricultural knowledge. In *Deep Roots: Rice Farmers in West Africa and the African Diaspora* (2008), Edda Fields-Black uses linguistic, archaeological, and historical evidence to demonstrate how tidal rice-growing technology developed among the Baga and Nalu of coastal Guinea in West Africa and how this technology spread to the rice industry in South Carolina and Georgia (see also Carney 2002.)

The unique slave system that emerged relied not only on the legal right of landholders to enslave but also on the widespread acceptance of **white supremacy**—the belief that nonwhites were biologically different, intellectu-

white supremacy: The belief that whites are biologically different and superior to people of other races.

ally inferior, and not fully human in a spiritual sense. Reflecting these ideas, the U.S. Census from 1790 to 1860 counted slaves as only three-fifths of a person. Only in 1868 did the Fourteenth Amendment to the U.S. Constitution put an end to this practice. Subsequently, the 1870 census was the first to count all people as whole people.

The term *white* was itself a construction, first appearing in a public document in reference to a separate race only in 1691 in Virginia. Colonial laws created and rigidly regulated **whiteness,** establishing sharp boundaries of who was white and who was not. Intermarriage was outlawed—a practice that the U.S. Supreme Court did not overturn until 1967. Mixing was punished by the loss of white status.

Anthropologist Pem Buck's *Worked to the Bone* (2001) documents the ways in which white privilege was invented in early 1700s Virginia to prevent rebellion among poor landless whites who were beginning to join with enslaved African workers against the European economic elite. Elites introduced a set of privileges reserved for whites—the right to own a gun, livestock, and land; the right to freedom at the end of indenture; the right to discipline blacks; and eventually the right to vote. These legal privileges were designed to ensure the cooperation of poor working whites and white indentured servants, who together constituted a majority of the early colonial populations, and to drive a wedge between the European and African laborers who had much in common.

Efforts to eliminate slavery spread rapidly but unevenly after the American Revolution (1775–83), culminating in the Civil War (1861–65) and President

FIGURE 6.8 *Left,* an advertisement for a slave auction, June 23, 1768. *Right,* a slave family picking cotton in the fields near Savannah, Georgia, ca. 1860s.

whiteness: A culturally constructed concept originating in 1691 Virginia designed to establish clear boundaries of who is white and who is not, a process central to the formation of U.S. racial stratification.

Abraham Lincoln's 1863 Emancipation Proclamation. Yet, long-established patterns of unequal treatment and entrenched ideas of white racial superiority persisted, providing the foundation for continuing inequality, discrimination, and white dominance. **Jim Crow** segregation laws throughout the South legally enforced the boundaries between whites and blacks in housing, education, voting rights, property ownership, and access to public services such as transportation, bathrooms, and water fountains. Vigilante white-supremacist groups such as the Ku Klux Klan, founded in 1866, emerged to enforce through violence and terror what they considered to be the natural racial order. Especially in the South, lynchings became a widespread means to intimidate blacks, enforce segregation, and ensure behavior that whites considered normal and appropriate. Between 1870 and the 1940s, thousands of African American men and women were tortured and brutally murdered (Brundage 1993).

The Rule of Hypodescent

Imposition of the rule of hypodescent has been key to drawing and maintaining boundaries between the races since the days of slavery, when one single drop of "black blood"—that is, one African ancestor—constituted blackness. *Hypo* literally means "lower." Through **hypodescent** the race of children of mixed marriages is assigned to the lower or subordinate category of the two parents—or, in many cases, the subordinate category of any one of many ancestors.

Hypodescent rules were enshrined in the laws of many U.S. states and backed by the U.S. Supreme Court. Consider the 1982 court case of Susie Phipps. Born looking "white," Phipps grew up assuming she was white. But when she requested a copy of her birth certificate in 1977, she found herself listed as "colored." A 1970 Louisiana law mandated that a person be designated black if his or her ancestry was one-thirty-second black—referring to any one of the thirty-two most recent ancestors. (This was an improvement over previous state hypodescent law, which set the threshold at one in sixty-four.) Phipps lost a court challenge to this categorization because the state produced evidence that she was three-thirty-seconds black—more than enough to satisfy the 1970 legal standard. Both the Louisiana Supreme Court and the U.S. Supreme Court refused to review the lower court's ruling and allowed the decision to stand (Jaynes 1982; Fluehr-Lobban 2006). Phipps's case reveals the process through which U.S. categories of race have been created and the tortured logic employed to assign individuals to particular racial categories. Also on full display are (1) the central role of the state in establishing and maintaining boundaries between the races it has constructed, and (2) the powerful influence of the legacies of slavery and past discrimination on the present (Omi and Winant 1994).

Although hypodescent is no longer enforced in law, it is still widely practiced in U.S. culture. A prominent contemporary example would be U.S. president

Jim Crow: Laws implemented after the U.S. Civil War to legally enforce segregation, particularly in the South, after the end of slavery.

hypodescent: Sometimes called the "one drop of blood rule"; the assignment of children of racially "mixed" unions to the subordinate group.

Barack Obama. His mother was a white woman from Kansas (she was also an anthropologist). His father was from Kenya in East Africa. They met as students in Hawaii, where Obama was born. Though 50 percent of his genes came from his father and 50 percent from his mother, the concept of hypodescent still shapes the way some people regard Obama's race.

Race and Immigration

For more than four centuries, the boundaries of whiteness in the United States have been carefully guarded, and a group's admission to that category has been rare and difficult. When the nation encountered diverse immigration from Asia and eastern and southern Europe beginning in the nineteenth century, debate raged about where the newcomers fit: Were the Chinese white? Were the Irish, Germans, Greeks, Italians, eastern Europeans, Jews, and Catholics really white, or were they biologically distinct from earlier immigrants from England, France, and the Nordic countries?

 The struggle to guard the boundaries of whiteness has been particularly intense at certain times, generating intense debate and sparking a sentiment of **nativism**—that is, the desire to favor native inhabitants over new immigrants. Nativists in the nineteenth century fought particularly hard to preserve the so-called racial purity of the nation's Anglo-Saxon origins. Riots, violence, discrimination, and anti-immigrant sentiment were commonplace. In the 1800s

nativism: Favoring certain long-term inhabitants over new immigrants.

a pseudoscience arose, called **eugenics**, that attempted to use scientific methodologies to prove the existence of separate races and, in particular, the superiority of the white "race" and the inferiority of all nonwhites.

Chinese and Irish Immigrants: What Race? Chinese immigrants first arrived in large numbers in the 1850s to work in California's gold mines, on its farms, and in railroad construction. Because they constituted the first group of Asians to come to this country, other residents struggled to place them in the U.S. racial hierarchy. European immigrant laborers saw the Chinese as competitors for jobs and branded them the Yellow Peril—a "race" that could not be trusted. Federal and state governments treated the Chinese immigrants ambivalently at best and often with great hostility.

Consider the 1854 California court case *People v. Hall*. In a lower court case leading up to this one, a Chinese man had provided eyewitness testimony to a murder committed by a white man, George W. Hall. Hall was convicted on the basis of this testimony. However, upon appeal, the California Supreme Court overturned Hall's conviction, claiming that the eyewitness had no standing in the court. The justices pronounced that the Chinese were "a race of people whom nature has marked as inferior, and who are incapable of progress or intellectual development beyond a certain point, as their history has shown; differing in language, opinions, color, and physical conformation, between whom and ourselves nature has placed an impassable difference" (Gross 2010). Thus, the Chinese were not white in the eyes of the law. Like African Americans of the time, they had no legal standing in the courts. Their eyewitness testimony was inadmissible.

Today most people consider Irish, Italians, Greeks, and eastern Europeans to be white, but none of these groups were received as white when they first came to the United States. They initially faced discrimination, prejudice, and exclusion because they were not Anglo-Saxon Protestants. When the Irish immigrants arrived in the 1840s and 1850s, they were poor, rural, Catholic, landless, and fleeing intense poverty and disease as a result of the Irish potato famine. Thus, they were seen as an inferior race (Ignatiev 1995). Similarly, the twenty-three million eastern and southern European immigrants who arrived in the United States between 1880 and 1920 (mostly Italians and eastern European Jews) were generally considered to be members of separate, inferior races—not white. Scientists, politicians, preachers, and the press warned against destroying the unity and purity of the United States by allowing their immigration. Together, eugenicists and nativists promoted the anti-immigrant National Origin Act of 1924: this legislation closed the doors to the large waves of immigrant workers who had been arriving in the United States in the nineteenth and early twentieth centuries. Over the next four decades, the legislation barred all but a few who were not of northern

FIGURE 6.10 Where did new Chinese immigrants fit in the U.S. racial hierarchy? Miners, including four Chinese, in California, ca. 1852.

or western European origins (Binder and Reimers 1995; Foner 2000). The act remained in effect until 1965.

Confronted with increasing immigration and diversity, the U.S. legal and political systems struggled for consistent definitions of who was white and who was not. Consider the 1923 U.S. Supreme Court case in which Bhagat Singh Thind, an upper-class Sikh immigrant from India, applied for U.S. citizenship. Despite the 1790 U.S. law limiting the right to naturalization (that is, becoming a citizen) to whites, Thind argued that as a part of the original "Aryan" or Caucasian race, he was white. Even though the justices agreed with his claim of Aryan or Caucasian ancestry, the Court found that Thind was not white as used in "common speech, to be interpreted in accordance with the understanding of the common man" (Lopez 2006, 66). Popular anti-immigrant and nativist sentiment had overcome even the pseudoscience of race prevalent at the time.

How exactly did the Irish, the Italians, and the eastern European Jews become "white"? Their increasing numbers, their intermarriage with members of other white groups, and their upward class mobility created conditions for inclusion in the white category. Karen Brodkin's book *How the Jews Became White Folks* (1998) offers additional insights into the whitening process of immigrants after World War II. At that time, the U.S. economy was emerging virtually unscathed from the war's destruction, unlike its competitors in Europe and Japan. And rapid growth in the U.S. economy was supporting an unparalleled expansion of the nation's middle class. Brodkin suggests that an extensive government program to reintegrate soldiers after the war paved the road to upward mobility for many U.S. citizens.

Indeed, the GI Bill of Rights provided a wide array of programs to sixteen million soldiers, who were primarily white and male. The benefits included

FIGURE 6.11 A 1903 cartoon from the magazine *Judge* illustrates anti-immigrant sentiment at the turn of the twentieth century. A tide of newcomers—Riff Raff Immigration—representing the criminal element of other countries washes up on American shores, to the displeasure of Uncle Sam, presenting a "danger" to American ideas and institutions.

preferential hiring, financial support during the job search, small business loans, subsidized home mortgages, and educational benefits that included college tuition and living expenses. Newly trained and educated veterans quickly filled the needs of the growing U.S. economy for professionals, technicians, and managers—jobs that offered opportunities for upward mobility and, thus, racial mobility. These educational opportunities, the dramatic rise in home ownership, and the expansion of new corporate jobs dramatically enlarged the U.S. middle class. The simultaneous elevation of living standards and financial assets of both native whites and new European immigrants softened earlier boundaries of whiteness and allowed the status of many immigrants to shift from racially nonwhite to ethnic white.

Middle Easterners Racial categories continue to be created and contested in the United States today. Where, for example, do people from the Middle East fit? Are Saudis, Iranians, Afghanis, Kurds, Syrians, Turks, and Egyptians "white," African American, or Asian? The shifting characterization of people from the Middle East—especially after the terrorist attacks of September 11, 2001—reveals another border region in the race debate and demonstrates how conceptions of race in the United States are constantly changing.

In a study of fourth graders in Brooklyn, New York, after the September 11 attacks, Maria Kromidas (2004) explores the way nine-year-old children engage issues of race, religion, and region to create racial categories, assign certain people (both children and adults) to them, and enforce those boundaries through language, humor, and social interaction.

Using the common U.S. Census categories, the school could be described as 28 percent black, 1 percent white, 46 percent Hispanic, and 25 percent Asian.

But these four categories do not reveal the diversity of the school and its neighborhood—a diversity that makes the students' formulations of race all the more complicated. Although the students and the surrounding community are predominantly African American and second- and third-generation Latino, a significant part of the population is composed of new immigrants from Nigeria, Bangladesh, Guyana, Jamaica, and the Dominican Republic.

In light of the events of September 11, students in the elementary school seem preoccupied with the potential danger from a perceived enemy—one they see racially as "brown, foreign, strange, and Muslim" (Kromidas 2004, 29). Though the children do not consider their Muslim classmates to be "evil" or "terrorists," they do take note of these classmates' identities as never before. Kromidas ("MK" in the dialogues below) notes in particular the equation of enemies with Indians, Pakistanis, or Afghanis, and eventually all Arabic ("Araback") people. Here we see a racial construction, a lumping together of unrelated people based on general phenotype—in this case, skin color.

Consider the following small-group student discussion:

EXAMPLE 1

SHERI: We were talking about who started it first, and if they kill a lot of white people. . . . I mean a lot of people we got to go to war right then.

MK: Who are they?

SHERI: The Indians.

MK: The Indians?

SHERI: I don't know—that's what I call them.

JONATHAN: The Pakistans!

MK: The Pakistans?

SODIQ: The Afghanistans!

MK: The Afghanistans?

JOSEPH: The terrorists.

Later that afternoon:

EXAMPLE 2

SHERI: I feel sorry for the Afghanistan people.

SUSANNA: Why do you feel sorry after what they did?

SHERI: Because they gonna die!
(*Most of the class breaks up with laughter.*)

LATISHA: (*standing up*) I feel happy!
(*laughter*)

LATISHA: No, no, no . . . because they want to kill our people, they're going to die too. They want to have a party when we die, so we should celebrate! [*referring to news clips of street celebrations in the Middle East after September 11*]

ANUPA: If they die, it will be better for us.

MK: Who are they?

ANUPA: The Araback people.

MARISELA: The Afghanistans have always hated the Americans. I know because I always watch the news.

EXAMPLE 3

LATISHA: The Indians, I call them Indians . . .

MK: Who?

LATISHA: The people that was in the airplane. They said that God told them to do this. (*throwing up her hands and moving her head in mock frustration*) Why would he tell them . . . ?

TEACHER: (*Interrupting*) You see, they had certain beliefs, but . . .
              (Kromidas 2004 18–19)

These conversations yield some interesting observations. First, the students have taken on images presented in the media and from the conversations of adults around them; second, the students manipulate those images to create patterns of exclusion in their own context. Through their conversations, language groups, social interactions, and friendship networks, the students seek to clarify boundaries and to include and exclude newcomers according to what they see as racial characteristics. In the racial maps of the United States, South-Asian Americans and Arab Americans do not have a clear place. Kromidas suggests that in the classroom, as in U.S. culture at large, the fourth graders of New York City are creating a new racial category and placing people in it. The category is generally defined as not white, not black, but brown; foreign, strange, Muslim, and possibly enemy.

Before September 11, "Middle Eastern" was not considered a separate race in the United States. Officially, the government's Office of Management and Budget includes people of Middle Eastern descent as whites, along with people of European and North African descent. But the **racialization** (that is, giving a racial character) of Middle Easterners in U.S. culture after September 11 suggests a movement away from whiteness as reflected in Kromidas's study of fourth graders in Brooklyn.

racialization: To categorize, differentiate, and attribute a particular racial character to a person or group of people.

What Is Racism?

Racism is a complex system of power that draws on the culturally constructed categories of race to rank people as superior or inferior, and to differentially allocate access to power, privilege, resources, and opportunities.

Types of Racism

Racism has multiple aspects that include individual and institutional components as well as the set of ideas—the ideology—that acts like glue to hold them together.

Individual Racism **Individual racism** is expressed through prejudiced beliefs and discriminatory actions. Being prejudiced involves making negative assumptions about a person's abilities or intentions based on the person's perceived race. Discriminating involves taking negative actions toward a person on the basis of his or her perceived race. Individual racism may be expressed through a lack of respect or through suspicion, scapegoating, and violence ranging from police brutality to hate crimes (Jones 2000). Individual, personally mediated acts of racism may be intentional or unintentional. They may be acts of commission (things that are done) or acts of omission (things that are left undone).

individual racism: Personal prejudiced beliefs and discriminatory actions based on race.

Institutional Racism Racism is more than individual prejudiced beliefs or discriminatory acts. Racism also includes **institutional racism**, sometimes called *structural racism*—patterns by which racial inequality is structured through key cultural institutions, policies, and systems. These include education, health, housing, employment, the legal system (legislatures, courts, and prison systems), law enforcement, and the media. Institutional racism originates in historical events and legal sanctions. But, even when outlawed, it can persist through contemporary patterns of institutional behavior that perpetuate the historical injustices (Jones 2000; Cazenave 2011; Feagin and Feagin 2011; Neubeck and Cazenave 2001).

institutional racism: Patterns by which racial inequality is structured through key cultural institutions, policies, and systems.

In the United States, stratification along racial lines is a legacy of discrete historical events that include slavery, Jim Crow legal segregation, expropriation of indigenous lands and immigration restrictions. Through these legal forms of institutional racism, the political, economic, and educational systems were organized to privilege whiteness. Today, despite the elimination of legal racial discrimination and segregation, patterns of inequality still break along color lines as a result of continuing individual and institutional racism. Such racism is evident in employment rates, income and wealth differentials, home ownership, residential patterns, criminal sentencing patterns, incarceration rates, application of the death penalty, infant mortality, access to health care, life expectancy, investments in public education, college enrollments, and access to the vote.

For example, the U.S. educational system has been a site for intense contestation over race and racism. In 1896—three decades after the end of slavery—the Supreme Court ruled in *Plessy v. Ferguson* that state-sponsored segregation, including in public schools, was constitutional as long as the separate facilities for separate races were equal. Across the South, individual white school administrators often refused, on overtly racist grounds, to allow children of color—black, Hispanic, Asian American—entrance to school buildings. But these individual actions alone did not constitute the total system of racism at work. They were systematically supported and enforced by government institutions: local boards of education, legislators, local police with guns and dogs, and court systems—including the U.S. Supreme Court.

Only in 1954 did the Supreme Court reverse itself in the case of *Brown v. Board of Education*, declaring unanimously that state laws establishing separate public schools for black and white students were unconstitutional and that separate educational facilities were inherently unequal. At the time, seventeen states, primarily across the South, required racial segregation. Sixteen prohibited it.

Contemporary racial disparities in school funding reveal how historical patterns of institutional racism can continue long after discrimination has been declared illegal (Miller and Epstein 2011). In 2003, the New York Court of Appeals, the state's highest court, found a long-standing disparity in state funding of public schools in New York City and suburban areas. New York City public schools, with high proportions of students of color, received an average of $10,469 per student, whereas schools in more affluent, predominantly white New York suburbs received $13,760 per student. The courts ordered New York State to increase its annual education budget by up to $5.6 billion to cover the costs of redressing this inequality while also providing $9.2 billion for capital improvement of New York City school buildings. The State of New York has yet to comply with these requirements.

Racial Ideology Racism relies on a third component—a set of popular ideas about race, or a **racial ideology**—that allows the discriminatory behaviors of individuals and institutions to seem reasonable, rational, and normal. Ideas about the superiority of one race over another—shaped and reinforced in the school system, religious institutions, government, and the media—caused people in the United States to believe that slavery was natural, that the European settlers had a God-given right to "civilize" and "tame" the American West, and that segregated schools were a reasonable approach to providing public education. As these ideas became ingrained in day-to-day relationships and institutional patterns of behavior, they ultimately provided the ideological glue that held racial stratification in place.

Today social scientists note that contemporary racial ideologies are much more subtle, often drawing on core U.S. values of individualism, social mobility, meritocracy, and color-blindness to make their case. So, for instance, in his book *Racism without Racists* (2010), sociologist Eduardo Bonilla-Silva critiques the contemporary calls in U.S. culture for color blindness—the elimination of race as a consideration in a wide range of institutional processes from college

racial ideology: A set of popular ideas about race that allows the discriminatory behaviors of individuals and institutions to seem reasonable, rational, and normal.

FIGURE 6.12 A racially segregated classroom in Monroe Elementary School, Topeka, Kansas, March 1953. Students Linda Brown (*front right*) and her sister Terry Lynn (*far left, second back*), along with their parents, initiated the landmark civil rights lawsuit *Brown v. Board of Education*.

admissions to the reporting of arrests by police. The ideology of color blindness suggests that the best way to end discrimination in the post–civil rights era is to treat individuals as equally as possible without regard to race. Bonilla-Silva warns that while the desire to transcend race by adopting a stance of color blindness appears reasonable and fair, the approach ignores the uneven playing field created by centuries of legal racism in areas such as wealth, property ownership, education, health, and employment. A color-blind ideology, Bonilla-Silva suggests, may actually perpetuate racial inequality by obscuring the historical effects of racism, the continuing legacy of racial discrimination, and the entrenched patterns of institutional behavior that undergird racism today.

In a country like the United States, which prides itself on being a meritocracy (a system that views people as a product of their own efforts and in which equal opportunity is available to all), the continuing existence of racism and skin-color privilege in the twenty-first century is difficult for many people to acknowledge. When the dominant culture celebrates the ideals of individualism and equal access to social mobility, it is ironic that for many people, success depends not only on hard work, intelligence, and creativity but also on the often unrecognized and unearned assets—cultural, political, and economic—that have accrued over hundreds of years of discrimination and unequal opportunity based on race.

Resisting Racism

Along with the history of individual and institutional racism, it is important to also acknowledge the long tradition of work against racism that continues today. Anthropologist Steven Gregory's ethnography *Black Corona*

MAP 6.4
Queens, New York

(1998) tells the story of the organized political resistance by a predominantly African American community in Corona, Queens, in New York City, when confronted by attitudes and policy expressions of racial discrimination. The African American community in Corona dates back to the 1820s, and it expanded under an influx of middle-class residents from Harlem in the first half of the twentieth century. By the 1970s, however, Corona, like many other urban U.S. communities, began to feel the devastating impact of globalization, particularly flexible accumulation, as New York City's economy deindustrialized. At this time, the city's economy moved from an industrial and manufacturing base to one driven by finance, information, and services (Baker 1995; Harvey 1990). As New York lost thousands of manufacturing jobs and billions of dollars in tax revenue and federal funds, residents of Corona struggled during the transition.

In the face of drastic government cutbacks to basic community services such as housing, education, and public safety, residents of Corona's LeFrak City—a public housing complex containing six thousand rental apartments—mobilized to demand sustained public investment in the maintenance and security of the property from their landlord, the City of New York. Confronting stereotypes of the apartment complex as a site of crime, welfare dependency, and family disorganization, African American parents in LeFrak City founded Concerned Community Adults (CCA), a community-based civic association, to engage in neighborhood improvement projects and strengthen relationships with the city's politicians and agencies. The CCA's Youth Forum organized neighborhood young people for social activities and leadership formation; together with the CCA, it worked to improve relations with the local police, who regularly harassed youth in the area. Through community-based action, LeFrak City residents worked with churches, community groups, and informal associations to establish their position as political actors, assert control over the neighborhood's physical condition, and insist on self-definition rather than accept the stereotypes held by surrounding communities and City leaders.

In the early 1990s, the Port Authority of New York and New Jersey—which controls the area's airports, bridges, and port facilities—announced plans to build an elevated light rail train between Manhattan's central business district and LaGuardia Airport that would cut directly through the heart of Corona's African American community. Residents had had extensive negative experiences battling the city over earlier plans to expand LaGuardia, which abuts Corona, that involved the loss of waterfront properties to the construction of runways, highway access, and exposure to the pollution of adjacent Flushing Bay. In its new plan, the Port Authority, representing the City of New York, argued that the city needed improved public transportation between Manhattan and LaGuardia to compete in the global economy and in the burgeoning

FIGURE 6.13 The history of race in the United States includes a strong tradition of resistance to individual and institutional racism. Here, demonstrators protest against unfair lending practices and mortgage foreclosures.

Raymond Codrington

Anthropologist Raymond Codrington has used the tools of anthropology to engage issues of race and inequality in a number of professional settings, including teaching, museum work, private consulting, and now in the world of public policy.

Today Codrington works as a senior research associate for the Roundtable on Community Change, which is a policy program of the Aspen Institute, an educational and policy studies organization based in Washington, D.C. The Aspen Institute was founded in the early 1950s in Aspen, Colorado, as a nonpartisan forum to convene prominent leaders from different U.S. sectors — arts, business, and academia — to address the pressing questions of the day. Aspen has since modified its seminar model to include a broader cross section of U.S. leaders working in areas of public policy, leadership, and social concern.

Codrington applies his skills as an anthropologist in Aspen's Program on Racial Equity. "Today we're working to help policy makers address race in their work. They're dealing with issues around poverty: how to alleviate poverty, how to address poverty. But they don't necessarily have a racial equity lens — a well-developed perspective on how race creates and maintains disparate outcomes for disadvantaged groups. So we convene people across sectors to think about the implications of race and racial equity for their work. Race is a difficult issue for a lot of people to talk about. The election of President Obama created a different challenge in our work because some people think, 'Why are we still having this conversation? Didn't people who are interested in racial equity get what they wanted? Let's move on.' But obviously, it's not that simple. Racism is still a very powerful factor in our culture and society."

Through the Program on Racial Equity, Codrington has helped develop a five-day leadership training curriculum that focuses on assisting senior leaders to develop a racial equity perspective — to think about how rac-

ism, particularly *structural racism*, impacts their work. "When we say 'structural racism,' we're talking about the intersections of public policies, institutional practices, and media representations. How do those things come together to create and maintain racial disparities in a broader context? So we need to look at the wider historical trajectory of racism to understand what has created structural racism today — how the law has codified racial disparities and how those disparities have become part of

Anthropologist Raymond Codrington

particular policy areas: criminal justice, education, unemployment, and wealth creation.

"For instance, *Plessy v. Ferguson* and *Brown v. Board of Education* are key cases in the U.S. legal system in the history of race that defined the way we think about access to public resources, access to public education. Once people have that history, they can begin to understand the root causes of these disparities. From there we can begin to give people a vocabulary, a road map, to let them know how to navigate the contemporary discussion about race."

Codrington notes that these training sessions often produce a significant cognitive shift—a different way of thinking about race and racism. "People come out of the seminar and say, 'OK, I think differently about race. I have different tools. I can talk about it in a different way. And that's going to help me in my work.' That kind of cognitive shift is an early-stage indicator, an early outcome. Then we're ready to work on mid-range, interim outcomes, such as making institutional changes in organizational leadership, communication, and programs. After all, that's what many people really want to know: What can I do with this knowledge?" Central to achieving these goals is the program's unique racial equity theory of change exercise. "It's basically a backward mapping exercise. People start out with a racial equity goal, perhaps to decrease incarceration rates of black youth by 20 percent by the year 2020. Then you think about what needs to be in place for you to address this goal. The idea is to get people to begin to develop a power map and power analysis of their community, institutional, and political context: What capac-

ities does their organization have? Are the right people involved? Where are their political allies and alliances? People come away with a much clearer sense of how to make concrete changes in the area of structural racism.

"The hardest part is the long-term policy changes—to see people introduce bills for policy change at the level of state legislature or more local levels. Those are the kinds of changes that our work is becoming more focused on now: longer-term, policy, and legislative changes.

"It's hard for people to really wrap their hands around race in a lot of ways. In these seminars I use every skill that I've mastered as an anthropologist to pull this off—everything from the initial contact with people we're going to work with, to the initial interview process, developing interview protocols, and developing rapport so people speak candidly about very difficult topics. You have a very short amount of time to gain people's trust and to get them to open up to you. To be able to read the room is essential. Being able to draw out some of the organizational and interpersonal dynamics is very helpful. So is being able to communicate what you see to colleagues who aren't anthropologists. As anthropologists we have a very different approach to getting a handle on what dynamics are in play in a particular group or a particular organization. The way anthropology brings together interviews, participant observation, lots of secondary research, and interaction definitely informs our work. Our ethnographic skills are always in play, which adds a much-needed level of analysis that ultimately helps our work become effective. We need all the tools we can get to work on racism and racial inequality."

global financial services industry. The elevated rail line through Corona, the argument went, would be good for the city's economy.

Corona residents warned that construction of this major infrastructure project through their community would not have any local benefit but instead would generate severe environmental consequences, lower the quality of life in the neighborhood, and divide and isolate portions of the community. They demanded that the rail line be built underground on property already owned by New York City between Corona and the airport that had been carved out to build the Grand Central Parkway years earlier. Local residents formed neighborhood committees and alliances with existing civic organizations, community groups, and churches. They engaged the city's public planning process and established alternative political forums outside the government's control to press for their case. They also created multicultural alliances with concerned groups in neighboring communities. Eventually the Port Authority abandoned the planned elevated train.

Gregory's ethnographic study of Corona's African American community reveals the power of local communities of color to mobilize and engage in political activism. It also demonstrates how such groups can contest the stereotypes of urban black communities and the practices of racial discrimination and exclusion, whether those involve housing, policing, or the environmental and community impacts of public infrastructure projects.

For a look at efforts to combat racism in a different context, see "Anthropologists Engage the World," on pages 228–29.

Race, Racism, and Whiteness

Popular conversations about race and racism tend to focus on the experiences of people of color. Whiteness is typically ignored, perhaps taken for granted. But analyzing race in the United States requires a careful look at whiteness. Anthropologists refer to "white" as an unmarked category—one with tremendous power, but one that typically defies analysis and is rarely discussed. Recent scholarship has been moving whiteness into the mainstream debates about race in the United States (Hargrove 2009; Harrison 1998, 2002a; Hartigan 1999; Marable 2002; Mullings 2005; Roediger 1992).

Although the events of the U.S. civil rights movement occurred well before most of today's college students were born, the media images of police blocking African Americans from attending white schools, riding in the front of the bus, sitting at department store lunch counters, or drinking from "whites-only" water fountains remain etched in our collective cultural memory. Although the overt signs declaring access for "whites only" have been outlawed and removed, many patterns of interpersonal and institutional behavior have resisted change (McIntosh 1989).

Initiating a Classroom Conversation about Race

Race and racism can be incredibly difficult topics of conversation in U.S. culture. How can the toolkit of anthropology help build relationships of rapport and trust that lead to deeper mutual understanding and opportunities for collective action?

Addressing issues of race and racism requires first opening up an honest conversation. In the classroom or in another setting on campus — perhaps your dorm, student organization, or religious group — write down your personal reflections and recollections about race and racism as provoked by the questions below. Then form discussion groups of four to five people. Make sure the groups are racially inclusive, if possible. Read and discuss what you have written, giving everyone a chance to participate, before exploring your conversation further.

1. What is your first recollection of race? of racism?
2. How would you describe the cultural environment in which you were raised: racially homogeneous? multiracial-multicultural? something else? What was the mix between home / community and school?
3. What patterns of race relations do you recall from high school? How much healthy social interaction was there across racial lines? What about interracial dating?
4. What patterns of race relations do you find on your college campus? Have you encountered race and racism on campus?
5. Complete this sentence: *The most important thing that our country needs to do NOW about race is* _____.
6. What obstacles do you encounter in discussing and addressing race and racism?

Now consider ways that the concepts of race and racism introduced in this chapter might help you understand the stories and experiences that emerge in these conversations.

Adapted from Fluehr-Lobban 2006.

"White Privilege" In her article "White Privilege: Unpacking the Invisible Knapsack" (1989), anthropologist Peggy McIntosh writes of "an invisible package of unearned assets" that are a legacy of generations of racial discrimination. Through these assets, whites have become the beneficiaries of cultural norms, values, mental maps of reality, and institutions. Unearned advantages and unearned power are conferred systematically and differentially on one group over others, whether those benefits lie in health, education, housing, employment, banking and mortgages, or the criminal justice system.

McIntosh articulates an extensive list of these privileges, ranging from the mundane to the profound. They include: (1) going shopping without being followed or harassed by store security; (2) using checks, credit cards, or cash and counting on skin color to not work against the appearance of financial responsibility; (3) seeing people of your "race" widely represented in the news, social media, and educational curricula; (4) swearing, dressing in second-hand clothes, or not answering letters or e-mails without having people attribute these choices to bad morals, poverty, or the illiteracy of your "race"; (5) feeling confident that you have not been singled out by race when a police officer pulls you over or an airport security guard decides to conduct a full-body scan; (6) criticizing the government and its policies without being considered an outsider.

As we have discussed in this chapter, since the early European settlement of North America, the boundaries of whiteness have been carefully constructed and guarded. Today the skin-color privileges associated with whiteness still pass down from generation to generation. They are simply harder to see. Acknowledging this fact enables us to analyze the functioning and effects of race and racism as a complete system.

As McIntosh writes, "For me white privilege has turned out to be an elusive and fugitive subject. The pressure to avoid it is great, for in facing it I must give up the myth of meritocracy. If these things are true, this is not such a free country, one's life is not what one makes it; many doors open for certain people through no virtues of their own" (1989, 12). Moving forward, McIntosh urges students to distinguish between (1) the positive advantages that we wish everyone could have and that we can all work to spread, and (2) the negative types of advantages that, unless challenged and corrected, will always reinforce current racial hierarchies.

Intersections of Race and Class It is important to note the powerful intersection of race and class. In *Living with Racism: The Black Middle-Class Experience* (1994), sociologist Joe Feagin and psychologist Melvin Sikes write about middle-class African Americans who, despite their class status, continue to face racial discrimination. In Chapter 11 on class and inequality, anthropologist Leith Mullings reflects on a similar dynamic in New York City's Harlem community. Though reflecting a privileged class status in comparison to other African Americans, the class advantages of middle-class African Americans still are limited by racial disadvantage. Because race and class intersect so deeply, improved class status cannot be assumed to bring a decrease in the experience of racial discrimination.

Whiteness is also stratified along deep, intersecting lines of class and region, gender and sexuality so that not all people of European descent benefit equally from the system of white privilege. In a study of a town she calls Shellcracker Haven, southwest of Gainesville, Florida, anthropologist Jane Gibson (1996) explored the process through which a community of poor whites has been systematically cut off from their local means of making a living. By imposing restrictions on fishing, gaming, and trapping as well as on agricultural activities—all of which benefit large-scale businesses—the Florida state government and its agencies have gradually prevented Shellcracker Haven's residents from making a living on the land or nearby water.

MAP 6.5
Florida

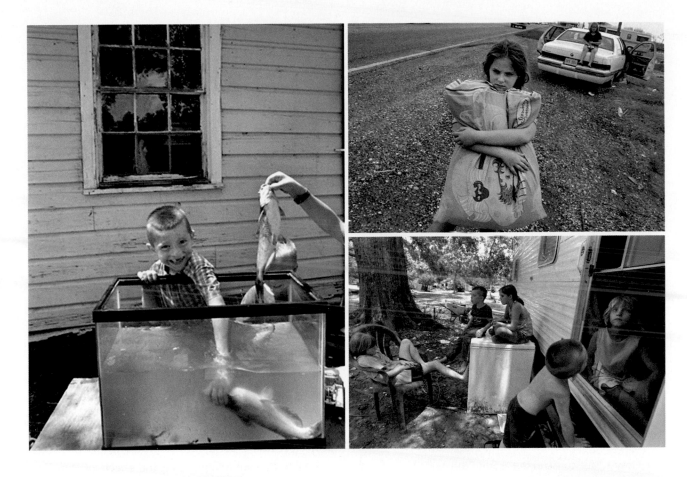

Gibson argues that these policies of disenfranchisement have been rationalized by stereotypes that state authorities promote. Such stereotypes portray the local people as "white trash," "swamp trash," and "crackers"; as dirty, skinny, shoeless, toothless, illiterate, and unintelligent. The stereotypes deflect attention from the skewed distribution of wealth and power and the uneven investments in roads, education, and health care that result from state policies. Poor whites are a subordinated group, distinct from successful middle- and upper-class whites in the state.

Gibson's study reveals that whiteness is not monolithic. Indeed, people who place themselves in this racial group experience a wide range of life chances. Poor whites in the United States comprise a mix of 22.3 million people, both urban and rural, who do not necessarily reflect the advantages of whiteness (Wray and Newitz 1996). The worst stereotypes portray poor whites as backward, inbred, lazy, illiterate, unintelligent, and uncultured. Epithets such as "redneck," "hillbilly," and "white trash" distance these whites from the middle-class social norms and economic success stereotypically associated with their whiteness (Hartigan 2005). Although the historical development, regional particularities,

FIGURE 6.14 Anthropologists of race in the United States have studied the often "unmarked" category of whiteness. The privileges of whiteness in the United States are not experienced uniformly, but are stratified along deep lines of class, region, gender, and sexuality.

and current circumstances vary among groups of poor whites, their poverty and social ostracism mark an extreme end of the U.S. class spectrum. In the current age of globalization, economic restructuring and global competition are further undermining the white privilege for many poor and working-class whites as manufacturing jobs leave the United States.

In this chapter we have begun our work as budding anthropologists to unmask the structures of power, starting with race and racism. We have seen

TOOLKIT

Thinking Like an Anthropologist: Shifting Our Perspectives on Race and Racism

As you encounter race and racism in your life — on campus, in the classroom, at the workplace, in the news, or in your family — thinking like an anthropologist can help you to better understand these experiences. As you untangle this knotty problem, remember to think about the big questions we addressed in this chapter:

- Do biologically separate races exist?
- How is race constructed around the world?
- How is race constructed in the United States?
- What is racism?

After reading this chapter, you should be better equipped to engage the challenges of race and racism. As you think back on the chapter-opening story about the impact of Hurricane Katrina on the population of New Orleans, how would you apply the ideas of this chapter to assist your analysis and inform your responses?

Hurricane Katrina was a dangerous storm, but its effects were a social disaster that disproportionately affected people along lines of race and class. Few would say that U.S. government leaders allowed the effects of Hurricane Katrina to occur because of individual prejudice or bigotry. But even though a catastrophic hurricane had been anticipated for New Orleans since 2001, the city, state, and federal governments had no effective evacuation plan. Why? In a city stratified by race and class, some residents had cars by which to leave the city and credit cards with which to pay for gas and hotel rooms. Others had to wait for the government to send buses, which arrived nearly a week later. Moreover, protective wetlands had been sold to developers, and the budget for maintaining and improving levees and pumps had been cut by 80 percent (Smith 2006; Marable 2006).

How do we make sense of what happened? Neil Smith suggests that there is no such thing as a natural disaster. Rather, he says, natural events become disasters for some people because of social factors, including race and social inequality. Can we imagine that the effects of Hurricane Katrina might reflect a type of structural racism buried in the practices and policies of our social institutions (which developed over hundreds of years of overt racial prejudice) that continue to affect where people live, how public infrastructure is funded, how government prepares for and responds to events, and how public needs are addressed?

Key Terms

race (p. 197)
racism (p. 197)
genotype (p. 200)
phenotype (p. 200)
colonialism (p. 203)
miscegenation (p. 208)
white supremacy (p. 214)
whiteness (p. 215)
Jim Crow (p. 216)
hypodescent (p. 216)

how flawed ideas of "race" serve as a rationale for very real systems of power built around racial stratification both in the United States and around the world. As globalization, particularly global migration, brings cultural systems of meaning and stratification into closer contact, your ability to analyze and engage dynamics of race and racism will prove to be increasingly important. In the following chapters we will consider other systems of power—including ethnicity, gender, sexuality, kinship, and class—and their points of mutual intersection with race.

nativism (p. 217)
eugenics (p. 218)
racialization (p. 222)
individual racism (p. 223)
institutional racism (p. 223)
racial ideology (p. 224)

For Further Exploration

American Anthropological Association. 1997. "Response to OMB Directive 15: Race and Ethnic Standards for Federal Statistics and Administrative Reporting." September. www.aaanet.org/gvt/ombdraft.htm. Response to revision of race categories in the 2000 U.S. Census form.

American Anthropological Association. 1998. "Statement on 'Race.'" May 17. www.aaanet.org/stmts/racepp.htm.

American Anthropological Association. *Race: Are We So Different?* www.understandingrace.org/home .html. Visit the AAA's online exhibit exploring an anthropological approach to race.

American Experience. 1986. *Eyes on the Prize: America's Civil Rights Movement 1954–1985.* Blackside. See the "Fighting Back (1957–1962)" segment on Southern school desegregation.

Aspen Institute. 2013. Roundtable on Community Change. www.aspeninstitute.org/policy-work/ community-change.

Duke, David Hughes, and John Duke. 2012. *From Silence to Recognition.* Documentary with interviews of Jewish students who faced discrimination by Emory University's School of Dentistry from 1948 to 1961.

Jones, Camara Phyllis. 2000. "Levels of Racism: A Theoretic Framework and a Gardener's Tale." *American Journal of Public Health* 90(8): 1212–15.

Race: The Power of an Illusion. 2003. California Newsreel. View the three-part television series on DVD, then visit the related PBS website at www.pbs .org/race/ for further discussions, exercises, and resources.

What can soccer teach us about ethnicity and nationalism? Here Germany's Jerome Boateng (*left*) challenges for the ball against his brother, Ghana's Kevin-Prince Boateng, during a 2010 World Cup soccer match in Johannesburg, South Africa.

p. 239

p. 241

p. 244

p. 247

p. 251

p. 264

CHAPTER 7

Ethnicity and Nationalism

When the World Cup soccer tournament opened in June 2010 in South Africa, teams from thirty-two nations carried the hopes and dreams of their supporters into the competition. Soccer stadiums filled up with fans painted in national colors, draped in national flags, and singing national songs and anthems. Other fans tuned in to television and radio broadcasts around the world, exulting and suffering along with the fates of their national teams. Over three years, 205 teams had battled through 848 matches to reach South Africa—the most extensive global tournament in history. At the time of the World Cup final, more than 700 million people gathered worldwide in pubs, restaurants, and crowded town squares to watch Spain play the Netherlands. What can we learn about ethnicity and nationalism from the World Cup?

Jerome Boateng and Kevin-Prince Boateng, two half-brothers born in Germany to a Ghanaian father and German mothers, both played in the World Cup—but for different national teams. Jerome played for Germany, the country of his birth. Kevin-Prince played for the Ghanaian national team, representing the country of his father's birth. What makes someone a member of a certain nation? The simple answer, it seems, should be birth. But in today's age of globalization, nationality is not so simple. The rules of FIFA, the world soccer federation, state that to play for a national team, a player must either be born in that country or have a parent or grandparent from that country. A player can also establish a new nationality by living in a new country for five years. But once a choice of nationality is made, it is irrevocable. As the son of an immigrant from Ghana, but born in Germany, Kevin-Prince could choose his nationality. In the World Cup, we see the complications of identity for children of immigrants and the changing rules of nationality on the international stage.

But what exactly is a nation? When Germany knocked England out of the World Cup, commentators in the United Kingdom lamented the death of the "ninety-minute nation" (Younge 2010). What did this mean? First, consider that England no longer exists as a separate nation. It is now part of the United Kingdom—along with Scotland, Wales, and Northern Ireland. In fact, the disappearance of England within the United Kingdom is a sore point for many of English descent. Their rival ethnic groups have gained political recognition in recent years. Scotland has a parliament; Wales and Northern Ireland have national assemblies. But politically, England has been subsumed into the United Kingdom.

The soccer pitch is one of the few places where English ethnic identity and nationalism can still be expressed. The game was born in England. In consideration of this, FIFA allows the English to continue fielding a World Cup team even without a nation. When the England team takes the field, English ethnicity and nationalism reemerge. The flag of England's patron saint, St. George, flies high over the prime minister's residence, temporarily replacing the Union Jack. Period costumes emerge on the streets of London. Traditional English songs resound in pubs. Through sports, the nation exists as long as England is playing. But at the end of a ninety-minute game, the "ninety-minute nation" returns to its place within the United Kingdom.

Let's consider another example. Midway through the World Cup, the French national team imploded as the world and the French nation watched. The whole team went on strike, refusing to practice before a crucial match that resulted in a humiliating, early exit from the tournament. What had happened? During the competition, a vitriolic rant by one of the team's stars, laced with ethnic comments, set off intense conflicts within the diverse French team—whose racial and ethnic composition reflects the country's colonial past and recent immigration. Indeed, immigration, nationality, and race are red-hot topics in France. With a long colonial past in Africa and Asia and significant recent immigration from these former colonies, France seethes with conflict over who is really French. Riots have erupted in immigrant neighborhoods. The national government recently banned Muslim women from wearing the veil in public. Thus, one must ask: Is it possible to "become" French? How long does it take? The difficult French national debates over ethnicity and nationalism were on display and under negotiation at the World Cup.

The World Cup is more than a series of soccer matches. As anthropologists, we know that sports are more than just a game. Yes, games happen in real time with dirt and sweat, tactics and strategies, wins and losses and ties.

But games are also symbolic, both for the players and for their fans. Victory and defeat, disappointment and heroism are wrapped up in a drama larger than life. Sports are a venue for the creation and negotiation of personal and national identity. They are sites of moral education about sportsmanship, leadership, the value of compromise, how to cope with victory and defeat, and how to work together with diverse people (MacClancy 1996). Wrapped up in an international competition like the World Cup are emotionally fraught matters: national identity and citizenship, the national and ethnic imaginations of people worldwide, the history of colonialism and independence, old rivalries, national pride, the expression of national character, and the negotiation of a people's place on the modern world stage. Moreover, the spectacle of the World Cup illustrates how the promotion of nationalism by the media, corporations, and national leaders has direct benefits for viewership, profit, and political power.

In this chapter we will explore ethnicity and nationalism from an anthropological perspective. In particular, we will ask three key questions:

- What does "ethnicity" mean to anthropologists?
- How is ethnicity created and put in motion?
- What is the relationship of ethnicity to the nation?

After reading this chapter, you will be able to understand and analyze the role of ethnicity and nationalism in your own life and in communities and countries worldwide.

What Does "Ethnicity" Mean to Anthropologists?

We hear the word *ethnicity* all the time. The press reports on "long-held ethnic conflicts" that shatter the peace in Ireland, Rwanda, Iraq, and Sri Lanka. We check boxes on college applications and U.S. census forms to identify our ethnicity or race. We shop in the "ethnic foods" aisle of our supersized grocery store to find refried beans, soy sauce, pita, and wasabi. Our use of *ethnicity* is not particularly consistent or terribly clear. In recent years in the United States, *ethnicity* has been increasingly substituted for *race* when describing group differences. *Ethnic* is often paired with *minority*, a term signifying a smaller group that differs from the dominant, majority culture in language, food, dress, immigrant history, national origin, or religion. But this usage ignores the ethnic identity of the majority. The same lack of clarity is true for our use of the terms *nation*, *nationalism*, and *nation-state*, all of which often blur together and at times seem indistinguishable from *ethnicity*.

Ethnicity as Identity

Over a lifetime, humans develop complex identities that connect to many people in many ways. We build a sense of relationship, belonging, and shared identity through connections to family, religion, hometown, language, shared history, citizenship, sports, age, gender, sexuality, education, and profession. These powerful identities influence what we eat, who we date, where we work, how we live, and even how we die. **Ethnicity** is one of the most powerful identities that humans develop: it is a sense of connection to a group of people who we believe share a common history, culture, and (sometimes) ancestry and who are distinct from others outside the group (Jenkins 1996; Ericksen 2010). Ethnicity can be seen as a more expansive version of kinship—the culturally specific creation of relatives—only including a much larger group and extending further in space and time. As we will see in this chapter, the construction of ethnicity, like kinship, is quite complicated, moving well beyond easy equation with biological ancestry. Ethnic identification beyond our immediate associations is primarily perceived, felt, and imagined rather than clearly documentable.

With the intensification of globalization and the increasing flows of people, goods, and ideas across borders, one might anticipate that the power of ethnicity to frame people's actions and to influence world events would diminish. Instead, ethnicity seems to be flourishing—rising in prominence in both local and global affairs. Why is it so powerful? When threatened or challenged, people often turn to local alliances for support, safety, and protection. Ethnicity is one of the strongest sources of solidarity available.

ethnicity: A sense of historical, cultural, and sometimes ancestral connection to a group of people who are imagined to be distinct from those outside the group.

As the effects of globalization intersect with systems of power at the local level, many people turn to ethnic networks and expressions of ethnic identity to protect their local way of life in the face of intense pressures of homogenization. As we will consider later in this chapter, ethnicity also can serve political purposes on the national and local levels as political elites and other ethnoentrepreneurs use calls for ethnic solidarity to mobilize support against perceived enemies inside and outside the nation-state. Rather than diminishing in the face of globalization, ethnicity emerges even more powerfully in specific situations of conflict, tension, and opportunity.

FIGURE 7.2 In what ways do stories, paintings, and even Thanksgiving turkey floats help create an American ethnic identity? *Left,* a 1914 depiction of the first Thanksgiving at Plymouth, Massachusetts. *Right,* the Tom Turkey float moves through Times Square during the Macy's Thanksgiving Day Parade, in New York City.

Creating Ethnic Identity

Anthropologists see ethnicity as a cultural construction, not as a natural formation based on biology or inherent human nature. Fredrik Barth (1969) describes ethnicity as the "social organization of cultural difference"; in other words, people construct a sense of ethnicity as they organize themselves in relation to others whom they perceive as either culturally similar or culturally different. Ethnic identity starts with what people believe about themselves and how others see them. Identity formation begins early and continues throughout our lives. People learn, practice, and teach ethnicity. Anthropologists who study it seek to understand how it is created and reinforced, how boundaries are constructed, how group identity is shaped, and how differences with others are perpetuated (Jenkins 2008). Who do you consider to be in your ethnic group? Who belongs to a different group?

Ethnic identity is taught and reinforced in a number of ways. One key method is the creation and telling of **origin myths**. By myth, we do not mean falsehood but rather a story with meaning. In the United States, the "American" origin myth includes stories of historical events—such as the landing of the *Mayflower,* the first Thanksgiving, the Boston Tea Party, the American

origin myth: A story told about the founding and history of a particular group to reinforce a sense of common identity.

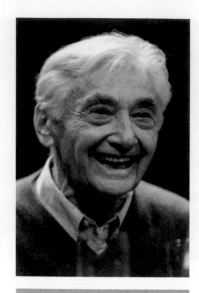

FIGURE 7.3 Social historian Howard Zinn, whose book, *A People's History of the United States*, challenges popular versions of the American origin myth.

ethnic boundary marker: A practice or belief, such as food, clothing, language, shared name, or religion, used to signify who is in a group and who is not.

genocide: The deliberate and systematic destruction of an ethnic or religious group.

situational negotiation of identity: An individual's self-identification with a particular group that can shift according to social location.

Revolution, the Civil War, the settling of the West—that are retold to emphasize a shared destiny as well as shared values of freedom, exploration, individualism, and multiculturalism. The American origin myth of the first Thanksgiving is ritually enacted each year with a national holiday. Schoolchildren produce dramas and artwork based on textbook stories. Families gather to feast, usually eating certain traditional foods. Nationally televised parades and sporting events add to the ritual's celebratory character. However, origin myths—like all elements of culture—are continuously promoted, revised, and negotiated. For example, recent years have seen more open discussion of the brutal conquest of Native Americans and, in books such as Howard Zinn's *A People's History of the United States* (2005), more challenges to classic textbook representations of the American origin myth.

People create and promote certain **ethnic boundary markers** in an attempt to signify who is in the group and who is not. These may include a collective name; shared cultural practices such as food, clothing, and architecture; a belief in common ancestors; association with a particular territory; a shared language or religion; and an imagination of shared physical characteristics. But ethnic boundaries are usually not clearly fixed and defined. Our social worlds rarely have distinct groups with clear boundaries. Not everyone imagined to be inside the group is the same; not everyone imagined to be outside the group is noticeably different. No group is completely homogeneous.

Identity, including ethnic identity, can be fluid and flexible, reflecting shifting alliances and strength over time and according to need (Ericksen 2010). People move between groups through marriage, migration, and adoption. Groups may vanish in situations of war or **genocide** (the deliberate and systematic destruction of an ethnic or religious group). New ethnic groups may come into existence—a process called *ethnogenesis*—when part of an existing group splits off or two groups form a new one.

Because ethnicity is not biologically fixed, self-identification with a particular ethnic group can change according to one's social location. This occurs through a process called **situational negotiation of identity**. For example, Kevin-Prince Boateng in our chapter-opening story could have chosen to be German, German-Ghanaian, Ghanaian, African, Afro-European, perhaps even a member of his father's local ethnic group in Ghana. At points during his life he may choose to identify himself with any of these, depending on the situation. Have you ever had the experience of identifying with a different aspect of your identity as you moved between groups or locations? As another example, the following section explores how immigrants from India to the United States undergo changing ethnic perspectives as they become Indian Americans.

Constructing Indian Identity in the United States The immigration experience profoundly affects ethnicity and ethnic identification. New immigrants reshape their home-country ethnic identification to build alliances and solidarity in their new host country. In her book *From the Ganges to the Hudson* (1995), anthropologist Johanna Lessinger explores the process by which a new Indian ethnic identity is created and publicly demonstrated through consumption, public festivals, and Indian immigrant media. Indian immigrants arrive in New York from all corners of their homeland, speaking different languages, following diverse cultural practices and religions, and reflecting class and caste stratifications. In India, a country of more than 1.2 billion people, these individuals would identify themselves as representing different ethnicities. But after arriving in New York as immigrants from India, they all begin the process of becoming Indian American.

Little India, a bustling shopping district in Jackson Heights, Queens, has become the symbolic center of Indian immigrant life and a key to the construction of Indian ethnic identity in the United States. Vibrant with the sights, sounds, and smells of India, the streets are lined with Indian grocery and spice shops, Indian restaurants, clothing and jewelry stores, travel agencies, music and video distributors, and electronics stores. Indian immigrants come from all parts of New York City and the metropolitan region to walk the streets of Little India and shop, eat, and take in the many symbols of "home."

MAP 7.1
New York / India

India, with a population of 1.2 billion, is home to people of many different ethnicities, shaped by geography, language, food, and cultural practices. But in New York City, Indian immigrants have created a wide-ranging ethnic infrastructure that supports and promotes the construction of a unified Indian ethnic identity in their new homeland. The infrastructure includes ethnic associations, religious temples, cultural societies, newspapers, television programming, and major public festivals. One of the largest festivals is the India Day Parade held in late August to mark India's nationhood and independence from British colonialism. Like the dozens of ethnic parade celebrations in New York each year, Indian immigrant community organizations, business owners, and hometown associations sponsor marching bands, singers, dancers, banners, and a vast array of colorful floats. In 2009, Shilpa Shetty (the Indian actress mentioned in the opening anecdote of Chapter 2) was the India Day Parade's grand marshal. In 2010, the parade featured the prime minister of Trinidad and Tobago, a Caribbean country to which many Indians were sent as laborers in the nineteenth century and from which many have migrated to New York. By including Indians of Caribbean descent, the parade organizers demonstrate their intention to unify the diverse diaspora of Indians now residing in New York City. Holding a public festival like the India Day Parade is a powerful way to stake a claim to a place in the multiethnic mosaic that is New York—to send a clear signal to all New Yorkers, including the political establishment, that Indians are here, are organized, and want to be taken seriously.

Ethnic boundaries are often fluid, messy, and contested. For example, exactly who is Indian American? Each year since 1994, the South Asian Lesbian and Gay Alliance (SALGA) has requested permission to march in the India Day Parade, only to be denied by parade organizers. Does this mean that gay men and lesbians of Indian ancestry are not Indian? Members of SALGA hold demonstrations each year along the parade route, holding signs that read "We are also Indians!" Despite the parade organizers' desire to build a broad-based Indian American identity and coalition, they are willing to declare SALGA not Indian enough to participate in the event. In this situation, sexuality becomes a more powerful boundary marker than country of origin. The rift over the India Day Parade is a very public and symbolic representation of the contestation of ethnic boundary markers—a struggle that reveals deep disagreements among Indian immigrants and many of their children—and the debate involved in defining who is Indian in the United States.

How Is Ethnicity Created and Put in Motion?

For most of the world's people, ethnicity is not a pressing matter in daily life. But it can be activated when power relationships undergo negotiation in a community or a nation. Then people call on shared ideas of ethnicity to rally others to participate in their causes, whether those causes involve ensuring self-protection, building alliances, constructing economic networks, or establishing a country. Ethnicity can also be activated by charismatic entrepreneurs of ethnicity who seek support from co-ethnics in their fight for political, economic, or military power against real or perceived enemies. The sections that follow illustrate how ethnicity can be harnessed for either harmful or beneficial outcomes.

Ethnicity as a Source of Conflict

The anthropological study of ethnicity requires an open-mindedness to new ideas of how ethnicity is formed and how it works—ideas that may be at odds with our everyday usage of the terms *ethnicity* and *ethnic groups*. Rogers Brubaker, in his book *Ethnicity without Groups* (2004), warns against "groupism" when studying ethnicity. Anthropologists may anticipate that we will work with clearly defined groups having fixed boundaries and homogenous membership who will act in a unified fashion. But this is not what we find on the ground as we explore ethnicity on the local level. Ethnicity is much more complicated, involving people with many perspectives, disagreements, and at times competing loyalties. The strong bonds of ethnicity that we associate with ethnic groups may wax and wane.

Why do the power and intensity of ethnicity harden and crystallize at certain times? When studying ethnic conflict, as in the cases of Rwanda and the former Yugoslavia that follow, Brubaker encourages paying attention to ethnic group–making projects. Such projects occur when ethno-political entrepreneurs—political, military, and religious leaders—promote a worldview through the lens of ethnicity. They use war, propaganda, and state power to mobilize people against those whom they perceive as a danger. Ethnicity may not even be the problem. Rather, the struggle for wealth and power uses the convenient narrative of ethnicity to galvanize a population to collective action. Once the wedge of ethnic difference has been driven into a population and used to achieve power, it can be self-perpetuating and extremely difficult to break (Ericksen 2010).

Mobilizing Ethnic Differences in Rwanda In 1994, the East African country of Rwanda was shattered by a horrific genocide involving two main groups, Hutu and Tutsi. Over a few months, as many as one million Tutsi and an unknown number of moderate Hutus died in a slaughter perpetrated by extremist Hutu death squads. In a country of only seven million people before the genocide, where Hutu made up 85 percent of the population and Tutsi 15 percent, how did this tragedy occur? How do Tutsi and Hutu, who have lived together in the region for generations and centuries, tell each other apart?

MAP 7.2
Rwanda

Before German and Belgian colonial rule in the early twentieth century, Hutu and Tutsi were distinguished mainly by occupation and social status. Hutu were primarily farmers; Tutsi were cattle owners. The two groups share a common language and religious affiliations. Intermarriage has been quite common. Children of mixed marriages inherited their fathers' identity. Although Tutsi were later stereotyped as taller and thinner than Hutu, it is not possible to distinguish between members of the two groups by looks alone.

In a common colonial practice used in countries worldwide, colonial governments chose one native group to serve as educated and privileged intermediaries between the local population and the colonial administration. The Belgian colonial government (1919–62) elevated Tutsi to the most influential positions in Rwandan society, to the exclusion of Hutu leaders. In an attempt to rationalize its prejudicial behavior, in the 1920s the Belgian colonial government hired scientists to measure Hutu and Tutsi anatomy—including skull size—so as to physically differentiate between the two groups. These flawed studies, based on the pseudoscience of eugenics (see Chapter 6) that developed in Europe and the United States, declared that Tutsi were taller, bigger brained, and lighter skinned—closer in physical form to Europeans and thus "naturally" suited to the role assigned to them by the Belgian colonial government.

To maintain and enforce this segregation, in 1933 the Belgian colonial government established a national identity card that included the category "ethnicity." Even after independence in 1962, Rwandan officials continued to use the identity card, forcing all citizens to be labeled as Hutu, Tutsi, Twa (a small minority population), or naturalized (born outside Rwanda). The cards were discontinued only in 1996 after the genocide.

Many Hutu resented the Belgians' decision to elevate Tutsi to power in the colonial government. Periodic protests in the early years of colonial occupation were followed by a major uprising against Tutsi elites in 1956. In 1959, the Hutu seized power and forced many Tutsi into exile in neighboring countries. At independence in 1962, the Hutu consolidated full power and implemented repressive policies toward the Tutsi. A full-blown civil war erupted in 1990. Subsequently, a 1993 United Nations–backed cease-fire collapsed when the plane of the Rwandan president, a Hutu, was shot down in April 1994.

What followed was an extensive genocide campaign by Hutu extremists who blamed Tutsi for the death of their president. Rwandan radio broadcast instructions to kill all Tutsi, including spouses and family members, as well as any Hutu moderates who were unwilling to cooperate. Hutu civilian death squads implemented the "Hutu Power" genocide program, a deliberate and seemingly long-planned extermination of Tutsi. As a result, Tutsi and moderate Hutu were killed largely by hand with machetes and clubs after local officials gathered them

FIGURE 7.5 Rwandan identity cards.

up into schools and churches. Hutu death squads used the Rwandan identity cards to identify Tutsi victims for extermination.

What role did ethnicity play in the Rwandan genocide? Western press and government reports referred to the extermination as "tribal violence," the result of "ancient ethnic hatreds" and a failed nation-state. However, we can see how colonial European policies constructed and enforced notions of difference between Hutu and Tutsi—including notions of physical and mental difference—that were not deep-rooted historical patterns but later served to rationalize genocide (Mamdani 2002). Indeed, the twentieth-century history of Rwanda reveals the ways in which local ethnic relationships can be broken down and reconstituted in long-lasting ways by a foreign superpower that uses ethnicity as a weapon to divide and rule and how those new patterns of ethnicity can be mobilized to fuel a struggle for economic, political, and military power.

Orchestrating Ethnic Conflict in the Former Yugoslavia The disintegration of the former Yugoslavia in the late 1980s and early 1990s led to a devastating civil war that harnessed ethnicity as a powerful weapon of conflict and hatred. The war began in 1992 among Catholic Croats, Orthodox Christian Serbs, and Bosnian Muslims as national political leaders scrambled for control over land and power. In direct contrast to journalistic accounts of the war, which traced its origins to ancient ethnic hatreds that condemned the country's people to an endless cycle of violence, Norwegian anthropologist Tone Bringa has offered a

MAP 7.3
Bosnia

different perspective. In her ethnography *Being Muslim the Bosnian Way* (1995), she declares, "The war was not created by those villagers. . . . The war has been orchestrated from places where the people I lived and worked among were not represented and where their voices were not heard" (5).

Beginning in 1987, Bringa conducted fieldwork in a diverse, Muslim–Catholic village in central Bosnia. She carefully describes the integrated social structures of daily village life—including the role of women, religion, and the family—and pays particular attention to the way Muslims practiced their faith. Bringa did not find a village populated with people who had always hated one another. They spoke the same language, went to school together, traded in the same local market, and shared village life as friends and neighbors. Bringa pointedly notes that despite the usual tensions any small community would face, these people of different faiths had lived together peacefully for five hundred years.

Significant change occurred in the community during the short time of Bringa's fieldwork. When she began her research, local Muslims based their identity on differences in religious practices from those of their Catholic neighbors. The emphasis was on practices such as scheduling of worship, prayer, and holiday celebrations, not on religious beliefs and convictions. However, these perceptions of self and others changed as war broke out and state leaders imposed new ethnic and cultural policies. Gradually, local Muslims were forced to identify less with their local community and more with the religious beliefs of other Bosnian Muslims, and they had to turn to the outside Muslim world as a source of solidarity and support.

When Bringa returned to the village in the spring of 1993—revealed in riveting scenes from her documentary film, *Bosnia: We Are All Neighbors* (1993)—to her horror she found that almost every Muslim home had been destroyed by Croat forces, with assistance from local Croat men of the village. All four hundred Muslims in the village (two-thirds of its population) had fled, been killed, or been placed in concentration camps. **Ethnic cleansing**—efforts of one ethnic or religious group to remove or destroy another in a particular geographic area—had destroyed the dynamic and peaceful fabric of village life that Bringa recalled from only a few years earlier. As she writes in the preface to her book, "my anthropological training had not prepared me to deal with the very rapid and total disintegration of the community. . . . [T]his war has made sense neither to the anthropologist nor to the people who taught her about their way of life" (Bringa 1995, xviii). Her second documentary, *Returning Home: Revival of a Bosnian Village* (Bringa and Loizos 2002), examines the return of some of the Muslim refugees and the attempt to reconstruct the village life that was destroyed during the civil war. In Bringa's account of Bosnian village life we can see the vulnerability of local ethnic identities to manipulation by outside political and military forces.

FIGURE 7.6 Bosnian Muslim women comfort one another near coffins of family members, victims of "ethnic cleansing," exhumed from a nearby mass grave.

Ethnicity as a Source of Opportunity

Ethnicity is not only mobilized to rally support in times of conflict. Ethnicity also can be mobilized to create opportunities, including engagement in everyday economics. Today ethnicity is being packaged and produced for a multibillion-dollar market: food, clothing, music, fashion, and cultural artifacts. People eat at ethnic restaurants, buy ethnic music, and decorate their homes and offices with ethnic furnishings. Perhaps you have some "ethnic" items in your dorm room or at home. John and Jean Comaroff, in their book *Ethnicity, Inc.* (2009), examine how the purposeful creation of ethnicity facilitates big business. The Comaroffs pay particular attention to the way ethnically defined populations are branding themselves and becoming ethno-corporations in order to capitalize on their ethnicity. Ethno–theme parks, cultural villages, and ecotourism all promote the ethnic experience to attract investors and customers. These are just a few pieces of the "Ethnicity, Inc." puzzle. (In contrast, for an example of a majority group's marketing of minority theme parks, see the group of images on the opposite page.)

Native Americans and the Ethno-Corporation The marketing of ethnicity is not uncommon globally, as marginalized indigenous groups seek to capitalize on their identity to attract investors and customers. Native Americans in the United States in recent years have established corporate entities to manage tribal land and invest tribal resources for the profit of their members, or "shareholders." Casinos have become big business, and the rise of casino capitalism has driven increasing opportunities for Native American groups to transition from "tribe" to "ethno-corporation." Sovereignty agreements signed long ago with the U.S. government allow the expansion of the gaming industry on native land. Outside venture capital is readily available to underwrite these new opportunities.

FIGURE 7.7 How can ethnic groups become ethno-corporations? Here, exterior and interior shots of the Pequot Foxwoods Resort, in Connecticut.

FIGURE 7.8 Each year, half a million tourists visit the Dai Minority Park in China's southwestern Yunnan Province. This is one of many ethno-parks owned and operated by members of China's Han majority (96 percent of the population), who market the nation's fifty-five ethnic minorities to a primarily middle-class Han clientele. Here tourists can live in Dai-style houses, eat ethnic meals, and participate in reenactments of ritual celebrations such as the water festival, pictured here, originally an annual three-day festival but now performed every day for the entertainment of visitors. How might ethno-theme parks benefit the Chinese government's goal of national unity? How do you think they affect the local communities?

The Comaroffs (2009) note the effects of ethno-corporations on Native American life and culture. Clearly, Native American ethnicity and culture are being cultivated and marketed to promote economic projects, both in the gaming industry and beyond.

Ethno-enterprises in turn cultivate ethnicity. The massive Pequot Foxwoods Resort in Mashantucket, Connecticut, for instance, not only runs a lucrative casino but also supports a library, archives, and linguistic collections of the Pequot Indians' "traditional culture." Conferences and workshops on Native American topics take place at the nearby Mashantucket Pequot Museum and

Research Center. In some places, Native American groups nearing extinction have been revived by a few remaining tribal descendants. The Comaroffs note that as these ethnically defined groups become more focused on profit seeking and are more successful as corporations, the question of membership becomes more controversial and requires careful regulation. Genetics, birthright, and ideas of ethnicity based on "blood" take on greater power than cultural ideas of ethnicity based on notions of belonging.

MAP 7.4
South Africa

Bafokeng, Inc., in South Africa For another look at ethnicity being mobilized for economic benefits, the story of one group in South Africa is remarkable for its corporate success. The Bafokeng, a Tswana nation in South Africa's North West province, trace their history in the area to the twelfth century. Between 1840 and the mid-1860s, their land was taken by white colonial settlers. Thereafter the Bafokeng, who could not own land under the new regime, went to work as laborers on the farms that had once been theirs; later they toiled in diamond mines to the south. Ultimately, though, to recover their land, the Bafokeng decided to try to buy it back. Pooling portions of their wage labor under the auspices of the Tswana king, and with a white German missionary serving as their proxy, the Bafokeng began a long-term strategy to repurchase their farms. Eventually, they reacquired thirty-three farms by the early twentieth century. To protect their land rights, the natives registered these farms under the name of the Royal Bafokeng Nation, Inc.—a private, corporate owner—not in the names of individuals.

Throughout much of the twentieth century, the Bafokeng engaged in complicated legal battles with the South African state to keep control over their land. Tensions rose dramatically when, in 1924, surveyors discovered that the Merensky Reef geologic formation that lay directly under Bafokeng land was the world's largest source of platinum metals and held significant deposits of chromite and graphite as well. Battles with the state and corporations over mining rights continued until the 1960s, when a deal was reached with a private company to provide the Bafokeng with royalties on all minerals extracted from their land. Once again, the Bafokeng placed their revenues into a communal trust. Since that time, they have invested their assets aggressively, transforming the Royal Bafokeng Nation into a massive ethno-corporation.

The extent of this corporation's scope is remarkable. Its rapidly diversifying array of businesses now includes mining and construction companies, investment companies, and even a premier soccer team—all held in the name of the Royal Bafokeng Nation (RBN). At home, it has invested heavily in jobs programs by establishing mid-size companies such as Bafokeng Civil Works, Bafokeng Brick and Tile, Bafokeng Chrome, Bafokeng Bakery, and a Bafokeng shopping center. The RBN has also invested in infrastructure such as roads, bridges, reservoirs, electricity, schools, and health clinics, and it has established a fund for Bafokeng individuals who are pursuing professional training or higher education.

Over time, the Royal Bafokeng Nation has become a wealthy corporate conglomerate with an extensive web of investments and holdings in South Africa and beyond. By 2004, mining contracts alone produced more than $65 million in profits. The ethnic group has become an ethno-enterprise—built, branded, packaged, and advertised on the Bafokeng ethnic name and identity.

Many scholars, politicians, and economists expected the RBN to wither away in the face of globalization, modernity, and the homogenizing influence of the capitalist economy. However, the RBN ethno-corporation has flourished. It provides a remarkable example of the ways in which ethnicity can be mobilized by stakeholders in identity-based businesses to create alternative strategies for survival and success in the global marketplace.

Despite their corporate success, all is not well within the Bafokeng nation itself. Questions regularly arise about who benefits from this version of "Ethnicity, Inc." Individual Bafokeng do not own shares in RBN, Inc. Its money is not distributed among members but is reinvested in the corporation. Despite investments in job programs, infrastructure, and education in the homeland, recent studies show that the Bafokeng have a 39 percent unemployment rate, 95 percent use pit latrines for toilets, and less than 13 percent have electricity. With extreme poverty rates, some observers refer to the Bafokeng as "a rich nation of poor people" (Comaroff and Comaroff 2009, 109). How would you assess the effectiveness of this mobilization of ethnicity by the Bafokeng?

Ethnic Interaction in the United States: Assimilation versus Multiculturalism

The United States has an extremely complicated history of dealing with people of different ethnic backgrounds. The relationship of "ethnic" and "American" (as applied to the United States) remains controversial today. From the outset, several factors made the United States one of the most ethnically diverse countries in the world: immigration from various regions in Europe, the importation of African slaves, and the conquest of Native American peoples. But this diverse population has experienced extremely different paths to incorporation into U.S. culture. In fact, these paths have often followed color lines that divide people of lighter and darker complexions.

Scholars have often used the **melting pot** metaphor to describe the standard path into U.S. culture. In the melting pot, minorities adopt the patterns and norms of the dominant culture and eventually cease to exist as separate groups—a process scholars call **assimilation**. Eventually all cooked in the same pot, diverse groups become assimilated into one big stew. According to this metaphor, tens of millions of European immigrants from dozens of countries with

melting pot: A metaphor used to describe the process of immigrant assimilation into U.S. dominant culture.

assimilation: The process through which minorities accept the patterns and norms of the dominant culture and cease to exist as separate groups.

myriad languages, cultures, and religious practices have been transformed into ethnic whites through marriage, work, education, and the use of English.

But in reality the melting pot has never been completely successful in the United States. Even the creation of whiteness, as we saw in Chapter 6, was often contentious and difficult, marked by intense rivalries and violence. Nathan Glazer and Daniel Patrick Moynihan's landmark study *Beyond the Melting Pot* (1970) found a failure to reach complete assimilation among European immigrants and their descendants as late as the third generation. For Africans, Native Americans, Latinos, and many Asian immigrants, the United States has been resistant to their assimilation into the dominant culture, regardless of their educational level or socioeconomic status.

The incredibly diverse flows of immigration to the United States since 1965 have made earlier familiar categories inadequate to capture the rapidly shifting ethnic character of the nation's population today. As discussed in Chapters 6 and 13 (on race and migration, respectively), immigrants and their children are creating new ethnic identities and new ways of becoming American. Today a multiculturalist narrative competes with the melting pot metaphor to represent the role of ethnicity in U.S. culture. **Multiculturalism** refers to the process through which new immigrants and their children enculturate into the dominant national culture and yet retain an ethnic culture. In multiculturalism, both identities may be held at the same time.

Tensions over which model will be dominant in the U.S. ethnicity story—assimilation or multiculturalism—are constantly rising to the surface. For example, attempts to establish English as the official language of towns, states, and even the U.S. federal government can be seen as (1) an effort to mandate language assimilation into the melting pot, and (2) a reassertion of the dominant culture's centrality against the rising trend toward multiculturalism (Rumbaut and Portes 2001).

What Is the Relationship of Ethnicity to the Nation?

Almost all people today imagine themselves as part of a nation-state. But this has not always been the case. **States**—regional structures of political, economic, and military rule—have existed for thousands of years, beginning in the regions now known as modern-day Iraq, China, and India. But the nation-state is a relatively new development. The term signifies more than a geographic territory with borders enforced by a central government. **Nation-state** assumes a distinct political entity whose population shares a sense of culture, ancestry, and destiny as a people. Though the term **nation** once was used to describe a

multiculturalism: A pattern of ethnic relations in which new immigrants and their children enculturate into the dominant national culture and yet retain an ethnic culture.

state: An autonomous regional structure of political, economic, and military rule with a central government authorized to make laws and use force to maintain order and defend its territory.

nation-state: A political entity, located within a geographic territory with enforced borders, where the population shares a sense of culture, ancestry, and destiny as a people.

nation: A term once used to describe a group of people who shared a place of origin; now used interchangeably with nation-state.

group of people who shared a place of origin, today the word *nation* is often used interchangeably with *nation-state*. **Nationalism** emerges when a sense of ethnic community combines with a desire to create and maintain a nation-state in a location where that sense of common destiny can be lived out (Gellner 1983; Wolf 2001; Hearn 2006).

Imagined Communities and Invented Traditions

Across the world over the past two hundred years, people have shifted their primary associations and identifications from family, village, town, and city to an almost universal identification with a nation or the desire to create a nation. Yet despite our contemporary assumptions that identification with an ethnic group or a nation has deep history, anthropological research reveals that most ethnic groups and nations are recent historical creations, our connection to people within these groups recently imagined, and our shared traditions recently invented.

Benedict Anderson (1983) conceived of the nation as an **imagined community**. He called it "imagined" because almost all of the people within it have never met and most likely will never meet. They may be separated by sharp divisions of class, politics, or religion and yet imagine themselves to have a common heritage and collective responsibility to one another and their nation. This sense of membership in an imagined national community can be strong enough to lead people into battle to protect their shared interests.

Anderson traces the imagined communities in Europe to the development of print communication in the capitalist economies that emerged in the eighteenth and nineteenth centuries. As people shared communication and information through newspapers and books published in a common language, Anderson suggests, they began to define themselves—to imagine themselves—as part of the same nation, the same community. Anderson's conception of imagined communities has become an essential analytical tool for thinking about nations and nationalisms.

Another view suggests that nations are invented. According to Eric Hobsbawm and Terence Ranger (1983), nations are not ancient configurations but instead are recent constructions with invented traditions. They may evoke a sense of deep history and inspire a broad sense of unity, but these nations are relatively new. For example, we imagine the French nation-state to have a deep and unitary history, but prior to the 1800s the French were a scattered collection of urban and rural people who spoke different languages, celebrated different holidays and festivals, practiced different religions, and held primary loyalty not to the French state but to their city, town, village, or extended family. It was two national infrastructure projects, launched in the early 1800s, that ultimately played key roles in inventing a French nation.

nationalism: The desire of an ethnic community to create and/or maintain a nation-state.

imagined community: The invented sense of connection and shared traditions that underlies identification with a particular ethnic group or nation whose members likely will never meet.

MAP 7.5
France

FIGURE 7.9 French classroom, 1829. What role can education play in creating a sense of common nationality?

What did these infrastructure projects involve? First, a new education system was introduced on a national scale. Its textbooks promoted a shared sense of French history, and perhaps most important, all schools used the Paris dialect of French as the medium of instruction. This created a standard national language—a lingua franca—that facilitated communication among the population. Second, the construction of an extensive network of roads and railways integrated rural areas into a national market economy. This new transportation infrastructure promoted the rapid flow of goods between agricultural and industrial sectors and allowed the regular movement of workers between countryside and city, thereby providing a national labor pool for France's growing economy. These national infrastructure projects proved crucial to transforming the diverse people living within the territorial boundaries of what is now modern-day France into a French people with a common sense of identity, history, language, and tradition (Weber 1976).

Anticolonialism and Nationalism

At times, efforts to imagine a national identity among a diverse group of people gain strength through the need—perceived or real—to join together against the threat of a common enemy. The outsiders—"others" who do not belong to the group—may be stereotyped along lines of religion, race, language, ethnicity, or political beliefs. War is the most dramatic strategy for evoking nationalism and mobilizing a population for the project of nation-building.

Tracing the Development of a Nation-State

The concepts of *nationalism* and *the nation* have shaped the modern world and are essential for understanding human history over the last two hundred years. Of the nearly two hundred nation-states in the world today, fewer than one-third existed in their current form forty years ago. Dozens of states were created in Central Asia and Eastern Europe following the collapse of the former Soviet Union and the breakdown of previously socialist states in the 1990s. Dozens more had been created after World War II as nationalist movements won independence from colonial powers in Asia, the Middle East, and Africa. Only a handful of the nation-states that exist today date back to the nineteenth century, and almost none have existed for more than two hundred years, certainly not in their present form.

Choose two or three countries, and trace their development to the current nation-state. Discussions of the formation of France, Rwanda, and Iraq in this chapter may offer guidance. Why have their borders changed? How have these nations been imagined and their traditions invented? Or consider the United States of America.

In 1776, at the signing of the Declaration of Independence, it consisted of only thirteen colonies along the Atlantic seaboard. The Louisiana Purchase in 1803 added the area for thirteen of the current states from Louisiana to Colorado. The Republic of Texas was an independent country from 1836 (when it broke away from Mexico) until 1845, when it voted to become part of the United States. In 1848, the United States paid Mexico $10 million for the territories constituting California and New Mexico. Hawaii and Alaska became the most recent additions to the United States when they were admitted in 1959. Puerto Rico, acquired from Spain in 1898, remains a Commonwealth controlled by the United States. Its population is fairly evenly divided between those who would like independence and those who wish to become the fifty-first state.

How have the many people who have lived in and immigrated to the territories now constituting the United States come to think of themselves as members of one nation? What are the complications of nation building for current nation-states whose boundaries encompass multiple ethnic groups?

Through much of the nineteenth and twentieth centuries, colonialism effectively constructed "the other" in the minds of people at home. Colonial governments, merchants, and missionaries represented those whom they were colonizing as backward, tribal, heathen, and violent—in other words, needing to be civilized, Christianized, and modernized. Through their colonial conquests, the emerging nation-states of Europe redrew the political borders of much of the world to suit their economic needs: they mapped out territorial boundaries without regard to local ethnic, political, economic, or religious realities.

Subsequently, the destruction of European economics during World War II (1939–45) weakened the colonial powers' ability to control their colonies.

National independence movements that had been gaining strength in colonies throughout Asia, Africa, the Middle East, Latin America, and the Caribbean before World War II were able to develop military capabilities and guerilla fighting tactics during the war and, subsequently, turned their efforts more fully toward liberating their countries from the colonial occupiers. The anticolonialist efforts led to a rise of nationalism in former colonies as disparate populations banded together to reassert local control.

As mentioned above, the territorial boundaries created by European colonial powers ignored local realities in favor of colonial economic and political interests. As a result, by the end of the colonial era few of the newly formed countries had homogeneous populations. Most now encompassed multiple ethnicities and identities within state borders that previously had not existed. Such disparities caused thorny problems for nationalist movements and for the nation-states that formed after independence. (Robbins 2011)

The Challenges of Developing a Sense of Nationhood

The following case studies from Zimbabwe, Iraq, and Argentina will expand your understanding of nation, nationalism, nation building, and the modern nation-state. Can you identify in these examples the key concepts introduced in this chapter?

Guerillas, Spirit Mediums, and Nationalism in Zimbabwe Zimbabwe was the last African colony to become independent (in 1980). In *Guns and Rain: Guerillas and Spirit Mediums in Zimbabwe* (1985), anthropologist David Lan examines the role of local religious beliefs and practices of ordinary people in the nationalist movement for liberation. In the rural Shona region of northern Zimbabwe bordering Mozambique, during the precolonial period, social life was organized around chiefs and chiefdoms. Local leaders were most often the direct descendants of a line of chiefs and kings, but their authority rested on their ability to bring rain to the farming communities under their protection and jurisdiction. This authority was traditionally legitimized through a public ritual led by the local spirit medium—a religious specialist who could communicate directly with the spirits of the ancestors. While in a trance, the spirit medium would be possessed by *Mhondoro*, the spirits of dead Shona kings and chiefs. Through the medium, these royal ancestors would confer their blessing and legitimacy on the new chief.

But during nearly one hundred years under British colonialism, the British administration usurped the role of selecting local chiefs. As a result, the chiefs, who no longer had the conferred support of the ancestors, lost much of their authority in the eyes of the local population. Spirit mediums, ignored and marginalized from the colonial political process, yet with their

MAP 7.6
Zimbabwe

own claims to authority through their ability to communicate with *Mhondoro*, often became points of resistance to colonial rule. When the struggle for independence began in the 1970s, guerilla fighters opposing the British needed the support of the local population, especially the rural farming population that made up most of the country. Lan tells of the strategic alliance formed in the north between guerilla fighters—many of whom were not Shona—and local spirit mediums to provide legitimacy, support, and protection to their struggle.

Through the alliance, spirit mediums drew on their deep history and connections in local communities to give legitimacy to the guerillas fighting against the British colonial occupation. Using elaborate rituals, the spirit mediums—possessed by *Mhondoro*—allowed the spirits of dead Shona kings and chiefs to recognize the guerillas as incarnations of royal warriors of the past and as legitimate leaders in the current liberation struggle. In the process, the spirit mediums placed combatants under the direct protection of the ancestors and thereby legitimized their cause in the eyes of the local communities. For a time, the power of the anticolonial guerilla fighters who brought guns supplanted that of the local chiefs who brought rain.

Anthropologist Lan records detailed interviews with fighters who vividly recounted how their ancestors protected and guided them to safety and victory. After liberation, the ancestors were celebrated by the common people in the streets and by the new national leaders as well. Banners and pictures of the ancestors hung in public places, and they were effectively installed as protectors of the new Zimbabwe. The liberation struggle had brought renewed, deep connections between tradition and modernity, past and present, ancestors and the living. The reinvented ethnic traditions merged with nationalist movements to promote and sustain Zimbabwe's anticolonialist struggles.

FIGURE 7.10 Enos Pondai, a spirit medium, was imprisoned by the colonial government of Rhodesia (now Zimbabwe) for resisting government authority and assisting guerilla fighters during the nation's war of independence.

Are There Any Iraqis in Iraq? Reflecting on the results of the March 2010 Iraqi national elections, a columnist for the *New York Times* wrote: "The aftermath of the vote . . . has emphasized that Iraq has not overcome its ethnic and sectarian divisions. Its newly elected political leaders—at times seemingly more divided than the populace—have been unable to form a government and choose a new prime minister" (Arango 2010).

Since the U.S. invasion and occupation of Iraq in 2003, news reports have featured stories of ethnic violence among Sunni, Shia, and Kurds—violence that the media portrays as the true obstacle to democracy and peace. The front pages of newspapers and the leads on evening news tell stories of seemingly endless and senseless suicide bombings, roadside explosives, armed militias, kidnappings, and assassinations. Elections are held, but the elected officials,

MAP 7.7
Iraq

torn by intense ethnic, religious, and political differences, are unable to form a functioning government. In the same way that the Western press typically reports what it describes as ethnic conflicts around the world—whether in Rwanda, Sudan, Sri Lanka, India, or the former Yugoslavia—deep and long-standing ethnic and religious cleavages in Iraq are blamed for an environment in which civil war is almost inevitable.

Why, after so many years of nation building with U.S. economic and military support, have the Iraqi people been unable to form a strong government and stop the violence? Aren't there any Iraqis in Iraq—people who would put the country first, ahead of other ethnic or religious differences?

As anthropologists, we are extremely interested in the formation of ethnicity, the way it is organized for political purposes, and the transformation of local identification with a particular ethnic group into a spirit of nationalism that seeks to create a nation-state as its full expression. Let's dig deeper into the complexities of ethnicity, religion, nationalism, and politics in Iraq.

Iraq does not have an ancient history as a nation. Although cities such as Baghdad have an ancient history in the region of Mesopotamia, sometimes called the "cradle of civilization," the country of Iraq did not exist before World War I. Even then, Iraq was not formed through local initiative. A secret treaty between France and Great Britain (the Sykes-Picot Agreement), signed during World War I, carved up their opponent, the Ottoman Empire, to form many of the countries we find in the Middle East today. The two European powers, with Russia's consent, drew national borders—including those of present-day Iraq—to meet their needs for economic access, trade routes, and political control. The powers mapped out these borders with little regard for the history, politics, religions, and ethnic makeup of the local populations.

With a mandate from the new League of Nations in 1920, the British established a monarchical government in the new state of Iraq and recruited and empowered leaders from the minority Sunni population to run the government. Members of the Shia and Kurd populations, excluded from leadership roles in the government, actively fought for independence from British colonial occupation. Britain subsequently granted full independence to Iraq in 1932 (with the exception of another brief military occupation during World War II), but the Sunni minority retained control of the government until the fall of Saddam Hussein in 2003.

After the U.S. military occupied Iraq in 2003, the people of Iraq inherited a collapsed state structure and confronted the prospects of "nation building" in a country under foreign occupation that had experienced decades of state-sponsored violence. Yet media representations of Iraq consistently traced its problems to the roots of ethnic conflict. Social scientists from many fields question these simple storylines that portray deep ethnic and religious hatreds as the cause of Iraq's current difficulties (Ericksen 2010). Ethnicity, they warn, should never be seen that simply or monolithically. A more careful examination may find that (1) ethnic and religious lines are not drawn so clearly, and (2) other identities based on factors such as region, family, and class—even international relations—may also play key roles in the unfolding of events. With a weak state unable to provide security to its population, people turn to other strategies for mobilizing support, safety, and the means for achieving a livelihood (Eller 1999).

Sports and National Identity in Argentina As discussed in the chapter opener, sports are more than just a game. Sports are a venue for creating and negotiating personal and national identity, imagining one's community, and inventing traditions (MacClancy 1996). In *Masculinities: Football, Polo and the Tango in Argentina* (1999), anthropologist Eduardo Archetti suggests that football (called soccer in the United States)—and, to a lesser extent, polo and the tango—has been key to the making of the Argentine national identity.

Argentina began as a country of immigrants. Between 1870 and 1914—at the same time that the United States experienced massive waves of immigration—six million European immigrants, rich and poor, arrived in Argentina. Most came from Italy and Spain, but together the newcomers represented dozens of European ethnic groups and nationalities all looking for a fresh start on the other side of the Atlantic Ocean. Thus, Argentina's rural and urban areas became places of intense ethnic and cultural mixing. Buenos Aires, the capital city, was completely transformed. What had been a premodern city on the edges of the world economy became a global, cosmopolitan center full of cultural connections and dislocations where Argentina intersected with the world. Imagining a national community with a sense of cohesion, connection, and identity out of this ethnic and cultural diversity would not be easy. Soccer would play a key role in the transformation. Archetti suggests that as Argentinians reinvented soccer, they invented themselves.

British immigrants had brought soccer to Argentina in the nineteenth century. The sport became so popular that by the 1920s, Argentina had established itself as a world soccer leader. In a few decades, soccer had been transformed from a foreign import to a national obsession, played with a unique style and passion.

Today football is the national sport, a passion that cuts across boundaries of class, region, race, and ethnic status. The soccer exploits of Argentina's local

MAP 7.8
Argentina

Haley Duschinski

For more than fifteen years, anthropologist Haley Duschinski has been conducting research on the ongoing conflict in Kashmir Valley, the homeland of the Kashmiri ethnic community. Located high in the Himalayas on the disputed border between India and Pakistan, Kashmir has become the most densely militarized zone in the world. More than 500,000 Indian security forces patrol the towns and villages, stationed in sandbag bunkers and sprawling camps as a massive popular uprising of Kashmiris resists Indian rule. Strikes, street protests, funeral processions, stone pelting, curfews, and tear gassing are everyday occurrences. And the use of lethal force by Indian security personnel against civilians—including human rights abuses, extrajudicial killing, disappearance, rape, and torture—has become commonplace. As Duschinski notes, "The militarization of Kashmiri society is absolutely pervasive—both in terms of the constant presence of the troops, and also in the way in which their presence has shaped all aspects of life."

Duschinski's long-term research in Kashmir has closely followed the shifting strategies of an independence movement to draw on notions of shared ethnic Kashmiri identity to mobilize for self-determination against the rule of the Indian state.

"There is a new generation of Kashmiris—the 1990s generation—who have grown up knowing only these conditions of state violence, crackdown, and protest. These young people are at the forefront of the movement today, driving it forward. Their ethnic identity—what it means for them to be Kashmiri—is largely defined by their shared experience of struggling against oppression, their shared experience of having to fight for the right to determine their own political futures. And they are developing different creative forms to articulate their demands and to express the complex realities of what it means to live life under occupation."

Their creative resistance strategies include everything from stone pelting at security forces, which is particular to young people on the streets, to protest demonstrations, mock trials and tribunals, documentation projects, and all kinds of artistic expressions. The movement now includes Kashmir's first rapper, MC Kash; its first novelist to reach a wide Western audience, Mirza Waheed; and its first graphic novelist, Malik Sajad. Kashmiri youth are also going into academia, including a new wave of Kashmiri graduate students studying anthropology at universities in India, the United Kingdom, and the United States.

In the last few years Kashmir activists have sought to engage an international audience, hoping to build international support for their movement. "Kashmiris largely reject the legitimacy of the Indian state in their homeland. Under the emergency laws, the state has been carrying out violence against them. The question is, How should people seek redress? Their only alternative has been to make legal appeals to the very state that has been respon-

Anthropologist Haley Duschinski during fieldwork in Srinagar, Kashmir Valley sible for carrying out the violations in the first place. And they do—they fight these human rights cases in the courts. I track these legal battles as part of my fieldwork. But they also recognize that the international community is another potential audience for their complaints and one that might be able to apply moral pressure on the Indian state to respond, not only to the legal claims but also to the political claims about the future of the region.

"India and Pakistan have pursued various forms of dialogue regarding the Kashmir conflict over the decades, but Kashmiris have had a hard time making the case that they should have a seat at that table, that their voices should be heard. Anthropology, by its nature, foregrounds and privileges the needs, priorities, and concerns of local people. This has real-world relevance in conflict situations, where people's local perspectives are often overlooked or seen as secondary to larger national security or geopolitical concerns.

What drew Duschinski, a native of a small town in South Carolina, to become interested in Kashmir? "The local economy of my hometown was completely dominated by a major nuclear weapons production site built in the 1950s and active throughout the Cold War. In high school, I became very politically active in opposition to it. It was part of my life from a very young age, which meant that I grew up always thinking about the state capacity for mass violence, thinking about how our national security program shapes people's lives, and thinking about my responsibilities as a U.S. citizen to my own country and to the rest of the world.

"I've always struggled to make sense of state violence in my own society, including direct violence of warfare as well as indirect violence of institutionalized racism, discrimination, and inequality that are structured into our democratic system. This led me, in college, to develop an interest in India—which is, after all, the world's largest democracy. Learning about political processes in India, especially patterns of state oppression and local community forms of resistance, helps me understand similar dynamics in my own society more clearly."

Duschinski relates the practice of anthropology to developing what the cultural critic Edward Said has called "wakefulness": "For me, this wakefulness comes from a fundamental commitment to the project of ethnography, which is grounded in participant observation. It comes through training yourself to live on the threshold between insider and outsider status so that you're fully participating in the world around you, but you're always constantly observing it, analyzing it, and critiquing it. You have to train your mind to see the world that way. You have to train your body to inhabit that space. Participant observation is not just a tool that we use during fieldwork. It becomes part of your way of being in the world.

"Wakefulness is about living in that state of constant awareness—and not just passively being there, but owning it, wanting to see the world against the grain, and being willing to describe what you see. This carries certain risks because it often means analyzing and interpreting situations in ways that run counter to dominant ideologies and the status quo. There's a revolutionary potential embedded in the heart of anthropology. And I think this is why many Kashmiri students appreciate the project of anthropology. Their homeland is a contested border territory, and they've grown up seeing the world from the margins, from the peripheries. The way they see the world does not fit neatly into nationalist narratives or dominant discourses. Instead, it fundamentally challenges them. Anthropology legitimizes that alternative standpoint, privileges it, calls for it. Anthropology trains you to inhabit that space and live your life there—awake."

FIGURE 7.11 Argentinian boys play soccer in a *potrero*—an outdoor lot. Has soccer helped Argentina became a nation?

and national teams are told and retold in living rooms, at bars, and at pickup games, and they are frequent topics in the press and popular novels. When the national team competes in tournaments abroad, or when players travel to perform for club teams elsewhere in the world, football becomes not only a forum for establishing a national identity but also a symbolic arena for representing Argentina and its citizens on the world stage.

When asked, Argentinians say that the most successful players and teams are those that faithfully mirror the authentic national style. This particular brand they trace to the *potrero*—the empty and uneven lots of confined outdoor spaces where neighborhood boys play after school without teachers or coaches. There one controls the ball by creative dribbling. In this unique social and spatial context, Argentina's boys develop the style of soccer that is unique to their country—a style not of efficiency, practicality, results, force, and goals, but of creativity, imagination, spontaneity, improvisation, inventiveness, and freedom. This style—the creation of beauty, joy, elegance, and the unexpected, the creation of the beautiful game—has become a symbolic expression of the national capabilities and potential of the Argentinian people.

As globalization creates flows of people, ideas, goods, and images across borders and builds linkages among local communities worldwide, we might anticipate that ethnicity and nationalism—which are associated with local and national identities—would have less capacity to shape people's lives and influence the way people make decisions. Instead, in many parts of the world we see an intensification of ethnic and national identities and related conflicts. Understanding the processes through which ethnicity and nationalism are imagined and mobilized and their traditions invented, often over relatively short periods, can provide a set of tools for analyzing the role of ethnicity in our world today.

Thinking Like an Anthropologist: Who Is an American?
In the opening story of the World Cup—one of the most global of all sporting events—and in the ethnographic examples throughout the chapter, we have seen how ethnic identity and nationalism continue to be imagined, built, nurtured, taught, learned, promoted, negotiated, and contested. And we have explored an anthropological perspective on three questions that connect the concepts of ethnicity and nationalism:

- What does "ethnicity" mean to anthropologists?
- How is ethnicity created and put in motion?
- What is the relationship of ethnicity to the nation?

Few of us are aware of the role of ethnicity and nationalism in our lives or how our culture works to promote them. As you learn to think like an anthropologist yourself, can you begin to see the process of ethnic identity construction at work in your own life and in the major debates of the culture that surrounds you? Consider these recent debates about who is and who is not an American:

- Despite an official "certificate of live birth" and other clear evidence that President Obama was born in the state of Hawaii on August 4, 1961, more than 25 percent of Americans surveyed in an August 2010 poll by the Pew Research Center claim that he is not a U.S. citizen. How is that possible?
- Some leading politicians want to change the Fourteenth Amendment of the U.S. Constitution. The amendment was passed after the Civil War to protect African Americans by ensuring that anyone born in the United States is granted full rights of citizenship. "Anchor babies," children born in the United States to Hispanic parents who are undocumented immigrants, are the target of these recent suggested changes to the Constitution. Some people fear that these babies are being "dropped as an anchor" so their parents can become citizens when their child attains the age of twenty-one. Do you think the U.S. Constitution should be amended to address this issue? Or is this debate simply a substitute for a larger struggle over who belongs to U.S. culture and who does not? How should a child's nationality and citizenship be defined?
- Plans to build an Islamic community center in lower Manhattan burst into the national awareness in August 2010. The center's organizers intended it as a place for healing and reconciliation after the tragedy of September 11 and as a symbol of American Muslims' determination to overcome the image of Islam as a violent religion. But certain enraged politicians denounced what they called the "Ground Zero mosque," demanding that it be stopped or moved away from Ground Zero. What role do ethno-political entrepreneurs play in an attempt to define Muslims as ethnic outsiders in the United States?

After reading this chapter, you should be better prepared with the anthropological tools to understand the ways ethnicity and nationalism work in your life and in your imagined communities—whether they are built around family, religion, hometown, ethnic group, or nation-state.

Key Terms
ethnicity (p. 240)
origin myth (p. 241)
ethnic boundary marker (p. 242)

genocide (p. 242)

situational negotiation of identity (p. 242)

ethnic cleansing (p. 248)

melting pot (p. 253)

assimilation (p. 253)

multiculturalism (p. 254)

state (p. 254)

nation-state (p. 254)

nation (p. 254)

nationalism (p. 255)

imagined community (p. 255)

For Further Exploration

Bloomberg, Michael. 2010. "Mayor Bloomberg Discusses the Landmarks Preservation Commission Vote on 45-47 Park Place." www.youtube.com/watch?v=kXm_fUDfJZQ&feature=related. The New York City mayor speaks about the proposed mosque and community center near the former World Trade Center site.

Bringa, Tone. 1993. *Bosnia: We Are All Neighbors.* Granada Television. Film of a Bosnian village studied by anthropologist Bringa before and after ethnic cleansing in 1993.

Bringa, Tone, and Peter Loizos. 2002. *Returning Home: Revival of a Bosnian Village.* Sage Film & Video (Sarajevo). Returning refugees attempt to restore community in their Bosnian village.

Daily Show with Jon Stewart. 2010, August 3. www.thedailyshow.com/watch/tue-august-3-2010/born-in-the-u-s-a-/. Segment on anchor babies, U.S. immigration, nationalism, and citizenship.

Gandhi. 1982. Goldcrest Films. Biographical film that includes anticolonial efforts to build a united India; the devastating strife between Hindus and Muslims; and the partition of India, Pakistan, and later Bangladesh.

Gourevitch, Philip. 1999. *We Wish to Inform You That Tomorrow We Will Be Killed with Our Families: Stories from Rwanda.* New York: Macmillan Picador.

Hotel Rwanda. 2005. Lions Gate Entertainment and United Artists. Movie about the dramatic rescue of Rwandans during the 1994 genocide.

United Nations. 1948. "Convention on the Prevention and Punishment of the Crime of Genocide." December 9. www.un.org/millennium/law/iv-1.htm.

Zinn, Howard. 2005. *A People's History of the United States: 1492–Present,* rev. ed. New York: Harper. A fresh look at American history and its origin myths.

Why are women underrepresented in the U.S. information technology field? The nonprofit group Girls Who Code wants to address the imbalance by teaching teenage girls to write computer code.

p. 272

p. 274

p. 279

p. 287

p. 292

p. 303

CHAPTER 8

Gender

In May 2012, Ellen Pao filed a sexual harassment and discrimination lawsuit against Kleiner Perkins Caufield & Byers (KPCB), a leading Silicon Valley venture capital firm where she had been a partner since 2005. Pao, a graduate of Princeton University, Harvard Business School, and Harvard Law School, claimed that in addition to experiencing unwanted sexual advances (followed by retaliation when she complained), she and other women at KPCB were consistently passed over for promotions and given a smaller share of corporate profits in comparison to the firm's male partners. Rather than highlighting an isolated incident, Pao's lawsuit illuminates patterns in gender dynamics in Silicon Valley and in the information technology industry as a whole. Despite KPCB's reputation for promoting women's corporate leadership, of thirty-eight investment partners in 2012, only nine were women. Only six of the top one hundred technology company chief executives were women. Nationally, only 25 percent of software engineers were women (Perlroth 2012).

The National Center for Women and Information Technology (2012) reports that women are underrepresented throughout the U.S. information technology field. Although 57 percent of all U.S. college graduates in 2010 were women, they held only 18 percent of degrees in computer and information sciences, down from 37 percent in 1985. Overall, women constituted only 25 percent of the computing workforce in 2011. These numbers are more striking when correlated with race: only 3 percent of the computing workforce comprised African American women; 4 percent Asian American women; and 1 percent Hispanic women.

Why are women underrepresented in jobs related to computers and information technology? How have these patterns in employment, pay, and promotion in Silicon Valley come about? What are the implications of these patterns for the lives and work of women and men? Attention to these questions of gender—that is, the characteristics associated with being a woman or man in a particular culture—is central to the practice of anthropology.

Since the pioneering work of Margaret Mead challenged U.S. cultural assumptions about human sexuality and gender roles (see Chapter 3), anthropologists, especially feminist anthropologists, have been at the forefront of attempts to bring the tools and analysis of anthropology to bear on crucial contemporary debates, social movements, and political struggles. Over the last forty years, **gender studies**—research into understanding who we are as men and women—has become one of the most significant subfields of anthropology. Indeed, anthropologists consider the ways in which gender is constructed as a central element in every aspect of human culture, including sexuality, health, family, religion, economics, politics, sports, and individual identity formation.

As we have seen throughout this book, people create diverse cultures with fluid categories to define complex aspects of the human experience. The same holds true for gender. Even biological sex is far more fluid and complex than people are taught. As we will see later in this chapter, nature creates diversity, not rigid categories. As globalization transforms gender roles and gender relations on both the local level and a global scale, anthropologists play an essential role in mapping the changing gender terrain of the modern world. In this chapter we will explore these issues in more detail:

- Are men and women born or made?
- Are there more than two sexes?
- How do anthropologists explore the relationship between gender and power?
- How is globalization transforming women's lives?

By the end of this chapter, you will be better prepared to understand the role that sex and gender play in the culture around you, including in the classroom, family, workplace, place of worship, and at the ballot box. You will also be able to apply anthropological insights into gender issues as they emerge in your own life—insights that will serve you well as boyfriends or girlfriends, spouses, parents, students, teachers, workers, managers, and community leaders in our increasingly global world.

gender studies: Research into the cultural construction of masculinity and femininity across cultures as flexible, complex, and historically and culturally constructed categories.

Are Men and Women Born or Made?

"That's just the way guys are," some women sigh when a man says or does some stereotypical "man" thing. "Women!" a man may exclaim, hands in the air, as if all the other guys in the room know exactly what he means. But what *do* they mean? Is there some essential male or female nature that differentially shapes the personalities, emotions, patterns of personal relationships, career choices, leadership styles, and economic and political engagements of women and men?

Distinguishing between Sex and Gender

Much of what we stereotypically consider to be "natural" male or female behavior—driven by biology—might turn out, upon more careful inspection, to be imposed by cultural expectations of how men and women should behave. To help explore the relationship between the biological and cultural aspects of being men and women, anthropologists distinguish between sex and gender. **Sex**, from an anthropological viewpoint, refers to the observable physical differences between male and female human beings, especially the biological differences related to human reproduction. **Gender** is composed of the expectations of thought and behavior that each culture assigns to people of different sexes.

sex: The observable physical differences between male and female, especially biological expressions related to human reproduction.

gender: The expectations of thought and behavior that each culture assigns to people of different sexes.

Historically, biological science has tended to create distinct mental maps of reality for male and female anatomy. Three primary factors have generally been considered in determining biological sex: (1) genitalia, (2) gonads (testes and ovaries, which produce different hormones), and (3) chromosome patterns (women have two X chromosomes; men have one X and one Y). Within this context, human males and females are said to display **sexual dimorphism**—that is, they differ physically in primary sexual characteristics as well as in secondary sexual characteristics such as breast size, hair distribution, and pitch of voice. Men and women on average also differ in weight, height, and strength. An average man is heavier, taller, and stronger than an average woman. Women on average have more long-term physical endurance and live longer.

sexual dimorphism: The phenotypic differences between males and females of the same species.

It is important to note, however, that in comparison to other animal species, human sexual dimorphism, particularly with regard to body size and voice timbre, is relatively modest (Fedigan 1982). On average, human males (U.S. average, 190 pounds) weigh about 15 percent more than females (U.S. average, 163 pounds) (Ogden et al. 2004). In comparison, male gorillas on average are double the size of female gorillas (Cawthon Lang 2005). In an extreme

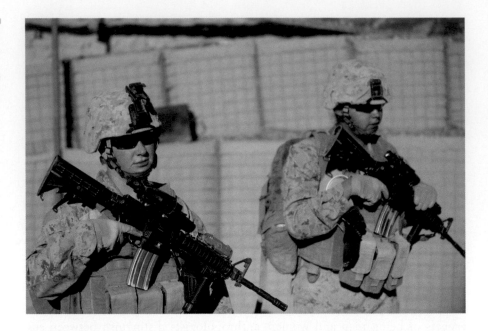

FIGURE 8.1 Gender roles, even those stereotypically associated with male strength and aggression, are in flux across the globe. Here, two women in the U.S. military patrol the front lines in Helmand Province, Afghanistan.

case of sexual dimorphism, among deep-sea anglerfish (*Cryptopasaras couesi*), the female can weigh as much as 10 kilograms (or 10,000 grams), whereas the male weighs only about 150 grams—1.5 percent the size of the females. Male anglerfish fuse their mouths to a female's skin and then gradually atrophy: they lose their digestive organs, brain, heart, and eyes, eventually becoming nothing more than a pair of gonads that release sperm in response to the female's egg release (Pietsch 1975).

Sexual dimorphism among humans is far from absolute. In fact, human male and female bodies are much more similar than different. Many biological characteristics associated with human sexual dimorphism fall along a continuum—a range—in which men and women overlap significantly. Not all men are taller than all women, though many are. Not all women live longer than all men, though most do. And as we will see later in this chapter, even primary characteristics of biological sex do not always fit into the two assumed categories of male and female.

Cross-cultural anthropological research challenges the assumed links between biology and behavior. Knowing a person's biological sex does not enable us to predict what roles that person will play in a given culture. In some cultures, people with two X chromosomes do most of the cooking, farming, public speaking, and ritual activity; in others, people with one X and one Y chromosome fill those roles. Alternatively, the tasks may be done by both but stratified by power and prestige. In many Western cultures, for instance, both XX and XY cook. But women tend to cook in the home, while men predominate as restaurant chefs. Clearly, this is not a biologically driven division of labor. What could be the cultural reasons?

Even roles stereotypically associated with male strength and aggression are in flux today. Women do heavy labor—like the women of Plachimada in this book's opening chapter who rise early to carry water drums miles from the well to their homes. In addition, the predominance of men in violence and warfare is shifting as militaries in many parts of the world rely on women soldiers to fly remote-controlled predator drones, launch missiles, and engage in firefights on the front lines of battle. Because biology cannot predict the roles that men and women play in a given culture, anthropologists consider how gender is constructed culture by culture, and they explore the implications of those constructions for the men and women in each context.

The Cultural Construction of Gender

Humans are born with biological sex, but we learn to be women and men. From the moment of birth we begin to learn culture, including how to walk, talk, eat, dress, think, practice religion, raise children, respond to violence, and express our emotions like a man or a woman (Mauss 1979). We learn what kinds of behavior are perceived as masculine or feminine. Thus, anthropologists refer to the **cultural construction of gender**.

Family, friends, the media, doctors, educational institutions, religious communities, sports, and law all enculturate us with a sense of gender that becomes normative and seems natural. For example, parents "do gender" with their children. They assign them boy or girl names; dress them in appropriately gendered clothing, colors, and jewelry; and give them the "right" haircuts. Parents even speak to their boy and girl children in different tones of voice. As we see gender being performed all around us, we learn to perform it in our turn. In these ways gender is taught, learned, and enforced.

Over a lifetime, gender becomes a powerful, and mostly invisible, framework that shapes the way we see ourselves and others (Bern 1981, 1983). Our relationships with others become an elaborate gendered dance of playing, dating, mating, parenting, and loving that reinforces our learned ideas of masculinity and femininity and establishes differing roles and expectations. Gender is also a potent cultural system through which we organize our collective lives, not necessarily on the basis of merit or skill but on the constructed categories of what it means to be a man or a woman (Rubin 1975; Lorber 1994; Cohen 2001; Bonvillain 2007; Brettell and Sargent 2009).

The following sections describe several ethnographic studies that explore the cultural construction of gender.

Teaching Gender in the United States: Boys, Girls, and Youth Sports Sports is a key cultural arena in which individuals learn gender roles. A study of young boys and girls playing co-ed T-ball provides insights into how gender in the United States is subtly and not-so-subtly taught, learned, and enforced through

cultural construction of gender: The ways humans learn to behave as a man or woman and to recognize behaviors as masculine or feminine within their cultural context.

Nature or Nurture?

Try this exercise, which aims to challenge your assumptions about how biology and culture—sometimes called nature and nurture—interact to shape us as men and women.

Write down the first things that come to mind in response to these questions: Women, if you woke up tomorrow and you were a man, how would your life be different? Men, if you woke up tomorrow as a woman, how would your life be different? Think about it. Start from the minute you wake up. Trace your morning routine, what you would wear, what you would eat, what you would do in the bathroom, what you would experience at school or the office, what would happen after work. Would suddenly being of the opposite sex change what you could normally do or say, or where you could go? Would people respond to you differently? Which differences would be determined by the change in your biology, and which ones by cultural expectations of what it means to be a man or a woman?

Women, if you woke up tomorrow and found that you were a man, how would your day be different?

youth sports (Landers and Fine 1996). T-ball is the precursor to baseball in which kids hit a ball off a stationary, upright plastic stick (a tee) rather than a ball thrown from a pitcher.

Landers and Fine found that T-ball coaches established a hierarchy of opportunity, training, and encouragement that favored boys over girls. Boys consistently received more playing time than girls, played positions (such as shortstop or first base) that provided more opportunities to touch the ball and develop their skills, and had more opportunities to practice hitting the ball at the plate. Boys frequently received coaching advice, while girls' mistakes went uncorrected. Parents and other players supported this hierarchy of training and opportunity and, along with the coaches, offered less or more encouragement along gender lines. For example, boys received more words of praise for their successes. These hierarchies were apparent not only between boys and girls, but within gendered groups as well. Among the boys, praise and opportunity were

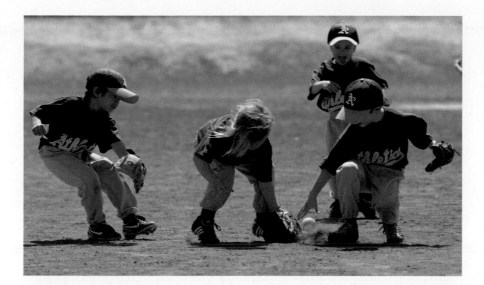

unequally distributed: those who were already stronger, faster, better coordinated, or more advanced in baseball skills were favored over those who were not as advanced. Moving beyond the T-ball experience, the researchers noted that ideal forms of masculinity and manliness are taught, learned, and enforced on the baseball field as well, promoting aggressiveness, assertiveness, competitiveness, physical strength and skill, and a drive to succeed and win (Landers and Fine 1996).

Did you ever participate in youth sports, either in the United States or in another country? If so, what was your experience like? Did your parents sign you up for certain sports—basketball, soccer, lacrosse, football, wrestling, ice hockey, dance, gymnastics, figure skating, cheerleading? If so, what role might their ideas of gender have played in their choice? Landers and Fine's study suggests that attributes stereotypically associated with boys such as athleticism, assertiveness, aggression, strength, and competitiveness are actively constructed along gender lines through a wide variety of youth sports. In considering their study, can you see the ramifications of such gender training on individuals' attitudes and behaviors as they become adults with responsible roles in family, work, and politics?

While recognizing the physical differences between men and women—modest as they are when considering the diversity of the whole human population—how do we factor in the role of culture in something like sports and athleticism? Gender enculturation in sports and physical play begins early and happens in varied settings. I remember taking my toddler son to the playground and watching as other parents encouraged their little boys to run, climb, and jump while urging their little girls to play nicely in the sandbox. Starting in everyday settings like this, perhaps we can begin to imagine the cumulative effects of parental expectations, peer pressure, and media images on girls' motivation to engage in intense physical activity and competition. As a result, sports may reflect less about real physical differences in speed, endurance, and strength and more about how a given culture constructs and maintains gender and sex norms. Perhaps becoming a world-class athlete depends more on opportunity, encouragement, coaching, nutrition, training facilities, and wealth than on being a man or a woman.

Today, as training and opportunities increase, women are closing the performance gap with men in many sports. But the persistence of inequality throughout sports culture precludes an accurate comparison between women and men athletes at the current time.

Constructing Masculinity in a U.S. High School Since the 1970s, gender studies have focused primarily on women. Recent studies, however, have begun to explore the gender construction of male identity as well as the broader construction of masculinity. The ethnography described here touches on several key aspects of this complex process.

C. J. Pascoe's ethnography *Dude, You're a Fag* (2007) explores the construction of gender—and particularly masculinity—in a suburban, working-class, racially diverse high school in north-central California. Calling someone a fag, what Pascoe calls "fag discourse," occurred almost exclusively among white male students in a daily banter of teasing, bullying, and harassment. Basing her conclusions on interviews with students, Pascoe found that calling someone a fag was not about whether someone was or was not gay; instead, it was directed at guys who danced like girls, cared about their clothing, seemed too emotional, or did something incompetent. In other words, white male students directed the epithet at other males who were not considered sufficiently masculine. Gay guys were tolerated as long as they were not effeminate, as long as they could throw a football around. Among the teenagers in Pascoe's study, fag discourse became a powerful tool for enforcing the boundaries of masculinity—a disciplinary mechanism for making sure "boys are boys" through the fear of abuse or violence.

Moreover, Pascoe points out that masculinity is not always associated with men. Girls can act masculine as well. She describes a group of "masculine" girls who play on the girls' basketball team and "perform masculinity" by the way they dress, display their sexuality, and dominate public spaces around the school. Jessie, a lesbian, is also president of the student council and homecoming queen. Her popularity appears to be related to her performance of masculinity. In these contexts, masculinity and dominance are linked to women's bodies, not to men's. Pascoe thus points out the ways in which both guys and girls can perform masculinity and girls can adopt masculinity to gain status (Bridges 2007; Calderwood 2008; Wilkins 2008).

Cartoon Commercials and the Construction of Gender

Do you still watch cartoons on Saturday morning? I want you to watch cartoons this weekend! Actually, I want you to watch the commercials in between the cartoons. These are directed at children who wake up early on Saturday mornings and plug in to the television for a few hours until their parents get up.

Children watch an average of 40,000 commercials a year on television (American Academy of Pediatrics 2006). This is a staggeringly high number, even though the Children's Television Act of 1990 limits commercials to 10.5 minutes per hour on the weekend and 12.5 minutes per hour on weekdays. (It jumps to 16 minutes per hour during prime time.) So kids watch a lot of commercials. What do they learn about gender on Saturday mornings?

When you view a commercial during this exercise, try to categorize it by target audience: boy or girl. You won't have a hard time with most. Pay attention to the gendering messages: colors, products, tone of voice of the models and voiceovers. On a recent Saturday morning I was amazed by how many commercials targeting girls were produced in pink, purple, and powder blue colors for toys ranging from bunnies to babies. Girls were encouraged to take care of small, cuddly, needy pets and babies, feed them, change their diapers, wipe their tears. Hovering mothers encouraged their efforts. The commercials for boys, in contrast, were produced in dark green, blue, and black. Loud voices, outdoor activities, motion, action,

What lessons do children learn about gender as they watch 40,000 commercials a year?

and adventure served to promote toy trucks, balls, guns, missiles, and warrior figures. What do you see when you watch? Make a list, and compare it with those of your classmates. Discuss how the media promote different constructions of gender.

If you are a male, think for a moment about how you establish and guard your own masculinity. Do your experiences have any similarities to those of the boys in Pascoe's study (either the aggressors or the targets)? Have your actions and experiences changed as you moved from high school to college? If you are a female, have you ever purposely adopted "masculine" attributes to gain status?

MAP 8.1
Mexico City

Machismo in Mexico The construction of male identity does not necessarily yield a rigid result, as the following study reveals. In *The Meanings of Macho* (2007), Matthew Gutmann examines what it means to be a man, *ser hombre*, for the men and women of a small neighborhood in Mexico City. Common conceptions of *machismo* as the concept has spread around the world feature stereotypes of self-centered, sexist, tough guys. When macho is applied to men in Latin America, especially working-class Mexican men, these stereotypes can also include insinuations of violence, drug use, infidelity, and gambling. However, Gutmann's research in a working-class community reveals a complex male world of fathers, husbands, friends, and lovers that does not fit the common stereotypes.

For the men whom Gutmann studied, machismo and masculinity constitute a shifting landscape. What it means to be a man (or a woman) in the community can depend on the particular man or woman or the particular circumstance. One of Gutmann's key informants, the elderly Don Timo, rails against effeminate men but has himself crossed stereotypical gender boundaries by actively helping to raise his children. Two other informants, Tono and Gabriel, who are tough young men, argue about a father's proper role in buying children's Christmas presents. These examples illustrate the fluidity of male identity in the population that Gutmann studied, and the quote below underscores his conclusions:

> When analyzing changing male identities in *colonias populares* in Mexico City, for example, categories that posit static differences in the male and female populations—the drunks, the loving mothers, the wife beaters, the machos, the sober family men, the submissive women—hinder one's efforts more than they assist them. Gender identities, roles and relations do not remain frozen in place, either for individuals or for groups. There is continuous contest and confusion over what constitutes male identity; it means different things to different people at different times. And sometimes different things to the same person at the same time. (Gutmann 2007, 27)

Ultimately, Guttmann discovered such complex male identities that he found it impossible to use any simple formula to describe a typical Mexican man, a Mexican urban working-class man, or a macho Mexican. Instead, he found the men in the community he studied to be working out their roles together with women, debating and deciding about household chores, child rearing, sex, the use of money, work outside the home, and the use of alcohol (Limon 1997; Parker 1999). How do these processes take place in your own family?

FIGURE 8.3 What does it mean to be macho? A couple and their baby on a stroll in Mexico City.

The Performance of Gender

Recently, anthropologists have moved from focusing on gender roles toward examining **gender performance**. Gender roles can mistakenly be seen as reflecting stable, fixed identities that fall in one of two opposite extremes—male or female. But anthropologists increasingly see gender as a continuum of behaviors that range between masculine and feminine. Rather than being something fixed in the psyche, gender is an identity that is expressed through action (Butler 1990).

My students, when identifying stereotypical masculine and feminine characteristics, often create something similar to the following list:

- *Masculine*: aggressive, physical, tough, competitive, sports oriented, testosterone driven, strong, unemotional
- *Feminine*: gentle, kind, loving, nurturing, smart, persuasive, talkative, enticing, emotional

But we know that both women and men can display any of these characteristics. And any individual may choose to display various characteristics at different times depending on the setting. A man may perform his masculinity—his gender—differently when watching football with his buddies than while out on a date.

Indeed, people regularly make choices about how they will express their gender identity, for whom, and in what context. This is why we say that gender is performed. A man may drive a truck to make a living but also gently change his baby's diapers and take her in a stroller to play in the park. A woman may

gender performance: The way gender identity is expressed through action.

FIGURE 8.4 What does this Viagra advertisement suggest about what it means to be a man in U.S. culture?

enjoy sewing dresses for her daughters but also dominate boardroom discussions as CEO of a company.

The recent explosion of Viagra use presents a dramatic example of the shifting of gender performance. Think about what it means to be a man in U.S. culture. Can an individual be a sexual, masculine man without an erection? Viagra was originally marketed to older men with erectile dysfunction. Lately, though, the target audience has shifted to include a younger generation of men perhaps dealing with performance anxiety in the face of sexually empowered women. Certainly, the marketing of Viagra fuels the culture's masculinity myth of the "real man" who is always ready for sex. But Viagra also ties ideas of men's sexual and social worth to an erect penis (Loe 2004).

Viewing gender as performance enables us to broaden our thinking beyond easy dichotomies and universal characteristics of "man" and "woman." Of course, stretching the norms of gender performance can pose challenges because the audience involved may not always accept the shifting gender roles. For example, a woman performing unorthodox gender identity may have difficulty being identified with her own gender group. Kath Weston (1991) shows how certain jobs, such as automobile repair, carry certain expectations of masculine gender performance, such as carrying a large tool case, expressing physical strength, and taking risks. The gender performance of women auto mechanics challenges common gender assumptions and may make it hard for other people to view them in the same group as women who choose more typically feminine-gendered employment.

Are men and women born or made? Anthropological research suggests that rather than looking for some essential male or female nature rooted in biology that shapes everything from personality to economic activity, a more fruitful exploration must consider the ways in which ideas of gender are constructed and performed in response to each culture's gender norms and expectations. In so doing, gender can be seen less as a naturally limiting framework and more as a set of fluid constructs and flexible choices. By taking this approach, we can more easily see that stratification based on gender is not fixed and natural; rather, it emerges as a result of decisions to arrange access to power, privilege, and resources in particular ways.

Are There More Than Two Sexes?

As our earlier discussion of sexual dimorphism indicated, primary characteristics of biological sex do not always fit neatly into the two assumed categories of male and female. Moreover, even when we can identify a person's biological sex, we cannot predict what roles that person will play in a given culture. The sections that follow make these points abundantly clear.

Case Study: Caster Semenya—Female Athletes and Gender Stereotypes

Caster Semenya (b. 1991) grew up in Masehlong, a rural South African village of subsistence farmers living in small brick houses and mud huts with little running water or electricity. In August 2009, at age 18, Semenya surprised the world by winning the gold medal in the 800-meter race at the track and field world championship sponsored by the International Association of Athletics Federations (IAAF) in Berlin, Germany. Within days, however, she was stripped of her medal and prize money. She was barred from international competition and plunged into a worldwide controversy and media frenzy.

What happened? Spurred by rumors promoted by sports blogs in South Africa, the Australian track and field association—whose runners Semenya defeated in Germany— filed charges that she was not a woman. These questions were not new. Despite her birth certificate showing the designation "female," as well as Semenya growing up as a girl and identifying herself as a woman, her powerful physique, vocal quality, and running prowess had frequently elicited questions from her competitors. According to her coach, Semenya sometimes addressed these challenges through a joint trip to the women's room with a member of the opposing team. But the IAAF investigation became an international incident. The IAAF subjected Semenya to a series of "gender tests" in which a panel of supposed experts—including a gynecologist, an endocrinologist, and,

FIGURE 8.5 South African runner Caster Semenya won a gold medal at the 2009 International Association of Athletics Federations track and field world championships in Berlin, Germany.

MAP 8.2
South Africa

surprisingly, a psychologist—attempted to determine her sex and her qualifications to run against other women in international competition. But how would they decide if she was a woman?

How would you decide?

Nearly a year later, the IAAF cleared Semenya to compete in international events against women. Her gold medal and her prize money were returned to her. The South African government had long since authorized her to compete in South Africa. The IAAF, however, refused to release the results of its inquiry, citing privacy issues. An unverified report of her gender test that was leaked to the press suggested that Semenya might have a common sex variation—specifically, female external genitalia matched with internal testes. Or perhaps she has a chromosomal variation. Like millions of others, Semenya might be intersexed, meaning that biologically she does not fit neatly into the category of male or female (Zirin and Wolf 2010).

Caster Semenya's experience raises important anthropological questions. These include not only how we ultimately distinguish between biological sexes (man and woman) but also how we understand gender—that is, what it means to be a man or a woman in a particular culture. Perhaps the uproar around Caster Semenya tells us even more about our cultural ideas of what men and women are supposed to be like—that is, it underscores the cultural construction of gender.

A Theory of Five Sexes

Biologist Anne Fausto-Sterling (1993) has proposed a theory that sheds light on the issue of fluidity versus rigidity in conceptualizing categories of biological sex and how they relate to gender identity. In her article "The Five Sexes: Why Male and Female Are Not Enough," Fausto-Sterling describes the middle ground between these two absolute categories. This middle ground encompasses a diversity of physical expressions along the continuum between male and female that once were labeled hermaphrodite and now are described as intersexed.

A review of medical data from 1955 to 2000 suggests that "approximately 1.7% of all live births do not conform to [the] ideal of absolute sex chromosome, gonadal, genital and hormonal dimorphism" (Blackless et al. 2000, 151). Using these statistics, we may estimate that millions of people are born as **intersexuals**—that is, as individuals who have some combination of male and female genitalia, gonads, and chromosomes. Fausto-Sterling identifies at least three major groups of intersexuals: Some have a balance of female and male sexual characteristics—for instance, one testis and one ovary. Others have female genitalia but testes rather than ovaries. Still others have male genitalia with ovaries rather than testes.

intersexual: An individual who is born with a combination of male and female genitalia, gonads, and/or chromosomes.

Most Western societies ignore the existence of middle sexes. More commonly, they legally require a determination between male and female at birth. Furthermore, since the 1960s, Western medicine has taken the extreme steps of attempting to "manage" intersexuality through surgery and hormonal treatments. According to the 2000 American Academy of Pediatrics policy statement on intersex surgery, "the birth of a child with ambiguous genitalia constitutes a social emergency" (American Academy of Pediatrics 2000, 138). Medical procedures—most performed before a child comes of age and can decide for him- or herself—aim to return intersexed infants to the cultural norm for heterosexual males and females, although about 90 percent of the surgeries make ambiguous male anatomy into female. Decisions are often based on the size of the penis: the smaller the phallus, the more likely the surgery will reassign the person as female. These interventions represent what French social scientist Michel Foucault ([1976] 1990) has referred to as *biopower*—the disciplining of the body through control of biological sex characteristics to meet a cultural need for clear distinctions between the sexes.

These medical interventions have faced increasing criticism both within the medical profession and among advocacy and support groups such as the Intersex Society of North America (www.isna.org) and Accord Alliance (www.accordalliance.org). Such groups have worked to educate the public and the medical community about the experiences of intersexed people, particularly about their right to control decisions about their sexual and gender identities. In 2006, *Pediatrics,* the journal of the American Academy of Pediatrics, published new guidelines that urge practicing greater patient-centered care, avoiding "elective" surgery until the person is old enough to make his or her own decision, and eliminating misleading and outdated language (such as *hermaphrodite*) that distracts from treating the whole person.

The presence of middle sexes suggests that we must reconceptualize one of our most rigid mental maps of reality—the one separating male and female. In the process, perhaps we will recognize that just as gender is culturally constructed, even our ideas of human biology have been culturally constructed as well. Acknowledgement of a diversity of physical expressions along the continuum between male and female may, in turn, allow for a less dualistic and more holistic approach to understanding the complex relationship between biology and gender.

Alternate Sexes, Alternate Genders
Cross-cultural studies show that not every culture fixes sexuality and gender in two distinct categories. Many cultures allow room for diversity. For example, even though India's dominant system for mapping sex and gender strongly emphasizes two opposite but complementary roles (male and female), Indian

culture also recognizes many alternative constructions. Hindu religion acknowledges these variations in myth, art, and ritual. Hindu myths feature androgynous and intersexed figures, and Hindu art depicts a blending of sexes and genders, including males with wombs, breasts, or pregnant bellies. In terms of Hindu ritual, the discussion below explores the role of one alternative group, known as *hijras*, in expressing gender diversity in India.

The Role of *Hijras* in Hindu Ritual *Hijras* are religious followers of the Hindu Mother Goddess, Bahuchara Mata, who is often depicted and described as transgendered. (The term **transgendered** refers to individuals whose gender identities or performances do not fit with cultural norms related to their assigned sex at birth.) Most *hijras* are born as men, though some may be intersexed. In *Neither Man nor Woman: The Hijras of India* (1998) and subsequent writing, Serena Nanda has analyzed these individuals and their role in demonstrating gender diversity.

Through ritual initiation and, for some, extensive ritual surgery to remove penis and testicles (an operation now outlawed in India), *hijras* become an alternative sex and gender. Culturally they are viewed as neither man nor woman, although they tend to adopt many characteristics of the woman's role. They dress, walk, and talk like women and may have sex with men. Because of their transgression of cultural and religious boundaries, they are at once both feared and revered. Many live in *hijra* religious communities on the margins of Hindu society. *Hijras* often face extreme discrimination in employment, housing, health, and education. Many support themselves through begging, ritual performances, and sex work. Violence against them is not uncommon, particularly against *hijra* sex workers.

At the same time, *hijras* are revered as auspicious and powerful ritual figures. They perform at weddings and at birth celebrations—particularly at the birth of a son. Not only do they bless the child and family, but they also entertain the celebrants and guests with burlesque and sexually suggestive songs, dance, and comedy. Their life in the middle ground between strong cultural norms of male and female contributes to their ritual power (Nanda 1998).

Reflecting on the place of *hijras* in Indian culture, Nanda writes:

> The *hijra* role incorporates many kinds of contradictions. *Hijras* are both men and women, yet neither men nor women; their ideal identity is that of chaste ascetics, yet they widely engage in sexual relationships; they are granted the power of the goddess and perform rituals in her name, but they are held in low esteem and are socially marginal. Yet, with all its contradictions and ambiguities,

transgender: A gender identity or performance that does not fit with cultural norms related to one's assigned sex at birth.

FIGURE 8.6 Hindu religious myth, art, and ritual acknowledge alternative gender constructions like this depiction of Ardhanari, an androgynous deity composed of Shiva and his consort Shakti.

the *hijra* role continues to be sustained by a culture in which religion still gives positive meaning to gender variance and even accords it a measure of power. (Nanda 2000, 39–40)

These insights underscore the potential for more complex understandings of sex and gender that move beyond assumptions of two discrete categories of male and female, masculine and feminine.

Two-Spirits in Native North American Cultures According to accounts written over the past one hundred years, many Native North American cultures have had traditions of gender diversity. Such traditions have allowed a gender alternative described in the anthropological literature as *berdache* and now more commonly referred to as Two-Spirits (Roscoe 1991; Williams 1992). Some of these transgendered men and women adopted roles and behaviors of the opposite gender. In certain cases, people considered them to have both feminine and masculine spirits. Often they were considered to have supernatural powers and thus held special privileges in the community.

In recent years the term *berdache*, introduced by French colonialists, has fallen into disrepute among scholars and activists. Since 1990 the term *Two-Spirits*, a direct borrowing from the Ojibwa language, has risen in popular and scholarly usage after being proposed by participants in the Third Native American/First Nations Gay and Lesbian Conference in Winnepeg, Canada. No common term exists across Native cultures for alternative gender patterns, nor are the historical or contemporary practices indicated by these terms by any means uniform. Instead, many different terms have served to represent local expressions of alternative gender and sexuality among Native Americans: for example, *winkte* (Sioux), *kwidu* (Tewa), and *nadleeh* (Navajo) (Jacobs 1997).

Current studies of sex and gender diversity in contemporary Native American communities attempt to de-romanticize the accounts offered by earlier anthropologists, historians, and other social scientists of a tolerant Native American life for those who were not heterosexual. These idealized views do not match the experiences of many gay, lesbian, transgendered, transsexual, or Two-Spirit Native Americans today who have experienced homophobia rather than acceptance both within and beyond their Native American communities (Jacobs 1997).

As stated throughout this chapter, nature creates diversity. And humans create diverse cultures. Thus, as the topics here have illustrated, biology does not fix in place gender roles, norms, performances, and patterns of interaction and stratification. Being cultural constructs, they all can change. These anthropological findings may challenge you to ask, "How might I work to expose and dismantle stereotypes and unequal structures of power

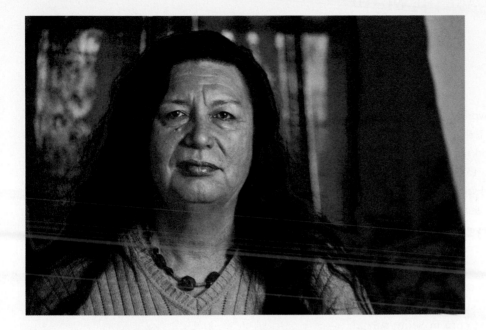

related to gender in my personal life, at school and in the workplace, and in U.S. culture more broadly?"

How Do Anthropologists Explore the Relationship Between Gender and Power?

Although gender may often be regarded as affecting individuals on a personal basis—for instance, how you negotiate relationships with people you date, study with, or work for—anthropologists also explore how gender structures relationships of power that have far-reaching effects. Understanding these processes becomes increasingly important as individuals and cultures experience heightened interaction in today's global age (Mascia-Lees 2009).

Meeting in 2000, the member states of the United Nations adopted eight Millennial Development Goals designed to eliminate the most extreme forms of global poverty and inequality:

1. Eradicate extreme poverty and hunger.
2. Achieve universal primary education.
3. Promote gender equality and empower women.
4. Reduce child mortality.
5. Improve maternal health.
6. Combat HIV/AIDS, malaria, and other diseases.
7. Ensure environmental sustainability.
8. Develop a global partnership for development.

Ida Susser

In the age of HIV / AIDS, how can women assert their right to safe sex and family planning? This is the central question of Ida Susser's most recent work in sub-Saharan Africa. Much of her life and career helps to frame the stakes of the problem. Susser is an engaged scholar working alongside communities on matters of gender, health, equality, and well-being. This work requires not only a diverse set of knowledge and skills, but also a commitment to helping those whom she studies.

From a young age, Susser became aware of social differences. "I was always interested in anthropology because of my background. I was born in South Africa under apartheid, and my parents were forced to leave for political reasons when I was age six. So I lived the life of an exiled immigrant from when I was very little.

"A nun taught me to read on the boat to England. We lived in Manchester, a section of old-fashioned houses on cobblestone streets, as old as Engels' descriptions of the same town. The sky was always foggy from industry, and the buildings and streets were black from soot. The whole experience was so different. But there in northern England I learned about working-class history. I think I approached my new neighborhood like an ethnographic experience, including when I went to visit people in their homes.

"At age twelve, my parents took me to India, and I remember vividly the misery and poverty. Then we moved to the United States when I was fifteen. It was terrible having to deal with the social cliques of my American high school!"

Susser attributes her interest in anthropology to these childhood experiences, because she sensed that this provided a way to understand social difference and inequality.

When Susser enrolled as an undergraduate at Barnard College in New York City in the late 1960s, the world was undergoing massive political upheaval, and college campuses were centers of activism and protest. Later, as a graduate student at Columbia University, "I was involved in the feminist movement, so I knew I wanted to study women's matters. At the time, Richard Nixon was talking about the Silent Majority. Who were the silent working class? Are they silent? What do they say when they're not silent? It was clear to me that the issue of gender was connected to labor, women's work. So first I went to the factory. Then I went to the neighborhood to understand how women organized their lives outside the factory."

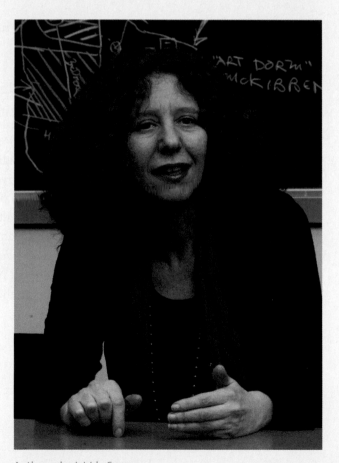

Anthropologist Ida Susser

Susser's research became the core of her first book, *Norman Street* ([1982] 2012), a classic ethnography of urban life in Brooklyn amid enormous social change. "I picked a white working-class population because the popular image was that they were patriarchal, against abortion, against welfare, against state funding. I wanted to understand where that idea of the white working class came from. This research happened at the time of the fiscal crisis in New York. It was huge. It was as big an event as 9/11. It was *the* transforming event. All kinds of services were being cut: food stamps, housing, fire engines, libraries. How could I do this work and not take that into account? So my research focused on how families fight back, how they struggle and address their problems."

Susser's engaged approach to anthropology seeks to help change the world she studies. "When I came to Brooklyn, I made it my job to support women in welfare and in organizing demonstrations, to support people raising funds, to stand up for people at City Hall. I never thought of myself as a fly on the wall. Anthropology teaches us that you learn about people by participating in their lives. From the beginning, I have believed that anthropologists are part of the community and they have to make practical decisions about what they are participating in and what they understand and what they want to engage."

Susser advises: "The task of the researcher is to document a problem and then place the issues within a broader theoretical framework. As a citizen of the world and a public intellectual, you see a problem and document. You use your disciplinary training to think through how social movements work and how they can achieve social transformation. How do you understand that on the ground? Then analyze the processes that may or may not have led to significant social changes!

"Of course, I do not believe in limiting the research to the grassroots local level. The analysis of the broader political situation requires interviews at City Hall and with corporate leaders as well as with the members of the working-class community."

In postapartheid South Africa around 1992, Susser became interested in community prevention of HIV and in gender relations. She found that no one was studying the relations of men and women in terms of HIV/AIDS. "We had a training program called Social Contexts of AIDS in 1996 in Namibia with Richard Lee and faculty at the University of Namibia, funded through a Fogarty Grant from Columbia University. We trained people to do fieldwork, to understand AIDS in context, to understand prevention, to address the question of stigma. We would observe and discuss how these issues are being addressed in Africa, what policies are in place. We worked with nursing faculty, pastors, and army personnel, and now they are running the show, doing their own research."

More recently, Susser helped to found Athena, a global network of individuals and organizations working to address the links among gender equity, human rights, and HIV/AIDS. Key to this work has been the development and distribution of a microbicide developed to protect women from contracting HIV. "Why is a microbicide so important for the gendered treatment of HIV/AIDS? The gel kills the virus but not the sperm, so women can still have children. People can still create families. One of the biggest disasters of AIDS is that it destroys the family, it destroys human relations." It is this careful analysis of the relationship of culture to health and particularly the gendered treatment of HIV/AIDS that Susser is helping to innovate.

As an engaged anthropologist, Susser uses her skills and training to bridge the gulf between the scientific community and local communities affected by HIV/AIDS. She works to analyze the social and political contexts in which people can bring about effective social change. And she works to ensure that new health and reproductive technologies fit with the desires and goals of local women and that young women have control over their reproductive lives and health.

As several of the United Nations goals indicate, improving the conditions of women held particular importance. Even though each goal included specific targets, in 2011 the United Nations Development Program reported that women's struggles for equality are far from complete.

A quick look at some statistics reveals the current contours of women's struggles worldwide: Six out of ten of the world's poorest people are women and girls. Two-thirds of all children unable to attend school are girls. The chance of dying because of pregnancy in sub-Saharan Arica is 1 in 16, but in the developed world it is only 1 in 3,800. Young women age 15 to 25 are being infected with HIV/AIDS three times faster than men in the same age group. Women are disproportionally affected by environmental degradation. And less than 16 percent of the world's parliamentarians are women (United Nations Development Programme 2013). It is not hard to conclude from these facts that gender plays a key role in power relationships on many levels and in many arenas. For a look at one anthropologist's efforts to address women's rights to safe sex and family planning in sub-Sarahan Africa, see the Anthropologists Engage the World feature on Ida Susser.

Revisiting Early Research on Male Dominance

As gender studies emerged in anthropology in the 1970s, one of the first targets of research was the apparent universality of male dominance across cultures. In searching for an explanation for what appeared to be women's universally low status, anthropologist Sherri Ortner (1974) proposed the existence of a pervasive, symbolic association of women with nature and men with culture (which was more highly valued). Ortner argued that the biological functions of reproduction, breast-feeding, and child rearing associated women with nature and placed them at a consistent disadvantage in negotiating relationships of power.

At the same time, Michelle Rosaldo (1974) saw the gender roles of men and women across cultures as being split between public and private spheres. Women, constrained by their role in reproduction, were confined to the private, or domestic, sphere—including the home, family, and childbearing. Men tended to dominate the public sphere—politics, economic exchange, and religious ritual. Because wealth and social status accrued to activities in the public sphere, men gained and maintained more power, privilege, and prestige than women did. Some scholars speculated that these patterns were rooted in the human evolutionary past—a proposition we will challenge later in this chapter. Others suggested that they might derive from men's superior physical strength. (See also Chodorow 1974.)

As scholars looked more carefully at women's lives in particular cultures, however, the picture became even more complicated. Previous assumptions about universal male dominance, including the gendered division of labor and uniformly separate spheres of activity and power, were revealed to be histori-cally inaccurate, overly simplistic in their reading of contemporary cultures, and prone to overlook the specific contexts of stratification and inequality (Leacock 1981). This was true not only for women's lives but for men's as well, where wealth, power, and prestige were stratified both within and between gender groups (Quinn 1977; Rosaldo 1980).

Feminist scholars also began to revisit earlier anthropological research. Perhaps not surprisingly, these scholars discovered the significant role of women in cultures that earlier anthropologists had reported to be uniformly dominated by men. In one important reconsideration of a classic anthropo-logical text, Annette Weiner (1976) revisited Bronislaw Malinowski's research on the Trobriand Islands, an archipelago of coral atolls just east of Papua New Guinea in the South Pacific. Malinowski (1922) had carefully detailed the Tro-briand economic system, which included a local exchange of yams and the now famous (in anthropology) Kula Ring, an elaborate exchange of cowry shell necklaces and armbands made as men circulated around the chain of islands. Later anthropological literature drew extensively on Malinowski's ethnographic descriptions of the Trobriand economy and related theories of exchange.

When Weiner reexamined the economic practices of the Trobriand Islands in the 1970s with an eye to the role of gender in shaping eco-nomic activity, she found that Malinowski's research was incomplete. In *Women of Value, Men of Renown: New Perspectives in Trobriand Exchange* (1976), Weiner describes the much more complex and significant roles of Trobriand Island women in economic exchange, kinship, and ritual life. Women engaged in an elaborate economic activity involving the exchange of bundles of banana leaves and banana fiber skirts as gifts made by women for other women in commemoration of individuals who had died. These exchanges were closely interconnected with the yam exchanges that Malinowski had described, but his failure to see the significance of the women's activity engendered an inaccurate view of them as inconsequen-tial to Trobriand economic life.

The emerging anthropological scholarship of gender in the 1970s provided new tools for Weiner to overcome gender blindness and, instead, see the full-ness of Trobriand culture. She wrote:

> Any study that does not include the role of women—as seen by women—as part of the way the society is structured remains only a partial study of that society. Whether women are publicly valued or privately secluded, whether they control politics, a range of eco-nomic commodities, or merely magic spells, they function within

MAP 8.3
Trobriand Islands

FIGURE 8.8 In contrast to Malinowski's earlier study (1922), why did feminist anthropologist Annette Weiner's research (1976) find Trobriand Island women engaged in significant economic activity, including the elaborate exchange of banana leaf bundles and banana fiber skirts (*left*), as well as participation in the yam harvest festival (*right*)?

gender stratification: An unequal distribution of power and access to a group's resources, opportunities, rights, and privileges based on gender.

that society, not as objects, but as individuals with some measure of control. (Weiner 1976, 228)

Weiner's example and admonition resonate throughout anthropology today. Attention to the processes and implications of the construction of gender has become standard for all ethnographic research. Today analysis of gender is not isolated to studies of women but occurs throughout the discipline in studies of both women and men. Furthermore, contemporary anthropological research acknowledges that gender cannot be viewed on its own but must be examined as it intersects with dynamics of race, class, and sexuality (Sacks 1989; Di Leonardo 1991; Stoler 2002; Mullings 2005; Moore 2011). This textbook reflects such an integration, including a full chapter on gender while incorporating attention to gender in all other chapters as well.

Gender Stereotypes, Gender Ideology, and Gender Stratification

The emphasis in gender studies on the cultural construction of gender challenges anthropologists to explore the dynamics of specific cultures to understand what processes serve to construct gender in each society. Today anthropologists are asking questions like these: What are the processes that create **gender stratification**—an unequal distribution of power in which gender shapes who has access to a group's resources, opportunities, rights, and privileges? What are the gender stereotypes and gender ideologies that support a gendered system of power (Brodkin 2007)?

Gender stereotypes are widely held and powerful, preconceived notions about the attributes of, differences between, and proper roles for women and men in a culture. Men, for instance, may be stereotyped as more aggressive, whereas women might be expected to be more nurturing. These stereotypes create important assumptions about what men and women might expect from one another. **Gender ideology** is a set of cultural ideas—usually stereotypical—about men's and women's essential character, capabilities, and value that consciously or unconsciously promote and justify gender stratification. Gender stereotypes and ideologies vary from culture to culture, though their effects may appear similar when viewed through a global lens.

We now consider two examples of the ways in which gender ideologies have influenced thinking in U.S. culture.

The Egg and the Sperm Emily Martin (1991) has explored the ways in which cultural ideas about gender—that is, gender ideologies—have influenced the way biologists have understood, described, and taught about human reproduction. In particular, Martin discusses what she calls the fairy tale of the egg and sperm. By examining the most widely used college biology textbooks at the time of her research, Martin found that the distinct roles of eggs and sperm were described in stereotypical ways, even if those descriptions did not match up with more recent scientific findings. The sperm was frequently described as the more active of the two:

> Take the egg and sperm. It is remarkable how "femininely" the egg behaves and how "masculinely" the sperm. The egg is seen as large and passive. It does not move or journey, but passively "is transported," "is swept," or even "drifts" along the fallopian tube. In utter contrast, sperm are small, "streamlined," and invariably active. They "deliver" their genes to the egg, "activate the developmental program of the egg," and have a "velocity" that is often remarked upon. Their tails are "strong" and efficiently powered. Together with the forces of ejaculation, they can "propel the semen into the deepest recesses of the vagina." For this they need "energy," "fuel," so that with a "whiplashlike motion and strong lurches" they can "burrow through the egg coat" and "penetrate" it. (Martin 1991, 489)

As this excerpt illustrates, the textbooks that Martin studied described the aggressive sperm as being propelled by strongly beating tails searching for the egg in competition with fellow ejaculates attacking and penetrating the protective barriers of the egg to fertilize the passive, waiting, receiving egg.

gender stereotype: A preconceived notion about the attributes of, differences between, and proper roles for men and women in a culture.

gender ideology: A set of cultural ideas, usually stereotypical, about the essential character of different genders that functions to promote and justify gender stratification.

FIGURE 8.9 Are the stories you have been told about the meeting of the sperm (blue) and egg drawn from biological research or cultural gender stereotypes?

Yet Martin cites biology research that reveals a very different dynamic. The tail of the sperm actually beats quite weakly and does not propel the sperm forward. Instead, the tail serves only to move the head from side to side enough to keep it from getting stuck on all surfaces except the egg. When the egg and the sperm do connect, the sperm is not the assertive aggressor. Rather, adhesive molecules on both create a chemical bond that keeps them attached. Then the sperm and egg work in tandem. The sperm secretes a dissolving fluid that allows it to move toward the egg's nucleus. At the same time, the egg draws the sperm in and actually moves its own nucleus to meet the sperm and better enable fertilization. Thus, rather than displaying active and passive roles, the egg and the sperm appear to be mutually active partners in an egalitarian relationship.

According to Martin, writing in the early 1990s, images of the egg and sperm found in popular and scientific writing have been commonly based on cultural stereotypes of male and female. Moreover, the scientific language of biology has promoted these gender stereotypes. Men are considered more active, vigorous, adventurous, and important than women, who are seen as passive, receptive, nurturing, and less valuable and significant. Martin warns that by reading stereotypical feminine and masculine behavior into our accounts of eggs and sperm, we enshrine these gender roles in nature—we make them seem natural. In turn, when this narrative becomes a common description of nature, it reinforces culturally constructed gender patterns, roles, and hierarchies. It is possible to express the effect of such a process of misinformation in this (mistaken) way: "Of course those characteristics of men and women are natural and normal—they show up at the very beginning with the behavior of the sperm and the egg!"

Martin also warns of the social risks of attributing human personalities to eggs and sperm—for instance, describing them like a human couple engaged in deliberate human activity to make a baby. U.S. culture continues to debate when "life" begins—at fertilization, at viability, or at birth. Describing the egg and sperm as engaged in intentional action—a key criterion for personhood—risks opening the door to more scrutiny of pregnant women and restriction of their health choices, from amniocentesis to abortion to fetal surgeries.

Man the Hunter, Woman the Gatherer Another familiar story that lies at the heart of U.S. gender ideologies is the tale of Man the Hunter, Woman the Gatherer. This fiction is frequently invoked to explain contemporary differences in gender roles by referencing the effects of human evolution. In our deep past, the story goes, human males—being larger and stronger than females—hunted to sustain themselves, their sexual partners, and their offspring (Lee and Devore 1968). Hunting required aggression, inventiveness, dominant behavior, male bonding, mobility, time away from the home, and less time with offspring—all patterns that we imagine have become hardwired into the human brain or imprinted on the human DNA. The ancient pleasure of killing animals supposedly shaped the human male psyche for aggression and violence and continues to drive men today. Women, in contrast, were gatherers (Dahlberg 1981). They collected fruits, seeds, and nuts and were more sedentary, home oriented, child centered, nurturing, cooperative, talkative, and passive.

This story, closely associated today with the field of evolutionary psychology, underlies much contemporary thinking about the origins and "naturalness" of gender relations. Contemporary gender roles, division of labor, and stratification of power, resources, rights, and privileges are assumed to have emerged directly from physical or mental differences that developed during human evolution. So, for instance, because early human males were hunters two million years ago, today modern human men prefer to go off to work, compete in the marketplace, and leave child rearing and housecleaning to the women. Quite simple, really—or is it?

Despite the popularity of this scenario in explaining contemporary male and female behavior, anthropological evidence does not support it. Yes, food foraging—hunting, scavenging, and gathering—was our ancestors' primary survival strategy for millions of years before the introduction of agriculture ten thousand years ago. Hundreds of thousands of people still live in societies where food foraging is a significant means of making a living. But no contemporary foraging societies or nonhuman primate groups display the division of labor described in the Man the Hunter, Woman the Gatherer story. In known foraging societies, women are not sedentary or passive members of the group (Stange 1997).

Though men appear to have done 70 percent of the hunting, it is not even clear that hunting was the foundational activity of early human groups. In fact, human patterns of group interaction more likely developed through the gathering and sharing of plant and seed resources. Archaeological evidence reveals that early hominid teeth were adapted to an omnivorous diet—most likely of plants, seeds, and meat, depending on what food was available in a particular season or area. Hunting would have contributed to this foundation when available, rather than the reverse. Meat may have been a part of the diet, but there is no conclusive evidence that our earliest human ancestors hunted prey themselves. Just as likely, they scavenged meat left behind by other predators (Fedigan 1986).

Anthropologists find no evidence to prove the existence of historical patterns of male dominance, including the protection of dependent women and children. Instead, contemporary food-foraging cultures and the archaeological record on gender roles reveal a highly flexible division of labor that enabled human groups to quickly adapt to changing conditions. In fact, a flexibility of roles rather than a clear division of labor may more properly define the key characteristic of male–female relationships over human evolutionary history. Based on the evidence currently available, Man the Hunter, Woman the Gatherer—such as Martin's description of the fairy tale of the egg and the sperm—appears to be a modern-day cultural myth about gender projected back onto human evolutionary history that serves to imbue contemporary gender patterns with an appearance of inevitability and "naturalness" (Fedigan 1986).

Despite the archaeological, physical, and cultural evidence that anthropologists have accumulated to debunk the Man the Hunter, Woman the Gatherer myth, still it is a daunting task to shake free of the popular idea in U.S. culture that men and women have some essential—and essentially different—nature that was shaped in our deep past. The stereotypical "boys will be boys" and "that's just a girl thing" approach to gender differences has become a powerful gender ideology, deeply ingrained in the day-to-day conversations, expectations, relationships, work patterns, pay packages, promotions, and political activities of contemporary life.

Perhaps it is simpler to believe that our genetic blueprint predetermines who we are as men and women. Perhaps this belief in the inevitability of gendered cultural patterns makes us feel better about the gender inequality structured into our cultural practices and institutions. Why try to change what is "inevitable and natural"? But if these cultural ways of thinking about gender mask the essential changeability of gender, then the burden lies more heavily on the individual, the community, and the body politic to challenge patterns of power, privilege, and prestige drawn along gender lines.

Enforcing Gender Roles and Hierarchies through Violence

Normative gender roles, identities, ideologies, and hierarchies are constructed and enforced through family attitudes, peer pressure, and institutional practices in education, media, religion, and the state. But they are also policed through gender violence. The term **gender violence** denotes forms of violence shaped by the gender identities of the people involved.

Globally, gender violence takes many forms. It includes verbal abuse, stalking, harassment, and any form of psychological or physical threat that evokes the fear of violence. Gender violence also includes rape, sex trafficking, dowry death, female infanticide, female genital cutting, and the battering and abuse of intimate partners and family members. (The latter is known in the United States as domestic violence.) In recent years, international attention has turned to gender violence during wartime, particularly sexual violence and the use of rape as a weapon of war. This form of brutality has been used against both women and men (Cahn 2004; Copelon 1995).

Whether occurring on college campuses or in the midst of war, gender violence reveals a destructive interplay between gender and other systems of power, including sexuality, race, ethnicity, and class.

Domestic Violence Domestic violence—sometimes referred to as intimate partner violence—is a widespread problem in U.S. culture. By this we refer to physical, sexual, or psychological harm by a current or former partner or spouse. Statistics reveal that one in four women in the United States will be abused by an intimate partner in her lifetime. Eighty-five percent of all domestic violence victims are women. Women are most often victimized by someone they know, not by a stranger. Women between the ages of twenty and twenty-four are at the greatest risk of nonfatal intimate partner violence. Intimate partner violence affects people of all ages, races, and classes, including both heterosexual and same-sex partners. (See the National Coalition Against Domestic Violence at www.ncadv.org, and the Domestic Violence Resource Center at www.dvrc-or.org.)

Violence or the threat of violence serves to maintain control over others in a systematic pattern of dominance. Rather than a primordial instinctive action, domestic violence is deeply rooted in cultural patterns of violence that are passed down from generation to generation. Witnessing violence against one's parents is the strongest risk factor in transmitting violent behavior from one generation to another. Studies show that boys who witness domestic violence are twice as likely to abuse their own partners or children as boys who do not witness such activity (Straus and Gelles 1990).

gender violence: Forms of violence shaped by the gender identities of the people involved.

FIGURE 8.11 The film *Boys Don't Cry* (1999) portrayed the real-life story of Brandon Teena, a transgendered man who was beaten, raped, and murdered by his male acquaintances when they discovered that he had female genitalia.

structural gender violence: gendered societal patterns of unequal access to wealth, power, and basic resources such as food, shelter, and health care that differentially affect women in particular.

Gender Violence on Campus Gender violence can occur in many contexts. For example, colleges and universities in the United States are not immune to the problems that arise at the intersection of gender, sexuality, and power. A study published by the U.S. Department of Justice reported that "young women at college face a greater risk of rape and other types of sexual assault than women in the general population or in a comparable age group" (Fisher, Cullen, and Turner 2000). In the college study, 90 percent of rapes were committed by someone the victim knew, usually a boyfriend, former boyfriend, coworker, classmate, friend, or acquaintance—a far higher percentage than in the general population. Although unwanted sexual contact and sexual threats may occur at bars, nightclubs, or work, almost all rapes and attempted rapes happen on campus. Almost 60 percent occurred in the victim's residence, 31 percent in other campus living quarters, and 10 percent in fraternities.

Violence against Gay Men and Lesbians Many gay men, lesbians, bisexuals, and transgendered individuals are targets of homophobia and violence. These types of gender violence, both verbal and physical, may serve as a form of discipline that asserts heterosexual gender norms on those who do not conform (recall the discussion of "fag discourse" earlier in this chapter). Transgendered people—those whose gender identities or performance do not fit with cultural norms related to their assigned sex at birth—are particularly vulnerable (Currah, Juang, and Minter 2006).

Structural Gender Violence In addition to interpersonal forms, anthropologists examine **structural gender violence**. This includes inequalities of wealth, power, privilege, and access to cultural resources that are stratified by gender. Poverty, hunger, and poor health impact victims' lives in violent and painful ways. The impact is often stratified along gender lines. These structural forms of gendered violence are largely invisible, rarely discussed, and too often dismissed as almost normal or inevitable (Merry 2008).

Challenging Gender Ideologies and Stratification

Women challenge and resist gender stereotypes, ideologies, inequalities, and violence directly and indirectly through creative local strategies, often building movements from the bottom up. Although lacking the global media attention or global solidarity afforded to international social movements, these local initiatives begin with women's culture-specific experiences (Abu-Lughod 2000). The following example provides a dramatic illustration of women challenging gender ideology, stratification, and violence.

Mothers of "The Disappeared" in El Salvador Between 1977 and 1992, the Central American country of El Salvador was torn by a brutal civil war. Threatened by calls for economic equality and political openness, the government unleashed military and military-related death squads in a campaign of violence and terror that targeted students, peasants, union leaders, and anyone else critical of its policies. All who expressed opposition to government policies were labeled subversive and subject to reprisal.

Over the course of the civil war the military assassinated, imprisoned, tortured, raped, and "disappeared" tens of thousands of El Salvadorans. One in every one hundred was murdered or disappeared. The late 1970s were marked by particularly brutal campaigns. Every morning, residents of the capital city awoke to the sight of dead bodies—visibly tortured—left lying in the streets or dumped on the outskirts of town by the death squads. Many were disappeared—that is, detained and never seen again.

The grassroots women's organization CO-MADRES (The Committee of Mothers and Relatives of Political Prisoners, Disappeared, and Assassinated of El Salvador) emerged against this backdrop. The committee was one of a number of "motherist" groups across Central America in which the mothers of victims mobilized for human rights and against violence. Originally founded in 1977 by nine mothers, CO-MADRES quickly grew to include teachers, workers, students, lawyers, housewives, and shopkeepers—still mostly mothers, but with a few fathers as well. CO-MADRES became one of the first groups in El Salvador to challenge the brutal actions of the government and the military.

MAP 8.4
El Salvador

Initially, the women of CO-MADRES focused on demanding information from government, military, and paramilitary groups about family members who had been incarcerated, assassinated, or disappeared. The women occupied government buildings, demonstrated in public parks and plazas, and held hunger strikes to exert pressure on the state. Searching for their missing relatives, they demanded access to prisons and prisoner lists, uncovered clandestine cemeteries, and formed alliances with international human rights groups to publicize the El Salvadoran government's atrocities.

As they became better organized, the women of CO-MADRES began to participate in movements for greater democratization, particularly demanding the inclusion of women at all levels of El Salvador's political decision-making bodies. Eventually, along with other feminist movements emerging globally, CO-MADRES began to address concerns about the prevalence of gender-based violence and rape and the absence of sex education and sexual autonomy for women in El Salvador.

CO-MADRES continued to work throughout the period of the El Salvadoran civil war despite attacks on the organization and its leaders by the government and its allies. CO-MADRES offices were bombed on multiple occasions. A majority of active CO-MADRES members and all of its leaders were detained, tortured, and raped: forty-eight were detained, five assassinated, and three disappeared. In El Salvador, rape became a common experience for the women activists of CO-MADRES and for urban and rural Salvadoran women whether they participated in a social movement or not.

CO-MADRES activist Alicia Panameno de Garcia, in an interview with anthropologist Lynn Stephen, shared how rape had become a widely used weapon of state-sponsored torture and how psychologically difficult it was to talk about it openly, even with other women victims.

ALICIA: Rape was one of those things we didn't really think about. We weren't really prepared for it happening to us. We didn't think that the military would systematically be using these practices. So the first few women were detained and they were raped and because we are taught that women are supposed to be pure, they didn't talk about that. They didn't say, "They did this to me."

L.S: They didn't talk about it?

ALICIA: Yes. But little by little we discovered it. The women started talking about it. They had to because it had consequences for their health. They needed medical assistance and when we would give people medical aid we started discovering that every one of the women had been raped. (Stephen 1995, 818)

Over time, the CO-MADRES members found that detained men were also being raped as part of their torture. The men were even more reluctant to talk about it than the women.

Eventually, CO-MADRES created a space for women to publicly discuss their experiences, to bring the sexual brutality of the military out into the open, and to talk about their fears—particularly that their husbands would abandon them. Working with other human rights organizations, the group began a process to hold the state accountable for these violations and call into question discriminatory legal codes that provided no rights to rape victims.

The story of CO-MADRES is just one example of the determined, creative, and often risk-filled efforts that women undertake across the globe to address gendered expressions of inequality, stratification, and violence. In an evolving response to their experiences in the midst of El Salvador's civil war, the women of CO-MADRES created a social movement that integrated traditional cultural expressions of femininity—ideas of motherhood, child rearing, and sacrifice for one's children—with direct confrontation of military death squads and government authorities as they demanded equality for women and sought to protect their families and their communities (Stephen 1995; Martin 1999; Molyneux 1999).

How Is Globalization Transforming Women's Lives?

Beginning in the 1980s, anthropologists turned their attention to the impact of globalization and flexible accumulation (see Chapter 12) on women and gender dynamics in local economies. At that time, women in many parts of the world were starting to migrate from rural areas to work in urban, coastal, export-oriented factories established by foreign corporations searching for cheap labor, low taxes, and few environmental regulations. As both local and national economies have continued to undergo rapid transitions, these women have had to negotiate between traditional gender expectations and the pressure to engage in wage labor to support themselves and their families (Mills 2003).

Impacts on Women in the Labor Force

Anthropological research spanning the 1980s through the early 2000s reveals that working women in various parts of the globe have experienced similar challenges at the volatile intersection of globalization and local realities (Mills 2003). The following summaries offer perspectives from Mexico, Malaysia, Cuba, Puerto Rico, the Dominican Republic, and Barbados.

Maria Patricia Fernandez-Kelly's *For We Are Sold, I and My People* (1983) provided an early picture of the incorporation of women into export-oriented factories as U.S. businesses shifted production across the Texas border to Juarez, Mexico. Though factory work in Juarez provided increased autonomy for women wage workers there, the U.S. corporations structured their employment opportunities to be irregular and short term. As a result, the factory work provided only temporary access to earnings. Fernandez-Kelly found a resulting intensification of female–male inequalities, rather than a lessening.

Aihwa Ong's *Spirits of Resistance and Capitalist Discipline* (1987) traced the experiences of rural Malaysian women who migrated to export-processing zones along the coast to manufacture electronics. This study brought to light the increasingly invasive surveillance and supervisory strategies used by management to discipline women workers in order to increase production efficiency. Ong's study also opened windows into women's resistance to exploitation: at times in the middle of the workday, women experienced episodes of spirit possession on the factory floor. Those who were possessed by a spirit often became angry and violent, screaming abuses at the factory managers and owners. Through the performance of spirit possession, these women engaged in a form of protest against their loss of humanity and autonomy on the factory floor.

Helen Safa's *Myth of the Male Breadwinner* (1995) provided a cross-cultural comparison of women's factory work in three Spanish-speaking Caribbean nations: Cuba, Puerto Rico, and the Dominican Republic. Safa explored whether women's entry into factory-based wage labor exposed them to greater exploitation as the targets of factory discipline and added to their domestic chores, or whether this work created greater autonomy, self-consciousness, and empowerment for the women. Her findings suggest that the effect of factory work on women varied according to their class, ethnicity, and culture.

Safa does suggest, however, that as women have increased their role in export processing, the primary location of patriarchy (male dominance) has shifted from the home to the workplace. Women now fall under the coercive power of the male factory owners and supervisors, in addition to having to negotiate roles and relationships with men at home.

Carla Freeman's *High Tech, High Heels* (2007) builds on the work of Fernandez-Kelly, Ong, and Safa in exploring the gendered production processes in export factories on the Caribbean island of Barbados. Women there work in the informatics industry: they do computer data entry of airline tickets and insurance claims, and they key in manuscripts for everything from romance novels to academic journals. Instead of toiling in garment or electronics sweatshops, these women enjoy working in cool, air-conditioned, modern offices. Freeman asks whether the comfortable conditions in the data-processing factories establish an improved position in the global economy for Barbadian women, or whether this new factory formation is simply another expression of women's exploitation through flexible accumulation.

Key distinctions separate the Barbadian informatics workers from those in other studies. They enjoy improved work conditions. As wives, mothers, and heads of households, rather than young, single, temporary sweatshop workers, they have won concessions from the company that include transportation, higher levels of job security, and more flexible work hours to care for their families. Freeman labels these women "pink-collar" workers because they fall between the blue-collar work done on the sweatshop factory floor and the white-collar work carried out in the higher-wage environment of the front office.

FIGURE 8.13 Globalization is reshaping the lives of working women as corporations search the world for cheap labor, low taxes, and fewer environmental restrictions. But are women reshaping globalization? *Clockwise from top left*: women labor in an automobile factory in Juarez, Mexico; an electronics factory in Penang, Malaysia; an international call center in Barbados; and a pharmaceutical plant in Puerto Rico.

MAP 8.5
Barbados

Despite the improved working conditions and social status for Barbadian women working in informatics, the company owners strive to extract maximum efficiency from them. Supervisors walk the floor and observe through glass windows to ensure continual surveillance. Managers calculate the keystrokes of each computer terminal. Wages are no higher than those of the typical sweatshop worker and in some cases are lower. The skills of data entry are not transferable to higher-wage clerical work. Women often need to take on additional work sewing, selling in the market, or working in beauty salons to support their families.

Freeman explores the ways in which the Barbadian women express their agency in the face of the informatics factory controls. These women use their status working with computers in air-conditioned offices to negotiate a different class status in the local community. They use clothing to fashion their local identities as well. Indeed, the women workers are preoccupied with fashion: they wear colorful, tailored skirt-suits with jewelry, high heels, and the latest hairstyles. With their clothes, these women perform a professional and modern gender identity that enhances their local reputations and distinguishes them from other low-wage workers in garment and textile factories.

Freeman's research adds to scholarly findings that women factory workers are not simply victims of the exploitative practices of flexible accumulation. Instead, by engaging these capitalist practices directly, women assert their own desires and goals in ways that transform the interaction between the local and the global (Richman 2001; England 2002).

Gendered Patterns of Global Migration

Globalization spurs the migration of women seeking to support themselves and their families, moving as never before within and between countries in a largely invisible flow. As revealed in the research of Fernandez-Kelly, Ong, Safa, and Freeman, tens of millions of women each year leave their homes and travel to urban areas to seek jobs in cities and export-processing factories in their own countries. Millions more leave developing countries in search of work abroad to support their families back home.

As an alternative to finding jobs in export-processing factories, many women immigrants work as nannies, cleaning ladies, maids, or home health aides in North America, Europe, Asia, the Middle East, and other developed regions. In so doing, they fill the shortage of what is known as "care work" in wealthy countries. This "global care chain" makes caregiving an international occupation in which the capacity of the world's poor—especially the world's poor women—to care is imported from the developing world to fill the expanding care deficit of the wealthy (Ehrenreich and Hochschild 2004).

Without these immigrant care workers, many other women in the developed world would be unable to go to work themselves (Hondagneu-Sotelo 2001).

Barbara Ehrenreich (Ehrenreich and Hochschild 2004) has suggested that the primary resource extracted from the world's poorer nations today is no longer oil, gold, or agricultural products. It is love. But while immigrant women care for the children and elderly of families in relatively wealthy countries, their absence creates a care deficit for their own children and elderly family members. This deficit serves to restructure the patterns of family, kinship, and care in the women's home countries (Chang 1998).

Anthropologists, whether studying gender, sexuality, kinship, race, ethnicity, religion, or any other cultural construct, seek to understand the rich diversity of human bodies and human lives, both past and present, to unlock the presuppositions that reside in mental maps of reality. As we analyze gender, we strive to unmask the structures of power that create unequal opportunities and unequal access to rights and resources along gender lines. These inequalities are far from natural, essential aspects of human life and human community. Rather, they are cultural constructs established in specific historical moments and cultural contexts. Through a careful analysis and exposure of gender as a culturally constructed system of power—not fixed and natural patterns of human relationship—anthropologists hope to participate in opening possibilities for all humans to live to their full potential.

Thinking Like an Anthropologist: Broadening Your View of the Cultural Construction of Gender

In this chapter we considered the story of Caster Semenya, the South African track star whose sex and gender became a point of international debate. As we have seen, sports are a powerful conveyor of gender norms, stereotypes, and ideologies. Through their key role in teaching boys to be boys and girls to be girls, sports illustrate the cultural construction of gender. As you think about Semenya's story, put it into perspective by reviewing the questions we have addressed in this chapter:

• Are men and women born or made?
• Are there more than two sexes?
• How do anthropologists explore the relationship between gender and power?
• How is globalization transforming women's lives?

Perhaps the controversy over Caster Semenya erupted not because of issues of biology but because she challenges the gender norms of what it means to be a male or a female, masculine or feminine. We have been taught that girls are not supposed to be so fast, strong, and muscular and that men are supposed to be the superior athletes. When women are strong, fast, aggressive, and competitive, something seems out of place—so out of place that some people may wonder if those individuals really are women.

Gender stereotypes, ideologies, and stratification create expectations and limitations on men as well. When men go against gender type—for example, when they are physically slow and noncompetitive—they can be subject to subtle jokes and not-so-subtle violence that enforces gender norms and reflects gender hierarchy among men.

In South Africa, Semenya was welcomed home like a hero, greeted by crowds at the airport, entertained by President Jacob Zuma, and honored by national hero Nelson Mandela. Sports have been central to South African politics over the last fifty years, both in the antiapartheid movement and in the struggle for national unity after the fall of the white South African government. Perhaps South Africans recognized the power to define biological norms as risky business after their experiences of being racially classified by white colonialists.

Gender performance and the response to it can be shaped by other systems of power as well. Is it possible that the challenges to Semenya drew international attention because she is an African woman from a poor rural village? Would she have been treated the same way if she were a wealthy white woman from the United States? As you utilize the anthropologist's tools from the chapters in this section on Unmasking the Structures of Power, consider how issues of gender, race, ethnicity, class, kinship, and sexuality may all intersect in the story of Caster Semenya or in any other story about sex and gender.

Key Terms

gender studies (p. 270)
sex (p. 271)
gender (p. 271)

For Further Exploration

Accord Alliance. 2013. www.accordalliance.org.

Brault, Brigitte, and the Aina Women's Filming Group. *Afghanistan Unveiled.* 2003. Women Make Movies. After the fall of the Taliban, young women document the experiences of women in Afghanistan.

Calling the Ghosts: A Story about Rape, War and Women. 1996. Directed by Mandy Jacobson and Karmen Jelincic. Bowery Productions. Jacobson and Jelincic document the experiences of women in Bosnia-Herzegovina and Croatia.

The Codes of Gender. 2009. Directed by Sut Jhally. Media Education Foundation. Jhally uncovers how contemporary advertising shapes masculine and feminine displays and poses in American popular culture.

Disappearing World TV series. 1990. "The Trobriand Islanders of Papua New Guinea." Directed by David Watson; consulting anthropologist, Annette Weiner. Granada Television International.

Ehrenreich, Barbara, and Arlie Russell Hochschild, eds. 2004. *Global Woman: Nannies, Maids, and Sex Workers in the New Economy.* New York: Holt Paperbacks.

Hondagneu-Sotelo, Pierette. 2001. *Domestica: Immigrant Workers Cleaning and Caring in the Shadows of Affluence.* Berkeley: University of California Press.

Intersex Society of North America. 2013. www.isna.org.

The Middle Sexes: Redefining He and She. 2006. HBO Undercover Video.

United Nations Development Programme. 2013. "The Millennium Development Goals: Eight Goals for 2015." www.undp.org / mdg /.

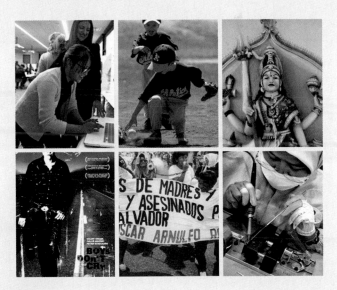

A Calvin Klein billboard uses sexuality to sell underwear.

p. 313

p. 317

p. 323

p. 327

p. 334

p. 342

CHAPTER 9
Sexuality

Sexuality is all around us in U.S. culture.

- People "do it."
- Scientists study it.
- Governments try to regulate it.
- Public school boards battle over sex education curriculums for teenagers.
- Commercials use sex to sell cars, beer, cosmetics, diamonds, and clothes.
- Pornography is the top Internet destination, constituting 25 percent of all search engine requests.
- Reality shows and daytime soap operas test the cultural boundaries of sexual innuendo, overt sex talk, and explicit sex scenes.
- Movies show glamorized young people conducting fanciful sexual relationships with little concern for the dangers of pregnancy, violence, or sexually transmitted diseases.
- Politicians battle over same-sex marriage while the courts consider its constitutional merits.
- Religious groups debate whether gay men and lesbians should be consecrated as ministers or rabbis.
- The U.S. military struggles to address the growing incidence of rape within its ranks as more women are assigned to active duty in combat zones.
- Public debates rage and anxieties soar about contraception, sexting, abortion, oral sex among teenagers, premarital sex, extramarital sex, and even whether the goal of sexuality should be procreation or pleasure.
- Erectile dysfunction drugs such as Viagra and Cialis promise sex whenever the mood strikes. (Just be sure to call your doctor if your erection lasts more than four hours!)

Sexuality is a profound aspect of human life, one that stirs intense emotions, deep anxieties, and rigorous debate. The U.S. population holds widely varying views of where sexuality originates, what constitutes appropriate expressions of sexuality, and what its fundamental purpose is. It is fair to say that our cultural norms and mental maps of reality are in great flux, and have been for several generations, in response to theological shifts, medical advances, and powerful social movements promoting the equality of women and gay, lesbian, bisexual, and transgendered individuals.

Sexuality involves more than personal choices about who our sexual partners are and what we do with them. It is also a cultural arena within which people debate ideas of what is moral, appropriate, and "natural" and use those ideas to create unequal access to society's power, privileges, and resources. Indeed, conflicts about sexuality often reveal the intersections of multiple systems of power, including those based on gender, religion, race, class, and kinship.

Anthropologists have a long but uneven history of studying human sexuality. Bronislaw Malinowski (1927, 1929) and Margaret Mead (1928, 1935), like other early anthropologists writing in the 1920s and 1930s, considered human sexuality a key to understanding the cultures they studied, so they wrote extensively about their research findings of human sexuality across cultures. Mead's work in the islands of the western Pacific challenged the assumption that U.S. attitudes about women, their gender roles, and expressions of sexuality were universal traits immutably fixed in human nature. After World War II, however, anthropological interest turned away from explicit attention to sexuality and focused instead on related issues of marriage, kinship, and the family. Since the 1970s, sexuality has reemerged as a key concern in anthropology, paralleling a rise of interest in the wider academic community spurred by the successes of the U.S. women's movement and the emergence of gay and lesbian studies (Weston 1993). Recently, anthropological scholarship has more intently considered the diverse expressions of sexuality in cultures worldwide, including Western cultures.

In this chapter we will examine the extensive body of work that anthropologists have compiled primarily in this latter period. In particular, we will consider the following questions:

- What is "natural" about human sexuality?
- What does a global perspective tell us about human sexuality?
- How has sexuality been constructed in the United States?
- How is sexuality an arena for working out relations of power?
- How does globalization influence local expressions of sexuality?

Despite all the sexuality in the air, Americans often struggle to find a common language with which to discuss it (whether in their personal lives, their families, their communities, the political arena, or the classroom) and often lack the theoretical and analytical frameworks to add depth to emotionally heated conversations. By the end of this chapter you should be able to discuss the role of nature and culture in shaping human sexuality. You should be able to recognize how norms of sexuality are created and used to organize the way cultures work. Furthermore, you should have a broader understanding of the vast diversity of human sexuality across cultures. And you should be able to incorporate anthropological insights as you seek to better understand the role of sexuality in your own life and in your relations with others.

What Is "Natural" about Human Sexuality?

Text three friends and ask them to define sexuality. You will most likely get three very different responses. Perhaps this is not surprising in a culture where sexuality is omnipresent but rarely discussed carefully. In 1998, U.S. president Bill Clinton famously said of his liaison with White House intern Monica Lewinsky, "I did not have sexual relations with that woman." He chose those words presumably because he and Lewinsky had not had intercourse. But did they have sex? Such careful word choice by a sitting president giving testimony under oath reveals the challenges of defining behavior that is not only a physiological process but also a cultural construction whose meaning can vary widely.

Consider the following data. A survey of college students in a large midwestern university, with results published in 2006, asked: "Would you say you 'had sex' with someone if the most intimate behavior you engaged in was . . . ?" The survey results showed that even college students do not agree about what "having sex" means. Kissing (2 percent) and petting (3 percent) clearly did not constitute having sex for almost all respondents. Oral "sex" (40 percent) constituted sex for many but not most. For 20 percent of respondents, anal penetration did not constitute having sex. Fully 99.5 percent of respondents indicated that vaginal intercourse did constitute having sex (Sanders and Reinisch 2006). As this study makes evident, even within one population group—college students at one university—there is disagreement over the meaning of the most physical aspects of sexual relations.

For the purposes of this chapter, we will define **sexuality** from two key perspectives. First, sexuality is the complex range of desires, beliefs, and behaviors that are related to erotic physical contact, intimacy, and pleasure. Second, sexuality is the cultural arena within which people debate ideas of what kinds of physical desires and behaviors are morally right, appropriate, and "natural" and use those ideas to create unequal access to status, power, privileges, and resources.

sexuality: The complex range of desires, beliefs, and behaviors that are related to erotic physical contact and the cultural arena within which people debate about what kinds of physical desires and behaviors are right, appropriate, and natural.

"Birds Do It, Bees Do It": The Intersection of Sexuality and Biology

The famous 1928 Broadway show tune by Cole Porter asserts, "Birds do it, bees do it. Even educated fleas do it. Let's do it, let's fall in love." Is it really that simple? Clearly, biology plays a key role in shaping sexuality, for sexuality includes distinct physiological processes. But how much of human sexuality is shaped by our nature? As we will see, exactly how our genetic inheritance shapes our desires, attractions, identities, practices, and beliefs is quite complicated and subject to heated debate.

People sometimes think that sexuality is the most "natural" thing in the world. After all, every species must reproduce or face extinction, right? Therefore, many assume that the sexual instincts and behaviors of other animals provide an indication of the natural state of human sexuality unencumbered by the overlays of culture.

Yet research reveals that human sexuality is actually a distinct outlier in the animal kingdom. In his article "The Animal with the Weirdest Sex Life" (1997), scientist and author Jared Diamond suggested that human sexuality is completely abnormal by the standards of the world's 30 million animal species and 4,300 mammal species. Diamond identified many ways in which humans differ from most other mammals, including the following examples:

- Most other mammals live individually, not in pairs, and meet only to have sex. They do not raise children together, and usually the males do not recognize their offspring or provide paternal care. In contrast, most humans engage in long-term sexual partnerships and often co-parent the couple's joint offspring.
- Most mammals engage in public sex, whereas humans, as a rule, have sex in private.
- Most mammals have sex only when the females of the species ovulate, at which time they advertise their fertility through visual signals, smells, sounds, and other changes in their behavior. Human women, however, may be receptive to sex not only during ovulation but also at other times during their menstrual cycle.
- All human women go through menopause, in which their ability to conceive children ends, long before the end of the human life cycle. But other mammals are fertile throughout their adult life, perhaps with a gradual deterioration as they age.
- Possibly most intriguing, humans, dolphins, and bonobos — a variety of ape — are the only mammals that have sex for fun rather than exclusively for reproduction. In fact, in contemporary U.S. culture, humans seem to do it mostly for fun.

FIGURE 9.1 Bonobos, dolphins, and humans are the only mammals that have sex for fun rather than exclusively for procreation.

By the standards of most mammals (including great apes, to whom we are most closely related), we humans are the sexual outliers. Despite the common belief that clues to the essentials of human sex drives and behaviors may be found in "nature," Diamond makes clear that humans have developed a sex life that lies far outside the natural framework of that of our mammal relatives. If other animals' sex lives do not provide clues to the roots of our sexuality, what can human biology tell us about the genetic and hormonal roots of sexual desire and sexual behavior?

One school of thought, which draws heavily on evolutionary biology, focuses on the ways in which human evolution has created biological drives that are embedded in the genes that shape the human brain and control the body's hormones. These drives work automatically—instinctively—to ensure the reproduction of the species. Human sexuality is thought to rely heavily on the expression of these biological drives.

Physical anthropologist Helen Fisher explores the complex biological roots of human sexuality in her book *Why We Love: The Nature and Chemistry of Romantic Love* (2004), in which she analyzes the relationship of body chemistry to human sensations of love. Fisher suggests that through evolution humans have developed a set of neurochemicals that drive an "evolutionary trajectory of loving" (93). These neurochemicals guide us through three distinct phases of falling in love: finding the right sexual partner, building a relationship, and forming an emotional attachment that will last long enough to raise a child. First, testosterone—found both in women and men—triggers the sense of excitement, desire, arousal, and craving for sexual gratification that we call lust. Then our bodies release the stimulant dopamine, and possibly norepinephrine and serotonin, to promote the feelings of romance that develop as relationships deepen. Eventually the hormones ocytocin and vasopressin generate the feelings of calm and security that are associated with a long-term partnership; Fisher calls these feelings attachment. These phases, she suggests, are built into our biological systems to ensure the reproduction of the human species, and they play key roles in shaping human sexuality.

Genetic science, despite remarkable developments that include the ability to map the human genome (the whole human genetic structure), still has limitations as a predictor of individual human sexual behavior. Yes, the frequency of certain behaviors in the human population may suggest an underlying biological component. But it is extremely difficult to directly trace links between specific genes and specific behaviors. So, for instance, despite widespread popular discussion of the topic, geneticists have not been able to identify a "straight" gene or a "gay" gene or any cluster of genes that determines sexual orientation.

Furthermore, we know that genes do not work in isolation from the environment. Our bodies and minds, which are not fully formed at birth, bear the imprint of both gene and environment. Beginning in the womb, our genes interact with the environment—the nutrients, sounds, emotions, and diseases that surround and infuse us. The exact effects of the interaction of biology and environment are extremely difficult to measure. Even within the parameters of Fisher's study, we cannot predict a particular man's level of sexual desire for a particular partner by measuring his level of testosterone. Attraction, desire, and even disinterest are not only biologically driven but also triggered by a vast array of cultural factors; these may include responses to the potential partner's

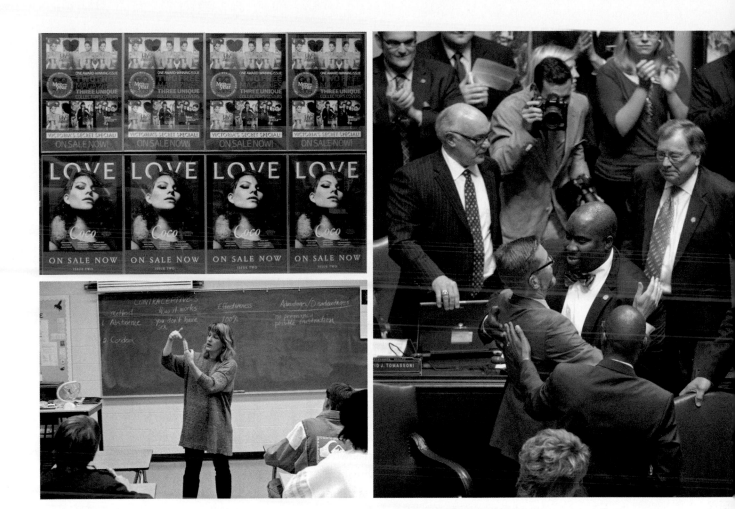

age, religion, class, race, education, and employment prospects. So, although biology clearly plays a role in human sexuality, exactly how it manifests itself in each individual and how it interacts with the environment and culture is not as clear as many popular descriptions of sexuality suggest.

Sexuality and Culture

A second school of thought, one we will consider in more detail throughout the rest of this chapter, focuses on the ways in which the people, events, and cultural environment around us shape—or construct—our sexual desires and behaviors. These feelings and actions may have roots in human evolution, but the constructionist perspective focuses on the process through which humans are enculturated from birth to channel these feelings and desires into a limited number of acceptable expressions. Culture shapes what people think is natural and normal. Parents, family, friends, doctors, religious communities, sex education classes, the media, and many other individual and institutional actors all play a role in shaping the

FIGURE 9.2 How do people, events, and the cultural environment around us shape our sexual desires and behaviors? *Clockwise from top left*: advertisements featuring sex and love; lawmakers congratulate Minnesota state senator Scott Dibble (*front left*), lead sponsor of Minnesota's gay marriage bill, after its passage, May 13, 2013; a sex education class at Kealing Junior High School, Austin, Texas.

way we express our sexuality and what those expressions mean to others. Thus, culture both guides and limits our sexual imaginations.

Constructionists also trace the ways in which, through culture, human groups arrange the diversity of human sexuality into a limited number of categories that are imagined to be discrete (such as homosexual and heterosexual, gay and straight), thereby masking the actual diversity of human expressions of sexuality. Where an individual is assigned within these categories has direct consequences for his or her life chances. Depending on the particular cultural construction of meaning surrounding human sexuality, not all sexual desires and behaviors may be considered equally acceptable. The meaning they acquire in a particular culture has the potential to affect access to social networks, social benefits, jobs, health care, and other resources (Harding 1998; Ore 2010).

It is important to note that the perspectives of evolutionary biology and cultural constructionism discussed in this section need not be mutually exclusive. Rather, they reflect different research emphases into the roots and contemporary expressions of human sexuality.

What Does a Global Perspective Tell Us about Human Sexuality?

A look at human sexuality over time and across cultures reveals significant diversity in (1) how, where, when, and with whom humans have sex, and (2) what certain sexual behaviors mean. This diversity challenges Western culture-bound notions and suggests alternative options for reinterpreting assumed cultural categories of sexuality. The discussions that follow offer examples of alternative constructions of sexuality in Suriname, Nicaragua, and Papua New Guinea.

Same-Gender "*Mati* Work" in Suriname

In the *Politics of Passion* (2006), cultural anthropologist Gloria Wekker explores the lives of black, working-class Creole women in the port city of Paramaribo, Suriname, a former Dutch colony on the northern coast of South America. Writing about the sexual choices Surinamese women make, Wekker (like Roger Lancaster and Gil Herdt in the studies described below) challenges the dominant thinking about sexual identity in Western scholarship and social movements by describing a much more flexible and inclusive approach specific to the local Paramaribo context.

Wekker's study focuses on *mati*—women who form intimate spiritual, emotional, and sexual relationships with other women. Wekker estimates that three out of four working-class black women in Paramaribo engage in "*mati* work" at some point in their lives, establishing relationships of mutual support, obligation,

MAP 9.1
Suriname

FIGURE 9.3 Women join a parade in the port city of Paramaribo, Suriname, on the northern coast of South America.

and responsibility with other women—sometimes living in the same household, sometimes separately, and often sharing in child rearing. In contrast to Western notions of fixed, "either/or" sexual identities, *mati* may engage in sexual relationships with both women and men—sometimes simultaneously, sometimes consecutively. Their relationships with men may center on having children or receiving economic support, but frequently *mati* choose a "visiting" relationship with men rather than marriage in order to maintain their independence.

Born in Suriname and trained as an anthropologist in the United States and the Netherlands, Wekker also writes about the transfer of *mati* work to the Netherlands. In recent decades, young Surinamese women have emigrated from the former colony to its former colonizer in search of economic opportunities. There, *mati* work has often developed in relationships between young immigrants and older black women of Surinamese parentage who have established Dutch citizenship. Wekker describes these relationships as often fraught with complicated power dynamics involving differential age, class, and citizenship status. Yet she notes that this *mati* work does not parallel European ideas of lesbianism.

Wekker pursues this distinction between conceptualizations of sexuality in Suriname and Europe in greater detail as she develops her analysis of *mati* work in Paramaribo. What steps, she asks, must anthropologists take to understand sexual relationships between people of the same gender cross-culturally without distorting what these relationships mean in their actual lives? Wekker argues that Western scholarship mistakenly links all sexual acts between individuals of the same gender to a notion of "homosexual identity"—a permanent, stable, fixed sexual core or essence, whether inborn or learned, that is counterposed to an equally fixed and opposite heterosexual identity. In the Western framework, a person is "either/or." The *mati* of Paramaribo, Wekker argues, approach their sexual choices very differently, regarding sexuality as flexible behavior rather than fixed identity. Their behavior is dynamic, malleable, and inclusive—"both/and"—rather than exclusive.

Wekker urges students of sexuality to not impose Western views about sexuality—what she considers "Western folk knowledge"—on the rest of the world but to understand sexuality in its local reality with the goal of rethinking same-gender behavior in cross-cultural perspective. Rather than thinking of one uniform expression of same-gender sexual behavior, she recommends focusing attention on the variation of people's behaviors. Furthermore, thinking cross-culturally, she argues that research and analysis of same-gender sexuality must recognize that the identical physical sexual acts between same-gendered people may be understood in multiple ways and have vastly different social significance in different cultures and historical periods (Wekker 2006, 1999; Brown 2007; Stone 2007). This point is also taken up by the following study of male sexuality in Nicaragua.

Machismo and Sexuality in Nicaragua

Cultural anthropologist Roger Lancaster explores similar themes in *Life Is Hard: Machismo, Danger and the Intimacy of Power in Nicaragua* (1994), in which he considers expressions of sexuality in a working-class neighborhood in Managua, Nicaragua, during the 1980s. In particular, he examined the concept of machismo—which can be defined as a strong, sometimes exaggerated performance of masculinity. This concept, which Lancaster sees as central to the Nicaraguan national imagination, shapes relationships not only between men and women but also between men and other men. Machismo creates a strong contrast between aggression and passivity. "Real" men—masculine men—are aggressive. But a real man's macho status is always at risk. Machismo must be constantly performed to retain one's social status.

Lancaster was particularly intrigued by the way machismo affects the sexual relations between men. Generally, in U.S. culture, any man who engages in a same-gender sexual behavior is considered gay. But in the Nicaraguan community that Lancaster studied, only the men who passively receive anal intercourse are pejoratively called *cochon*—"queer, faggot, gay." The *machista*, the penetrator, is still considered a manly man—an *hombre-hombres*—under the rules of machismo. For it is the *machista*'s role to achieve sexual conquest whenever possible with whoever is available. The active partner acts out machismo, enhancing his status by dominating a weaker person. Among Nicaraguan men, the intersection of sexuality

MAP 9.2
Nicaragua

and power creates a culturally constructed system of arbitrary and unequal value for male bodies in which machismo privileges the aggressive, assertive *machista* penetrator over the passive, receptive, penetrated *cochon*.

Lancaster points out that in Nicaragua the same acts that in the United States would be seen to reveal one's "essential" homosexuality—desire for and sexual activity with someone of the same sex—are interpreted differently. In fact, active, aggressive men enhance their masculinity and macho status, even if they engage in same-gender sexual activity (Lewin 1995; Rouse 1994; Perez-Aleman 1994).

Boy-Inseminating Ritual Practices in Papua New Guinea

Like Lancaster's work in Nicaragua, cultural anthropologist Gil Herdt's fieldwork among the Sambia (a pseudonym for a small group of people in the eastern highlands of Papua New Guinea) raises another challenge to Western assumptions that same-gender sexual activity undermines gender identity, making gay men effeminate and lesbians masculinized. According to Herdt (1981, 1987, 1993), the Sambia believed that adult men needed to supply boys with semen to ensure their development into manhood. This belief served as the foundation for a ritual practice of boy-insemination that was fully accepted throughout the culture.

Over several years of ceremonies conducted in men's ritual lodges, boys performed fellatio on older men in order to receive their semen. This ritual exchange, Herdt's informants explained, created masculinity, made young men into warriors, and prepared them for marriage to women. Studies conducted by anthropologists in other areas of New Guinea showed similar concerns with the power of liquids—semen, mother's milk, coconut milk—to carry meaning (Herdt 1999). However, the means of transferring the semen (including anal intercourse or direct application to the skin) and its power varied by group.

Herdt's study revealed that the exchange of semen between older and younger men, an act that would be associated with homosexuality in the United States, actually strengthened the young Sambian men's masculine identity. The same-sex initiation did not threaten their heterosexual identity and desire or make other members of the culture consider them effeminate. In fact, performing fellatio with older men was considered to be an essential act that strengthened younger men and prepared them to transition out of a feminized childhood dominated by mothers and other women (Brewis 2000; Flanagan 1986; Knauft 1987).

The studies in Suriname, Nicaragua, and Papua New Guinea are representative of the vast array of cross-cultural research that cumulatively has been called the ethnocartography of human sexuality (Weston 1993), mapping the global scope of diverse human sexual beliefs and behaviors. This ethnocartography marks a period in the anthropology of sexuality that built

MAP 9.3
Papua New Guinea

on the premises that (1) cross-cultural attention to the practices and beliefs of others can yield a deeper analysis of one's own culture, and (2) awareness of the broad panorama of human life offers opportunities for reexamining what seems normal and natural in one's own cultural practices. After reading about the previous three studies, in what ways are you challenged to rethink your own conceptions of human sexuality?

We turn now to consider the unique construction of human sexuality in the United States.

How Has Sexuality Been Constructed in the United States?

Anthropology strives to make the unconscious patterns and practices that frame our daily lives conscious so that we can examine them, make clearer assessments about how culture shapes our imaginations, expectations, and opportunities, and consider a more complete range of possible options.

In many of the studies discussed throughout this chapter, we see expressions of sexuality that do not fit the dominant Western model that limits discussion to two categories: **heterosexuality**, or attraction to and sexual relations between individuals of the opposite sex; and **homosexuality**, or attraction to and sexual relations with members of the same sex. At times in Western cultures this heterosexual-homosexual binary may be supplemented by discussions of **bisexuality**, or attraction to and sexual relations with members of both sexes, and **asexuality**, or lack of attraction to others. The term *transgender* has emerged in recent decades to describe people whose gender identity or gender expression differs from the sex they were assigned at birth (Valentine 2007). But these latter categories are less frequently considered. As we will see, historical and cross-cultural research suggests that the dual category system of heterosexuality and homosexuality has a uniquely Western cultural history.

The Invention of Heterosexuality

Popular conversations about sexuality in the United States often focus on same-gender sexuality. This may not come as a surprise. As discussed in Chapter 6, contemporary conversations about race tend to center on the experiences of being black, Hispanic, or Asian and avoid discussing being white, even though whiteness is the central racial category around which all others have been organized. Likewise, in popular discussions and academic studies of sexuality, talk of different-gender eroticism (heterosexuality) often is overwhelmed by discussions of same-gender eroticism (homosexuality). This emphasis has left heterosexuality largely forgotten and unmarked. In recent years, the anthropology of sexuality has worked to shift scholarly attention to focus on the norm (heterosexuality) and the process by which the particular expression of heterosexuality prevalent in U.S. culture today became the norm (D'Emilio and Freedman 1998).

Historian Jonathan Katz (2007) argues that heterosexuality as it is practiced and understood in contemporary U.S. culture is a fairly recent invention. The respected *Oxford English Dictionary Supplement* lists the first U.S. usage only in 1892. Because words provide clues to cultural concepts, Katz suggests that the lack of earlier citations in popular or scientific venues in the United States indicates that heterosexuality had not achieved widespread cultural currency in the nineteenth century.

Does this mean that women and men in the United States were not engaging in opposite-gender sexual activity prior to the invention of this word? Katz suggests instead that heterosexuality as we think of it is not the same as reproductive intercourse between a man and a woman. Instead, what we call heterosexuality today is a particular arrangement between the sexes that although not excluding reproductive intercourse, also involves ideas about the practice and purpose of sex that have not always been socially authorized. So, for instance, the early references to heterosexuality often referred to it as a perversion of the natural order because of its association with sex for pleasure rather than for procreation. The Victorian ideal of sexuality, heavily influenced by Christian teachings, considered sex to be for procreation alone. (The Victorian era generally corresponds with the life of the British monarch Queen Victoria [1837–1901].) In this view, sex for pleasure represented a danger to the purposes of God. Masturbation — clearly nonprocreative — was considered a life-threatening, depleting form of self-abuse.

Only in 1892 did the translation of German psychiatrist Richard von Krafft-Ebings's influential work *Psychopathia Sexualis* first introduce to the U.S. scene the modern sense of "heterosexuality" as erotic feelings for the opposite sex and "homosexuality" as erotic feelings for the same sex. This marked a significant shift in the scientific community, supported by a growing number of medical doctors, toward the new idea of sexuality for pleasure rather than exclusively for procreation. The rapidly expanding number of newspapers, books, plays, films, restaurants, bars, and baths associated with the rising consumer culture in the early twentieth century reinforced the gradual shift toward the sex-for-pleasure concept.

Sexology A scientific study of sexuality, called *sexology*, began to emerge in the United States in the late nineteenth century. This activity played a central role in the establishment of heterosexuality as the dominant erotic ideal and in the gradual process of dividing the U.S. population into distinct heterosexual and homosexual groups. Sexology sought to understand the essence of human sexuality as it was expressed naturally through sexual behavior. Sexologists trusted that this scientific knowledge of human sexual behavior would enable them to look beyond cultural variations in sexual practices to perceive the underlying nature of sexuality across cultures. In the twentieth century, elaborate scientific studies led by prominent scholars of sex such as Alfred Kinsey, Shere Hite, and William Masters and Virginia Johnson utilized interviews, questionnaires, observation, and participation to explore the sexual lives of thousands of primarily white U.S. residents. Their studies produced surprising results.

Alfred Kinsey (1894–1956), a Harvard-trained biologist and zoologist, produced two of the most famous studies, *Sexual Behavior in the Human Male* (Kinsey, Pomeroy, and Martin 1948) and *Sexual Behavior in the Human Female* (1953). Based on data gathered from thousands of subjects, Kinsey and his collaborators suggested that human sexuality was much more diverse than was commonly assumed. In fact, rather than finding a sharp dichotomy between heterosexuality and homosexuality, his studies revealed a continuum of sexual behavior. Taking into account his respondents' experiences—including the frequency of certain sexual activities, sexual responsiveness to same and opposite genders, fantasies, dreams, and feelings—Kinsey's team placed people along a continuum of sexual feelings and behaviors. This so-called Kinsey Scale plotted exclusively heterosexual behavior on one end of the spectrum and exclusively homosexual behavior on the other, with various points in between.

Kinsey and later sexologists found that human sexuality does not fit into simplistic categories. Rather, it is marked by diversity, flexibility, and fluidity. In a break with earlier sexologists and widespread public opinion at the time, Kinsey rejected the claims that humans represent two discrete populations, heterosexual and homosexual. "Only the human mind invents categories and tries to force facts into separated pigeon-holes. The living world is a continuum" (Kinsey, Pomeroy, and Martin 1948, 639). Kinsey noted that his studies showed same-gendered attraction, fantasies, and experiences to be much more common than previously thought. Furthermore, he found that sexual behaviors could shift over the course of a lifetime, spanning both heterosexual and homosexual activity (Hubbard 1990).

Despite their arguments for the recognition of diversity and flexibility in human sexual behavior, Kinsey's reports contributed in two ways to the establishment of heterosexuality as the dominant erotic ideal in U.S. culture. First, by placing heterosexuality and homosexuality on opposite ends of his scale, Kinsey reinforced the cultural assumptions that these were opposite and irreconcilable categories. Additionally, his studies' reliance on quantitative results reinforced the emerging popular and scientific consensus that because it was the sex most people were having, heterosexuality was the functional norm for human sexuality (Katz 2007; Hubbard 1990).

Over the course of a century, heterosexuality gradually came to be seen as the norm—the presumed "natural" state—against which to judge all other expressions of sexuality in U.S. culture. Today cultural notions of sexuality are in flux, yet a particular version of heterosexuality continues to be constructed and contested.

Within this context, we now consider the role of weddings in shaping contemporary conceptions of human sexuality in the United States.

"White Weddings"

White Weddings: Romancing Heterosexuality in Popular Culture (2008), a study by sociologist Chrys Ingraham, is not a book about wedding ceremonies. It is about wedding culture and what the author calls the "wedding industry"—the vast network of commercial activities and social institutions that market 2.3 million weddings a year in the United States. The wedding industry and the wedding culture, Ingraham argues, provide insights into how U.S. culture gives meaning to marriage and, in the process, constructs contemporary understandings of heterosexuality.

Constructing Heterosexuality It's hard to turn on the television, log on to the Internet, or check out at the local grocery store without encountering some reminder of U.S. society's fascination with weddings. Bridal magazines, popular tabloids, television shows, and commercials in every medium saturate the culture with images of a spectacle of excess that will, they promise, lead to everyone's fairy-tale ending of "happily ever after." Wedding consultants push wedding announcements, bridal showers, wedding halls, floral arrangements, diamond rings, rehearsal dinners, reception halls, gifts and favors, caterers, photographers, bands, limousines, and glamorous honeymoons to romantic destinations. Wedding registries orchestrate the delivery of just the right gifts of kitchenware, china, household furnishings, and every appliance imaginable. The average bridal gown (mostly made in third world garment shops by women who will never have a white wedding), including alterations, headpiece, and veil, will cost $1,811 (2008 figures). The average U.S. couple will spend more than $27,852 (in 2008) on their "big day." Altogether, the annual $80 billion dollar wedding industry wields enormous social and economic power.

Ingraham reminds her readers that brides are not born. They are made. Every girl in U.S. culture, almost from birth, is bombarded with cultural symbols and messages about what it will take to have her very own white wedding. Barbie dolls and other toy-industry favorites model the perfect bride, complete with accessories (including Ken?) for the perfect white wedding. Disney movies, feature films, and television shows celebrate weddings as key life moments (and central plot devices) and essential cultural symbols. Every broadcast season features a spate of elaborate made-for-television weddings, especially on shows struggling in the ratings.

From childhood, girls are tutored in preparation for the "you may kiss the bride" moment, learning to apply makeup, wear high heels, send valentines, go on dates, and select a prom dress. Boys learn to buy flowers and corsages, wear tuxedos, pay for dates, lead during the first dance, buy an engagement ring, and initiate sex. But no matter where you think human sexuality originates, it is clear that these behaviors do not occur in nature. They are constructed in culture. The wedding industry and wedding culture—the romantic idealization of the wedding ritual—enculturate boys and girls, men and women, about what to do, when, and with whom, in order to lead up to that perfect day. Weddings, Ingraham suggests, and the elaborate rituals that lead up to them over a lifetime, are not only exuberant public celebrations of romantic love. Weddings are also key cultural institutions through which we learn what it means to be heterosexual.

Inequality and Unequal Access What do weddings tell us about the construction of heterosexuality in U.S. culture? Building on recent feminist scholarship, Ingraham suggests that white weddings, and the marriages that result, offer insights into the gendered power dynamics embedded in the normative patterns of heterosexuality that have developed since the late nineteenth century. These power dynamics disadvantage women while being largely obscured by the idealism and romance that U.S. culture wraps around these institutions. Historically, the institution of heterosexual marriage included legal stipulations that effectively made women the economic and sexual property of their husbands. This assumption continues to be ritualized in contemporary U.S. weddings by the father "giving away" the bride to her soon-to-be husband, exchanging the woman between two men.

Today patterns of inequality are less visible but no less significant. Although not legally sanctioned, assumptions about the proper role and relative value of men and women within the context of heterosexuality promote inequalities in the home. There, the gendered division of labor means that frequently the woman carries a double workload as a wage earner while simultaneously bearing primary responsibility for domestic work and child rearing. In the workplace, usually still dominated by male leadership, women receive unequal pay for equal work, are promoted less often than men, and are targets of sexual harassment.

Ingraham selected the book title *White Weddings* to highlight the issues of class and race that also are embedded in the workings of the wedding industry and the fairy tale of the wedding ritual. White weddings are not available to all. The women sewing wedding dresses, the young men mining diamonds, and the staff serving dinner on the Caribbean honeymoon island cannot afford a white wedding. Nor does the industry depict a diverse population in its advertising, insinuating that white weddings are primarily for white folks. Actually, most Americans cannot afford the average U.S. wedding; they incur significant debt for the ceremony and honeymoon to launch their marriage.

Weddings are often romanticized as rituals of love and commitment, but the question of who can or cannot marry has consequences under the law. In the United States, legally sanctioned marriages convey a wide assortment of federal and state entitlements that are unavailable to those who are unmarried—another example of the use of heterosexuality to organize social life. Advantages are extended in areas as wide-ranging as inheritance rights, tax benefits, health care access, Social Security and other retirement benefits, hospital visitation rights and health care decisions, housing benefits, and insurance coverage. In this context, heated debates about who should be able to marry have implications beyond the realm of moral disagreements. These debates signal profound challenges to an underlying system of power and privilege based on the assumption that heterosexuality, and a particular version of it, is the cultural norm.

Ingraham suggests that the idealized version of weddings and married life—full of love, purity, morality, and affluence—maintains an illusion of well-being in patterns of relationship between men and women that, in reality, may or may not be present. Our romance with this illusion (what the author calls the *heterosexual imaginary*), so heavily promoted by the wedding industry and the institutions of wedding culture, misleadingly encourages us to assume that the patterns of heterosexuality that we have inherited are natural, timeless, and unchanging. In reality, they are culturally constructed, recently invented, and malleable. As such, humans have the ability to make their own choices about the organization of their most intimate relationships, about the way the division of labor will be shaped between men and women, family responsibilities shared, gender roles assigned, and economic and cultural resources allocated.

This process of contestation is already under way, with significant cultural implications. The stability of heterosexuality as the norm for social and sexual relationships is being challenged by many dynamics today: women's increasing economic independence, the necessity for two-career households to support the family, the presence of feminist and gay rights movements, the legal recognition of same-sex partnerships and marriages in some U.S. jurisdictions, the availability of contraception and abortion, changing norms of gender and sexuality, rising divorce rates, and the strengthening of laws against domestic and sexual violence. At the same time, some religious and secular movements are working to reinforce many of the heterosexual norms symbolized by white weddings (Gardner 2011). The cultural renegotiation of socially acceptable patterns of relationship and sexuality leaves very few in the United States untouched.

In the second edition of her book, Ingraham reflects on the wrenching and at times risky process of evaluating the sacred, valued rituals and institutions of weddings. Her writing elicited responses of appreciation along with expressions of anger, resistance, and dismissal. Clearly, the critique of the dynamics underlying U.S. weddings and marriages caused discomfort for many, and for some the attack felt quite personal. These responses, Ingraham offers, may signify the crucial need to analyze one of the most powerful rituals in U.S. culture and one of the most significant locations for constructing relationships and patterns of power (Ingraham 2008; Milkie 2000; Siebel 2000).

Lesbian and Gay Commitment Ceremonies

The debate about same-sex weddings is one arena where the contestation of U.S. norms of sexuality is thoroughly engaged. In *Recognizing Ourselves* (1998), anthropologist Ellen Lewin opens a window into both the personal and the political dynamics of gay and lesbian commitment ceremonies. Drawing on interviews with more than fifty couples and on her own attendance at dozens of ceremonies, Lewin recounts the stories of U.S. couples wrestling with what it meant to get "married" in a 1990s culture that legally restricted same-sex marriage in all fifty states. Focusing on the actual rituals designed by couples, Lewin unveils the ways these invented rituals foster both continuity and creativity in a culture by integrating themes of love, tradition, kinship, community, authenticity, and resistance (Lewin 1998; Kennedy 1999).

Denied legal status by the state and often rejected by religious communities, the couples in Lewin's study created rituals to recognize themselves—to celebrate their love and to call their communities to participate in supporting their relationships. Their stories include a lesbian couple's "traditional" Jewish wedding in which the "bride" wore a white wedding dress and the "groom" a tuxedo; a hippie gay couple saying their wedding vows privately on their favorite beach to avoid the consumerism of typical heterosexual weddings; and another couple who gave their wedding a country-and-western theme.

FIGURE 9.6 How are contemporary understandings of sexuality being shaped by the highly symbolic ritual of marriage? Here, a couple exchanges rings at their wedding ceremony.

Rituals of Resistance and Acceptance Lewin reflects on the multiple roles that commitment ceremonies play in the gay and lesbian community, serving as rituals of resistance and as rituals of acceptance. For some in the study, commitment ceremonies, holy unions, and weddings were a form of resistance against the cultural norms and legal standards that denied gay men and lesbians the recognition of their lives and loves in ways readily provided to heterosexuals. Their public performances allowed them a chance to speak of their anger and sorrow, to refuse to be marginalized and mistreated, and to challenge the dominant patterns of heterosexuality and gender stratification in mainstream U.S. culture. Many also saw their ceremonies as part of efforts to legalize same-sex marriage and advocate for the legal, health, and economic benefits associated with heterosexual marriages.

For others, their commitment ceremonies expressed more personal and intimate feelings, including their wish to formalize their bonds of love in sacred and special ways, acknowledge their intensifying personal connections, and make their commitments public. Here Lewin discovered a distinct sense that commitment ceremonies were rituals of acceptance and conformity. By participating in public ceremonies long reserved for heterosexual couples, gay men and lesbians claimed their place in the wider society, acknowledging that they were already part of local communities, schools, families, and workplaces—that they belonged. For these couples, commitment ceremonies became a statement and celebration of their inclusion in mainstream U.S. culture.

Lewin states that for the couples she interviewed, the ritual performances of both resistance and acceptance were not always consciously done or carefully thought through. Nor were the dynamics of resistance and acceptance always mutually exclusive. Instead, she reflects on a subtle process of cultural change present in the planning and celebration of commitment ceremonies that embodied multiple meanings reflecting the diverse individuals, unique couples, and complex emotions involved.

In the preface to her book, Lewin reflects on her own ceremony of commitment to her partner in their Reform Jewish synagogue. Although initially hesitant about the idea, after years of "free[ing] ourselves from the negative messages and assaults on self-esteem generated by attempts to 'measure up' in the eyes of straight society, and questioning the underlying standards and assumptions of 'institutionalized heterosexuality' so powerfully represented in weddings," Lewin experienced the dramatic effects of communal ritual, long studied by anthropologists. She wrote:

> Still, it was hard for us to explain, to ourselves or to others, why we wanted to have a ceremony. Looking back on the decision, it

seems that we longed to share our discovery of one another with the world, or some little piece of it; we wanted to make the fact of our relationship public and official, even though there seemed to be nothing that required us to do so. (Lewin 1998, xvi)

After completing interviews with dozens of gay and lesbian couples, Lewin concluded:

> [T]he stories couples told me added to the feelings produced by my own ceremony, convincing me that normalization of gay relationships effected through wedding rituals cannot help but have a profound impact on the ways lesbians and gays view ourselves and on the views others adopt toward us. (Lewin 1998, xix)

As we noted earlier in the chapter, human sexuality encompasses not only desires, beliefs, and behaviors related to erotic physical contact, intimacy, and pleasure, but also a cultural arena in which people (1) promote and contest ideas of what kinds of physical desires and behaviors are morally right, appropriate, and "natural." The studies by Ingraham and Lewin challenge us to consider the ways in which contemporary understandings of sexuality—as expressed through the highly symbolic ritual of marriage—continue to be shaped, invented, and contested in U.S. culture.

Federal Law and Public Opinion

Indeed, intense debates about marriage equality and same-sex marriage continue today, both in the United States and around the world. Public opinion of same-sex marriage continues to shift in U.S. culture, especially among younger generations. Federal and state laws also continue to change. Over the past decade, a series of U.S. states have legalized same-sex marriage while others have passed legal restrictions.

In June 2013 the U.S. Supreme Court ruled unconstitutional the 1996 U.S. federal law, the Defense of Marriage Act (DOMA). DOMA had declared marriage to be the legal union between one man and one woman; ensured that no state could be forced to recognize the marital rights of gay or lesbian couples married in another state (a right granted to all heterosexual marriages); and restricted federal benefits to heterosexual couples only. The restricted benefits included Social Security survivor benefits, the right to file joint tax returns, and access to government employee health insurance. The overturning of DOMA after seventeen years placed opposite-sex marriages and same-sex marriages on equal footing in the eyes of the U.S. federal government for the first time.

Placed in historical perspective and in light of our anthropological perspectives on the fluidity and malleability of human sexuality, perhaps we can view these shifts not as some new and surprising contestation of age-old "natural" patterns of sexuality, but as the most recent rethinking of human sexuality in U.S. culture. If so, we might then be better prepared to analyze the underlying intersections of sexuality and power in our own personal and political lives.

How Is Sexuality an Arena for Working Out Relations of Power?

As we have noted, sexuality is more than an expression of individual desires and identities. French social scientist Michel Foucault (1978, 103) described sexuality as "an especially dense transfer point for relations of power." By this he meant that in every culture, sexuality—like race, ethnicity, class, and gender—is also an arena in which appropriate behavior is defined, relations of power are worked out, and inequality and stratification are created, enforced, and contested.

Indeed, cultural institutions ranging from governments to religious bodies attempt to regulate many aspects of sexuality. These aspects include marriage and divorce; monogamy and polygamy; age of consent; definition of incest; reproductive rights; and the rights of gay men, lesbians, bisexuals, and transgendered persons; as well as pornography, sex trafficking, and prostitution. A consideration of "who is allowed to do what with whom and when" exposes the intersections of sexuality and power in a culture. Attention to intersectionality—the way systems of power interconnect to affect individual lives and group experiences—offers a fundamental shift in the way social scientists study inequality and stratification, including the way we think about sexuality. In this section we consider several case studies that reflect on these intersections historically and in contemporary life, globally and in the United States.

Colonialism and Intersections of Sexuality, Race, Class, and Nation

Cultural anthropologist Ann Stoler explores sexuality as an arena for working out power relations. Her book *Carnal Knowledge and Imperial Power* (2010) is a historical study of the ways sexuality served as a tool for enforcing social boundaries under European colonialism. In particular, Stoler explores the strategies that European colonizers used to control the sexual practices, or carnal knowledge, of people under their rule. By controlling sexuality, colonizers sought to establish clear boundaries of European identity and thereby protect their rights to the profits of colonialism and their privileges as members of what they considered to be the dominant race.

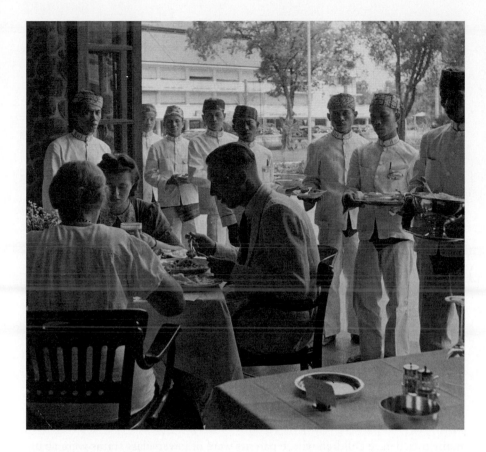

FIGURE 9.7 Who bedded and wedded with whom was not left to chance in European colonies. Physical and social boundaries in all areas of life were hardened to discourage racial mixing of colonists with the colonized, as depicted in this photo, circa 1940, of a Dutch colonialist family eating in Java, Indonesia, while a group of Indonesian waiters attend to them.

Through extensive historical research on colonial activities from the early 1600s into the twentieth century, Stoler reveals the essential role of intersections of sexuality, race, class, and nationality for understanding the colonial enterprise. Questions of "who bedded and wedded with whom" were not left to chance in the colonies of Spain, Portugal, France, England, or Holland. Leading corporations such as the Dutch East India Company painstakingly wrote, clarified, and implemented rules for sexual liaisons and marriage relations. For example, in the two centuries from 1622 to 1822, the Dutch restricted the immigration of European women to Asia. Bachelor European male employees were recruited but then prohibited from marrying women of the colonies. Instead, these male employees were encouraged to live with imported slaves or native concubines — but not to marry. Colonial legislation ensured that these women, along with the children of their liaisons, would have no right to claim citizenship in the colonial homeland or any rights and privileges as spouses or children of colonial subjects.

Later, when restrictions on the immigration of European women were lifted, their domestic, economic, political, and sexual lives in the colonies were restricted in gender-specific ways. Physical and social boundaries between

European women and native men were hardened to discourage racial mixing. Colonized men, in particular, were portrayed as a sexual danger to the racial purity of women of the colonial community, despite the nearly total absence of reports of sexual violence by native men against European women.

Gender-specific sexual sanctions, especially as they related to race, delineated lines of power between European men and women in the colonial endeavor. Colonial administrators considered this strict control of sexual practices crucial to maintaining distinct communities of Europeans with clear racial and class boundaries.

The colonial boundaries that were intended to distinguish communities of colonizers from their colonial subjects were, in reality, much more complicated, fragile, fractious, and fluid than intended. The children of mixed-race relationships, for instance, posed a challenge to the preferred rules of colonization and threatened to blur the colonial divide. Which children would become citizens? Which ones would be relegated to the position of colonial subjects? Which ones would be granted access to the privileges of colonizers, and which ones would be labeled illegitimate—doomed to ambiguous social status and economic disadvantage? These difficult questions vexed colonial administrators who were expected to keep the lines clear. Because all mixed-race children shared some European heritage, decisions about their status as citizens or subjects often hinged on more than their perceived race. Often what mattered most was their parents' class position within the colonial enterprise. Ultimately, many mixed-race children whose parents were of lower-class status were abandoned by the colonial powers.

Within the European colonial community, tensions of class, religion, and power created divisions that threatened the intended boundaries. For example, company officials, bankers, military leaders, planters, workers, and missionaries expressed different visions of empire. Ultimately, boundaries between the colonizers and the colonized proved unenforceable. Stoler points out that in the Dutch-controlled colonial territory of Java, nearly 75 percent of those granted European legal status by 1900 were of mixed race, revealing a significant blurring of intended boundaries.

Stoler's analysis of European colonial practices indicates that attitudes toward sexual practices are not always shaped solely by carnal desires. Systems of economic, political, and colonial power exert significant influence on the ways desires are expressed and understood as sexuality intersects with dynamics of race, class, and nationality. These dynamics remain evident today, as we will see in the following discussions.

Intersections of Race and Sexuality for Black Gay Women

As previously discussed, one's sexual identity is shaped by its intersection with other dynamics of power, including race, class, gender, age, and religion.

Sociologist Mignon Moore's book *Invisible Families* (2011) explores the impact of the intersection of race and sexuality on the identities, relationships, and families of black gay women in the United States. Moore notes that, historically, race has framed black women's political, economic, and religious identities (see also Higgenbotham 1992; Dill 1983). And whereas many middle-class white lesbian couples experience sexuality as the primary framework that shapes their identity, many in the black lesbian community (including African American, Afro-Caribbean, and African immigrant women) find that race—perhaps as much as, if not more than, sexuality—is the primary framework that shapes their identity.

In an interview with Moore, Zoe Ferron (a pseudonym), an African American woman born in 1960 in Brooklyn, New York, reflected on how the identities of race, gender, and sexuality described her:

> If I had to number them one, two, three? Probably Black and lesbian—real close, to be honest with you. I don't know which would come up as one. Probably Black. Woman last. . . . Because that is just what it is. People see your Blackness, and the world has affected me by my Blackness since the very inception of my life. . . . My sexuality is something that developed later on, or I became aware of later on, [because] I think *it's always been what it's been*, but I think that it was just something that developed in my psyche. But being Black is something that I've always had to deal with: racism since day one and recognizing how to navigate through this world as a Black person, and even as a Black woman. (Moore 2012, 33)

The intersection of race and sexuality becomes particularly meaningful as black gay women participate in black or gay communities that define themselves around just one of these statuses.

Moore notes that prior to the 1980s, gay sexuality in racial minority communities was rarely articulated in public settings. And only infrequently was it recognized as a component of the community's larger experiences of discrimination and struggle. Instead, openly gay sexuality was perceived to flout notions of "respectability"—virtue, modesty, discipline, responsibility—that had developed within the black middle class and that its leadership promoted as important tools to combat racist stereotypes in the workplace, political arena, and family life (Shaw 1996; Wolcott 2001). Moore points to a strong reluctance during that period by gay blacks to challenge community expectations about respectability by creating families together.

In the intervening years, same-gender sexuality has become an increasingly public issue in U.S. culture through prominent debates about same-sex marriage, the rights of gay men and lesbian adults to adopt children, and the rights

FIGURE 9.8 A couple share a laugh while playing cards with their daughter and son at home in Chicago, Illinois.

of lesbians and gay men to serve openly in the military. At the same time, recognition of same-sex relationships and families has increased in the black community, and black political and religious leaders have begun to address issues related to gay sexuality as matters of civil rights and fairness. Relationships once hidden from families and communities have gradually moved into the public sphere, where the participants can be celebrated as gay women and men and can openly form unions and raise families.

How do the women in Moore's study navigate the black middle-class politics of respectability in order to both live their sexuality openly and maintain strong community connections? Moore suggests that by risking the disruption of this particular version of respectability, black women who live openly as lesbians—forming families, getting married, becoming mothers, and raising children—offer an alternative manifestation of respectability at the intersection of sexuality and race.

Can you see how the intersection of race and sexuality may differentially affect one's life choices and opportunities? In your own life, how is your sexuality shaped by its intersection with other systems of power—perhaps age, gender, race, class, or religion?

Sexuality and Power on U.S. College Campuses

In what ways do sexuality and power intersect on your college campus? If, as anthropologist Eric Wolf argues (see Chapter 2), every relationship is embedded in complex dynamics of power, how do you personally navigate intersections of sexuality with gender, age, class, race, or religion? Has your college or university created opportunities to discuss matters of sexuality?

Certainly, attention to **sexual violence** on college campuses has increased (Sanday 1990). Terms such as *date rape* and *domestic violence* have become part of the national conversation (see also Chapter 8), and many colleges and universities have implemented policies on sexual harassment and sexual conduct. Still, many women experience sexual harassment, violence, and rape while in college (Fisher, Daigle, and Cullen 2010). While these policies attempt to address extreme expressions of the intersection of power with sexuality, conversations about sexuality can be far more wide-ranging.

Antioch College: From "*No* Means *No*" to "*Yes* Means *Yes*" In the early 1990s, when many colleges were beginning to articulate sexual offense policies, a small liberal arts college in the U.S. Midwest gained national attention for its unusual policy. Most sexual offense policies start with the assumption that "*No* means *no*." Most legal definitions of rape assume that if a woman does not consent or is incapable of consent for any reason, then any sexual activity with her is considered rape. However, Antioch College in Ohio developed a different type of policy. It was initiated by students; developed by a task force of students, faculty, and administrators; and promoted in mandatory training workshops for all students. The policy went beyond "*No* means *no*" to mandate that participants must receive an explicit "yes" at every step of the encounter. Both participants must negotiate and agree to everything.

According to the policy, "Obtaining consent is an on-going process in any sexual interaction. Verbal consent should be obtained with each new level of physical and / or sexual contact / conduct in any given interaction, regardless of who initiates it. Asking 'Do you want to have sex with me?' is not enough. The request for consent must be specific to each act." Among the policy's specific provisions are the following:

MAP 9.4
Ohio

- The person with whom sexual contact / conduct is initiated is responsible to express verbally and or physically her / his willingness or lack of willingness when reasonably possible.
- If someone has initially consented but then stops consenting during a sexual interaction, she / he should communicate withdrawal verbally and / or through physical resistance. The other individual(s) must stop immediately.
- To knowingly take advantage of someone who is under the influence of alcohol, drugs, and / or prescribed medication is not acceptable behavior.

- If someone verbally agrees to engage in specific contact or conduct, but it is not of her/his own free will due to any of the circumstances stated below, then the person initiating shall be considered in violation of this policy:
- The person submitting is under the influence of alcohol or other substances supplied to her/him by the person initiating;
- The person submitting is incapacitated by alcohol, drugs, and/or prescribed medication;
- The person submitting is asleep or unconscious;
- The person initiating has forced, threatened, coerced, or intimidated the other individual(s) into engaging in sexual contact and/or sexual conduct. (cited in Cameron 1994)

Antioch's policy drew criticism from many people who considered it excessively intrusive. But linguistic anthropologist Deborah Cameron, who studied the effects of the policy on campus (1994), found that rather than creating awkwardness and uncertainty, for many students the new policy promoted a more elaborate language for talking and thinking about sex. The policy also appeared to have improved some students' sex lives in the process.

The Antioch policy presents a challenge that requires a dramatic shift in thinking about intimate sexual encounters. It also commands a new attention to shifting the power dynamics that underlie current patterns of gender and sexuality in the culture at large. Imagine if all forms of coercion—physical and

FIGURE 9.9 Students at Antioch College, in Ohio, which gained national attention for its unusual policy on sexual conduct on campus.

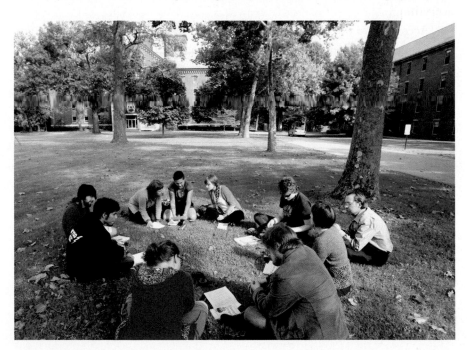

Creating a Code of Sexual Conduct

What are your rules for sexual conduct? How do you expect others to treat you in intimate situations? What are your expectations about a healthy intersection of sexuality and power?

All colleges now have sexual offense policies or sexual harassment policies that spell out their expectations for how men and women on campus should behave toward one another. The high incidence of sexual harassment and date rape has forced colleges to become more explicit in expressing their expectations and more proactive in ensuring that all students understand what constitutes appropriate and inappropriate behavior.

Federal legislation has mandated that colleges be much more transparent about conditions on campus and develop avenues for addressing allegations of sexual violence. These policies include guidelines for filing complaints and responding to charges that are brought within the university community.

Consider drafting a code of sexual conduct for your college, either on your own or with classmates. Be sure to include clear expectations for behavior, requirements for training members of the community, and procedures for addressing breaches of the code. Then compare your policy to what your college actually has in place. You will be able to find your college's policy on its website. How do the two differ? Why do you think the areas of similarity and difference arise? If you find the policy inadequate, consider strategies you can take as an individual or with others to effect change.

psychological coercion; the pressure of norms, obligations, and expectations; and the fear of ridicule or abandonment—were removed from the equation, enabling people to engage in sexual intimacy only when they really wanted to. What if "yes" really meant "yes" (Friedman and Valenti 2008)?

How Does Globalization Influence Local Expressions of Sexuality?

Globalization has significantly influenced local expressions of sexuality, and this effect is evident in many arenas. For example, time-space compression (see Chapter 1) is facilitating the movement of people—particularly men—within countries and across national borders in search of sexual pleasure. In addition, disruptions of local economies are pushing women to find wage labor to support themselves and their families. And international campaigns for gay and lesbian rights, often initiated in Western countries, are shaping a global conversation about sexuality and the human rights of sexual minorities worldwide. At the same time, groups opposing gay and lesbian sexuality are promoting their own agendas on a global platform.

These transformations suggest that individual expressions of sexuality and local understandings of sexuality are undergoing dramatic shifts as they intersect with economic policies, immigration practices, and political movements at the national, regional, and international levels influenced by processes of globalization (see Curtis 2009). The following studies offer insights into the potential for close linkages between your life and the lives of men and women around the world through the arena of human sexuality. This is an arena that most of us view as deeply personal but that today crosses national borders in the company of economic flows, immigrant journeys, international tourism, and global rights campaigns.

Beach Resorts, Dominican Women, and Sex Work

The current era of globalization has seen a dramatic rise in **sex tourism**—trips organized through the tourism sector to facilitate commercial sexual relationships between tourists and local residents in destinations around the world, including Brazil, Costa Rica, the Dominican Republic, Cuba, Kenya, the Philippines, and Thailand. Built on the infrastructure of the tourism industry (including airlines, hotels, restaurants, and local transportation), today sex tourism involves millions of sex workers in a multibillion-dollar industry.

Cultural anthropologist Denise Brennan's ethnography, *What's Love Got to Do with It?* (2004), explores the impact of globalization on Sosua, a beautiful beach town on the northern coast of the Dominican Republic in the Caribbean. Sosua has become a prime destination for white male European sex tourists. Internet advertisements and chat rooms draw them in with images of beautiful beaches, luxurious accommodations, and inexpensive sex with Afro-Caribbean island women. The globalized tourism industry provides a seamlessly integrated product, as package tours purchased in Europe bundle airfare, hotels, meals, and entertainment. Corporate owners of the resort hotels are frequently the same foreign airline companies that recruit and deliver the tourists to Sosua.

Yet the booming industry does not benefit everyone. Despite the allure of development through globalization, little of the sex tourism money reaches local Dominican hotels, restaurants, or other businesses. Local workers still toil for low wages, while European nationals are brought in by the resorts to fill well-paid management positions. Over the years, the well-funded foreign tourist hotels have largely undermined the local tourist industry: they monopolize tourists' expenditures by providing all-inclusive package tours, thereby depriving local businesses of income from the tourist trade. In fact, most of the tourist money never leaves the travel companies' home bank accounts in Europe.

Sosua also attracts young women who migrate from across the Dominican Republic to seek opportunities through the sex trade that flourishes around the luxury hotels. These mostly poor, rural, black women hope to reap some of the

sex tourism: Travel, usually organized through the tourism sector, to facilitate commercial sexual relations between tourists and local residents.

MAP 9.5
Dominican Republic

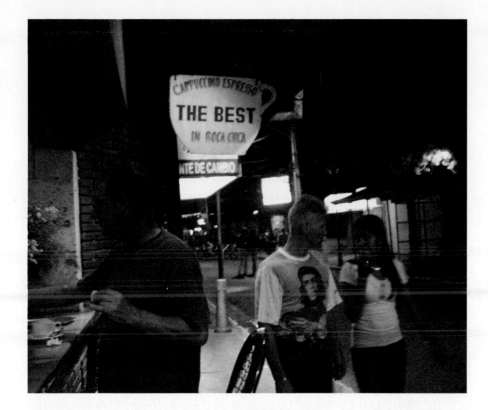

FIGURE 9.10 A European tourist walks with a local woman along a strip of nightclubs and hotels in the beach resort of Boca Chica, Dominican Republic, known as a hot spot for commercial sex tourism.

benefits of globalization, too, through **sex work**—that is, providing commercial sexual services to foreign tourists. If white European sex tourists have fantasies of sexual pleasure with exotic native women, the women of the Dominican Republic have their own fantasies. They believe that the money they earn will help release them and their families from the hardships of life in their largely rural, underdeveloped country. Even more fantastical, they hope to marry one of these tourist men—who they imagine will help them acquire a European visa, take them away, and enable them to escape their world of poverty and limited opportunities. If they can find romance along the way, all the better.

sex work: Labor through which one provides sexual services for money.

Brennan describes how sex work is more than a survival strategy for these women. Sosua's sex workers have developed an advancement strategy. In essence, they are working to make the transnational links created by foreign investment come alive for themselves just as for the European tourists. Brennan's careful storytelling depicts women who are not powerless victims of sexual violence and exploitation in the sex tourism industry; instead, they actively attempt to create a better life for themselves through it.

Unfortunately, the globalization deck seems stacked against these women. For one thing, prostitution is not legal in the Dominican Republic. With no legal protections, sex workers frequently become the victims of extortion and harassment by local police. On a larger scale, globalization affects sex tourists and sex workers in radically different ways, providing completely different possibilities for fulfilling their fantasies. Marriage, a visa to Europe, and financial security rarely materialize for the women in Sosua. Instead, globalization as expressed through sex tourism reproduces and reinforces the unequal relations that existed previously between men and women of different nationalities. In doing so, it also reinforces inequality along lines of gender, race, class, and nationality. At its roots, sex tourism relies on these inequalities of the globalized economy to satisfy the fantasies of tourists from developed countries and to maximize profits for corporate shareholders.

"Anthropologists Engage the World," on pages 342–43, highlights cultural anthropologist Patty Kelly and her research among sex workers in Mexico. It provides another example of the complicated ways in which sexuality intersects with other dynamics of power and the flows of globalization.

Sexuality, Language, and the Effects of Globalization in Nigeria

The tendency of globalization to intensify connections across national boundaries may generate opportunities for greater cooperation on issues of mutual concern affecting people in disparate parts of the world. But this capacity to bridge barriers also has the potential to homogenize—to shape global discourses that blur distinctions and smooth over differences—in a way that may put local indigenous expressions at risk.

In *Allah Made Us: Sexual Outlaws in an Islamic African City* (2009), linguistic anthropologist Rudolf Gaudio presents an ethnographic study of the language practices of *'yan daudu*, feminine men in the northern Nigerian (Hausa-speaking) city of Kano. *'Yan daudu* are one group of *masu harka*, a code term for "people who do the deed"—that is, men who have sex with other men. *'Yan daudu* are men who act like women: they cook, serve food, sing, dance, or work as prostitutes. Over the years, their role has been publicly recognized in northern Nigerian culture. But with the introduction of strict Islamic sharia law, which forbids same-gender sexuality, in recent years *'yan daudu* have faced increased persecution, harassment, and marginalization on account of their gender and sexual nonconformity. As international campaigns for gay rights intersect with Nigerian culture, the resulting conversations risk drawing local expressions of human sexuality into a national and international debate that links them to so-called Western decadence and new forms of colonialism considered unacceptable by the Nigerian government.

Unlike most Western conceptions of sexuality, *masu harka* and *'yan daudu* do not see homosexual behavior as incompatible with marrying women, forming families, and having children. Nor do they necessarily consider their sexuality incompatible with their Muslim faith. Gaudio met many who are observant Muslims and some who have taken the *hajj*, a pilgrimage to the Muslim holy city of Mecca that is required of every believer who can manage the journey. For some

MAP 9.6
Nigeria

FIGURE 9.11 Have international debates about human sexuality put local expressions at risk? Here *'yan daudu* dancing at a party in Kano, Nigeria. The men's faces have been disguised to conceal their identities.

Patty Kelly

How might an anthropologist study sexuality in an age of globalization? Cultural anthropologist Patty Kelly conducted fieldwork in a Mexican brothel.

Sex work is legal in one-third of the states of Mexico. The Zona Galactica brothel, where Kelly conducted her fieldwork, is located in Chiapas in southern Mexico. Sex work there is legal—run and regulated by the state. To study and analyze commercial sex in a globalizing world, Kelly spent a year with the Zona Galactica's 140 women sex workers, their clients, and the government administrators who run the brothel.

Kelly arrived in Chiapas during a time of popular unrest. Dramatic economic changes associated with globalization and supported by the Mexican government were disrupting the agricultural life of rural farmers, or *campesinos*. Pushed off their land by large-scale agribusiness, many were migrating to cities in search of work but finding themselves competing with other rural migrants and poor urban dwellers for the same low-paying jobs in factories, as servants, or in the informal economy.

The Zona Galactica provided an alternative employment option within the local service economy that in many cases provided a more secure, predictable, and better-paid living. At the Zona Galactica, Kelly found that some women were satisfied with their jobs. They could set their own hours, decide their own rates, and choose what services they would provide. Others would have preferred doing other work if they could have found it. But all the women used the brothel to make a decent living, get health care, build a sense of community, and develop a sense of dignity. The men who visited the brothel were mostly local working-class men, along with a few truckers passing through the area. As a result, the sex workers often forged relationships with their customers over time. Such relationships enabled the women to negotiate better terms and work with more dignity.

Overall, Kelly found that these women held more open-minded and practical attitudes about sexuality than even their middle-class Mexican female counterparts.

At the Zona Galactica, Kelly built a particularly strong relationship with Lydia, who eventually became the central figure in her ethnography. Kelly's book, *Lydia's Open Door: Inside Mexico's Most Modern Brothel* (2008b), is a vivid account of life and work in the sex trade. It sets this topic amid the larger struggles against impoverishment, landlessness, and political upheaval that the women of southern Mexico face every day. Key to Kelly's portrayal are the heartfelt interactions with Lydia, who became her friend and key informant; Lydia taught Kelly about the life of a sex worker but also invited Kelly home to her shantytown on the hilly outskirts of the city to generously share holiday meals far beyond her means.

Sadly, Lydia died of HIV/AIDS shortly after Kelly's fieldwork stay and before the book's publication. Kelly was moved by the way Lydia's fellow women sex workers honored her memory, including pooling their money to purchase a coffin so that Lydia's twin sons would not have to give their mother a pauper's funeral. Kelly reflects that it

Anthropologist Patty Kelly celebrates her birthday with a cake at her field site—a brothel in Chiapas, Mexico.

is these moments of community and solidarity that exemplify the lives of sex workers in the Zona Galactica.

Kelly's writing challenges stereotypes about prostitution by examining sex work in the Zona Galactica as one type of work in a wide spectrum of women's labor. Though rarely framed in this way, she notes that women often use their bodies, intimacy, and sexuality to perform various kinds of gendered work. Sometimes women's use of sexuality is explicit, as with Lydia and her colleague sex workers. But sexuality also comes into play in other kinds of workplaces. Waitresses dress, act, and talk in a sexualized manner, hoping that the allure of sexuality will bring them bigger tips. Most restaurants and many offices hire women receptionists in the belief that the women's sexuality will please the customers and clients. Sexuality is also on display in corporate offices in negotiations over roles, promotions, and power in the hierarchy. By seeing the women of the Zona Galactica within the broader spectrum of sexuality in work, Kelly urges her readers to understand the choices made by the women of the brothel without passing moral judgments. Can we consider sex work as a reasonable way for poor women living in the economic scarcity of the Chiapas region of southern Mexico to earn a living and support their families?

Kelly encourages a rethinking of the U.S. public policy debate over the criminalization of sex work. "Legalizing and regulating prostitution as the Mexican state has done in the Zona Galactica has its own problems—it stigmatizes sex workers (mostly by requiring them to register with the authorities), subjects them to mandatory medical testing that is not always effective, and gives clients and workers a false sense of security (with respect to sexual health and otherwise). But criminalization is worse. Prostitution will continue, even if illegal. But when criminalized, women will have fewer protections and less control over their work as they are forced to conduct it in the shadows."

In an editorial published by the *Los Angeles Times* and syndicated nationally, Kelly (2008a) built on her experiences in Mexico to take the bold step of advocating the decriminalization of sex work in the United States: "I have met hundreds of men who have paid for sex. Some seek any kind of sex; others want certain kinds of sex; a few look for comfort and conversation. Saying that all sex workers are victims and all clients are demons is the easy way out. Perhaps it's time to face this fact like adults (or at least like Mexico)—with a little less moralizing and a good deal more honesty."

Reflecting on the value of fieldwork and the study of anthropology, Kelly offers, "Anthropology is a unique way to see such vitally important aspects of ordinary people's lives. The ethnographic methods brought me closer to the perspectives of the people I lived and worked with. I was able to use concepts from geography, gender theory, and political economy to analyze sex work in Zona Galactica. I think anthropology allows us to see the world differently, to recognize that long-held individual and collective beliefs can be changed if we come to understand each other in a more relative sense. Really, only by exposing ourselves to other people's way of life can we hope to achieve this kind of examination of ourselves and our own culture."

of these men, the pilgrimage to Mecca may enable them to establish status and respectability in the international arena that they could not achieve on their own at home, where many other Nigerians consider them to be outlaws and deviants.

An In-Group Dialect Challenges Dominant Norms *'Yan daudu* use language, their bodies, clothing, food, and media such as movies and videos to play with the conventional meanings of male and female, masculine and feminine. As a linguistic anthropologist, Gaudio pays particular attention to their use of language as a tool with which to challenge the dominant norms of northern Nigerian culture. *'Yan daudu* have developed their own local language called *yaren harka*, the "dialect of those who do the deed." *Yaren harka* is a secret in-group code drawn from the common Nigerian Hausa dialect; through this code they tease, flirt, and toss around sexual innuendos in a way that is inaccessible to outsiders. In an environment where *'yan daudu* occupy positions of disadvantage and marginalization, the *harka* dialect provides an opportunity to build community and solidarity.

But the *harka* dialect also becomes a site for competition among *'yan daudu*. Because opportunities for material success are limited, internal competitions may emerge among *'yan daudu* for material and symbolic resources. These can include admiration, attention, or "boyfriends" and "husbands." Thus, among *'yan daudu*, language becomes a way to compete. Linguistic skill, creativity, and nimbleness provide the keys to success. The *harka* dialect enables *'yan daudu* to banter about sexuality while disguising their intentions within common, day-to-day language.

Are *'yan daudu* gay? This question is not easy to answer. *'Yan daudu* are feminine men. In contrast, Gaudio takes note of another group of *masu harka*, referred to as "civilians"—masculine men who seek to meet other men. Some "civilians" dress, talk, and act like *'yan daudu*—like women—in private. But by seeking out *'yan daudu*, these "civilian" men can continue to perform their masculinity in public and avoid the threat of discovery. Clearly *'yan daudu* and "civilian" lifestyles challenge the rigid categories of gay and straight, heterosexual and homosexual, that underlie most Western constructions of gender and sexuality.

Globalization's Homogenizing Influence *'Yan daudu* sexual practices in northern Nigeria are complicated by the effects of globalization. Most African countries achieved their independence from European colonial powers in the 1960s and 1970s, and memories of those incursions are still fresh in Africans' collective memory. Moreover, the awareness of new forms of economic, military, political, and cultural domination that have emerged since the end of colonialism are ever present. Like many Africans, many Nigerians regard homosexuality as part of the wave of Western influences that have been flooding their country and continent for well more than a hundred years.

Most national governments in Africa do not consider the practice of homosexuality as authentically African—certainly not the way homosexuality is framed in international scholarly and activist discourse. These governments see the push for recognizing gay sexual rights as a human right as simply a new front of Western imperial domination. One exception to this perspective is South Africa, where gay rights were included in the new constitution of 1994.

Gaudio's ethnography of *masu harka* shows diverse expressions of sexuality on the local level. The presence of *'yan daudu,* for example, challenges the notion that Africa is devoid of indigenous sexual minorities. But the emergence of an international movement for gay rights threatens to undermine the diversity of local expressions of human sexuality. Gaudio notes that Western scholars and international activists often presume that the international movement's categories can be applied with relative ease from one linguistic and cultural setting to another. However, forcing the conversation into restrictive, binary categories of heterosexuality and homosexuality endangers the continued existence of local sexual expression by placing those indigenous expressions into a debate about foreign influence, imperialism, and so-called Western decadence.

The emerging antigay rhetoric unifies Muslim fundamentalist, Christian orthodox, and evangelical groups. It threatens to close off the possibility of recognizing the diversity of sexual desires, practices, and identities of individuals and local communities that may have previously operated outside the Western-oriented, homosexual-heterosexual framework. In so doing, it reveals the power of globalization to introduce narrower, homogenizing perspectives on the many and varied expressions of human sexuality found in cultures around the globe (Gaudio 2009; Harris 2009; Leap 2010).

As we have seen throughout this chapter, human sexuality is more than the personal choices we make about our sexual partners and how we express our erotic desires. The anthropological lens and a global perspective have enabled us to see that sexuality is a complex relationship between individuals as well as between individuals and the larger culture. We have examined how elements of human sexuality are culturally constructed—formed in relationship to particular people, cultural norms, and expectations. Rather than representing sharply drawn, fixed, and oppositional identities representing two discrete categories, sexuality is diverse, flexible, and fluid.

But we have also seen that the construction of human sexuality—how it is perceived and valued—is a highly contested process. Debates rage and decisions are made about human sexuality that affect people's life chances and access to power, privileges, rights, and resources. Certain rights or benefits may be granted or restricted based on assumptions about sexual preferences or sexual behavior. Given this reality, within anthropology sexuality has become a key cultural location for analyzing, understanding, and contesting stratification and inequality, including the ways sexuality intersects with other systems of power, such as race, gender, ethnicity, nationality, religion, kinship, and class.

TOOLKIT

Thinking Like an Anthropologist: Sexuality in Your Life

Sexuality is all around us. Turn on the television, search the Internet, check out at the grocery store, or drive down an interstate highway, and you will find sexuality all around you in reality shows, websites, magazines, and billboard advertisements. At times in U.S. culture, the presence of sexuality is so pervasive as to be overwhelming. In such an environment, how do you begin to make sense of what sexuality means for you on a personal level and for U.S. culture on a political level? Remember to consider the big questions that have organized this chapter:

- What is "natural" about human sexuality?
- What does a global perspective tell us about human sexuality?
- How has sexuality been constructed in the United States?
- How is sexuality an arena for working out relations of power?
- How does globalization influence local expressions of sexuality?

Although anthropology may not be able to help you decide whom to date or when to do what and where, it does offer a set of tools—perspectives and insights—that may help you think more clearly about what it all means, what the cultural frameworks are within which you negotiate your desires and decisions, and what your full range of options may be when you consider your sexuality within a global perspective. Questions of sexuality run deep in U.S. cultural conversations. Having thought through key issues of sexuality from an anthropological perspective, are you better prepared to engage in the debates and advance the conversation?

Key Terms

sexuality (p. 311)
heterosexuality (p. 320)
homosexuality (p. 320)
bisexuality (p. 320)
asexuality (p. 320)
sexual violence (p. 335)
sex tourism (p. 338)
sex work (p. 339)

For Further Exploration

Columbia University. 2013. Go Ask Alice. www.goaskalice.columbia.edu. Columbia University's health service website, Go Ask Alice, provides reliable and accessible information about health, including sexuality, sexual health, and relationships.

The Education of Shelby Knox. 2005. By Marion Lipschutz and Rose Rosenblatt. Cine Qua Non / InCite Pictures. Documentary about a teenager from a Southern Baptist family in Lubbock, Texas, who takes a True Love Waits (chastity) pledge but eventually becomes an activist for comprehensive sex education.

It Gets Better Project. 2010. www.itgetsbetter.org. Website created by sex advice columnist Dan Savage with his partner, Terry, in the wake of several well-publicized cases of young people bullied into suicide. This website is intended to inspire hope for LGBT youth facing harassment. It features videos of moral support from political figures and entertainers who remind teenagers tormented by others about their sexuality that it indeed does get better.

LaFont, Suzanne. 2002. *Constructing Sexualities: Readings in Sexuality, Gender and Culture.* Upper Saddle River, NJ: Prentice Hall.

Schwartz, Pepper, and Virginia Rutter. 1998. *The Gender of Sexuality: Exploring Sexual Possibilities.* Altamira Press.

Southern Comfort. 2001. Directed by Kate Davis. Next Wave Films. A poignant documentary about the life of Robert Eads, a female-to-male transsexual living in rural Georgia. The painful tragedy of Eads's story is that he is dying of ovarian cancer and is denied treatment by two dozen doctors who feared harm to their reputations.

Stop Raping Our Greatest Resource: Power to Women and Girls of Democratic Republic of Congo. 2013. http://drc.vday.org. Hundreds of thousands of women in eastern Congo have been victimized by rape used as a weapon in the ongoing warfare in this African country. This website includes videos, photographs, and descriptions of women's efforts to break the cycle of violence and establish a women's shelter and leadership training school.

Jeffrey Harrison, once a highly requested sperm donor, with a biological daughter in Los Angeles, California.

p. 355

p. 361

p. 365

p. 367

p. 372

p. 380

CHAPTER 10

Kinship, Family, and Marriage

In November 2005, the *New York Times* published a story about Danielle of Seaford, New York, and JoEllen of Russell, Pennsylvania, titled "Hello, I'm Your Sister. Our Father is Donor 150." These two teenagers, whose mothers conceived them through artificial insemination, had recently found each other through the Donor Sibling Registry: a website that facilitates connections between "donor-conceived" offspring and their donor-parents. Meanwhile, in Venice, California, Jeffrey Harrison read the same *New York Times* story. In the late 1980s, Harrison had earned $400 a month donating sperm to the California Cryobank. He was Donor 150. By agreement, the Cryobank had kept his identity anonymous over the ensuing years. Now he was surprised to be reading a story about these two young women conceived with his sperm. Fifteen months later, on Valentine's Day, Mr. Harrison contacted Danielle and JoEllen to reveal his identity.

This story exposes key questions about our most important human relations, relations that we sometimes call "family" and that anthropologists have explored under the category of kinship. Who is "related" to whom? Who decides? Is kinship biological, or can family be chosen? Is Jeffrey Harrison indeed the father of Danielle and JoEllen, or is he simply their common donor? How would you interpret the father role of Jeffrey Harrison in comparison to that of the father who raised Danielle, or to JoEllen's two mothers? Who actually constitutes "family"?

Humans live in groups. As a species, we rarely live alone or in isolation. Kinship—the creation of relatives—is perhaps the most effective strategy humans have developed to form stable, reliable, separate, and deeply connected groups that can last over time and through generations.

kinship: The system of meaning and power that cultures create to determine who is related to whom and to define their mutual expectations, rights, and responsibilities.

nuclear family: The kinship unit of mother, father, and children.

Kinship is the system of meaning and power that cultures create to determine who is related to whom and to define their mutual expectations, rights, and responsibilities. Of course, humans also form groups through work, religion, education, and politics. But none compare to the power of families and kinship networks to provide support and nurture, ensure reproduction of the next generation, protect group assets, and influence social, economic, and political systems.

Kinship groups are often assumed by many in western cultures to have a biological basis and to arise around the **nuclear family** of mother, father, and children. But when we examine these assumptions in a cross-cultural context, they show themselves to be a Euro-American ideal that not even those cultures have realized. Kinship groups come in a variety of shapes and sizes: We trace our connections through biological ancestors. We create kinship relations through marriage and remarriage. We adopt. We foster. We choose families of people who care about us. Sometimes we even imagine everyone in our nation to be part of one big, related, kinship community.

In the twenty-first century, we are vividly aware of new forms of family life as kinship relations shift, closing off familiar patterns and opening up new ones. The image of a family with mother, father, two kids, and a dog gathered around the dining room table every evening for a home-cooked meal and conversation may be familiar as a cultural icon, but for many people the experience of family is more complicated as families are taken apart, reconstructed, and blended. New reproductive technologies—including artificial insemination, in vitro fertilization, and surrogacy—continue to stretch our ideas of kinship and families by showing how human culture, through science and technology, is shaping biological relationships.

Although the term kinship may be unfamiliar to you, the subject material is not. Through kinship studies, anthropologists examine the deepest and most complicated aspects of our everyday lives—our relationships with people closest to us, including our mothers, fathers, brothers, sisters, grandparents, cousins, husbands, wives, and children. These are the people we live with, eat with, count on for support, and promise to take care of when they are in need. We pour our emotions, creative energy, hopes, and dreams into these relationships. Many of the most emotionally vibrant moments of our lives—from joy and love to anger and pain—occur at the intersection of individual and family life: birthdays, holiday celebrations, shared meals, weddings, illnesses, and funerals. Through kinship, we see our lives as part of a continuum. We look back to see the history of the people we come from, and we look ahead to imagine the relatives and families yet to be.

At the same time, kinship is deeply intertwined with forces beyond the everyday activities of family and home. In our families, we also learn basic patterns of human behavior—how to treat one another, how to act in groups, how to navigate differences of age, gender, ethnicity, and sexuality. This enculturation shapes our lives outside the household, including the way we think about gender roles, the division of labor, religious practices, warfare, politics, migration, and nationalism. Because cultural norms, values, and social structures can always be changed, kinship and family also become places of contestation, experimentation, and change that reflect and shape debates within the larger culture.

The study of kinship is one of anthropology's unique innovations for thinking about how culture works. In this chapter, we will explore the following questions about kinship.

- How are we related to one another?
- Are biology and marriage the only basis for kinship?
- Is a country like one big family?
- How is kinship changing in the United States?

We will examine the many strategies people use to form kinship groups, and we will consider the implications of kinship's changing expressions in the twenty-first century. By the end of the chapter you should be ready to interpret your own family tree—not simply by creating a list of relatives, but also by considering how those ties are formed and the role that kin play in shaping who you are as an individual and as a member of society. You will also be prepared to understand and analyze the ways debates about kinship shape important aspects of our individual and collective lives locally, nationally, and globally.

How Are We Related to One Another?

Who are you related to? As we saw in Chapter 5, all humans are closely related genetically, sharing more than 99.9 percent of our DNA. Despite this close biological "kinship" among all humans, closer to home we tend to organize our personal relationships more specifically through systems of common biological descent, marriage, love, and choice. As you will discover throughout this chapter, cultures have a variety of ways of organizing kinship relationships. Some will be familiar to you, and others will not. All are equally valid.

Descent
One way that humans construct kinship groups is by tracking genealogical descent. In descent groups, primary relationships are with consanguineal relatives (what U.S. culture refers to as "blood" relatives). These would include your

descent group: A kinship group in which primary relationships are traced through consanguine ("blood") relatives.

mother, father, sister, brother, grandparents, and grandchildren, as well as your uncles and aunts who are your parents' siblings—but not your uncles and aunts who are married to your parents' siblings. **Descent groups** are often imagined as long chains of connections from parents to children that reach back through many generations to a common ancestor or group of ancestors.

Early anthropological studies through the mid-twentieth century assumed the descent group to be central to the social structure of most nonindustrial cultures outside Europe and North America (Malinowski 1929, 1930; Fortes 1949; Radcliffe-Brown 1950; Evans-Pritchard 1951). Anthropologists of that period expected to find extended descent groups that stretched back over many generations and worked together. Such groups were considered key to understanding each culture's economic, political, and religious dynamics because of the way kinship underlies large social networks extending beyond the immediate family into all aspects of cultural life. We will consider one classic example, the Nuer, in the following section.

In contrast, most European and North American cultures do not use descent to organize social groups. Although we may keep track of our ancestors over a few generations, generally we have not constructed large social networks based on kinship connections. In the United States, perhaps the Rockefellers and the Kennedys might loosely qualify. They stretch back over a few generations, tracing roots to a much more recent common ancestor (either John D. Rockefeller or Joseph Kennedy); and although now subdivided into smaller segments, they still maintain strong enough connections to function together at times on common economic, social, political, or ritual activities and projects. But such descent groups are extremely rare in North America.

Anthropologists distinguish two types of descent groups: clans and lineages. **Lineages** can clearly demonstrate genealogical connections through many generations, tracing the family tree to a founding (apical) ancestor. **Clans** likewise claim connection to a founding ancestor, but they do not provide the same genealogical documentation. Descent groups may be *matrilineal,* constructing the group through the mother's side of the family, or *patrilineal*, tracing kinship through the father's side. Both matrilineal and patrilineal patterns reflect *unilineal* descent because they build kinship groups through either one line or the other. In contrast, *ambilineal* descent groups—including Samoans, Maori, Hawaiians, and others in Southeast Asia and the Pacific—trace kinship through both the mother and the father. This alternative pattern is sometimes called *bilateral* or *cognatic.*

Most people in the world practice patrilineal descent as their primary strategy to track kin group membership. At the same time, most people still build kinship networks bilaterally through both parents, even when tracing descent unilineally. Are you aware of how your own family traces descent?

lineage: A type of descent group that traces genealogical connection through generations by linking persons to a founding ancestor.

clan: A type of descent group based on a claim to a founding ancestor but lacking genealogical documentation.

The Nuer of Southern Sudan The Nuer people of southern Sudan in north-east Africa constitute a classic representation of the descent group. British anthropologist E. E. Evans-Pritchard studied this group in the 1930s (Evans-Pritchard 1951). At the time of his research and until the latter part of the twentieth century, the Nuer were primarily a pastoral, cattle-herding people that moved between settlements throughout the year to adapt to rainy and dry seasons. The Nuer constituted a patrilineal descent group: both boy and girl children were born into the group, but membership could only pass to the next generation through the sons who inherited membership through their fathers. Nuer clans were *exogamous*—meaning that marriages within the group were not permitted. Large clans were divided into lineages, although lineages were extensive enough to spread over several villages.

Cattle were the center of Nuer economic life. They were owned by men, but they were milked by women as well as by boys who had not yet come of age and been initiated into the descent group. A successful marriage proposal often required the groom to provide cattle in exchange for the bride.

The patrilineal kinship structures of clans and lineages provided the primary structure for Nuer political and economic activity. In the villages, the lineages collectively owned land, fisheries, and pastures. Ceremonial leadership of Nuer group life was organized under sacred ritual leaders, but these individuals did not control the social networks built around kinship and cattle, so they were not the driving force in Nuer culture (Stone 2009).

FIGURE 10.1 What does a descent group look like? *Left*, a chief (*standing*) and his sons, photographed by Bronislaw Malinowski; they represent the core of a patrilineal descent group in the Trobriand Islands. *Right*, a Kennedy family portrait, Hyannis, Massachusetts, 1930s, including, seated second from left, future U.S. attorney general Robert Kennedy; center, future U.S. president John F. Kennedy; second from right, family patriarch Joseph Kennedy Sr.

Searching for Kinship Patterns As early anthropologists gathered kinship data from cultures worldwide, they developed a limited number of general categories that facilitated comparison. Despite vast geographic distances and language differences, only four primary systems were identified to classify relatives in the parental generation: *lineal, bifurcate merging, generational,* and *bifurcate collateral.* When beginning with the ego's generation (the ego being the central character and starting point in tracing kinship relationships—for example, you in your own family tree), anthropologists found only six different ways of organizing relatives, in which the variation centered on the classification of siblings and cousins. Each of these six were named after a key group in which the pattern occurred: Eskimo, Iroquois, Hawaiian, Crow, Omaha, and Sudanese (Figure 10.3).

Generalized systems of kinship classification can be very useful for identifying and comparing broad patterns of social structure. But anthropologists have found that actual, local kinship patterns do not always match the generalized models. The ways in which human groups trace connections between generations—in other words, how they construct genealogies—can be messy and far from exact. Genealogies are full of gaps, interruptions, disruptions, uncertainties, and imagined or assumed connections. Some groups have extensive genealogies, but even these carefully constructed records may be partly mythical and based on limited recollections or partial history. In contrast, other groups have extremely shallow genealogical memories that span only two or three generations. Segments of these descent groups may no longer live together or act together. Other relatives may have been forgotten or excluded from the main line through conflict. Political, economic, and/or military upheaval may have disrupted collective memory and records. Or kinship patterns may have changed over time as groups adapted to external pressures. As a result, these groups' knowledge of individual ancestors and even whole generations may have been lost.

Once again, the Nuer are an excellent example. Despite representing one of the six key cross-cultural variations in kinship studies (Sudanese), their day-to-day kinship practices did not exactly match the clear patrilineal descent model that might be imagined on a Nuer family tree. Evans-Pritchard determined that the Nuer inherited formal group membership through patrilineal descent, but he and Kathleen Gough ([1971] 2001), who revisited the study a generation later, found that most Nuer individuals continued to trace kinship relations through both parents. These bilateral kinship relationships created by marriage were often just as important as those created through descent. Specifically, while women married into the Nuer descent group and produced children for that group, they also provided their children with close connections to kin on the mother's side, particularly the mother's brother. This pattern often occurs in patrilineal groups.

MAP 10.1
The Nuer Region of East Africa

FIGURE 10.2 The Nuer, of the Sudan, are a classic representation of a descent group. *Top left,* a Nuer man, his sons, and cattle outside the family homestead, 1930s (photo by E. E. Evans-Pritchard). *Top right,* a Nuer family homestead, 2007. *Bottom left,* Nuer men leaping (beside Evans-Pritchard's tent) in a dance that often took the form of mock battles between village groups. Dances accompanied marriages and provided courtship opportunities for Nuer youth. *Bottom right,* Nuer women dancing in the bride's family homestead at a contemporary Nuer wedding.

FIGURE 10.3 Kinship Naming Systems Early anthropologists identified only six general patterns worldwide for classifying relatives when beginning with the ego's generation: Eskimo, Hawaiian, Sudanese, Omaha, Crow, and Iroquois.

SOURCE: http://anthro.palomar.edu/kinship

ESKIMO

1 = Father	5 = Brother
2 = Mother	6 = Sister
3 = Aunt	7 = Cousin
4 = Uncle	

The Eskimo kinship naming system is the most common in Europe and North America. Only members of the nuclear family are given distinct terms. Aunts and uncles are distinguished from parents but not by side of the family. All cousins are lumped together.

HAWAIIAN

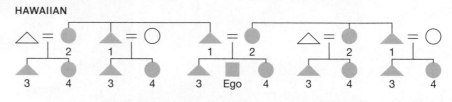

1 = Father and father's brothers	3 = Brothers and male cousins
2 = Mother and mother's sisters	4 = Sisters and female cousins

The Hawaiian system is the least complicated. The nuclear family is deemphasized, and relatives are distinguished only by generation and gender.

SUDANESE

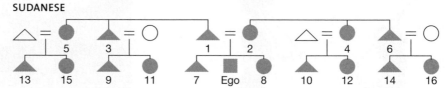

The Sudanese kinship system is the most complex. Each category of relative is given a distinct term based on genealogical distance from ego and the side of the family. There can be eight different cousin terms, all of which are distinguished from ego's brother and sister.

When Gough revisited Evans-Pritchard's original study, she suggested that local events in the 1930s may have affected Nuer kinship practices at the time. During the time of Evans-Pritchard's research in the 1930s, the Nuer were resisting British colonial occupation of the Sudan. In addition, they were involved in a conquest of the neighboring Dinka ethnic group. Additional intense conflicts existed among Nuer groups. Gough suggests that these tensions, conflicts, and disruptions may have intensified Nuer attention to kinship and marriage patterns as they attempted to reinforce group identity and assimilate outsiders. Gough also suggests that the particular expressions of kinship recorded by Evans-Pritchard may have been adaptations to political and economic conditions rather than an entrenched, changeless kinship norm (Gough [1971] 2001; see also Stone 2009).

OMAHA

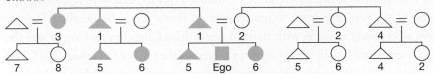

1 = Father and father's brothers
2 = Mother and female on mother's side
3 = Females on father's side
4 = Males on mother's side
5 = Male siblings and parallel cousins
6 = Female siblings and parallel cousins
7 = Male cross cousins
8 = Female cross cousins

The Omaha, Crow, and Iroquois naming systems trace kinship through unilineal descent—either patrilineally or matrilineally—so distinguishing between cousins takes on importance. The Omaha system is typical of kinship patterns traced through patrilineal descent.

CROW

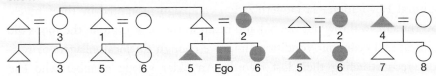

1 = Father and father's brothers
2 = Mother and mother's sisters
3 = Female on father's side
4 = Male on mother's side
5 = Male siblings and parallel cousins
6 = Female siblings and parallel cousins
7 = Male cross cousins
8 = Female cross cousins

The Crow system is typical of kinship patterns traced through matrilineal descent.

IROQUOIS

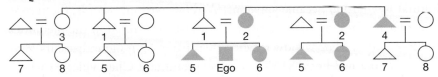

1 = Father and father's brother
2 = Mother and mother's sister
3 = Female on father's side
4 = Male on mother's side
5 = Male parallel cousins
6 = Female parallel cousins
7 = Male cross cousins
8 = Female cross cousins

The Iroquois kinship system can be traced either matrilineally or patrilineally. Note the same term is used for father and father's brother and for mother and mother's sister, reflecting shared membership in lineages.

Kinship, Descent, and Change in a Chinese Village As Gough found in her Nuer study, political factors can shape efforts to construct kinship—a pattern I also uncovered in my own research in a Chinese village. When I conducted fieldwork in the late 1990s, I thought I had found a classic, Nuer-style patrilineal descent group. Ninety percent of the men in the village had the surname Chen and traced their origins back to the founding Chen—the apical ancestor—who they believed had settled in the area more than seven hundred years earlier. The village children, boys and girls, were all named Chen.

But the Chen daughters were all to be married out to men in neighboring villages. The Chen men were to marry women from the same neighboring villages who would move in with them at home. The Chen family temple was the largest ancestral hall in the village and served as the center for venerating Chen ancestors. Until the 1960s, village lands, including agricultural plots and fisheries, were held in common by the Chen lineage, which acted like a small corporation. Male elders allocated access to the collectively owned village property to the other males in the descent group during an annual lineage meeting.

The village appeared to be a textbook case of a patrilineal Chinese decent group. But kinship is always a bit more complicated and interesting than anthropologists first imagine. In the late 1960s, family and temple ancestral records were destroyed as part of a national political movement called the Cultural Revolution—a modernization campaign promoted by the Chinese government to throw out the old and bring in the new. Only in the 1990s did political and economic conditions improve enough for local villagers to consider reconstructing their lost records. An older village member who had become a university professor in the provincial capital accepted the task of writing and publishing a local village history book called a *zhupu* ("gazetteer"). His research included an effort to reconstruct the village genealogy and the Chen line of descent. Funding came from villagers working abroad, particularly in the United States.

When the research was complete, however, the devastating impact of the Cultural Revolution became apparent. Without written records, the reconstructed genealogy relied primarily on oral histories stored in the memories of village elders. Many vividly recalled their parents' and grandparents' generations. Some had heard stories of a few prominent Chen villagers whose earlier travel, business success, or scholarship had made them famous in the villagers' collective memory. Of course, the apical ancestor, his sons, and a few of their immediate descendents had been remembered. Unfortunately, most of the generations prior to 1900 had been left blank. The genealogical details, if they had ever existed, had been destroyed during the Cultural Revolution.

Migration has also challenged the Chen descent group's ability to maintain kinship connections, especially in the context of the current global age. In fact, fully 70 percent of the villagers—most between the ages of eighteen and forty—have left China since the early 1980s to seek their fortunes in the United States, Japan, South America, Canada, and Europe. Some return to visit their hometown. Most marry and have children in their new host country. According to the rules of the patrilineal descent group, all children born to villagers working abroad still belong in the descent group, and males can pass on

MAP 10.2
Fuzhou

FIGURE 10.4 Chinese family ancestral hall outside Fuzhou, China, built with money sent by villagers working abroad.

that membership to the next generation. But faced with such a massive out-migration and global diaspora of the lineage, how would they keep track as villagers migrated halfway around the world?

New York is the primary international destination for the village's immigrants. There, with the support of village leaders in China, immigrants have created a village hometown association to rebuild and strengthen hometown kinship ties. The association enables villagers to reconnect, provide mutual support, share information, and use their kinship networks to improve their immigrant experience. Association leaders also keep track of fellow villagers, their marriages, and their offspring. They report these developments back to the Chen family elders in China for proper recording. Through this process, long-held village strategies for kinship formation and group building are adapting to the challenges of wide-scale international migration, spurred by globalization. Modern communication and transportation technologies are enabling Chinese villagers to innovatively extend their notions of patrilineal descent, both spatially beyond China's national boundary and temporally forward into the future.

Certainly the forces of globalization, including migration and time-space compression, are placing stress on kinship systems worldwide. This is occurring as members of kinship groups relocate temporarily or permanently to nearby factories or jobs in other countries to seek improved economic and educational opportunities or to avoid natural disasters and political upheavals. Although generalized kinship categories developed by an earlier generation of anthropologists have provided insights into broad patterns of kinship, anthropologists who study kinship today confront more fluid kinship patterns maintained through flexibility and creativity.

Marriage and Affinal Ties

A second way humans form kinship groups is through marriage—what anthropologists refer to as **affinal relationships**. Unlike the construction of kinship groups through descent, which links direct genealogical ancestors and descendents, marriage builds kinship ties between two people who are (usually) not immediate biological kin. Marriage also creates a relationship between the spouses' respective kinship groups, called "in-laws" in U.S. culture. The new kinship group created through marriage is linked through affinity and alliance, not through shared biology and common descent.

Something like marriage exists in every culture, but its exact form and characteristics vary widely—so widely, in fact, that it is difficult to say that any one characteristic is universal. **Marriages** create socially recognized relationships that may involve physical and emotional intimacy, sexual pleasure, reproduction and raising of children, mutual support and companionship, and shared legal rights to property and inheritance. The bond of marriage may also serve to create connection, communication, and alliance between groups.

Marriages take many forms, including arranged marriages and companionate marriages. **Arranged marriages**, orchestrated by the families of the bride and groom, continue to be prominent in many cultures in Asia, the Pacific, the Middle East, and Africa. Arranged marriages are even common among some religious groups in the United States and, in a sense, among some segments of the upper class who send their children to elite private schools to meet future partners and encourage in-group marriage. These traditional marriages ensure the reproduction and continuation of the kinship group and build alliance with other kin groups. Thus the couple's parents may view the economic and political consequences of marriage alliance as being too important to the larger kinship group to be left to the whims of two young people. In this context, marriage becomes a social obligation and a symbol of commitment to the larger group rather than a mechanism for personal satisfaction and fulfillment. Alliance marriages of this sort require extensive negotiation to balance the needs of the group and the intimate personal feelings of the individuals being married. Bonds of affection may develop in an arranged marriage, but this is not the primary goal.

What about Love? Today marriage patterns are changing rapidly. Younger generations are increasingly thinking of love, intimacy, and personal pleasure—

affinal relationship: A kinship relationship established through marriage and / or alliance, not through biology or common descent.

marriage: A socially recognized relationship that may involve physical and emotional intimacy as well as legal rights to property and inheritance.

arranged marriage: Marriage orchestrated by the families of the involved parties.

not social obligation—as the foundation on which to build families and kinship relations. Love—and what anthropologists call **companionate marriages**, which are built on love—is the ideal to be achieved.

Romantic love appears to be present in cultures worldwide. For decades, many anthropologists and other scholars considered romantic love to be a luxury and a unique product of modern Western cultures or other global elites. You may find it hard to imagine that anthropologists have largely ignored romantic love in their cross-cultural studies, particularly when considering classic love stories like those of Tristan and Isolde in France, China's Jade Goddess, the Indian Kama Sutra, or the Greek love poems of Sappho. A review of 166 ethnographic studies, however, reveals that even though anthropologists have not focused on romantic love, their research has encountered it in many cultures. William Jankowiak and Edward Fisher's (1992) study found references to love in 147 of the 166 studies, an overwhelming 89 percent. And, they claim, the absence of references to love in the others is more likely a result of oversight by the original researchers rather than the absence of romantic love in the cultures.

Jennifer Hirsch's (2007) study of love in a small western Mexican town examines the rise of companionate marriage at the intersection of love and globalization. In response to migration, economic exchange, and the time-space compression of communication technology such as telephones and the Internet, love and intimacy are being transformed as globalization links a poor, rural community with its wealthy neighbor to the north, the United States. The population of Degollado, Jalisco—fifteen thousand people according to the 2000 census—varies according to the season. In the spring and summer, many residents migrate north of the border to do agricultural and construction work

FIGURE 10.5 Young people's ideas about marriage in Degollado, Jalisco, Mexico, are shifting under the influence of globalization. In the Procession of Absent Sons each winter (*right*), residents of Degollado welcome home those who migrate north of the U.S. border to work, part of a festival atmosphere in which young people explore possibilities for love and marriage.

companionate marriage: Marriage built on love, intimacy, and personal choice rather than social obligation.

MAP 10.3
Degollado

in the United States. When they return in the winter, they bring back dollars, baseball hats, electronics, and trucks. In a festival atmosphere, young girls promenade around the plaza in the hopes of evoking a marriage proposal. "The economy of love is intricately interwoven with the political economy of migration" (Hirsch 2007, 94).

In interviews with local women residents and those who had relocated to the United States, Hirsch found a distinct shift in the description of marriage. For older women, love came from living well together, and successful marriage involved fulfilling one's roles and obligations: men brought home the money; women cooked, washed, cleaned, and raised the children. In contrast, younger women measured a good marriage relationship by its level of intimacy and trust, as well as by mutually pleasurable sex. But Hirsch also found that companionate marriage and the emphasis on love do not lessen inequality in marriage or tensions about who earns the money and who gives the orders. Instead, the emphasis on love appears to provide a modernizing sheen to continuing gender inequalities by glossing them over with sexuality and intimacy.

Ethnographic research has uncovered similar developments in the relationship between love and marriage in many other parts of the world, such as Malaysia (Chan 2006), Papua New Guinea (Wardlow 2006), China (Yan 2003), Egypt (Inhorn 1996), and Brazil (Rebhun 1999; Gregg 2003). In these areas, research reveals diversity in local expressions of companionate marriage but shows that young people increasingly frame marriage in terms of love, in contrast to the marriage patterns of their parents (Hirsch 2007). Consider for a moment how your own views on marriage compare to those of your parents and grandparents.

polygyny: Marriage between one man and two or more women.

polyandry: Marriage between one woman and two or more men.

monogamy: A relationship between only two partners.

Monogamy, Polygyny, and Polyandry Cultural rules, often inscribed in law, may determine who is a legitimate or preferred marriage partner. They may even determine how many people one can marry. Historically, some cultures, such as the Nuer of Sudan or the Brahmans of Nepal, practiced **polygyny**—several marriages involving one man and two or more women. In a few cultures, including the Nyar of India and the Nyimba of Tibet and Nepal, **polyandry** has been common—marriages between one woman and two or more men. Most marriages in the world demonstrate **monogamy**—marriage (usually) between one man and one woman.

Even where monogamous marriages are the norm, it is common for people to marry more than one person in their lifetime. How does this happen? Marriages may be interrupted by divorce or death. In these cases, individuals who marry again reflect a process called *serial monogamy* in which monogamous marriages follow one after the other.

Incest Taboos Just as some form of marriage exists in essentially all cultures, likewise all cultures have some form of **incest taboo**, or rules that forbid sexual relations with close relatives. Such taboos relate to nuclear family members: parents and children, siblings, and grandparents and grandchildren. Incest taboos also affect marriage patterns. A few historical examples of brother-sister marriage exist: among the Inca of Peru, among certain traditional Hawaiian groups, and among ancient Egyptian royalty (perhaps to preserve family control over wealth and power). But these cases are rare. Incest taboos universally prohibit marriage between siblings and between parents and children. But can a person marry a cousin? Let's explore that question more closely.

Beyond the nuclear family, incest taboos vary from culture to culture. In some contemporary cultures, including parts of China, India, the Middle East, and Africa, *cross-cousins* (children of a mother's brother or father's sister) are preferred marriage partners, but *parallel cousins* (children of a father's brother or a mother's sister) are excluded. Even in the United States, incest rules regarding marriage between cousins vary from state to state. Nineteen states allow *first-cousin* marriages (between the children of two siblings). More distant cousins are not excluded from marriage under U.S. law. Former New York City mayor and presidential candidate Rudy Giuliani, for example, was married to his *second cousin* for fourteen years before getting divorced. No other country in the Western world prohibits first-cousin marriage. Moreover, although it is illegal in the United States to marry a *half-sibling* (a brother or sister with whom one shares a parent), this is not illegal in many other cultures. Can you think of anyone in your family or a friend's family who is married to a cousin?

Even though the incest taboo is universal, its origins are unclear. Some scholars have suggested that the taboo arises from an instinctive horror of sex with immediate family members that developed during our evolutionary history (Hobhouse 1915; Lowie [1920] 1961). But studies of primates do not reveal a consistent incest taboo that humans might have inherited (Rodseth et al. 1991). Furthermore, if this instinctive horror existed, then it seems likely that humans would not need to create taboos to restrict incest.

Other theories have addressed the issue from different perspectives. For example, anthropologist Bronislaw Malinowski (1929) and psychologist Sigmund Freud (1952) both suggested that incest taboos might have developed to protect the family unit from sexual competitiveness and jealousy, which would disrupt cooperation. However, neither scholar could substantiate this claim with historical or contemporary ethnographic data. Another theory suggests that incest taboos arose out of concern that inbreeding would promote biological degeneration and genetically abnormal offspring (Morgan [1877] 1964). However, incest taboos predate the development of population science and the understanding of human genetics.

Even using contemporary genetic information, the science does not support the assumptions behind the incest taboo. For instance, incest does not create defective genes. If a harmful trait runs in the family, systematic inbreeding will increase the possibility of the defective gene being passed along and amplified in the gene pool. But long-term systematic inbreeding over many generations has few actual historical human examples. Genetic studies of consanguineous unions show some increased risk of congenital defects, but only within the studies' margin of error. These risks are actually less than the risk of congenital defects in children whose mothers are over the age of forty; yet this older population is not prohibited from marrying or giving birth (Bennett et al. 2002). Therefore, despite the universal existence of incest taboos, the extent of the taboos varies widely and no consensus exists as to their origins or exact purpose.

Other Marriage Patterns Beyond explicit incest taboos, all cultures have norms about who is a legitimate or preferred marriage partner. In some groups, including most descent groups, marriage tends to reflect **exogamy**, meaning marriage to someone outside the group. Other groups practice **endogamy**, requiring marriage inside the group. Although kin group exogamy is more prevalent, endogamy exists in numerous cultures. It is practiced, for example, within the Indian caste system and within whole ethnic groups, as evidenced by both historical and contemporary U.S. marriage patterns.

In the United States, we practice *kindred exogamy*: we avoid, either by force of law or by power of tradition, marriage with certain relatives. At the same time, we also follow clear patterns of class and race endogamy. Indeed, most marriages occur between people of the same economic class and within the same "race" (U.S. Census Bureau 2010). As noted in Chapter 2, interracial marriages were outlawed for most of U.S. history, and only in 1967 did the U.S. Supreme Court rule that antimiscegenation laws are unconstitutional. Although interracial marriage is legal today, intense patterns of racial endogamy continue.

Most monogamous marriages occur between one man and one woman, but there are important exceptions, including female marriage among the Nuer of Sudan and the Nandi of Kenya. Today same-sex marriage has gained increasing acceptance globally, being recognized in the Netherlands (2001), Belgium (2003), Spain (2005), South Africa (2006), Norway (2009), Sweden (2009), Argentina (2010), Iceland (2010), Portugal (2010), Denmark (2012), France (2013), Brazil (2013), Uruguay (2013), New Zealand (2013), and United Kingdom (2013). In North America, Canada legalized same-sex marriages in 2005. In the United States, as of 2013 same-sex marriages are recognized in Massachusetts, Connecticut, Vermont, New Hampshire, Iowa, New York, Washington, D.C., Maryland, Maine, and Washington State, California, Delaware, Minnesota, and Rhode Island.

exogamy: Marriage to someone outside the kinship group.

endogamy: Marriage to someone within the kinship group.

FIGURE 10.6 While interracial relationships are legal in the United States today, intense patterns of racial endogamy (within the same group) continue. Here, Mildred and Richard Loving embrace at a press conference the day after the U.S. Supreme Court ruled in their favor, June 13, 1967, in *Loving v. Virginia*, overturning Virginia's laws banning interracial marriage. And John Lawrence (*left*) and Tyron Garner (*right*) attend a press conference in Houston, June 26, 2003, after the U.S. Supreme Court in *Lawrence v. Texas* struck down the Texas ban on gay sex as an unconstitutional violation of privacy.

Whether arranged or not, and whether monogamous, polygynous, or polyandrous, marriages may be accompanied by an exchange of gifts—most commonly, bridewealth and dowry—used to formalize and legalize the relationship. Though most contemporary Western cultures view marriage as an individual matter entered into by a couple who are romantically in love, in many non-Western cultures marriages focus on the establishment of strategic alliances, relationships, and obligations between groups—namely, the bride's kin and the groom's kin. Bridewealth and dowry gifts formalize and legalize marriages and establish the relationship between these groups.

Bridewealth—common in many parts of Africa, where it often involves the exchange of cattle, cash, or other goods—is a gift from the groom and his kin to the bride's kin. Often thought of as a means to compensate her family for the loss of the bride, bridewealth agreements also establish reciprocal rights and obligations of the husband and wife, give legitimacy to their children, and assign the children to the husband's family. Even with the exchange of bridewealth, though, marriages may not always remain stable. Incompatibility, infertility, and infidelity can threaten the marriage agreement and trigger a return of the bridewealth. In this way, bridewealth can stabilize the marriage by establishing a vested interest for both extended families in the marriage's success (Stone 2009).

Through a **dowry**, the bride's family gives gifts to the husband's family at marriage. Common in India, a dowry may be part of a woman's family inheritance that

bridewealth: The gift of goods or money from the groom's family to the bride's family as part of the marriage process.

dowry: The gift of goods or money from the bride's family to the groom's family as part of the marriage process.

the woman and her new husband can use to establish their household. In many cases, dowries may be seen as compensation to a husband and his family for taking on the responsibility of a wife, perhaps because of women's relatively low status in India or because upper-class and upper-caste women are not supposed to work. Today gifts often include personal and household items. Compulsory dowries are no longer legal in India (since 1961). But dowries are still quite common as part of the public process of transferring rights and legitimizing alliances. In some unfortunate instances where the dowry is considered insufficient, the bride may become the victim of domestic violence. In extreme cases this may lead to the murder or suicide of the bride, sometimes through bride burning or self-immolation. Such practices have come under severe criticism and are the target of human rights campaigns by groups inside India and in the international community that are committed to protecting the rights and lives of Indian women (Stone 2009).

Are Biology and Marriage the Only Basis for Kinship?

Cross-cultural ethnographic research reveals diverse strategies for constructing kinship ties that do not require direct biological connection or marriage alliances. As you will see, the range of strategies underscores the fluid, socially constructed aspect of kinship in many cultures.

Houses, Hearths, and Kinship: The Langkawi of Malaysia

Among Malay villagers on the island of Langkawi, studied by Janet Carsten in the 1990s, kinship is not only given at birth but also is acquired throughout life (Carsten 1997). The Langkawi house and its hearth — where people gather to cook and eat — serve as places to construct kinship. In particular, Langkawi kinship is acquired through co-residence and co-feeding. In the local thinking, "blood" and other bodily substances are formed by eating food cooked at home. Other bodily substances, explicitly breast milk and semen, are regarded as forms of blood. Thus a husband and wife gradually become more similar by living and eating together. Sisters and brothers have the closest kinship relationship in childhood because they grow up in the same household eating the same food; but as they marry and move out of the shared home, their "blood" becomes less similar.

The Malay ideal is to marry someone close in terms of genealogy, geography, social status, or disposition. But perhaps because of the Langkawis' history of mobility, as well as the arrival of settlers in their outlying region of the Malay state, local notions of kinship have allowed new people to become close kin by living and eating together. For example, many children in the community have

MAP 10.4
Langkawi

grown up spending significant time in homes with adults other than their birth parents. This fostering has been common for nieces, nephews, grandchildren, and others who are welcomed into the foster family and treated on an equal basis with those born into the family.

In addition, Langkawi understandings of fostering have often included expressions of hospitality in the community, whether one is a short-term or long-term visitor, a visiting student or a distant relative. Villagers assume that all those who live together and eat together, regardless of their backgrounds, gradually come to resemble one another physically. The ideal guest—successfully fostered—stays for a long time, becomes part of the community, marries a local person, and raises children. In this way, the individual fully enters the kin group. This flexible process has built kinship relations that do not require the connection of biology or marriage. Instead, "[h]ouses and their hearths are the sites of the production of kinship" (Carsten 1997, 128; Carsten 2004; Peletz 1999; Stone 2009).

Cousins by Choice: Asian Youth in Southall, England

Who are your cousins? Are they all biologically related to you? Not necessarily. For example, the youth in Southall, an ethnically diverse suburb of London, England, call one another "cousin" as a way to build strong connections across ethnic, religious, and cultural boundaries. These connections enjoy the strength of kinship and friendship combined.

FIGURE 10.7 Among the Langkawi in Malaysia, kinship is created by sharing meals prepared in the family hearth and living together in the same house. *Left*, Langkawi children eat together near the family kitchen. *Right*, a Langkawi child and her maternal great-grandmother sit together, becoming kin, on a house ladder.

Dana Davis

Dana Davis's research in a shelter for battered women, written up in her book *Battered Black Women and Welfare Reform* (2006), offers insights into the creative process that people use to construct fictive kinship relationships during times of need.

"Since most of the women spent up to three months at the shelter, they came to know each other very well, and the relationships they developed lasted well beyond shelter life. Because the escalation of violence in women's lives caused family ties to disintegrate, women . . . attempted to recreate the family that was lost due to violence" (Davis 2006, 154).

Reflecting on her fieldwork in a recent interview, Davis recalled, "Doing research in the battered women's shelter was very intense. But it was amazing to be around people who at least at that moment had made the decision to leave a battering relationship. They were actually feeling phenomenally empowered. But then felt disempowered as a result of their encounter with the welfare system."

Davis's fieldwork took place immediately after the 1996 passage of the U.S. federal Personal Responsibility and Work Opportunity Reconciliation Act (PRWORA). This legislation sought to restructure the welfare system by limiting the length of time recipients could receive benefits, imposing stricter conditions for food stamp eligibility, reducing assistance to immigrants, and instituting recipient work requirements. In the case of the shelter women, these policies were applied without regard to their experience of violence and abuse, the actual availability of jobs, or the women's efforts to keep their children safe. From Davis's perspective, many of the law's requirements made it more difficult for women in the shelter to access the governmental support they and their families needed. In addition, Davis found that the

women experienced a racism deeply intertwined with public welfare programs and in the actions of program administrators. As a result, after experiencing violence in their personal lives, the women felt they faced a kind of structural violence—violence enacted by the welfare system and its staff. Confronted by these conditions, women turned to the construction of fictive kin to create their own social safety net.

"I always think of fictive kinship as rooted in Carol Stack's work. But I also experienced that process in my own life, having 'sisters' and 'aunts' and 'uncles' who became part of my extended family, people for whom there were mutual obligations. The battered women actually had a structure of who could be who in their networks. People

Anthropologist Dana Davis

employed at the shelter became uncles and aunts. By naming them that, they then did things that were against shelter rules, including going to people's houses, babysitting their kids, doing stuff for them. When they left the shelter, women named other women in the shelter 'sister.' They informally adopted other people's children. The relationships came with mutual obligations for food, money, and services. Some women couldn't afford to get a phone when they moved out to their own apartments. But another woman would get the phone, and someone who was her 'sister' could use that phone number when looking for a job. They were constantly negotiating kinship relationships. They were also negotiating psychological reparative relationships because of the violence and disconnections they had experienced."

Reflecting on her intimate work with women in the shelter during her research, Davis remembered, "There were people I helped individually. I bought food. I went with women to social services. I used my knowledge about human rights violations to urge women to file human rights complaints when they were experiencing what they perceived as demoralizing forms of structural violence when they went to the welfare office.

"What I found so fascinating was the things that women expected me to do as a result of their perception of my power. In fact, I did have more power than they did. Informants are pretty savvy. They know the research world and they wanted me to tell people stuff—meaning policy makers and people who could give the women some immediate relief from their desperation. And they didn't want me to clean it up, which is a slightly awkward and different dilemma.

"One woman was bulimic. She would just stick her finger down her throat to vomit and get people's attention, which she learned to do in foster care when she was being sexually abused. Then she wanted me to go to the department of housing to talk to the director about her bulimia and ask the director to help get her an apartment.

"It's hard to imagine having to go generate the performance of another person's pain. But the women wanted me to translate their experience. I didn't think twice about it at the time. I went right over to the housing department and spoke to the director—who was really quite nice—and I said, you know, this woman, she's going to start gagging and throwing up unless she gets a house. Of course it didn't help her get a house, but I did what she asked me to. It wasn't until I began writing about how desperate the circumstances made these women, that I understood more deeply why they were completely fine with the sensationalization of their experiences. It's all about how you manage depravation through revelation. How you tell your story.

"In hindsight, I would say that I didn't do research on battered women, per se. I would say I did research on neoliberalism [see Chapter 12]. Since the women were experiencing the direct effects of U.S. welfare reform policies, I was really looking at the impact of privatization and neoliberalism, through the lens of battered women. I was talking to real people about something that is ideological and economic and global while at the same time very personal. My research on battered women sat at the intersection of neoliberalism, race, and gender, and at the intersection of intimate violence and structural violence."

In talking about what she hopes for anthropology students, Davis said, "I want students to think outside their own boxes. Anthropology has an accumulation of ethnographic data that helps us see things differently. But anthropology doesn't just help you understand the diversity of the world. It should help you think critically about your own perceptions of the world. Every conversation about cultural anthropology needs to work back to the question, 'How do you now interpret yourself and your community's behavior?'"

MAP 10.5
London

Southall, sometimes referred to as Britain's South Asian capital, is home to Sikhs (the majority), Muslims, Hindus, Caribbean immigrants, and whites (primarily Irish). In Britain, these ethnic minority communities are often viewed as separate groups made up of people who are essentially the same and who pass down their cultures from generation to generation without significant change. In contrast, Southall youth are creating more diverse, inclusive notions of community and culture, connection and kinship. According to anthropologist Gerd Baumann, who studied Southall youth in the 1990s, these youth are less locked into the dominant ideas of ethnic, cultural, and religious difference and are more open to the possibility of a connected Asian community. "Cousins are friends who are kin and kin who are friends," said one of the youths Baumann interviewed (1995, 734). A cousin may be related by biology or through choice. Southall youth may encourage their parents to let them go out because they are going out "with their cousins." Or they may line up cousins for protection against possible street violence because family takes care of family. In the process, Southall's youth are expanding the idea of kin across boundaries of religion, ethnicity, and culture.

FIGURE 10.8 Youth in Southall, outside London, call one another "cousin" to build connections across boundaries of ethnicity, religion, and race.

Why has the kinship term *cousin* been so successful for constructing kinship ties in Southall? Because *cousin* is common in many of the languages and immigrant cultures represented in the community, people of diverse backgrounds share some common expectations about what being a cousin means. Biological cousins, like any biological alliances, are not always reliable in times of intense need. So the possibility of adding other, more trustworthy, cousins to one's kinship network is very attractive. And success in constructing cousins has led to further experimentation. In Southall, the power of *cousin* derives from the blurring of lines of kinship and friendship. Kinship carries a sense of obligation and loyalty; friendship affords the power of choice and preference. Together they generate a blend of moral expectations that establishes a unique foundation for relatedness. Using the term *cousin* provides an opening to build connections, alliances, and deep relations among people of often extremely different backgrounds (Helweg 1998; Shaw 1998).

Creating Kin to Survive Poverty: Black Networks near Chicago, Illinois

Kinship can even be a means to survive poverty, as Carol Stack's *All Our Kin: Strategies for Survival in a Black Community* (1974) demonstrates. This ethnography is a classic in anthropological kinship studies. Through deep involvement in an impoverished urban African American community called the Flats in a town outside Chicago, Stack uncovered residents' complex survival strategies based on extended kinship networks.

Although the federal government's 1965 Moynihan Report "The Negro Family: The Case for National Action" had branded the black family as disorganized, dysfunctional, and lost in a culture of poverty of its own making, Stack found otherwise. She uncovered a dynamic set of kinship networks based on mutual reciprocity through which residents managed to survive conditions of intense structural poverty and long-term unemployment.

These kinship networks included biological kin and *fictive kin*—those who became kin. They stretched among households and across generations, extending to include all those willing to participate in a system of mutual support. People provided child care. They loaned money to others in need. They took in children who needed a foster home for a while. They borrowed clothes. They exchanged all kinds of things when asked. They cared for one another's sick or aging family members. Despite survival odds stacked against them in a community with few jobs, dilapidated housing, and chronic poverty, residents of the Flats succeeded in building lifelines for survival through their extended kinship networks (McAdoo 2000; Taylor 2000).

For another look at black women's strategies for establishing kin relationships, see "Anthropologists Engage the World" on pages 368–69.

MAP 10.6
Chicago

Mapping Kinship Relationships: Tracing Your Family Tree

Kinship is constructed. Exactly how it is constructed can vary from culture to culture. For example, families can be formed on the basis of biology, marriage, and / or choice. Thus strategies for building kinship and identifying relatives can be complicated. In this exercise, you trace your family tree. Keeping in mind what you've read in this chapter, let's see what you can learn about how your family has constructed kinship relationships.

Getting Started

An abbreviated list of symbols used to create a genealogical kinship chart is given below. The chart starts with a key individual, the central character, who is referred to as the "ego" and serves as the starting point in tracing kinship relationships. In your family tree, you are the ego.

How can you learn about your family tree and kinship history?

Symbol	Meaning	Symbol	Meaning
Characters		*Kin Abbreviations*	
Δ	male	M	mother
○	female	F	father
□	individual	B	brother
	regardless of sex	Z	sister
/ (✕, ∅)	deceased	H	husband
▲, ●, ■	ego of the	W	wife
	diagram	D	daughter
		S	son
		C	cousin

Symbol	Meaning
Relationships	
=	is married to
≠	is divorced from
~	co-habitates with
≁	is separated from / does not co-habitate with
|	is descended from
⊓(⊓)	is the sibling of
⊙	adopted-in female
⊿	adopted-in male

Research Strategies

In gathering information about your family history, many sources are available. Interview family members. Search family records to see what might already exist. Old family papers and record books can be very useful: for instance, family Bibles often have records written in them, and photographs may have names or dates noted on the back. Search for family burial plots; census and voter rolls; birth, marriage, and death certificates; wills; land deeds; and immigration and military records. Consult genealogy websites, and consider using an online program that allows members of your family to add information to your tree.

Kinship Language in Comparative Perspective

Language can tell you a lot about kinship. Anthropologists compare genealogical kin types to various cultures' actual kinship terms. For example, Americans use the term *uncle* to cover a wide range of kin, including a mother's brother (MB), a father's brother (FB), a mother's sister's husband (MZH), and a father's sister's husband (FZH). In this context *uncle* does not differentiate biological descent from marriage relationships, nor does it distinguish by age.

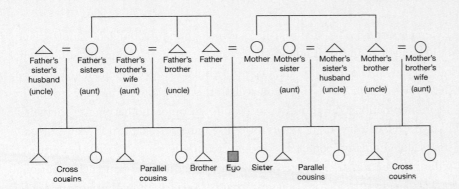

FIGURE 10.9 Nuclear Family Kinship Chart This typical kinship chart of a nuclear family is labeled both with genealogical kin type and with the culturally specific kinship terms used in the United States. Your family may not fit this pattern, but it provides a place to start building your own family tree.

In contrast, Chinese terminology calculates kinship much more carefully. It distinguishes paternal and maternal relatives as well as birth order within generations and biological versus affinal descent. The Chinese do not have a generic term for "uncle." Instead, unique terms denote a father's older brother as opposed to his younger brother. A distinction also exists between a father's brothers and a mother's brothers, as well as between a father's sister's husband and a mother's sister's husband.

Father's older brother: *bofu* 伯父
Father's younger brother: *shufu* 叔父
Father's sister's husband: *gufu* 姑父
Mother's brother: *jiufu* 舅父
Mother's older sister's husband: *yifu* 姨父

Kinship terminology reflects different calculations within the culture about the role of these relatives in the life of the ego. In much of China, the extended family (*jia* 家) and lineage (*zu* 族) have played a pervasive role in economics, politics, and religion. As a result, kinship roles and obligations are carefully traced and implemented.

As you develop your own kinship chart / family tree, try using kin types rather than kin terms to make your family tree as specific and informative as possible. The simplicity of contemporary U.S. kinship terminology reflects the dominant role of the nuclear family that focuses on father, mother, and children as the key kinship relationships. Uncles and aunts, regardless of their genealogical kin type, play a limited role in child rearing, economic support, and inheritance. With kinship calculated bilaterally (that is, with equal weight on the mother's and the father's side of the kinship chart), there is no need to differentiate kinship terminology at this level.

Interpreting Your Family Tree

Families are more than lines on a family tree. Families represent stories, interesting people, power dynamics, even mysteries. What story does your family tree tell? Your family tree reflects educational patterns, geographic relocations, and inheritance flows. It has grown and been pruned through biology, marriage, and choice. Some branches likely are well preserved, and others might be missing. Who has been cultivating and pruning the tree and who has the records now?

As a budding anthropologist, you are interested in what patterns your family tree reveals.

Is a Country Like One Big Family?

References to the nation often invoke metaphors of homeland, motherland, fatherland, and ancestral home. These concepts consolidate political force and build a sense of common nationality and ethnicity. Indeed, Benedict Anderson, in *Imagined Communities* (1983), marvels at the ability of nation-states to inspire a common national or ethnic identity among people who have never met, most likely never will meet, and have little in common socially, politically, or economically. Yet many people feel so connected to their country that they are even willing to die for it. How does this idea of the "nation" gain such emotional power? Janet Carsten (2004) suggests that nationalism draws heavily on ideas of kinship and family to create a sense of connection among very different people.

Like membership in many families, citizenship in the nation generally derives from birth and biology. Citizenship may be conveyed through direct descent from a current citizen. Another key pathway to membership in some nations, available to immigrants and other outsiders, like membership in many other families, is through marriage. Over time, members of the nation come to see themselves as part of an extended family that shares a common ancestry and a deep biological connection. As the boundaries blur among kinship, nationalism, and even religion, these powerful metaphors shape our actions and experiences (Carsten 2004). The next two sections illustrate how experiences related to the concepts of kinship and the nation can differ dramatically from one culture to another.

MAP 10.7
Punjab

Violence, Kinship, and the State: Abducted Women in Western Punjab

The relationship between kinship and the nation-state can be highly complex, especially under conditions of violence. Anthropologist Veena Das (1995), known for her work on violence, suffering, and the state, has explored these complicated linkages in the aftermath of the disastrous partition of India and Pakistan in 1946–47. Over the course of fifteen months following partition, widespread violence struck cities, towns, and the countryside. Fanatic Hindus, Muslims, and Sikhs carried out kidnappings, rapes, lootings, and other atrocities against members of groups other than their own. More than half a million people were left dead in the name of religion and in the service of patriotic fervor.

Das focuses on the more than one hundred thousand women who were abducted and the many more who were raped during the mayhem. Their abduction and rape created a moral and practical crisis, both for families and for the state. Within families of West Punjab, where most of the abuses occurred, kinship norms traditionally placed high values on purity and honor to help regulate sexuality. Thus, women who were violated and abducted during the violence were seen to bring shame on themselves and their families. In fact, Das documents widespread stories, particularly among men, who honored the memory of women relatives who chose death rather than sexual violation. These women were considered heroic martyrs.

After the conflict, the governments of both countries set a high priority on recovering the "sisters and daughters" who had been abducted so they could be restored to their families of origin. Over several years, however, numbers of abducted women had married, become pregnant, borne children, and even converted to their abductor-husbands' religion. Yet the return of these women and children became a matter of national honor. The Indian and Pakistani governments passed legislation invalidating their marriages and conversions and forced them to leave their new families behind.

Despite each state's sense of victory in restoring its national kinship honor, the women's families of origin did not always share this satisfaction. For example, many returning women were quietly married off to any relative who would take them. Their children—conceived during abduction—were rarely claimed as legitimate kin. Both the women and children were left out of family genealogies and stories.

Overall, the return effort yielded contradictory outcomes. The state celebrated the return of abducted sisters, daughters, and their children as a sign of the restoration of the national family and the upholding of its paternal role to protect its family members. But the state's actions conflicted with local kinship norms. Family honor was not restored by the return of the abductees, but rather compromised by the sexual violations these women had experienced. Although the state sought the return of its rightful members as an act of purification to restore national honor, local families, confronting the abducted women's perceived pollution, sought to restore family honor by pushing the women away and silencing their stories. In these contradictory outcomes, we see how kinship can serve as an arena in which other structures of power exert domination.

Reproducing Jews: Issues of Artificial Insemination in Israel

In another nation as well, Israel, we can see how women serve as key players in defining and maintaining kinship connections. Susan Kahn's (2000) ethnography *Reproducing Jews: A Cultural Account of Assisted Conception in Israel* provides a dramatic contemporary example of the powerful intersection among reproduction, kinship, religion, and the state. For historical and religious reasons, Jewish women in Israel feel great pressure to reproduce the family and the nation. Israel's national health policies heavily favor increased reproduction. The national health insurance, for instance, subsidizes all assisted reproductive technologies. It does not promote family planning services to prevent pregnancy. Today the country has more fertility clinics per person than any other nation in the world, and it was the first to legalize surrogate motherhood.

Kahn's study examines a small but growing group of single Jewish mothers who are giving birth through artificial insemination. Because Jewishness passes down matrilineally from mother to child, what happens when a child is conceived through assisted reproductive technologies? These matters are of vital importance to the reproduction of Judaism and the state of Israel and, thus, are subject to intense debate by Jewish rabbis and Israeli state policymakers alike. Some scenarios are straightforward. For instance, in the eyes of the Israeli state any offspring conceived through artificial insemination and born to unmarried Jewish women are legitimate citizens. The line of descent and religious inheritance through the mother is clear. As evidence, the state provides these unmarried mothers with a wide range of support, including housing, child care, and tax breaks.

But other scenarios spur complex disagreements about religion and nationality. What is the effect on citizenship and religious identity when non-Jewish

MAP 10.8
Israel

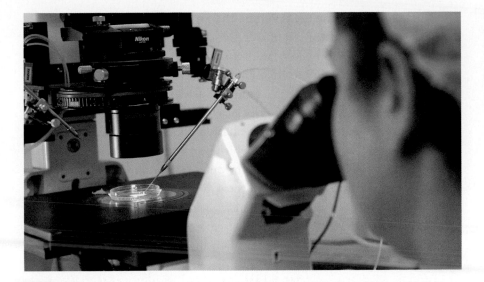

men donate sperm to Jewish women? Who is considered to be the father—the sperm donor or the mother's husband? When Jewish women carry to term eggs from non-Jewish women, who is considered to be the mother—the donor of the egg or the woman who carries the egg to term? The situation is equally complicated if a non-Jewish surrogate mother carries the embryo of a Jewish woman that was fertilized by a Jewish man through in vitro fertilization.

Much is at stake in these arguments for the Jewish religion and for the state of Israel. The decision about kinship in these cases of assisted reproductive technologies intersects with heated debates about how Judaism is reproduced and how Israel is populated. In fact, the decision has implications not only for the Jewish religion but also for notions of ethnic and national belonging and for the pathways to legal citizenship in the state of Israel (Finkler 2002; Nahman 2002; Feldman 2001; Stone 2009).

How Is Kinship Changing in the United States?

Many people see the 1950s-style nuclear family (represented in classic television shows such as *Leave It to Beaver*) as the traditional model of kinship in the United States. The father-husband-breadwinner went to work each day outside the home, while the mother-wife stayed home to take care of the household, raise the children, and be the ideal companion. They owned their own single-family house in the suburbs and functioned as a separate, private family unit. In many ways, this view of the nuclear family has become entrenched as the standard against which to judge other family forms (Schneider 1980).

The Nuclear Family: The Ideal versus the Reality

The nuclear family concept acquired a particular history in Western industrialized cultures. This occurred as families adapted to an economic system that required increased mobility to follow job opportunities wherever they might lead. Though people are born into a **family of orientation** (in which they grow up and develop life skills), when they reach adulthood they are expected to detach from their nuclear family of orientation, choose a mate, and construct a new nuclear **family of procreation** (in which they reproduce and raise their own children). These "detachable" nuclear family units are extremely well adapted to a culture that prioritizes economic success, independence, and mobility over geographic stability and intergenerational continuity.

Historical studies suggest that the place of the nuclear family as the cornerstone of U.S. culture may be more myth than reality (Coontz 1988, 1992). Although the nuclear family came into prominence during a unique period of economic expansion after World War II, before that time it had not played a major role in the kinship history of the United States. The idealized nuclear family of the twentieth century did not exist for the early colonists and only emerged as a result of industrialization in the nineteenth century. Even at its height in the mid-twentieth century, participation in the nuclear family model was far from universal. It was limited to a minority of Americans, particularly those in the white middle class (Coontz 1988, 1992; Carsten 2004; Stone 2009).

Current kinship patterns in the United States are changing rapidly, just as they are in many other parts of the world. In a wide variety of newly constructed family forms and kinship networks, biology is becoming less central and personal choice is becoming more important (Figure 10.12).

Though the divorce rate has been 50 percent for more than three decades, today in the United States we are creatively renegotiating kinship after divorce. Blended families are constructing new relationships to include step-parents, step-children, step-siblings, multiple sets of grandparents, and extended households of former spouses. Unmarried couples are living together. Same-sex couples are having or adopting children. Families are supplementing biological connections and affinal marriage connections with alternative family forms based on friendship, respect, and mutual support. These patterns reflect new residential and interpersonal relationships that contrast sharply with the imagined privacy and separation associated with the nuclear family ideal.

Chosen Families

People in the United States are increasingly creating kinship through choice. Step-parents, step-children, and step-siblings, as well as families with adopted children, are choosing to construct blended families with deep, enduring bonds. New reproductive technologies are yielding families of choice through in vitro

---

family of orientation: The family group in which one is born, grows up, and develops life skills.

family of procreation: The family group created when one reproduces and within which one rears children.

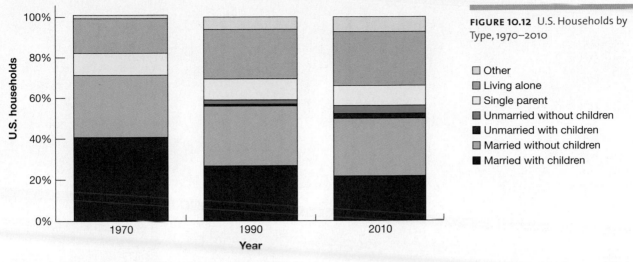

FIGURE 10.12 U.S. Households by Type, 1970–2010

☐ Other
◼ Living alone
☐ Single parent
◼ Unmarried without children
◼ Unmarried with children
◻ Married without children
◼ Married with children

SOURCE: http://www.census.gov/hhes/families/data/families.html

fertilization, artificial insemination, and surrogacy. These patterns cut across all social classes and ethnic groups.

Kath Weston's (1991) ethnographic study of the construction of gay and lesbian families in San Francisco in the 1980s, *Families We Choose*, provides an example of creating kinship through choice. For many gay men and lesbians, "coming out" is a uniquely traumatic experience, especially when the revelation of one's sexuality and life choices generates hostility from close friends and family. When parents, siblings, and other close relatives cut off the kinship ties that U.S. culture suggests should be permanent and enduring, gay men and lesbians have turned to chosen families instead.

Not surprisingly, chosen families come in many shapes and sizes. Gay and straight friends, biological children, children adopted formally and informally, and former lovers all can become kin. Close friends can become family. Support networks and caregivers can take the place of biological kin and become kin themselves. Weston finds this to be a particularly common experience for those who provide care through intense illness, such as AIDS. Love, compassion, and the hard work of care over time make kinship very real in chosen families. This is a crucial development, especially when biological kin ties are inadequate or have failed completely.

Weston's study reminds us not to assume that the natural characteristics of biological kinship ties are better than the actual behavior of chosen families. In the absence of functional, biologically related families, Weston points out, chosen families take on the characteristics of stability, continuity, endurance, and permanence to become "real" (Bolin 1992; Lewin 1992).

FIGURE 10.13 Increasingly people are creating kinship through choice. Here, a gay couple in Chengdu, China, share their home with their adopted son, daughter-in-law, and grandson.

The Impact of Assisted Reproductive Technologies

Discussions of new technologies that assist in human reproduction have filled the popular media, religious publications, courtrooms, and legislative halls of government. Such technologies include sperm and egg donation, in vitro fertilization, surrogacy, and cloning. Their emergence raises questions about the rights of parents and of children born with this assistance, as well as the impact of these innovations on our ideas and experience of kinship and family. Culture, in the form of medical technology, is now shaping biology. The long-term implications for kinship are unclear but deserve consideration (Franklin 1997).

Reproductive technologies are not new. Most, if not all, cultures have had techniques for promoting or preventing conception or enabling or terminating pregnancy. These have included fertility enhancements, contraceptives, abortion, and cesarean surgeries. Over the last thirty years, technological developments have opened new avenues for scientific intervention in the reproductive process and the formation of kinship. DNA testing can now determine the identity of a child's father with remarkable certainty, erasing uncertainty about paternity. Medical tests can now identify the sex of unborn children, a practice that has become problematic in parts of India and China where a strong cultural preference for male children has led to early termination of many female fetuses (Davis-Floyd 1997). As the following examples illustrate, when reproductive technologies become increasingly specialized, the implications for cultural constructs such as family and kinship become progressively more complex.

Artificial Insemination and In Vitro Fertilization Artificial insemination with donated sperm is now quite common in cases where an individual or a couple is infertile or where a woman wants to get pregnant without the participation of a man. Artificial insemination is relatively simple, inexpensive ($200 to $400), and successful 30 percent of the time with fresh sperm and 15 percent of the time with frozen sperm. Sperm can be provided by the legal father or by an anonymous donor.

In vitro fertilization is much more complicated and expensive, with fees topping $25,000 for one treatment. After an egg is fertilized in a laboratory petri dish, the resulting embryo is implanted in a woman's uterus—either the biological mother's or a surrogate's. In vitro fertilization procedures are less successful (14 percent) than artificial insemination with fresh sperm, often requiring multiple attempts and sometimes ultimately not working. Some women find the process so stressful that advocates have suggested the procedure's real beneficiaries are the highly paid medical professionals, not the couples who desperately want children and undergo the procedure with expectations that give them what is often false hope (Raymond 1993; Bonaccorso 2009).

Surrogacy In vitro fertilization has increased the number of surrogate mothers, a development that further complicates ideas of kinship. This complex situation first came to light in 1987 when Marybeth Whitehead, a surrogate mother, sought custody of Baby M in a widely publicized U.S. legal case. She had contracted with William Stern and his wife to have a child using his donated sperm, but subsequently she sought to break the contract and keep the child. After a protracted legal battle, two separate New Jersey courts awarded custody to Stern. The case raised key questions for understandings of kinship: Who was the mother? If Whitehead was the mother, why would the courts grant custody to the father? Can a woman give away her "biological" motherhood through a written contract? Is the man who simply provides sperm more of a father than the woman who provides the egg, carries the fetus, and gives birth to the child is a mother? (See Raymond 1993; Kahn 2000; Teman 2010.)

Surrogate mothers earn about $10,000 for carrying a child to term. But Helena Ragoné's (1994) study of surrogate mothers in the United States found that most were not motivated by financial gain. Most were not poor. In fact, most were working-class women with modest incomes. They reported being motivated by the desire to give the gift of a child to a couple who could not have one of their own. Ragoné's study, however, raised key ethical concerns about the power dynamics involved when wealthy couples hire working-class women to bear their children. What are the implications of wealthy women buying or renting the rights to the bodies of women who are less economically well off in order to satisfy a desire for reproduction? How does a particular culture separate the economic, biological, and emotional issues involved in surrogacy? These are the difficult questions that women are facing with the rise of new assisted reproductive technologies.

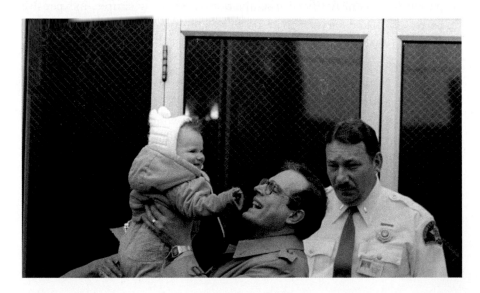

FIGURE 10.14 But who is the mother? William Stern holds his daughter, then known as Baby M, after her visit with her birth mother, Mary Beth Whitehead, who acted as a paid-surrogate mother for Stern and his wife but refused to give up custody after the girl was born.

Cloning Cloning—the creation of genetically identical copies of cells or whole organisms—has not been used to reproduce humans. It has, however, successfully served to reproduce sheep, goats, mice, rats, cats, rabbits, cattle, and many other species (Franklin 2007). Therapeutic cloning of human cells is an active area of research that involves the use of embryonic stem cells—cells taken from embryos for research into treatments for degenerative diseases and for use in medicines and transplants. Ethical issues for research on human embryos and human cloning are extremely complicated and controversial.

Natural human cloning occurs with the birth of identical twins (Stone 2009). But human cloning as a new reproductive technology aimed at reproducing humans would be a radical transformation of the relationship of biology and culture (through technology). From an anthropological perspective, radical technological interventions over the past twenty years—from fertility treatments and genetic testing to mapping the human genome and cloning—are transforming the field of kinship studies, redefining the boundaries between nature and culture, and suggesting the need to reshape basic understandings of kinship.

Families of Same-Sex Partners

Gay and lesbian couples are not new in U.S. culture, but recently they have become more open about their sexual orientation and their relationships. At the same time, many other people are having an increasingly open discussion about gay men, lesbians, and same-sex marriage. Television shows and movies routinely include gay characters. Rosie O'Donnell and Ellen DeGeneres have children whom they raise with their women partners. The Episcopal Church ordained the first openly gay bishop, Eugene Robinson, who is in a committed, long-term relationship. And when a high school in Louisiana cancelled its senior prom in 2010 rather than allow a graduating student to bring her girlfriend as her date, a group of parents organized an alternative prom so the girls could attend. These examples demonstrate a growing recognition of same-sex relationships in numerous U.S. cultural arenas.

However, the cultural debate about homosexuality and same-sex marriage in the United States is intense and by no means settled. Within the debate we can see the contestation of cultural norms and values. Opponents raise concerns that these alternative kinship patterns will cause the breakdown of the traditional family and that the acceptance of homosexuality will lead to social disorder. Echoing their concerns, in 1996 the U.S. Congress passed the Defense of Marriage Act, eventually repealed in 2013, which forbade federal government recognition of same-sex marriages. At the same time, as noted earlier, a growing number of states have legalized same-sex marriage, recognized same-sex marriages conducted in other states, and registered civil unions, thereby enabling same-sex couples to qualify for many of the same social benefits that are available to heterosexual couples in those locales.

Drawing on generations of cross-cultural research on kinship, marriage, and the family, in 2004 the American Anthropological Association issued the following statement:

> The results of more than a century of anthropological research on households, kinship relationships, and families, across cultures and through time, provide no support whatsoever for the view that either civilization or viable social orders depend upon marriage as an exclusively heterosexual institution. Rather, anthropological research supports the conclusion that a vast array of family types, including families built upon same-sex partnerships, can contribute to stable and humane societies. (American Anthropological Association 2004)

From an anthropological perspective, these discussions about same-sex marriage illustrate the changing patterns of kinship in the United States. Looking cross-culturally, we see that there is no single definition of marriage, but many. As anthropologist Linda Stone notes, "From a global, cross-cultural perspective, those who seek same-sex marriage are not trying to redefine marriage, but merely to define it for themselves, in their own interests, as people around the world have always done" (Stone 2009, 271).

A similar response might reassure those who worry that changing kinship patterns, particularly the shift away from the nuclear family, will undermine traditional family values. Concern over the breakdown of the traditional family often centers on increasingly high divorce rates, a rise in teen pregnancy, and a growing number of children living in poverty because they reside in single-parent households. However, in historical comparison, some kinship patterns that today appear strikingly different—especially when compared to the ideal of the nuclear family—may not represent such dramatic change after all. Consider the following observations. Teen pregnancy rates have declined since their peak in 1957. Although 20 percent of all children in the United States live in poverty today—a very troubling statistic—in 1900 the same percentage of children lived in orphanages, often because parents were too poor to raise them at home. And although current divorce rates are high, marriages in earlier generations did not last any longer. In 1900 the average life expectancy for men was 46.3 years, compared to 76.2 in 2010. Women in 1900 could expect to live an average of 48.3 years, compared to 81 in 2010 (U.S. Center for Disease Control, 2013). Because of significantly shorter life expectancies, earlier marriages tended to be cut short by a spouse's death,

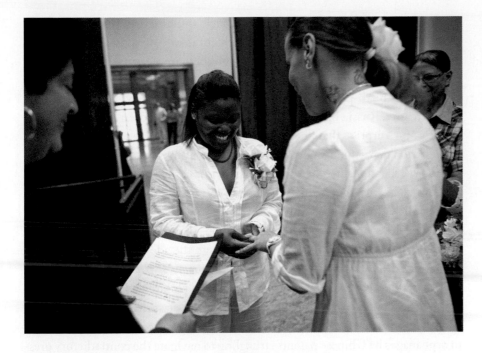

FIGURE 10.15 Nastassia Heurtelou (*left*) and Luz Heurtelou (*right*) were married at the Brooklyn Clerk's Office, July 24, 2011, when New York became the sixth U.S. state to legalize same-sex marriage.

not by divorce. As a result, the proportion of children raised in single-parent households in 1900 was similar to the proportion today (Coontz 1992, 1997).

Although it is possible to find and interpret statistics that might support opposing sides in the debate over changing marriage and family patterns, one point is undeniable: marriage, family, and kinship are cultural constructs, and as such they are subject to change. You are certain to see even more change in these arenas during your lifetime.

Transnational Adoptions

The process of adoption—the legal transferring of children for parenting purposes—and the experiences of adopted children and their families offer further insight into the social construction of kinship and the creation of chosen families. At the same time, the recent rise in transnational adoptions offers insights into the influence of globalization on the construction of kinship across national borders.

Global Trends and Structural Players In the United States, by 2007 intercountry adoptions represented 14 percent of all adoptions, the third-largest source after adoption by relatives and those organized through a U.S. child welfare agency. Fully 19,509 out of 136,001 U.S. adoptions in 2007 were arranged across national borders. The top five "sending" countries were China (5,453), Guatemala (4,728), Russia (2,310), Ethiopia (1,255), and South Korea (939). Globally, not all countries permit international adoption of their children.

Even those that do allow such adoptions, such as China and Korea, have well-established rules and strict procedures (Kim 2010). In contrast, Guatemala has significantly curtailed its adoption program in recent years in response to abuses that include the trafficking of children bought or stolen from their Guatemalan birth parents (U.S. Department of Health & Human Services 2012). In 2013, Russia banned adoptions of Russian children by U.S. citizens.

It is no surprise that the power of government offices, welfare agencies, immigration departments, and other institutions shapes the movement of people based on age, nationality, gender, and class. In this context, the exchange of babies creates a global market in which children in certain countries become commodities for consumption by parents in other countries. Research by sociologist Sara Dorow explores this complicated intersection of economics, politics, national identities, race, gender, and class created through the adoption process.

In *Transnational Adoption: A Cultural Economy of Race, Gender, and Kinship* (2006), Dorow traces the journey of Chinese children adopted by U.S. parents as they cross geographic, cultural, ethnic, and class divides. Most children adopted from China have been abandoned in public spaces or secretly delivered to orphanages by Chinese parents struggling to navigate the contradictory pressures of (1) a strong cultural preference for sons and (2) government-enforced family planning policies that seek to limit families to one child. In traditional Chinese exogamous marriage patterns, daughters marry out into another family. Sons then provide the only guaranteed source of long-term labor and financial security, especially for rural families. These patterns directly conflict with the government's one-child-per-family policy if the firstborn child is a girl. Even allowing rural families to have a second child if the first is a girl has not eliminated female infanticide or the abandonment of girl babies.

China provides no legal channel for parents to put their children up for adoption. As a result, Dorow estimates that several hundred thousand abandoned babies, almost all girls, are in the care of Chinese orphanages at any given time. An even larger number have been adopted by Chinese families in China. Moreover, fully 95 percent of intercountry Chinese adoptions are girls.

Transnational adoption may be viewed as a series of individual stories: for example, a Chinese mother gives up her baby; the baby is adopted and moved; a U.S. mother seeks a baby and successfully completes the adoption process. But Dorow advocates a more comprehensive and global view of the process—a view that incorporates cultural norms and values, the political contexts of the sending and receiving countries, economic factors, and a vast array of institutions and individual actors that combine to create a new form of international immigration. Dorow's multisited, global ethnography encompasses eighty interviews with adopting parents and other participants in the adoption process plus fieldwork in Minnesota, San Francisco, and eight locations in China.

FIGURE 10.16 Globalization is shaping kinship as families are constructed across national borders. Here, couples from the United States wait at the U.S. embassy in Guangzhou, south China, to get visas for their newly adopted Chinese children.

Tracing the paths of the children through the adoption process, she encounters a complicated array of orphanages, administrators, government offices, tourist hotels, adoption agencies, translators, facilitators, advocacy groups, social workers, support groups, adoptive families, and the children themselves. All play a role in a circuitous, expensive (adoptive families pay $20,000 on average), and public process of creating the intimate experience of kinship.

What is the process by which Chinese girls become others' kin through transnational, transracial adoption? Through adoption, Chinese babies—usually between five and twenty-four months old—are transported from some of the country's poorest and most marginal regions to live with primarily white, middle- and upper-class families in one of the world's most developed countries. Certainly the race and class of their adoptive families eases the assimilation process. But the transnational flow of bodies reflects the unevenness of globalization, because uneven economic and political opportunities separate Chinese and U.S. families.

Is a "Clean Break" Possible? One attraction of Chinese adoptions is the imagination of a "clean break" between the family of birth and the family of adoption. Public records of biological parents rarely exist for abandoned Chinese babies, significantly curtailing the likelihood of later attempts to reclaim the children or reestablish contact. The new parents become indisputably permanent and legal parents. And with the passage of the 2001 U.S. Child Citizen Act, children adopted abroad are automatically granted U.S. citizenship upon their return with citizen parents to the United States. The Act dramatically streamlines the process of adoption, citizenship, and, in the eyes of adoptive parents, assimilation into their new families, culture, and nation. Many adoptive parents also believe that Asian children are more easily assimilated into white families than children of Latino, Native American, or African descent, including African American babies—thus facilitating the "clean break" from country and culture of origin.

But Dorow's research questions whether such a clean break is possible. After all, the transition is not easy for many children or their adoptive families. Where do adopted Chinese babies belong? Born in China, are they Chinese? Adopted by U.S. families, are they American? Are they Chinese American? Many Americans assume that leaving a poor family in a developing country and moving to a relatively rich family in a developed country will automatically bring the child a better life. But haunting questions remain. Why were these girls abandoned? Where will they fit in the architecture of race and class in their new communities? Confronted with these complications, how are Chinese girls made kin?

Dorow traces the many strategies that adoptive parents and their children take to navigate the in-between space that adoptive children inhabit between U.S. and Chinese culture. These strategies include participating in Chinese cultural celebrations, maintaining contact with Chinese orphanages, participating in support groups or groups of children adopted from the same agency, and even making return visits to China. Such activities help to restore a sense of history in the face of the many silences and gaps related to birth parents, birth family, ancestry, and home village. Although the whiteness and class privilege of most adoptive families ease the transition of these adopted children into the U.S. racial framework, Asian children of white parents still are marked as nonbiological kin. "Are these your real kids?" adoptive parents are often asked. Friends and neighbors, classmates and teachers still read race and kinship in the bodies of these adopted children (Yngvesson 2003).

Dorow challenges all those "touched by adoption"—the extended network of people who are affected by adoption and whose lives affect the adoption experience—to "reimagine an intimate geography of difference" (Dorow 2006, 269) that can better bridge the contradictions of race, class, and nation. The adoption process creates possibilities for transformative new patterns of kinship and belonging if those involved can embrace difference while resisting the limitations imposed by assumed categories of race, family, and nation. By looking beyond the borders of difference, transnational and transracial adoption holds out possibilities to reimagine a global kinship focused on belonging rather than dislocation (Volkman 2005; Dorow 2006; Kim 2007).

Today changes in the nuclear family, the rise of families of choice, the increase of same-sex marriages, advances in assisted reproductive technologies, and the expansion of transnational adoptions are reshaping views of kinship and family in the United States. These changes do not necessarily indicate a general decline or improvement of family life or moral values. However, they do reveal a shift of kinship patterns away from a biologically defined, nuclear family model toward other models based on choice, flexibility, and fluidity (Stone 2009; Coontz 1992).

TOOLKIT

Thinking Like an Anthropologist: Kinship in Personal and Global Perspective

We experience kinship all the time, although we may not use that term to describe it. For example, kinship is frequently in the news, as the following examples illustrate:

- In January 2011, Lilliana Ramos, a single mother and undocumented immigrant who had lived in the United States for twenty-one years, was detained and deported to Mexico, leaving her three children, eleven-year old Karleen, sixteen-year old Ashley, and nineteen-year-old Brian—all U.S. citizens—to fend for themselves in Oregon.
- In 2005, U.S. courts ruled that the husband of Terry Schiavo was more immediate kin than her parents, and therefore he could make the decision to remove her life support after she had spent fifteen years in a vegetative state, even though her parents begged him not to do it.
- The divorced parents of twenty-eight-year-old U.S. Army soldier Jason Hendrix, killed by a roadside bomb in Iraq, battled over who would choose his burial plot. His father won the case, based on the custody agreement in a 1991 divorce settlement and the Army's long-standing policy of awarding a soldier's remains to the oldest living relative.

These cases offer just a glimpse of how cultural understandings of kinship intertwine with national laws and how prominent kinship matters have become part of the national conversation in the United States.

Kinship is close to home, for it comes alive in the people we live with, eat with, play with. It is vital as we experience the most dramatic periods of our personal lives. You will continue to make kinship and family relationships—perhaps through marriage, having children, and choosing close friends who ultimately become family. Thinking like an anthropologist can help you to better understand these experiences. And in today's globally interconnected world, having an understanding of the vast diversity of kinship patterns may help you navigate relationships with classmates, friends, family, and colleagues. As you do so, keep in mind the questions that have guided our discussion in this chapter:

- How are we related to one another?
- Are biology and marriage the only basis for kinship?
- Is a country like one big family?
- How is kinship changing in the United States?

In thinking about the two teenagers at the beginning of the chapter, how can we apply this chapter's ideas to better understand their situation and, more generally, any future changes in the constructs of kin and family? Who is related to whom? Who decides? Is kinship primarily biological, or can family be chosen? Who constitutes your own family? As you traced your family tree, did you see that kinship is not only about creating a list of relatives, but also about understanding the many ways those ties are formed and the role that kin play in shaping you as an individual and as a member of society? These tools of anthropological analysis will become increasingly important as the concept of kinship continues to change in cultures across the globe during the twenty-first century.

Key Terms
kinship (p. 350)
nuclear family (p. 350)
descent group (p. 352)

For Further Exploration

Bridewealth for a Goddess. 2000. By Chris Owen, with Andrew Strathern. Ronin Films. An elaborate religious ritual in the Western Highlands of New Guinea in which men seek protection through marriage to a powerful goddess.

Coontz, Stephanie. 1988. *The Social Origins of Private Life: A History of American Families 1600–1900.* New York: Verso.

———. 1992. *The Way We Never Were: American Families and the Nostalgia Trap.* New York: Basic Books.

———. 1997. *The Way We Really Are: Coming to Terms with America's Changing Families.* New York: Basic Books.

Holtzman, Jon D. 2000. *Nuer Journeys, Nuer Lives: Sudanese Refugees in Minnesota.* Boston: Allyn & Bacon. As a result of the civil war in Sudan, some Nuer refugees now live in Minnesota. Holtzman discusses changes in Nuer lifestyle since Evans-Pritchard's time and in the context of global migration.

The Nuer. 1971. Produced by Robert Gardner and Hilary Harris for The Film Study Center at Harvard University. CRM / McGraw-Hill Films. Classic film portraying the traditional, cattle-centered life of the Nuer of Sudan.

Saheri's Choice: Arranged Marriage in India. 2002. Films for the Humanities and Sciences, Princeton, NJ. A contemporary arranged marriage seen through the life story of an Indian girl.

An Orioles baseball game at
Baltimore's Camden Yards.

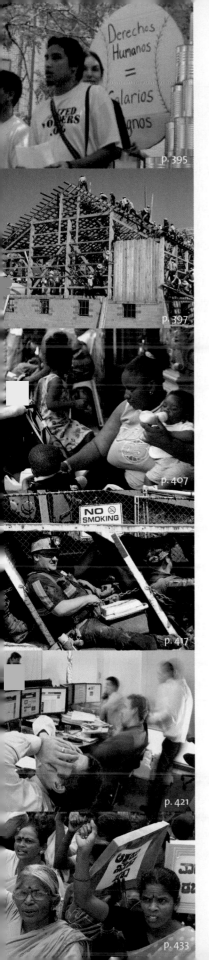

p. 395

p. 397

p. 407

NO SMOKING

p. 417

p. 421

p. 433

CHAPTER 11

Class and Inequality

What can you learn about class and inequality in U.S. culture through the lens of professional baseball? Many of us spend hours at ballparks tracking balls and strikes, hits, stolen bases, great fielding plays, batting averages, and earned run averages, or consuming hot dogs, peanuts, popcorn, soda, and beer. But as anthropologists, let's dig deeper and explore the economic and social relationships—which we will refer to as *class*—of those involved in making the game happen.

Consider a Baltimore Orioles game at Camden Yards Stadium. On the field, the top-paid Orioles player in 2012, outfielder Nick Markakis, earned $12.3 million. That averages out to about $95,000 a game, or $22,500 for each at bat. Numerous lesser-known players made the league minimum of $400,000 for the entire season. Collectively, the Orioles players earned $102 million in 2012. Baltimore manager Buck Showalter earned $1.5 million for the season. The four umpires each earn between $120,000 and $350,000 per season depending on their years of experience. In contrast, what do you suppose the security guards and grounds crew earn?

From your seat in the stands, you may be able to infer some things about class and inequality from those around you. You may not know the other spectators' average income and wealth, but stadium seating reflects the ability to pay, with the most desirable seats escalating in price as they get closer to the field and home plate. At Camden Yards, standing-room tickets in right field—the least desirable—cost $9 in 2012, while box seats behind home plate cost $140. Some people are happy to see one game a year; others buy season tickets. With the average ticket price at $23, a family of four averages $92 to see a game—not to mention parking,

MAP 11.1
Baltimore

refreshments, and souvenirs. If each person gets a hot dog, soda, and popcorn, a family can easily spend $150 to $200 on a trip to the game.

Curiously, the two extreme ends of the class spectrum in Camden Yards are largely invisible.

Peter Angelos, lead owner of the Orioles, is by far the richest man in the stadium. He built his reputation as a lawyer representing labor unions and their members, then amassed a fortune as lead litigator in several high-profile civil lawsuits. Angelos purchased the Orioles with several partners in 1993 for $173 million. By 2012, the franchise was worth $460 million and had $206 million in operating revenues.

At the opposite extreme are the day laborers who clean the stadium long after the cheering crowds have left. In 2002 these men and women earned $4 an hour, and many lived in homeless shelters near the stadium. Over the next two years they collaborated to form the United Workers Association (UWA), and in 2004 they began a three-year campaign against Angelos and the Maryland Stadium Authority, owner of Camden Yards, seeking a living wage — the minimum hourly wage necessary to meet basic needs such as food, housing, clothing, health care, and transportation. Under pressure from UWA, student groups, and religious communities, Angelos initially agreed to pay the Baltimore City living wage. But by 2005 the workers' hourly wage had increased to only $7, far below what was promised.

Becoming desperate, by summer 2007 eleven stadium cleaners and their supporters announced that on Labor Day they would begin a hunger strike. Rallies at local churches and a statewide educational tour built public support, drew media attention, and ratcheted up pressure for a fair settlement. On the Friday before Labor Day, the governor announced a commitment to pay a state living wage and his expectation that all state agencies and contractors would abide by it. That same day, the Maryland Stadium Authority board voted to guarantee the stadium cleaners the state living wage of $11.30 an hour.

Although this vote signaled a victory for UWA and its supporters, earning $11.30 an hour for the full year in 2009 would still have barely broken the federal poverty line of $22,050 for a family of four. It is hardly enough to live a decent life by typical standards in the United States, where the middle-class dream includes a stable and well-paying job, decent housing, a healthy lifestyle, time for recreation and leisure, and the ability to raise children who will be more prosperous than their parents.

Our brief examination of the baseball game reveals indications of class differences in U.S. culture. Yet of all the systems of stratification and power, class may be the most difficult to see clearly and discuss openly. In previous chapters we have considered stratification along lines of race, ethnicity, gender, and sexuality. In this chapter we will explore the systems of class and inequality that exist in the United States and elsewhere: how they are constructed, how class intersects with race and gender, and how inequality affects individuals' life chances.

By **class** we refer to a system of power based on wealth, income, and status that creates an unequal distribution of the society's resources—usually moving surpluses steadily upward into the hands of an elite. Systems of class stratify individuals' life chances and affect their possibilities for upward social mobility.

In this chapter we will consider the following questions:

- Is inequality a natural part of human culture?
- How do anthropologists analyze class and inequality?
- How are class and inequality constructed in the United States?
- What are the roots of poverty in the United States?
- Why are class and inequality largely invisible in U.S. culture?
- What is caste, and how are caste and class related?
- What are the effects of global inequality?

By the end of the chapter, you will understand how systems of class work and how they affect your life chances and those of others. You may also be motivated to engage in efforts to change systems of inequality if you so choose. As you prepare for a career in the global economy and a life in this global age, being able to analyze the effects of class and inequality will prove an essential tool in your anthropological toolkit.

class: A system of power based on wealth, income, and status that creates an unequal distribution of a society's resources.

Is Inequality a Natural Part of Human Culture?

Inequality exists in every contemporary culture, though not to the extremes of Peter Angelos and the stadium cleaners in Baltimore. Each society develops its own patterns of stratification that differentiate people into groups or classes. Such categories serve as the basis for unequal access to wealth, power, resources, privileges, and status. As discussed in earlier chapters, these systems of power and stratification may include race, ethnicity, gender, and sexuality. In addition, systems of social class create and maintain patterns of inequality, structuring the relationships between rich and poor, between the privileged and the less well off. But are stratification and inequality intrinsic to human culture?

Egalitarian Societies

As we will consider further in Chapter 12, for thousands of years, until the development of agriculture approximately 10,000 years ago, the primary human economic and social structure—certainly among our *Homo* species—has been hunting and gathering. This type of structure has promoted **egalitarian societies** based on the sharing of resources to ensure group success with a relative absence of hierarchy and violence within or among groups. Most modern humans who have ever lived have been hunter-gatherers.

Archaeological evidence suggests that human evolutionary success relied on cooperation and the sharing of food, child rearing, and hunting and gathering responsibilities, not on hierarchy, violence, and aggression. After all, building a system of **reciprocity** in which group members equally share the bounty of the moment has long-term benefits for sustaining the group. Members can then expect the generosity to be reciprocated (Knauft 1991). Although contemporary economic relations tend to be organized around the exchange of money for services, patterns of reciprocity still exist. You may take class notes for someone who returns the favor—reciprocates—at a later date. You may give someone a ride or walk their dog or share your lunch with the understanding that at some point in the future your favor will be reciprocated. In these instances, members of our extended "group" share their resources of time, food, or other amenities for the long-term benefit of sustaining the group. Can you think of other ways you engage in reciprocity with people in your group? (See Chapter 12 for a longer discussion of reciprocity.)

Anthropologists have studied egalitarian societies among contemporary hunter-gatherer groups such as the Ju/Hoansi of Africa's Kalahari region (Lee 2003), as well as the Canadian Inuit and the Hadza of Tanzania (Marlowe 2010), among many others. Efforts to establish more egalitarian systems of economic and social relations have also occurred within highly stratified societies.

egalitarian society: A group based on the sharing of resources to ensure success with a relative absence of hierarchy and violence.

reciprocity: The exchange of resources, goods, and services among people of relatively equal status; meant to create and reinforce social ties.

FIGURE 11.2 Reciprocity in action: an Amish community gathers to raise a barn.

The Amish (Hostetler 1993) and Hutterite (Hostetler 1997) communities in the United States are good examples on a small scale.

Hutterites, a small Christian sect, live primarily in rural North American communities and make their living mostly through agriculture. They own all property collectively and provide for individual members and families from the community's common resources. Families live in separate homes owned collectively by the community and take their meals in a common dining room. The Amish, also a small North American Christian group, are known for their simple lifestyle and their rejection of labor-saving devices that might make them less reliant on the community. The Amish maintain a cooperative economic and social structure that revolves around the church, based heavily around reciprocity. Perhaps the best-known example is the distinctive Amish practice of collective barn raising in which the entire community gathers to rapidly erect a barn for one family, an act of reciprocity that is returned many times over as barns are raised throughout the community over the years.

Ranked Societies

Anthropologists also recognize **ranked societies,** where wealth is not stratified but prestige and status are. In these societies, positions of high prestige—such as chief—are largely hereditary. Because only certain individuals can occupy

ranked society: A group in which wealth is not stratified but prestige and status are.

these positions, the social rank of the society is set regardless of the skills, wisdom, or efforts of other members.

Chiefs usually do not accumulate great wealth, despite their high prestige. In fact, their lifestyle and standard of living may not vary significantly from those of any other member of the group. Group members offer gifts of tribute to the chief, but these are not kept and hoarded. Instead, the chief redistributes the tribute to group members. This act of gift giving—a form of **redistribution**—ensures his or her prestige while also preserving the well-being of all group members. The chief's rank and status are reinforced not through accumulation of wealth but through reciprocity and generosity. Ranked societies have existed in most parts of the world, but anthropologists have most carefully studied those in the islands of the South Pacific (Petersen 2009) and along the Pacific Northwest coast of North America (Boas 1966).

One redistribution ceremony famous in the field of anthropology is the **potlatch** practiced among the Kwakiutl of the Pacific Northwest. Among this Native American group, the chief would establish and reestablish claims to prestige and status by holding an elaborate feast and gift-giving ceremony—a potlatch. He would give guests all of his personal possessions, including extra supplies of food, cooking pots, blankets, weapons, and even boats. What was not given away might be destroyed as a sign of the chief's great capacity. The more elaborate the gift giving, the more status and rank the chief gained in the community. The chief's generosity also applied pressure on his guests to reciprocate in like manner, or even more elaborately in a later ceremony (Boas 1966). In a practical sense, the potlatch served to distribute key community resources of food and clothing broadly among group members. As a ritual ceremony, it represented a tradition among the Kwakiutl and other ranked societies in which social status is established not by wealth and power, but by the prestige earned via one's capacity for generosity.

Contemporary patterns of cooperation, sharing, collaboration, and reciprocity draw on patterns of behavior central to human evolutionary success over millions of years. In contrast, social patterns of entrenched hierarchy and stratification emerged much more recently in the human story.

The extreme stratification in today's world is a fairly recent development. Anthropologists trace its roots to the rise of intensive agriculture and populous market towns, where relatively small groups of elite merchants and landholders were able to accumulate wealth. Stratification and inequality became more pronounced in industrialized capitalist economies over recent centuries, and this uneven development appears to be accelerating under the forces of globalization, further concentrating wealth in the hands of the few. Still, countries

redistribution: A form of exchange in which accumulated wealth is collected from the members of the group and reallocated in a different pattern.

potlach: Elaborate redistribution ceremony practiced among the Kwakiutl of the Pacific Northwest.

FIGURE 11.3 Women of the Makah Nation on the U.S. Pacific Northwest coast prepare salmon steaks for a potlatch, a communitywide redistribution ceremony and feast.

such as Norway, Sweden, and Denmark have made efforts to narrow stratification through a system of redistribution that uses taxation of wealth and generous social benefits. Even the United States, the country with the most extreme inequality of any current advanced industrialized country (Stiglitz 2012), also uses a progressive tax rate, requiring higher-income earners to pay a higher tax rate to more equally disperse the costs of government services. We will further explore the development of stratification and inequality in the current era of globalization via analysis and statistical evidence throughout this chapter and in Chapter 12.

How Do Anthropologists Analyze Class and Inequality?

We turn now to consider four key theorists of class and inequality. European social philosophers Karl Marx and Max Weber, writing in the nineteenth and early twentieth centuries in the context of the Industrial Revolution, are separated by a century from French sociologist Pierre Bourdieu and U.S. anthropologist Leith Mullings, whose late twentieth-century writings are based in the context of a much more complicated and advanced capitalist economic system.

Theories of Class

Each theorist discussed below responds to the unique social and economic challenges of his or her time and offers key analytical insights that allow anthropologists today to more deeply investigate the realities of class and inequality. As you read about each theorist, consider how you might apply their key concepts to understanding the social class relationships and inequality in our opening story about the baseball game.

Karl Marx: Bourgeoisie and Proletariat Karl Marx (1801–1882), perhaps the most widely read theorist of class, wrote against a background of economic change and social upheaval. During the nineteenth century, rapid economic changes and new government policies brought massive social upheaval and dislocation to western Europe. As the Industrial Revolution swept through the area, government policies restricted poor rural families' use of common village lands. (In England, these were called Enclosure Acts, because they enclosed the commons.) Deprived of access to land they had depended on for farming, grazing, and gathering, rural people migrated to urban centers to seek jobs in the expanding industrial factories.

Marx's analysis of the increasing inequalities in the emerging capitalist economy of nineteenth-century Europe distinguished between two distinct classes of people. The **bourgeoisie**, or capitalist class, owned the **means of production**—the factories, machines, tools, raw materials, land, and financial capital needed to make things. The **proletariat**, or working class, lacked land to grow their own food, tools to make their own products, and capital to build workshops or factories. Unable to make their own living, they sold their work—their labor—to capitalists in return for wages.

Marx identified labor as the key source of value and profit in the marketplace. Owners sought to constantly increase their income by forcing workers to toil faster, longer, and for lower wages, thereby reducing the cost of production and increasing the difference between the production cost and the sale price. The surplus value created by the workers could then become profit for the owner. In this relationship, capitalists increased their wealth by extracting the surplus labor value from workers. Recognition of these two fundamentally different positions within the economy—two different classes—was essential to Marx's understanding of power relations in a culture.

bourgeoisie: Marxist term for the capitalist class that owns the means of production.

means of production: The factories, machines, tools, raw materials, land, and financial capital needed to make things.

proletariat: Marxist term for the class of laborers who own only their labor.

FIGURE 11.4 Can you apply Marx's understanding of class to a fast-food restaurant? At a typical McDonald's, the cashier makes $7.25 an hour for a full-time annual wage of $15,080 with no benefits. The store manager, who makes closer to $40,000 annually plus benefits, serves the owner by ensuring that the most surplus labor value possible can be extracted from the workers (PayScale 2012).

Today anthropologists apply Marx's ideas to analyze class and power in contemporary society while acknowledging that capitalism has grown much more complex since Marx's time. Intense competition has grown among capitalists, notably between those in the manufacturing and financial sectors. Small business owners and farmers now own the means of production, technically making them part of Marx's bourgeoisie, but they do not possess the same access to capital as others in that class. The working class—the proletariat—is divided, with conflicts along lines of race, gender, and ethnicity. Moreover, increasing global circulation of capital is drawing local cultures and communities into class-based relationships that were not present even a generation ago.

Many contemporary social scientists recognize a middle class of professionals and managers (white-collar workers) that has emerged between capitalists and the working class (blue-collar workers). But others who take a more strict Marxist view of class argue that professionals and managers are still members of the proletariat (Durrenberger and Erem 2010; Buck 2009). They may have more power in the workplace and substantially higher incomes, but they still sell their labor to the bourgeoisie. These managers, government officials, military, police, and even college professors receive special privileges from the bourgeoisie. But it is worth the price to gain the cooperation of this middle class in organizing, educating, and controlling the working class, thereby maximizing the extraction of profits by the capitalist class.

Along with Friedrich Engels, Marx wrote the *Communist Manifesto* (1848) as a political pamphlet urging workers to recognize their exploited class position and to unite in order to change the relations between proletariat and bourgeoisie emerging in the capitalist system. Marx noted, however, the extreme difficulty for workers to develop a class consciousness—a political awareness of their common position in the economy that would allow them to unite to change the system. Why? Because their continuous struggle simply to make ends meet, as well as the creative means used by the bourgeoisie to keep the proletariat divided, work against a unified challenge to the stratification of society.

Max Weber: Prestige and Life Chances Max Weber (1864–1920), like Marx, wrote against the backdrop of economic and social upheavals in western Europe caused by the expansion of capitalism during the Industrial Revolution. In analyzing the emerging structures of stratification, Weber added consideration of power and prestige to Marx's concern for economic stratification of wealth and income. By **prestige**, Weber referred to the reputation, influence, and deference bestowed on certain people because of their membership in certain groups (Weber [1920] 1946). Thus certain occupations may hold higher or lower prestige in a culture—for instance, physicians and farm workers. Prestige, like wealth and income, can affect life chances. Prestige rankings affect the way individuals are treated in social situations, their access to influential social networks, and their access to people of wealth and power (Table 11.1).

Weber saw classes as groups of people for whom similar sets of factors determine their life chances. By **life chances**, Weber referred to the opportunities that individuals have to improve their quality of life and realize their life goals. Life chances are determined by access not only to financial resources but also to social resources such as education, health care, food, clothing, and shelter. Class position—relative wealth, power, and prestige—determines access to these resources. According to Weber, members of a class share common life chances, experiences, and access to resources, as well as similar exposure and vulnerability to other systems of stratification.

Pierre Bourdieu: Education and Social Reproduction Pierre Bourdieu (1930–2002) studied the French educational system to understand the relationship among class, culture, and power ([1970] 1990). Throughout much of the world, education is considered the key to upward social mobility within stratified societies. **Social mobility** refers to the movement of one's class position—upward or downward—in stratified societies. Theoretically, the *meritocracy* of education—whereby students are deemed successful on the basis of their individual talent and motivation—should provide all students

---

prestige: The reputation, influence, and deference bestowed on certain people because of their membership in certain groups.

life chances: An individual's opportunities to improve quality of life and achieve life goals.

social mobility: The movement of one's class position, upward or downward, in stratified societies.

TABLE 11.1 Top 20 Occupations by Prestige, United States and China

Rank	United States	Score	China	Score
1	Physician	86.05	Mayor	92.9
2	Lawyer	74.77	Government minister	91.4
3	Computer scientist	73.7	University professor	90.1
4	University professor	73.51	Computer engineer	88.6
5	Physicist	73.48	Judge	88.3
6	Chemist	73.33	Court prosecutor	87.6
7	Chemical engineer	73.31	Lawyer	86.6
8	Architect	73.15	Engineer	85.8
9	Biologist	73.14	High-ranking governmental or political party member	85.7
10	Scientist	73.09	Scientist	85.3
11	Dentist	71.79	Translator	84.9
12	Judge	71.49	Revenue officer	84.9
13	Engineer	70.69	Social scientist	83.9
14	CEO	70.45	Doctor	83.7
15	Geologist	69.75	Computer software designer	83.6
16	Psychologist	69.39	Writer	82.5
17	Aerospace engineer	69.22	Reporter	81.6
18	Manager, medicine and health	69.22	Real estate developer	81.5
19	Clergy	68.96	Director / manager of state-owned enterprise	81.3
20	Civil engineer	68.81	Manager of investment company	81.1

SOURCE: **United States:** National Opinion Research Center. 2009. *General Social Surveys, 1972–2008: Cumulative Codebook*. Chicago: University of Chicago. http://publicdata.norc .org:41000/gss/documents/BOOK/2008%20GSS%20Codebook.pdf; **China:** Xinxin Xu. 2013. "Changes in the Chinese Social Structure as Seen from Occupational Prestige Ratings and Job Preferences." Translated by Yihan Feng. *Sociology Research* 3.

social reproduction: The phenomenon whereby social and class relations of prestige or lack of prestige are passed from one generation to the next.

an equal opportunity. Instead, Bourdieu's research uncovered a phenomenon of **social reproduction** in the schools. Rather than providing opportunities for social class mobility, Bourdieu found that the educational system helped reproduce the social relations that already exist by passing class position from generation to generation in a family. What factors in schools work against the meritocratic idea and instead serve to limit a person's life chances? First (as we might expect from Marx and Weber's ideas of class), a family's economic circumstances make a difference. But Bourdieu identified two additional key factors: *habitus* and cultural capital, which are both reinforced in schools.

habitus: Bourdieu's term to describe the self-perceptions and beliefs that develop as part of one's social identity and shape one's conceptions of the world and where one fits in it.

Bourdieu described *habitus* as the self-perceptions and beliefs that develop as part of one's social identity and shape one's conceptions of the world and where one fits into it. *Habitus* is taught and learned at an early age and is culturally reinforced through family, education, and the media. It is not fixed or predetermined, but it is so deeply enculturated that it becomes an almost instinctive sense of one's potential. *Habitus* emerges among a class of people as a set of common perceptions that shape expectations and aspirations and guide the individual in assessing his or her life chances and the potential for social mobility. Life decisions—for instance, the choice of college education or career—are made on the basis of the family's *habitus.*

To get a sense of the pervasiveness of *habitus,* think for a moment about your own situation. Why have you chosen to attend college, and what major are you pursuing? Might certain concerns of class or money be influencing your educational and career paths? How might this *habitus* also influence your choice of friends and, perhaps someday, a marriage partner?

cultural capital: The knowledge, habits, and tastes learned from parents and family that individuals can use to gain access to scarce and valuable resources in society.

Cultural capital is another key to the social reproduction of class. Bourdieu defined **cultural capital** as the knowledge, habits, and tastes learned from parents and family that individuals can use to gain access to scarce and valuable resources of society. For example, family wealth can create cultural capital for children. With enough money, parents can provide their children with opportunities to travel abroad, learn multiple languages, take music lessons, join sports clubs, go to concerts and museums, have enriching summer experiences, and build social networks with others who have similar opportunities. These opportunities build the social skills, networks, and sense of power and confidence that are essential for shaping class position and identity in stratified societies. Family wealth allows children to perpetuate cultural capital, including high motivation and a sense of possibilities that are crucial for academic success. Schools reward cultural capital. In the process, schools reproduce social class advantage.

The U.S. public school system is heavily influenced by cultural capital. From an early age, students are split into separate tracks based on standardized test performance and teacher evaluations. Around sixth grade, for example, students are separated into the mathematics track that will lead either to Advanced Placement Calculus their senior year in high school or to remedial or regular math. Selective colleges often screen positively for applicants with AP Calculus credits. As a result, decisions made in sixth grade affect students' college possibilities. Did you know this? Some people with cultural capital do know. A study of middle-school math groups in Boston public schools reveals the way mathematics tracking tends to reproduce class in the classroom. Of the students in the accelerated math track, 60 percent had fathers with a doctorate and 33 percent had fathers with a master's degree. Just 5.6 percent had fathers with only a high school degree. Of the students in remedial math, 50 percent had fathers with a high school diploma or less (Useem 1992).

How would you assess your own level of cultural capital? Be aware that cultural capital can also shape the way others see you. Do you have the social skills, experiences, and exposure to travel, music, art, and language that will make you an interesting colleague, one capable of building social networks for success on the job? Can you identify ways in which your level of cultural capital would provide an advantage or disadvantage in scenarios such as succeeding in a job interview, obtaining health care, finding an apartment, or getting a date?

Leith Mullings: Intersectionality among "Race," Gender, and Class In recent years, Leith Mullings's work on intersectionality has led anthropologists to reexamine class by analyzing the deep connections among class, race, and

MAP 11.2

gender. Building on the field's long history of holistic ethnographic studies of local communities, Mullings offers an intersectional approach: she asserts that class, in the United States and many other areas, cannot be studied in isolation but, instead, must be considered together with race and gender as interlocking systems of power. **Intersectionality** provides a framework for analyzing the many factors—especially race and gender—that determine how class is lived and how all three systems of power and stratification build on and shape one another.

In the 1990s Mullings led a study, The Harlem Birth Right Project, on the impact of class, race, and gender on women's health and infant mortality. The study focused on central Harlem, at that time a vibrant, primarily African American community in northern Manhattan, New York City (Mullings 2005; Mullings and Wali 2001). Of particular concern, infant mortality rates in Harlem were twice the rate of New York City's overall. Previous studies (e.g., Schoendorf, Hogue, and Kleinman 1992) had demonstrated that African American women in the United States, at every socioeconomic level, have more problematic birth outcomes than white women regardless of social class. Even college-educated African American women experienced infant mortality at twice the rate of college-educated white women. This observation suggested that factors other than education and social status were at work.

Mullings's research team gathered data through participant observation in community organizations and other sites in Harlem, as well as through surveys, in-depth interviews, and life histories with pregnant women and women with children. On the basis of their data, the team examined how the underlying conditions of housing, employment, child care, and environmental factors, as well as the quality of public spaces, parks, and even grocery and retail stores might affect the health outcomes being reported in Harlem, where both working-class and middle-class women lived. Since the early 1990s, Harlem has been hard hit by dramatic changes in New York City's economy. Manufacturing jobs with middle-class wages have been lost to flexible accumulation (see Chapters 1 and 12), as New York City–based companies relocate production overseas. Meanwhile, job growth in the metropolitan area has occurred in the high-wage financial sector and in the low-wage service sector. Throughout the 1990s, government social services were cut back while public housing and transportation were allowed to deteriorate.

The effects on working-class and middle-class women in Mullings's study were notable, with increased physical and mental stress, especially for pregnant women. For working-class women, inadequate, overpriced, and poorly maintained private and public housing forced many women and their children to be constantly on the move, searching for affordable housing and sharing living

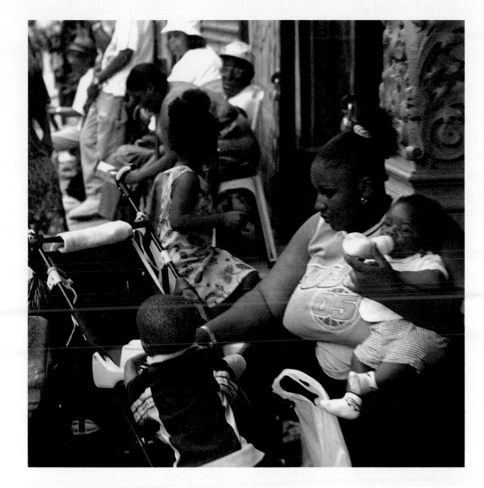

FIGURE 11.6 Mother and children, Harlem, New York. How do class, race, and gender intersect to affect people's life chances?

spaces with friends and relatives to make ends meet. The need to regularly fight for needed repairs drained time and energy from hard-working women holding multiple low-wage jobs while juggling work and child care. A shortage of steady, well-paying jobs meant that women had very little income security or benefits, so they often pieced together a living from multiple sources. Middle-class women, many of whom were employed in the public sector, were also increasingly subject to layoffs as local governments downsized. The study also found that heavy pollution in the Harlem area, including airborne pollutants from a sewage treatment plant and six bus depots, contributed to elevating the child asthma rate to four times the national average (Mullings 2005; Mullings and Wali 2001).

The Harlem Birth Right Project illustrates a powerful application of the intersectional approach to understanding class and inequality. It reveals how inequality of resources (class), institutional racism, and gender discrimination combine to affect opportunities for employment, housing, and health care in the Harlem community. It also shows how these factors link to elevated health problems and infant mortality.

Leith Mullings

Leith Mullings first encountered anthropology as an undergraduate at Queens College, City University of New York, through the teaching of Hortense Powdermaker. During the civil rights movement—when across the South, people were being beaten by policemen, bitten by dogs, and doused by fire hoses—she was hearing from Powdermaker about the anthropological challenge to appreciate differences: different kinds of people, different cultures, different ways of being. "One day she shared an experience of doing fieldwork in Melanesia, dancing with the local people and thinking, 'If my family (some of whom lived in the South) could see me dancing with the natives, what would they think?' I was impressed by the way anthropology changed the way she saw the world. This was one of the things that drew me to anthropology."

Now a distinguished professor at the City University of New York Graduate Center and president of the American Anthropological Association, Mullings has become well known for her work on intersectionality—analyzing the intersection of race, class, and gender—which she has put to work in her ethnographic fieldwork, including a groundbreaking project on health disparities in Harlem, New York.

"One reason I became interested in the Harlem project was the opportunity to undertake a study that embraced community collaboration in research. Community collaboration refers to involving the community in guiding research in a wide variety of ways.

"For example, the researchers formed a Community Advisory Board (CAB), composed of people who lived or worked in Harlem. The CAB suggested that instead of recounting the data in the traditional format—unemployment, female-headed households, numbers of people on welfare—that we report the same data in a more positive way—for example, how many people are employed, how many are not on welfare. In other words, to emphasize the strengths of the community.

"The CAB also advised us to consider the ways people resisted and the ways people attempted to overcome the circumstances they found themselves in. For instance, they suggested that we do ethnography in Housing Court (which was in lower Manhattan). There I encountered Harlem women on their own, bravely confronting the lawyers of their landlords in order to hold on to shelter for themselves and their children. That was one of the ways in which we discovered how much insecure housing negatively affects health and well-being.

"The CAB also pointed us to the lines at Legal Aid as people tried to prevent their children from being placed in the problematic special education track. Filing complaints of police brutality and job discrimination, or informing the City about landlords who did not provide heat or hot water, are all ways people tried to better their lives that are not obvious to the casual observer. They don't show up in the news. They don't show up in the statistics. Major social movements such as the civil rights movement or people

Anthropologist Leith Mullings

marching against police brutality may make the news. The day-to-day struggles people wage are often not apparent. We may not have directly encountered this without community collaboration."

Since its popularization in the early 1980s, intersectionality has become a key theoretical approach within anthropology and other social sciences but one that requires careful analysis of local realities. "What is not addressed in many statements of intersectionality is how to analyze the intersection of race, class, and gender. What is their relationship? In some circles it has become a mantra. Many scholars reiterate Race, Class, Gender: Intersectionality. But the real work lies in understanding how at a particular moment these three indices of inequality articulate.

"I believe that class is prefigurative. Race and gender have various degrees of salience in different historical conditions, societies, or locations.

"Sometimes one trumps the other. For example, in the contemporary United States, gender subordination results in some limitations for elite women. But in most instances, class trumps: access to huge resources allows them all kinds of privileges and freedom unimagined by most men or women.

"To put intersectionality to work, when you read a newspaper, encounter situations, or interact with people, think—and this is a hard concept—what are the axes of stratification that affect the opportunities of the people involved. Start by thinking about whiteness, for instance: What are the privileges that whiteness brings, whatever the class? What obstacles do people of different classes, races, and/or genders confront? What does it mean in their lives? What does that mean for their opportunities?

"Take something so minor as trying to get a taxi. It is often difficult for black people of any class to catch a cab in New York City. A cab driver will frequently pass a black person by to pick up a white person. Race is the first thing the drivers see. Taxi drivers cannot always read class. People do not always "wear" their class. A number of elite black people have had trouble getting cabs, famously the

actor Danny Glover or former New York City mayor David Dinkins. But as an older black woman, I can get a taxi to stop more often than my son Michael, a tall, good-looking, dark-skinned black man, who can rarely get a cab to stop. The intersection of gender and race make it more difficult for him to get a taxi.

"These are daily inconveniences. But think about how it works on a broader level: trying to find a job or housing, or even to purchase a car. White and black 'testers' with virtually identical resumés and qualifications have been sent to job interviews; 20 to 25 percent of the time blacks and Latinos were 'treated less well' and often not called back for interviews or offered lesser jobs and lower pay than their counterparts with the same qualifications. Studies (see Marable 2000) have demonstrated that African Americans with financial circumstances identical or superior to whites have been denied loans or are offered mortgages with less favorable terms."

In thinking about anthropology as a toolkit for life, Mullings offers the following observation: "Anthropology is important because anyone living in today's world will have to learn to live with many different kinds of people. We live in a global, transnational world in which few places are isolated. Anthropology also encourages looking beneath the appearance to the underlying structure. You don't have to become a professional anthropologist. But it is a way of being in the world. It is an important lens through which to understand today's world.

"The skills of participant observation are key. Being an anthropologist is like having canine hearing because you are automatically observing and analyzing what is going on around you. It provides you with a new perspective and a more sophisticated understanding of what is going on right next to you.

"My children hated going to the movies with me because I immediately have an analysis and they just wanted to watch the movie.

"But in the end this is what makes us anthropologists, eyes wide open."

Mullings points out the many forms of collaboration that women in Harlem use to resist these structures of inequality and survive in their chosen community. Calling this the Sojourner syndrome, she links the agency of contemporary African American women to the life story of Sojourner Truth. Truth was born into slavery in the late 1790s and was emancipated in 1827 after experiencing physical abuse and rape and watching many of her children be sold away from her. Subsequently she became an itinerant preacher for the abolition of slavery, building coalitions with white abolitionists and later participating in the early women's rights movement. The stories of the women in Harlem today, like Sojourner Truth's, reflect the determination and creativity required to overcome interlocking constraints of racism, sexism, and class inequality.

Applying Theory to Practice: Observing Class at a Baseball Game

Let's return to the anecdote at the beginning of the chapter. Can you see ways to apply the theoretical concepts introduced by Marx, Weber, Bourdieu, and Mullings to analyze a Major League Baseball game and the economic and social dynamics at work in Baltimore's Camden Yards stadium? Can you recognize a stratification of classes based on control over the means of production as Marx suggested? Where do Peter Angelos, the Orioles manager, the players, and the stadium workers fit? How do you assess the differential life chances of those assembled in the stadium? How does class affect their life chances for education, health, and financial security? Does prestige play a role in differentially shaping their life chances? How do *habitus* and cultural capital affect the social mobility of each person? And how do systems of stratification such as race, gender, and class intersect in this context? Because class is so rarely discussed in U.S. culture, these questions may seem difficult to pursue. But by asking these questions about a baseball game—or any cultural activity, group, or institution—you begin to develop the tools necessary to think like an anthropologist.

How Are Class and Inequality Constructed in the United States?

Our national myth tells of the United States as a "classless" society with open access to upward social mobility for those who are hardworking and talented, including the potential to rise from rags to riches in a single generation. This is the cultural story we tell, but is it reality? In fact, in the United States one's life chances are heavily influenced by the class position of one's family—the financial and cultural resources passed from generation to generation. What are the chances that a homeless person sweeping the Orioles stadium someday will be able to afford a box seat behind home plate or an apartment near the stadium? What are the chances that her child will become as well educated or as wealthy as Peter Angelos' child?

In the fall of 2011, issues of class and inequality burst into U.S. national headlines as the Occupy Wall Street (OWS) movement established encampments in cities across the country and made famous their slogan, "We Are the 99%." OWS pointed to the increasing inequality in the United States and the growing advantages of the wealthiest. Though OWS spurred conversations about class and inequality in the ensuing months, class has been and continues to be one of the most mystifying concepts in U.S. culture. It is rarely discussed and largely off the radar screen. In fact, most people do not have an accurate picture of where they and their families fit into the nation's class structure. Do you think you do? A Pew Research Center poll in 2008 showed that 53 percent of Americans consider themselves to be middle class, including 40 percent of those making less than $20,000 a year and one-third of those making more than $150,000 a year. As many as 21 percent of respondents considered themselves to be upper class (Pew Research Center 2008). In a 2007 CNN poll, 40 percent reported that they were or would soon be among the richest 1 percent of the U.S. population (cited in Sacks 2007).

Both quantitative and qualitative research reveal that stratification by class is very real and significantly affects people's life chances. In fact, class stratification in the United States is not new. The Founding Fathers who signed the Declaration of Independence and drafted the U.S. Constitution were among the richest men in the thirteen colonies at that time. George Washington was one of the largest landholders. As the young nation's territories spread westward, opportunities for upward social mobility were plentiful for certain portions of the population, but not for Native Americans, blacks, and most women. Access to wealth, power, prestige, and the resources of U.S. society were stratified not only by race and gender but also by class. Income and wealth inequality narrowed after World War II as an economic boom spurred a growing middle class, particularly among European Americans, and as government benefits such as the GI Bill for returning soldiers created opportunities for a new segment of the population to attend college and own homes. But since the mid-1970s, inequality has been increasing as income and wealth have concentrated at the upper end of the economic spectrum.

A Look at the Numbers

Economic statistics provide a sobering picture of inequality in the United States today. They also reveal the increasing concentration of income and wealth at the top rungs of the class ladder. In reviewing statistics related to class, we examine both income and wealth.

Income Income is what people earn from work, plus dividends and interest on investments along with rents and royalties. (A dividend is a payment by a corporation to its shareholders of a portion of corporate profits. Interest is a fee paid

income: What people earn from work, plus dividends and interest on investments, along with rents and royalties.

TABLE 11.2 Average U.S. Household Income by Percentage of the Population, 2011

Percentage of U.S. Population	Household Income Range	Number of Households
Top 5%	Above $186,000	6,054,200
Top 20%	Above $101,582	24,216,800
Second 20%	$64,434–$101,582	24,216,800
Middle 20%	$38,520–$62,434	24,216,800
Fourth 20%	$20,262–$38,520	24,216,800
Bottom 20%	Less than $20,262	24,216,800

SOURCE: U.S. Census Bureau. 2013. Historical Income Tables: Income Inequality, Table H-1 All Races. www.census.gov/hhes/www/income/data/historical/inequality/index.html.

for the use of borrowed money—for example, interest paid on a bank savings account. Rent refers to payment to an owner as compensation for the use of land, a building, an apartment, property, or equipment. Royalties are income based on a percentage of the revenue from the sale of a patent, book, or theatrical work paid to the inventor or author.) Table 11.2 shows a breakdown of average household income in the United States for 2010. Do you know where your family fits in the national income range?

Income patterns reveal the way power is distributed in a society. As Table 11.3 illustrates, income distribution among the U.S. population shows a heavy concentration at the top. Although the median income in the United States in 2010 was just over $50,000 (meaning that half of the nation's households earned more than that and half earned less), the top 5 percent of households received 21.3 percent of all income. The top 20 percent received 50.2 percent of all income, while the bottom 20 percent received only 3.3 percent. The bottom 40 percent totaled only 11.8 percent of all income. These gaps have widened substantially over the past four decades.

Furthermore, the gap between people at the top end of the income scale and the average worker has skyrocketed over the past five decades (Figure 11.7). In 1965, the salaries of corporate CEOs averaged 18 times the pay of an average worker. By 2000, immediately following the 1990s stock bubble, that number had skyrocketed to an astonishing 411 times the average worker's pay, though by 2011 (following the 2008 financial crash), the number had dropped to 209 times. In comparison, in 2005 in Europe the ratio was only 25 to 1. In 2008, in the United States, as many as 13,480 people earned $10 million or more.

TABLE 11.3 Distribution of U.S. Household Income, 1967 versus 2011

	Top 5% of Population	Top 20% of Population	Bottom 40% of Population	Bottom 20% of Population
1967	16.3%	43%	15%	4.1%
2011	22.3%	51.1%	11.6%	3.2%

SOURCE: U.S. Census Bureau, 2013. Historical Income Tables: Income Inequality, Table H-2 All Races. www.census.gov/hhes/www/income/data/historical/inequality/index.html.

The top 400 earners averaged $344 million in 2007, though the number dropped to $202 million each in 2009, reflecting how much of their income came from the stock market (U.S. Internal Revenue Service 2009).

Wealth Wealth is another key indicator of the distribution of power in a society. By **wealth** we mean the total value of what someone owns—including stocks, bonds, and real estate—minus any debt, such as a mortgage or credit card debt. If wealth were evenly distributed, every U.S. household would have had $380,000 in 2007. But wealth is not evenly distributed. As Table 11.4 shows, in 2009 the top 1 percent of U.S. households (representing three million people) controlled 35.6 percent of the nation's wealth. The next 19 percent (including managers, professionals, and small business owners) controlled 51.6 percent. The bottom 80 percent of the population (comprising wage and salary workers),

wealth: The total value of what someone owns, minus any debt.

FIGURE 11.7 Average U.S. CEO Pay vs. Average Worker Pay, 1965–2011

SOURCE: www.epi.org/publication/ib331-ceo-pay-top-1-percent

TABLE 11.4 Distribution of Private Wealth in the United States, 2009

Percentage of Population*	Percentage of Private Wealth	Number of People
Top 1% of Population	35.6%	3,000,000 people
Next 19% of Population	51.6%	57,000,000 people
Bottom 80% of Population	12.8%	240,000,000 people

*Total U.S. population in 2009 = 300,000,000.

SOURCE: Economic Policy Institute. 2011. *The State of Working America*. Washington, DC: Economic Policy Institute.

owned just 12.8 percent of the nation's wealth. Fully 24 percent of U.S. families have no wealth or are in debt.

It is evident that wealth is even more unevenly distributed than income and that the gap is widening. Since 1976, wealth has increased by 63 percent for the wealthiest 1 percent of the population and by 71 percent for the top 20 percent. Wealth has decreased by 43 percent for the bottom 40 percent of the U.S. population (Economic Policy Institute 2011). The widening gap has multiple causes. First, shifts in the U.S. tax code have lowered the top tax rate from 91 percent in the years from 1950 to 1963, to 35 percent from 2003 to 2012, allowing the wealthy to retain far more of their income (Tax Policy Center 2012). Second, wages for most U.S. families have stagnated since the early 1970s. Moreover, credit card, education, and mortgage debt have skyrocketed. Finally, the collapse of the housing market beginning in 2007 dramatically affected many middle-class families who held a significant portion of their wealth in the value of their home. By 2012, fully 31 percent of all homeowners owed more on their mortgages than their homes were worth (Zillow 2012).

Despite our society's cultural images of the United States as a nation of stockholders, Wall Street as a democratizing institution, and the stock market as a place of economic empowerment, the actual distribution of stocks in the U.S. population tells another story. The top 1 percent of all U.S. households owns 38.3 percent of all stocks. The top 10 percent owns roughly 81 percent. The bottom 90 percent owns just over 18 percent of the stocks held by households in the United States (Table 11.5). Fully 50 percent of U.S. households own no stocks. Even among those who do hold stocks, most own them through pension and retirement funds, where they are not accessible for general use.

A closer look at other types of wealth—including equity in businesses, pensions, and homes (principal residence)—also reveals the concentration of wealth among the upper classes of U.S. society. The bottom 90 percent of the population is better represented in pension funds and principal residence,

TABLE 11.5 Wealth Distribution in the United States, by Asset Type

	TYPE OF ASSET			
	Stocks	Business Equity	Pensions	Principal Residence
Top 1% of Population	38.3%	62.4%	14.4%	9.4%
Next 9% of Population	42.9%	30.9%	44.8%	29.2%
Bottom 90% of Population	18.8%	6.7%	40.8%	61.5%

SOURCE: G. William Domhoff. 2012. "Power in America: Wealth, Income, and Power." *Who Rules America?* http://sociology.ucsc.edu/whorulesamerica/power/wealth.html.

but the top 10 percent of the population is nonetheless proportionally more heavily represented in every area.

In another surprising statistic about the transfer of wealth from generation to generation, only 1.6 percent of Americans receive $100,000 or more in inheritance. Another 1.1 percent receives $50,000 to $100,000. The rest of the population— 97.3 percent—receives no inheritance whatsoever (Domhoff 2012).

Wealth is also stratified by race, as Table 11.6 shows. Reflecting the devastating long-term effects of slavery and Jim Crow segregation on the African American community, as well as the difficult immigration experiences of most of the U.S. Hispanic population, white households have accumulated 15 times the net worth of black and Hispanic households.

Most Americans struggle to identify the distribution of income and wealth in the United States and to locate their position within it (Norton and Ariely 2011). After reviewing the quantitative data on income and wealth stratification in the United States, can you identify pieces of information that were particularly surprising to you? Does the statistical picture correspond with the picture of U.S. society that you imagined? Do you have a clearer sense of where you and your family currently stand? Although statistics and quantitative data provide a broad overview, we turn now to several case studies that explore class and income inequality in local contexts and their impact on the life chances of real people in local communities.

Ethnographic Portraits of Class in the United States

Anthropologists have studied the construction of class and its effects across the spectrum of U.S. culture—in rural, urban, and suburban settings and in relationship to race and gender. Ethnographic portraits like those presented below

TABLE 11.6 Median* Income and Wealth by Race in U.S. Households, 2007

Race	Median Income	Median Wealth (Net Worth)
White	$50,000	$143,600
Black	$30,000	$9,300
Hispanic	$35,000	$9,100

*Median = the number separating the top half from the bottom half of the distribution.

SOURCE: G. William Domhoff. 2012. "Power in America: Wealth, Income, and Power." *Who Rules America?* http://sociology.ucsc.edu/whorulesamerica/power/wealth.html.

personalize the numbers we have just seen, putting faces to statistics and bringing real-life stories into the discussion.

Poor Whites in Rural Kentucky In *Worked to the Bone: Race, Class, Power, and Privilege in Kentucky* (2001), anthropologist Pem Davidson Buck provides a dynamic introduction to intersectionality. She analyzes the intersections of class, race, and gender through the history of the poor white population in two rural Kentucky counties. Here the privileges often associated with whiteness in the United States have been severely limited by class. Buck traces the development of an economic system built on tobacco cultivation, coal mining, and manufacturing that has created a class hierarchy in which "sweat is made to trickle up" (Buck 2001, 13). In other words (reflecting Marx's theory), the surplus value of workers' labor drains upward into the hands of successive layers of elites.

Numerous historical events and processes contributed to this development. The construction of race in Kentucky through slavery, sharecropping, and Jim Crow legislation served to persuade European laborers that they should value their whiteness and attach their primary identities with the white elite rather than build solidarity with laborers of other races. The dispossession of Native Americans from their land consolidated elite control over the territory's natural resources. Later, poor and working-class whites were enticed by the elites with promises of white privilege to view all newcomer groups (such as Jews, Catholics, Irish, and later immigrants) with suspicion as outsiders, ethnic "others," and "white trash," rather than as potential allies in the struggle for fair value, wages, and compensation for their work.

Buck writes about life in central Kentucky from a personal perspective. She and her husband bought land in the rolling farm country, choosing to not pursue careers but to buy land and try to live off of it. They grew food in their garden, raised goats and dairy calves, and took various jobs shoveling corn

MAP 11.3
Kentucky

FIGURE 11.8 Miners in Hazard, Kentucky, sit in a "break car" that will carry them down a coal mine shaft for their daily work shift. How does their sweat "trickle up"?

or stripping tobacco on a large farm to make ends meet. He eventually took a job with a plumbing and heating supply company, and later they started a small plumbing and heating business of their own. All told, they spent twelve years living under the poverty line and producing most of their own food.

> It was while fixing plumbing leaks, lying on my back under kitchen counters, soldering pipes while wedged between bottles of cleaning fluids, that I learned about the view from under the sink. I often found myself in fairly wealthy homes, looking up from under the sink at the lady of the house and thinking about her life. She had furniture I could not afford, dressed her children from stores I never entered, and complained about leaking plumbing at a time when what few pipes we had in our own house froze and burst with remarkable regularity. (Buck 2001, 2)

It is this view "from under the sink" that Buck brings to her analysis—the view of the farmhands, handymen, factory workers, and students struggling to make ends meet despite endless hours of back-breaking work. It is the view of people who see clearly how their sweat trickles up to enhance the lives and economic success of others who are already better off.

Buck places Kentucky's economic development within the context of national economic trends and the global economy. Whiteness has been a continuously evolving smokescreen, she claims, adjusted and readjusted to the changing needs of the elites as the drainage system has been reorganized:

> We are presently in . . . a period of intense competition, this time between elites around the world struggling to control the global economy. The consequences of that struggle are now filtering into

the middle class, although they have been affecting people lower in the drainage system since the late 1970s. Whiteness no longer provides protection from the consequences of policies that make larger and larger portions of the United States into a Third World labor force. Nor does middle-class status provide complete protection. (Buck 2001, 221–22)

Through her analysis, Buck draws connections between class and race in U.S. culture. The construction of class, as she chronicles in her reflections on her community in central Kentucky, has relied on a complex manufacturing of what it means to be white. But as the local economy of the rural United States becomes further integrated into the global economy, and as the sweat of local workers trickles further and further up, even the privileges of whiteness are not enough to protect those who live at or below the poverty line and whose fingers are already "worked to the bone."

Downward Mobility: The Middle Class and the Working Poor Wealth and poverty mark the extremes of a fluid class continuum, but the expected trajectory up the ladder—the core of the so-called American dream—often eludes U.S. families. Social mobility does not always involve movement up the class ladder. News stories, television shows, movies, newspapers, and magazines rarely publish articles about the downwardly mobile. This is a "hidden dimension of our society's experience because it simply does not fit into our cultural universe" (Newman 1999, 9). Instead, our cultural narrative is a story of a meritocracy where "worthy individuals rise to the top and the undeserving fall by the way side" (243).

Katherine S. Newman has written a trilogy of books that reveal the vulnerabilities of the U.S. middle class and the obstacles to success for the working poor. Newman's books are *Falling from Grace: Downward Mobility in the Age of Affluence* ([1988] 1999), *Declining Fortunes: The Withering of the American Dream* (1993), and *No Shame in My Game: The Working Poor in the Inner City* (1999). In *Falling from Grace*, Newman explores the economic and psychological struggles of 150 families who strive to maintain their class position in U.S. culture. She interviewed managers, air traffic controllers, factory workers, and displaced homemakers (women and men who have worked primarily in the home but are no longer financially able to continue); she traced their vulnerability to moving down the economic ladder as a result of job losses, relocation of jobs overseas, and divorce (Kingfisher 2001).

What are the effects on the psyche when hard-working, moral individuals spiral downward—that is, when they "fall from grace"? Newman notes that many do not blame the failure of the economic system; instead, they blame their own failure, personal defects, and unworthiness.

Ten Chairs of Inequality

To dramatize the distribution of wealth in the United States, find ten friends and ten chairs. Each chair will represent 10 percent of the nation's wealth, and each person will represent 10 percent of the population. Place one friend in each chair to visualize what an even distribution of wealth would look like. Now pick one of your friends and give her seven chairs. This shows the proportion of wealth held by the top 10 percent of the population. In fact, if your friend's arm represented the top 1 percent of the population, her arm alone would have almost four chairs (about 33 percent). Your other nine friends get to share the remaining three chairs.

How does it feel to be in the group of nine or to be the one person in the top 10 percent? This exercise reveals the dynamics of the stratification of power through wealth in U.S. society. But it also offers potential insights into social mobility. What are the chances the nine people sharing three chairs will be able to move into a situation in which they each have seven chairs? What conditions would need to exist for that social mobility to happen?

Ten Chairs of Inequality

Adapted from Tamara Sober Giecek. 2013. "The Ten Chairs." Teaching Economics As If People Mattered. www.teachingeconomics.org.

In *No Shame in My Game*, Newman asks why, in a nation of great prosperity and wealth, people who work full time are still poor (Wacquant 2002; Durrenberger 2001). She examines obstacles facing the working poor—those who often work more than full time to make ends meet and for whom minimum-wage jobs are not enough to pull themselves or their families out of poverty. Many people in the United States believe that urban poverty is a result of lack of motivation, welfare dependency, and a poor work ethic (see "The 'Culture of Poverty': Poverty as Pathology," p. 422); but Newman challenges this vision as a gap in our understanding of urban environments and inner-city economies. In these milieus she has found a broad array of hard-working citizens for whom hard work does not pay off, who struggle to provide for their families, who are one paycheck away from financial disaster. According to Newman, the main determinant of class position and social mobility is not one's work ethic, but structural barriers that have created an increasing gap between the life chances of the well educated and highly skilled and those of high school dropouts (see "Poverty as a Structural Economic Problem," p. 423).

Wealth, Inequality, and Wall Street Although many anthropologists study the most marginalized members of a culture, recently a number of research projects have "studied up" (Nader 1972; Savage and Williams 2008): they have investigated power elites and cultural decision makers ranging from elite scientists (Gusterson 1996) and Wall Street executives (Tett 2010) to government officials (Brash 2011). In *Liquidated: An Ethnography of Wall Street* (2008), anthropologist Karen Ho relates how she went to work in a Wall Street investment bank to understand the inner workings of Wall Street in the 1990s during one of its biggest boom periods. Why, she asks, in a time of record corporate profits and soaring stock prices, do we see rapid downsizing, layoffs, and dismantling of the social safety net? She focuses on the surprising fact that when corporations lay off workers and downsize, not only do the companies' stock prices go up but the stock values of the investment banks go up as well.

Ho points to a transformation of the corporate culture of Wall Street: the desire for profits is not new; what is new, she finds, is a disconnect between what is considered best for the corporation and what is best for most of its employees. Today employees seldom benefit from corporate success. Instead, the benefits go to stockholders. Ho suggests that a "new cultural code for doing business" on Wall Street—characterized by a relentless search for unending profits and combined with government deregulation of the financial services industry—rewards efforts to make money, not to make goods and services. Witness in recent years the willingness of commercial banks and investment houses to bundle and resell so-called toxic assets, including the high-risk mortgages that played a key role in the 2008 market meltdown and Wall Street collapse. Ho claims that Wall Street participated in its own dismantling through mergers and liquidations within the financial community itself as large companies consumed smaller ones, downsized, and laid-off employees to maximize their own stock values. Ho regards the collapse of Wall Street banks and investment houses in 2008 not so much as a surprise or anomaly, but as a predictable result of Wall Street culture, values, and workplace models.

Despite the U.S. national myth of a classless society, both quantitative and qualitative research studies expose the depth of inequality and stratification as well as the obstacles to social mobility. Although class stratification is not new, historical research suggests it is also not inevitable. Inequality has been shown to not be "essential" in human communities. By examining both statistical and ethnographic material, anthropologists seek to reopen a conversation about the roots of inequality—the obstacles to greater opportunity, social mobility, and improved life chances in a culture that is reluctant to discuss class.

What Are the Roots of Poverty in the United States?

Why do people live in poverty in the United States—one of the wealthiest countries in the world? Anthropologists have actively engaged academic and public policy debates surrounding this conundrum. Policy debates often place responsibility for poverty on the bad habits of the individual or the lack of fair opportunities created by the economic system. The actual roots of poverty must be clearly understood if the experience of poverty is to be eliminated or ameliorated.

The 2011 report of the U.S. Census Bureau found 46.2 million people—15 percent of the U.S. population—living in poverty (U.S. Census Bureau 2011). This is the largest number in the fifty-one years that poverty statistics have been tracked. Twenty percent of U.S. children live in poverty. The 2011 U.S. government's poverty line for single adults stood at $10,890 in pretax income and $22,350 for a family of four. Many scholars consider the poverty line calculations, developed in 1964, to be unrealistic in today's economy; instead, they calculate a poverty line at 50 percent higher to be a more useful representation of people's standard of living.

Poverty rates vary by race. Hispanics have a 25.3 percent rate, representing 13,244,000 people. Non-Hispanic whites are at 9.8 percent, with 19,171,000 people below the poverty line. The black poverty rate is 27.6 percent, which includes 10,929,000 people. The Asian poverty rate is 12.3 percent or 1,973,000 people (U.S. Census Bureau 2011). Our discussions of the history and contemporary expressions of race and racism in the United States in Chapter 6 helped shed light on these disparities. Despite prevalent media representations of inner-city poverty among communities of color, it is important to note that the largest group of the nation's poor are white and live in rural and suburban areas (Figure 11.10).

What are the root causes of poverty? Anthropologists and other social scientists have articulated numerous theories to explain poverty's origins and persistence. In the United States, two key theories have focused on poverty as pathology and poverty as a structural economic problem.

The "Culture of Poverty": Poverty as Pathology

Theories of poverty as pathology trace ongoing poverty to the personal failings of the individual, family, or community. Such theories see these failings as stemming from a combination of dysfunctional behaviors, attitudes, and values that make and keep poor people poor. Anthropologist Oscar Lewis called this a "culture of poverty." His research in Mexico (1959) and the United States (1966) suggested that certain ways of thinking and feeling lead to the perpetuation of poverty among the poor. Lewis argued that children growing up poor in a highly class-stratified economic system were particularly vulnerable to developing feelings of marginality, helplessness, and dependency that would shape their value system, worldviews, aspirations, and character and make it difficult for them to escape poverty.

Lewis's work focused primarily on the impact of poverty in the developing world. But his research and theory of a culture of poverty became attractive to policy makers in the United States. Although many scholars, including anthropologists, discredited this theory on the grounds that it blamed the victims of poverty for structural problems beyond their control, the theory formed the basis of key social policies during the latter part of the twentieth century.

Beginning in the 1960s many social scientists, social workers, and government officials adopted the culture of poverty theory. Key among them was Daniel Patrick Moynihan, who in 1965 submitted a report to President Lyndon Johnson titled "The Negro Family: The Case for National Action," commonly known as the Moynihan Report. Moynihan's report attempted to trace the root causes of poverty in African American communities to cultural patterns despite the evident structural causes of inequality and discrimination built into Jim Crow and segregation laws. By the 1980s and 1990s, debates around the

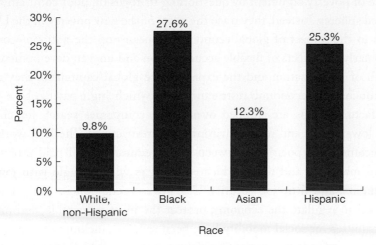

FIGURE 11.10 People in Poverty by Race, 2011

SOURCE: www.census.gov/hhes/www/poverty/data/incpovhlta/2011/table3.pdf

"culture of poverty" transformed into discussions of an urban "underclass." It was suggested that the pathologies displayed by this underclass—including crime, welfare dependency, and female-headed households—continued the cycle of poverty for urban African American communities (Wilson 1987).

Poverty as a Structural Economic Problem

Theories of poverty as pathology have been strongly criticized within anthropology. As a distinct counterpoint, proponents of poverty as a structural problem trace its roots to dysfunctional aspects of the economic system. These theories place more responsibility on the failure of government to address fundamental economic patterns that have forced people into poverty and not provided a means out.

Many anthropologists have critiqued the "culture of poverty" theory, beginning with a series of essays edited by Eleanor Burke Leacock (1971). If there are no jobs, inadequate education and health care, and systematic failure to invest in the infrastructure of impoverished neighborhoods and communities, then poverty cannot be changed by changing attitudes and values. What are often considered to be characteristics of a culture of poverty are actually characteristics of poverty itself; they have nothing to do with the attitudes, values, and life choices of those forced to live in poverty. As discussed earlier, Leith Mullings (2005) and others have challenged the depiction of a complacent and ghettoized underclass by pointing to the resilient and determined efforts made by the poor to overcome the dire economic, social, and political conditions that they face.

Anthropologists Judith Goode and Jeff Maskovsky (2001) challenge the culture of poverty argument by questioning its focus on poor communities as isolated spheres. Instead, they trace the roots of the new poverty in the United States to the impact of global economic processes on the nation's economy, particularly the effects of flexible accumulation and uneven development. The growth of globalization and the expansion of global capitalism, they argue, has launched an economic restructuring in which high-paying, blue-collar manufacturing jobs are shipped overseas as companies search for cheaper labor, lower taxes, and fewer environmental restrictions. The U.S. workforce has become more polarized between highly educated, well-paid professionals and managers and under-educated workers who struggle with low pay, no benefits, and little job security. U.S. government policies and programs designed to regulate the economy, protect the most vulnerable, and provide opportunities for social mobility have been reduced, including public education, housing, and investment in infrastructure—roads, bridges, water systems, and power grids.

Goode and Maskovsky warn that as poverty and inequality grow, those most deeply affected—including the one in four U.S. children who live in poverty (U.S. Census Bureau 2009)—remain largely hidden and disappear from national awareness. In response, they encourage a new awareness of the many ways in which poor people engage in collective and individual strategies to survive. They call for anthropologists to engage in ethnographic research that contributes to the grassroots efforts of the poor (Dudley 2000; Anglin 2002). In addition, they call for adequate public investment in affordable housing, health care, education, and nutrition programs to create a framework whereby individual initiative can more readily succeed.

Discussions about the root causes of poverty continue today in both popular conversations and policy circles. Intense debate continues, for instance, on the appropriate role of government in addressing problems of persistent poverty. Arguments often draw on the distinction between seeing its roots in a culture of poverty or in a long-term structural problem of exclusion. Can poverty be addressed through improved housing, provision of health care, education, and the creation of living-wage jobs (the structural causes), or must perceived patterns of dependency on government programs and services be addressed to confront an underlying culture that holds people back? You will encounter these questions in conversations with classmates and coworkers, and you will influence these debates at different points in your life—perhaps as you undertake community service as a college student or later as you engage in the U.S. political process.

FIGURE 11.11 How is flexible accumulation shaping U.S. inequality? Laid-off factory workers of the closed Doosan Bobcat plant, Bismarck, North Dakota, symbolically leave behind steel-toed work boots in the parking lot as they exit the plant for the final time.

Why Are Class and Inequality Largely Invisible in U.S. Culture?

As previously discussed, the U.S. national origin myth (see Chapter 7) consistently promotes themes of meritocracy and social mobility as central to U.S. national identity. Despite this claim to a culture of equal opportunity, the review of economic data in this chapter has revealed the existence of class and inequality in U.S. society as well as the disturbing reality that inequality is increasing. Even with the statistical evidence of class in America, attention to this pattern of stratification is minimal and inequality remains largely invisible. Why?

The Role of the Media

Anthropologist Gregory Mantsios (2003) suggests that the media play a significant role in hiding class stratification in the United States by largely ignoring it. In an analysis of news articles, Mantsios found that only one in every five hundred *New York Times* stories addressed poverty. In a broader review, using the *Reader's Guide to Periodic Literature*, Mantsios found that only one article in every one thousand addressed poverty. Instead, the media focus on promoting a narrative of the United States as a meritocracy and an egalitarian society.

Mantsios's analysis further shows that depictions of poor people tend to be stereotypical: as welfare cheats, drug addicts, or criminals. Panhandlers ask for handouts. Con men try to trick others out of their hard-earned money. The poor need charity to get through holidays such as Thanksgiving and Christmas. The poor frequently are blamed for their own misfortune, charged with having bad attitudes and lacking effort. Their poverty is portrayed as a bad habit that is inescapable. Poverty and class divisions are described as strange and abnormal—as aberrations of true American life, not as a reflection of the structure of the nation's economic system.

Mantsios argues that perhaps more than government, religion, or educational institutions, the media is the most influential force in shaping public awareness. On average, he points out, U.S. residents watch twenty-eight hours of television a week. Television, movies, radio, and now the Internet define our cultural tastes, shape our historical narratives and our national identity, and circumscribe the range of possibilities we see for ourselves.

Class is particularly invisible in U.S. television programming. Programs rarely portray poverty. Poor people are absent or ignored. Instead the typical television series presents a homogenized version of the upper middle class designed to represent "everyone." Living in a generic upper-middle-class neighborhood, everyone is a cop, a doctor, a lawyer, or a business executive. Even those with blue-collar jobs are portrayed as middle class. Everyone is well off and, if not rich already, aspiring to be so. Among the cool young people who inhabit these communities, difference and stratification arise from beauty and sexuality, not from jobs, income, or wealth. Even reality television shows—from *American Idol* to *Survivor* and *Top Chef*—portray "ordinary people" who seek wealth and glamour through achieving fame and celebrity (McGrath 2005).

Moreover, Mantsios asserts, the media shape the idea of the middle class. Newspapers, television, and movies all promote the idea that viewers and readers are part of the upwardly mobile portion of society, part of the affluent in-group. Business reports, stock picks, fashion pages, wedding announcements, even ski reports convey the message that the concerns of the wealthy are the concerns of us all. The wealthy—including celebrities and sports and entertainment superstars—are represented as fascinating and benevolent. Corporate empire builders and investment wizards are seen as role models (with a few bad apples giving the wealthy a black eye now and then).

Mantsios argues that these portrayals blur the divisions created by class and inequality. In this context, the nation's diverse population becomes one big middle class. Working-class, blue-collar workers and their jobs—supervised, unskilled, or semiskilled labor—are portrayed as increasingly outmoded and irrelevant in the global economy, even though 50 percent of all U.S. workers hold blue-collar jobs. It's no wonder, then, that the poor are rarely seen.

Voluntary Isolation

In addition to the media's reluctance to show the hard realities of poverty, we can identify a tendency in part of the population to isolate itself from exposure to the lower class. Anthropologist Setha Low explores the recent development of gated communities—neighborhoods protected with walls, gates, security guards, entry codes, and key cards designed to control the social environment. As Low points out in *Behind the Gates: Life, Security, and the Pursuit of Happiness in Fortress America* (2004), wealthy and middle-class residents create these enclaves, now estimated to represent 10 percent of all homes in the United States, to ensure spatial distance from others whom they consider less desirable.

Forty years ago, before the rise of gated communities, members of these middle and upper-middle classes led a massive flight from urban areas to the suburbs in an attempt to distance themselves from the poverty, crime, and decay associated with city life. Today residents who can afford homes in gated communities—including retirees and commuters who work in the city—attempt to enhance their sense of safety by extending their isolation and insulation. Wealth and income allow this particular segment of U.S. society to wall themselves off from others, providing the illusion of enhanced security while reinforcing the replication of cultural capital through interactions limited to a certain class of the population.

Low reflects that many in the U.S. population have experienced an increasing sense of insecurity over the past thirty years, particularly after the September 11 attacks. Primary responses and solutions have included increased policing in public venues, armed guards in private venues, enhanced surveillance technologies, walling, and gating. Communities attempt to use gates to protect their children, reduce crime, control the environment, keep out "others," and ensure quality services and amenities for residents. Low's interviews also reveal that residents of gated communities symbolically use the gates to ward off the unknown—unemployment, loss of loved ones, and downward mobility.

Low suggests that in many ways the gates and walls may be counterproductive. By increasing isolation, the gates also produce fear. Life lived behind the walls is life lived in an enclave as if under siege—constantly guarded and locked up, protected from dangers real and imagined. Furthermore, the walls and gates not only shut others out but also shut residents in. In this way walls and gates increase social segregation, limit interaction across classes, deter broad-based civic engagement, and inhibit social connectedness, ultimately undermining the very efforts to create safety through community that the walls and gates were originally intended to promote and secure (Sullivan 2006; Walklate 2005).

The Consumer Culture

The consumer culture provides yet another explanation for the invisibility of class in the United States. Despite falling incomes over the past thirty years, many families have been able to maintain at least the experience of a middle-class lifestyle. They accomplish this by working more (especially women, who have entered the workforce in increasing numbers), borrowing money in mortgages against the value of their homes, running up credit card debt, and taking out more student loans to pay for their own or their children's college education.

Though income and wealth have not increased for the vast majority of the nation's population, people have been able to consume as if they were upwardly mobile—at least until the collapse of the housing bubble in 2007 and the meltdown of financial markets beginning in late 2008. At that point, banks began to foreclose on homes that were no longer worth as much as the owners had borrowed against them. Credit card interest rates skyrocketed, and credit lines were reduced. Still, total credit card debt in 2012 was $865 billion (Board of Governors of the Federal Reserve System 2012a), a sign of the extent to which the population continues to consume as if it were middle and upper class even when annual income does not support this lifestyle. Fully 46.7 percent of U.S. households carried a balance on their credit cards, with an average of nearly $16,000 per indebted household. Perhaps more surprising, in 2010 student loan debt surpassed total credit card debt for the first time, climbing to $1 trillion in 2012 and revealing the shifting burden of educational expenses into long-term debt (FinAid 2013). Total mortgage debt in mid-2012 stood at a staggering $13.4 trillion (Board of Governors of the Federal Reserve System 2012b). These sobering statistics reveal the ways consumer spending has been supported by mortgage, credit card, and education debt, thereby masking the growing inequalities of income and wealth in the United States (Williams 2004).

The role of class is rarely discussed but present everywhere in U.S. society, as is the attempt to "consume" class. In *Consuming the Romantic Utopia: Love and Cultural Contradictions of Capitalism* (1997), sociologist Eva Illouz suggests that even love and romance are shaped by class—both by financial capital and by cultural capital. As a college student, you experience this tension all the time. Dating is expensive. Romance takes time and money. How do you show you are in love? The rituals of love—the acts that are expected to show affection and cultivate romance—depend on the ability to shop and buy. You need the right clothes, haircut, makeup, perfume or cologne, shoes, birth control. You need a gym membership to stay fit or diet pills to stay skinny. The rituals of romance, including food, drinks, movies, gifts, and travel, all require money. A romantic dinner out is expensive. Even a romantic dinner at home may require extra expense for wine, candles, and special music to complete the ritual.

Class even shapes our choice of romantic partners. We often think of love as a spontaneous act of emotion, good chemistry—a matter of the heart. But why do we feel that connection? Research shows that people are likely to marry someone of their own race (see Chapter 2). Discounting Hollywood movies, how likely is it that you would marry someone outside your class? Finding someone of a similar background who has the same cultural capital and knows the same language and symbols of romance—someone of the same class—strongly influences our choices of romantic partners. What has your own experience been in this regard?

As you develop your skills as a budding anthropologist, clearly seeing the outlines of class and its effects on you and the people around you may require extra effort. Media—from movies to television to the press—largely ignore the existence of income inequality and the gaps between wealth and poverty. Consumption patterns, fueled by deep indebtedness through credit cards, home mortgages, and educational loans, mask class differences at least on the level of acquisition of consumer goods. Perhaps this cultural tendency to mask class and inequality—to make them invisible—is one reason the abrupt rise of the Occupy Wall Street movement in the fall of 2011, with its class-revealing slogan "We Are the 99%," surprised so many people. But perhaps the same tendency to make class invisible explains why the movement fell so quickly from the media's public eye once protestors were removed from the spaces they physically occupied in parks and town squares. Nonetheless, a careful understanding and analysis of class will prove to be a crucial tool in your toolkit as you attempt to understand the complexities of the global world in which you live.

What Is Caste, and How Are Caste and Class Related?

caste: A closed system of stratification in a society.

achieved status: Social position established and changeable during a person's lifetime.

ascribed status: Social position inherited, assigned at birth, and passed down from generation to generation with enforced boundaries.

Caste, like class, is a system of stratification. It organizes members of a culture into hierarchically ranked groups with unequal access to the rewards and privileges of society. But unlike class systems, which theoretically allow some social mobility, **caste** is a closed system of stratification. Class is largely an **achieved status**—established and changeable during a person's lifetime. In contrast, caste is an **ascribed status**—inherited, assigned at birth, passed down from generation to generation with rigidly enforced boundaries among caste groups.

Caste in India

The most carefully described example of caste exists among the Hindus of India. Their complex caste system reflects the influences of religion, Indian social and economic relations, the nation's experience of colonialism, and recent processes of globalization.

Textbook descriptions of India's caste system trace its origins back two thousand years to Hindu religious texts, rituals, and beliefs that divided the population into four *varna*, or castes. Each caste was associated with particular

FIGURE 11.12 *Visvamitra Visits Vasishtha's Hermitage, Kulu, Punjab Hills, 1700* depicts representatives of all four Hindu varna, or castes: Vasishtha—the hermit-*Brahmins*; Visamitra-*Ksyatriyas*—the soldier/ rulers; *Vaisyas*—the agricultural workers/merchants; and *Shudras*— the laborers and artisans.

occupations and was ranked according to its purity in following Hindu ritual practices. *Brahmins* were scholars and spiritual leaders. *Ksyatriyas* served as soldiers and rulers. *Vaisyas* were agricultural workers and merchants. *Shudras* worked as laborers and artisans.

Completely outside and below these castes were other marginalized groups, including the "Untouchables," or **dalits** (literally, "broken people"). *Dalits* were assigned the most spiritually polluting work: cleaning latrines, collecting garbage, tanning leather. Social and religious stigma led to their physical separation from the rest of the community. They were considered so polluted that they were forbidden to use upper-class wells or temples. Members of the upper classes believed that simply touching a *dalit* would contaminate them; even touching a *dalit*'s shadow was considered unclean.

These religious beliefs have provided a rationale for an inflexible system of inequality and stratification, locking people into a caste for life. Though the caste hierarchies were established on religious principles, the resulting system established powerful long-term political, economic, and social implications.

Recent scholarship (Prashad 2001) explores a more complicated history of the Indian caste system than most textbooks present. Studies of local Indian communities suggest that caste has no uniform expression across India. The nation has an immense geographic range and a diverse population, with more than 4,600 distinct ethnic groups. Patterns of stratification within those communities could not be traced to a uniform application of ancient Hindu ritual texts. Instead, patterns

FIGURE 11.13 Indian boys and men of the Untouchables, or *dalits*, working with hides in a lime pit at a tannery, circa 1946.

MAP 11.4
India

of stratification vary widely. Caste has served not only as a cultural, religious, or political system but also as a structure for organizing economic exploitation.

Although caste predates European expansion into India and British colonial rule, the arrival of the Portuguese in 1498 and later British colonial efforts radically reshaped the system and made it more rigid. Colonial land laws removed certain groups, particularly *dalits,* from their ancestral lands and put them to work as street sweepers and leather workers. Segregation of employment groups created a stereotyped version of caste relations. By replicating in the Indian caste system patterns of class that were prominent in England, the British colonial power reshaped Indian castes as a mechanism for administering the enormous colony and extracting wealth generated there for the benefit of the British Empire (Prashad 2001).

India's caste system continues to change. Discrimination on the basis of caste is now illegal, having been outlawed in the constitution written after India gained independence in 1949. *Dalits* and other oppressed groups now are provided special protections and affirmative action programs to overcome the effects of centuries of exploitation. In the political realm, caste identity and consciousness at times have served for mobilizing allies and votes. In 1997, India elected its first *dalit* president, K. R. Narayanan. Caste distinctions have been blurred, especially in some urban areas.

India's recent economic transformations mean that new occupations and social mobility are undermining the power of caste boundaries to maintain a system of stratification. But the deep inequalities of the caste system persist, and changes are uneven. In public settings, caste boundaries are breaking down—for instance, in inter-caste dining. But in private—for instance, in arranged marriages—and particularly in rural areas, caste patterns remain strong. Moreover, the historical advantages of higher-caste groups have not been dismantled; this is especially evident in rural areas, where 70 percent of the population lives. Most of India's 160 million *dalits*—one-sixth of the population—continue to be agricultural workers who live in poverty. Few live in cities. The vast majority are illiterate, and only a handful participate in the industrial workforce or other Indian economic sectors (such as technology, telecommunications, and finance) that are becoming more integrated into the global economy.

From Caste to Class

As India participates more in the global economy, certain sectors of the economy and certain regions of the country, particularly urban areas, are seeing the hierarchy of caste shift toward a hierarchy of class, beginning a transition from a society organized by an ascribed status to one organized by an achieved status. Yet, despite these economic changes and *dalit*-led movements for civil rights at the local, regional, and even national levels, the nation's deeply rooted inequalities continue to preserve power and privilege for the upper classes while

FIGURE 11.14 Demonstration for women's rights and *dalit* rights in Bangalore, India, 2009, highlighting the intersection of gender and caste.

inhibiting most *dalits* and lower-caste members from participating fully in the country's economic and social life (Deliege 2011; Guilmoto 2011).

Globally, the spread of globalization and worldwide market economies has been speeding the transition from caste systems to class systems. After all, capitalism and the forces of globalization mean that workers must be able to move freely from place to place in response to changing economic conditions. Workers have to be able to transition within professions to match up with changing jobs. The rigidity of a closed caste system stands in stark contrast to and in direct conflict with the demands of the global economy. The rigidity of the caste-based, ascribed status hierarchy is gradually shifting to a class-based (achieved) status system. Yet patterns of inequality remain extremely slow to change.

What Are the Effects of Global Inequality?

Globalization has produced unprecedented opportunities for the creation of wealth, but it has also produced widespread poverty. This uneven development is a central characteristic of the global capitalist system. Because it affects every corner of the world, it will be increasingly important for you as a global citizen to understand its impact.

Statistics reveal the extremes of uneven development. For example, in 2013 the world had 1,426 billionaires, up from 937 billionaires in 2010 (Geromel 2013); yet, with the exception of China, global poverty has increased over the past twenty years. Today 40 percent of the world's population lives in poverty, defined by the United Nations (UN) as income of less than $2 per day.

One-sixth of the world's population—877 million people—lives in extreme poverty, surviving on less than $1 each day. The UN has calculated that if household wealth were divided equally on a global basis, using 2000 data each household would have roughly $20,000. Instead, the report found that 2 percent of the world's population owns more than half of all wealth on the entire planet. The wealthiest 20 percent of the world's population receives 75 percent of the total global income (Davies et al. 2007).

The Gini index developed by the World Bank provides a global picture of inequality by comparing the per capita gross national income—total income produced by the economic activity of a state—of the world's economies. The World Bank classifies countries as high income ($12,196 or more per person), upper middle income ($3,946 to $12,195), lower middle income ($996 to $3,945), or low income ($995 or less). According to the Gini index, the gap between rich and poor countries has grown in recent years and continues to widen (Map 11.5). Although the index provides a comparison of country averages, it does not take into account inequality within countries. Even the poorest countries have an elite organized around political, economic, or military power. The richest countries, as we have seen in the United States, have an increasing number of people living in poverty. What does this mean in concrete terms?

Growing global inequality affects the life chances of the world's population on many fronts, including hunger and malnutrition, health, education, vulnerability to climate change, and access to technology. Hunger is indeed a global problem. Although there is enough food in the world to feed everyone, it is unevenly distributed. Every day 870 million people go hungry—one out of every eight—according to the UN World Food Programme. Two hundred million children under age five are malnourished (World Food Programme 2013).

Health and mortality are also serious problem areas. Preventable infectious diseases such as malaria, measles, and HIV/AIDS kill millions each year in poor countries. People are more likely to die in infancy in low-income countries—and eleven times more likely to die at birth than in wealthy countries. Moreover, people live longer in high-income countries, averaging a seventy-eight-year life span compared to fifty-eight in low-income countries (World Food Programme 2013).

Access to education, a gateway to economic advancement, is also uneven. Basic literacy varies widely between high- and low-income countries. In addition, the digital divide prevents the majority of the world's inhabitants from participating in technological advances that are transforming the world's economy.

Climate change also affects the rich and poor unequally. Those with financial and political resources can buy safety, living outside areas that are vulnerable to natural disasters. A recent example from the United States underscores

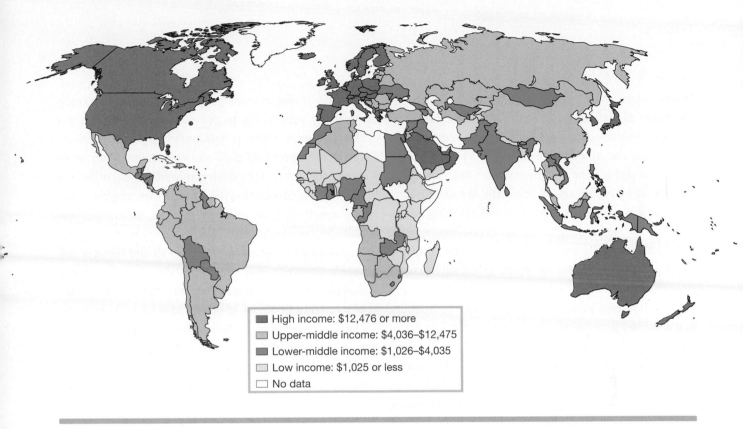

High income: $12,476 or more

Upper-middle income: $4,036–$12,475

Lower-middle income: $1,026–$4,035

Low income: $1,025 or less

No data

MAP 11.5 The World by Income, 2011

SOURCE: http://data.worldbank.org/income-level/OEC

this point: anthropologist Neil Smith, when examining the effects of Hurricane Katrina on the people of New Orleans, called it an "unnatural disaster" because the storm's most severe effects were caused by the government's failure to adequately build and maintain the city's levee system, not by the storm itself. New Orleans residents experienced Katrina's effects unevenly along lines of class as well as race and gender (Smith 2006).

Throughout this chapter we have explored the complexity of class stratification and inequality both within the United States and globally. Despite the centrality of class-based stratification in the dynamics of globalization and its powerful effects on individuals' life changes and possibility for social mobility, class arguably remains the most overlooked of the systems of power we have considered in this textbook. Careful attention to the theoretical approaches to class adopted by anthropologists, including ethnographic research and data analysis, will position you to more fully engage issues of income and wealth inequality as you participate in a rapidly globalizing world.

Thinking Like an Anthropologist: Observing the Dynamics of Class through Baseball and Beyond

In our chapter-opening story, we began to tease out the dynamics of class through the context of a baseball game. Baseball is perhaps the quintessential all-American sport. Millions of kids grow up playing Little League baseball, going to games with their parents, and watching games on television. Kids and adults join fantasy baseball leagues, and adults check the box scores online or talk about the latest games with colleagues at the office. High schools celebrate their teams' exploits. Cities promote the local baseball franchise as central to the community's identity. But what lies underneath the surface in the business of baseball?

Having read this chapter, you are now better prepared to analyze this iconic U.S. cultural activity through the lens of class. For underneath the bright lights, celebrity, and adoring fans of a Major League Baseball game lies a set of unequal relationships. And these differences—starkly revealed by comparing the lives of team owner Peter Angelos and the day laborers who clean the Baltimore Orioles stadium—translate into significantly different access to services, resources, and life chances. Our discussion in this chapter has expanded from the baseball context to explore the following questions:

- Is inequality a natural part of human culture?
- How do anthropologists analyze class and inequality?
- How are class and inequality constructed in the United States?
- What are the roots of poverty in the United States?
- Why are class and inequality largely invisible in U.S. culture?
- What is caste, and how are caste and class related?
- What are the effects of global inequality?

As systems of class stratification create widening inequality, your ability to perceive, analyze, and discuss class will become increasingly important. Class affects life chances in almost all realms of culture, including other sports, the restaurant industry, universities and other elements of the education system, health care, religious organizations, housing, government services, and many others that you can identify. How do these systems of class and inequality affect your own life chances and those of the people closest to you? As you consider these issues, you may be motivated to engage in efforts to reshape systems of inequality. Certainly, as you prepare for a career in the global economy and a life in this global age, being able to analyze the effects of class and inequality will be an essential tool in your anthropological toolkit.

Key Terms

class (p. 395)
egalitarian society (p. 396)
reciprocity (p. 396)
ranked society (p. 397)
redistribution (p. 398)
potlatch (p. 398)
bourgeoisie (p. 400)
means of production (p. 400)
proletariat (p. 400)
prestige (p. 402)
life chances (p. 402)
social mobility (p. 402)
social reproduction (p. 404)
habitus (p. 404)
cultural capital (p. 404)
intersectionality (p. 406)
income (p. 411)
wealth (p. 413)
caste (p. 430)

achieved status (p. 430)

ascribed status (p. 430)

dalits (p. 431)

For Further Exploration

Board of Governors of the Federal Reserve System. 2012. "Mortgage Debt Outstanding." www.federalreserve.gov.econresdata/releases/mortoutstand/current.htm.

Class Matters. 2005. New York: Times Books. www.nytimes.com / pages / national / class / index.html. A year-long series of articles and features (print and online) and interactive graphics (online) developed by the *New York Times* to explore the impact of class in U.S. culture.

Domhoff, G. William. 2012. *Who Rules America?* http://sociology.ucsc.edu/whorulesamerica/power/wealth.html. Website by sociologist William Dumhoff explores issues of wealth and power.

Economic Policy Institute. 2013. *The State of Working America.* http://stateofworkingamerica.org. The Economic Policy Institute's annual publication.

FinAid. 2013. "Student Loan Debt Clock." www.finaid.org/loans/studentdebtclock.phtml.

Inequality.org. 2013. www.inequality.org. A website established by the Institute for Policy Studies, a Washington, D.C.–based think tank focusing on economic inequality.

Roosevelt, Franklin Delano. 1944. "Economic Bill of Rights" (speech). www.youtube.com / watch?v=3EZ5bx9AyI4. Roosevelt's proposal for a "second bill of rights" for U.S. citizens.

Sacks, Peter. 2007. *Tearing Down the Gates: Confronting the Class Divide in American Education.* Berkeley: University of California Press.

Statistic Brain. 2013. "Credit Card Debt Statistics." www.statisticbrain.com/credit-card-debt-statistics/.

Stiglitz, Joseph. 2012. *The Price of Inequality: How Today's Divided Society Endangers Our Future.* New York: Norton.

United Nations Development Programme. 2013. "The Millennium Development Goals: Eight Goals for 2015." www.undp.org/mdg/. The UN established eight goals toward eliminating global poverty by 2015.

United Nations. 1948. The Universal Declaration of Human Rights. www.un.org/en/documents/udhr/index.shtml. Established in 1948, in the aftermath of the atrocities of World War II, to articulate an international agreement about what fundamental rights should be available to all humans.

Yes! 2013. www.yesmagazine.org. Magazine that provides in-depth analysis of global economic and environmental issues, stories about real people confronting these challenges, and suggestions for how to become engaged in finding solutions.

How is globalization reshaping the world in the twenty-first century? Here, a delegation of officials and agricultural experts from fourteen French-speaking African countries visits a tropical fruit–processing facility in south China. China has become Africa's largest trading partner and the top source of direct aid and investment as the Chinese search for agricultural products and raw materials for their rapidly expanding population and economy.

Where does your chocolate come from? A young man on an eastern Côte d'Ivoire farm breaks cocoa pods to extract the beans used to make chocolate.

p. 442

p. 445

p. 451

p. 451

p. 465

p. 465

CHAPTER 12

The Global Economy

Do you know where your last chocolate bar came from?

Today's global economy is a complex network of exchanges and connections that reach far beyond the candy machine outside your classroom or the store across the street. A piece of chocolate, a cup of coffee, or an iPod link the wealthiest resident of a world capital or a student at an elite college to a subsistence farmer in Africa or a factory worker in China. In today's world we are all deeply connected. Let's use the chocolate bar to illustrate this point.

Côte d'Ivoire, West Africa, exports 40 percent of the world's cocoa, which is used to make chocolate. Much of the country is covered in tropical forest, amid which are plantations carved out by farmers using hand tools. Seven million Côte d'Ivoirians make a living farming cocoa and coffee. Although the global price for cocoa—set on the commodities market in New York City—is relatively high, Côte d'Ivoire's farmers see little return for their work. The bulk of the profits go to transnational agricultural corporations, such as U.S.-based Cargill and Archer Daniels Midland (ADM) and the Swiss firm Barry Callebaut. These corporations buy cocoa beans and process them into chocolate products to be eaten worldwide. Few local farmers in Côte d'Ivoire have ever eaten a chocolate bar.

In recent years, Côte d'Ivoire has been riven by poverty, civil war, and conflict over cocoa and coffee revenues. In a fiercely contested election in 2010, Alessane Ouattara defeated incumbent Laurent Gbagbo for the presidency. Gbagbo's corrupt regime had relied on high taxes on cocoa and coffee farmers to subsidize its excesses and to fund Gbagbo's paramilitary hit squads. The election of Ouattara, a former deputy director of the International

MAP 12.1
Côte d'Ivoire

Monetary Fund (IMF), gave Côte d'Ivoirians hope of a more secure and prosperous future. But Gbagbo refused to acknowledge his loss in the election and remained ensconced in the presidential palace. By clinging to power and stirring ethnic violence, Gbagbo pushed the country toward civil war.

To undercut Gbagbo's financial base, Ouattara called on international corporations to embargo Côte d'Ivoire's coffee and cocoa exports, claiming that Gbagbo used profits from the sales to fund his armed resistance. Giant U.S. agribusiness corporations eventually pledged to cooperate, but refused to allow independent inspection of their exports. Many nongovernmental organizations (NGOs) charged that Côte d'Ivoire was circumventing the embargo by shipping its coffee and cocoa overland to neighboring Mali and Burkina Faso, which were reselling the goods to the same corporations.

As fighting between Gbagbo's and Ouattara's supporters escalated in 2011, the French military, returning to its colonial role, stormed the airport outside Abidjian, the country's economic capital and primary port. The French had established a colony in Côte d'Ivoire in 1840 to enter the ivory trade and build coffee and cocoa plantations. Even after Côte d'Ivoire's independence in 1960, however, the French maintained a strong economic and military presence there. In the hopes of limiting violence in the civil war, France joined with the United Nations (UN) to create a demilitarized zone stretching across the country. French and UN soldiers then isolated the presidential palace, still occupied by the defeated Gbagbo until forces loyal to new president Ouattara forced Gbagbo from the residence and arrested him. Despite

FIGURE 12.1 What role have chocolate revenues played in the recent conflict in Côte d'Ivoire? Here, soldiers loyal to newly installed president Alassane Ouattara patrol after the arrest of former president Gbagbo.

continuing hostility between supporters of Gbagbo and Ouattara, in 2012 the country's economy began to recover. Cocoa production began to stabilize in response to the global demand for chocolate (North 2011, Monnier 2013).

The conflict in Côte d'Ivoire reveals many of the complex dynamics of today's global economy: (1) the interconnectedness of farmers in rural West Africa with chocolate eaters and coffee drinkers worldwide; (2) the tension-filled relationship between nation-states and transnational corporations; (3) the strategic military interventions, often by former colonial powers, that serve to police local political affairs and global economic flows; (4) the power of global financial markets to determine the price of coffee and cocoa, and thus the quality of life of small farmers; and (5) the link between consumers and producers through global commodity chains that have shattered notions of distinct national territories.

To fully understand the modern world economy, we must examine the concept of an economy as well as the historical developments that underlie today's global economy. In this chapter we will explore the following questions:

- What is an economy, and what is its purpose?
- What are the roots of today's global economy?
- What role has colonialism played in forming the modern world economic system?
- What is the relationship between the nation-state and the corporation in the global economy?
- What are the dominant organizing principles of the modern world economic system?
- How does today's global economy link workers with consumers worldwide?
- Is today's global economic system sustainable?

By the end of the chapter you should be able to analyze the major economic patterns of the contemporary global economy and assess its underlying principles. Armed with this information, you will be better prepared to make choices about your own lifestyle as a consumer and to engage in debates about how to create a sustainable economic system as the growing human population places increasing pressure on Earth's resources.

What Is an Economy, and What Is Its Purpose?

At the most basic level, an **economy** is a cultural adaptation to the environment—a set of ideas, activities, and technologies that enable a group of humans to use the available land, resources, and labor to satisfy their basic needs and, if

economy: A cultural adaptation to the environment that enables a group of humans to use the available resources to satisfy their needs and to thrive.

organized well, to thrive. Thus, an economic system is a pattern of relations and institutions that humans construct to help collectively meet the needs of the community. Of course, today the concept of an economy seems much more complicated. But what is an economy at its core?

Production, Distribution, and Consumption

Anthropologist Yehudi Cohen (1974) refers to an economy as a set of adaptive strategies that humans have used to provide food, water, and shelter to a group of people through the production, distribution, and consumption of foodstuffs and other goods. In the following sections, we will explore the varied ways humans have produced, distributed, and consumed as part of their economic activity. In particular, we will consider distinctive modes of production, ranging from food foraging to industrialism; general patterns of distribution and exchange; and the emergence of a global economy that has transformed both production and distribution, as well as patterns of human consumption.

Over the course of history, humans have developed various economic strategies to survive in diverse environments. Cohen (1974) suggests five primary adaptive strategies that developed at different times and places: food foraging, pastoralism, horticulture, agriculture, and industrialism. By reviewing these strategies, we begin to understand that the current consumption-based global economy—with its emphasis on industrial production (even in agriculture), consumption, and technology—is only one of many possible variations.

From Foraging to Industrial Agriculture: A Brief Survey of Food Production

Food Foraging Before the domestication of plants and animals around eleven thousand years ago, all humans were **food foragers**. We made our living by hunting, fishing, and gathering nuts, fruit, and root crops; in fact, we evolved into our current physical form as food foragers. Mobility was key: small, egalitarian groups followed the movement of large animals and the seasonal growth of fruits, vegetables, and nuts to secure their survival. Throughout human history, food foragers have ranged over a remarkable variety of habitats, from the most hospitable to the most extreme.

Today fewer than 250,000 people make their primary living from food foraging. Most food foragers now incorporate farming and the domestication of animals as well. The remaining food foragers often live in the most marginal of Earth's environments—cold places, forests, islands—where other economic activity and other strategies for food production are not sustainable. Recent food foragers include the Inuit (Eskimos) of Canada and Alaska, Native Australian aborigines, and inhabitants of African and South American rainforests.

food foragers: Humans who subsist by hunting, fishing, and gathering plants to eat.

FIGURE 12.2 *!Kung san* men forage for food in the Kalahari Desert of northeast Namibia.

Two classic ethnographies examine recent food forager communities. Richard Lee's *The Dobe !Kung* (1984) explores the history and life patterns of the *!Kung san* people living in the Dobe region of the Kalahari Desert in southern Africa. Also, Colin Turnbull's *The Forest People* ([1961] 2010) considers the Mbuit and Efe people living in tropical forests along the equator of Central and East Africa in what is now the Congo; they hunt elephants and other big game with spears, bow and arrow, and large nets. It is important to emphasize that stereotypical gender divisions of labor—which assume that men hunt and women both gather food and care for children—do not match the reality of food-foraging communities such as those studied by Lee and Turnbull (see Chapter 8).

FIGURE 12.2 *!Kung san* men forage for food in the Kalahari Desert of northeast Namibia.

Pastoralism, Horticulture, and Agriculture Cohen identifies three adaptive strategies for food production in nonindustrial societies: pastoralism, horticulture, and agriculture. The earliest evidence of food production can be traced to approximately eleven thousand years ago in the region surrounding the Tigris and Euphrates Rivers (the Fertile Crescent) in what is modern-day Iraq. These strategies for food production led to more permanent human settlements that facilitated the development of tools and pottery and the specialization of human trades.

pastoralism: A strategy for food production involving the domestication of animals.

horticulture: The cultivation of plants for subsistence through nonintensive use of land and labor.

slash and burn agriculture: A practice of clearing land for cultivation. Also called *swidden farming*.

agriculture: An intensive farming strategy for food production involving permanently cultivated land.

Pastoralism involves the domestication and herding of animals for food production. Goats, pigs, sheep, cattle, llamas, horses, and camels may be raised and herded to support the family or extended community (although pastoralism today is often combined with hunting and gathering and horticulture). Pastoralism usually involves herders moving livestock seasonally between high- and low-altitude grazing areas—a process referred to as *transhumance*—while other community members remain at home. The Nuer of Sudan, studied by E. E. Evans-Pritchard (see Chapter 11), are perhaps the best-known group for whom pastoralism (paired with small-scale agriculture) was a key component of their economic strategy.

Horticulture is the cultivation of plants for subsistence through a nonintensive use of land and labor. Horticulturalists use simple tools such as sticks and hoes to cultivate small garden plots. Land is generally rotated in and out of use to exploit more fertile ground. Horticulturalists frequently employ **slash and burn agriculture**—also called *swidden farming*—to clear land for cultivation, kill insects that may inhibit crop growth, and produce nutrient-rich ash that serves as fertilizer. Communities that rely on horticulture tend to be fairly sedentary, remaining close to their sites of food production. Horticulture is frequently combined with hunting, gathering, and pastoralism to provide the communities' basic needs.

In addition to the Fertile Crescent, early evidence of agricultural activity exists in Pakistan's Indus River Valley, China's Yellow River Valley, and the Nile Valley of Egypt, as well as in Mexico and the Andes region of South America. **Agriculture** requires an intensive investment in farming and well-orchestrated land-use strategies. Irrigation, fertilizer, draft animals, and machinery such as plows and tractors provide the technology and labor for successful agriculture. Irrigation systems may include the terracing of hillsides and the channeling of rainfall and natural watercourses through carefully constructed pathways in an elaborate manipulation of natural resources. Through agriculture, humans produce enough food on permanently cultivated land to satisfy the immediate needs of the community and to create a surplus that can be sold or traded.

Exact catalysts for the emergence of agriculture alongside hunting and gathering and pastoralism are unclear. But the effects of increased food production promoted a more sedentary lifestyle, an increased population size, and the founding of permanent settlements and population centers. Towns and cities created markets to facilitate local and long-distance trade of agricultural surpluses and craft products. Specialists such as blacksmiths, carpenters, stonecutters, and weavers established small businesses in market towns to serve the surrounding territories.

Whereas hunter-gatherer societies tended to be largely egalitarian, the rise of intensive agriculture in nonindustrial cultures led to social stratification.

Social distinctions included large landholders, wealthy merchants, and owners of small businesses, as well as peasants and landless tenants working on large farms and estates as wage laborers. Anthropologists consider peasants to be small-scale rural farmers whose agricultural surpluses are transferred upward to support the dominant elites and others who do not farm but whose goods and services are considered essential (Wolf 1966).

Industrial Agriculture Intensive agricultural practices began with the introduction of plows, draft animals, and irrigation. But recent years have seen the rise of **industrial agriculture**, which involves a massive mechanization of farming and the mass production of foodstuffs. In fact, in the twentieth century, agricultural production shifted from individual farms and farmers to large corporate-run farms, or agribusinesses, that rely on the intensive use of machinery (such as tractors and combines), irrigation systems, pesticides, and fertilizers.

industrial agriculture: Intensive farming practices involving mechanization and mass production.

As the world's population continues to expand, pressure to increase global food production intensifies. Recent decades have seen remarkable progress in feeding the world population. Although portions of the world continue to face famines and food shortages, these are not a result of inadequate food production but, rather, unequal distribution of the food that is produced.

Despite increased food production, industrial agriculture and agribusinesses have yielded complicated results. For example, chemical fertilizers and pesticides pose dangers to workers and to local water resources. Antibiotics that keep poultry and livestock healthy in industrial production facilities seep into the human food chain. Genetic engineering reduces crop diversity, making crops more susceptible to harsh weather and pests in the long term. Food irradiation poses potential safety and health hazards. Overall, industrial agriculture requires extremely high energy input to support machinery, irrigation, pesticides, fertilizer, and transportation costs. In many cases, more calories—units of energy—are required in the production process than the food actually provides when it is consumed.

Over the last fifty years, the introduction of industrial agricultural practices by transnational corporations has transformed the role of small farmers and peasants in the global economy. Agribusinesses in many parts of the world have pushed many formerly self-sufficient, small-scale farmers off the land in order to mechanize the preparation of fields, planting of seeds, application of fertilizers and pesticides, and harvesting. As a result, even though the industrialization of farming has yielded dramatic increases in global food production, fewer people work in agriculture and the displaced rural populations are moving to urban centers in search of wage labor.

Despite the advances in pest- and weather-resistant crop varieties and the dramatic recent increase in output, world food production faces increasing stress

FIGURE 12.3 A Chinese-owned farm in Angola, southern Africa, produces corn for export to China, a reflection of industrial agriculture in today's global economy.

today. For example, global climate change is creating less predictable growing conditions, and rapid population growth is straining available food supplies. As a result, wealthy food-importing nations such as China, Korea, Japan, India, and Saudi Arabia are buying up agricultural land and water resources in the fertile nations of Africa (ranging from Egypt to the Sudan to the Congo and Angola) to ensure exports of wheat, rice, and corn to support their own populations. With such activity by foreign countries, will Africa's countries be able to feed themselves in times of environmental and economic instability (Brown 2011)?

All adaptive strategies are subject to the limitations of the natural environment. **Carrying capacity** is the number of people who can be supported by the resources of the surrounding region. The carrying capacity of land for food foragers, pastoralists, horticulturalists, or lower-intensity agriculturalists is more locally limited. But in most cases, farming generates a higher carrying capacity than food foraging because the labor-intensive activity of farming supports more extensive human settlements.

Given the expansion of industrialism, including industrial agriculture, the impact of economic activity has more global consequences today. What is Earth's carrying capacity? Can the planet support our projected population growth and consumption of natural resources? Can our contemporary economy

carrying capacity: The number of people who can be supported by the resources of the surrounding region.

meet current human needs, given the planet's carrying capacity? We will consider these questions as we explore the modern world economic system over the remainder of this chapter.

Distribution and Exchange

All cultures have developed patterns for the distribution and exchange of goods and information produced by their members. In fact, the exchange of goods and ideas appears to be central to the workings of culture, establishing patterns of interaction and obligation among people. Anthropologists recognize three main patterns of exchange: market exchange, reciprocity, and redistribution. All are embedded in the everyday workings of almost every culture.

Market Exchange Today patterns of distribution and exchange are heavily influenced by economic markets that facilitate the buying and selling of land, natural resources, goods, services, labor, and ideas. Contemporary markets range in size and scope from village markets in India to the New York Stock Exchange on Wall Street. Though some people may **barter**—that is, exchange goods and services one for the other—most contemporary economic transactions are based on an exchange medium, or some form of money. In recent human history, the medium of exchange has varied. Items such as salt, precious stones, shells, livestock, precious metals such as gold or silver, coins, and most recently paper money have served to make payments for goods and services. By two thousand years ago, coins had become a common method of exchange in urban centers in Asia, Africa, and Europe and along long-distance trade routes, facilitating the expansion of trade across vast distances (Davies 2005; Wolf 1982).

barter: The exchange of goods and services one for the other.

Reciprocity Reciprocity involves an exchange of goods and services among people of relatively equal status. Such exchanges, including gift giving, create and reinforce social ties between givers and receivers, fulfill social obligations, and often raise the prestige of the gift giver. For example, the sharing of food resources, whether in earlier hunter-gatherer groups or among contemporary families, builds a sense of community, fulfills social obligations to the group, and raises the prestige of the provider. Anthropologists identify three types of reciprocity defined by the social distance between exchange partners: generalized reciprocity, balanced reciprocity, and negative reciprocity (Sahlins [1974] 2004; Service 1966).

Generalized reciprocity encompasses exchanges in which the value of what is exchanged is not carefully calculated and the timing or amount of repayment is not predetermined. Generalized reciprocity is common among close kin or close friends, serving as an expression of personal connection while reinforcing family and social networks. You may often experience generalized reciprocity without

reciprocity: The exchange of resources, goods, and services among people of relatively equal status; meant to create and reinforce social ties.

recognizing it: offering to take someone to the airport without expecting exact or timely reciprocity; borrowing a pen or sheets of paper; offering some of your food to a friend. Likewise, parents provide for their children—food, shelter, education, clothes, protection—without calculating the value or expecting repayment on predetermined terms. They give these gifts out of a sense of love and responsibility. Any expectation of reciprocity tends to be general, not specific—looked for in the form of love or respect rather than a specific amount of cash.

Balanced reciprocity occurs between people who are more distantly related. This type of exchange includes norms about giving, accepting, and reciprocating. The giver expects the gift to be accepted and then to receive something in return. The recipient has an obligation to accept the gift (or is otherwise considered rude or ungrateful) and reciprocate promptly with a gift of equal value. The goal of exchanges based on balanced reciprocity is to build and maintain social relationships, often beyond the immediate kin group. A classic example is the gift exchanges of the Trobriand Islanders' Kula Ring discussed in Chapter 3. Contemporary examples might include gifts between friends and close associates, such as birthday presents, dinner invitations, or even picking up a round of drinks after work. Participants in these relationships of exchange have an obligation to reciprocate and to do so proportionally to the gift that they have received.

Negative reciprocity refers to a pattern of exchange in which the parties seek to receive more than they give, reaping a material advantage through the exchange. Whereas general and balanced reciprocity are based on relationships of trust and familiarity, negative reciprocity occurs among people who are strangers, antagonists, and enemies with opposing interests. Through hard bargaining, cleverness, deception, or cheating, the parties hope to minimize their cost and maximize their return. Extreme cases of negative reciprocity may include the use of force to achieve one's goals despite an imminent threat of retaliation. Familiar contemporary examples include e-mail scams that offer to share an inheritance if recipients send their bank account information; Wall Street investment managers who offer high returns but ultimately steal their clients' money; or predatory mortgage lenders that offer housing loans at interest rates the borrower cannot afford to repay, ultimately taking the borrower's money and home through foreclosure.

Redistribution Finally, **redistribution** is a form of exchange in which goods are collected from the members of the group and reallocated in a different pattern. Redistribution requires the collected goods to flow through a central location—a chief, a storehouse, or a central government—where it can be sorted, counted, and redistributed. In small-scale societies, redistribution brings prestige to the community leader as food and goods collected from the leader's supporters are reallocated for supporting the general populace or establishing alliances with outside groups. A classic example in the anthropological literature is the potlatch (see Chapter 11). You have experienced redistribution directly if in your family

redistribution: A form of exchange in which accumulated wealth is collected from the members of the group and reallocated in a different pattern.

FIGURE 12.4 What are our expectations for exchanging gifts and favors? *Top left*, a family sits down for breakfast in Afghanistan, an expression of *generalized reciprocity*. *Bottom left*, a birthday party represents a form of *balanced reciprocity*, exchange designed to build and maintain social networks. *Right*, Wall Street investment manager Bernard Madoff, convicted in 2009 of bilking investors of 65 billion dollars through the promise of high returns, an example of *negative reciprocity*.

those who work outside the home share their wages with those who do not in order to provide all members with food and shelter. And if you receive a paycheck for a job, your taxes are part of the U.S. government's system of redistribution.

Redistribution may increase or decrease the inequality of wealth and resources within a group. In fact, many cultures have **leveling mechanisms**—practices and organizations that level out resources within the group. In the United States, for example, as in many other nation-states, redistribution is enacted through local, state, and federal tax codes. The government collects money (more from those with greater resources) and then reallocates and redistributes the nation's wealth to provide services (e.g., the military) and infrastructure (e.g., roads and bridges). Leveling mechanisms enact a cultural commitment to the collective

leveling mechanism: Practices and organizations that reallocate resources among a group to maximize collective good.

good that seeks access to safety, health, education, food, and shelter for all group members irrespective of class.

The extent and direction of redistribution is constantly debated. How much should successful people contribute to ensure that other members of society have an opportunity to be successful as well? Patterns of redistribution may also shift wealth upward. For instance, the U.S. government has used taxpayer money to rescue failing Wall Street financial firms during the 2008 market crash and to subsidize profitable oil companies and agribusinesses. The government also assesses lower taxes on capital gains on investments—a benefit accruing largely to the wealthy—than on income earned from wages.

Having reviewed general concepts of production, distribution, and exchange, we now turn to the roots of today's global economy. It has fundamentally transformed patterns of production, distribution, exchange, and consumption and the ways humans interact through economic systems.

What Are the Roots of Today's Global Economy?

Recent centuries have intensified the integration of all humanity into an interconnected global economy. Although images from *National Geographic* magazine or Discovery Channel programs often imply that human history is a story of isolated tribes with little or no outside contact or exchange, anthropological research tells a different story. It is one of connection and encounter, not isolation.

Economic anthropology—the study of human economic activity and relations—views the world through the lens of movement rather than through the perspective of fixed and discreet groups. The key characteristics of today's global economy are mobility and connection. But not all of these connections have been smooth and easy. Many have been—and still are—contentious and unequal.

Early Long-Distance Trade Routes

In 1492 Christopher Columbus sailed from Spain in search of a sea route to Asia. Many scholars regard Columbus's voyage as the symbolic beginning of the modern world economic system. His journey across the Atlantic certainly launched the encounter between Europe and the Americas. But by that time, European elites were already aware that China and India dominated world economic activity. Europe stood on the periphery.

More than two thousand years ago, long-distance trade routes connected Asia, the Middle East, Africa, and Europe in a dynamic international network of economic exchange (Wolf 1982; Frank 1998; Braudel [1979] 1992; Abu-Lughod 1989; Schneider 1977). Camel caravans traveled along the Silk Route from China through India and the Middle East. From there, overland trade routes led into

FIGURE 12.5 Long-distance trade routes have connected Asia, the Middle East, Europe, and Africa for over two thousand years. Here, the Tabula Rogeriana, a map of trade routes through north Africa, Europe, the Indian Ocean, and much of Asia, written in Arabic and attributed to the Arab geographer Muhammad al-Idrisi, 1154.

North Africa and Europe, energizing Mediterranean ports such as Alexandria, Venice, Rome, and Constantinople. In the first millennium C.E., sea routes extended trade along the Arabian Peninsula and down the eastern coast of Africa. Regular maritime trade linked coastal regions around the Indian Ocean, China, and Southeast Asia. Arab traders had established trade routes, economic exchange relations, and local communities throughout Asia. Camel caravans moved gold, salt, and slaves from West Africa across the Sahara to North Africa and the Middle East. An Arab slave trade predated the European trans-Atlantic slave trade by seven hundred years, transporting slaves of diverse origins from West and North Africa, the Mediterranean, Persia, England, Ireland, and eastern Europe at different times between the eighth and the nineteenth centuries (Lydon 2009).

Movement was slow, but long-distance trade moved luxury items such as silk, spices, tea, and gunpowder across vast territory encompassing Asia, the Middle East, Europe, and Africa. Marco Polo traveled the Silk Route from Venice to China and back again along already-existing land and sea trade routes. His journey took twenty-four years (1271–1295). Ibn Battutah, an Islamic scholar-official from Morocco in North Africa, began a pilgrimage to Mecca in 1325 and traveled to Constantinople, the Middle East, Southeast Asia, and China as well as West Africa before returning home in 1349. Tales of Marco Polo and Ibn Battutah's journeys have been preserved, but most likely they reflect the experiences of many others who also journeyed along long-distance trade routes long before Columbus sailed west from Spain in 1492.

In 1405, eighty-seven years before Columbus voyaged to the Americas, a seven-foot-tall admiral named Zheng He set sail from Fuzhou, China, with a fleet that would have dwarfed Columbus's three ships. Fully 317 ships and

27,870 sailors made the first of seven voyages between 1405 and 1433, sponsored by China's Ming emperor. Zheng He's fleets visited thirty-seven countries throughout the South Seas of Asia, the Middle East, and down the eastern coast of Africa, linking into existing patterns of trade, exchange, and connection. At each stop Zheng He's fleet encountered the far-reaching networks of overseas Chinese that had existed for hundreds of years. His voyages illustrate the extensive global economic system that already existed by 1400 and China's pivotal role as the world's economic powerhouse (Frank 1998). China led the world in the production and export of silk, porcelain ceramics (china), tea, fruit, drugs, cotton, tobacco, arms and powder, copper and iron products, zinc, and cupronickel (Frank 1998; Aub-Lughod 1989). Before long, Europe's elite were seeking greater access to China's desirable commodities.

European Traders Buy Their Way In

By the time Columbus sailed in 1492, Europe's elite needed more than a shorter trade route to Asia to enter the world economy. They needed a way to buy themselves in. Although China wanted or needed very little from the West, Europeans increasingly sought its export commodities. As a result, European trade in Asia created surpluses for China, whose exports constantly surpassed its imports. China demanded payment of all deficits in silver and gold, setting off an intense global competition for these scarce resources.

As a result, acquisition of silver and gold was high on the Europeans' agenda in the Caribbean and the Americas. They systematically plundered the Mayan and Aztec kingdoms as well as the indigenous populations as they conquered the continent. Local populations were forced into slave labor to extract precious minerals, as at the lucrative silver mines in Peru. Between 1500 and 1600 the supply of silver in circulation in Europe increased eightfold (Robbins 2005). The gold and silver plundered from the Americas enabled Europeans to buy a seat on the economic train based in Asia. As a result, between 1500 and 1800, massive quantities of silver flowed eastward across the globe to China. By the mid-1800s, frustrated by the drain on their national treasuries, European powers moved to alter their trade imbalance with China through military action. This action began with the first Opium War in 1839, in which Britain forced China to accept opium grown on British plantations in India in lieu of silver (Frank 1998; Spence 2013).

What Role Has Colonialism Played in Forming the Modern World Economic System?

Europe's global economic engagements between 1500 and 1800 relied primarily on extensive maritime trade within the existing global economic system. The American colonies were an important exception. They served as a harbinger of colonial expansion in the rest of the world in the nineteenth and early twentieth centuries. In fact, the European conquest of the New World—the Caribbean and the Americas—launched an era of colonialism that eventually touched every corner of the globe.

Under **colonialism**, colonial powers redrew the map of the world and fundamentally reorganized the political and economic balance of power on a global scale. Europeans' advanced military weaponry and strategies, developed through years of continental warfare and naval battles, gave them an advantage that enabled them to dominate others in the colonial era.

Beginning in the 1500s, European colonialism played a pivotal role in establishing the framework for today's global economic system. Patterns of trade in slaves, sugar, furs, and cotton, enforced through military interventions, drew together the people, politics, economics, and even diseases of Europe, Africa, and the Americas in a triangle of previously unimaginable, highly unequal, and long-lasting relationships of exchange. Even today, we can find traces of many of these connections in the global economy—for example, the French military operating in Côte d'Ivoire in the story that opened this chapter.

colonialism: The practice by which a nation-state extends political, economic, and military power beyond its own borders over an extended period of time to secure access to raw materials, cheap labor, and markets in other countries or regions.

The Triangle Trade

The **triangle trade** that emerged in the 1500s among Europe, Africa, and the Americas involved an extensive exchange of goods, people, wealth, food, diseases, and ideas that transformed the economic, political, and social life on both sides of the Atlantic (Map 12.2). It also brought western Europeans the resources they needed to grow their national economies and expand their role in international trade.

triangle trade: The extensive exchange of slaves, sugar, cotton, and furs between Europe, Africa, and the Americas that transformed economic, political, and social life on both sides of the Atlantic.

Sugar Europeans established a plantation economy in the Caribbean and South America to produce sugar for export to Europe. Although sugarcane was originally domesticated in the South Pacific, early merchants had carried sugar along trade routes through India, the Middle East, and the Mediterranean. Columbus had carried sugar to the Caribbean, which, along with Brazil, offered an ideal climate for sugarcane cultivation. But now, plantation production transformed sugar from a luxury item to a key component of the European diet. Sugar also sweetened three other key commodities in the triangle trade—all stimulants (drugs)—coffee, tea, and cocoa (Mintz 1985).

Slaves The expansion of sugarcane plantations by the Spanish and Portuguese could not be sustained by the local populations in the Caribbean and South America because they were decimated by European diseases and the grueling conditions of forced labor. So plantation owners turned to the African slave trade to supply their labor needs. Between the sixteenth and eighteenth centuries, millions of Africans were sold into slavery and transported across the

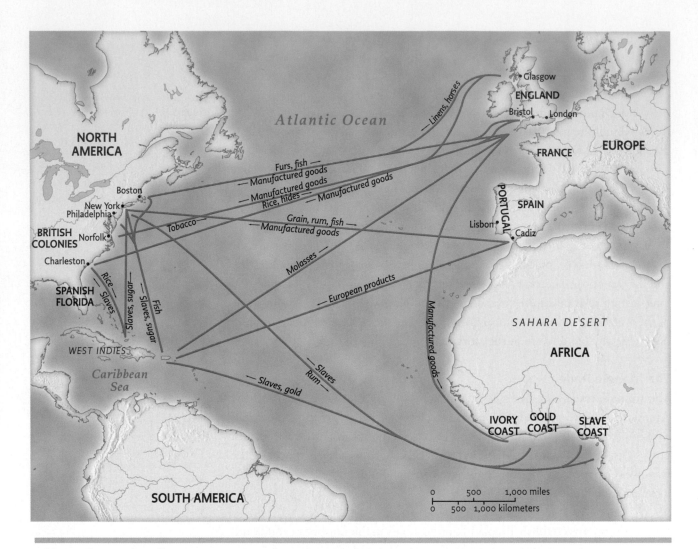

MAP 12.2 The Triangle Trade

Atlantic to work on sugarcane plantations in the Caribbean and South America. Later, rising demand for cotton for England's textile industry required more laborers for cotton plantations in the southern region of what is now the United States. This pressure further stimulated demand for African slaves. Many Africans — perhaps millions — died in the traumatic passage across the Atlantic, and millions more died in inhuman conditions of incarceration and slavery after arriving in the Americas.

Slavery has existed at many times in human history, often based on differences in religion or ethnicity or involving prisoners of war. Evidence reveals that at the time of the Europeans' arrival in West Africa in the sixteenth century, an active slave market already existed (Alexander 2001). Europeans and others, including

Arab traders from the Middle East, linked into it to purchase slaves. (Trade in African slaves to the Middle East may have begun as early as the eighth century C.E. and extended into the nineteenth century.) But the enslavement of Africans in the Americas drew on a unique framework in which skin color served as the marker for enslavement. The uncompensated labor of African slaves, extracted under brutal conditions, subsidized the economic growth and development of Europe and the American colonies for more than 350 years.

Furs In North America, the fur trade, particularly in beaver pelts, pulled the continent into the global economy. European trappers established trading relationships with Native Americans, swapping beaver pelts for European finished products such as guns, metal tools, and textiles. The fur trade was not as lucrative as the Asia trade in spices, silk, or porcelains, but an active European market for fur coats and hats created steady demand.

The production and consumption of beaver fur transformed North America. The European demand for fur drove the European expansion deeper into the North American continent. Native settlement patterns were severely disrupted, as were local agricultural practices and economic activities. Conflicts between the British and French drew indigenous populations into colonial wars. European germs devastated a population that had no immunity to European diseases (Wolf 1982).

FIGURE 12.6 Beginning in the early seventeenth century, the fur trade pulled North America into the global economy. European fur traders barter with Native Americans in this engraving after a detail from Gauthier and Faden's "Map of Canada," 1777.

The decimation of the indigenous populations in North and South America and the Caribbean (estimated by some scholars to be as many as fifteen million people), combined with the relocation of millions of Africans and the arrival of millions of European immigrants, transformed the human population of the New World over a period of a few centuries. Furthermore, the large-scale migration of Europeans and the forced migration of Africans had lasting repercussions on their home communities as well (Wolf 1982; Robbins 2005).

The Industrial Revolution

The **Industrial Revolution** in the eighteenth and nineteenth centuries drove the next phase of European colonial activities. As European economies, led by Great Britain, shifted toward machine-based manufacturing, the new industries relied heavily on the raw materials, cheap labor, and open markets of the colonies. Numerous factors contributed to this phenomenon.

The Colonies' Essential Role In the emerging capitalist economy, the globalizing effects of improved communication and transportation drew together the lives of rural farmers and miners in the colonies with factory workers in industrializing nations. Urban textile factories in England replaced home-based systems of manufacturing and pulled rural peasants into urban wage-based jobs. Cheap cotton from plantations in the southern United States and India stimulated production. The steam engine, iron making, and new forms of power generation increased industrial production. Larger and faster steam-powered ships transported significant quantities of raw materials, food, and finished products from port to port. And railroads provided transportation between port cities and interior areas, moving rural workers to urban factories, raw materials from mines and farms to ports, and finished products to markets across continents.

At the same time, Europe's expanding cities, combined with growing colonies, provided markets for goods produced in Europe's factories. The huge profits from the trans-Atlantic triangle trade provided the capital infusion necessary to fund Europe's industrial transformation.

Competition under Capitalism Industrial expansion of the capitalist economy created intense competition among European countries for raw materials, cheap labor, and markets. Throughout the nineteenth and early twentieth centuries Great Britain, France, the Netherlands, Belgium, Russia, and Japan all raced to divide nonindustrial regions of the world into colonies that would secure their economic growth. In the process, European countries redrew the political map of the world and restructured the global economy to serve their expanding industrial activities.

Industrial Revolution: The eighteenth- and nineteenth-century shift from agriculture and artisanal skill craft to machine-based manufacturing.

Colonial spheres of influence were established over much of Asia, Africa, and the Middle East. In Asia, British military intervention forced China into a series of unequal treaties that granted Great Britain and later the United States, France, and Germany special rights to trade and legal protection within China. (These privileges continued until the communist revolution in 1949.) Hong Kong and Macau were ceded to the British and Portuguese, respectively. By the late nineteenth century, Japan began to establish Asian colonies, first in Taiwan (1895) and eventually including most of East Asia, including the eastern seaboard of China. (Japan's colonial enterprise was only ended by its 1945 defeat in World War II.)

The colonial division of Africa was extremely abrupt. In 1884–85, fourteen countries gathered at the Berlin Conference in Germany to negotiate a settlement in the competition for African resources. Representatives of Germany, Portugal, France, and England took the lead—accompanied by Spain, Russia, Belgium, Turkey, and the United States—in carving up the African continent into fifty colonies. No African representatives were present.

Previously, only coastal Africa had been colonized. Eighty percent of the continent was still locally controlled. But the Berlin Conference forced a division of people and resources in the interior, drawing new political boundaries along natural features such as rivers, mountains, and ports without regard to ethnicity, language, history, village, or family. These boundaries have continued to shape political, economic, and cultural life in Africa long after African liberation movements brought an end to colonialism following World War II (see the Rwanda discussion in Chapter 7).

Anticolonial Struggles

Local populations resisted colonialism with mixed success. Independence movements utilized strategies of rebellion, resistance, and negotiation to achieve their goals. These included nonviolent actions such as those led by Mohandas Ghandi in the Indian struggle against British colonialism, as well as violent uprisings such as those in the Algerian quest for independence discussed below. Frequently, external factors such as wars, economic crises, and international pressures aided independence movements by creating conditions for their success.

National Independence Movements In the Americas, independence movements on both continents brought changes. The United States declared independence from Great Britain in 1776, eventually winning independence through the Revolutionary War. The people of Haiti, a highly profitable Caribbean French colony known for its sugarcane, coffee, cocoa, indigo, and cotton plantations, declared independence in 1804 and became the first independent former colony to be ruled by people of African descent. In Latin America, Brazil declared independence from Portugal in 1822. By 1825, most of Spain's colonies in South America had achieved independence.

In Asia, Japan not only successfully resisted European colonial efforts but also established its own colonial enterprise. It occupied Taiwan for fifty years (1895–1945), Korea for thirty-five years (1910–45), and China beginning with the invasion of Manchuria in 1931 and expanding to much of eastern China through World War II. During the war, the Japanese military overran European and American colonies in Asia, including Indonesia, Malaysia, Vietnam, Cambodia, Laos, Burma, Hong Kong, and the Philippines.

Ultimately, World War II created conditions for the success of national independence movements and the collapse of the colonial system. For example, Japanese occupation destroyed much of the European colonial infrastructure in Asia and inspired organized national resistance movements. These forces led efforts toward national independence when the war ended. On a global scale, the war-ravaged economies and political institutions of the European colonial powers could no longer sustain their colonial enterprises, especially in the face of organized resistance movements. Between 1945 and 1990, more than one hundred former colonies gained their independence.

The Algerian Experience Gillo Pontecorvo's riveting film *The Battle of Algiers* (1965) captures universal aspects of the brutal anticolonial struggle through the lens of the Algerian movement for independence from France. The French, who were active colonialists in West and North Africa, ruled Algeria from 1830 to 1962.

Set in the Algerian capital, *The Battle of Algiers* focuses on the narrow streets of the casbah, the old Turkish city within Algiers. This area became the site of violent conflict between pro-independence guerillas of the National Liberation Front (NLF) and the French military. Between 1954 and 1962, two million young Frenchmen served as soldiers in Algeria. More than twenty thousand died. Unable to convince the French to withdraw, the NLF launched terrorist attacks against the French settler population, setting off bombs in public places and killing French policemen. In retaliation, French paratroopers stormed the casbah, sealing in the Algerian population and ferreting out NLF leaders and supporters through interrogation, torture, assassination, and bombings.

After independence, ties between the two countries remained complicated. Independence brought massive migration from Algeria to France. More than one million French colonial settlers, along with Algerian Muslims who served as soldiers in the French military, were "repatriated" (relocated) to France for

MAP 12.3
Algeria

FIGURE 12.7 Algierian residents do battle against the colonial French military in *The Battle of Algiers*, 1965.

their safety. In succeeding years, many poor rural Algerians also migrated to France to find work in the expanding postwar economy.

In Algeria, *The Battle of Algiers* has become popular as a tale of the anticolonial struggle that threw off French control after 132 years of colonial administration. But in France, screening of the film was not allowed until 2001, thirty-six years after its release. Its graphic portrayal of French troops created discomfort with French complicity in the widespread torture of Algerian nationalists. The torture included beatings, electric shock, waterboarding, and extrajudicial killings. The French commander in Algiers during the uprising called these techniques a "cruel necessity" in the battle against the terror tactics of nationalist guerillas (Harries 2007).

Pontecorvo's film reflects a brutal but not uncommon path toward independence at the end of colonialism following World War II. In 1980, Zimbabwe became the last African country to achieve independence from the European colonial powers. In Asia, however, only toward the end of the twentieth century did Britain return Hong Kong (1997) and Portugal return Macau (1999) to China. But as we have seen in the opening story about Côte d'Ivoire, and as we will see throughout the remainder of this chapter, despite the formal end of the colonial era, patterns of relationship established under colonialism—from migration and economics to military involvement—continue to influence both former colonies and colonizers.

The Modern World Economic System

With the end of the colonial era, many people believed that the former colonies—wealthy in natural resources and freed from colonial control—would see rapid economic growth. But such growth, as well as diminished poverty and the possibility for income equality, has proved to be elusive. Why have patterns of inequality established under colonialism persisted into the current era?

Conflicting Theories Modernization theories, which became popular following World War II, predicted that with the end of colonialism the less developed countries would follow the same trajectory as the industrialized countries and achieve improved standards of living. Certainly, the rise of industrial capitalism in Europe beginning in the late eighteenth century had spurred spectacular advances in production and a sense of optimism in the possibilities for dramatic material progress—in other words, **development** (Larrain 1989). As decolonization approached, politicians and economists in industrialized nations began to strategize about how to develop the economies of the colonies of Britain, France, Portugal, and other European powers (Leys 1996). The modernization model was assumed to be the key. Progress, modernization, and industrialization would be the natural path of economic development throughout the global capitalist economy, though this process would need nurturing through foreign aid and international investment.

After World War II, policy theorists and planners believed that scientific and technological expertise could help replicate the European and North American style of development across the globe. Through an array of new international aid agencies and financial institutions, such as the World Bank, the IMF, and the UN, wealthy nations worked with emerging national governments in former colonies to develop programs they hoped would stimulate growth, alleviate poverty, and raise living standards. Development projects often emphasized state investment in infrastructure as an engine of economic growth, focusing on the construction of ports, roads, dams, and irrigation systems (Cowen and Shenton 1996).

The underlying philosophy of post–World War II development efforts put faith in the inevitability of human progress: with the right economic policies

modernization theories: Post–World War II economic theories that predicted that with the end of colonialism, less-developed countries would follow the same trajectory toward modernization as the industrialized countries.

development: Post–World War II strategy of wealthy nations to spur global economic growth, alleviate poverty, and raise living standards through strategic investment in national economies of former colonies.

and economic stimulation, all or most societies would follow the same trajectory toward greater accumulation and standards of living. This faith in universal progress assumed that development efforts would facilitate shifts from poverty to wealth by transforming local economic activity from agriculture to industry; subsistence lifestyles to capital accumulation and mass consumption; kinship-based social and economic relations to contract-based ones; and, ultimately, tradition to modernity. In many early development efforts, anthropologists helped tailor projects to local needs as they designed, implemented, and evaluated programs to alleviate poverty and human suffering (Edelman and Haugerud 2005).

But by the 1960s, scholars began to question the Western development model. Despite the end of colonialism, less developed countries, even those with rich natural resources, did not experience modernization and economic growth. Many local and national economies remained stagnant or lost ground in the international economy. Many took on increasing international debt to keep their economies stable in the postcolonial era.

At this time, **dependency theory** emerged as a critique of modernization theory. Scholars from Latin America, in particular, argued that a new kind of colonialism—**neocolonialism**—had emerged (Cardoso and Faletto 1969; Frank 1969). Dependency theorists argued that despite the end of colonialism, the underlying economic relations of the modern world system had not changed. These scholars introduced the term **underdevelopment** to suggest that poor countries were not poor because of some fundamental structural flaw (such as inadequate natural resources), but because participation in the global economy left them underdeveloped. It was still structured to extract resources from less developed countries and transfer them to developed, industrialized countries. Thus, dependency theorists argued, underdeveloped countries should break their dependency on the global economic system and build up and protect their own self-sufficient national economic activities.

Core and Periphery Immanuel Wallerstein (1974) introduced to these debates a *modern world systems* analysis. Wallerstein characterized the nations within the world economic system as occupying core, semiperiphery, and periphery positions (Map 12.4). The **core countries**—primarily industrialized former colonial states—dominate the world system, extracting cheap labor and raw materials from periphery countries and sending them to the industrialized core. Finished products, with value added in the manufacturing process, are then returned to markets in the periphery. Core countries control the most lucrative economic processes, including the financial services sectors.

Periphery countries—among the least developed and least powerful nations—serve primarily as sources of raw materials, agricultural products,

dependency theory: A critique of modernization theory that argued that, despite the end of colonialism, the underlying economic relations of the modern world economic system had not changed.

neocolonialism: A continued pattern of unequal economic relations despite the formal end of colonial political and military control.

underdevelopment: The term used to suggest that poor countries are poor as a result of their relationship to an unbalanced global economic system.

core countries: Industrialized former colonial states that dominate the world economic system.

periphery countries: The least developed and least powerful nations; often exploited by the core countries as sources of raw materials, cheap labor, and markets.

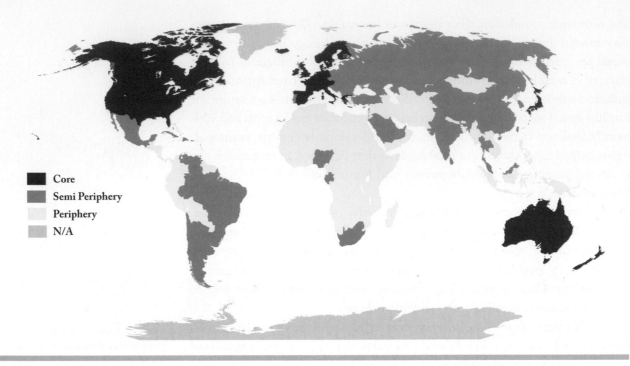

MAP 12.4 The Core/Periphery Division of the World

- ■ Core
- ■ Semi Periphery
- □ Periphery
- ■ N/A

cheap labor, and markets for the economic activities of the core. Established patterns of economic, political, and military relationship ensure the steady transfer of wealth, natural resources, and human resources from the periphery to core, contributing to underdevelopment. **Semiperiphery countries** occupy a middle position. They may have developed some industry, draw resources from the periphery, and export manufactured products to the core and periphery, but they lack the economic and political power of the core.

Core and periphery are not necessarily geographically isolated from one another. Wallerstein suggests that peripheral areas often exist within core countries as pockets of poverty amid generally high standards of living. In the United States, the Appalachian mountain region (see discussion of Pem Buck's book *Worked to the Bone* in Chapter 11) might be considered a periphery within a core country: it has abundant natural resources of coal, timber, and water but intense poverty, poor education and health care, and limited infrastructure. Core areas also exist within periphery countries. These include urban centers (ports and capital cities), dominated by the economic, military, and political elite, that provide linkages between core countries and the often more rural people in the periphery. Abidjian, Côte d'Ivoire, could be considered a core area within a periphery country, serving to connect rural cocoa farmers and the global chocolate trade.

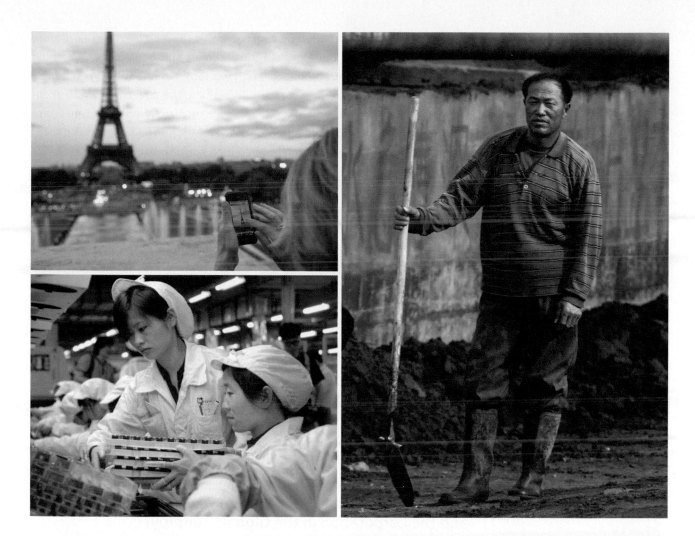

Over the past forty years, globalization has complicated the neat categories of Wallerstein's theory. Capital, goods, people, and ideas flow less predictably today between a geographically defined core and periphery. But the realities of uneven development and entrenched inequality persist. Fully 80 percent of the world's population still lives in developing nations decades after the end of colonialism. The failure of economic development strategies since World War II to advance the economic conditions of most former colonies, combined with dramatically uneven development, have raised significant questions about the appropriate strategies for addressing structural imbalance in the global economic system and related problems of poverty, hunger, illness, and environmental degradation going forward.

Development In recent years development has become contentious within the field of anthropology. Although development remains a foundational strategy

FIGURE 12.8 Where does your iPhone come from? The journey of an iPhone illustrates Wallerstein's concepts of core, semi-periphery, and periphery. *Clockwise from right*: A worker at a rare earth mine in Inner Mongolia; rare earth elements are vital to the manufacturing of electronics, including iPhones. Factory workers at the Foxconn plant in Shenzhen, south China, where most iPhones, iPads, and other Apple products are made. A woman takes a photo of the Eiffel Tower in Paris, France.

of powerful international organizations as well as most governments of poor nations, many scholars question its ultimate goals and beneficiaries (Escobar 1991, 1995; Gupta and Ferguson 1997; Ferguson 1997). In response, broader indices have been created to more holistically evaluate the effects of development strategies by augmenting the previous reliance on strictly economic measures such as gross domestic product. One such measure is the UN Development Program's Human Development Index, which considers improvements in life expectancy, literacy, formal education, political participation, and access to basic resources (Edelman and Haugerud 2005).

Despite disagreements within anthropology about the overall effectiveness of development strategies, today many anthropologists work in the field of development, at the World Bank, UN agencies, the Inter-American Development Bank, and smaller development-oriented NGOs. But the failure of the development model to significantly alleviate global poverty has led other anthropologists to explore alternatives to development. These approaches include efforts to localize projects and de-link them from the global marketplace; draw on community and indigenous knowledge; establish fair trade markets; and deepen local involvement in economic and policy decisions. These efforts are often linked to local social movements, NGOs, and civil society groups; they focus on developing practical experiences for raising living standards that can then be expanded to broader contexts (Cavanaugh, Wysham, and Aruda 2002).

What Is the Relationship Between the Nation-State and the Corporation in the Global Economy?

Over the past hundred years, the corporation has increasingly challenged the nation-state (which dominated the colonial era) for supremacy in the global economy. We can trace this change through the history of two economic models that dominated the U.S. economy (and beyond) during the twentieth century.

From Fordism to Flexible Accumulation

In 1914 Henry Ford, the founder of Ford Motor Company, a U.S. automobile manufacturer, experimented with a new strategy for profit making within the industrializing economy of the United States. Ford is famous for refining the factory assembly line and the division of labor that facilitated efficiency in industrial mass production. Perhaps equally significant, at a time when many U.S. manufacturers were exploiting immigrant workers with low wages and long work hours to maximize profits, Ford took a different approach.

Ford made several key innovations. Most important, he introduced a $5, eight-hour work day—a living wage that he hoped would create a worker who was loyal to the company, dependable on the job, and cooperative with management in the grueling, repetitive work environment of the assembly line. Ford also believed that every Ford worker should be able to buy a Ford car. Higher wages and shorter hours, he felt, would create a new pool of consumers with the income and leisure to purchase and enjoy a car. Ford sought to form a new

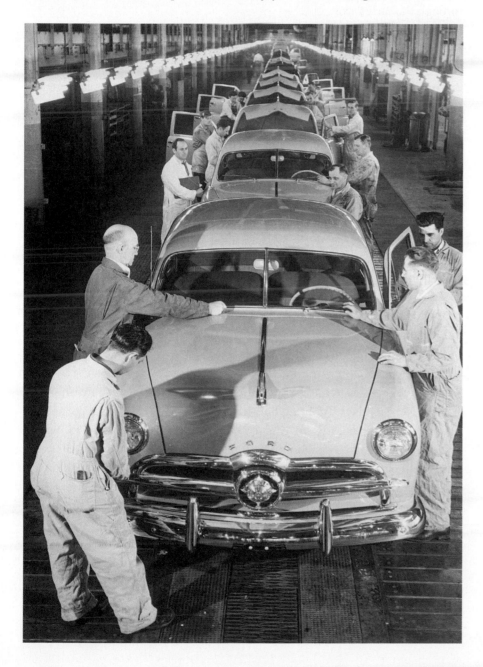

FIGURE 12.9 What can an old car teach us about the global economy today? Here, assembly line workers put the finishing touches on 1949 Ford sedans at the height of Fordism in the United States.

social compact between labor and capital that would benefit his corporation. These were the central aspects of **Fordism**.

Fordism took hold firmly after World War II with growing cooperation among corporations, labor, and government. The latter stepped in to regulate corporate responsibility for worker health and safety and, eventually, environmental impact. Wages and benefits, along with corporate profits, rose steadily through a long postwar boom that drove a rapid expansion of the middle class through the early 1970s.

However, industrial economic activity in the late 1960s and 1970s began to shift away from the Fordist model toward what geographer David Harvey (1990) has called strategies of flexible accumulation. At this time, corporate profits faced increasing pressures as European and Japanese economies recovered from the devastation of World War II and the "tiger" economies of newly industrializing nations (such as South Korea, Taiwan, Hong Kong, and Singapore) entered global competition. An oil crisis in 1973 further strained economic production in core countries, and a simultaneous global recession left many corporations seeking new strategies to enhance their profits.

Flexible accumulation refers to the increasingly flexible strategies that corporations use to accumulate profits in an era of globalization. In particular, these strategies include *offshoring* (relocating factories anywhere in the world that provides optimal production, infrastructure, labor, marketing, and political conditions) and *outsourcing* (hiring low-wage laborers in periphery countries to perform jobs previously done in core countries). By so doing, corporations could bypass high production costs, organized labor, and environmental laws in the core industrial cities and core countries.

Under flexible accumulation, corporations—even highly profitable ones—began to eliminate jobs in old core industrial centers such as New York, Chicago, and Detroit. Instead, they opened factories "offshore" in places such as Mexico, the Caribbean, South Korea, and Taiwan. In the 1980s they began to relocate factories to China to take advantage of even lower wages, lower taxes, and weaker environmental restrictions. Today Walmart has more than five thousand factories in China producing goods for its stores worldwide. Recent strikes by Chinese workers demanding higher wages and better working conditions have led some corporations to relocate again, opening new factories in Thailand, Cambodia, Vietnam, and Bangladesh. Over the past forty years, strategies of flexible accumulation have transformed the local factory assembly line into a global assembly line.

Global Cities To manage global production, corporations created international headquarters. As part of this process, a number of old industrial centers reinvented themselves as command centers for global production. This phenomenon began with New York, Tokyo, and London and subsequently included Los Angeles, Chicago, Miami, Hong Kong, Sydney, Paris, Amsterdam, and Buenos Aires. All of these cities had experienced the loss of industrial manufacturing in the 1970s and 1980s. Now these **global cities** (Sassen 2001) provide corporations with the physical infrastructure and human resources required to run a corporate headquarters: local transportation, international airports, regional rail networks, reliable power grids and water supplies, and modern communication systems, as well as skilled accountants, lawyers, information technology specialists, and marketers.

global city: A former industrial center that has reinvented itself as a command center for global production.

Outsourcing of Jobs

New communication technologies have enabled corporations to outsource many jobs to developing areas. Since the 1990s, companies have been outsourcing software design, airplane reservations, data processing, radiology readings, and data analysis. The call center industry—those people at the 800 numbers we call for help with an electronic device or to make rental car and airline reservations—has been aggressively pursuing low-cost options across the globe.

Call centers once located in Kansas and Nebraska now operate in India and the Philippines. They attract college graduates with English language skills who earn 30 to 50 percent of what a U.S. worker would earn for the same job. Recently, call centers in the Philippines have been expanding as Indian centers shift to the development of information technologies and software that require a higher level of education. With 350,000 call center workers,

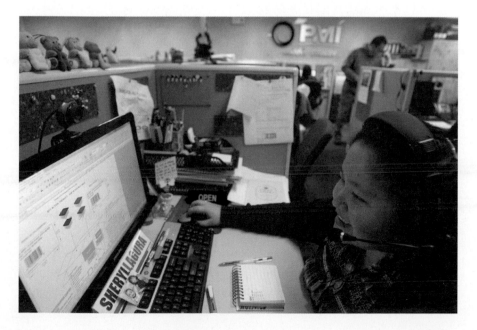

FIGURE 12.10 Who answered your last call for tech support? Here, a call center agent in the Philippines talks to a client in the United States, an example of how jobs are being outsourced from core countries to low-wage destinations under flexible accumulation.

the Philippines has surpassed India to become the largest call center operator in the world—for now (Patel 2010).

Under flexible accumulation, corporations will continue to search for the lowest costs through offshoring and outsourcing. They will follow the money trail to countries with pockets of low-wage English speakers, whether in China, Vietnam, Egypt, Mexico, Eastern Europe, or South America.

What Are the Dominant Organizing Principles of the Modern World Economic System?

Flows of capital, goods, and services associated with flexible accumulation have built on old colonial patterns and have made use of advances in transportation and communication technologies (time-space compression). But other forces also help integrate all people and nations into one free market with minimal barriers. These forces include powerful international financial institutions such as the World Bank, the IMF, and the World Trade Organization (WTO); international trade agreements such as the former Global Agreement on Trade and Tariffs (GATT); and regional agreements such as the North American Free Trade Agreement (NAFTA) or the Asia-Pacific Trade Agreement (APTA). Drawing on an economic philosophy called neoliberalism, these institutions and agreements have created a strong international financial and policy framework, one that promotes an even deeper integration of nations and local communities into a modern world economic system.

Capitalism, Economic Liberalism, and the Free Market

The work of the Scottish economist and philosopher Adam Smith (1723–1790) and the British economist John Maynard Keynes (1883–1946) provided key intellectual counterpoints that have shaped economic debates about the functioning of capitalism in the twentieth century. In *The Wealth of Nations* (1776), Adam Smith promoted economic liberalism through his ideas of laissez-faire ("leave it alone") capitalism. In Smith's view, free markets and free trade, being liberated from government intervention, would provide the best conditions for economic growth: they would unleash competition to maximize profits. In contrast, Keynes later argued that capitalism would work best when the government had a role in moderating the excesses of capitalism and ensuring the basic welfare of all citizens (Keynes [1936] 2007).

U.S. president Franklin Delano Roosevelt relied on Keynesian economic philosophy in his approach to the Great Depression of 1929–41. His administration initiated government programs such as the Works Progress Administration to put unemployed Americans back to work, and the Social Security program to ensure the basic welfare of all American people, especially the elderly and most vulnerable.

After World War II, leading Western governments applied Keynesian economic philosophy in rebuilding their war-torn economies and establishing development projects to stimulate growth in former colonies. Keynesian economics began to lose popularity in the 1970s in the wake of a global recession. But today it maintains a role in certain government policies—those that (1) stimulate economic activity through public investment in infrastructure projects and the employment of civil servants while also (2) seeking to regulate the excesses of corporate and financial activities and moderate the most extreme effects of capitalism on the population through the provision of a social safety net and investment in health, education, and housing.

Neoliberalism

Economic liberalism, building on Smith's philosophy, has reemerged since the 1970s as a guiding philosophy for the global economy. This **neoliberalism**, associated with conservative fiscal and political policies in the United States, views the free market—not the state—as the main mechanism for ensuring economic growth. Neoliberal policies focus on promoting free trade on a global scale, eliminating trade barriers, and reducing taxes, tariffs, and all government intervention in the economy. Neoliberalism promotes the privatization of public assets (such as publicly owned utilities and transportation systems) and an overall reduction, if not privatization, of government spending on health, education, and welfare.

neoliberalism: An economic and political worldview that sees the free market as the main mechanism for ensuring economic growth, with a severely restricted role for government.

Since the 1980s, powerful international financial institutions have promoted neoliberal policies. These institutions are the IMF, the World Bank, and the WTO, which was founded in 1995 to replace the GATT. The Allied nations established the IMF and the World Bank after World War II to regulate financial and commercial relations among the industrial powers. The IMF and the World Bank were also charged with providing loans for modernizing national economies ravaged by the war; in this role they often subsidized national development efforts, including infrastructure projects such as ports, roads, dams, and irrigation systems. Particularly since the 1980s, IMF and World Bank programs have promoted free trade, free markets, and reduction of the state's role in local and international economics.

Structural Adjustment During the 1980s and 1990s, global financial institutions emphasized structural adjustment loans as a key, though controversial, mechanism to address poverty and development in poorer nations. Structural adjustment loans seek to stabilize a country's long-term economic development. They require fiscal austerity measures, a reduced role for the state in the economy, and a restructuring of national trade and tariff policies so as to create freer access to local markets. These loans also require receiving governments to (1) eliminate agricultural and manufacturing subsidies and price supports on essential commodities such as food and oil, (2) reduce government spending on health, education, and social services, (3) privatize state-owned enterprises, and (4) deregulate financial and labor markets.

In the 2001 documentary film *Life and Debt*, filmmaker Stephanie Black explores the recent economic history of the Caribbean island of Jamaica. Her research examines the effects of IMF and World Bank structural adjustment programs on the day-to-day life of Jamaicans and on the Jamaican government's efforts to establish economic independence after three hundred years of British colonialism (1655–1962).

Since the withdrawal of British financial support at the end of colonial rule, Jamaica's government has had to turn to international lenders to provide short-term cash infusions to support basic services. The loans and their high interest rates carry requirements to restructure the Jamaican economy, reduce price supports for basic foods, cut back on education and health care spending, and reduce barriers to international trade—all strategies intended to stabilize the economy and enhance growth through participation in global trade. But the promised benefits failed to materialize. Jamaica's local economic production in key agricultural sectors has in fact been undermined by subsidized, low-cost imports—for instance, subsidized milk products from the United States. Jamaica has ultimately become saddled with more than $4 billion in external debt that it does not have the capacity to repay.

MAP 12.5
Jamaica

Pros and Cons of Neoliberal Policies Debates continue over the effectiveness of neoliberal policies. The failure of IMF and World Bank policies to avert economic crises in Asia and Latin America in the 1990s called into question the long-term benefits of neoliberal policy prescriptions on a global scale. In particular, there is skepticism in many countries over the notion that facilitating competition and profit making through free trade, free markets, and privatization promotes improved economic opportunities for most of the world's people. Much of Latin America has repaid debts to the IMF and has rejected neoliberal economic strategies. The World Social Forum, an annual international meeting of social movements and NGOs, explores alternatives to neoliberal economic policies and the negative aspects of globalization.

Protests against the WTO in Seattle, Washington, in 1999 launched a global movement to resist neoliberal policies and what many critics consider to be the unequal application of international trade standards (Graeber 2002). At the WTO meetings in Cancun, Mexico, in 2006, developing countries refused to ratify new international trade treaties because of perceived inequalities of

FIGURE 12.11 What are the best steps to build a healthy economy? Here, protestors in Madrid, Spain, demonstrate against government austerity measures, 2012.

global trade standards. The refusing countries especially objected to the protection of subsidies to farmers in the United States and Europe, who export subsidized farm products at lower costs that undermine the receiving countries' local agricultural projects and small independent farmers.

But in Europe, several nations (Greece, Spain, Portugal, and Ireland) are currently struggling to adapt to mandates for austerity imposed by the IMF and the European Central Bank in return for loans made to stabilize their national economies. Widespread protests by affected workers, especially in Greece, have threatened the stability of national governing coalitions that agreed to the externally imposed restrictions. Leaders of underdeveloped countries, scholars, and activists have argued that these policies are the centerpiece of an ever-evolving global economic system that promotes uneven development and ensures that wealthy countries remain wealthy and poor countries remain poor (Sachs 2005; Krugman 2009; Stiglitz 2010).

The debate over neoliberal and Keynesian economic strategies continues to rage in the United States after the financial collapse of 2008 led to the so-called Great Recession. Followers of Keynesian economics—often associated with political liberals and moderates—argue for greater regulation of financial markets, increased consumer protections, an expanded healthcare safety net, and heavy investment in infrastructure projects to put people back to work. Followers of neoliberalism—primarily associated with conservatives—seek lower taxes, smaller government, faster debt repayment, and reduced regulation to stimulate economic activity by businesses. Crucial debates continue over efforts to privatize Social Security, Medicare, and Medicaid and to reduce government support for education. Have you experienced any of the effects of these debates, perhaps in reduced government funding of your high school, college, or university, an increase in your student loan rate, or expanded health care access?

How Does Today's Global Economy Link Workers with Consumers Worldwide?

Through much of recent human history, markets have been places where farmers and craftsmen, traders and consumers exchange products, ideas, information, and news, linking local communities to one another and to communities at greater distances, enabling all to benefit (Polanyi [1944] 2001). Today local markets are more deeply integrated as social and material commodities often flow across national borders (Hannerz 1996). Although **commodity chains**—the hands an item (commodity) passes through between producer and consumer—used to be primarily local, globalization has extended their span across territories and cultures, intensifying the

commodity chain: The hands an item passes through between producer and consumer.

connection between the local and global in ways previously unimaginable (Haugerud, Stone, and Little 2000). Tsukiji Fish Market, the largest fish market in the world today, is a prime example.

Tsukiji: Fish Market at the Center of the World

Standing in the heart of downtown Tokyo, Japan, Tsukiji Fish Market is the center of a massive global trade in seafood and a cultural icon of Japanese cuisine. Each day sixty thousand traders gather to auction bluefin tuna from Maine, eel from southern China, octopus from West Africa, salmon from Canada, and shellfish from California; these then make their way into the restaurants, supermarkets, and homes of Japanese people across the country. Tsukiji Fish Market feeds the city's 22 million people and many more throughout Japan. But Tokyo and the Tsukiji Market are also command central for an intricate global trade in seafood.

The Japanese people's desire for sushi and sashimi has established Japan as the world's main market for fresh tuna. And Japanese cultural influence has spurred the consumption of sushi in other countries. At the same time, rising demand in Japan has led to overfishing and the decimation of the local tuna fishery. Forty years of time-space compression have facilitated an extension of the tuna commodity chain to previously unconnected places and people. Advances in transportation and communication—refrigerated trucks and cargo jets traveling international routes, along with cell phones, faxes, and the

MAP 12.6
Tokyo

FIGURE 12.12 Where does your fish come from? Here, a tuna fish auction at Tsukiji Fish Market, Tokyo, Japan, 2007.

Internet—have promoted an integrated network of fishermen, buyers, and shippers. The search for the perfect tuna has now expanded to the North Atlantic, the Mediterranean, and Australia.

Anthropologist Theodore Bestor's study (2004) of the transnational tuna trade, particularly in Atlantic bluefin tuna, takes him to coastal Maine and the Mediterranean coast of Spain. Fishing boats returning from the Atlantic Ocean dock at marinas along the eastern seaboards of Canada and the United States. There they meet with Japanese buyers who assess the quality of the catch. The sale is based on the latest prices on the Tokyo market. High-quality tuna is packed in ice, and refrigerated trucks deliver it to an airport to be shipped to Tokyo for the next day's market at Tsukiji.

Bestor's focus on Atlantic bluefin tuna allows a more complex view of global markets. The stories of these global commodity chains—what Appadurai (1986) calls tracing the "social life of things"—illustrate how the modern world economic system works. Tsukiji Market and the movement of tuna to it enhance our understandings of Wallerstein's ideas of an integrated, but increasingly complicated, world system. Goods, money, ideas, and even people (or, in this case, tuna) flow from periphery to core. But assumptions of a fixed core and periphery, as well as expectations of a predictable flow of raw materials, are called into question. In the story of tuna and sushi, natural resources flow to consumers at the center of the global market and at the end of the global commodity chain. But in this story Japan is the core. The Atlantic seaboards of North America and Europe are the periphery (Bestor 2001, 2004; Stevens 2005; Jacobs 2005).

Do you eat sushi? Have you wondered where the raw fish comes from and how it gets to your local restaurant or market while still fresh? The next time you see sushi displayed for sale, consider asking the store manager or restaurant owner about the commodity chain that links a fisherman to your dinner.

"Friction" in the Global Economy

To examine the complicated dynamics of the global economy, cultural anthropologist Anna Tsing (2005) has focused on what she names "friction"—the messy and often unequal encounters at the intersection of the local and the global, including the role of transnational corporations, international development agencies, local and national governments, and global trade regulations. She examines the destruction of rainforest in Kalimantan, Indonesia, on the island of Borneo. Recently the dense tropical forests and swamp lands have been clear-cut and burned to satisfy a global demand for timber, to open lands for mining, and to create agricultural land for palm oil plantations. (Palm oil is a common ingredient in foods, cosmetics, household products, and biofuels.) Today transnational corporations use uncontrolled burns to clear rainforests at the rate of an equivalent of three hundred football fields each day.

The Travels of a Chocolate Bar

Anthropologists have often traced the movement of commodities such as silver, sugar, fur, tea, and coffee to reveal the global connections—political, economic, military, and social—that link producers and consumers, rural and urban communities, and people and nations on opposite sides of the world. For example, Sidney Mintz's classic work *Sweetness and Power: The Place of Sugar in Modern History* (1985) explores the way sugar historically transformed economic and social relations among Europe, Africa, and the Americas. In general, the movement of commodities illuminates the human dimensions of globalization that are often obscured by distance and marketing. Do you know where your chocolate, tea, coffee, and sugar come from? Who made these products? What are their lives like? How are you connected to the people who harvested those crops in another part of the world?

Igor Kopytoff (1986) has suggested that all commodities have a biography, and Arjun Appadurai (1986) has urged anthropologists to consider the "social life of things." To return to our opening story, consider writing a biography of a chocolate bar. Buy one and put it on your desk. What are the ingredients? Where do they come from? Start with cocoa, the primary ingredient, and Côte d'Ivoire, which produces more than 40 percent of the world's cocoa. Ask yourself the following questions:

- What are the working and living conditions of the people who produce the cocoa?
- How is it produced? Are child laborers involved?
- How do the producers get the cocoa to market?
- How are the prices set?
- Which international corporations dominate the chocolate trade? Who regulates it?
- How is chocolate marketed?
- Where did you buy it?
- How much profit does a store owner make on a bar of chocolate?
- Are there hidden costs that are not included in the price you paid? Consider underpayment of labor; environmental impact; government subsidies that are direct (to the company) and indirect (infrastructure such as roads, ports, bridges, and water systems); and the health care costs created by harvesting, transporting, processing, or eating the food. How are these costs obscured?

For further information, read the report *Hot Chocolate* (2007) produced by Global Witness. If you would rather research your morning cup of coffee than your afternoon bar of chocolate, start by watching the documentary *Black Gold: Wake Up and Smell the Coffee* (2006).

Where does your chocolate bar come from?

Tsing's ethnography focuses on the complex interactions and frictions among the many players in Kalimantan. We can list some examples:

- International corporations seek profits for shareholders by conducting widespread logging and mining to feed an expanding global market.
- Indonesia's military dictatorship conspires with corporations to gain a share of profits.
- Local residents resist destruction of their native lands. Other residents participate with the corporations in hopes of getting rich.
- Indonesian environmental activists link local residents to international networks of NGOs working on environmental and human rights campaigns.
- Foundations based in the West invest in development projects to improve the living conditions of those affected by landscape conversion and to promote community-based natural resource management.
- UN meetings in New York address the impact of environmental degradation on quality of life.
- Scholars study conditions on the ground and the forces driving the multiple global projects that touch down in Kalimantan.

Tsing's notion of friction pushes anthropologists to recognize that the global interconnections associated with the world systems model are complicated and full of friction. Indeed, encounters between powerful economic forces and corporate actors, on one hand, and real-life individuals, households, communities, and regions, on the other hand, are often awkward, unstable, and unequal. They bring people together across different cultures, social and economic statuses, and worldviews. In Tsing's study of Kalimantan, the transformation of the natural environment brings into tension dozens of players with different motivations. She argues that ethnographers must address the total array of global connections that shape local realities (Tsing 2005; McKay 2006).

Chinese Restaurants and the Global Economy

Have you ever wondered why chicken with broccoli is so cheap in your local Chinese restaurant? Or how the Chinese restaurant workers got to the little town or big city where your college is located? The answer lies along a street called East Broadway in Chinatown on the Lower East Side of Manhattan. There an entire migration industry draws Chinese immigrants from the rural villages of the Fuzhou area of southeastern China to New York City and sets them on the move again to a Chinese restaurant near you.

Located along East Broadway are a cluster of services that facilitate the movement of Chinese immigrants. These services provide for their daily needs as they make their way from a rural Chinese economy built around farming and fishing to a U.S. restaurant economy in one of the world's most developed countries. Offices for immigration lawyers, English language classes, driving schools, and producers of legitimate and illegitimate documents stand alongside doctors' offices, pharmacies, clothing stores, and gambling parlors. East Broadway's human smugglers help undocumented immigrants make their way across national borders. Phone card sales booths help workers keep in touch with family back in China. MoneyGram and Western Union wire transfer offices send money back to family members in the home villages. Key to this migration industry are two dozen employment agencies that match newly arrived workers with Chinese restaurants across the country and another dozen long-distance buses that deliver Fuzhounese to those restaurants.

This global flow of Fuzhounese is fraught with frictions. Chinese human smugglers charge more than $70,000 to bring a person to the United States, leaving immigrants with huge debts that may take years to repay. Restaurant owners rely on vulnerable, underpaid workers to make their profit margins on inexpensive dishes such as chicken with broccoli. Workers often live and work in the restaurants, putting in twelve- to fourteen-hour days, six or seven days a week. They suffer from emotional stress and the physical strain of grueling work, plus the isolation of living in a foreign land. New York's Chinatown becomes a place for rest and recuperation between stints at a far-off restaurant. The so-called Chinatown buses provide the link that moves workers between out-of-town jobs and the support system of the migration industry along East Broadway. As many as fifty thousand individuals are circulating through this Chinese restaurant industry at any given time.

The movement of rural men and women from Chinese villages to the far reaches of the United States illustrates the deep interconnectivity of people in the modern world economic system. The demand for inexpensive Chinese food in Omaha, Nebraska, can pull a young Chinese farmer across an ocean to help fill the demand of a global labor market and pursue her dream of wealth and happiness for herself and her family. That is the story behind your next dish of chicken with broccoli (Guest 2011).

Is Today's Economic System Sustainable?

Today we have an economic system of astounding complexity. Our economic activity surpasses anything we might have imagined even fifty years ago. The global economy integrates all of the world's people to one extent or another into a global system of exchange. But does it work well for everyone? What are the criteria we might use to assess its effectiveness?

Successes and Failures

The global economy has achieved remarkable success over the past sixty years. For example, gross national income of the global economy rose from around $1 trillion in 1960 to nearly $70 trillion in 2010. The same period saw a 50 percent increase in school enrollments and a drop in infant mortality rates of more than 60 percent. And life expectancy nearly doubled over the last century, reaching 67.2 years in 2010 (Moran 2006).

But the outlook is not all rosy. In 2010 the world had nearly one billion people going hungry each day and living in absolute poverty. Another 1.7 billion people live in relative poverty, attempting to survive on the equivalent of $2 a day. Six million children die of malnutrition each year. Clearly, global inequality continues to increase (Moran 2006). Is the current trajectory of the global economy sustainable? And what can anthropologists contribute to addressing these questions? These issues constitute the focus of the work of environmental anthropologist Emilio F. Moran, featured in "Anthropologists Engage the World," on pages 482–83.

The Human Ecological Footprint

Since at least the time of the earliest human settlements and the development of farming and pastoralism, humans have had an impact on their local environments. Human impact increased with an expanding population and was accelerated by the Industrial Revolution. Over the past sixty years, we have transformed our relationship with nature, and now our impact is being felt on a planetary scale.

The UN estimates that the world population, which was 2.5 billion in 1950, will increase from 7 billion in 2012 to 10.1 billion by 2100. Each day, we add 220,000 people. Each day, human consumption increases while available natural resources decrease. How will we sustain an almost 50 percent increase in global population when current resources are already overused? As this crisis deepens, how will your life be directly affected? What personal and collective strategies can you imagine for addressing the emerging problems?

Accelerating climate change is already evident, and the human contribution to the environmental crisis is clear. Agricultural yields are being affected by rising temperatures and increased greenhouse gases in the atmosphere. Food shortages are increasing despite intensive farm mechanization, chemical fertilizers, and pesticides. Carbon emissions from burning oil and gas are heating the planet and acidifying the oceans. At the 2009 global climate conference in Copenhagen, Denmark, 167 nations endorsed an agreement that acknowledged the need to

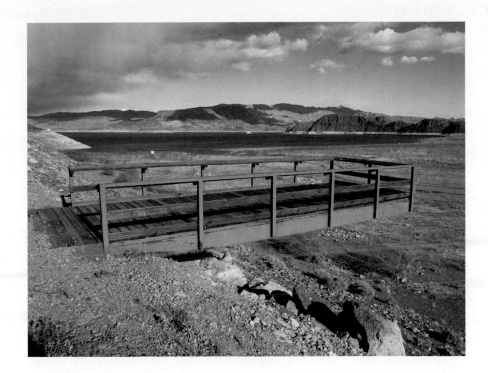

FIGURE 12.13 What is the carrying capacity of planet Earth? Here, a pier juts out into the air over Lake Mead, Nevada, where a severe long-term drought has lowered water levels more than 80 feet below normal.

cut global emissions drastically to hold the overall increase in global temperatures below 2 degrees Celsius (3.6 degrees Fahrenheit). Meeting this goal was recognized as essential to avoid a global ecological catastrophe. But so far, global temperatures have already risen eight-tenths of a degree Celsius, and humans continue to pour record amounts of carbon into the atmosphere (McKibben 2010, 2012).

The scramble for natural resources—especially freshwater, oil, and coltan (a scarce metal ore used in cell phones and other electronic devices)—pits wealthy nations against poor nations. The ice sheets in the Himalayas that provide drinking water for billions of people in Pakistan, India, Burma, and Indo-China are shrinking from global warming. Underground aquifers that provide freshwater to billions more in China and the Middle East are being depleted faster than nature can replenish them. Environmental trends do not bode well for the global economy using today's technologies.

Humans have a huge ecological footprint. Production, distribution, and consumption have been transformed in the contemporary global economy (Table 12.1). And consumerism is driving a dramatic expansion of the human ecological footprint. Studies suggest that as early as 1980 humans began to use more resources than the planet could regenerate. By 2000, our consumption of the world's resources stretched above 50 percent of sustainable levels. In other words, at our current rate of consumption, it would take 1.5 Earths to sustain our rate of resource consumption and absorb our pollution using prevailing

Emilio F. Moran

> We have in the past 50 years, changed nearly every aspect of our relationship with nature.
>
> —Emilio Moran (2006, 1)

Environmental anthropologist Emilio Moran has built a career studying the human dimensions of global climate change, initially through fieldwork in Brazil's Amazon Basin and today as distinguished professor of anthropology and environmental sciences at Indiana University Bloomington and director of the Anthropological Center for Training and Research on Global Environmental Change. In recognition of his leadership in this area, Moran has won a Guggenheim Fellowship, been named a fellow of the American Association for the Advancement of Science, and in 2010 was elected to the National Academy of Sciences.

Moran's interest in climate change began during his doctoral fieldwork on the environmental impact of the construction of an immense highway across Brazil's Amazon Basin. He hitched rides with construction crews and studied systems ecology, geography, tropical soils, and the basics of slash and burn (swidden) farming. Ultimately, his anthropological training led him to examine the impact on local communities as highway construction spurred the migration of people and changed the Amazon. "I was looking at people from very different backgrounds from all over Brazil being thrown together into new communities where they had to negotiate everything from religious practices to leadership structures and what crops to grow, thereby changing the landscape."

Moran emerged from this period of fieldwork convinced of the need for an interdisciplinary approach to the study of global climate change. "Anthropologists must be concerned with the entire experience of humankind, combining humanistic and scientific approaches, rigorous observation, measurement, and illustration. We have to use a variety of methods to understand what is happening to the land and the people. We have to think about the physical environment, the rainfall, soil types, the crops that are grown, as well as locating people historically and sociologically. It's not only about culture. People live in a real landscape—they first have to survive in order to hope to thrive. Your job as an anthropologist includes trying to observe what's going on in people's physical world.

"To really engage in the climate debates and research, anthropology students today need to learn the science of whatever part of ecology they want to engage with. I did it studying soils and agriculture to start with, and then systems ecological modeling. You can go through other windows. You can go through demography; you can go through earth systems science—many, many avenues. But you must know the science if you want to be part of this conversation. Otherwise you're talking to yourself. We have to learn some skills that we don't typically get in anthropology.

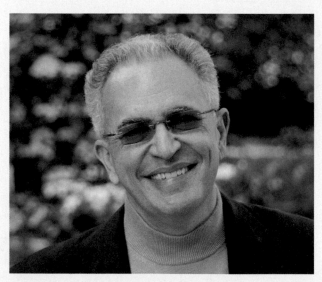

Anthropologist Emilio Moran

"When I created the Anthropological Center for Training and Research in 1992, climate scientists were asking social scientists to join them in understanding global dimensions of environmental change. But the scientific debates in general were too far removed from the realities of people and what they do. The climate models were all of these global circulation models that could not include human activity and decisions. So I created a center to emphasize the anthropological concern for the human dimensions of global climate change and to train social scientists of all varieties to use key technologies for climate research. For instance, satellite remote sensing is widely used by climate scientists. It provides a particular way of looking at landscape change. But anthropologists ask different questions than many scientists. When I look at a remote sensing image of a tiny little two-hectare field in the Amazon, I want to know what's happening in every one of those pixels in that field. What is happening in the process of swidden farming? And I want to track through time how that field changes, how it's planted or abandoned. In the field of climate science, particularly as it related to remote satellite imaging, nobody had done that before. We were bringing a unique contribution to the way science was done. People had sampled pixels because they're all interested in broad questions, for instance about soil fertility. But we wanted to know: Is it growing coffee, or pepper; how has the field changed over time; when did it go fallow? To answer these questions you have to do a lot of fieldwork. This is not done in a lab. You go into the field to interpret the data from the satellite digital data. The anthropology comes in as you do a lot of fieldwork about how people use the land. That information—coupled with the remote sensing image—enhances what you are able to tell from the satellite data. That's a contribution to the study of climate change, a contribution using an anthropological perspective."

In discussing the role of anthropology in the study of global climate change, Moran urges, "We have to make the decision to engage in these conversations as equal partners. If we're going to be equal partners, we have to be able to understand what the other one is saying and challenge them by having competence in climate science. Otherwise they're going to dismiss what we say because we don't understand the science. Anthropologists can be the bridge between the social sciences and the natural sciences. That's what everybody is looking for today in the environmental field. Ideally, every investigation of an environmental system should be a joint effort between social and natural scientists. But if we are invited to the table, we need to have the skills to really be part of that team on an equal basis."

In his book *People and Nature* (2006), Moran looks ahead at the climate challenges facing the world. "One of the challenges before us is how to re-conceptualize the interactions between people and nature. One step forward is to think organically, as organisms-in-nature, bringing our own versions of meaning to it in accordance with our histories. Dichotomous thinking led us to think of people as apart from nature and charged with controlling nature for human purposes—and crucially, as distinct from the inherent dynamics of the Earth system itself. . . . What happens to the air we breathe, the water we drink, and the land upon which we depend for our food matters. If we take care of it, it will nurture us—and if we damage its capacity to provide us with sustainable goods and services, and the comfort of aesthetic beauty, we will put ourselves at risk. We cannot do this alone, but it must be a partnership of trust in human communities bound by covenants that favor life over material accumulation, that favor dignity for members of the community and the pleasures of taking care of each other, and nature, as the highest good. We need to re-conceptualize our relations with each other, and with nature—and to think of human agents as organic parts of nature" (2006, 8–9).

TABLE 12.1 Energy Consumption in Selected Countries, 2008

Country	Total[a]	Per capita[b]
World	493.0	73.6
United States	100.6	330.4
China	85.1	64.6
Russia	30.4	216.2
Japan	21.9	171.8
India	20.0	17.5
Germany	14.4	174.3
Canada	14.0	422.4
France	11.3	180.3
Brazil	10.6	54.1
United Kingdom	9.3	151.0

[a] Total consumption figures are in quadrillion Btu.

[b] Per capita consumption figures are in million Btu.

SOURCE: U.S. Census. The 2012 Statistical Abstract, Table 1383. www.census.gov/compendia /statab/2012/tables/12s1383.pdf.

technologies. By the year 2030, estimates suggest, we would need two planets to sustain our economic activity. This is what scientists call ecological overshoot, when human demands on nature exceed the planet's ability to provide. The results are depletion of freshwater systems, the buildup of carbon dioxide in the atmosphere, collapsing fisheries in the oceans, and diminishing forest cover (Global Footprint Network 2013).

World on the Edge

Time is short. Scholars in many fields are asking if we have come to the crisis point where our model of economic growth is leading to ecological collapse. Our current economic system risks pushing us closer to the edge. Although most residents of developed countries have been shielded from the worst effects of these changes, people in poorer countries, particularly in coastal and low-lying regions, are already hard hit. For example, Bangladesh's coastal flood plain has been repeatedly inundated with monsoons, flooding, and devastating erosion. Even the United States is experiencing an increased incidence of droughts, heat waves, and damaging storm fronts.

Perhaps the biggest test of the global economy and its underlying principles will be its sustainability. Can we sustain the current pace of economic growth? Is it within the planet's carrying capacity? Is it reasonable to think that through modernization all people will attain a middle-class lifestyle when we know that if everyone on the planet had the same ecological footprint as an American, the global lifestyle would require five Earths to support?

If we are on the edge, we are not yet over the cliff. But significant changes are needed to reestablish the balance between humans and our planet. We must slow population growth. We must stabilize the global climate by rapidly shifting from petroleum-based, carbon dioxide–producing energy sources to renewable fuels such as wind and solar power. Perhaps most fundamental, we need to reassess the culture of consumption that considers the acquisition of capital as a measure of self-worth and compensates for a lack of capital by buying on credit. In the twenty-first century, we will need to redefine the key threats to the future of humanity (Korten 2001). These are not terrorism but population growth, climate change, hunger, water shortages, costly oil, poverty, rising food prices, the collapse of nation-states, and a lack of will to address these challenges urgently (Brown 2011).

As students, you can engage these issues on an individual and an institutional level. You can conserve energy and water, plant trees, use public transportation or a bike rather than a car, reduce how much you consume, and consider the hidden costs in all products that you buy. You can educate yourself about the threats to the future of your friends, family, and future generations. Beyond changes in your lifestyle, you can engage these issues through the institutions around you. Challenge your college to conserve energy, recycle, invest in solar and wind power on campus, invest its endowment in renewable energy companies rather than carbon-generating oil companies, and offer courses on the relationship between economics and the environment. Find creative ways to engage religious institutions, local governments, stores, and corporations to adjust their institutional practices and cultures. Change, whether personal or institutional, is not easy. But it may not be a choice.

TOOLKIT

Thinking Like an Anthropologist: Situating Yourself within the Global Economy

Globalization of the world economy has transformed the way we live. If you wish, you can touch just about anyone anywhere in the world in the next twenty-four hours by phone, e-mail, or air travel. Communication and transportation advances have enabled companies to move their production facilities around the world in search of cheaper labor costs, lower taxes, and fewer environmental restrictions—what we call flexible accumulation. Factories move offshore to make clothing and electronic goods. Offices spring up around the world to process X-rays, book airline reservations, and offer technical support. This new global factory and global assembly lines mean that much of what we eat, wear, drive, and communicate with has traveled across national borders and oceans to reach our table, closet, driveway, or desktop.

As you analyze the global economy and your connection to it, consider again the questions we raised at the beginning of the chapter:

- What is an economy, and what is its purpose?
- What are the roots of today's global economy?
- What role has colonialism played in forming the modern world economic system?
- What is the relationship between the nation-state and the corporation in the global economy?
- What are the dominant organizing principles of the modern world economic system?
- How does today's global economy link workers with consumers worldwide?
- Is today's global economic system sustainable?

Our opening story of chocolate in Côte d'Ivoire highlighted both the complexities of the global economy and the connections it facilitates among people, states, and corporations worldwide. Chocolate—like coffee, tea, sugar, a laptop, or a smartphone—reveals both (1) the incredible potential of our globalized economy to create connections, and (2) the unwelcome consequences of globalization that lead to imbalances and inequalities.

We have asked whether the global economy works well. Is it sustainable? How can we ensure the adequate distribution of resources necessary for human life—food, clean water, shelter, and health care? These are questions you will have to answer in your lifetime. And you will answer them by the life choices you make. For, with the continuing intensification of globalization, we are all connected in a web of constraints and opportunities. Perhaps your engagement with the global economy is not constrained by poverty, illiteracy, or violence. But it may be constrained by cultural expectations—for instance, group and peer pressure about what you need to fit in, dress well, eat right, and travel from place to place. Do you really have the choice in U.S. culture to not consume? How you address these constraints and opportunities will make a difference.

The good news is that there are many points at which to intervene in the current patterns of the global economy, whether you work to save the forests, recycle, support fair trade, reevaluate your consumption patterns, organize to support the rights of workers around the world, or become an engineer focusing on clean manufacturing or a scientist developing renewable energy sources. Thinking like an anthropologist will help you to analyze your choices in a more informed and responsible way.

Key Terms

economy (p. 443)
food foragers (p. 444)
pastoralism (p. 446)
horticulture (p. 446)
slash and burn agriculture (p. 446)
agriculture (p. 446)

For Further Exploration

The Battle of Algiers. 1965. Directed by Gillo Pontecorvo. Allied Artists Corporation. Riveting film about Algerian anticolonial struggle against France.

Black Gold: Wake Up and Smell the Coffee. 2006. By Marc Francis and Nick Francis. Speak It / Fulcrum. Documentary on the global coffee trade.

Fish Is Our Life. 1994. Directed by Peregrine Beckman. Documentary Educational Resources. Companion to Theodore Bestor's book *Tsukiji: The Fish Market at the Center of the World.*

Global Footprint Network. www.footprintnetwork.org. Assess your global footprint.

Global Witness. 2007. *Hot Chocolate: How Cocoa Fueled the Conflict in Côte D'Ivoire.* www.globalwitness.org /sites/default/files/pdfs/cotedivoire.pdf. Report on chocolate in Côte d'Ivoire.

Life and Debt. 2001. Directed by Stephanie Black. Tuff Gong Pictures. Documentary on the effects of the global debt crisis on Jamaica.

Roger & Me. 1989. Directed by Michael Moore. Dog Eat Dog / Warner Bros. The deindustrialization of Flint, Michigan, as General Motors closes its automobile factories in an early stage of flexible accumulation.

The Story of Stuff. 2007. By Annie Leonard. www .storyofstuff.org. An online animated documentary film exploring the contemporary cycle of production, distribution, and consumption, and its impact on the global environment.

350.org. www.350.org. Movement of grassroots environmental activists, including student chapters on college campuses across the United States.

Yes! Magazine. www.yesmagazine.org. Alternative strategies for a sustainable world.

Egyptians hold up pictures of missing relatives after the *al-Salam Boccaccio 98* ferry disaster in the Red Sea, 2006.

p. 492

p. 493

p. 497

p. 502

p. 512

p. 523

CHAPTER 13
Migration

In the predawn hours of February 3, 2006, the Egyptian ferryboat *al-Salam Boccaccio 98*, overloaded with 1,414 passengers, capsized in the rough waters of the Red Sea. It was on a routine 120-mile trip, carrying mostly Egyptian migrant workers home from Saudi Arabia. About an hour after departure, fire erupted on the ship's three lower decks. As crew members fought the fire, accumulating water caused the ship to list severely. Passengers scrambled across the deck in an unsuccessful attempt to balance the boat, but it continued to roll over and began to sink. By the time Egyptian navy rescue teams arrived nearly ten hours later, 1,027 passengers had died, marking the worst maritime accident in Egypt's modern history. Only 387 passengers survived.

In Safaga, Egypt, families gathered on the docks and near the ferry company offices, awaiting news of their children, siblings, parents, cousins, and friends returning from Saudi Arabia. The first rescue boat, carrying only 125 survivors, arrived nearly twenty-four hours after the *al-Salam 98* was reported missing. Rumors quickly circulated regarding the extent of the disaster. Most of the migrants traveling on the ferry would not be returning home.

Government investigations of the tragedy revealed that the *al-Salam 98*—a thirty-five-year-old Egyptian ferry, built in Italy and sailing under a Panamanian flag—had been carrying forged safety certificates, defective life rafts, too few winches to lower life rafts, uncharged fire extinguishers, and life jackets with expired validity. The *al-Salam 98* had regularly sailed overloaded, often carrying as many as 2,000 people.

489

MAP 13.1
Red Sea

The ferry passengers on the *al-Salam 98*, as on most days, were mainly poor or working-class young people returning home to Egypt after stints as temporary guest workers in Saudi Arabia's construction, agriculture, restaurant, and domestic service sectors. Like other Gulf states, Saudi Arabia has a severe shortage of workers for low-skill jobs. In fact, the nation meets its labor needs by recruiting laborers not only from Egypt but also from Pakistan, India, Sri Lanka, Nepal, and the Philippines. Egypt sends approximately 2.7 million citizens abroad to work each year, more than 900,000 to Saudi Arabia alone. With a weak Egyptian economy, political uncertainty, and pockets of extreme poverty, sending a relative abroad to work becomes a key economic strategy. When people cannot find decent work at home, they look elsewhere—even across national borders.

As we will see, these patterns of migration are expanding across the globe, spurred by the process of flexible accumulation, time-space compression, and uneven development of the contemporary global economy. Migration itself is stretching the network of human interaction and creating new opportunities for encounter and exchange, linking cultures, ideas, and institutions while creating opportunities for people to relocate and expand beyond long-term networks of kinship and religious, political, and ethnic identities. Consider these examples:

- Thousands of Filipino women domestic workers can be found in Hong Kong's central square every Sunday, their day off.
- Rural Africans relocate to larger African cities to raise money to support family and community back home.
- Japanese Brazilians return "home" to work in the Japanese automobile industry.
- Indian migrant workers struggle under restrictive work laws in Gulf states such as Bahrain that keep them isolated and vulnerable to exploitation by employers.
- "Coyote smugglers" lead Mexicans across the U.S. border into Arizona.
- Chinese "snakeheads" smuggle rural Chinese onto container ships bound for the United States, where many end up working in the Chinese restaurant business.

The sinking of the *al-Salam 98* was a devastating tragedy, but the migration story of its Egyptian passengers is not unique. Their journeys play out on overcrowded boats, trains, planes, and buses and by foot in every country, bringing individuals from their home communities to new places in search of work or refuge from hostile conditions. The tragedy of the Egyptian ferry highlights the massive and often precarious global movement of people, and it raises fundamental questions about migration in today's world:

- Why do people move from place to place?
- Who are today's migrants?
- Where do people move to and from?
- How is immigration affecting the United States today?

With so much migration, it is often hard to remember that each journey encompasses the hopes and dreams of one person, his or her family, and perhaps an entire community. This chapter introduces many of the concepts, themes, and dynamics that anthropologists consider when examining the interconnections between migration and globalization, as well as case studies of specific immigrant groups and individuals. By the end of the chapter, you will be able to apply these perspectives to understand the important migration process that is transforming individual lives and our world in the twenty-first century.

Why Do People Move from Place to Place?

Humans have been on the move since our species' earliest days, seeking out better living conditions for themselves and their families. Humans eventually migrated out of Africa across continents into the Middle East, Europe, and Asia; they ultimately crossed oceans to reach Australia and the Americas. Humans have moved in search of better hunting grounds, pastures, fields, natural resources, and climate. They have moved to avoid conflict, violence, predators, and natural disasters. Some, such as early explorers Marco Polo and Ibn Battutah, traveled along long-distance trade routes that linked much of the world well before Columbus's time. Others were forced to move against their will—for example, to serve the needs of colonialism on plantations and in mines, including millions in the trans-Atlantic slave trade. Clearly, movement is a fundamental characteristic of the human experience.

The past thirty years have seen one of the highest rates of global migration in modern history, not only between countries but within them as well. The powerful effects of globalization have stimulated migration from rural areas to urban areas and from less developed countries to more developed countries. At the same time, time-space compression (see Chapter 1) has transformed the migration experience: rapid transportation and instantaneous communication enable some migrants to travel more cheaply and quickly, and to still stay connected with folks back home, in ways that were impossible for earlier migrant generations. Flexible accumulation also stimulates migration by disrupting local economic, political, and social relationships while linking local communities to global economic processes. In 2010 the United Nations (UN) estimated that there were 214 million international migrants, plus hundreds of millions more moving within their own national borders (UN Department of Economic and Social Affairs, Population Division 2009). The Chinese government estimates that more than 230 million people migrate internally in that one country alone (Liang 2012).

But why do people migrate? And why do they choose certain destinations? These decisions are rarely random or frivolous. In fact, most people in the world never migrate. Only 3 percent move beyond national borders. With seven billion people on the planet today being drawn into an ever-thickening web of global interactions, we might ask why so few people are migrating. And with such uneven distribution of wealth and standards of living in the contemporary global economy, why are so few people moving to make a better life? In fact, the decision to migrate requires the confluence of a variety of factors—factors that anthropologists identify as pushes and pulls, bridges and barriers.

Pushes and Pulls

The decision to migrate and the chosen destination are often shaped by **pushes and pulls**. People are *pushed* to migrate from their home community by poverty, famine, natural disasters, war, ethnic conflict, genocide, disease, or political or religious oppression. Even some development policies may push people to move: for example, some may have to relocate to make room for a hydroelectric dam that is essential to the country's economic development. (This has been the case in areas throughout the world, including Panama's Bayano dam, China's Three Gorges dam, and Malaysia's Batang Ai dam.) Those who are forced to migrate are often termed refugees. Other people are pushed to migrate by a lack of

pushes and pulls: The forces that spur migration from the country of origin and draw immigrants to a particular new destination country.

opportunities in their home community. Indeed, the uneven development in the global economy stimulates much of today's global migration. Frustrated by their inability to achieve life aspirations and meet the needs of their families at home, many people seek opportunities elsewhere. Still others migrate to keep up with successful immigrant neighbors who send money back home to support family, build a house, or pay for family members' education (Portes and Rumbaut 2006).

Destinations are not chosen randomly, nor are all destinations equal. When considering migration, people are *pulled* to certain places by job opportunities, higher wages, educational opportunities for themselves and their children, access to health care, or investment opportunities. Family and friends who have already migrated provide encouragement and connections. At the same time, media such as television, music, and film, along with powerful advertising, promote the desire to live a Western middle-class, consumer-oriented lifestyle. The manufacturing of this desire (see Chapter 2) sweeps across the globe to motivate people who dream of fulfilling this vision by moving abroad. China and India alone hold 37 percent of the world's population (2.4 billion together), and their rapidly expanding economies have drawn hundreds of millions into the search for a middle-class lifestyle and its status symbols—a television, a car, and a refrigerator. Indeed, at the beginning of the twenty-first century, more and more people are eagerly entering the globalizing world economy.

Bridges and Barriers

To understand global migration flows, we must look beyond the push and pull factors to examine the **bridges and barriers** that influence who moves and where they go. Despite strong pushes and pulls, migration is not a journey easily undertaken. There are many barriers to such movement. Migrants need a high

FIGURE 13.1 Global migration today takes many forms. *Left to right:* Women line up outside an employment agency in Manila, Philippines, seeking jobs as domestic workers in Middle Eastern countries. Croatian Serb refugees flee Bosnia and Herzegovina in 1995. A camp for Somalis displaced by drought and famine, in Mogadishu, Somalia, 2011. A family scavenges in the ruins of their home in Fengjie, China, one of many towns eventually submerged by the massive Three Gorges Dam.

bridges and barriers: The factors that enable or inhibit migration.

level of motivation and a good deal of ingenuity to get started. Migration often requires learning a new language and adapting to a new culture. It means leaving family, friends, and religious communities. And it can be expensive, requiring upfront expenditures for passports, visas, and transportation, as well as fees paid to recruitment firms or smugglers. Even though globalization has promoted an increased movement of goods, money, and information, the free movement of people is still discouraged. Governments go to great lengths to regulate borders (with varying degrees of success), using passports, visas, border patrol agents, and immigration inspectors to determine who may leave and who may enter.

My own research, published in *God in Chinatown: Religion and Survival in New York's Evolving Immigrant Community* (2003), focuses on migrants from towns and villages near Fuzhou in southeast China. In recent years, these individuals have come in large numbers: first to New York to work in Chinese restaurants, garment shops, and construction trades; and now spreading across the United States as they open take-out restaurants and all-you-can-eat buffets. As much as 50 to 70 percent of the population in many similar Chinese towns and villages has migrated out, and perhaps hundreds of thousands of them have come to and through New York City.

Of the 1.3 billion people in China, why have people from the Fuzhou City area decided to migrate out of China? And why do so many go to New York City? The pushes are the same for Fuzhounese as they are for many rural people

FIGURE 13.2 East Broadway, Chinatown, New York, the central business district for new immigrants from Fuzhou, China.

in China—small incomes, difficult farm labor, limited opportunities for upward mobility or education. And the pulls of New York City—in this case, the tremendous need for low-wage workers—exist in many big cities, not only in the United States but also in countries much closer to China.

What bridges enable this migration flow, and what barriers must Fuzhounese overcome as they seek to relocate ten thousand miles across the Pacific Ocean? In the back of a Chinese restaurant in New York City, I interviewed Chen Dawei, age nineteen, who had come from Fuzhou one year earlier and whose story sheds light on the Fuzhounese immigrant experience:

MAP 13.2
Fuzhou City

> I didn't really want to go to America. But everyone else my age had already gone. I didn't want to seem stupid. My parents really wanted to send me. They have a little shop on the main street. We aren't poor. But we don't make much money either. Making $1,500 a month as a delivery man for a Chinese restaurant in the United States sounds really good when your family is lucky to make that much in a whole year back home. I really didn't want to go. But people kept calling to say how well they were doing. Both of my uncles were already in the U.S. Lots of people were sending money back home. And people who got green cards would come back and build a nice home for their family.
>
> So my dad arranged with a snakehead (smuggler) to send me to New York. It cost $65,000. We borrowed some from my uncles. And some from friends who had already gone to New York. The rest we borrowed at really high interest. It will probably take me four or five years to pay it all off.
>
> My trip was easier than a lot of my friends'. At least I didn't have to spend time on a boat or get smuggled across the border from Mexico. The snakeheads got me a tourist visa to Hong Kong. Then they took me to Thailand, Turkey, and Amsterdam. I flew into JFK Airport. The snakeheads had arranged a visa from a fake company, so I didn't have any problem getting through immigration. Do I like it here in New York? It's kind of boring. Since I've been here I've been working non-stop. Mostly in Chinese restaurants, six days a week. New York, Milwaukee, Asheville, and Maryland. Lots of places. I've got to pay off my debt, so I keep working. I send some money home to my parents when I can. Someday I want to open my own restaurant.

Chen Dawei's story highlights important bridges and barriers to migration. Consider the following aspects of his story, all of which illustrate bridges.

chain migration: The movement of people facilitated by the support of networks of family and friends who have already immigrated.

Like most immigrants, Fuzhounese come to New York City because someone from their family or hometown is already there. Family and friends create **chain migration** as networks of people who have already immigrated to a new place encourage and support other immigrants who follow. They may share information, loan money, or even support visa applications and sponsor legal migration. Moreover, *communication technology* stimulates the exchange of information between earlier immigrants and those considering the journey. Phone calls, videos, letters, e-mails, and wire transfers of money all link sending and receiving areas. *Geographic proximity or distance* makes certain journeys more or less difficult and precarious (in this sense, it can act as either a bridge or a barrier). Contiguous borders are easier to cross. But as in the Fuzhounese case, expanding *transportation networks* and increasingly inexpensive international flights facilitate migration along certain corridors.

Yet immigrants cannot randomly cross borders, for official barriers stand in their way. Most noticeable are *government immigration policies* that regulate borders and place restrictions on who comes in and out of the country. To address this problem, in many countries legal immigration is brokered through *recruitment agencies* that negotiate between workers and employers to arrange visas and travel. These recruiters channel qualified professionals into high-skill jobs such as nursing or information technology as well as low-skill jobs such as domestic work, agriculture, construction, and factory work. When the need for workers cannot be met legally, *smugglers* guide undocumented working-class immigrants, like Chen Dawei, across national borders under the radar of governments.

hometown association: An organization created for mutual support by immigrants from the same home town or region.

In some immigrant flows, *supportive organizations* such as **hometown associations** (organizations created for mutual support by immigrants from the same hometown), religious communities, or refugee placement groups encourage migrants, sponsor immigration, and help to resettle newcomers in the receiving country. Other bridges for immigration include *media* (such as television and film) and *advertising* that familiarize immigrants with particular destinations. Immigration can also be influenced by *political connections* between countries based on *colonial histories,* or by current patterns of *aid and investment* and cultural ties such as *religion* and *language.*

Recalling the Egyptian migrant workers who were traveling on the *al-Salam 98,* similar language, culture, and religion have served as bridges for their migration to Saudi Arabia. Moreover, Saudi labor recruiters actively seek out willing workers, and the Egyptian government allows them to leave and return easily. The Saudi government welcomes them legally as temporary workers. And regular transportation routes across the Red Sea provide speedy—although in the *al-Salam 98* case, tragically unsafe—passage.

Remittances and Cumulative Causation

Individuals generally do not make migration decisions on their own, as in Chen Dawei's case. Who migrates and where they go is usually a group decision embodying the family's hopes and dreams entrusted to one member considered most likely to succeed. Family resources are assembled to support the migration. Sacrifices are made as husbands, spouses, or children are sent ahead to establish an economic foothold and diversify the family's opportunities. Once settled, the immigrant sends home income in **remittances** (resources transferred from migrants working abroad to individuals, families, and institutions in their country of origin).

Remittances have a significant impact on migrants' families, communities, and even national economies. These include both economic (monetary) resources and social remittances such as ideas, behaviors, identities, and social capital (Levitt 2001). Globally, economic remittances in 2010 were estimated to be $440 billion, including $325 billion sent by migrants to developing countries, although they are often undercounted because of the widespread informal transfers of cash through friends, family, and other middlemen (International Migration Organization for Migration 2012). Again recalling this chapter's opening story, a high percentage of the more than 2.7 million Egyptians who work abroad send remittances back home. In 2009, these remittances totaled $7.8 billion, or 5 percent of Egypt's total national income (International Organization for Migration 2010). Most remittances support the basic needs

remittance: Resources transferred from migrants working abroad to individuals, families, and institutions in their country of origin.

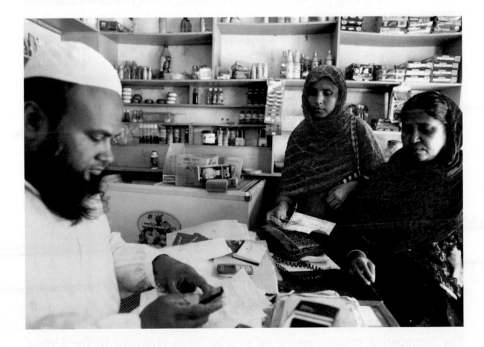

FIGURE 13.3 A woman and her daughter send a remittance to family through an agent at a general store just north of Dhaka, capital of Bangladesh.

of families back home—food, shelter, and education—but they may also support public works and institutions in the local community. Immigrants contribute to infrastructure projects such as senior centers, schools, roads, and water systems. They support hometown associations, churches, temples, and mosques. A smaller percentage of remittances are invested in business enterprises. For many labor immigrants, remittances guarantee a place to return to if things don't work out or for their retirement years. In these cases, remittances provide not only an economic foundation but also an investment in social status.

In many communities worldwide, like the areas around Fuzhou, China, so many of these factors come together that immigration has actually become a way of life. It reflects a dynamic called **cumulative causation**, in which migration comes to be expected. On a visit to a rural town outside Fuzhou, I was invited to give a lecture at an English-language prep school. Since the 1980s, as many as 70 percent of the residents in this area have emigrated to the United States. The forty teenagers in my classroom were all excited to have a native English speaker to practice with, and as an anthropologist I am always happy to have a chance to learn more about the local culture. "Why are you studying English?" I asked them. "To go to America!" they answered. When I opened their textbook, I found it filled with chapters on typical Chinese restaurant phrases: *Do you want fried rice or white rice? Do you want your chicken and broccoli spicy or not spicy?* The students were all preparing not only to go to America, but to work in Chinese restaurants there! For these young people, as for Chen Dawei, immigration is more than just a possibility. Because their communities harbor a culture of migration, these young people may prepare for this likelihood for years. As they grow up they expect to follow their parents and siblings, uncles and aunts, and neighbors and friends in leaving home in search of a better life through immigration.

Each immigrant's journey is unique in some way. Yet each journey entails certain elements that can be helpful in analyzing the migration process. If you or someone in your family is an immigrant, or perhaps someone else you know, how might the key concepts of pushes and pulls, bridges and barriers help you to understand their immigrant journey more deeply? See Table 13.1 for a summary of these factors.

cumulative causation: An accumulation of factors that create a culture in which migration comes to be expected.

Who Are Today's Migrants?

Globally, immigration includes people from a wide variety of class backgrounds, ranging from refugees fleeing war or natural disaster, to unskilled workers with little education, to well-educated doctors and elite corporate businesspeople. The immigration debates raging on evening news programs in the United

TABLE 13.1 Why Do People Move from Place to Place?

Pushes	Bridges and Barriers	Pulls
Poverty	Migration chains	Job opportunities
Famine	Communication technology	Higher wage levels
Natural disasters	Geographic proximity or distance	Educational opportunities
War	Transportation networks	Access to health care
Ethnic conflict	Government immigration policies	Investment opportunities
Genocide	Recruitment agencies	Family and friends
Disease	Smugglers	Media, such as television, music, and film
Political or religious oppression	Supportive organizations	Consumer-oriented advertising
Unfavorable development policies	Religious networks	
Lack of job opportunities	Political connections	
	Colonial histories	
	Foreign aid and investment	
	Language and cultural ties	
	Remittances	
	Cumulative causation	

States might give the impression that all migrants to the United States are poor, undocumented, and from Mexico. But these impressions would be wrong. Most migrants to the United States are not poor, uneducated, unemployed, or undocumented. Migration to the United States is a journey more frequently undertaken by those with education, job skills, and financial resources—and the motivation—that set them apart from the majority of their fellow citizens. Even those who come illegally tend to have skills and education levels above their home country's national average. Indeed, the rigors of the migration process self-select the brightest and the best (Portes and Rumbaut 2006).

Types of Immigrants

To begin to analyze the migration experiences of so many people in so many parts of the world, immigration scholars often focus on immigrants' economic roles, whether as laborers, professionals, entrepreneurs, or refugees. Although not applicable to every immigrant journey, these categories delineate certain patterns that constitute a general framework for analysis and comparison.

labor immigrant: A person who moves in search of a low-skill and low-wage job, often filling an economic niche that native-born workers will not fill.

guest worker program: A policy that allows labor immigrants to enter a country temporarily to work.

Labor Immigrants **Labor immigrants**, like the Fuzhounese, move in search of low-skill and low-wage jobs, filling economic niches that native-born workers will not fill. Labor immigrants constitute the majority of migrants in the world today. They may be legal or illegal, but they are drawn by employment opportunities that, though limited, provide jobs at higher wages than are available in their home economies. In many countries, labor immigrants enter under temporary **guest worker programs** that grant the right to work for limited periods but deny long-term rights and privileges.

In the United States, labor immigrants are key to the success of agriculture, restaurants, hotels, garment production, and meat processing. Have you ever thought about who launders the hotel sheets and towels, cuts up the chicken in your grocery poultry section, picks the peaches at the fruit stand, or washes the dishes in your local diner? Have you ever wondered why you can eat Chinese food at such reasonable prices? Labor immigrants, legal and illegal, are part of our everyday lives. Without them, many businesses would have to close their doors or raise wages (and thus prices) and offer benefits to attract native-born workers.

The Egyptian workers on the *al-Salam 98* were labor immigrants. Their experience, and that of other workers who migrate to Saudi Arabia, illustrates the fact that labor immigrants' working conditions can be quite difficult. These workers must have signed, binding contracts before entering Saudi Arabia. Workers may not switch jobs or leave the country without their employer's permission. Many times, the employer holds their passports to ensure compliance. Because this practice puts the employer in a position of tremendous power over the workers, there have been many complaints about abusive practices. In particular, some women domestic workers have charged that employers keep them employed against their will under abusive conditions. As temporary workers, with limited legal rights, they are vulnerable to exploitation. Despite these problems, hundreds of thousands of Egyptians continue to immigrate to Saudi Arabia in hopes of improving their own and their families' economic situation.

professional immigrant: A highly trained individual who moves to fill an economic niche in a middle-class profession often marked by shortages in the receiving country.

brain drain: Migration of highly skilled professionals from developing / periphery countries to developed / core countries.

Professional Immigrants **Professional immigrants** are highly trained individuals who move to fill economic niches in middle-class professions marked by shortages in the receiving country. A key component of the professional immigrant category is university students trained in Western-style professions who lack opportunities to implement their training at home. This migration is often referred to as a **brain drain**, for many of the most highly skilled professionals trained in developing countries are enticed by wages and other opportunities to relocate to developed countries. This migration is doubly devastating: not only are the talents of these professionals lost to the home country, but so is the investment in their education and training.

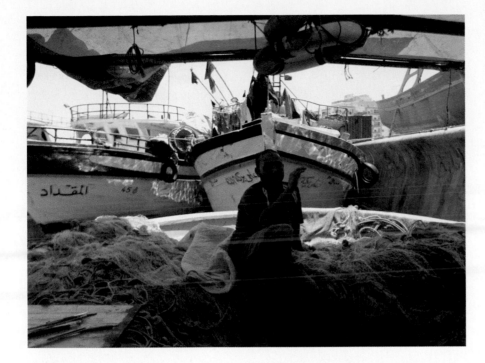

FIGURE 13.4 An Egyptian migrant worker in Benghazi, Libya, explains his work on a fishing boat. Most fishermen in Benghazi are from Egypt.

In the United States today, professional immigrants include doctors, nurses, engineers, and information technology specialists, among others. Hospital corporations in developed countries establish recruitment centers in developing countries to attract health care professionals and prepare them for immigration to fill shortages. Nursing schools in the United States, for instance, cannot train enough nurses to staff the nation's hospitals and expanding nursing home facilities. As a result, tens of thousands of Filipino, Indian, and Caribbean nurses and doctors have come to the United States as professional immigrants. In fact, hospitals in Africa face a critical shortage as health care professionals are recruited to fill shortages in Europe. These middle-class immigrants move not only to gain better salaries but also to enjoy better working conditions.

Significant numbers of Indians have come to the United States as professional immigrants. Already prepared for relatively privileged positions in India, these are ambitious, middle-class people with training in economics, medicine, nursing, engineering, or management. Once in the United States, if they receive the proper credentials, they work in these fields; moreover, their children attend college and often focus on science, information technologies, engineering, business, law, or medicine. If unable to obtain the proper credentials, professionals from other countries may face the prospects of downward mobility in the immigration process, working in less desirable jobs for a short period or permanently.

One distinct advantage that Indian immigrants bring is a combination of social capital and access to financial capital. **Social capital** (language skills,

social capital: Assets and skills such as language, education, and social networks that can be mobilized in lieu of or as complementary to financial capital.

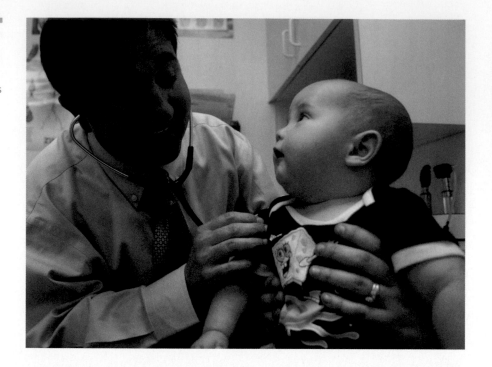

education, and social and kinship networks) enables them to quickly enter the U.S. economy. Access to financial capital (either their own money or funds borrowed through extended family networks) provides resources for success as professionals or entrepreneurs. Although many Indian immigrants come from the professional class at home, they have chosen to launch entrepreneurial careers in small, local, family-run retail stores, hotels, or motels in the United States (Lessinger 1995).

Another kind of professional immigrant emerges at the extreme upper end of globalization activity. The expansion of transnational corporations requires elite professional immigrants who are willing to relocate for long periods or to routinely travel from country to country as part of the workweek. These professional immigrants, sometimes called "cosmonauts" because of their constant, jet-set movement through Earth's atmosphere, constitute a small fraction of the global migration flow, but they have caught the attention of many scholars and journalists because they represent the hyperactivity of movement made possible by contemporary globalization (Ong and Nonini 1997).

Entrepreneurial Immigrants Entrepreneurial immigrants move to new locations to conduct trade and establish businesses. On a global scale, Chinese entrepreneurs are perhaps the most famous for practicing the art of buying and selling: they establish businesses as merchants, restaurateurs, and small shopkeepers in countries worldwide. In the United States, Koreans have been

entrepreneurial immigrant: A person who moves to a new location to conduct trade and establish a business.

particularly successful in establishing groceries, liquor stores, dry cleaners, and other small businesses in urban areas such as Los Angeles, Washington, D.C., Baltimore, and New York City. These "middleman minorities" have taken over businesses catering to low-income groups, often in central cities. Immigrant entrepreneurs usually utilize ethnic connections to mobilize the financial capital needed to start businesses. They borrow from family and friends. Revolving loan funds are common in these communities as networks of immigrants pool resources that are borrowed at interest, repaid, and borrowed again.

In addition, ethnic connections nurtured in ethnic neighborhoods link entrepreneurs with co-ethnic labor migrants. These connections enable the entrepreneurs to find the cheap labor they need to compete in the U.S. marketplace. The connections also provide labor immigrants with avenues to use their social capital to locate jobs in an ethnic economy that may not be available to them in the mainstream economy. However, sometimes these connections have a downside: such co-ethnic relations may also open opportunities for more established immigrants to exploit newcomers under the guise of ethnic solidarity (Guest and Kwong 2000).

In his ethnography *Money Has No Smell* (2002), the anthropologist Paul Stoller writes about the networks of Muslim West African street vendors and merchants in New York City. These individuals ply their trade selling socks, gloves, and videos on city sidewalks, and they import African art and textiles to sell in markets and small shops in Harlem, along Canal Street, and in fairs and cultural festivals across the country—a trade we will discuss further in Chapter 17. These young men extend centuries-old traditions of long-distance trade across the Atlantic, often making regular return trips to buy merchandise and visit family. Describing the importance of social networks in this community, Stoller writes:

> For a person like Issifi Mayaki, nothing is more important than his social relations—the viability of family, the maintenance of mutually nurturing friendships, the endurance of networks based and built on relations of mutual trust. With varying degrees of effectiveness, Issifi and his brother traders have continuously negotiated and renegotiated their social lives. In so doing, they have established new trading partnerships and have dissolved others. They have mastered the culture of capitalism as they have reinforced the traditions of long-distance African trading. They have staked out individual space in a market culture as they have engaged in a cooperative economics dictated by Islam and by long-standing West African commercial practices. They have adapted to the unfamiliar stresses of city life in New York as they have reaffirmed their African identities. (2002, 178–79)

FIGURE 13.6 Have you noticed immigrant entrepreneurs where you live or go to school? Here, shoppers browse African merchandise displayed by West African street vendors in New York City.

refugee: A person who has been forced to move beyond his or her national borders because of persecution, armed conflict, or natural disasters.

Entrepreneurial migrants have been on the move for thousands of years along local, regional, and long-distance trade routes. Contemporary globalization has only increased the volume of entrepreneurial activity and enhanced entrepreneurs' ability to engage in their trade in places farther from home.

Refugees Refugees constitute a fourth type of immigrant. These are people who have been forced to migrate beyond their national borders because of political or religious persecution, armed conflict or other forms of violence, or natural or human-made disasters. To be officially recognized as refugees under international treaties, they must usually demonstrate to a foreign government a well-founded fear of persecution or physical harm. The UN estimated a total of 15.4 million refugees worldwide in 2010 (UN High Commissioner for Refugees 2012).

In the 1990s immigrants from the former Soviet Union made up the largest refugee group arriving in the United States (Orleck 1999). These included a large number of Jews escaping anti-Semitism, ethnic violence, and economic convulsions after the collapse of communism. Although many Soviet Jews chose to resettle in Israel, a large number of others chose the United States, drawn by family connections as well as by economic and educational opportunities. A high proportion of these immigrants were academics, scientists, professionals, and technical workers—an elite class among immigrant groups—but many in this first generation suffered downward mobility after migration as they struggled to transfer professional skills and credentials across cultures and languages. Being white Europeans, however, they were able to leave behind their minority status in the former Soviet republics and assimilate into the U.S. racial majority.

Their resettlement was assisted by the strong network of sponsors and support agencies established by earlier waves of Jewish immigrants. In fact, Jewish refugee resettlement agencies played a significant role in the immigrants' choice of country, city, and even neighborhood. In the United States, the Hebrew Immigrant Aid Society (HIAS)—established in the late nineteenth century to resettle an earlier generation of Jewish immigrants—channeled Jews from the former Soviet Union into Jewish communities and social networks in New York and Los Angeles. Working with other Jewish agencies, such as the New York Association for New Americans (established after World War II to resettle Holocaust survivors) and Jewish Vocational Services and Jewish Family Services in Los Angeles, HIAS settled refugees in permanent housing and provided job training and placement, language instruction, social activities, and mental health programs. The agencies also assisted these immigrants in accessing federal subsidies to ease housing, job training, and educational costs, as the U.S. government had admitted them under full refugee status (Orleck 1999; Gold 1995).

Although refugee status technically applies to those who seek asylum in another nation, the experiences of **internally displaced persons** can be just as devastating. These migrants' experiences mirror those of international refugees, except they take place in the migrants' own countries. For example, much attention has highlighted the ethnic and religious conflict in Darfur, Sudan, where millions of displaced persons have been forced into refugee camps inside the country and in neighboring Chad and the Central African Republic. Worldwide, the UN estimated 26.4 million internally displaced persons in 2011 (Internal Displacement Monitoring Center 2012).

At the same time, a much larger and longer conflict in the Republic of the Congo has been largely ignored in the international press. Known in many quarters as "Africa's world war" because it has involved nine nations and twenty armed groups, the conflict in the mineral-rich Congo erupted after ethnic violence and genocide in neighboring Rwanda spilled across the border in 1994. Fighting between Rwandan combatants and homegrown militias joined by forces from Uganda destabilized the country and led to the overthrow of long-term dictator Mbutu and an intense civil war from 1998 to 2003—the bloodiest war since World War II. Four million people have died in the Congo since 1998, half of them children under age five. Hundreds of thousands are now internally displaced persons who continue to flee violence, poverty, and disease (Human Rights Watch 2012).

internally displaced person: A person who has been forced to move within his or her country of origin because of persecution, armed conflict, or natural disasters.

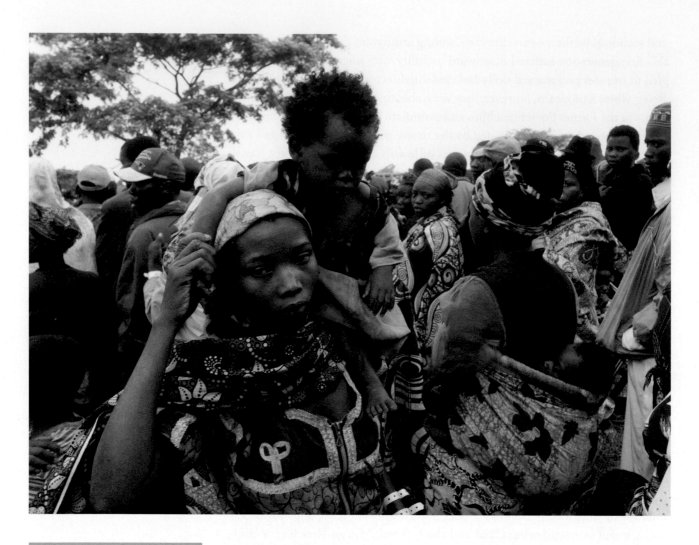

Women and Immigration

Just as the current global age is experiencing increased migration, it is also seeing larger numbers of women in all four immigrant categories. This is a result of economic globalization. For example, as discussed in Chapter 8, the growth of export processing zones has feminized global factory work as women migrate both within their countries and across national boundaries. By 2010, according to UN statistics, 105 million women immigrants were living abroad, nearly matching the 109 million immigrant men (UN Department of Economic and Social Affairs, Population Division 2009). In some receiving countries, such as the United States, women immigrants are now in the majority.

Anthropologists have been at the forefront of research about women immigrants, challenging scholars in all fields to see migration as a *gendered process*—one that affects both men and women, but often in distinctly different ways. Just as women reshape immigration patterns, the immigration experience also reshapes gender roles and gender relations (Hondagneu-Sotelo 1994; Mahler and Pessar 2001). Through migration, many women enhance their economic and social status as they take jobs, expand social networks, access social institutions, and gain new personal freedom. As a result, not just women but also husbands, children, parents, and other kin must adjust to shifting gender roles and family patterns. Also through migration, some immigrant men may lose status in public and domestic spheres — perhaps through diminished economic power, an unfamiliar status as a racial or ethnic minority, or being undocumented in their new country. In these ways, migration has a transformative effect on gender roles for both women and men.

Recently, anthropologists and other immigration scholars have turned particular attention to the complicated lives of women labor immigrants — both legal and illegal, both those migrating by choice and those forced to migrate through sex and labor trafficking. The increasing numbers of domestic workers are particularly vulnerable, often experiencing domestic violence and sexual abuse. But they are also particularly powerful, holding a central financial role in supporting their families back home and in providing the hard currency that developing countries need to repay global debts (Constable 2007). Pierrette Hondagneu-Sotelo's ethnography *Doméstica* (2001), for example, examines Mexican and Central American immigrant women who work as nannies and housekeepers in Los Angeles. This is an area where urban and suburban homes are joining factories as the primary places for new immigrants to find work. As the globalizing economy places ever-greater time pressure on the managerial class, they are hiring immigrant laborers to mow their lawns, clean their homes, and care for their children. The low-wage, off-the-books labor of Mexican and Central American immigrants, particularly women, has become so ubiquitous that it goes unnoticed as they subsidize the lifestyles of middle- and upper-class working families (Sassen 1998).

Immigrant Generations

The children of immigrants also have been the focus of a growing body of research. Both scholars and public policy experts are carefully observing how this expanding population will become part of U.S. culture (Kasinitz et al. 2008; Portes and Rumbaut 2001; Zhou and Bankston 1998). Immigration scholars generally distinguish among first-, 1.5-, and second-generation immigrants. The **first generation** comprises immigrants who left their home countries as adults. Their children born and raised in the new host country are the **second generation**. The term **1.5 generation** refers to children born in the home country who then migrate with their parents and grow up in the new host country. Depending on the age at migration, these children experience a doubly complex enculturation process, negotiating two cultures during adolescence and

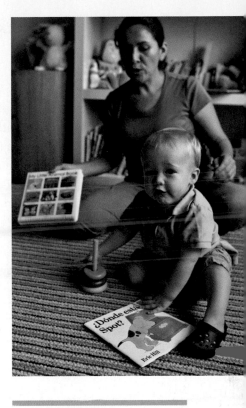

FIGURE 13.8 *Donde está Spot?* Elas Tarazona, an immigrant from Central America, works as a nanny for a U.S. family and teaches Spanish as a second language to William.

first-generation immigrant: A person who left his or her home country as an adult.

second-generation immigrant: The child of immigrants who is born and raised in the new host country.

1.5-generation immigrant: The child of immigrants who is born in the family's home country but at a young age moves with his or her parents to a new host country.

An Immigrant Interview

Interview an immigrant of any age, gender, and national-ity. Ask to hear his or her immigration story. Listen for the key migration concepts discussed in this chapter: pushes and pulls, bridges and barriers, and immigrant type. Ask about the person's incorporation experience in the new country, and explore immigration-related issues such as gender and the second generation. How are gender roles different in the new country? What are the expectations of members of the second generation, and how does their life differ from that of their immigrant parents? Analyze this story, and then synthesize it in a short essay using the first person.

often serving as cultural brokers for their parents—for instance, translating between English and their home country language.

Anthropologist Ana Aparicio explores the local community-organizing and political activism of second-generation Dominicans who are now teenag-ers and young adults in the Washington Heights area of New York City. Unlike their parents, whose identity and political activity included both the Domini-can Republic and New York, the second generation is deeply engaged in New York's local issues because that is where they were raised and educated. In her ethnography, *Dominican-Americans and the Politics of Empowerment* (2006), Aparicio highlights how these young activists have mobilized their own com-munity to address issues of education, police brutality, civic participation, and the lack of services and public investment. These second-generation young people also resist the typical racial-ethnic classifications found in U.S. society. As we discussed in Chapter 7, these people negotiate their identity situationally, moving back and forth among being Latino, Dominican, black, or more gener-ally people of color. This sophisticated awareness of racial hierarchies and power enables them to build coalitions and organize across racial-ethnic lines, particu-larly with Puerto Rican and African American New Yorkers. (See "Anthropol-ogists Engage the World," on pp. 510–11.)

Where Do People Move To and From?

Globalization has transformed the spatiality of the world economy and has intensified the volume and types of movement occurring within and across political boundaries (Trouillot 2003). But not every country is equally affected

MAP 13.3
Contemporary Global Migration
Patterns

by today's global flows of migrants. Some are primarily sending countries; others are primarily receiving countries. Moreover, not all migration occurs across borders. Thus, a truly global perspective on migration must include both international and internal migration.

International Migration

International migrants, or migrants who cross borders, exist across the globe, but they largely relocate to more developed countries. Of the 214 million international migrants in 2010, 70 million (33 percent) lived in Europe, 61 million (28 percent) in Asia, and 50 million (23 percent) in North America. Only 9 percent of international migrants lived in Africa, and 3 percent each in Latin America and the Caribbean and Oceania (U.N. Department of Economic and Social Affairs 2012). Map 13.3 shows the primary migration flows for receiving and sending countries.

In one remarkable flow of international migration, residents of the Kingdom of Tonga, an independent Pacific island nation of 100,000 people, have been leaving in large numbers for New Zealand, Australia, and the United States since 1965. Cultural anthropologist Cathy Small has traced the migration of one extended family and its agricultural village community as more than one-third of its population relocated to California between 1965 and 1995. In her ethnography, *Voyages: From Tongan Villages to American Suburbs* (1997), Small asks why so many people would leave a place that has free medical care,

Ana Aparicio

Ana Aparicio thought she had a problem. She recounts, "When I entered graduate school, I was active in community organizing and found it difficult to balance that work with my studies." Her advisor helpfully suggested that she marry the two. And so she launched an ethnographic research project on youth and political mobilization in New York City's Washington Heights community. Aparicio's work among first- and second-generation Dominican Americans has since provided her a unique view on how globalization is experienced and shaped by young people.

Aparicio's work centers squarely on the roles that youth have undertaken in transforming their community and the world. "One organization I worked with was founded by youth, in their teens and early twenties. Now it is the largest Dominican-focused organization in the country, with multiple offices. For me, it is not just that youth are the future of the community or nation, but that they are living and active in the present."

In her research, Aparicio found that the ground on which community activism takes place had changed dramatically, adding a transnational component to youth politics. "As part of my project I traveled to the Dominican Republic with youth leaders from New York to work with political parties there. What we saw in the DR was that it was the younger folks who were interested in engaging with and had the most to say about issues like sanitation pick-up, park maintenance, and gang violence. Then back home in Washington Heights, they recognized large gaps in how city resources were being allocated to different neighborhoods."

A key moment arrived in 2000 when the organization held its tenth annual conference. Youth leaders were concerned about New York State's announcement that it would cut 40,000 summer youth jobs. The budget crisis coincided with the death of Amadou Diallo, an unarmed twenty-three-year-old Guinean immigrant shot by police officers, and the growth of the prison-industrial com-

plex that kept many of their minority contemporaries in detention. Youth leaders saw these events and developments as related. They went to the state capital in Albany and successfully helped to lobby for summer employment funds to be reinstated. In doing so, Dominican American youth forged racial identities that disrupted the older generation's tendency to distance themselves from African Americans. These youth, Aparicio argues, "challenged racism and offered an antiracist language to redefine their communities."

The year 2000 also saw local chapters of political parties from the Dominican Republic campaigning to the nearly half a million Dominicans in New York City ahead of presidential elections. Caravans lined the streets of Washington Heights. It might have seemed odd to see posters and stickers promoting political candidates from

Anthropologist Ana Aparicio

another country, but Aparicio observed how Dominicans demonstrated vested interests in issues facing their home country. Second-generation youth groups ran voter-registration drives and were especially vocal about fighting racism and calling attention to social justice issues facing the working poor.

Aparicio felt that much of the literature on Dominicans seemed to be missing what she was seeing in her work with youth organizers. Their struggle for social justice in their communities was also a struggle to reshape prevailing notions of community, citizenship, race, ethnicity, and nationhood. Aparicio found that "the second generation is pivotal in deciding the racial and ethnic identification of families and communities." What makes this process novel is that identification doesn't just develop through living in the adopted nation; it also arises through an interaction with the Dominican homeland.

"I have two tracks of research," Aparicio explains. "First, I am interested in the relationship between policy and racial and ethnic disparities in areas like the construction industry and access to health care. Second, I study immigrants and community development and politics. It is easy to see the policy side in statistical data, but to understand how policy is experienced on the local level you have to use an ethnographic toolkit. I want to know how people engage with and change these processes."

In her teaching, Aparicio regularly encounters students with a broad range of career interests. "Students who major in public policy, education, and political science often find immigration policy and data about the incorporation of immigrants in the United States easy to comprehend. But the processes behind housing and home-ownership, graduation rates, political involvement—that takes anthropology. I like to encourage students to use an anthropological lens to explore their world."

As Aparicio reminds her students, "Anthropology takes a lot of preparation and practical knowledge." Still, some of her most memorable mishaps and fortunate encounters have been the result of unexpected happenings. Some of the most valuable fieldwork data in Aparicio's work came outside of scheduled interviews—from fortuitous street encounters with demonstrators, for example. These kinds of experiences underline the importance of long-term research and the ethnographic endeavor to understand the everyday life of others.

free elementary education, a 99 percent literacy rate, a low crime rate, and no history of civil war or conflict, and where every family owns a home. According to her findings, the desire to receive remittances (considered a push from family at home), the pull of the U.S. labor market, and bridges that include strong religious networks and U.S. immigration laws favoring reunification of family members are all important factors. But the key to Tongan immigration is the increasing gap between Tongan aspirations and opportunities. Small's research suggests that as wave after wave of Tongans migrate abroad, in the foreseeable future the number of Tongans living abroad will surpass the number remaining at home.

Reflecting strong trends of the past forty years, nearly 20 percent of all international migrants live in the United States. The U.S. total of nearly 40 million foreign-born residents in 2010 was the highest total of any nation in the world, and migration to the United States has continued at an average rate of 1.2 million annually since 2000 (U.S. Census Bureau 2012). Other countries, however, have a much higher percentage of immigrants in their population than the 12.4 percent of the foreign-born U.S. population. As of 2005, 25.9 percent of Saudi Arabia's 24.6 million people was foreign-born, primarily guest workers (like those in the story of the Egyptian ferry) who do not have permanent legal status. Ireland's foreign-born population in 2005 was 14.1 percent; Canada's, 18.9 percent; Australia's, 20.3 percent; Switzerland's, 22.9 percent; Israel's, 39.6 percent; Hong Kong's, 42.6 percent; Kuwait's, 62.1 percent; and Qatar's, 78 percent (UN Department of Economic and Social Affairs, Population Division, 2009). Table 13.2 presents data on migrant populations in absolute numbers.

TABLE 13.2 Migration Stock by Major Area of Origin and Destination, 2010 (in millions)

Origin	DESTINATION						
	Africa	Asia	Europe	Latin America and Caribbean	North America	Oceania	TOTAL
Africa	15.5	4.0	7.7	0.0	1.7	0.4	29.2
Asia	1.0	46.1	19.0	0.3	14.2	2.0	82.6
Europe	0.8	7.8	37.3	1.5	9.0	2.4	58.7
Latin America and Caribbean	0.0	0.6	3.9	4.6	23.5	0.1	32.8
North America	0.1	0.5	0.9	1.0	1.4	0.2	4.1
Oceania	0.0	0.1	0.3	0.0	0.3	0.9	1.6
Other	1.8	2.1	0.9	0.2	0.0	0.1	5.1
TOTAL	19.3	61.3	69.9	7.7	50.0	6.0	214.2

SOURCE: UN Department of Economic and Social Affairs, Population Division. 2012. "Migrants by Origin and Destination: The Role of South-South Migration." Population Facts. www.un.org/esa/population/publications/popfacts/popfacts_2012-3_South-South _migration.pdf.

Malian Migrants: Reshaping Globalization from the Ground Up Though international movements of people between continents and across oceans often capture public and scholarly attention, today significant movement occurs between neighboring countries. In *Migrants and Strangers in an African City* (2012), anthropologist Bruce Whitehouse examines the large-scale migrations happening within Africa as people move in response to poverty and uncertainty. Whitehouse focuses on migrants from Mali, a large West African nation of 16 million people. Though landlocked, Mali's position at the center of regional trade networks crisscrossing West and North Africa has a long history. Today, Malians, along with hundreds of thousands of other West Africans, increasingly have been on the move. Some have settled in developed Western countries such as France, Spain, and the United States, or in Asian cities such as Dubai, Bangkok, Hong Kong, and Guangzhou. Most, however, have relocated within the African continent—notably to Senegal, Côte d'Ivoire, Burkina Faso, Gabon, Congo, and South Africa.

Whitehouse begins his ethnography with the story of a small town in southern Mali that he calls Togotala. The town lies on an arid plain between

MAP 13.4
Mali

desert to the north and forest to the south. The harsh environment brings regular drought and then a three-month rainy season during which torrential downpours threaten to erode the area's fragile soil. With agricultural production being inadequate to meet the immediate needs of the Togotala population, and with no development assistance from the Malian government, the community has a history of producing merchants who enter the regional trade networks in order to send remittances home to support their families and the community at large. The influence of merchant remittances is evident in the larger cinderblock homes that have been constructed in Togotala's central district, a school for children in grades 1 to 9, a water tower run by solar power to pump water to communal faucets throughout the town, a landline phone system, a health clinic, and several modern mosques. These local developments are concrete testimony to Togotala's deep connection to the world beyond its borders, and they hint at the creative individual responses that literally bring home the benefits of the global economy.

Twice daily, battered buses arrive in Togotala carrying goods and passengers and providing the town's primary link to the outside world. A ride south to Mali's capital, Bamako, connects Togotala's merchants to an extensive transport network through which they can reach more distant destinations. Whitehouse traces some of Togotala's residents southward to a large Malian community in Brazzaville, capital of the Republic of Congo. A port city of 1.5 million residents on the northern bank of the Congo River, Brazzaville serves as the country's administrative, manufacturing, and financial center. It is also a transfer point for agricultural products, wood, rubber, and other raw materials coming from upriver onto the Congo-Ocean railroad that links Brazzaville to the seaport of Pointe-Noire. French colonialists originally brought West Africans to Brazzaville in the 1800s to serve as soldiers, porters, laborers, and messengers. But West Africans succeeded in creating parallel economic networks of merchants, traders, laborers, blacksmiths, leatherworkers, and traditional storytellers—economic networks that survived the end of colonialism in 1960. Today, a large community of Malians, mostly Muslim, work in Brazzaville as importers, shopkeepers, street vendors, entrepreneurs, and merchants in the diamond and jewelry trades.

Despite their long history in Brazzaville, Malians are treated as outsiders and strangers, segregated by language, social organization, and religion. Under these conditions, a strong connection to home enables the migrant Malians to resist the experience of exclusion from key local spaces, whether political, economic, social, or religious. From the vantage point of life in Togotala, Whitehouse easily portrays why people seek employment outside the community. More difficult to understand is why they come back so frequently and continue to be active in Togotala economics, politics, and social life.

FIGURE 13.10 Entrepreneurial immigrants from Mali have built a vibrant community in Brazzaville, Republic of Congo.

From the perspective of Malian life in Brazzaville, the choice to maintain an intense and direct connection to home becomes more understandable. The connection enables them to maintain a sense of place and belonging despite the local marginalization and in the face of increasing mobility and spatial separation from their families and home community.

Migrants, including the merchants of Togotala and other entrepreneurs across Africa, reveal creative individual responses to the intensification of interaction that is occurring worldwide. Actions by migrants such as the Egyptians on the *al-Salam 98* or the Malians in Brazzaville—less powerful people whose stories are often ignored in the grand narrative of globalization—reveal the determined, entrepreneurial strategies that local people employ to bring the benefits of the global economy to their communities and to reshape globalization from the ground up.

Internal Migration

internal migration: The movement of people within their own national borders.

Whereas international migration involves migration across borders, **internal migration** refers to the movement of people within their own national borders. For example, disruptions of rural life such as farm consolidation by agribusiness or development projects such as dams and roads stimulate migration. In addition, urban-oriented development programs and the establishment of large-scale export processing zones in developing countries have provided the pulls for significant internal migration from rural to urban areas to fill the new labor needs. (This is the case in countries such as Mexico, Guatemala, Brazil, South Korea, China, Thailand and Bangladesh.) Moreover, women workers, sought after by factory owners in export processing zones, constitute a high proportion of internal migrants.

Advantages and Disadvantages of Internal Migration within China China today is gripped by economic transformations and the widespread migration—both internal and international—that often accompanies such change. Since the early 1980s, the country has been rapidly modernizing, experimenting with a mixture of capitalism and state control of key sectors of the economy. As a result, private investment and private ownership are on the rise. They have combined with direct investments by overseas Chinese and massive state investment in infrastructure to spur the growth of China's cities, particularly in coastal provinces. The construction boom and the growth of industry in cities, along with the increasing income disparity between urban and rural dwellers, has pulled seasonal and long-term labor migrants from rural to urban areas. Downtown areas of both large and small cities have seen the emergence of day-labor pools as these migrants shop their physical labor for wages, which are so scarce in rural areas (Solinger 1999; Zhang 2001; Liang 2012).

Special economic zones for export processing have been springing up along China's coasts since 1982 in an effort to attract foreign capital and boost industrial production (Solinger 1999). Shenzhen, once a sleepy border village between Hong Kong and Guangzhou (Canton), is perhaps the most vivid example of this policy. Today it is one of China's leading manufacturing centers for exported goods, providing easy access to Hong Kong's port and transportation hubs as well as drawing tens of thousands of internal migrants to work in its factories. Shenzhen's economic success, however, also reveals the vulnerable position of low-wage migrant laborers in developing countries as they sweat on factory floors at very low wages and with few environmental or safety protections. Studies show evidence of internal migrant laborers returning to their rural hometowns with long-term physical illnesses and injuries from their sweatshop work (Chang 2008).

MAP 13.5
Shenzhen

Shenzhen also reveals the vagaries and economic logic of globalization's flexible accumulation strategy. For nearly three decades China's factories, situated in export processing zones, have provided lower-wage labor, lower taxes, and fewer environmental restrictions than other developing countries in Asia and Latin America. Jobs and production have expanded as these conditions attract foreign investment and draw internal migrants. But as China's economic conditions have improved and workers have become better organized, many in the workforce are unwilling to work for such low wages and under such brutal conditions. As a result, wages have been creeping up. Recent trends show factories now shifting out of China to Bangladesh, Thailand, Cambodia, and Laos as globalization facilitates the search for export processing zones that will provide cheaper labor and other lower production costs.

Transnational Migration: Effects on Families and Communities Back Home

In another phenomenon of globalization, time-space compression—notably, advances in communication and transportation—has transformed the migration experience by tying migrants more closely to their families and communities back home. The dominant story of previous generations often had migrants leaving one country and settling permanently in a new country, largely cutting off ties with their country of origin and assimilating to the new home country. But for many migrants today, relocating no longer entails the abrupt rupture of ties between sending and receiving communities. Many migrants travel back and forth, send money through Western Union, talk regularly with family and friends by telephone, and share videos and movies. Phone cards that provide hours of service for $10 or $20 have replaced the $1 a minute international calls of a generation ago.

This practice of maintaining active participation in social, economic, religious, and political spheres across national borders has been called **transnationalism** and its participants *transnational immigrants*. Recent research on earlier waves of migration reveal a level of transnationalism evident even one hundred years ago as European immigrants to the United States exchanged letters and money, made return trips, arranged marriages, and supported family migration across the Atlantic (Foner 2000). Contemporary globalization has intensified the webs of interaction, lowered the cost of travel and communication, and speeded up the exchange of people, information, and money, thereby enabling some migrants to enjoy a lifestyle that spans national borders.

Ethnographer Robert Smith (2006) has documented the transnational political lives of Mexicans living on Long Island, New York, who maintain deep involvement in their hometown in Puebla, Mexico. These immigrants have established a hometown association in Long Island that raises money for school construction, road repair, and other infrastructure projects back home in Mexico. Leaders of the hometown association keep in regular contact with fellow villagers in Long Island and actively solicit their support for the needs of the home community. These villagers, who may be citizens of both the United States and Mexico, also actively participate in local Mexican politics. They vote. They lobby. They meet with Mexican officials who visit the United States. And some based in Long Island actually serve on their Mexican community's town council, flying to Mexico for meetings and bringing the concerns of other transnational Mexican migrants into the affairs of their hometown.

Return Migration

Return migration refers to immigrants who, having settled in a new receiving country, reverse course and return "home," sometimes in the same generation and sometimes in later generations. In the early twentieth century, for example, hundreds of thousands of Japanese migrated to Brazil, Peru, Argentina, and other Latin American countries to escape a deep economic recession and to avail themselves of expanding economic opportunities in new lands. Despite being marginalized as foreigners, the Japanese immigrants settled in, learned new languages, built homes and businesses, and established families. Decades later, in the early 1990s, nearly 250,000 of the 2 million Nikkeijin — overseas Japanese — living in Latin America returned to Japan, pushed by an economic downturn and pulled by a severe labor shortage in Japan.

Confronted by manufacturing industries collapsing for lack of workers, and unable to attract native Japanese to jobs that young people especially considered unappealing, the Japanese government established preferential immigration policies — bridges — for the Nikkeijin, assuming that they would integrate better than migrant workers from China, Korea, India, and Iran. Indeed, the Nikkeijin, many of whom had maintained a strong sense of Japanese identity in Latin America, saw an opportunity for economic success in a return to what they considered their homeland. Much to their surprise, though, the returning Nikkeijin did not receive a warm welcome. Instead, many permanent Japanese viewed them as "foreigners," as intruders and cultural strangers.

Brazilian Japanese: Creating a New Ethnic Niche after Return Migration

In *Brokered Homeland* (2002), Joshua Hotaka Roth examines the return migration experiences of these Japanese Brazilians. Roth documents not only the ways in which Japanese policies and practices intensified the Nikkeijin marginalization, but also the Japanese Brazilians' creative responses to their rejection by mainstream Japanese society. Roth's research reveals how a wide array of mediating institutions—employers, labor brokers, politicians, journalists, and government agencies—established barriers to Nikkeijin reentry into Japanese life. For instance, although they were legal immigrants and visa holders, few Brazilian Japanese held Japanese citizenship. As a result, the government denied them access to a wide range of public services generally available to the Japanese population, including health insurance, pensions, social welfare, and unemployment insurance.

Faced with often intense cultural and structural marginalization, a few Nikkeijin returned again to Latin America. Still others continued to travel back and forth as "transnational commuters" or "yo-yo migrants" (Ishi 2003). But most Brazilian Japanese remained in Japan. Counter to their original intentions of reintegration into Japanese culture, now many of them have strategically accentuated their Brazilian identities, constructing their own cultural forms and a unique ethnic community. Carving out their own ethnic niche, Japanese Brazilians—many unattached to Brazilian culture while residing in Brazil—have embraced Brazilian cultural forms in Japan: waving Brazilian flags, dancing the samba, and joining Brazilian musical bands. More significant, they have launched Japanese Brazilian businesses and local media outlets, even constructing a cultural center to teach Brazilian music and dance in the community.

Over time, Roth notes, Japanese Brazilians are becoming a permanent ethnic group in Japan. These migrants, who are the children and grandchildren of Japanese born in Japan, have returned to contribute to an increasingly multicultural homeland, enriching Japanese culture in the process. As the Japanese Brazilian return migrants establish their own identity in Japan, Roth predicts that these new cultural forms may even eventually become part of what it means to be Japanese (Goodman 2004; Howell 2004; Yamanaka 2003).

How Is Immigration Affecting the United States Today?

Immigration is one of the most controversial issues in the United States today. After all, immigrants are coming to the United States in numbers not seen since the last great wave brought Italians and eastern European Jews from 1880 to 1915. Although as many as one million immigrants may enter the United States legally each year, hundreds of thousands more enter illegally. The U.S.-Mexico border is increasingly defended and militarized, becoming one of the most heavily guarded borders in history.

Although migration has always been a part of the U.S. national origin story, the country's record is mixed, as a deep ambivalence about immigration has often come to the fore. Where do you think immigrants should fit in the nation's story? Are you and your family immigrants?

Immigration and the National Origin Myth

Immigration is a central component of the U.S. national origin myth. Many people in the United States like to trace their national roots to the pilgrims who landed in the *Mayflower* at Plymouth Rock in Massachusetts in 1620, migrating to these shores to escape religious persecution in Europe. Two hundred years later, the Irish fleeing the 1840s potato famine arrived to help build the country's roads, canals, and transcontinental railroad. Germans, Italians, and eastern European Jews followed in the late nineteenth and early twentieth centuries, escaping political and religious persecution and economic instability while searching for the fabled streets paved with gold. The "melting pot" received these immigrants, and the Statue of Liberty lifted its torch in New York harbor in welcome. The words of Emma Lazarus's poem are indelibly etched in the popular imagination as a symbol of that era and of the nation's generosity toward and reliance upon immigrants:

> *Give me your tired, your poor,*
> *Your huddled masses yearning to breathe free,*
> *The wretched refuse of your teeming shore.*
> *Send these, the homeless, tempest-tost to me,*
> *I lift my lamp beside the golden door.*

Of course, the actual immigrant story is more complicated. Certainly, immigration provided new opportunities for many new arrivals. But they did not arrive in an empty land. For the indigenous population of the Americas, immigration brought not opportunity but destruction. Nor did all those who came to the Americas come of their own free will.

The Spanish settled the southeastern area and explored the southern reaches of the continent all the way to California long before the Plymouth or Jamestown settlements sprang up. But today the Spanish language they left behind is considered a foreign language. Subsequently, the massive westward internal migration led by European immigrants was facilitated by the rapid spread of infectious diseases and by a state-sponsored genocide of Native American peoples. Moreover, the African slave trade, driven by a need for labor in the sugar, cotton, and tobacco plantations of the South, forced the involuntary migration of millions of Africans to the United States, where they worked as slaves without compensation to build a nation. And the Irish, viewed as poor, Catholic, and racially inferior, were targeted in the 1840s and 1850s with gang violence and ostracism.

 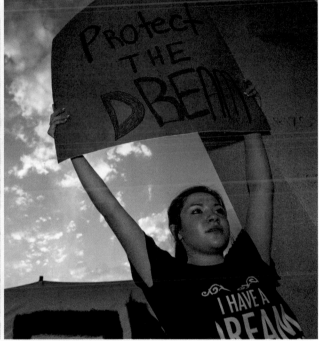

FIGURE 13.11 *Left,* Minuteman volunteers armed with binoculars and pistols watch the U.S./Mexico border near Bisbee, Arizona, for signs of undocumented immigrants, 2005. "Future generations will inherit a tangle of rancorous, unassimilated, squabbling cultures with no common bond to hold them together, a certain guarantee of the death of this nation as a harmonious 'melting pot.' The result: political, economic and social mayhem." —from About Us at www.minutemanproject.com. *Right,* a student in Phoenix, Arizona, demonstrates for the DREAM Act, a proposal to legalize children brought to the United States by undocumented parents. "If the United States is 'a country of immigrants,' why are so many people worked up about new immigrants today? My family works hard. Most of my classmates are immigrants. We're the future of America!" —eighteen-year-old student, Baruch College, The City University of New York.

From 1882 until 1943, under the federal government's Chinese Exclusion Acts, the Chinese were the only immigrant group excluded on the basis of national origin (see Chapter 6). Clearly, the nation was not entirely welcoming to all newcomers.

The anti-Chinese sentiment codified in the Chinese Exclusion Acts marked a shift in American attitudes toward immigrants as earlier arrivals from Britain and France looked down even on later European arrivals, specifically those from southern and eastern Europe, as watering down the original "stock" of the U.S. population. In 1921, following the peak of Italian (largely Catholic) and eastern European (largely Jewish) immigration, Vice President Calvin Coolidge stated, "America must be kept American," signaling his desire to limit future immigration from those regions. In 1924 the U.S. Congress passed the National Origins Act, which severely restricted immigration from all but western and northern European countries. Subsequently, the intense period of globalization and labor migration at the end of the late nineteenth and early twentieth centuries came to a halt, followed by a period of protectionism, isolationism, and nationalist fervor that lasted until 1965.

Immigration since 1965

Since 1965, when the United States radically changed its immigration policies, a rising tide of immigrants has been arriving again on the nation's shores. Coming from a vast array of countries and cultures, by their sheer numbers and diversity they are transforming cities, suburbs, and rural areas and are affecting schools, religion, politics, and health care. In cities such as New York and Los Angeles, the foreign-born immigrant population is close to 40 percent. Together with their U.S.-born children, this group constitutes more than 20 percent of the U.S. population (U.S. Census Bureau 2012).

Today's immigrants differ in many ways from those of a century ago. Post-1965 immigration—particularly the unprecedented numbers from Latin America and the Caribbean, but also from Asia, Africa, and the Middle East—has transformed the nation's racial-ethnic composition. Prior to 1950, fully 90 percent of immigrants were from Europe. By early in the twenty-first century, 50 percent were from Latin America and 25 percent were from Asia, areas where globalization has produced especially uneven results (Suarez-Orosco 2003). See Table 13.3 on page 524 for a comparison of immigrants' countries of origin in 1900 versus 2011.

Other demographic trends are revealing as well. In 2001 Hispanics surpassed African Americans for the first time as the largest minority group in the United States. Asians have shown the most rapid growth, increasing eightfold from 0.5 percent to 4 percent since 1960. The number of professionals and the changing settlement patterns also distinguish today's immigrants. Though many immigrants arrive with limited education or skills, a higher proportion now already have professional skills and college degrees, drawn to the United States by knowledge-intensive sectors of the economy. Fully 50 percent of today's immigrants continue to settle in traditional gateway cities such as New York, Chicago, Los Angeles, San Francisco, Houston, and Miami; but some are also finding jobs and settling in middle America—from the Rocky Mountains to the Great Plains to New England, including rural areas and suburban enclaves (Foner 2003).

Immigrants from the Middle East have changed the religious and cultural landscape of many parts of the United States over the past thirty years. In *All American Yemeni Girls: Being Muslim in a Public School* (2005), education scholar Loukia K. Sarroub examines the educational experiences of the children of immigrants from Yemen, a small oil-rich country near Saudi Arabia. Along

FIGURE 13.12 Despite the prominence of immigrants in the U.S. national origin myth, the country has not entirely welcomed all newcomers. *Clockwise from left:* Chinese migrants came to the U.S. West Coast in the 1850s to work in agriculture, mining, and railroad building but gradually came to be perceived as "The Yellow Peril"—dangerous competition with European immigrants for jobs. "Where the Blame Lies": in this 1891 anti-immigration cartoon, Uncle Sam surveys an immigrant horde in New York Harbor. The crowded intersection of Orchard and Hester Streets on New York City's Lower East Side, 1905.

TABLE 13.3 Ten Largest Foreign-Born Populations in the United States, 1900 to 2011

1900	2011
1. Germany	1. Mexico
2. Ireland	2. China
3. Canada	3. India
4. Great Britain	4. Philippines
5. Sweden	5. Dominican Republic
6. Italy	6. Cuba
7. Russia	7. Vietnam
8. Poland	8. South Korea
9. Norway	9. Colombia
10. Austria	10. Haiti

SOURCE: 1900 data from U.S. Census Bureau. 1999. "Profile of the Foreign Born Population in the United States: 1997," www.census.gov/prod/99pubs/p23-195; 2011 data from Migration Policy Institute. "Top Ten Countries of Birth of New Legal Permanent Residents, Fiscal Year 1986 to 2011." MPI Data Hub. www.migrationinformation.org/datahub/historicaltrends.cfm.

with other, larger numbers of Middle Eastern immigrants, these Yemenis have settled in Dearborn, Michigan. Though their parents live much as they did in Yemen, the Muslim teenage girls navigate multiple worlds and systems of belief as they make their way through the Dearborn public schools. They are simultaneously Yemenis, Muslims, Americans, daughters of immigrants, and high school students. With their bodies covered except for face and hands, they negotiate a balance among their homes, mosques, and schools as they try to be "good Muslim women," "good Yemeni daughters," and "good Americans." Sarroub's ethnography reveals the challenge facing the nation's public schools in this era of intense immigration and the crucial role of public education as a place for immigrants to explore what it means to be American.

Debates over Inclusion

Never before has the United States received immigrants from so many countries, with such a variety of economic and social backgrounds and so many motivations for migration. In fact, the diversity of the current immigrant population challenges fundamental assumptions about how newcomers are incorporated into the host society. How much multiculturalism and cultural diversity

FIGURE 13.13 Practitioners prepare for a religious ritual at the Church of the Lukumi Babulu Ayea, a Santería congregation started by Cuban and Haitian immigrants in Hialeah, Florida. The U.S. Supreme Court ruled that the city of Hialeah could not ban the church's animal sacrifices.

are desirable? To what extent should the dominant culture accommodate the newcomer, and to what extent should immigrant groups change to match the dominant culture? In the United States, these questions generate heated debates on topics as varied as the use of English as an "official" language, public school holidays, parental and child rights, religious practices, and health practices. The following examples are just a small sample of the broad range of issues under debate.

A Santería Church in Florida Consider the legal case of *Church of the Lukumi Babulu Ayea v. City of Hialeah* in Florida, which involved a religious issue. A legal battle erupted when the town of Hialeah, Florida, passed laws in 1987 to ban animal sacrifices after learning that Cuban and Haitian immigrants intended to start a Santería church there. The church's religious rituals would include slaughtering goats, chickens, pigeons, ducks, and turtles. Santería, a religion that is common in parts of the Caribbean, combines elements of Catholicism and West African spiritualism. Worshippers communicate through trances and spirit possessions with powerful spirits called Orishas, who play an active role in the worshippers' lives. Animal sacrifices are considered essential to please these Orishas, to facilitate communication with them, and to ensure support from them.

After public hearings in which some residents condemned the Cuban and Haitian immigrants as sinners who needed to be saved by Jesus, the Hialeah city council passed an ordinance criminalizing the killing of animals outside slaughterhouses for any purpose other than food consumption. The council made explicit exemptions, however, for Jewish ritual slaughter and for hunters, exterminators, and local farmers, among others. After a six-year court battle, the U.S. Supreme Court ruled in favor of the Cuban and Haitian congregation, stating that "although the practice of animal sacrifice may seem abhorrent to some, religious beliefs need not be acceptable, logical, consistent, or comprehensible to others in order to merit First Amendment protection" (cited in Shweder 2003, 280). The Court further ruled that the city could not make laws designed to discriminate against the religious practices of one particular group (Shweder 2003).

Muslim Taxi Drivers in Minnesota In 2002 the Metropolitan Airports Commission (MAC) of the Minneapolis St. Paul International Airport in Minnesota began to receive formal complaints about its taxi service. Some taxi drivers, many of whom were Muslims from Somalia, were refusing to take passengers who were carrying alcohol, claiming that their religion did not allow them to consume or transport alcohol. Their refusals, prohibited by local taxi ordinances, were disrupting taxi pickups, delaying passengers, and drawing increasing numbers of complaints. Disciplinary action for refusing to take a fare—being sent to the back of a two- to four-hour taxi queue—did not seem to be effective despite the economic and practical hardship imposed. And attempts to use special bags to cover the alcohol, often purchased in airport duty-free shops, have met resistance from passengers and drivers (Pierce 2008).

The MAC's airport director has sought input from the Somali community, the local Muslim association, taxi drivers, and passengers in trying to resolve the matter. What do you think should be done? How would you formulate a solution? Who would you talk to? What information would you need about the drivers' immigration experiences and religious beliefs to make a good decision? Is there a compromise?

Thinking more broadly, how far do you think a host society should go to accommodate newcomers? Where is the proper line between the melting pot's assimilationist approach and a multicultural approach (see Chapter 7)? Some scholars (e.g., Brimelow [1995]) argue that the United States receives too many immigrants, that the melting pot is overflowing, and that the nation's cultural unity is at risk. Yet studies of the immigrant second generation (the children of immigrants) have shown their deep integration into mainstream U.S. culture. Children of immigrants, with few exceptions, fully incorporate into their parents' country of choice and feel little allegiance or connection to their parents' country of origin (Portes and Rumbaut 2001).

Today the United States continues to be one of the top destinations for international migration, both documented and undocumented. Labor immigrants, professional immigrants, entrepreneurs, and refugees arrive in the country ready to work and contribute to the economy and overall society. But immigrants bring diversity of beliefs and practices as well, a diversity that has the potential for reshaping the dominant patterns of cultural thinking and action. How do you assess the risks and benefits? How is immigration directly affecting your life?

Thinking Like an Anthropologist: Assessing the Advantages and Disadvantages of Migration

As you encounter the challenges and opportunities of migration—studying with classmates from other countries, working with people in multinational corporations, socializing or working with immigrants, reading about immigrant experiences in the newspaper, debating immigration policies, or yourself being a migrant away from home inside or outside your native country—thinking like an anthropologist can help you to better understand these experiences.

Now that you have read this chapter, how would you apply its ideas and analysis to gain a more complete understanding of the tragic sinking of the *al-Salam 98*? Reconsider for a moment the key questions posed at the beginning of the chapter:

- Why do people move from place to place?
- Who are today's migrants?
- Where do people move to and from?
- How is immigration affecting the United States today?

Then reconsider the chapter's opening story. Why are Egyptian migrants leaving home to work in Saudi Arabia? What are the pushes and pulls, the bridges and barriers? Who actually migrates? How does their migration affect their families and home communities? Can these migrants become part of Saudi culture? Then remember that the story of the Egyptian migrant workers is reenacted in countless other migration journeys across the globe.

As we discussed in Chapter 12, globalization stimulates migration because it creates uneven development: some areas develop rapidly, others fall behind. These areas may be in close geographic proximity, such as Egypt and Saudi Arabia or the United States and Mexico. They also may be far apart, such as New York City and Fuzhou, China. They may be linked by common language, religion, regional transportation and communication networks, and complicated political histories. Regardless of distance and national boundaries, globalization facilitates the movement of people, particularly to satisfy the pulls of the labor market. But these seemingly overwhelming migration flows are quite controversial. Some people, particularly in developed countries, see immigration as threatening to their "way of life." Anti-immigrant sentiment is strong in the United States, Europe, Australia, and Japan, which are all immigrant-receiving areas. Despite the increasingly free flow of goods, services, and money around the globe, national immigration policies have resisted the flow of people. As you practice thinking like an anthropologist, how do you think this tension within globalization will be resolved?

Key Terms

pushes and pulls (p. 492)
bridges and barriers (p. 493)
chain migration (p. 496)
hometown association (p. 496)
remittance (p. 497)
cumulative causation (p. 498)
labor immigrant (p. 500)
guest worker program (p. 500)
professional immigrant (p. 500)
brain drain (p. 500)
social capital (p. 501)

For Further Exploration

Peter Brimelow. 1995. *Alien Nation: Common Sense about America's Immigration Disaster*. New York: Random House.

A Day without a Mexican. 2004. Directed by Sergio Arau. Xenon Pictures. A film about what happens in California when all the Mexicans disappear for a day.

Foner, Nancy. 2000. *From Ellis Island to JFK: New York's Two Great Waves of Immigration*. New Haven, CT: Yale University Press. Scholarly introduction to U.S. immigration from the late nineteenth century to the late twentieth century.

The Internal Displacement Monitoring Centre. www .internal-displacement.org. Online source of current information about internally displaced persons.

Lost Boys of Sudan. Documentary film (2004. Directed by Megan Mylan and Jon Shenk. Actual Films / Principe Productions) and book (by Mark Bixler. 2006. Athens: University of Georgia Press) about a group of more than twenty thousand boys displaced and orphaned during the Sudanese civil war from 1983 to 2005.

The Other Side of Immigration. 2009. Directed by Roy Germano. Roy Germano Films. Explores the Mexican side of the Mexico-U.S. migration.UN Department of Economic and Social Affairs, Population Division. www.unpopulation.org. Extensive data on international migration.

UN High Commissioner for Refugees. www.unhcr .org/statistics/populationdatabase. Online source of current information about international refugees.

An Egyptian protestor takes a photo with her mobile phone while chanting slogans in Tahrir Square, Cairo, December 2012.

p. 533

p. 544

p. 551

p. 557

p. 559

p. 566

CHAPTER 14
Politics and Power

Throughout 2011 and 2012, the Middle East and North Africa were roiled by antigovernment demonstrations, strikes, marches, and rallies, as well as by sometimes violent responses from police, militaries, and pro-government demonstrators and militias. What has become known as the Arab Spring spread quickly from Tunisia to Egypt, eventually including a civil war in Libya and uprisings in Syria, Bahrain, Yemen, Morocco, Algeria, Iraq, Jordan, and Oman.

The revolution in Egypt caught the world's attention as tens of thousands of young people faced off against the police and soldiers defending the repressive regime of Hosni Mubarak, who had been Egypt's president for thirty-three years. The protestors hurled rocks and paving stones against tear gas and bullets, eventually toppling the Mubarak government and creating an opening for a dramatic shift in the political environment and power structure of Egypt, one of the cornerstones of the region's politics.

The movements for social change across the region were marked by new forms of political protest and mobilization. Laptops, the Internet, and search engines enabled a generation separated by national borders to find out about anything going on anywhere, easily bridging the local and the global. Cell phones, flip cameras, Twitter feeds, and Facebook pages brought a new dynamic to the creation of social networks and mass mobilizations as individuals previously separated by geography and political borders found new ways to link together, posting a constantly refreshed stream of YouTube videos of marches, celebrations, violence, and atrocities.

In Egypt, these elements of time-space compression facilitated the cooperation of social networks, student organizations, religious movements, unionized factory workers, and soccer clubs. Global interconnections appeared everywhere. Leaders of the April 6 Youth Movement traveled from Egypt to Europe to learn the nonviolent strategies of the Serbian Youth Brigade, named Otpar, that had helped topple Serbian dictator Slobodan Milosevic in 2000. Egyptian youth also studied the work of American political scientist Gene Sharp (1993), who promoted nonviolence as the most effective means to undermine a police state that might otherwise respond to violent resistance with repressive tactics. An Egyptian executive for Google, Wael Ghonim, established a Facebook group, named We Are All Khaled Said, in honor of a young Egyptian man who had been beaten to death by Egyptian police. The group became the central organizing location for tens of thousands of young Egyptians who were determined to change the life chances and political possibilities of their fellow citizens (Abu-Lughod 2012; Ghannam 2012; Hamdy 2012; Hirschkind 2012).

Power is often described as the ability or potential to bring about change through action or influence—either one's own or that of a group or institution. Indeed, power is embedded in all human relationships, whether that power is openly displayed or carefully avoided—from the most mundane aspects of friendships and family relationships to the myriad ways humans organize institutions and the structural frameworks of whole societies (Wolf 1982).

The Greek philosopher Aristotle spoke of humans as political animals. By this he meant that we live with other people in communities through which we strive to organize ourselves to achieve the good life—not as hedonists seeking the maximization of individual pleasure, but as a collective partnership (*koinonia*) seeking the good life, virtue, and beauty through community. The presence of politics and relations of power in the ebb and flow of daily life makes it a central focus of anthropological study. Although uprisings such as the Arab Spring may draw attention to the most public, dramatic, and sometimes violent aspects of politics, anthropologists also consider the multiple local forms of politics—the careful political interactions and activities that occupy much of daily life and are essential in making a community a decent place to live (Gledhill 2000; Kurtz 2001; Lewellen 2003).

Throughout this book we explore power and its intersections with culture. We work to unmask the structures of power built on ideologies of race, gender, ethnicity, and sexuality and the institutions of kinship and religion. We also examine the power dynamics of the world economy and the stratifications of class. In this chapter, we explore power as it is expressed through political systems and processes: the way humans have organized themselves in small groups, the role of the state in national and international politics, and the ability of people (nonstate actors) to engage in politics and exercise power through individual

FIGURE 14.1 Who has power? Wael Ghonim, a high-level employee of Google Egypt and one of the leading members of the Egyptian opposition, leaves his apartment in Cairo.

action and social movements outside the direct control of the state. We consider the historical and contemporary approaches that anthropologists have taken toward these crucial issues and the ways in which globalization is shifting the dynamics of power and politics on local and global levels. In particular, we will examine the following questions:

- How have anthropologists viewed the origins of human political history?
- What is the state?
- How is globalization affecting the state?
- What is the relationship among politics, the state, violence, and war?
- How do people mobilize power outside the state's control?

While reading this chapter, you will analyze many expressions of politics and the ways in which aspects of power are expressed locally and globally today. You will consider how political anthropology can help you think more deeply about your own expressions as a political creature, including the ways you negotiate human relationships on the interpersonal, group, community, national, and global level. You will examine the changing role of the state in local, national, and global affairs and the ways humans mobilize collectively through social movements to challenge the power of the state and the effects of globalization by advocating for social change and human rights. Finally, you will consider an anthropological debate about the roots of violence in human culture. The skills you acquire in this chapter will be valuable additions to your toolkit for living as a political actor and an engaged citizen in today's global world.

How Have Anthropologists Viewed the Origins of Human Political History?

Over the course of history, humans have organized themselves politically by using flexible strategies to make their groups and communities a better place to live. Our earliest human ancestors appear to have evolved in small, mobile, egalitarian groups of hunter-gatherers. It is in these types of groups that core human characteristics and cultural patterns emerged.

For nearly a century, beginning in the late 1800s, anthropologists studying politics and power focused primarily on small-scale, stateless societies, attempting to understand human political history through the political activities of contemporary hunter-gatherers, pastoralists, and horticulturalists. But beginning in the 1960s, as nation-states emerged to dominate political activity on a global scale, the anthropological gaze shifted significantly to encompass more complex, state-oriented societies and the process by which local settings are politically incorporated into a larger context.

The specialization called *political anthropology* took clear shape after World War II as anthropologists such as Meyer Fortes and E. E. Evans-Pritchard (1940), as well as other British social anthropologists (e.g., Turner 1957; Gluckman 1954), examined the local political systems of Africa. Others looked closely at the political systems of the Middle East and Asia (Leach 1954; Barth 1959) and the indigenous people of the Americas (Redfield 1941; Wallace 1957). These highly detailed studies of local political systems rarely placed the communities in a larger context, despite being conducted at a time when colonialist powers had imposed nonindigenous governing structures in much of the world.

As they undertook these studies of politics in many cultures, anthropologists attempted to create a common language, a typology that would enable them to communicate across cultural areas and compare and contrast their findings (Gledhill 2000; Lewellyn 2003). The political anthropologist Elman Service (1962) famously classified the vast and varied world of political systems into four basic types: bands, tribes, chiefdoms, and states. Although infrequently used today, this framework shaped a generation of anthropological thinking about political systems. Service proposed that political systems develop through a natural, evolutionary progression from simple to complex and from less integrated to more integrated, with patterns of leadership evolving from weaker to stronger. Subsequently, when states emerged as the dominant political actors on the world stage, the examination of bands, tribes, and chiefdoms, anthropologists hoped, might provide insights into the origins and fundamental nature of the state.

Bands

Anthropologists have used the term **band** to describe small, kinship-based groups of food foragers who move over a particular territory while hunting and gathering. Through archaeological evidence and the study of a few remaining band societies, anthropologists have identified key characteristics of band organization and leadership. A band might range in size from twenty to several hundred people depending on the time of year and the group's hunting and ritual cycles. Bands break up and re-form regularly in response to conflicts among members and the formation of new alliances.

Small, close-knit bands served as the primary way of life not only for our modern human ancestors but also for the entire genus *Homo*, including *Homo habilis*, *Homo erectus*, and early *Homo sapiens*. As a result, evolutionary biologists suggest that life in the band shaped the development of our earliest human characteristics and cultural patterns.

Politically, bands are highly decentralized, with decisions made primarily by consensus. Leaders emerge for a task at hand (organizing the hunt, moving the campsite, negotiating a conflict), with their leadership position resting on their skill, knowledge, generosity toward others, and level of respect within the band. With limited resources to compete for, bands have minimal stratification of wealth and power. But perhaps more important, the active cooperation required among diverse groups of relatives and nonrelatives in order to successfully adapt to an unpredictable and shifting landscape may have

FIGURE 14.2 Qaanaaq Greenland dog teams and Inuit hunters traveling to a hunt. Once food foraging was the primary way of life for humans and our ancestors, but today food foragers are limited to the most remote areas of the planet.

band: A small kinship-based group of foragers who hunt and gather for a living over a particular territory.

embedded in humans a tendency toward egalitarian social and political organization rather than hierarchy.

In his book *Hierarchy in the Forest: The Evolution of Egalitarian Behavior* (1999), evolutionary biologist Christopher Boehm explores what life in bands can tell us about whether humans are fundamentally hierarchical or egalitarian. Drawing on ethnographic studies of contemporary and historical hunter-gatherer bands, as well as tribes, chieftains, and states and archaeological findings, Boehm argues that the sharing of scarce resources, including food, was for hunter-gatherer bands the most economically efficient—indeed, essential—economic strategy. And this strategy could only be sustained through egalitarianism. Cooperative gathering of foods, coordinated game hunting, and reciprocal sharing went hand in hand with resisting hierarchy and domination as successful adaptations for humans living in hunter-gatherer bands. As a result, over the course of human evolutionary history, hunter-gatherer bands and tribal communities generated an egalitarian ethos that promoted generosity, altruism, and sharing while resisting upstarts, aggression, and egoism.

In hunter-gatherer and other small-scale communities, which served as the political and economic framework for much of human existence, members invest an enormous effort to suppress hierarchy and enhance cooperation. The resulting egalitarianism made the hunter-gatherer lifestyle possible as people worked as a group to assert dominance over anyone who tried to establish himself or herself as a leader. While other close primate kin—and perhaps humans themselves—may instinctively form social dominance hierarchies (that is, patterns of interpersonal domination) with alpha individuals presiding over them, the evidence of egalitarian hunter-gatherer societies provides a crucial insight into an alternative or complementary pattern that emerged during the time human interaction was shaped by life in small bands. Boehm argues that this social environment lasted long enough to shape innate human tendencies toward cooperation. Although hierarchical tendencies are present in egalitarian social systems, evidence reveals that hierarchical tendencies are regularly balanced out and even overcome as the weak work together to compensate for, and even dominate, the strong in order to create egalitarianism and effective community.

Despite serving as the predominant economic, social, and political structure over the course of human evolution, by the mid-twentieth century only a few bands of food foragers remained. These groups were living in the most remote areas of the planet: the rainforests of South America, the arctic tundra of North America, and the deserts of Africa and Australia.

Tribes

The term *tribe* is frequently used in contemporary media when describing conflict among groups within a state. Media coverage of civil wars or internal conflicts—particularly in parts of Africa, the Middle East, Asia and the Pacific—frequently refers to tribal conflicts, tribal warfare, tribal factions, rifts, and alliances. In these instances, *tribe* is usually a reference to a loosely organized group of people acting together, outside the authority of the state, under unelected leaders and "big men"/"strong men" and drawing on a sense of unity based on a notion of shared ethnicity.

Most popular references to tribes carry connotations of primitive, uncivilized, and violent people who engage in conflict based on "ancient" tribal factions and hatreds. These faulty characterizations reflect the ethnocentric perspectives of observers who operate from inside a state framework. Their characterizations perpetuate the deeply problematic evolutionary assumption that less complex political organizations are naturally less effective, stable, rational, and civilized.

As originally formulated (Service 1962), the term *tribe* referred to a culturally distinct population, often combining several bands, that imagined itself as one people descended from a common ancestor and organized around villages, kin groups, clans, and lineages. Tribes appear to have emerged between ten and twelve thousand years ago as humans began to shift from food foraging to pastoralism and horticulture. Like bands, tribes are largely egalitarian, with a decentralized power structure and consensus decision making. Leaders do emerge, sometimes called "village heads" or "big men" (Sahlins 1971), who garner the support of followers in several villages. But their power is limited. It is built and maintained through the leaders' personal achievements—such as success in war, conflict resolution, group organizing, and generosity of feasts and gifts—rather than awarded through political institutions.

Anthropologists have identified confederacies of tribes in Central Africa and on the Central Plains of North America that worked together to coordinate hunting, preserve the peace, or defend against perceived outside threats. Perhaps most famous is the Iroquois Confederacy formed by five distinct but closely related indigenous groups in the northeastern United States and Canada: the Mohawk, Oneida, Onandaga, Cayuga, and Seneca. Although the Iroquois Confederacy appears to predate European colonial activity in the Americas, confederacies are often formed at the demand of colonial powers, which prefer to deal with defined political groups rather than people on the move with shifting leadership and allegiances. The confederacy structure enabled colonizers to streamline the process of colonial control for trade and treaty making (Snow 1994).

FIGURE 14.3 A replica of the eighteenth-century Hiawatha belt that records the agreement of the first five nations of the Iroquois Confederacy to live in peace (Smithsonian object no. 269056). The center tree symbol represents the Onondaga, where Hiawatha, the peacemaker, planted the Tree of Peace under which the leaders of all five nations buried their weapons of war.

tribe: Originally viewed as a culturally distinct, multiband population that imagined itself as one people descended from a common ancestor; currently used to describe an indigenous group with its own set of loyalties and leaders living to some extent outside the control of a centralized authoritative state.

chiefdom: An autonomous political unit composed of a number of villages or communities under the permanent control of a paramount chief.

In recent centuries, independent tribal peoples largely have been eliminated; they have been conquered and incorporated into the nation-states that have come to dominate the global political landscape. Today no groups operate totally outside the framework of the state. Even a weak state or a failed state directly influences all those living within its borders. In this context, today we might define a **tribe** more accurately as an indigenous group of people with its own set of loyalties and leaders living to some extent outside the direct control of a centralized, authoritative state. In many cases, current discussions use the term *ethnic group* instead of *tribe* (Ferguson 2011).

Chiefdoms

Within Elman Service's evolutionary typology of political systems, the **chiefdom**—an autonomous political unit comprised of a number of villages or communities under the permanent control of a paramount chief (Carneiro 1981, 45)—represented a transitional form between the simpler political structures of tribes and the more complex political structures of states. As in bands and tribes, the social relations of the chiefdom were built around extended kinship networks or lineages. The chiefdom might encompass thousands of people spread over many villages.

Unique to chiefdoms, leadership was centralized under a single ruling authority figure—a chief who headed a ranked hierarchy of people, asserted political control over a particular territory, and held the authority to make and enforce decisions. In parts of Polynesia, for instance, chiefs functioned as full-time political specialists, resolving conflicts and organizing collective economic activity. The permanent position of chief endured from generation to generation, often passing through direct descent and inheritance from father to son or through other kinship relationships. Religious rituals and beliefs often served to confirm the chief's authority.

Through feasts and festivals such as the potlatch (see Chapter 11), the chief gathered a portion of the collective bounty of the chiefdom's harvest or hunt and redistributed the communal wealth to the populace, thereby symbolically and practically reinforcing his or her central role among the people. Though group members' access to power and resources depended on one's hierarchical relationship to the chief, the process of redistribution served a central role in moderating inequality and limiting conflict within the chiefdom.

Micronesia: Adapting Political and Social Structures to an Island Ecology

As mentioned early in this section, humans have always applied flexible strategies to improve life in their communities. In *Traditional Micronesian Societies* (2009), political anthropologist Glenn Petersen explores the creative adaptation of Micronesian social and political structures to the particular ecological challenges of island life. Micronesia is an archipelago of thousands of mostly small islands in the South Pacific that are often separated by hundreds of miles. The islands are extremely fertile with abundant fresh water, food, vegetation, and marine life. Normally, they are ideal places to live and can support a sizable population relative to their land mass.

MAP 14.1
Micronesia

But the islands are also highly susceptible to catastrophic storms and droughts generated by fluctuating weather patterns over the Pacific. Droughts can easily devastate the vegetation and population of smaller islands. And the storm surge associated with a direct strike by a typhoon can inundate the typical Micronesian island, which is a coral atoll less than fifteen feet above sea level. Such a surge can completely saturate the island's gardens with saltwater, causing a disaster that may require several years of intensive labor to rehabilitate. Although the frequency of devastating droughts or typhoons is unpredictable, their occurrence every twenty years or so has made an indelible mark on Micronesian political and social structure.

Petersen documents how over time Micronesians have developed an elaborate social and political organization that enables them to survive and quickly recover from natural disasters. Because of the distance between islands and the irregularity of weather patterns, devastation on one island may not touch neighboring islands. Thus, Micronesian social and political structures allow survivors to travel to other islands to find relief and support from extended kinship-based networks while they rehabilitate gardens at home. Key to this arrangement are the matrilineal clans widely dispersed among multiple islands that systematize the relations of reciprocity needed to overcome natural catastrophes.

The dispersed matrilineal clans, headed by chiefs, are organized in a hierarchically nested structure, with multiple levels fitting into one another. Clans, the highest-level and most expansive groups, are geographically dispersed over many islands and multiple communities. Clans include many subclans—smaller groups spread over a more limited area—and lineages, which are local groups of kin who live near one another. Lineages may have fewer than fifty members and are usually organized around the control and cultivation of specific plots of land. One becomes a member of a particular group primarily through birth into the mother's clan.

By means of this elaborate structure, every Micronesian is a member of both a local lineage and a dispersed clan that includes local lineages on many islands. This arrangement yields a complex political identity, as each person is a member of two related but separate systems of government. First, each Micronesian lives in and belongs to a local community with its own government and chief. Each community may in fact have multiple lineages associated with dispersed clans, though usually one is recognized as senior to the others. In addition, each Micronesian belongs to a dispersed matrilineal descent group with its own chiefly system.

During times of catastrophe, this dual political and social system provides a highly effective adaptation to natural disasters. Even when faced with personal tragedy and the destruction of home and garden, each Micronesian is able to rely on interpersonal networks on other islands for survival and assistance. Each Micronesian knows that he or she can move in with relatives on another island or may be expected to invite displaced relatives into his or her own home while they reconstruct their gardens, homes, lineages, and lives. This kind of support can be found on islands large and small. In fact, on larger, higher islands that are less vulnerable to drought and typhoon, feast-making is central to lineage and community life. Feasts, which feature the sharing and redistribution of community surpluses, such as the potlatch discussed earlier in Chapter 11, enable individuals and groups to build prestige. But they also serve as mechanisms for supporting families, lineages, and communities in times of crisis.

Violence and Conflict Resolution in Micronesia Petersen takes particular note of the impact of the Micronesians' elaborate social and political structures on the patterns of violence and conflict resolution within their society. Micronesian culture celebrates the warrior role, holding warriors and martial skill in high regard. In fact, a central role of the chief involves preparing the group for warfare and conflict. Warfare is always seen as a possible, sometimes unavoidable means for resolving disputes. The potential for conflict over scarce resources intensifies during times of natural disaster, drought, and flood. But Petersen argues that Micronesians employ these capacities for organized violence as deliberate strategies for maintaining peace. Preparing for war serves as a deterrent, reminding people of the potential costs and spurring the development of an extensive repertoire of ways to avoid warfare and violence.

Thus, while Micronesian culture places elaborate emphasis on the role of warriors and martial skill, these are, in the language of the central island Pohnpei, considered *tautik* ("little service"). Held in greater honor in traditional Micronesian culture are what the Pohnpeians call *taulap* ("great service"): generosity of spirit, duty to one's kin, and the ability to produce food and other goods in quantities that enable gift giving and feasting. These values are reflected and embedded in the elaborate social and political structures of dispersed matrilineal clans that provide a nonviolent means for moving people from resource shortage to resource availability, even during times of great crisis.

FIGURE 14.4 Micronesian islanders confront the effects of natural disasters—like this home destroyed by a typhoon (*left*)—with creativity, signs of aesthetic beauty, and flexible kinship structures. In this context, generosity of spirit, duty to one's kin, and the ability to produce food and other goods in quantities that enable gift giving and feasting (*right*) are held in higher esteem than martial skill or the role of the warrior.

Putting Typologies in Perspective

Though the typology of bands, tribes, chiefdoms, and states provided a basis for cross-cultural comparison, Service's framework has frequently proven too simple to capture the complexity and diversity of political practices and institutions that are reflected in ethnographic studies and the archaeological record. For instance, evidence now clearly suggests that across human history, groups of bands, tribes, and chiefdoms were never as isolated or homogenous as mid-twentieth-century anthropologists proposed. In contrast, today we argue that movement, encounter, exchange, and change have been the hallmarks of human groups, both small and large, throughout human history.

Nor could twentieth-century political systems always be considered trustworthy representations of the human past, recent or distant. Certainly, by the time anthropologists began to enter the field in the late nineteenth century to document and classify people and their political systems, European colonial expansion—including often violent encounters—had transformed peoples and their political structures across the globe. Colonialism, the slave trade, the conquest of indigenous peoples of the Americas, military activity, missionary efforts, and global trade deeply influenced every political arrangement from the most populous urban setting to the most rural village. It is safe to say that anthropologists have not observed a band, tribe, or chiefdom that has not been influenced by colonialism, the power of the state, and the forces of globalization.

Today no political arrangement of band, tribe, or chiefdom can operate outside the pervasive influence of the state. As a result, political anthropology has turned from a primary focus on small-scale, stateless societies to consider both the structures and processes of the state, the ways individuals and local settings are politically incorporated into the larger framework of the state, and the developing position of the state in global affairs.

What Is the State?

state: An autonomous regional structure of political, economic, and military rule with a central government authorized to make laws and use force to maintain order and defend its territory.

As states took on an increasingly central role in shaping the local communities that anthropologists traditionally studied, political anthropologists turned their ethnographic attention to the state itself. Today we typically define the **state** as an autonomous regional structure of political, economic, and military rule with a central government authorized to make laws and use force to maintain order and defend its territory. Some loosely configured states existed as early as five thousand years ago in Mesopotamia and Egypt, and somewhat later in China, Japan, the Indus Valley, and portions of the Americas. Throughout most of human history, however, people organized themselves primarily through less centralized, flexible bands, tribes, and chiefdoms.

The global landscape of contemporary states that now dominates local, regional, and international affairs reflects the impact of Western expansion over the past five hundred years, particularly European imperial and colonial expansion (see Chapter 12). European colonialists deployed economic, political, and military force to redraw the political borders of much of the world to meet colonial economic needs. In this process, the colonial powers carved states and territories out of geographic areas inhabited by indigenous groups who were previously organized along lines based more on local kinship, political, and economic relations.

Few states are older than the United States, which officially formed in 1783. In fact, most of the states in the world today did not exist before World War II—certainly not in their current configurations. Most gained independence from colonial rule only in the decades immediately following World War II. By 2012, there were 196 independent states in the world.

The Modern Western-Style State

The type of state that has emerged since the sixteenth century, built largely on a Western model and expanded through colonization and globalization, developed with certain unique characteristics (Giddens 1985). Unlike earlier forms of the state, such as China's, which had relatively porous borders and loose administration, modern states feature a central administration designed to penetrate the everyday social life of its citizenry. A standing army asserts control over a carefully defined territory. Administrative, communication, and military infrastructures define and enforce the state's borders. The state, rather than a big man or chief, serves as the source of laws and law enforcement. People of all classes within the bounds of the state acquire an identity as citizens who owe allegiance primarily to the state, not to local networks based on kinship, religion, or ethnicity (Asad 1992).

Externally, modern states compete economically and militarily with other states for resources and territory. Internally, each state seeks to establish a monopoly on the legitimate use of force within a territorial domain (Weber [1919] 1965). For example, it enlists citizens' cooperation and pacifies resistance through expanded administrative power in police forces, the judicial system, tax collection, and regulatory regimes (Giddens 1985). It also accomplishes these objectives via surveillance techniques and institutions such as prisons, hospitals, and asylums, through which individuals classified as deviant from the cultural norm are removed from mainstream society and disciplined (Foucault 1977).

One unique contribution of political anthropologists to the study of the state has been a focus on the processes of the state rather than its institutions and structures. Rather than seeing the state as a completely autonomous, territorially defined entity with fixed institutions, structures, and procedures, political anthropologists have asked how the state came into being, how it was established as the ultimate authority managing all other institutions and social relations, and how each state has been uniquely constructed and organized by people and their cultural norms, values, symbols, and mental maps of reality.

Despite the illusion that the state is fixed, cohesive, and coherent, states are in fact constantly being shaped and reshaped through daily interactions with individuals, communities, nonstate institutions, social movements, and other states. From this perspective, we can see that states are actually quite fluid, contested, and even fragile (Sharma and Gupta 2006).

How does the state become the ultimate authority within a particular territory? Anthropologists suggest that the state becomes real in the imaginations and experiences of people as it is encountered in a particular space. This spatialization of the state (Ferguson and Gupta 2002)—the perception that the state fills a particular space, encompasses all aspects of culture, and stands above all other elements of the society—is produced through mundane

FIGURE 14.5 When does the state become real to you? Consider the particular spaces in which you encounter the state. *Left to right:* passport control at O'Hare Airport, Chicago; a courtroom in Santa Fe, New Mexico; a voting booth in Ciudad Juarez, Mexico; the construction site of a bridge over the Danube River between Romania and Bulgaria; and a street in Melbourne, Australia, where firefighters race to an emergency.

hegemony: The ability of a dominant group to create consent and agreement within a population without the use or threat of force.

bureaucratic state practices. The state is encountered in everyday acts of governance: mail delivery, tax collection, mapping, surveys, issuance of passports, jury duty, voting, notarization, distribution of food to the poor, distribution of pension checks to the elderly. Through these routine and repetitive acts, the state comes to feel all-encompassing and overarching—a dynamic that Ferguson and Gupta call "vertical encompassment." Representations of the state on the television and radio, as well as in the newspapers or movies, all contribute to the construction of the state as concrete and real. These representations reinforce the conception of the state as the primary institutional form through which social relations—family, community, civil society, economic exchange—are experienced.

Aspects of State Power

The rituals and routines of the state also include overt practices of coercion. In fact, political philosopher Max Weber argued in 1919 that the fundamental characteristic of a state is its ability to establish a monopoly on the legitimate use of force in a particular territorial domain (Parsons 1964). States exert coercive power not only through military and police forces but also through the guarding and regulating of borders, the determining of criteria for citizenship, and the enforcing of discipline through rules, regulations, taxation, and the judicial system.

State power is also established through **hegemony**, which is the ability of a dominant group to create consent and agreement within a population without the use or threat of force (Gramsci 1971). How is this done? As discussed in Chapter 2, cultural institutions of government, media, schools, and religions shape what group members think is normal, natural, and possible, thereby influencing and limiting the scope of human action and interaction. Group members develop a way of seeing the world—a set of beliefs about what is normal and appropriate—that subconsciously limit their life choices and chances. As discussed in Chapter 7, states reinforce this hegemony by promoting intense feelings of nationalism (a sense of shared history, culture, language, destiny, and purpose, often through invented traditions of holidays, parades, national songs, public ceremonies, and historical reenactments) to promote the perception of the state as a unified entity.

The hegemonic aspect of power can make group members discipline their own behavior, believing and acting in certain "normal" ways (often against their own interests), even without threat of punishment for misbehavior (Foucault 1977). Within the hegemony of ideas, some thoughts and actions actually become unthinkable and undoable. Others seem reasonable, necessary, and desirable; these include collective actions for the greater good of the "nation," even going so far as killing and being killed. Some modern states, however, are unable to gain the cooperation of their populace through consent and must resort to coercion. Where do you see this dynamic at work in the world today?

How Is Globalization Affecting the State?

Today globalization presents serious challenges to the state, particularly in terms of flexible accumulation, time-space compression, and expanding migration. The boundaries of the state—its influence and control over internal and external affairs—appear to be shrinking in the face of pressures related to globalization and the neoliberalizing global economy.

International Nonstate Actors Challenge State Sovereignty

In a global economy with increasing flows of people, money, goods, and ideas, state borders are becoming more porous. As a result, states are increasingly struggling to control who and what enters and leaves their territories. State sovereignty—the right of the state to maintain self-determination within its borders—is being challenged by powerful international nonstate actors.

As discussed in Chapter 12, international financial institutions such as the World Bank, the International Monetary Fund, and the World Trade Organization, backed by the world's most developed economies, are pressuring states to adopt neoliberal economic policies. These policies include free markets; free trade; the free movement of goods, capital, and ideas; and access to local markets for transnational corporations. Furthermore, to receive development loans from international financial institutions, developing countries are required to privatize state-owned infrastructure such as ports, water systems, utilities, and transportation and to reduce state funding for social services, health care, and education. These changes, it is suggested, while lessening the state's ability to control what flows across its borders, will enhance the state's ability to compete in the global economy.

Economic restructuring promoted by international financial institutions and implemented by the state has yielded a flourishing of civil society. This is evident in the phenomenon of people joining together to form local organizations and movements to protest the social upheaval and uneven development that has accompanied the institution of neoliberal economic policies. These nongovernmental organizations (NGOs), sometimes called **civil society organizations**, have become key players in challenging state policies and in creating space through which activists can work together to access resources and opportunities for their local communities.

civil society organization: A local nongovernmental organization that challenges state policies and uneven development, and advocates for resources and opportunities for members of its local communities.

Civil Society Organizations Gain a Global Reach

One key strategy of civil society organizations has been to join forces with transnational movements and networks to transform local problems and conflicts into part of a global project for rights and resources. By linking up with groups outside their national borders, local civil society organizations are able to join forces with other activists, networks, and campaigns, such as Amnesty International, Human Rights Watch, Africa Watch, or World Vision and even international agencies like the United Nations. These linkages enable the civil society organizations to advocate for local environmental concerns, women's rights, human rights, and indigenous rights—issues that also transcend the borders of the state.

Communication and transportation advances associated with time-space compression—from cell phones to Facebook, Twitter, and YouTube—facilitate the formation of these transnational networks. This process not only promotes the flow of observers, advisors, and participants in meetings and conferences but also stimulates global information flows of on-the-ground developments and organizing strategies. Working together, the international coalitions mobilize international sentiment and bring pressure to bear on

FIGURE 14.6 Activists from an Indonesian civil society organization perform during a protest against the policies of the World Trade Organization, 2008.

nation-states to address problems occurring within their borders. In this way, the coalitions challenge the ultimate claims of state sovereignty over affairs within state borders.

Tanzania: The Maasai Demand Political Rights and International Recognition Anthropologist Dorothy Hodgson documents the rise of civil society organizations in Tanzania, East Africa, in *Being Maasai, Becoming Indigenous: Postcolonial Politics in a Neoliberal World* (2011). The Maasai have traditionally lived as seminomadic pastoralists raising cattle on the open rangelands of Tanzania and Kenya. Marginalized within their own nation, first by colonial governments and later by the postcolonial state established after independence from Britain in 1961, the Maasai live on the economic and political periphery. They suffer from low levels of education, limited access to health care, and high levels of poverty.

Though the Maasai lifestyle has been changing and pastoralist economic patterns diversifying to include cultivation, trade, and wage labor, the Maasai have remained largely invisible to state planners. These bureaucrats have viewed the Maasai rangelands as "unoccupied" and have frequently sold or leased them to investors and developers.

Spurred by increasing land loss and impoverishment, beginning in the 1990s Maasai and other pastoralists in northern Tanzania began to create NGOs in an attempt to assert their political rights to resources and recognition and to represent themselves in negotiations with state and international entities. More than one hundred NGOs were created in slightly more than a decade. Key to

MAP 14.2
Tanzania

FIGURE 14.7 Maasai women in Tanzania address issues of poverty and livelihood through a micro-enterprise producing local handicrafts.

their strategy was a decision to represent themselves as "indigenous" in order to build alliances in the international indigenous rights movement. The move generated hostile responses from their own government, which had sought to downplay any ethnic divisions within the country. But the claim of indigenous rights established the Maasai as prominent actors with the United Nations and other international human rights bodies and attracted millions of dollars of funding for the NGOs from a wide array of international organizations focused on the plight of "first peoples."

Unfortunately, the rapid influx of outside funding and attention generated tremendous internal tensions in the Maasai community. Rifts developed among activists along lines of gender, generation, and class, and between the younger educated men who tended to run the NGOs and the rural, uneducated, grass-roots communities they represented. By the early 2000s, Maasai NGOs strategically shifted themselves away from identification with indigenous rights. Instead, they cultivated a new reputation as advocates on the issue of livelihood: What cultural rights, land rights, political recognition, and services were necessary to preserve the pastoralist livelihood of the Maasai people? Through this shift, they successfully struck a new balance between two goals. They continued to advocate for Maasai political rights in relationship to the state government. But they also developed a new identity as civil society organizations dedicated to serving their people through the delivery of services and economic resources.

Hodgson, a long-time observer of Maasai culture with a deep knowledge of northern Tanzania (2001, 2005), reflects on the broader significance of these creative and often challenging projects. She notes that the Maasai efforts to address impoverishment and marginalization reveal central trends and tensions prevalent in many developing nations as local communities explore avenues for political action in a local context shaped both by the legacies of colonialism and by contemporary neoliberal economic and political policies (Homewood 2012; Lesorogol 2012).

What Is the Relationship among Politics, the State, Violence, and War?

Perhaps no use of power is more troubling and challenging than violence, the "bodily harm that individuals, groups and nations inflict on one another in the course of their conflicts" (Ury 2002, 7). Conflict happens on the playground, in the classroom, in the boardroom, and on the battlefield. As we look globally today, we seem to be experiencing a period during which violent conflict is not sporadic, but permanent—a time of continuous war in one place or another involving extraordinarily sophisticated tools and weaponry (Waterston 2009).

Are Humans Naturally Violent or Peaceful?

Underlying many discussions and debates about politics, war, and peace is the question of whether humans are naturally violent or peaceful. Is there something in the human evolutionary past that predisposes modern humans to behave in a particular way when confronted with conflict?

The main arguments can be simplified into three generalizations. First, organized human violence can be seen as a natural expression of the inherent human condition. In this view, human aggression and violence may be attributed to physiological factors such as testosterone, DNA, and neural wiring. Or a natural tendency toward violence may be conceived of as a reasonable adaptation to the frustrations of drives, though an adaptation that only manifests itself when survival is at issue. A second conception of violence considers humans to be inherently peaceful. In this view, violence arises through cultural practices and patterns that overwhelm basic human nature. A third scenario places the roots of human violence in between nature and culture. So, for instance, humans may be naturally prone to violence but culturally capable of avoiding it. Or humans may be naturally peaceful and only culturally provoked into for-saking their nature. Another option posits that these two alternatives are evenly matched. As described earlier, for instance, Micronesians employ their capaci-ties for organized violence as a deliberate means for maintaining peace, prepar-ing people for warfare and conflict as a form of deterrent to war and a reminder of the detrimental effects of violence.

Challenging the Myth of Killer Apes and Aggressive Humans Some who see violence and war as a legacy of our evolutionary past point to a common myth about aggressive primates and killer apes as evidence. If aggression, com-petition, and violence are part of our primate relatives' evolutionary develop-ment, they argue, then these impulses must be deeply ingrained in human nature as well. According to this view, natural levels of aggression, competition, and violence linked to genes and hormones must be generated internally and instinctively released in social relations. Conflict, then, naturally drives individ-uals farther apart into competing and warring groups.

Physical anthropologist Frans de Waal (2002), reviewing studies of living primate macaques, chimpanzees, and bonobos, points out patterns of behav-ior that directly challenge this myth. De Waal notes, for instance, that for social animals such as primates, this pattern of conflict and distancing would lead to everyone living alone, yielding an ineffective pattern of social relationships for individuals who rely on social cooperation for survival. In the primate social groups de Waal has reviewed, a far more complicated dynamic emerges in times of conflict. Rather than increased distance, reconciliation occurs on a regular basis. In fact, increased attraction is regularly observed between opponents after fights. Researchers have identified this reconciliation mechanism in twenty-five separate primate groups, revealing powerful inclinations toward reconciliation among individuals who have a great deal to lose if their relationship deteriorates. Among bonobos, a primate group closely related to humans on a genetic level, sex is used to resolve conflicts. Bonobo conflicts and tensions occur in all com-binations of female and male. So do reconciliations. Bonobos have a high rate of reconciliation and a low rate of violence.

De Waal suggests that among primates there are various options for resolv-ing conflicts, including avoidance, tolerance, and aggression. These options are employed at various times depending on the situation, the partner, and the stakes. According to de Waal, primate studies indicate that "aggression [is] not . . . the product of an inner drive but . . . one of the options that exists when there is a conflict of interest" (24). Ultimately, researchers may find that aggres-sive primate behavior has a genetic component; but this component does not operate in isolation, nor is it necessarily dominant. Equally natural among pri-mates are mechanisms for cooperation, conflict resolution, rechanneling of aggression, and reconciliation (de Waal 2002).

FIGURE 14.8 Are humans naturally violent or peaceful? Despite the myth of killer apes and aggressive humans, primate studies reveal that increased attraction is regularly observed between opponents after a conflict. Here, two female bonobos reconcile after a fight.

The State and War

Although genetically controlled impulses for war are hard to isolate and clearly identify, significant contemporary anthropological research has been conducted on the ways in which war and violence are complicated, learned social processes (Besteman 1996, 2002; Gusterson 1996, 2004; Farmer 2003; Lutz 2001; Ferguson 2002; Waterston 2009). Over the past one hundred years, war has become far more than waging hand-to-hand combat or pulling a trigger at close range—actions that we might associate with aggression driven by hormones. Instead, modern warfare and violence are considerably more premeditated and calculated, relying on computers, satellites, missiles, GPS tracking, and airborne drone strikes.

Today anthropologists study a highly militarized world in which violence and war seem normalized and permanent. Warfare has become the most visible of all human political institutions that reveals the state's pursuit of power. As we will see in Carolyn Nordstrom's work later in this chapter, warfare can no longer be viewed as a local military phenomenon. Indeed, modern warfare is embedded in a global system of war making. This fact pushes anthropologists to study the intersection of multiple factors that play a role in constructing warfare and violence as a reasonable means for resolving conflicts. These factors may be as disparate as economic stratification, ethnic identity formation, migration, weapons manufacturing and trade, the imbalance between weak states and strong states, and resource shortages involving oil, water, and land (Nugent and Vincent 2004).

Militarization A growing body of anthropological literature has focused on **militarization**—the contested social process through which a civil society organizes for the production of military violence (Lutz 2004; see also Geyer 1989; Bickford 2011). Catherine Lutz, an anthropologist of militarization, in *Homefront: A Military City and the American Twentieth Century* (2001), describes how the processes of militarization include not only the production of material objects such as bullets, bombs, tanks, planes, and missiles but also the glorification of war and those who make war, as states seek to shape their national histories and political culture.

Lutz warns that left unchecked, militarization threatens to shape other aspects of cultural institutions to its own ends. For example, it influences research in physics, information technology, and psychology; it affects national budget priorities; it impacts discussions and debates about gender and sexuality, race and citizenship, privacy and security; and it limits what can be discussed in the news, online, or in the classroom.

Sociologist C. Wright Mills, in his classic study *The Power Elite* (1956), warned that building an expansive military structure and the industrial capacity to support it—a military industrial complex—ultimately would lead to a "military definition of reality" in which human interactions would be seen through the logic of warfare and violence. War would become the "common sense of the nation." The central elements of this militarized thinking include cultural assumptions that defense is the first need of every organism; that human beings are naturally aggressive and territorial; that force is the primary means to get things done in the world; and that if one weapon creates security, then a thousand weapons create more security. The fact that these assumptions seem reasonable to many people in a society were evidence to Mills of the power of militarized culture to shape the way people think.

Lutz suggests that ultimately, militarization creates a kind of hegemony of thinking: It limits what is perceived as normal and natural, what can and cannot be said or done. It identifies some people as allies and others as enemies. It dehumanizes and demonizes to make hating and killing seem logical, normal, and appropriate (2004).

Constructing Soldiers, Constructing War How would you answer the following questions: Are soldiers born or made? Is it possible that if war must be constructed, soldiers must be constructed, too? In *Fallen Elites* (2011), Andrew Bickford explores the process of militarization, particularly the process by which soldiers are made—and unmade—by the state. Bickford's work sheds light on how states make soldiers in order to make war.

Bickford studied the life histories of military officers and border guards of the former East Germany who have been living in postunification Germany

FIGURE 14.9 How does popular culture glorify war and those who make war?

MAP 14.3
Germany

since the fall of the Berlin Wall in 1990. Originally stationed by the U.S. military as a soldier on the front lines in Berlin toward the end of the Cold War in 1984, Bickford returned after reunification as an anthropologist. He found himself at interviews, meals, and meetings sitting across the table from his recent enemies, some of whom readily admitted that given the opportunity, in the earlier era they would have shot and killed him without hesitation. After all, he had been a member of the U.S. military—an enemy. Now demobilized by the unified German military, however, these formerly powerful elites of the hard-line communist East German military participated in Bickford's anthropological study. How could matters of life and death have shifted so easily?

No one is born a soldier, argues Bickford. As the demobilized East German officers in Bickford's study reveal, soldiers who are made can also be unmade. Soldiers do not come prepackaged and ready to fight, kill, and die. Instead, individuals must be made into soldiers through processes of enculturation that teach them to fear, hate, and kill—processes that define particular people as the enemy, as a dangerous, mortal threat.

Because soldiers become the flesh-and-blood actors performing on behalf of the state, Bickford notes how crucial it is for the state to construct a powerful ideal of the soldier—an ideal imbued with characteristics of courage, honor, strength, and duty. This ideal becomes the preeminent symbol of the state and its power. In the process, the hero soldier comes to represent the ideal citizen who embodies the state's key values and worldview.

The construction of soldiers as model citizens happens in numerous ways. States formally honor the memory of soldiers—individuals who were fathers, grandfathers, brothers, uncles, husbands, boyfriends (and less often but no less honorable, mothers, grandmothers, sisters, aunts, wives, girlfriends). States also promote the character of soldiers, representing in mythologized language and ritual their heroic deeds in defense of the state: their service as strong and virtuous warriors, protectors, and conquerors—indeed, as powerful agents of life and death, yet also as simple men and women with a job to do to protect their families, their nation, and its way of life. Creating the ideal of the soldier, argues Bickford, is essential to the process of militarization, linking that ideal to notions of citizenship, national identity, and the honor and legitimacy of the state.

Exploring the Complex Life of Dangerous Things

Anthropologist and physician Paul Farmer suggests that to understand how deeply war and violence have become insinuated into human culture, anthropologists must trace the complicated life of "dangerous things" (Waterston 2009). Try this mental exercise: Think of an object of war—

perhaps a bullet, a gun, a landmine, a remote sensing device. Imagine its dangerous life. When it reaches the battlefield, how did it get there? Consider how it is designed, tested, manufactured, paid for, and delivered. Who sells it?

In the case of war, the dangerous object is embedded in a network of actions and decisions. Who sends soldiers into battle? Who chooses the enemy? Who provides the food, hospitals, toilets, cafeterias, and health care supplies to support the soldiers? How is intelligence gathered and surveillance conducted? How is the public convinced or required to provide funding and other support for this process?

What role do movies, video games, holidays, parades, and memorials play in creating an environment in which violence is perceived as a reasonable means to resolve conflict? How do we learn to hate certain people and not others — enough to consider firing a bullet at them?

When we carefully consider the life of a dangerous object such as a bullet, we can begin to see the complex cultural production of the act of firing a gun that goes far beyond any instinctive need to resolve conflict through violence.

FIGURE 14.10 What is the life of a dangerous thing like a rifle, a bullet, or a bomb? *Clockwise, from top left:* The Colt Defense factory in Hartford, Connecticut, makes the M16 and M4 rifles, the rifles of choice of the U.S. military. A gun poised and ready, in a refugee camp in Lebanon. The Eleventh International Defence Industry Fair, in Istanbul, Turkey, in 2013, attracted 781 companies from 82 countries.

Anthropology on the Front Lines of War and Globalization

The fact that today's world is rife with conflict presents anthropologists with many opportunities to study current cases of warfare and violence in the context of pressures from globalization. Anthropologist Carolyn Nordstrom's work exemplifies contemporary anthropological contributions to this kind of study. Nordstrom focuses on the real, messy, local experiences of violence, resistance, survival, and creativity in actual communities where war occurs, not in the comfortable offices and remote institutions of military officials and political leaders. At the same time, she turns a spotlight on the complex web of local and foreign interactions and actors that drive war and make warfare a global phenomenon.

MAP 14.4
Mozambique

In Mozambique Between 1989 and 1996, Nordstrom made multiple visits to war-torn areas of Mozambique, a southeast African country wracked by a fifteen-year civil war after independence from Portugal that claimed a million lives, mostly civilian. To reach rural and forested regions, she traveled with bush pilots making airlifts into war zones. In contrast to typical journalistic war reports, Nordstrom experienced firsthand the low-intensity conflict called "terror warfare," perpetrated by rebel guerillas and Mozambican government soldiers, that targeted the country's civilian population through military attacks, hunger, and displacement.

These destructive forces of warfare targeted the basic structures of Mozambican community life: hospitals, schools, and government offices, as well as teachers, health care professionals, religious authorities, and community leaders. By destroying and disrupting the institutions, practices, and key practitioners of local culture, the forces of violence sought to destroy the local population's political will.

In her ethnography of civil war in Mozambique, *A Different Kind of War Story* (1997), Nordstrom recounts the determined creativity that local populations employed to combat this terror and violence. In one village heavily targeted and frequently overrun by troops of both armies, most community leaders and service providers had fled as refugees to avoid potential assassination. Most resources and infrastructure had been destroyed. During the first severe attack on the village, however, one remaining health care practitioner gathered up as many medical supplies as she could carry and hid in the nearby bush until the soldiers left. Though the soldiers knew her name and searched for her, the villagers kept her secret, kept her safe. On the front lines of battle, soldiers passed through the village regularly in subsequent months. Yet the health worker remained, hiding her medical supplies, living a nomadic life on the outskirts of the area, and being protected by the villagers, who continued to carry their ailing members to her for treatment.

These actions by the health worker and the villagers are emblematic of the creativity that Nordstrom's research finds to be the most potent weapon against war—the determination to survive and resist, to continually

FIGURE 14.11 With globalization, an extensive network of individuals and industries circles the globe from one war to the next. *Clockwise, from top:* United Nations High Commissioner for Refugees workers distribute blankets to Syrian refugees along the Jordanian-Syrian border, 2012. Members of the media mark their flak jackets as gunfire rings out near the Tripoli Hotel in Lebanon, 2011. An Australian mercenary trains rebel recruits in Myanmar.

refashion and reconstruct one's self, community, and world. Nordstrom concludes her ethnography by suggesting that if, as early political philosophers such as Thomas Hobbes proposed, violence is the "natural state" of human affairs when political institutions collapse, then war-torn regions such as Mozambique should be rife with scenes of aggression, acts of self-preservation, and individual attempts at survival in a dog-eat-dog world. Instead, Nordstrom consistently found people who resisted and defeated the political violence of war by attending to the day-to-day matters of their community—sharing food, healing wounds, repairing lives, teaching children, performing rituals, exchanging friendship, rebuilding places, and creatively reconstructing the everyday patterns that constitute a meaningful life (Englund 1999; Honwana 1999; Richards 1999).

A Comparative Study In a later book, *Shadows of War* (2004), Nordstrom makes the case that standard notions of local wars fought by local actors over local issues are largely fiction. Through a comparative study of war and violence in Mozambique, Sri Lanka, South Africa, and Angola, she instead traces the extensive global networks of individuals and industries that feed and fuel local violence and war. Mercenary soldiers, foreign strategists, arms suppliers, businesspeople, black marketeers, smugglers, humanitarian relief workers, researchers, propagandists, and journalists all circle the globe, moving from one war to the next. Multitrillion-dollar international financial networks support warfare. Illegal drugs, precious gems, weapons, food supplies, military training manuals, and medicines are products moved by international networks of legitimate and illegitimate businesses and agencies that profit from the business of war.

Thanks to globalization, the business of war now operates on a worldwide scale. It influences both the architects of war, who primarily engage the battle from a distance, and the people who suffer the consequences on a war's front lines. Discussing the local people impacted by the business of war, Nordstrom notes that theirs are not the typical war stories recounted in the media. When war is portrayed only through the prism of weapons, soldiers, territory, and strategic interests won or lost, a more significant reality is ignored: the heroic efforts of people on the front lines who resist and maintain life in the face of violence and death (Finnstrom 2005).

How Do People Mobilize Power Outside the State's Control?

Systems of power, including the state, are never absolute. Their dominance is never complete. Even when a culture's dominant groups and institutions are very powerful in terms of their ability to exercise force or to establish control through hegemony, they do not completely dominate people's lives and thinking. Individuals and groups with less power or no power may still contest the established power relationships and structures through political, economic, religious, or military means and challenge and change cultural norms, values, symbols, and institutions. This power is a potential that anthropologists call **agency**.

In such displays of human agency, we see the way culture becomes the realm in which battles over power are waged; where people contest, negotiate, and enforce what is considered normal and what people can say, do, and even think. Because of human agency, cultures do not remain rigid and static. They change.

Efforts to change cultural patterns take various forms, which we will consider further. Human agency may be expressed through individual strategies of resistance, such as the "weapons of the weak" discussed in Chapter 2, collective efforts such as social movements, and alternative institutions to the state such as those based on religion.

agency: The potential power of individuals and groups to contest cultural norms, values, symbols, mental maps of reality, institutions, and structures of power.

Social Movements

Social movements are collective, group actions in response to uneven development, inequality, and injustice that seek to build institutional networks to transform cultural patterns and government policies. Social movements engage in contentious politics, usually outside the mainstream political process, to address specific social issues, although they usually do not seek to overthrow the social order. The study of social movements is interdisciplinary, engaging not only anthropologists but also sociologists, political scientists, and historians.

social movement: Collective group actions in response to uneven development, inequality, and injustice that seek to build institutional networks to transform cultural patterns and government policies.

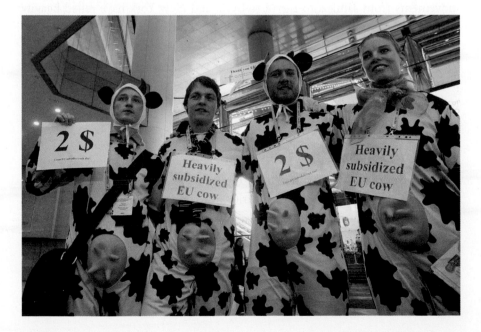

FIGURE 14.12 Activists dressed as cows protest the European Union's farm export subsidies, 2005.

Anthropological analysis of social movements emerged forcefully after the turbulent 1960s and 1970s. During that period, the developed countries of Europe and North America had experienced intense grassroots mobilization around civil rights, women's rights, the environment, gay and lesbian rights, and antiwar movements. During the same period, anticolonialist and nationalist movements and insurgencies had erupted in poorer regions of the globe (Edelman 2001).

Recently, the anthropological analysis of social movements has focused on the responses of local communities to the forces of globalization. Factors such as the worldwide movement of capital and production through flexible accumulation, the increasing migration within and across national borders, and rapidly increasing yet uneven rates of development have spurred the emergence of social movements as local communities organize to protect their land, environment, human rights, and cultural identities in a changing economic and political context. Simultaneously, time-space compression has facilitated increased communication and cooperation among individuals, social movements, and NGOs, thus creating opportunities for a "globalization from below" (Falk 1993, 39).

As part of this phenomenon, as we discussed above in terms of Hodgson's ethnography of the Maasai, actors who operate outside the formal institutions of the state and beyond the control of dominant global financial entities (such as the World Bank, the International Monetary Fund, and the World Trade Organization) utilize social media and social networking to build transnational activist networks and alliances. Through these mechanisms, their combined efforts address inequality, environmental degradation, and human rights abuses (Nash 2005; Juris 2008). Within the past several years, for example, social movements from Tunisia to Egypt to Syria and New York have relied heavily on social media to challenge political, economic, and military systems of power. (Recall, for example, the chapter-opening discussion of the Arab Spring.) In the following sections, we consider several types of social movements: rural peasants in Costa Rica, U.S. people of color who find themselves vulnerable to environmental pollution, and urban Occupy Wall Street protestors seeking greater economic egalitarianism.

Rural Social Movements In the last thirty years, rural social movements have drawn anthropologists' attention as farmers engage in creative political struggles to resist the impact of globalization on their land, livelihood, and way of life. As one example, Marc Edelman's *Peasants against Globalization* (1999) examines the activism of the rural poor in Costa Rica, Central America, during the 1980s and 1990s. Edelman recounts a story that reflects the beleaguered experience of rural agricultural workers elsewhere across the globe in recent decades.

Exploring the Balance of Power in Human Relationships

Human political engagements encompass every relationship in our lives. You don't have to be running for elected office or participating in a social movement to be involved in politics. Every relationship has a power dynamic. In some, you have power over the other person. In others, someone has power over you. Or the dynamic of power may shift back and forth depending on the circumstance.

Make a list of all the relationships and interactions you have in the course of a day: with family, friends, teachers, students, employers, coworkers, shop owners, waiters, government officials. Or watch a television show or a movie and observe the relationships of power represented there. Now describe the way power is balanced in each relationship you experience or observe. How is power organized? Can you see the intersections of age, gender, income, race, religion, sexuality, and / or citizenship? What political negotiations are present in these relationships? Consider how these political dynamics were established and how they might be changed. Must they continue indefinitely as they are?

Having gained independence from Spain in 1821, Costa Rica is one of the most politically stable countries in the Americas. By the early 1980s, Costa Ricans had built a strong, economically self-sufficient democracy and taken the radical step of abolishing the nation's military in order to invest in programs of national development. Such programs aimed to provide education, health care, tariff protections for local products, and price supports for basic foodstuffs to ensure a basic livelihood for all citizens. The programs also provided government-backed loans to farmers to stabilize agricultural production.

During the mid-1980s, however, Costa Rica was drawn into the civil wars of its neighbors, serving as a key ally of the United States on the Central American peninsula as war and upheaval spread in Nicaragua, Guatemala, and Panama. Simultaneously, a debt crisis affecting most of Latin America shook Costa Rica's economy and spurred rapid inflation. Under the auspices of providing foreign aid to an ally, the U.S.-sponsored Food for Peace program delivered massive quantities of subsidized corn, wheat, and rice—purchased from U.S. farmers—to the Costa Rican market. The subsidized food, however, undercut Costa Rican farm prices, making it increasingly difficult for local farmers to sell their own products at the price needed to break even.

Ultimately, these changes in the Costa Rican food market drove many small-scale farmers out of business, lowered the country's overall food production, and ended its history of food self-sufficiency. Structural adjustment loans offered by the International Monetary Fund and the World Bank to help Costa Rica through the crisis required the government to eliminate price

MAP 14.5
Costa Rica

FIGURE 14.13 A farmer holds a puppet of Costa Rican president Laura Chinchilla during protests in the capital, San Jose, over new property taxes on agricultural land, 2012.

supports, tariff protections, and government-backed loans while drastically reducing investments in health care and education. These measures further deepened the country's crisis.

Edelman retells the stories of local, small-scale farmers—often called peasants in the anthropological literature—and their national umbrella group, UPANACIONAL, as they fought these threats to their way of life. The peasants marched, blocked highways, and held street demonstrations. They built alliances with wealthy farmers, lobbied national politicians, and promoted charismatic activist figures into national prominence to speak on their behalf. In fact, the rural farmers that Edelman depicts challenge many traditional stereotypes of peasants. In the face of difficulties tied to both national and international policies, they reveal themselves to be worldly, outspoken, forward thinking, creative, persistent, and proud, refusing to be silenced or sidelined.

The climax of the Costa Rican peasants' collective action and direct pressure tactics came as several dozen farmers and movement leaders occupied government buildings in June 1988. At the conclusion of the standoff, the activists were arrested; however, the negotiated settlement extracted a government commitment to provide access to low-interest credit for Costa Rica's rural farmers. This was a significant victory in response to the peasants' demands. Edelman concludes that the Costa Rican peasants may not have stopped the effects of globalization on their nation's rural population, but through collective action they were able to soften the harshest blows (Gudmundson 2001; Welch 2001).

Occupy Wall Street Anthropologists seek to understand how social movements arise, mobilize, and sustain themselves. Even though conditions of inequality and injustice are widespread in many parts of the world, the activation of movements for social justice occurs in only certain situations. Anthropologists have investigated the material, human, cognitive, technical, and organizational resources necessary for social movements to succeed (McAdam, McCarthy, and Zald 1996). Recent attention has turned to the **framing process** of movements—specifically, how shared meanings and definitions arise to motivate and justify collective action.

Actions by the Occupy Wall Street movement beginning in September 2011 illustrate the role of the framing process. How did Occupy protestors capture the attention of a nation (and beyond) and build a consensus for social action? What factors led to their success? Organizers of the movement had been involved in planning well before September 2011. The financial crisis of 2008, precipitated by reckless speculation on the part of big banks and investment companies, had created an underlying instability in the U.S. economy and intensifying recriminations in the political sphere. But when protestors occupied Zuccotti Park near Wall Street in lower Manhattan on September 17, 2011, they did not have the benefit of a parallel dramatic change in the nation's economic, social, or political conditions. There were two keys to their success, both related to framing. First was the framing of the movement as simultaneously virtual and physical. And second was a framing of their cause under the banner "We Are the 99%."

Anthropologist Jeffrey Juris, who studied Occupy Boston, has examined both the core identity of the Occupy movement and the cultural and technological mechanisms that sustained its momentum. The interplay between virtual and physical forms of protest has been key. Social media drew a diverse group of people with shared concerns—in this case, over economic inequality—into shared physical spaces. Listservs, websites, and collaborative networking tools facilitated new patterns of protest that built on and resonated with more traditional forms. Social media served a key role in keeping the physical outdoor protests and occupations alive, vibrant, and relevant. In the process, not only did the physical occupations become a protest tactic, but also the "physical and communal embodiments of the virtual crowds of individuals aggregated through the viral flows of social media" (Juris 2012, 269).

Another key to Occupy's success rested on framing the movement's cause under the banner "We Are the 99%." With this simple phrase, Occupy Wall Street gradually focused public discourse on questions of the fundamental fairness of the U.S. and global economy in light of rapidly growing conditions of inequality over the past forty years that have steadily transferred wealth from 99 percent to 1 percent of the nation's population. Despite growing calls by political leaders and media critics demanding that Occupy Wall Street activists put forward specific policy proposals to address the problems they were

framing process: The creation of shared meanings and definitions that motivate and justify collective action by social movements.

Melissa Checker

Melissa Checker not only studies movements for social justice, she also participates in them. "In college I worked in organizations for low-income housing and rights for the homeless. I saw students involved in recycling and ecological awareness campaigns. But I thought environmental issues were largely a white middle-class cause. I did not consider the environment a question of social justice.

"Beginning with my research about a group of Hasidic Jewish, Latino, and African American activists in Brooklyn, New York, who successfully opposed the installation of a massive garbage incinerator in their neighborhood, I had to rethink that assumption. What has become clear to me over the years is that people of color bear a disproportionate burden of our nation's toxic waste. And I realized that any new movement for environmental justice would have to incorporate many issues: not only concern for air, water, and soil, but also for the basic community resources that people of color did not have access to."

Checker conducted fieldwork for her doctoral dissertation in a poor, rural, predominantly African American community near Augusta, Georgia. This community was struggling with the effects of decades of toxic waste dumping by local factories. The toxins were taking a terrible toll on the environment, seeping into people's homes and destroying their health. Checker published her research results in *Polluted Promises: Environmental Racism and the Search for Justice in a Southern Town* (2005), a powerful account of local activism as a community of color built a social movement to challenge the deep and troublesome connections between race and environmental pollution.

Checker volunteered at the main grassroots organization while conducting her anthropological research, working hand in hand with local community members in the hopes of giving back to the community, not simply extracting information for her dissertation. Toward the end of her book, Checker cites Martin Luther King Jr.,

who wrote from a Birmingham jail, "The passage of time alone does not bring change." Checker's account documents just such a long struggle: three decades of painstaking work by a community to improve living conditions and stop the industrial pollution of its environment. Ultimately, Checker found, stakes for the community were much higher than ridding their neighborhood of chemical contaminants. Organizers also challenged persistent and commonplace forms of racial discrimination that blamed bad health, education, and economic conditions on the victims.

Checker says she became an anthropologist because she wanted to work with people, not sit behind a desk. "In my fieldwork with activists, I don't say a lot. I hang back and listen. I think that catches them off guard. Usually as an academic or a white person, people expect you to try to tell them what to do. But anthropology trains you to be a listener, to find out from people what they want. The questions emerge from what the people are saying. This surprises people. Many researchers apply for grants or publish work without ever asking what a community wants or needs." Checker considers this attentiveness to the desires and perspectives of

Anthropologist Melissa Checker

local people a quintessential part of the anthropological toolkit.

Conducting research that engages difficult community issues is not always easy. When she finished writing her book, Checker shared the manuscript with residents. "I was taught in graduate school you should show your work to the people you work with so they see how they're represented," she explains. "It was terrifying, but I was shocked at how well it went." Not everyone was pleased, however. "I thought it was fair to also send the manuscript to the corporation the community was opposing. In response, their attorney wrote me a letter threatening me with defamation and libel. My publisher terminated my book contract and said I was on my own. With the help of an attorney I eventually found a new publisher, but the experience demonstrated the potential consequences of writing about powerful forces in this country."

Today Checker maintains close ties to members of the community. All the royalties from her book go directly to the community, which helps in a practical way. At the same time, her book has become a valuable document that community members use for telling their story. Far more than a doctoral dissertation or an ethnography of fieldwork, her book has become a tool in their struggle.

Checker has long done double duty as an academic and a freelance journalist. "I want to channel my activism by writing for different audiences. During fieldwork, announcing myself as a journalist was a way to ingratiate myself to the community. They didn't necessarily have time for me as an anthropologist, but they had time for me as a journalist. Now it's part of my commitment as an engaged anthropologist. It's helpful to my academic work to write differently for wider audiences. In journalism I find you have to be more dramatic; you have to have a hook, though I'm careful not to overstate things. However, some situations are urgent and deserve broad public attention. For instance, recently I broke a story about the history of a radioactive brownfield site using leaked documents I obtained. In my writing I try to show different perspectives on complicated problems to reach a wide audience. I think people appreciate that complexity. A field like anthropology is uniquely situated to tell ordinary people's stories. We should be able to share them with the widest possible audience."

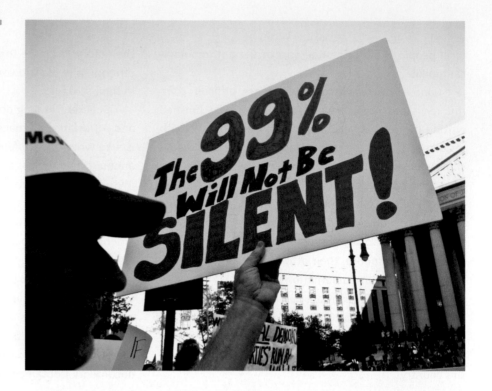

FIGURE 14.14 Occupy Wall Street protestors successfully framed the debate against corporate greed and social inequality with their motto, "We Are the 99%."

decrying, the movement steadfastly refused. Instead, its members focused on the underlying issue of inequality framed in their motto, "We Are the 99%."

Activists recognize that sustaining a consensus for action will depend not only on the underlying economic conditions and openness of the political system to change, but also on the movement's ability to continue to successfully frame its identity. However, Juris suggests that movements such as Occupy Wall Street can pursue multiple paths. While continuing to develop alternative models of democratic self-organizing that directly challenge state policies, such movements also can recognize the possibility for indirectly shaping policy debates by influencing wider political discussion. Writing in the spring of 2012, Juris noted that Occupy Wall Street had already contributed to a shift in public discourse. The framing process of Occupy has successfully highlighted growing inequality and the influence of financial and corporate interests in the economy and politics. At the same time, Occupy has functioned as a laboratory for the production of alternative forms of democracy and community (Juris 2012, 261).

Alternative Legal Structures

In addition to overt social movements and subtle, nonovert forms of resistance, it is possible to challenge structures of power in an arena where the state usually holds clear authority: in matters of the law. But how do people organize alternative legal structures outside the direct control of the modern state? What gives authority and legitimacy to alternative structures if they are not enforceable by the state's coercive power? Legal anthropologist Hussein Ali Agrama spent two years conducting ethnographic research on local courts and councils in Cairo, Egypt, to explore these questions (Agrama 2010, 2012).

Islamic Fatwa Councils in Cairo, Egypt Agrama compared the operations of two key local sources of legal authority: (1) the Personal Status courts operated by the Egyptian state and (2) the Al Azhar Fatwa Council, independently established in 1935 and one of the oldest and most established centers of Islamic authority. In the busy and crowded Personal Status courts, Egyptians of all walks of life appear before a judge, an official of the state, who makes legally binding rulings that draw on the Egyptian Constitution and legal codes that are based on the principles of Islamic Sharia (law). In the equally busy and crowded Fatwa Council, held in a spacious room located at the main entrance to the Al Azhar mosque, seekers approach Islamic legal scholars and interpreters of Islamic law, or muftis, for religious answers about matters of daily life. The muftis respond freely with legally nonbinding answers to anyone who asks. Their decision is called a fatwa—a response to a question about how to live ethically and rightly.

MAP 14.6
Cairo

In comparing these two court systems, Agrama encounters a startling dynamic. Both deal with an overlapping set of issues heavily focused on matters of marriage, sex, divorce, reconciliation, and inheritance. Both draw their decisions from Islamic Sharia, although the Personal Status courts engage Islamic law through the Egyptian Constitution and legal code, whereas the muftis refer directly to Sharia and other Islamic traditions in their fatwas. What interests Agrama is that despite these basic similarities, the petitioners' responses to the authorities' rulings are markedly different. The legally binding judgments of the Personal Status court are generally looked on with great suspicion. People go to great lengths to avoid the consequences of the court's decisions despite the state's ability to coerce obedience to its judgments. In distinct contrast, the Fatwa Council exercises great authority even though seeking decisions from the Council is not obligatory, a fatwa is not legally binding, and once issued, a fatwa does not have to be obeyed. In fact, petitioners can seek more than one fatwa on the same issue if they wish. But Agrama's research finds that petitioners take fatwas very seriously, following the decisions even if they entail great difficulty or unhappiness—this despite no identifiable institutional enforcement mechanism.

FIGURE 14.15 Fatwa council at the Al Azhar Mosque, Cairo, Egypt.

What accounts for the differentiation between Personal Status courts and the Fatwa Council? And how does a given fatwa acquire its authority without the threat of coercive force like that which the state makes available to the Personal Status courts? To understand the authority of the fatwa, Agrama explores the complex interactions and expectations between seekers of fatwas and the muftis that issue them. Contrary to popular impressions, fatwas are not merely designed to dispense points of correct doctrine in obedience to prescriptions found in Islamic Sharia. Rather, the mufti seeks to apply Islamic tradition and law to resolve particular problems, identify an effective solution, and point the seeker toward a path forward. The process includes significant perplexities and uncertainties: the fatwa seeker arrives perplexed by his or her life situation, and at least initially the mufti is uncertain about how to respond. In this context, the mufti typically begins by asking for further information in an attempt to fully understand the context and facts as presented. The fatwa seeker approaches the mufti with the hope that he will have the skills to point the way out of the trouble, to offer a way forward—to discern and speak the right words.

In the end, both seeker and mufti share a collective responsibility for the success of the fatwa: the mufti must be sure to speak the right words, and the seeker must apply them correctly. Although the consequences of an incorrect fatwa may be most damaging for the seeker during his or her lifetime, the mufti is believed to bear responsibility for the outcome in the hereafter. Ultimately, the fatwa is pronounced in order to put the questioner on the right path forward, to offer direction and facilitate a journey on which the seeker can advance within the range of doctrine toward a Muslim ideal. Agrama suggests that it is careful and personal navigation of these complexities that engenders trust and conveys legitimacy on the muftis and their fatwas.

Despite the overarching presence of the state (Ferguson and Gupta 2002) and, in this case, the explicit presence of a state-run court, individuals and communities consistently seek alternative frameworks of authority through which to organize their lives. Agrama's study of the bustling Al Azhar Fatwa Council in Cairo provides one compelling example and sheds light on local practices of the fatwa—practices that are increasingly popular within Egyptian society and the Muslim world more generally, yet are frequently misunderstood in the West.

In the opening story of the Arab Spring and in the ethnographic examples presented throughout this chapter, we have seen the remarkable diversity of strategies that humans use to exercise power through the medium of politics. Although the political upheaval in North Africa and the Middle East readily draws the focus of the world media, Agrama's work in Cairo reminds us that human political activity occurs at many different levels during the course of daily life. Whether through the politics of the state, acts of war, social movements, or small-scale resistance that James Scott labeled weapons of the weak, we have considered how anthropologists examine power and politics and the cutting edges of political activism that will continue to draw their interest in the future.

Thinking Like an Anthropologist: Applying Politics to Daily Life and Beyond

In each chapter of this book, we have investigated how human cultures construct, engage, and negotiate systems of power. We have considered the role of influential ideologies and structures of race, gender, ethnicity, class, kinship, and religion. In this chapter, we have explored how power is expressed and organized through political systems and processes. Politics exist in every human relationship and every community, large or small. People are constantly negotiating the interpersonal and institutional balances of power.

As we saw in the chapter-opening story, politics is not necessarily separate from daily life. We don't have to run for political office or start an online petition to be involved in politics. At its most basic level, politics encompasses all of the ways we organize ourselves to achieve what we most desire for our community: our family, friends, classmates, fellow citizens, and fellow inhabitants of planet Earth. As you learn to think like an anthropologist about politics and power, remember the opening questions that we have used to frame our inquiries:

- How have anthropologists viewed the origins of human political history?
- What is the state?
- How is globalization affecting the state?
- What is the relationship among politics, the state, violence, and war?
- How do people mobilize power outside the state's control?

If, as it appears, humans do not have an overwhelming and uncontrollable biological drive toward aggression and violence, then unlimited avenues open up to explore strategies for addressing problems that confront us today. These strategies include cooperatively engaging the challenging issues of our schools, communities, nations, and world and developing political responses that take into account the unique cultural dynamics of local communities and specific groups.

As a new generation of social activists around the globe develops social networking and social media strategies for expressing their concerns and attempting to influence the systems of power and politics, the networked nature of these movements also means that you, as a college student, have every possibility of becoming an anthropologist who engages the world.

Key Terms

band (p. 535)

tribe (p. 538)

chiefdom (p. 538)

state (p. 542)

hegemony (p. 544)

civil society organization (p. 546)

militarization (p. 552)

agency (p. 559)

social movement (p. 559)

framing process (p. 563)

For Further Exploration

Checker, Melissa. 2005. *Polluted Promises: Environmental Racism and the Search for Justice in a Southern Town*. New York: NYU Press.

How to Start a Revolution. 2011. Directed by Ruaridh Arrow. www.howtostartarevolutionfilm.com. Featuring Gene Sharp and his impact on social movements and uprisings around the world.

Nordstrom, Carolyn. 2004. *Shadows of War: Violence, Power, and International Profiteering in the Twenty-First Century*. Berkeley: University of California Press.

Sharp, Gene. 1993. *From Dictatorship to Democracy: A Conceptual Framework for Liberation*. East Boston, MA: Albert Einstein Institution. Nearly two hundred methods of nonviolent resistance from rude gestures to mock funerals.

Ury, William. 2002. *Must We Fight? From the Battlefield to the Schoolyard, a New Perspective on Violent Conflict and Its Prevention*. San Francisco: Jossey-Bass.

What is religion? Buddhist monks march through the streets of Yangon, Myanmar, in 2007 to protest actions of the military government.

p. 579

p. 583

p. 587

p. 589

p. 599

p. 608

CHAPTER 15
Religion

In September 2007 thousands of barefoot, saffron-robed Buddhist monks marched through the streets of Yangon (Rangoon), the capital of Myanmar, leading dramatic demonstrations to protest the repressive policies and abusive practices of Myanmar's military government. A surprise decision to increase fuel prices by as much as 500 percent had sent the cost of everything (from rice and eggs to cooking oil and transportation) skyrocketing—and this in a country where the average annual income is less than $300. Students and workers had launched the earliest protests, but government forces quickly cracked down, searching homes, detaining demonstrators, and arresting movement organizers.

With resistance largely beaten down, dynamics across the country changed when government riot police shot at and beat several monks during protests north of the capital. Suddenly monks took to the streets everywhere. Because Myanmar's 400,000 Buddhist monks and 75,000 Buddhist nuns are deeply revered, both by civilians and by the military, the arousing of this religious network reignited popular demonstrations. Within weeks thousands of silent monks marched in procession for miles through the streets of Yangon. Cheering crowds created a protective cordon on either side of them, offering water, food, and physical protection as they faced off with government forces.

In one of the most dramatic moments of the demonstrations, one monk marching at the front of the procession held his black wooden begging bowl upside down as the group paraded in front of government military forces. Almsgiving is a religious obligation for Buddhists. In this primarily Buddhist country, giving alms—including food—to Buddhist monks, which they receive daily in their black begging bowls, is one of the most profound acts of religious ritual. By turning over their bowls, the monks symbolically refused to receive alms from the authorities, the military, and their supporters. With this simple gesture they matched their street demonstration with a religious boycott, effectively excommunicating their opponents from the practice of their faith.

Religion plays a central role in human life and human culture. Through the study of religion, anthropologists engage some of the deepest, most difficult, and most enduring human questions—about meaning, difference, power, love, sexuality, mortality, morality, human origins, and kinship. Religion has been a central interest of anthropologists since the beginning of our field. Research about religious beliefs and practices worldwide has explored an amazing diversity of symbols, rituals, myths, institutions, religious experts, groups, deities, and supernatural forces. As you read about diverse religions in this chapter, some beliefs and practices may seem quite familiar. Others may be surprising or unexpected. Many might stretch your basic assumptions of what religion is and does. For example, does the idea of ten thousand Buddhist monks leading protest marches seem strange to you?

Religion offers a rich vein of material for exploring the complexity of human culture, including systems of belief and systems of power. It is perhaps the hottest topic in the world today as globalization brings different traditions, beliefs, and practices into contact. In the United States, immigration over the past five decades has transformed the religious landscape (Figure 15.1). Temples, mosques, gurdwaras, and retreat centers now join churches and synagogues in small towns and big cities across the country. College campuses, too, reflect an expanding religious diversity. As people of different religious traditions encounter one another in neighborhoods, schools, and other public institutions, lively debates take place about education, zoning, health care, public security, and civil rights. These encounters create the potential for tension and misunderstanding on school boards, zoning committees, and town and city councils, as well as in civic associations and even college classrooms. But they also offer opportunities for interfaith encounters, learning, and engagement. An anthropological understanding of religion can help you to navigate and engage this changing landscape.

In this chapter, we will consider the anthropological approach to understanding the many groups, beliefs, and practices that are called religion. In particular, we will examine the following questions:

- What is religion?
- What tools do anthropologists use to understand how religion works?
- In what ways is religion both a system of meaning and a system of power?
- How is globalization changing religion?

FIGURE 15.1 Religion in the United States

Extensive public polling in the United States reveals shifts in religious demographics in response to globalization and immigration patterns. In particular, the United States is experiencing a decline in the total percentage of Protestant Christians that parallels a growth in Catholic Christians from Latin America; Muslims from the Middle East, South Asia, and Africa; Orthodox Christians from Eastern Europe and the Middle East; Hindus from India; and Buddhists from China, Southeast Asia, and East Asia.

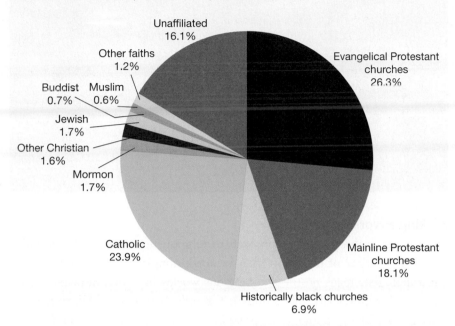

SOURCE: *Pew Forum on Religion & Public Life. 2008. http://religions.pewforum.org/reports/.*

By the end of the chapter, you will be able to investigate and analyze religion using the tools of an anthropologist. You will be better able to understand religion in your own life, in the growing religious pluralism of the United States, and in diverse religious expressions around the world. These skills will be increasingly valuable tools for living and working in the twenty-first century.

What Is Religion?

When anthropologists talk about "religion," what are we really talking about? Since the beginning of the discipline, anthropologists have been attempting to create a universal definition that might apply to all religions' local manifestations. But the vast global diversity of unique local expressions makes defining religion a difficult task. Is there something present in all cultures that we can call religion?

FIGURE 15.2 What is religion? At the 600-year-old Prasanna Ganapathy Temple in Bangalore, India, a Hindu priest performs ritual blessings of new cars, auto rickshaws, and motorbikes to bestow divine protections on car and owner.

Seeking a Working Definition

The unique anthropological approach to religion begins with the everyday religious practices of people in their local communities. Through fieldwork, anthropologists focus on the real religious worlds in which humans experience religion physically and express it through their actions. We may study a religion's history, theology, scriptures, and major figures, but we do so to understand their meaning and significance in the life of a community of people. Religion is not theoretical in people's daily activities. People make sense of the world, reach decisions, and organize their lives on the basis of their religious beliefs. Starting from these beginning principles, anthropologists also explore the myriad ways religion intersects with other systems of power, whether economics, politics, race, gender, or sexuality. And we explore how local religious expressions may be connected to larger religious movements or institutions.

Anthropologists have compiled a vast and diverse set of data on religious beliefs and practices worldwide. But are there any common characteristics that apply in every situation? In general, we find that all local expressions of religion combine some, but not necessarily all, of the following elements:

- Belief in powers or deities whose abilities transcend those of the natural world and cannot be measured by scientific tools.
- Myths and stories that reflect on the meaning and purpose of life, its origins, and humans' place in the universe.

- Ritual activities that reinforce, recall, instill, and explore collective beliefs.
- Powerful symbols, often used in religious rituals, that represent key aspects of the religion for its followers.
- Specialists who assist the average believer to bridge everyday life experiences and the religion's ideals and supernatural aspects.
- Organizations and institutions that preserve, explore, teach, and implement the religion's key beliefs.
- A community of believers.

As a working definition, we might then say that a **religion** is a set of beliefs based on a unique vision of how the world ought to be, often revealed through insights into a supernatural power, and lived out in community. (For an overview of the distribution of adherents to major world religions today, see Figure 15.3. Considering the range of religions shown there, perhaps you can begin to imagine the challenge inherent in creating a working definition to cover such a broad spectrum.)

As social scientists, anthropologists have largely been uninterested in questions of any religion's ultimate truth or falsity. Instead, we understand that religious worlds are real, meaningful, and powerful to those who live in them. Our task is to carefully make those worlds come alive for others by capturing their vivid inner life, sense of moral order, dynamic public expressions, and

religion: A set of beliefs based on a unique vision of how the world ought to be, often revealed through insights into a supernatural power and lived out in community.

FIGURE 15.3 Religion in Global Perspective
This chart shows estimated relative distribution of adherents to the major world religions. It is worth noting, however, that few countries collect data on religious beliefs and practices and, as we will discuss, local religious expressions may not neatly fit these categories.

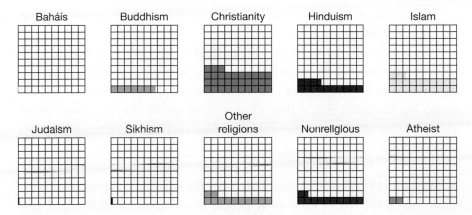

SOURCE: *Adherents.com. 2012. www.adherents.com/Religions_By_Adherents.html.*

interactions with other systems of meaning and power—whether those religious expressions occur in a remote Chinese village temple or the most famous Catholic cathedral in Rome (Bowie 2006).

Local Expressions and Universal Definitions

Attention to local religious expressions complicates anthropologists' efforts to create a universal definition of religion. In a religious studies course, you would likely use a textbook that allocates one chapter for each of the largest world religions, including Christianity, Islam, Hinduism, Buddhism, Chinese religion, Sikhism, Judaism, and others. Each chapter might include an overview of the religion's history, theology, scriptures, major figures, and formal institutions. Under such an approach, drawing broad comparisons among the major religions can prove helpful in providing a general picture of the world's most established religious traditions and in understanding each religion's ideal expression. At the same time, it may obscure the creative and flexible ways people actually practice their religion that may diverge from the ideal.

Indeed, local expressions and creative adaptations are often at the heart of anthropological research because they reveal how people make a religious tradition come alive in their own context. Let's consider Islam for a moment. Muslims and non-Muslims alike generally regard Islam as highly uniform wherever it is practiced—as a religion that would consistently manifest its core characteristics and definition regardless of location. For example, all Muslims are expected to follow the Five Pillars of Islam: making a declaration of faith, saying prayers five times a day, performing acts of charity, fasting during the holy month of Ramadan, and undertaking a pilgrimage to Mecca. In addition, all Muslims revere the authority of the Quran and the Prophet Muhammad. But on the local level, Muslims frequently expand these formal borders and develop modes of popular expression that may include distinctive devotional practices, life-cycle rituals, marriage customs, ritual clothing, and forms of veiling.

Awareness of the ways in which Muslim life and religious practice vary locally can offer an important insight to an anthropologist conducting research or to anyone seeking to build relationships across religious boundaries. The examples that follow illustrate the possibilities for local variation within a religious tradition that is often assumed to be universal in its expressions.

A Muslim Saint Shrine Across India, certain popular expressions of Islam push the boundaries of what many people would consider traditional Islam. One example is Husain Tekri, a Muslim saint shrine, or *dargah*, named in

FIGURE 15.4 Hindu and Muslim pilgrims at the Husain Tekri shrine in northern India breathe in incense to access the healing powers of the shrine.

memory of the martyred grandson of the Prophet Muhammad. (A **martyr** is a person who sacrifices his or her life for the sake of his or her religion.) Pilgrims from across northern India come to this shrine to remember Husain Tekri, to venerate the Muslim saints, and to participate in healing rituals. (A **saint** is an individual considered exceptionally close to God who is then exalted after death.) Husain Tekri is part of the religious healing circuit of northern India along which both Hindu and Muslim pilgrims travel as they seek the saint or deity with the specific power to cure their ills.

Pilgrims to Husain Tekri may stay for a day or settle in nearby lodges and remain for days, months, or a year. They come in search of healing from suffering, illness, and financial ruin, and relief from the presence of evil spirits (*haziri*). The main daily ritual activity is the burning and distribution of *loban*—rock-like chunks of incense sold at the shrine and thrown onto red-hot coals eight times a day. As the white smoke of *loban* billows from the braziers, pilgrims—both men and women —are engulfed in the cloud, breathe in the smoke, symbolically consume the *loban,* and absorb its potency. Through pilgrimage and the ritual consumption of *loban*, pilgrims access the healing powers of the shrine. There, they believe, the power and mercy of the martyred Husain and his family enable them to escape their sick bodies, their mental anguish, and the malevolent spirits possessing them.

martyr: A person who sacrifices his or her life for the sake of religion.

saint: An individual who is considered exceptionally close to God and is exalted after death.

Surprisingly, pilgrims to the shrine of Husain Tekri are of many religious backgrounds, not only Muslim but also Hindu, Sikh, and Jain. Seeking healing across religious lines is actually a common occurrence in many parts of India, as pilgrims of various faiths try multiple religious systems to find the most successful means of healing, especially for illnesses beyond the powers of mainstream medicine (Bellamy 2011).

Amma's Healing Room Also in India, another local practice involves the healing powers of just one individual: a woman named Amma. In a small courtyard in the southern Indian city of Hyderabad, this Muslim healer meets forty or fifty patients a day. They come to her for healing from all manner of mental, spiritual, and physical illnesses brought on by evil spirits and forces.

As at the saint shrine of Husain Tekri, people of many faiths come to Amma—Hindus, Muslims, even a few Christians, directed by word of mouth or drawn to her healing room by the green flag of a saint shrine flying above the courtyard. They come to be cured of illnesses that seem beyond the power of their medical doctors or that require treatments beyond their financial means. At a low table in her healing room, surrounded by dozens of patients and disciples, Amma listens to each patient's problems and writes healing charms and remedies (such as verses from the Quran, numbers, or names of God) on an amulet, often a small fabric pouch or metal box hung on the right upper arm or around the neck for spiritual protection.

Amma's healing room crosses seemingly rigid boundaries of religious categories. In one sense, it does so in terms of the ease and comfort with which

FIGURE 15.5 Amma (*right*), a Muslim healer, in Hyderabad, India, writes out charms and remedies at her healing table for pilgrims afflicted by mental, spiritual, and physical illnesses.

practitioners of various faiths seek healing in the same place. In another sense, it does so because a female Muslim healer takes a position of spiritual leadership that in Islam would usually be reserved for men (Flueckiger 2006).

The examples above suggest that what are often considered clearly defined, universally uniform, and consistent world religions actually can be flexible and innovative at the local level. Certainly the pilgrims of Husain Tekri and the visitors to Amma's healing room consider their practices to be mainstream local religious activity. From an anthropological perspective, such local expressions of religion are no less complete, meaningful, or true than those taught in the most elite Muslim madrassa, Buddhist monastery, or Christian school of theology.

What Tools Do Anthropologists Use to Understand How Religion Works?

Anthropologists have developed a set of key insights about how religion works that serve as a toolkit for understanding religion as we experience it in our fieldwork. These concepts may prove useful to you in thinking about religion in your own life and in your community, nation, and the world.

Anthropological theories of religion have been deeply influenced by the ideas of nineteenth- and twentieth-century philosophers Émile Durkheim, Karl Marx, and Max Weber. All three examined the connection between religion and the political and economic upheavals of their time: an Industrial Revolution that spurred massive shifts in land relationships throughout western Europe; large-scale rural to urban migration; and high levels of unemployment, poverty, and disease. Through their writing, Durkheim, Marx, and Weber reshaped the study of religion, moving from the theological and cosmological orientation that dominated pre-twentieth-century European and North American thinking to focus on the role of religion in society. These thinkers inspired generations of anthropologists who have expanded and refined their theories.

Émile Durkheim: The Sacred and the Profane

Émile Durkheim (1858–1917) was a French sociologist who explored ideas of the **sacred** (holy) and the **profane** (unholy), as well as the practical effects of religious **ritual**. His work in these areas has provided key analytical tools for social scientists seeking to understand common elements in different religious movements and the practical application of religious ideas in the social life of religious adherents.

sacred: Anything that is considered holy.

profane: Anything that is considered not holy.

ritual: An act or series of acts regularly repeated over years or generations that embody the beliefs of a group of people and create a sense of continuity and belonging.

Developing the notion of a fundamental dichotomy between sacred and profane, Durkheim defined religion as "a unified system of beliefs and practices relative to sacred things, that is to say, things set apart and forbidden—beliefs and practices which unite into one single moral community called a Church, all those who adhere to them" ([1912] 1965, 62). Durkheim saw religion as ultimately social—something practiced with others—not private or individual. Through the collective action of religious ritual, group members reaffirm, clarify, and define for one another what is sacred and what is profane. Durkheim's famous study *Elementary Forms of Religious Life* (1912) examined the religious beliefs and practices of Australian aborigines (the indigenous population), which he and others believed to be the most primitive culture of the time and, thus, closest to religion's original forms. The aboriginal "elementary" religious beliefs and practices, he believed, could reveal the most basic elements of religions and shed light on religion's evolution into present forms.

As western European societies experienced radical transformations in the late nineteenth and early twentieth centuries, Durkheim turned to the rising problem of *anomie*—an alienation that individuals experience when faced with physical dislocation and the disruption of social networks and group values. He wondered how society would overcome this crisis and reestablish its essential cohesion. Durkheim argued that religion, particularly religious ritual, plays a crucial role in combating anomie and addressing larger social dynamics of alienation and dislocation by creating social solidarity, cohesion, and stability. He saw religion as the glue that holds together society's many different pieces. Through ritual, Durkheim believed, society is able to regenerate its sense of social solidarity. Ritual defines and reinforces collective ideas of the sacred and profane. Thus, through ritual, the community's sense of cosmic order is reaffirmed, its social solidarity is regenerated, and the group's continued survival and growth are ensured.

Durkheim's work has influenced many anthropologists who have explored the role of ritual in religions and in the wider society. As we will see, the focus on how religion is lived out daily and enacted through ritual has become a cornerstone of the anthropological approach to the study of religion.

Religion and Ritual

Anthropologists of religion have paid particular attention to the role of ritual. Through attention to its central role in religion, anthropologists are aware that religion is not so much talked about as it is *performed* in public displays, rites, and rituals; not so much thought about as it is *danced* and *sung*. Rituals embody the beliefs, passions, and sense of solidarity of a group of people. They make beliefs come alive. When performed repeatedly over years and generations, rituals, as Durkheim suggested, create a sense of continuity and belonging that defines a group and regenerates its sense of solidarity, history, purpose, and meaning.

Rites of Passage French ethnographer and folklorist Arnold van Gennep (1873–1957) first theorized a category of ritual called **rites of passage** that enacts a change of status from one life stage to another, either for an individual or for a group (van Gennep [1908] 1960). Religious rites of passage are life-transition rituals marking moments of intense change, such as birth, coming of age, marriage, and death.

Audrey Richards (1899–1984), a pioneering British woman in early male-dominated British anthropology, observed and recorded one such rite of passage in 1931 among the Bemba people of Zambia, Central Africa. Their elaborate ritual, called the *chisungu*—a coming-of-age ceremony for young teenage women after first menstruation and in preparation for marriage—was danced in eighteen separate ceremonies over one month in a ritual hut and the surrounding bush. Over fifty special *chisungu* songs and forty different pottery emblems were involved. The *chisungu*, exclusively a women's ritual, was performed to provide magical protection to the girl and her family from the physical dangers of puberty and the magical dangers associated with the first act of intercourse in legal marriage. Within the rituals, older women also passed down the songs, sacred stories, sacred teachings, and secret lore of the Bemba womanhood, marking a clear change of status within the tribe from girl to woman (Richards 1956).

Victor Turner (1920–1983) built on Richards's pioneering work to explore why rituals and rites of passage are so powerful across religions and cultures. Drawing on his own research in Africa and on extensive comparison of cross-cultural data, Turner theorized that the power of ritual comes from the drama contained within it, in which the normal structure of social life is symbolically

rite of passage: A category of ritual that enacts a change of status from one life stage to another, either for an individual or a group.

MAP 15.1
Zambia

FIGURE 15.7 *Left,* anthropologist Audrey Richards at work in Zambia, ca. 1931. *Right,* girls kneeling during the *chisungu,* a coming-of-age initiation ceremony among the Bemba people of Zambia. Have you experienced a coming-of-age ritual or other rite of passage?

dissolved and reconstituted. He identified three primary stages in all rites of passage. First, the individual experiences *separation*—physically, psychologically, or symbolically—from the normal, day-to-day activities of the group. This may involve going to a special ritual place, wearing special clothing, or performing actions such as shaving one's head. The second stage, **liminality**, involves a period of outsiderhood during which the ritual participant is set apart from normal society, existing on the margins of everyday life. From this position the individual can gain a new perspective on the past, the present, or the future and thereby experience a new relationship to the community. The final ritual stage, *reaggregation* or *reincorporation*, returns the individual to everyday life and reintegrates him or her into the ritual community, transformed by the experience of liminality and endowed with a deeper sense of meaning, purpose, and connection to the larger group (Turner 1969).

Turner believed that all humans experience these rites of passage and that the experiences shape their perceptions of themselves and their community. Through them, he asserted, humans develop **communitas**: a sense of camaraderie, a common vision of what constitutes the good life, and perhaps most important, a commitment to take social action to move toward achieving this vision. Turner felt that the universal practice and experience of ritual reveals at the root of human existence an underlying desire for community and connection. Based on his cross-cultural investigation of the practice of rituals and rites of passage, Turner suggested that at the center of all human relationships there is a deep longing for shared meaning and connection, not a desire for self-preservation or material gain.

Have you experienced a rite of passage such as van Gennep, Richards, and Turner describe? Perhaps you have traversed these ritual stages of separation, liminality, and reincorporation at some point in your life—at a coming-of-age ceremony in your own religious tradition, or at a wedding or funeral. If so, can you recall the feeling as you put aside the mundane rhythms of everyday life, entered a liminal space set apart from normal society (perhaps in a church, synagogue, mosque, temple, gurdwara, wedding hall, or funeral parlor set aside for sacred rituals), and then reentered the regular flow of the world with a new outlook or thinking a bit more deeply about the meaning of life? Perhaps, then, you also have an idea of the sense of communitas that Turner suggests emerges from these common experiences that all humans share at some point in their lives.

Pilgrimage Turner applied his thinking about rites of passage to the study of religious pilgrimage, which he considered to be a unique form of religious ritual. Pilgrimage rituals, like those to Muslim saint shrines in northern India discussed previously, exist in religions around the world. In a **pilgrimage**, adherents travel to sacred places as a sign of devotion and in search of transformation and

liminality: One stage in a rite of passage during which a ritual participant experiences a period of outsiderhood, set apart from normal society, that is key to achieving a new perspective on the past, future, and current community.

communitas: A sense of camaraderie, a common vision of what constitutes a good life, and a commitment to take social action to move toward achieving this vision that is shaped by the common experience of rites of passage.

pilgrimage: A religious journey to a sacred place as a sign of devotion and in search of transformation and enlightenment.

enlightenment. For example, all Muslims are obliged to perform, if life circumstances allow, the *hajj* pilgrimage to Mecca. Jews, Christians, and Muslims all
have pilgrimage sites in Jerusalem. Many Hindus travel to the holy city of Vara-
nasi (Benares) to bathe in the Ganges River. Daoists climb Mount Tai in eastern
China. The pilgrimage journey, Turner suggested, involves the same process of
separation, liminality, and reincorporation associated with other rites of passage.
Similarly, pilgrimage creates a shared sense of communitas among those who
undertake the journey, even if years or entire generations separate the pilgrimages.

For Turner, life in society is a process of becoming, not being; it is a process of change. He maintained that rituals, pilgrimages, celebrations, and even
theatrical performances facilitate this process and have the potential to initiate and foster change, not only in the individual but in the larger culture as
well (1969).

"The Abominations of Leviticus" The British anthropologist Mary Douglas (1921–2007), like Richards and Turner, began her studies of ritual in Africa.
Subsequently, she applied her insights to Western cultures by drawing parallels

between the ceremonies and ritual practices of African cultures and those of Christianity and Judaism. In *Purity and Danger* (1966), Douglas explored the ways that Durkheim's notions of sacred and profane—for Douglas, purity and danger—are deeply embedded in Western traditions.

In a famous chapter called "The Abominations of Leviticus," she examined the ritual practices of Jewish dietary laws. She approached this study with the following questions: Why are some animals considered clean and others unclean in God's eyes, according to the Book of Leviticus in the Hebrew scriptures? Do these practices reflect medical concerns about eating pork that might be infected by trichinosis? Do they reflect ethical guidelines about the treatment of animals? Are they arbitrary religious prescriptions? After concluding her study, Douglas argued instead that these codes reflect a deep-seated desire for order in the midst of the social chaos that confronted the Hebrew people of that time.

Historically, in the period when the dietary codes were written, the Hebrew people struggled with their return from captivity and exile. The codes helped define the community and make clear who was a Jew and who was not. In this way, they protected the community from the dangers of foreign influence. How could they create order out of chaos? And how could they keep God's commandments constantly in mind? The dietary laws, Douglas suggested, are a command to be holy. Thus, they became a metaphor of holiness. Keeping the dietary laws daily became a ritualized meditation—a reminder of the holiness of God, who is always present in their lives.

Douglas maintained that keeping the Jewish dietary laws plays the same role today. The ritual rules of dietary discipline serve as a regular reminder of who God is and who the individual is in relationship to God. These rituals are a kind of meditative practice that regularizes moments of liminality in the course of daily life. Are there similar practices or requirements in your religious tradition that serve as a reminder, a command to be holy? Do you observe religious dietary restrictions? Do you wear certain clothes or jewelry? Do you wear a cross or a bindi or a hijab? Do you style your hair in a certain way? Are you called to daily prayer during the day or at night? Do you say a prayer before meals? If you answer yes to any of these questions, perhaps you can personally assess Douglas's insights. And perhaps you have a sense of the power that ritual action can hold in a person's or a group's daily life.

Karl Marx: Religion as "the Opiate of the Masses"

Karl Marx (1818–1881) was a German political philosopher. He is primarily known for his *Communist Manifesto* (1848) and *Capital* (1867), a radical critique of capitalist economics emerging in western Europe in the nineteenth century (see Chapter 11). However, Marx was also highly critical of the role of religion in society, famously calling religion "the opiate of the masses" (Marx and Engels 1957). What did he mean?

In a time of economic upheaval and intensifying social stratification, Marx warned that religion was like a narcotic: it dulled people's pain so they did not realize how serious the situation was. Religion, Marx argued, played a key role in keeping the proletariat—the working poor—from engaging in the revolutionary social change that he believed was needed to improve their situation.

Marx's statement that religion is "the opiate of the masses" fits within his larger social analysis. He believed that throughout human history, economic realities have formed the foundation of social life and have generated society's primary dynamics, including class stratification and class struggle. He called this economic reality the "base." In his view, the other institutions of culture (including family, government, arts, and religion) arise from and are shaped by economic reality and the deep tensions of economic inequality and class struggle.

FIGURE 15.9 German political philosopher Karl Marx.

The role of these institutions, including religion, according to Marx, is to mask the material conditions and exploitation at the economic base and to contain—or provide a controlled release for—the tensions generated by class difference and class conflict. Religion, which Marx also called "the sigh of the oppressed," could provide to the downtrodden a sense of consolation that the sufferings of this life would end and be rewarded in heaven, thereby offering divine justification for the economic status quo. In Marx's view, religion provided an opiate—a painkiller—to undermine the masses' impulses to resist exploitation and change the social order.

Marx's overall focus on economics and power has pushed anthropologists to consider the relationship between religion and power. Contemporary studies move beyond Marx's idea that religion is merely an illusion that blinds people to economic realities. Studies like those of Robin Root (2009) and Charlene Floyd (1996) (considered later in this chapter), while not drawing directly on Marxist theory, examine how religion can play a complex role in systems of power—both by exercising power through economic resources and the mobilization of religious personnel, and by resisting systems of oppression through alternative ideas, symbols, and resources. The role of the Burmese monks in the chapter-opening story is relevant in this context. As they brought the city of Yangon to a stop in support of human rights activists, they revealed the way religion can exercise its more material power and be a positive force for change in the underlying economic and political order.

Religion and Cultural Materialism Anthropologist Marvin Harris (1927–2001) built on Marx's analysis of the base, or infrastructure, and the way in which the material conditions of a society shape its other components. Harris's

MAP 15.2
India

theory of **cultural materialism** argued that material conditions, including technology and the environment, determine patterns of social organization. In this view, human culture is a response to the practical problems of earthly existence. In *Cows, Pigs, Wars, & Witches* (1974), Harris turned this perspective toward many perplexing questions of why humans behave in certain ways—including why Hindus venerate the cow, Jews and Muslims abstain from eating pork, and some people believe in witches. Harris proposed that these practices might have developed in response to very practical problems as people sought to adapt to the natural environment.

Have you ever wondered why cows are considered sacred in India? Harris approached this question not through personal immersion in the worldviews of Indian Hindus, but rather by exploring larger environmental forces—the cultural ecology—that might promote this cultural practice. If you visit India you will find zebu cows—a scrawny, large-humped cattle species found in Africa and Asia—wandering freely about city streets and rural areas. These cows randomly eat food from market stalls, graze on sidewalk shrubs, and defecate indiscriminately. In a country with deep pockets of poverty and malnutrition, why are these cows left to roam and not slaughtered for nutritious, protein-rich dinner beefsteak?

Eating beef is prohibited in Hinduism, as is eating all meat. The cow, in Harris's view, became a symbolic representation of *ahimsa*—the practice of nonviolence and respect for the unity of all life that is key to Hinduism, Buddhism, and Jainism. How this tradition began is unclear, but today the holy mother cow is a symbol of health and abundance, and its image appears throughout Indian culture in media such as posters, movies, and carvings. The symbol also has a literal presence on streets and in fields.

Harris suggests that religious prohibitions protecting the cow have overwhelming practical applications in a culture that relies on agricultural production. Cows, after all, produce calves that grow up to be oxen, which Harris calls the tractor, thresher, and family car of the Indian agricultural system. Without an ox, a family has no way of planting, harvesting, preparing, or transporting its crops. Without an ox, a family loses the capacity to farm and eventually loses its land. Cows also produce vast quantities of dung, almost all of which can be recycled into fertilizer and cooking fuel. Religious dedication to *ahimsa* protects this resource even under the most difficult economic conditions. No matter how hungry the family may be in one season, keeping the cow alive ensures long-term survival.

For Harris, religiously based practices that appear to function in opposition to sound nutritional practices or economic development strategies may in fact be very rational cultural adaptations to the surrounding ecology. In India, the cow is extraordinarily useful. Its protection, especially during difficult economic times, may be essential to the long-term stability and survival of the Indian people and culture.

Think about any other religion, perhaps one you already have an affiliation with. Can you apply the perspectives of Marvin Harris's cultural materialism to any of its practices and beliefs? Can you begin to imagine how certain material conditions of everyday life may have shaped patterns of religious belief and practice?

Max Weber: The Protestant Ethic and Secularization

Max Weber (1864–1920), a German sociologist, philosopher, and economist, considered religious ideas to be a key for understanding the unique development of societies worldwide and the rise of industrial capitalism, particularly in western Europe. Why, he asked, did this highly rationalized, systematized, and industrial form of capitalism emerge in Europe and not in another part of the world?

Unlike Marx, who considered that economics ultimately shapes society, Weber believed that ideas, including religious ideas, can be equally powerful. His book *Sociology of Religion* (1920) was the first sociological attempt to compare the world's religions. In it, Weber suggested that Asian religious beliefs and ethical systems had stood in the way of capitalist economic growth

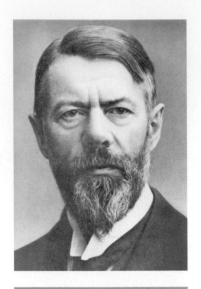

FIGURE 15.11 German sociologist and philosopher Max Weber.

there and had kept Asian economies from developing along the western European path. China, India, and other cultures had developed aspects of modern capitalism even earlier than western Europe did; but without a certain kind of ideological support, a more advanced capitalism had not evolved in Asia. Weber suggested that economic innovations alone could not explain the different paths.

In *The Protestant Ethic and the Spirit of Capitalism* (1905), Weber suggested that the ascetic values of self-denial and self-discipline that developed in western European Protestantism provided the ethic that was necessary for capitalism to flourish. Certain Protestant sects, including Calvinists, felt that it was important to express their religious beliefs and values in a daily lifestyle of thrift, discipline, and hard work. In these ideas, Weber found evidence of the ethical and psychological framework necessary for the success of industrial capitalism. He did not dismiss the role of economics in shaping the social dynamics of western Europe, but he argued that ideas, including religious ideas, may at times equally influence the economic direction of a society.

Also key to the development of Western capitalism, according to Weber, was an increasing systematization and rationalization of religious ideas. As Western Christianity evolved, this increasing rationality brought a decline of practices based on tradition, ritual, and magic. Weber saw these developments echoed in society at large: rationalization led to bureaucracies with clear, intellectual, and systematized rules that replaced tradition, sentiment, and charisma as the operating system in social institutions. Weber imagined an evolution of rationalization in religion that led from (1) traditional religion based on magic and led by shamans; to (2) charismatic religion based on the persuasive power of prophets such as Buddha, Jesus, and Moses; and, finally, to (3) rational religion based on legal codes of conduct, bureaucratic structures, and formally trained religious leaders. He anticipated that this evolutionary process would be almost inevitable. But he warned that as society became more rationalized, it also risked becoming more secular—less religious—and thus losing the very spirit that had driven its success and development.

Scholars have debated Weber's secularization thesis for many years (Stark 1985; Asad 1993; Casanova 1994; Berger 1999). Certainly in Western Europe today, religious identification among native-born residents continues to sink to record lows. In contrast, the United States stands as a striking exception to this pattern in industrialized countries, as religious beliefs and practices remain strong in both the native-born and the immigrant populations. Polls consistently show that nearly 90 percent of the U.S. population believe in God and more than 80 percent identify with a particular religion (Pew Forum on Religion & Public Life 2012). Even the assumed separation of church and state in the United States is far from absolute. Battles continue over the teaching of evolution in the science curriculums of public schools, fans at public high school football games in Texas rise to recite in unison the Christian Lord's Prayer, and crowds at New York's Yankee Stadium stand during the seventh-inning stretch for a moment of silence to remember those serving in the U.S. military and then sing "God Bless America." In these instances, religious sentiments infuse public and political life, and public rituals of civil society take on sacred status (Bellah 1980).

Moreover, widespread revivals of religious ideas, organizations, and movements around the world in the face of increasing modernization—and at times in resistance to the homogenizing influences of globalization and Western culture—provide additional evidence that modernization does not always lead to secularization. The rise of fundamentalist movements in Islam, Hinduism, and Christianity, for instance, suggest that Weber's secularization theory may have limited predictive value.

Shamanism

As we saw above, Weber considered the first stage in the evolution of rationalization in religion to involve traditional religion led by shamans. Indeed, more formal religious organizations with trained specialists and elaborate moral rules and ritual practices are fairly recent in human history, spanning two to three thousand years at most with the rise of Hinduism, Buddhism, Judaism, Christianity, and Islam. Throughout much of human history, the religious needs of human communities have been served by **shamans**—part-time religious practitioners with special abilities to connect individuals with supernatural powers or beings. The term *shaman* derives from the name given to healing specialists among the seminomadic people of Siberia, but it has since been applied to healers, spiritualists, witches, and witch doctors in cultures worldwide.

Shamans live as part of the local community, participating in daily activities and work, but are called on at times to perform special rituals and ceremonies. They often gain their powers through special training or experience, passing through a journey or test of spirit such as illness, isolation, physical pain, or an emotional ordeal. Through rituals involving prayers, meditation, songs, dance, pain, or drugs, shamans enter a trance, often at will. While entranced, they implore deities and powers to take action or to provide special knowledge and power that may assist individuals or the community at large: healing, medicinal advice, personal guidance, protection from illness or other attack, fortune telling, and control over the weather.

Anthropologist Laurel Kendall studied both the public and private rituals of women shamans in a small rural community in South Korea. In the opening scene of her book, *Shamans, Housewives, and Other Restless Spirits* (1985), Kendall describes a *kut*—a public shamanistic ritual. This event was officiated by

shaman: A part-time religious practitioner with special abilities to connect individuals with supernatural powers or beings.

MAP 15.3
South Korea

several women shamans who, through a dramatic performance involving costumes, music, dances, and trancelike states, called upon local gods, deceased ancestors, and related spirits, including warriors and generals; the shamans pleaded, cajoled, and bribed them to help those in the present world to address problems with troublesome children, drunken husbands, economic struggles, illness, and other maladies and to fight off threats by meddling ghosts and spirits. Each shaman invoked certain deities with whom she had developed a special relationship, and they in turn inhabited her during the ritual trances, dances, songs, and mediation. During such events, deities often weep, lament, and console the living through the words and actions of the shamans.

Kendall notes that public shamanistic rituals represent a professionalization of Korean household religion. Whereas trained and initiated shamans lead public rituals, in the home untrained and uninitiated women frequently engage the same deities and spirits on behalf of their husbands and children in an attempt to diagnose and heal the family's ills—from illness to crop failure. In this Korean household religion—a complex blend of elements of Buddhism, Daoism, and Confucianism—both shamans and housewives, Kendall argues, take on not only the role of ritual specialists but also of creators of meaning for their families and communities (Kendall 1985, 1988; Spencer 1987; De Vos 1987).

Although the role of the shaman is generally associated with small agricultural or seminomadic societies, shamans today often relocate to contemporary urban settings along with their immigrant communities. A variation of the shaman role also occurs in more formal religious organizations, as trained religious specialists there seek to (1) intervene with their deities on behalf of adherents or (2) assist adherents in practices of prayer and meditation through which they seek healing or guidance.

Religion and Magic

Anthropology has a long history of studying cultures where magic is practiced and witches are real. **Magic** involves the use of spells, incantations, words, and actions in an attempt to compel supernatural forces to act in certain ways, whether for good or for evil. Magic is part of cultural practices in every part of the world. And religion, almost everywhere, contains some components of magic.

In *The Golden Bough* (1890), anthropologist James Frazer (1854–1941) distinguishes between imitative magic and contagious magic. **Imitative magic** involves a performance that imitates the desired result, perhaps manipulating a doll or some other representation of the target of magic in the belief that the action will have direct imitative effect. **Contagious magic** centers on the belief that certain materials—perhaps clothing, hair, fingernails, teeth—that

magic: The use of spells, incantations, words, and actions in an attempt to compel supernatural forces to act in certain ways, whether for good or for evil.

imitative magic: A ritual performance that achieves efficacy by imitating the desired magical result.

contagious magic: Ritual words or performances that achieve efficacy as certain materials that come into contact with one person carry a magical connection that allows power to be transferred from person to person.

FIGURE 15.12 The success of J. R. R. Tolkien's Lord of the Rings trilogy and J. K. Rowling's Harry Potter series has revealed a vast appetite in Western culture for magic, witches, and wizards, at least in their fantastical literary and cinematic form.

have come into contact with one person carry a magical connection that allows power to be transferred from person to person.

In this section we consider the work of E. E. Evans-Pritchard, who sought to understand witchcraft and magic in East Africa; Paul Stoller, who apprenticed with a sorcerer in West Africa; and George Gmelch, who traces the belief in magic in contemporary U.S. society.

E. E. Evans-Pritchard: Rethinking the Logic of Magic

E. E. Evans-Pritchard (1902–1973), a British anthropologist who conducted extensive fieldwork in Africa's southern Sudan region, challenged Weber's rationalization thesis that assumed modernization and the rise of science would bring increasing rationality in a culture and its religious practices, thereby leading to a decrease in practices of magic. Instead, Evans-Pritchard's research among the tribal Azande people from 1926 to 1930 found that their use of magic was not an irrational expression but a component of a highly organized, rational, and logical system of thought that complemented science in understanding the way the world works.

In *Witchcraft, Oracles and Magic among the Azande* (1937), Evans-Pritchard describes in careful detail the elaborate religious system of the Azande in which magic, witchcraft, and poison oracles are central elements in daily life and conversation. The Azande trace all misfortunes to witchcraft. Their witchcraft does not involve rituals, spells, or medicines. Instead, it is a psychic power that may be used consciously or unconsciously by a witch—a woman or a man—to

MAP 15.4
Azande region, South Sudan

cause misfortunes or death. Witchcraft is inherited from a parent, and a witch's body contains a witchcraft substance (which the Azande described to Evans-Pritchard as an oval, blackish swelling or bag near the liver of a witch) that cannot be detected during life but can be found during an autopsy.

Magic among the Azande, in contrast to witchcraft, is performed consciously through rites, spells, the preparation of herbal medicines, and other magical techniques. Magic has its own power and can be used to combat witchcraft. If people perceive that magic is being deployed against them, they may consult a witch doctor—mostly men—who will use magic and medicines to try to thwart the work of the witch. Witch doctors are formally taught the knowledge of rituals and medicines as they are initiated into what amounts to a professional association. In the most extreme cases—those involving matters of life and death, and those that have ended up in court—the witch doctor may consult a poison oracle. As described to Evans-Pritchard, the poison oracle is created by administering a dose of poison to a chicken, and its subsequent death or recovery exposes the innocence or guilt of the accused witch. Poison oracles may also be used to ascertain answers to questions posed by the witch doctor to resolve the case. The witch identified as the source of the evil witchcraft is then asked to cease the witchcraft but may claim ignorance and proceed to plead with his or her own stomach—the location of the witchcraft in the body—to stop.

Witchcraft, Oracles and Magic among the Azande is considered one of the outstanding works of anthropology in the twentieth century. It not only stands as an exquisitely detailed ethnography but also provides the basis for rethinking the role of magic in society. Evans-Pritchard challenges the ethnocentric views of Western scholars who dismiss magical practices as irrational and illogical when compared to modern, rational, Western scientific strategies for accumulating knowledge of the external world. He contends instead that Azande ideas that may seem exotic, strange, and irrational to Europeans in actuality formed consistent, comprehensive, and rational systems of thought within the context of the Azande's daily lives and social structures.

Among the Azande, magic explained things that did not make sense otherwise, particularly the experience of misfortune; it provided an alternative theory of causation that supplemented the theory of natural causation. Magic helped explain what could not be explained by scientific study of nature. Evans-Pritchard presented the case of a wooden granary structure that collapsed and injured several people seated underneath it. Science could explain how insects had damaged the wood, which led to the collapse. But science could not explain the misfortune of why the people who were injured were sitting in a particular location at a particular time. For the Azande, witchcraft and magic could explain the misfortune.

Evans-Pritchard argued that the Azande saw no contradiction between witchcraft and empirical knowledge. For them, witchcraft and magic provided a rational and intellectually consistent explanation for what science cannot explain. Belief in witchcraft only appears inconsistent and irrational, Evans-Pritchard chided his Western colleagues, when they are arranged like museum objects on a shelf and examined outside the context of daily life.

Paul Stoller: "In Sorcery's Shadow" In the ethnography *In Sorcery's Shadow* (1987), anthropologist Paul Stoller and his co-author Cherl Olkes extend Evans-Pritchard's commitment to respect and understand others' systems of knowledge, even when they may at first appear irrational, unreasonable, and incomprehensible. Stoller takes Evans-Pritchard's work on magic and sorcery (another term for witchcraft) to a deeper personal level through direct engagement in the beliefs and practices of those he studied.

In the late 1970s Stoller arrived in the Songhay region of the Republic of Niger, West Africa, determined to learn about the role of religion in community life there. Through intensive fieldwork covering five visits over eight years, his deep involvement in a world of magic, spirits, sorcery, and spirit possession prevalent in the Songhay and surrounding regions eventually led him to be initiated as a sorcerer's apprentice. He memorized magical incantations. He ate special foods needed for his initiation. He ingested medicinal powders and wore magical objects to protect him from antagonistic sorcerers. And he

FIGURE 15.13 A sorcerer preparing a written tablet for a customer in the Songhay region of Niger.

MAP 15.5
Songhay region, Niger

indirectly participated in an attack of sorcery that temporarily paralyzed the intended victim (1987, ix).

His fieldwork led him to reflect on the transformative and deeply personal experience of conducting research into people's religious worlds:

> Long-term fieldwork and field-language fluency are two important ingredients in the recipe I am compiling. But the most important ingredient, I am convinced, is deep respect for other knowledge, other worlds, and other people. . . . For me, respect means accepting fully beliefs and phenomena which our system of knowledge often holds preposterous. I took my teachers seriously. They *knew* that I used divination in my personal life. They *knew* that I had eaten powders to protect myself. They *knew* I wore objects to demonstrate my respect for the spirits. They *knew* I had an altar in my house over which I recited incantations. They liked the way I carried my knowledge and power and taught me more and more. (1987, 228)

Stoller's fieldwork came to an abrupt end, however, when he experienced an attack by spirits sent against him by a powerful village sorceress. Suffering the debilitating physical effects of the sorceress's attack, Stoller fled the village and West Africa, returning home to the United States to finally rid himself of the illness.

> But ethnographers can go too far. They can pursue the other's reality too hotly, crossing a line that brings them face to face with a violent reality that is no mere epistemological exercise. If they know too much, they must swear an oath of silence. If they reveal what they shouldn't, they may be murdered. (1987, 229)

Not every anthropologist apprentices with a sorcerer or is attacked by one. In this regard, Stoller's experience as an anthropologist of religion is an outlier in the field. But the anthropological commitment to long-term, in-depth participant observation brings many of us into close contact with the beliefs, practices, and emotions of those whom we study, an intimacy that often reveals the vibrant power of religion in their lives that leaves one marked by the encounter. Is it possible to comprehend someone's religious beliefs and practices without accepting that they are real—at least for the believer?

George Gmelch: Baseball Magic In case reading about the work of Evans-Pritchard and Stoller leaves you relieved that you live in a Western world that relegates belief in magic to children's books and movies, research by anthropologist and former Minor League Baseball player George Gmelch may surprise you. It turns out that beliefs and practices of magic are not so unfamiliar in U.S. culture.

Gmelch's study of baseball in the United States (1992) explores the rituals, taboos, and sacred objects of magic that are in almost constant use. He finds that they reflect the kinds of beliefs and activities that are prevalent in all sports.

Baseball players use charms such as special clothes or jewelry. Moreover, Gmelch found, players believe that good magic is contagious. If it worked before, and if the player uses the same ritual again, perhaps the magical conditions for success can be re-created. Thus, players repeat certain actions to help them succeed: Pitchers touch the bill of their cap, wear good-luck charms, or never touch the foul line between home plate and first base when moving between the pitcher's mound and the dugout. Batters wear the same shirt or underwear, or use the same movements over and over again in the batter's box, to capture the magic of previous success.

In baseball, Gmelch found magical thinking to be most prevalent in situations with the most uncertainty. These especially involved pitching and batting, where success rates (the best hitters rarely succeed more than 30 percent of the time) are markedly lower than in fielding (where players successfully complete well over 90 percent of the plays).

Have you ever noticed certain ritual-like movements while watching close-ups of batters and pitchers during televised baseball games or other sporting events? Do you yourself have special charms or practices or clothes that you

FIGURE 15.14 Magic rituals, taboos, and sacred objects are used constantly in American sports. *Left,* Boston Red Sox designated hitter David Ortiz adjusts his gloves before every swing, drawing upon a notion of contagious magic to bring him good luck while batting. *Right,* former New York Mets reliever Turk Wendell's magical practices included always leaping over the baseline when walking to the mound, brushing his teeth between innings, chewing black licorice while pitching, and wearing a necklace decorated with the teeth of wild animals he had hunted and killed.

believe will bring you good luck during games, exams, dates, and so on? What about jewelry or ornaments?

Anthropology challenges us to understand the beliefs and practices of others from within their own cultural framework. By making the strange familiar, we may then also make the familiar strange. In other words, we may take what seems natural and normal in our own lives and see it through new eyes.

The study of religion often forces anthropologists to address personal issues of identity, belief, and objectivity in ways that many other areas of study do not. Is it possible to fully understand a religion without being a practitioner? Can someone remain objective if he practices the religion he studies? Anthropologists of religion consider these important questions when conducting fieldwork and writing about their experiences. Through any experience of intensive fieldwork we risk challenging, transforming, and possibly shattering our own worldviews even as we risk influencing those of the people we study. These dynamics are particularly volatile in the study of religion.

In What Ways Is Religion Both a System of Meaning and a System of Power?

Many people in Western cultures think of religion as a system of ideas and beliefs that are primarily a personal matter. In the United States, for instance, doctrines asserting the separation of church and state promote an ideal of the separation of religion from politics. But as we saw in Chapter 2, any analysis of a cultural system that focuses solely on its underlying meanings risks ignoring the ways that power is negotiated within the system and how it engages other systems of power within the culture. This observation applies to our study of religion as well.

Religion and Meaning

symbol: Anything that signifies something else.

Building on the themes of Max Weber's *Protestant Ethic and the Spirit of Capitalism*, anthropologist Clifford Geertz (1926–2006), in his essay "Religion as a Cultural System" (1973), suggests that religion is essentially a system of ideas surrounding a set of powerful **symbols**. Hindus, for example, consider the cow sacred because by protecting it they symbolically enact the protection of all life. Other widely recognized religious symbols include the cross for Christians, the Torah scroll for Jews, and the holy city of Mecca for Muslims. For Geertz, each symbol has deep meaning and evokes powerful emotions and motivations in the religion's followers. Why?

FIGURE 15.15 A Jewish worshiper holds up a Torah scroll to receive a blessing at the Western Wall, Judaism's holiest prayer site, in Jerusalem's Old City. How does an object made of paper and ink become a powerful symbol with deep religious meaning?

These symbols acquire significance far beyond the actual material they are made of. Objects made of wood, metal, rock, or paper come to represent influential explanations about what it means to be human and where humans fit in the general order of the universe. Symbols, with their deep pool of meaning, create a sense of order and resist chaos by building and reinforcing a larger worldview—a framework of ideas about what is real, what exists, and what that means.

We can see symbols at work in various religious contexts. For Christians, the bread and wine served at the communion ritual are more than actual bread and wine. They symbolically recall the death and resurrection of Jesus, the power of God to overcome death, and the promise to Jesus's followers of everlasting life beyond the suffering of this world. Communion also recalls the fellowship of all Christian believers who share in the benefits of God's sacrifice, a sense of connection with people around the world. For Jews, the Torah scroll is more than a composite of paper and ink. It represents the holy word of God as revealed through the prophets, the story of a covenant between God and the people of Israel, an agreement that in return for faithfulness God will provide liberation from captivity, the establishment of a nation of people, and abundant life. For Hindus, the cow requires veneration because it represents the Hindu practice of *ahimsa*—nonviolence toward all living things. In a practical sense, this means that no leather may enter the temple and all shoes must remain outside the temple door. Even these acts are symbolic of Hindus' belief that all life is sacred and that attention to this fact will transform the practicing individual and lead to his or her reincarnation as a more sentient being.

Geertz comments that these symbols and their underlying conceptions of reality become so matter-of-fact in the religious context, expressed in familiar rituals and doctrines, that believers feel their presence helps them move beyond mundane matters and experience what is "really real." Believers may have contact with the religious world only briefly or irregularly, especially in comparison with the ordinary world that they experience every day. Yet through the power of religious symbols, they feel that the religious world is truly real. Religious practice, ritual, and symbols provide access to that ultimate and sought-after reality.

Anthropologists encounter symbols and their powerful effects in numerous areas of our field, but the use of symbols in religious belief and practice is particularly pervasive and rich. As we will consider next, as anthropologists work to analyze the ongoing vitality of religion in today's globalizing age, understanding the ways symbols are constructed and given meaning and authority will be a valuable skill for navigating an increasingly interconnected world.

Religion and Power

Anthropologist Talal Asad, in his book *Genealogies of Religion* (1993), criticizes Geertz's explanation of religion. Asad bases his inquiry on questions such as these: How did religious symbols get their power? Who or what gave them their authority? What gives religion the power and authority to have meaning in people's lives? After all, Asad asserts, symbols do not have meaning in and of themselves. He suggests that religion and religious symbols are actually produced through complex historical and social developments in which power and meaning are created, contested, and maintained. What historical processes have given the cross, the Torah, the *hajj*, and the cow their symbolic power? Without understanding these particular **authorizing processes**, Asad claims, we cannot understand what really makes religion work.

Asad argues that most definitions of religion are not universal. Instead, he claims, they are the creations of Western scholars based on western European ideas of what religion is and how it works—in particular, the way Christianity has developed in relationship to the state. Such scholars look for Western ideas of religion in the spiritual and ritual practices of other cultures. Asad warns that these attempts to create a universal definition impede an understanding of religion in other parts of the world. For instance, he suggests that Weber's assumptions that religions become increasingly rationalized as societies modernize, and that societies become increasingly secularized as a sharper

authorizing process: The complex historical and social developments through which symbols are given power and meaning.

Visit to a Religious Community

Choose a religious community that you would like to visit, either by yourself or with other members of your class. Contact the organization to arrange a visit at a time when you can participate in a public ritual, perhaps a worship service, festival, or parade. Be sure to find out what attire is appropriate for visitors.

During your visit, consider how the concepts introduced in this chapter can serve as tools for analyzing and understanding what you see.

1. Do you see examples of sacred and profane objects / acts during your visit (Durkheim)?
2. Can you recognize ways in which ritual promotes a sense of communitas by leading members through separation, liminality, and reincorporation (Turner)?
3. Is Marx's critique of religion as "the opiate of the masses" relevant to the event you attend?

4. Can you identify particular symbols (Geertz) unique to this religious community and determine their meaning? What do you think gives them their power and authority (Asad)?
5. How does power make itself evident during your visit? What power relationships do you observe?
6. Can you identify any ways in which globalization influences the religious beliefs and practices that you observe?

If appropriate, interview a religious leader and/or a member of the religious community during your visit. Use the interview to explore these questions further and to gain deeper insight into what you observe.

If you attend with other classmates, compare your reflections after the visit. Be sure to reread the appropriate sections of this chapter to see which concepts come alive in more detail now that you have observed the activities of a religious community from an anthropological viewpoint.

---

separation develops between religion and the state, are rooted in the way Western Christianity has developed—not in a universal pattern that we can assume exists in religions worldwide.

In the case of Islam, religious beliefs and political power are intricately intertwined in many countries, and national governments may seek to impose a version of Islamic religious law, called Sharia, through mechanisms of the state. Asad suggests that in these cases, Western understandings of the essential nature of religion that assume increasing secularization and separation of church and state may lead scholars and casual observers to dismiss other expressions of religion as irrational and backward. Instead, these other religious expressions are simply different—outside the normative definition of religion established in Western scholarship. Asad states that scholars of religion must beware the power of universal definitions to obscure local realities. They must carefully examine local expressions of religion, how those expressions developed over time, and what has given those expressions the power and authority to be so meaningful to believers (Asad 1993).

As you begin to think like an anthropologist of religion, try to examine religious symbols from the perspectives of both Geertz and Asad. As you consider religious symbols in the culture around you—perhaps in your own religious tradition—can you begin to appreciate the power of symbols to evoke intense emotions and motivations that put believers in touch with what feels "really real"? Can you begin to consider the ways in which particular symbols have been constructed, given meaning, and authorized through particular historical and cultural processes? The "Your Turn" exercise on page 601 will give you an opportunity to transform these new insights into analytical tools.

Blurring the Boundaries between Meaning and Power

The work of both Geertz and Asad has influenced contemporary anthropological research on religion. We now consider local examples of religious activities and organizations in which meaning and power are intertwined and the boundary between religion and other social systems of power is not rigid. As we consider these studies, can you begin to see how analyses of both meaning and power are essential in achieving a comprehensive picture of the role of religion in culture?

China's Religious Revival In recent years, a religious revival has been spreading across China in urban and rural areas. After years of attempts by the Chinese government to eradicate religious practices, especially popular folk religious activities, today the Chinese population is rebuilding temples, restoring graves, and re-creating religious festivals. The Chinese state officially recognizes Buddhism, Daoism, Protestant Christianity, Catholicism, and Islam, and all are experiencing growth and revitalization. However, the most vibrant expansion of religious activity is among practitioners of Chinese popular religion—a tradition that incorporates elements of Buddhism, Daoism, and the veneration of family and village ancestors.

The Black Dragon King Temple complex in Shaanbei, China, is the center of one such revival. Formerly a small, isolated shrine in the early 1980s, it is now a large temple complex with many buildings and year-round activity. The temple has become a catalyst for religious revival, the revival of folk cultural traditions, and the development of community economic activity. It also serves as a site for negotiating the relationships among popular religion, the Chinese state, and the surrounding rural agricultural society.

Village religious life throughout China today includes elaborate public funerals, weddings, grave sweeping, the burning of spirit paper money for

MAP 15.6
Shaanbei

FIGURE 15.16 Crowds attend the Black Dragon King Temple annual festival, in rural Shaanbei, China. How would anthropologists examine the intersection of religion with other systems of power in this scene?

ancestors, the avoidance of hungry ghosts (ancestors who have no family looking after them), and seeking favor from a wide variety of deities. Each village has at least one god, sometimes more, and the area's deities are ranked according to their *ling*, or magical efficacy (in other words, how well they are able to get the job done). People pray to these gods for practical benefits in times of trouble, to resolve conflicts, to protect the souls of sick children, to heal illnesses and maladies, to offer advice on matters ranging from matchmaking to business dealings, and to send rain in times of drought.

The village temples become the central location for praying, presenting offerings, buying incense and spirit paper money, performing public rituals, and hosting religious festivals. Villagers may pray to many gods—any they think may be able to help them. Visiting different temples and shrines in several villages is quite common; people believe this practice will not incite the wrath of jealous gods as long as individuals offer proper thanks when requests are successfully granted and problems resolved.

The revival of popular religious life has generated activities well beyond the temple. Temple festivals have spurred the rebirth of opera performances, storytelling, folk dances, and a wide variety of other folk cultural traditions. China's overall economic growth translates into increased donations as both local worshippers and visiting pilgrims contribute to temple renovations, sponsor rituals and festivals, and make gifts to honor the gods. Temple activities in turn generate income for the entire community.

Key to the Black Dragon King Temple's success is an active and effective temple leadership committee. At its head is Lao Wang, a visionary, energetic, and enterprising local resident. The temple association builds and maintains the temple and its structures, manages its funds, stages festivals, and negotiates with other social organizations and players. In addition, the temple leadership channels a portion of its economic proceeds to the construction of better roads, irrigation systems, and schools in the community. Such civic engagement has elevated the temple leaders' position in community affairs. In today's China, some people become part of the local elite by getting rich, whereas others are elevated through moral leadership. In this atmosphere, the temple leadership's economic activities and political influence have earned them status as part of the local elite. Through the success of their religious organization, the temple association—and particularly Lao Wang—has become the most influential nongovernmental organization in the area, a powerful civic organization operating completely outside the realm of the Chinese state.

The experience of the Black Dragon King Temple reveals the surprising power of popular religion in contemporary China. Rural religious communities are carving out spaces of civic activity apart from the operations of the Chinese government, reviving and re-creating rural traditions in the face of modernization and urbanization throughout China. They are reasserting and negotiating avenues of autonomy in what has been a highly centralized political system (Chau 2006; Guest 2003).

Religion and Revolution in Mexico Religion scholar Charlene Floyd's research (1996) on the role of the Catholic Church in a revolutionary movement in the Chiapas region of southern Mexico provides another example of how meaning and power are expressed in religion. Chiapas is one of the poorest states in Mexico, where most children do not finish primary school and many homes have no running water. The people are poor, but the land is rich: it holds large reserves of oil and natural gas, provides most of the country's hydroelectric power, and supports half of its coffee crop. The tension between an impoverished people, on the one hand, and rich natural resources extracted by Mexico's state and corporations, on the other, has not always found a smooth resolution.

In the early hours of January 1, 1994, some of the poor people of Chiapas, calling themselves Zapatistas (after the Mexican revolutionary Emiliano

Zapata), covered their faces with bandanas and ski masks, marched into four Chiapas cities, and declared in a dramatic manifesto, "Today we say enough is enough!" Stunned by the uprising, the Mexican government and the economic leaders of Chiapas quickly accused the Catholic Church of inciting the rebellion. In particular, they blamed one of the bishops of Chiapas, Samuel Ruiz García, and his *catequistas*, or lay teachers. But how could a Catholic bishop and a group of lay teachers be accused of inciting a rebellion? Did they actually do so? In considering these questions, we must explore the Church's role in Mexican society.

Today, 90 percent of Mexicans identify themselves as Catholic, a faith that has been a key component of Mexican national identity ever since Spanish colonizers forcibly imported it five hundred years ago. In certain periods of Mexican history, religion and politics have been closely aligned. For example, a Catholic priest, Father Miguel Hidalgo y Costilla, is credited with providing the initial spark for the Mexican independence movement in 1810. Calling on the name of Mexico's indigenous saint, the Virgin of Guadalupe, Father Hidalgo challenged his parishioners by asking, "Will you free yourselves?" Despite periods of alignment, Mexican history has seen ongoing tensions between the powerful institution of the Catholic Church (which has been one of Mexico's largest landholders) and the Mexican state. The Church has been involved in political movements in Mexico before, but did it have a role in the 1994 uprising in Chiapas? A quick look at recent church history may shed light on this question.

In 1959 Pope John XXIII called for a Vatican Council to modernize the Catholic Church. By the end of this conference (1962–65), commonly called Vatican II, the Catholic Church had begun a dramatic revolution in theology and practice. In an attempt to redefine the Church as "the people of God" rather than an institution, Vatican II moved to make local congregations more accessible to the layperson. Congregations were allowed to worship in their own local language rather than Latin. Priests and lay members were encouraged to open the Church more fully to the world, using the Church as an instrument of liberation in people's lives, as a servant to the poor rather than an ally of the politically powerful.

Bishop Samuel Ruiz García, head of the Diocese of San Cristobal de las Casas in Chiapas, where the Zapatista uprising occurred, attended Vatican II and a subsequent meeting in 1968 of Latin American Catholic leaders. He returned to Mexico determined to implement the new theology of liberation: he would put the Church to work to better the life conditions of the one million primarily indigenous people in his diocese. The diocesan program for training lay teachers, called *catequistas*, transformed its curriculum from a primary focus on Church doctrine, scriptures, law, liturgy, and music to include concerns of community life and social needs. By the time of the Zapatista uprising, the *catequistas* had grown from seven hundred to eight thousand.

Most were now elected by their local indigenous communities; they were deeply involved not only in traditional Catholic religious education but also in the empowerment of indigenous people in their struggles against poverty. *Catequistas* developed prominent roles as community and political leaders, accompanying their constituents in efforts to eradicate poverty and landlessness in Chiapas and to open the state's political process to greater participation from people at the grassroots.

Were Bishop Ruiz and the *catequistas* responsible for the 1994 Zapatista uprising? No accusations have been proven of a direct role in the Zapatista leadership. But did the *catequistas'* theology of liberation, expressing the Catholic Church's desire for the empowerment of indigenous people and the elimination of poverty, provide moral support and practical training to communities engaged in this struggle? If so, then the Catholic Church of Chiapas provides an instructive example for anthropologists—of how we must consider the role of religious ideas, symbols, and engagements with other systems of power to understand religion in all its fullness (Floyd 1996).

Swaziland's Churches: Religious Health Assets in Fighting HIV/AIDS

Research suggests that across Africa, religious organizations—particularly Christian churches—manage as much as 70 percent of all medical assets, including urban hospitals and rural health clinics (Root 2009). As the following discussion illustrates, the potential role of local congregations in health promotion in Swaziland reveals churches to be not only places of spiritual life but also significant health assets.

Swaziland is a small, landlocked, primarily agricultural country in southern Africa. It has one of the highest rates of HIV infection in the world, with fully 26 percent of Swazis between the ages of 25 and 49 testing HIV positive. As a result, life expectancy is only thirty-three years, and 34 percent of children under age 18 live with neither parent. Swaziland has an estimated 6,500 local church congregations—one for every 183 people. In comparison, the country has one HIV testing and counseling facility for every 6,180 people and one antiretroviral treatment site for every 45,400 people. In this dire context, recent research (Root 2009) has been exploring the current and potential role of Christian churches—not as places for worship and prayer, but as key community health assets. Fieldwork reveals that churches function as places where health can be promoted, treatment encouraged, and social, material, and spiritual support provided.

MAP 15.8
Swaziland

HIV infection among Swazi women is particularly high. Forty-nine percent of Swazi women age 25 to 29 are HIV positive. And because Swaziland is an intensely patriarchal society, women's rights within the family are severely limited and their role in public affairs is even more circumscribed. Gender inequality is stark. Even the family homestead can be a place of particular vulnerability, stigmatization, and discrimination for HIV-positive individuals. In this environment, it is very difficult for anyone to disclose their HIV symptoms and seek treatment (Whiteside et al. 2006).

In the midst of this health care crisis, churches are complex social spaces. They can be sites for stigmatization, but they also provide alternative spaces for women to deal with their HIV infections. In fact, women make up the majority of churchgoers in Swaziland. Churches can provide networks of material support that women may not receive on their homesteads. Just as important, churches can promote alternative narratives of self-understanding that allow women to imagine disclosing their HIV status. Indeed, research shows that disclosure may be a key to treating and preventing the spread of disease. Women who disclose their HIV status in the church community have the possibility not to be shunned and dismissed. Instead, they may be called courageous for daring to make their problem public and asking for help. As a result, local church congregations in many locations where health clinics are rare and HIV testing is rarer still are becoming key avenues for health education, health promotion, and reduced stigma and discrimination.

These "religious health assets" (Cochrane 2006) play tangible and intangible roles in the public health enterprise, mobilizing the symbolic and material power of Christian communities to promote concrete interventions in the health outcomes of rural Swazis. For more discussion of how churches intersect with women's health needs in Swaziland, see "Anthropologists Engage the

Robin Root

Medical anthropologist Robin Root began her career conducting research on HIV risk among female electronic factory workers in Malaysia (see Chapter 6). She then switched her geographic focus to southern Africa, where she began to explore the role of religious communities in the fight against the spread of HIV / AIDS.

"I got involved in Swaziland through a chance encounter with a missionary on a fourteen-hour nonstop flight on my way to an AIDS conference in Capetown, South Africa. I was struck by a project he was working on in a rural area of Swaziland doing really small-scale attempts to foster income-generating projects for AIDS widows: trying to grow small gardens, small-scale irrigation projects. And his wife ran a foster home for AIDS orphans in the town. It completely connected with my interest in medical anthropology and applied health programs.

"Swaziland challenges me intellectually, physically, emotionally, and spiritually. The extremes of human existence—good and evil, rich and poor—are put in such stark relief with one of the highest HIV infection rates in the world. Life expectancy is about forty years. This means that Swazi middle age is equivalent to when we might be sophomores in college. It puts what we consider the normal aspects of life into stark relief. It's such a high-vulnerability setting.

"I knew very little about Swaziland before I began my research. So I walked to fifty family homesteads and conducted a household impact questionnaire. I wanted to get a baseline understanding of information about family composition, religion, marriage, HIV views and knowledge, and economics.

"One of the things I found was that Christianity in particular was playing a complicated and, in a way, progressive role in addressing many aspects of HIV. Swazi pastors are really on the front lines, especially in rural areas. They want to address the death and dying of their congregations. They want whatever resources they can use—financial, educational, and informational.

"Stigma is one of the greatest impediments to treating HIV in Swaziland. People are afraid to let others know they are infected because of the potential social fallout. But some pastors are using their pulpit and their homestead visitation—they spent a lot of time going from homestead to homestead because people were not healthy enough to go to church—to strengthen religious beliefs and sometimes to encourage support for those family members who are unwell. As individuals who are in many ways as authoritative in their culture as physicians are in ours, they had a powerful role.

"Of course this was not always easy. One HIV-positive pastor I interviewed had not disclosed his HIV status to his congregation. Even though he had set up two churches explicitly to address the needs of people with HIV / AIDS. He knew the very thing that would get them to get antiretroviral [ARV] treatment would be to disclose his status and encourage them to seek treatment by explaining that he

Anthropologist Robin Root (*right*) in Swaziland

was still alive because of ARVs. But as he told me, 'the very moment I were to disclose, people would flee my church and say I'm not a man of God. I've got HIV.' That was the problem. Feeling that this was exactly what it would take to get people to get the ARVs but fearing that the church he set up to help them would dissolve in the aftermath.

"Churches are in many ways women's spaces. Men certainly attend as well. But churches are places where women can gather other than at the homestead where they reside. They can create underground networks of communication around, for example, encouraging someone who looks unwell to go to the clinic to get medication. Reaching out to provide food. Providing information about where to go to get medicine. These are some of the concrete ways church-based networks intersect with HIV/AIDs. When the rural health clinic is four miles away from these communities, how are they to get transport if they haven't the money for transport or are too unwell to go themselves? Though having elements of stigmatizing processes as well, churches and church networks can provide the space and social relationships for conversations to occur in rural areas where pastors and parishioners, and community care supporters, can encourage people to get tested, adhere to drug regimens, care for sick neighbors. This is where the church comes in.

"The work in Swaziland has changed me in many ways. Perhaps the most profound is that I came to believe there is evil, with a capital E. I didn't believe that before. By evil I mean both the global structural processes that impoverish millions in violent and inexorable ways as well as the other human practices, such as stigma, that stand in the way of getting people the treatment they need. I can't comfortably sit back and let that play out.

"The importance of expanding our Western notion of biomedicine as 'intervention' based has become clear as well. Effective health care is more than scientific. It is fundamentally social. The relationship between the health personnel and patient affects whether the patient understands the instructions, takes the medications regularly, and returns for a follow-up health visit. Medicines affect people's well-being through social relationships. If those relationships aren't managed well, then the biomedical mechanisms won't be effective.

"Conventional health policy and programming aims to provide medicines that people will take and then get well. But making medications affordable and accessible, while essential, is not enough. Handing people condoms and telling them to go use them is not really adequate to prevent HIV infection. How do you address the questions of power and intimacy and sex that affect condom use in the local culture? It is here that an anthropologist can be valuable if he or she can navigate and negotiate the different knowledge systems that biomedical and nonbiomedical practices represent, realizing that people may draw upon all sorts of human and material resources in the face of sickness and death.

"When I'm on the ground in Swaziland, I find myself, intentionally and not, becoming an intersection between conventional public health/biomedical information about HIV/AIDS and experiences of HIV/AIDS that are specific to that setting and those communities. Then when I'm back home in the United States I continue to be that intersection, but I'm not living it day to day. I'm writing about it and always trying to understand what role I can play to help empower the very vulnerable people I've worked with in Swaziland to tackle the health crisis they are facing."

World" on pages 608–09. After reading about Robin Root's work, think back to the discussions of religious expression in China and Mexico, as well as your own visit to a religious community. In what ways do those different religious contexts exemplify the blurring of boundaries between meaning and power?

How Is Globalization Changing Religion?

The forces of globalization—especially migration and time-space compression—are stretching and shaping religions and religious practices. Increasing immigration sometimes means that whole communities—their beliefs, religious architecture, religious leaders, and even their gods—relocate across national boundaries. Travel is broadening the encounters of people of different faiths. At the same time, information about religion is more widely available, and communication technologies enable religious institutions to transform their strategies for cultivating and educating participants. Cities, especially those serving as immigrant gateways, are generally the focal point of this increasing encounter. It is here that new immigrants revitalize older religious institutions and construct new ones, often establishing deep ties to home and sophisticated networks of transnational exchange.

Revitalizing the Catholic Church in the United States

Throughout the United States, Catholic churches are being rejuvenated as immigration from heavily Catholic countries brings new membership, worship styles, social needs, and political engagements. A wave of rallies in major cities across the United States in 2005 in support of reform of U.S. immigration laws received key institutional and organizational support from local Catholic churches with encouragement from the U.S. Catholic leadership. Indeed, the Church saw as a key human rights issue the reuniting of families across the border and eliminating opportunities for the exploitation of vulnerable, low-wage workers. At the same time, today's immigrants are reshaping the Church's future—just as immigrant waves from Ireland, Germany, and Italy did in the nineteenth century.

Mexican Catholicism in New York City In New York City, Mexican immigrants have reshaped many of the city's Catholic churches. Over the past twenty years, hundreds of thousands of Mexicans, many undocumented and the vast majority Catholic, have arrived in New York to work in low-wage jobs in restaurants, groceries, construction, and the nearby agricultural industry on Long Island. In the process, these immigrants have brought their home-country religious practices and particularly their devotion to Our Lady of Guadalupe.

FIGURE 15.18 How are religious practices crossing national borders in a global age? Every December Mexican Catholic immigrants in New York City march carrying portraits of Our Lady of Guadalupe, patron saint of Mexico.

The miraculous appearance of the Virgin Mary, mother of Jesus, in 1531 in Guadalupe, Mexico, in the body of an indigenous person has become a symbol of the Mexican nation and of the special blessings Mexicans have received from God.

Across New York's Catholic churches, images of the Virgin of Guadalupe are prominently displayed. Within parishes, Guadalupano committees have formed to meet new members' needs and political concerns. The root of these committees is Association Tepeyac, a Mexican Catholic immigrant organization created in New York by a Mexican Catholic religious order to advocate for immigrant rights, services, and legalization. Tepeyac draws on the symbolic power of the Virgin to galvanize its movement. In this context, the Virgin of Guadalupe links and mobilizes Mexicans more than language, ethnicity, social class, or common nationality. She is a symbol of Mexican national identity but also represents a universal Catholic commitment to human rights. The Virgin is venerated as a protector of the poor, oppressed, and weak. Tepeyac supports and links Guadalupano committees in local churches and takes the lead in advocating for immigrant rights, particularly a general amnesty for undocumented workers.

The arrival of Mexican Catholics has brought increased attention to the plight of undocumented workers and has built new symbolic and practical links across the U.S.–Mexico border. On December 12 each year since 2002, thousands of Mexican Catholic immigrants walk in procession down New York City's Fifth Avenue to St. Patrick's Cathedral to celebrate the Feast Day of Our Lady of Guadalupe. Organized by Association Tepeyac and the Guadalupano committees, the procession in New York is the culmination of a torch run that begins in the Basilica Church of the Virgin of Guadalupe in Mexico City. Each year, Mexican Catholic devotees carry a lit torch and a portrait of the Virgin across the U.S.–Mexico border, through the large Mexican immigrant populations across the southeastern United States (including in Alabama, Georgia, and North Carolina), and culminate their pilgrimage in New York City. Calling themselves "messengers of a people divided by a border," the torch runners combine an expression of religious devotion to the Virgin of Guadalupe with advocacy for the reform of U.S. immigration laws.

Through their devotional practices, Tepeyac and the Guadalupano committees articulate an alternative citizenship. This citizenship is not subject to the temporary and seemingly capricious laws of a foreign country. Rather, it is one in which all people are equal in the eyes of the Mother of God, represented in her manifestation as the Virgin of Guadalupe. Today, as globalization stimulates the international movement of people, nation-states may resist that movement through immigration policies that create disjunctures for family members living on opposite sides of a border or for undocumented immigrants living on the wrong side of the law. For these immigrants, as revealed in the story of

FIGURE 15.19 Every year, Mexican Catholics carry a lit torch and a portrait of the Virgin of Guadalupe from Mexico City to New York, combining religious expression with political advocacy for reform of U.S. immigration laws.

Tepeyac and the Guadalupano committees, religion can provide both a symbolic and a material healing of the rift created by the states' response to globalization and cross-border flows of immigrants (Galvez 2009).

Relocating Rituals and Deities from the Home Country

Globalization is transforming the ritual practices of religious communities large and small as congregations adapt to their members' mobility and the lively flow of ideas, information, and money across borders. These dynamics have rapidly spread the religious practices of a small, local, village Daoist temple in rural China to New York and beyond through a network of Chinese restaurants opening across the United States. Today, thanks to globalization, the village temple's adherents and their local god have become international border-crossing immigrants.

Immigrant Chinese Gods A few years ago, I walked into a little temple just off Canal Street in Manhattan's Chinatown as part of a project to map the

Chinese religious communities in New York City (Guest 2003). Women and men, young and old, crowded into the noisy and smoky old storefront space, lighting incense, chatting with old friends, and saying prayers at the altar. Most were from the same small village in southeastern China, outside the provincial capital of Fuzhou. They had opened this temple to continue their religious practices in the United States and to serve as a gathering place for fellow immigrant villagers who lived and worked in and around New York City. Here immigrants can reconnect with friends and relatives from their hometown, participate in rituals of devotion to their deities, and build networks of fellow devotees they may not have known before arriving in New York.

For a highly transient population, the temple serves as a center for exchanging information about jobs, housing, lawyers, doctors, employment agencies, and more. It operates a revolving loan fund for members to pay off smuggling debts or start up a take-out restaurant. Through the temple, members contribute to building their home temple and support other charitable projects in their home community back in China. Despite the undocumented status of many of these immigrants, the temple provides a way to participate in civic activities and express themselves as contributing members of the community in much the same way that Tepeyac and the Guadalupano committees do for New York's Mexican immigrants.

I later visited the home village temple in China to learn about village life and local religious traditions. One evening as I prepared to leave, the master of the temple expressed disappointment that I had not been able to meet the temple's spirit medium, a young woman who had a special relationship with the village's local god. He explained that on the first and fifteenth day of each lunar month, the local god possesses her and speaks through her to interpret the villagers' dreams and answer their questions: What name should I give my child? What herbal remedy will cure my ill? Will this woman be a good match for my son? When should I try to be smuggled out of China to the United States? I shared the master's disappointment at this missed opportunity and readily accepted his invitation to return on a future visit.

A year later I did return. The spirit medium, however, was gone. She and her husband, the temple master informed me, had moved to the United States and were now working in a restaurant in a place called "Indiana." I was disappointed again, but I expressed my concern that their departure may have disrupted a key element of temple life. The master then told me this story:

> Actually she still does it—only now it's from Indiana. Our believers work in restaurants all over the United States and some are still here in China. When they want to ask the advice of the god, they just pick up their cell phones and call. The spirit medium keeps

careful records of their questions and dreams. Then on the first and fifteenth of the lunar month, just as always used to happen when she was here, she goes into a trance. The god leaves our temple here in China and flies to Indiana to possess her. Her husband then asks all the questions and writes down the answers. When the possession is over, the god returns to our village, and the spirit medium and her husband return all the phone calls to report the wisdom of the god. (personal interview)

Perhaps the look on my face and my one raised eyebrow alerted the master to my initial skepticism. "We can feel the god leave here every time," he said. "Really. Why don't you believe that? In America you have lots of Christians who believe the Christian god can be everywhere in the world at the same time. Why can't ours?"

The more I thought about it, the more I wondered why the local god of a village in China couldn't also be in Indiana. As an anthropologist of religion, I was reminded once again that religious practices and beliefs in today's age of globalization continue to be fluid and adaptable. After all, humans are adaptable, and so are their cultural constructions. Religion is a vibrant example of this core anthropological insight.

Thinking Like an Anthropologist: Religion in the Twenty-First Century

After reading this chapter, you should have a deeper understanding of some of the approaches anthropologists take to understanding the role of religion in people's lives and in communities large and small. These insights can serve as a toolkit as you consider expressions of religion in other countries and at home in the United States.

Think again about the Buddhist monks' protest that opened the chapter, and recall the key questions we have asked about religion:

- What is religion?
- What tools do anthropologists use to understand how religion works?
- In what ways is religion both a system of meaning and a system of power?
- How is globalization changing religion?

After reading the chapter, can you apply the writings of Durkheim, Marx, Weber, Geertz, and Asad to events in the real world? Can you see concepts of sacred and profane, ritual, rite of passage, communitas, symbol, and power emerge in the actual expressions of religion in Myanmar?

Despite the symbolic power and dramatic physical presence of the Buddhist monks' protests in 2007, a brutal military crackdown put an end to the demonstrations just a few days later. Yet despite the short-term setback, in hindsight one may consider the long-term effects these religious actions may have had on more recent events. The monks' protests demonstrated deep opposition within Myanmar society to the military government—not only by students and workers, but also by 500,000 religious professionals who wielded both symbolic power and a willingness to engage in direct action. In a country where the military government was unaccustomed to organized resistance, the monks demonstrated that through their religious networks they are organized, meet regularly, enjoy an independent communication network, honor their vows of obedience to an authority other than the government, and articulate an alternative vision of a just and peaceful society.

National elections held the following year (2008) were considered by most observers to be rampant with fraud. But shortly afterward, the government began to introduce economic and political reforms that have brought a positive transformation to Myanmar. The changes include dramatic success by the main opposition party in April 2012 elections. What role might the 2007 religious protests have played in creating the environment for political and economic developments in the ensuing years?

Key Terms

religion (p. 577)
martyr (p. 579)
saint (p. 579)
sacred (p. 581)
profane (p. 581)
ritual (p. 581)
rite of passage (p. 583)

liminality (p. 584)

communitas (p. 584)

pilgrimage (p. 584)

cultural materialism (p. 588)

shaman (p. 591)

magic (p. 592)

imitative magic (p. 592)

contagious magic (p. 592)

symbol (p. 598)

authorizing process (p. 600)

For Further Exploration

Dialogue at Washington High. 2007. By the Jewish-Palestinian Living Room Dialogue Group. Dialogue. Documentary film of Jewish and Palestinian teens who model connecting with the "other."

Lambek, Michael, ed. 2008. *A Reader in the Anthropology of Religion*, 2nd ed. Malden, MA: Blackwell.

Morris, Brian. 2006. *Religion and Anthropology: A Critical Introduction*. New York: Cambridge University Press.

Number Our Days. 1977. Directed by Lynne Littman. Direct Cinema. Documentary film by anthropologist Barbara Myerhoff of creation of ritual in a Jewish senior center in California.

The Pew Forum on Religion & Public Life. www .pewforum.org. This website explores the intersection of religion and public affairs in the United States and globally through surveys, demographic analysis, and social science research.

The Pluralism Project. www.pluralism.org. Twenty-year-long Harvard University project to document the changing U.S. religious landscape. Of particular interest, Case Studies in Religious Pluralism explore critical incidents of religious interaction in contemporary U.S. context.

Stoller, Paul, and Cheryl Oakes. 1987. *In Sorcery's Shadow: A Memoir of Apprenticeship among the Songhay of Niger*. Chicago: University of Chicago Press.

What makes someone healthy? The oldest twins in the world, sisters Ena Pugh and Lily Millward of Garthbregny, Wales, turned 100 on January 4, 2010, to much fanfare. The national papers touted the sisters' simple lifestyle, love of laughter, close family ties, exercise, religious faith, and good deeds. "Great-grandmother Lily revealed the secret of their long life is 'laughter and having a joke with each other.' She said 'We used to work on the farm all day, but we would enjoy ourselves.' 'It was a lot of fun and sociable. We've been very lucky and we have always been in good health' " (Daily Mail 2010).

p. 625

p. 631

p. 633

p. 635

p. 637

p. 638

CHAPTER 16
Health and Illness

When we hear about people who live to a ripe old age, such as the twins on the opposite page, we tend to attribute their longevity to good genes or a healthy lifestyle. But is that the whole picture? What is the total range of factors that lead to good health? Let's look at another region of the world to get a broader perspective.

North of the Texas–Mexico border, half a million people live in impoverished communities called *colonias*. Established in the 1950s to house migrant Mexican workers brought to work on America's farms, *colonias* now are permanent settlements. Located largely outside incorporated towns and cities, many lack municipal services of water, sewage, paved roads, and public transport. Fully 64 percent of residents were born in the United States, including 85 percent of those under age 18. Still, residents of *colonias* struggle to maintain their health. They have limited access to health care, and what they receive lacks continuity between visits. As of 2011, 80 percent had no health insurance. The Texas Department of State Health Services reported incidences of dysentery, cholera, and hepatitis A in the *colonias* far above the state average. Tuberculosis rates were double the state average and four times the U.S. national average. Asthma and bronchitis were common ailments, as were mosquito and tick-borne illnesses such as dengue fever and lyme disease. Even Hansen's disease, also known as leprosy, continued to occur (Ramshaw 2011).

What accounts for the health disparities between the hundred-year-old British twins and the residents of the *colonias*? Conventional wisdom attributes health and longevity to a combination of "good genes" and good behavioral choices: eating right, not smoking, drinking in moderation, avoiding illegal drugs, exercising, and even flossing. These criteria mesh with core American values of individualism, personal responsibility, and the benefits of hard work and clean living. But are these factors sufficient to explain health and longevity—or the lack of it? Getting sick is a part of life. Everyone experiences colds, fevers, cuts and bruises, perhaps a broken bone. But some people get sick more often than others. Death and dying are part of life; but some people suffer more and die sooner, while others are healthier and live longer. Anthropologists are interested in knowing why.

In this chapter we will explore anthropologists' growing interest in health and illness. Although these concerns have deep roots in our discipline, the specialization of *medical anthropology* has grown immensely since the 1980s as our discipline's key research strategies—intensive fieldwork, extensive participant observation in local communities, and deep immersion in the daily lives of people and their local problems and experiences—have proven profoundly effective in solving pressing public health problems.

Medical anthropologists employ a variety of analytical perspectives to examine the wide range of experiences and practices that humans associate with disease, illness, health, and well-being—both today and in the past. We study the spread of disease and pathogens through the human population (known as epidemiology) by examining the *medical ecology*: the interaction of diseases with the natural environment and human culture. Looking more broadly, medical anthropologists use an *interpretivist approach* to study health systems as systems of meaning: How do humans across cultures make sense of health and illness? How do we think and talk and feel about illness, pain, suffering, birth, and mortality? *Critical medical anthropology* explores the impact of inequality on human health in two important ways. First, it considers how economic and political systems, race, class, gender, and sexuality create and perpetuate unequal access to health care. Second, it examines how health systems themselves are systems of power that promote disparities in health by defining who is sick, who gets treated, and how the treatment is provided.

Medical anthropology's holistic approach to health and illness—examining epidemiology, meaning, and power—assumes that health and illness are more than a result of germs, individual behavior, and genes. Health is also a product of our environment; our access to adequate nutrition, housing, education, and health care; and the absence of poverty, violence, and warfare.

In this chapter we will explore the following questions:

- How does culture shape our ideas of health and illness?
- How can anthropologists help solve health care problems?
- Why does the distribution of health and illness mirror that of wealth and power?
- How is globalization changing the experience of health and illness and the practice of medicine?

By the end of the chapter, you will understand how anthropologists approach the study of health and illness and how these concepts vary across cultures. You will be able to recognize how your own conceptions of health and illness are a cultural construction. You will be able to critically analyze both the systems of power that shape access to health care and the way in which health systems create and exacerbate inequalities within and between populations.

FIGURE 16.1 Globally, people have created a vast array of healing practices, all intricately intertwined with local cultural understandings of disease, health, illness, and the body. *Left*, a clinical assistant performs an ultrasound sonogram on a pregnant woman. *Right*, an Indian healer provides a villager with an ayurvedic massage.

How Does Culture Shape Our Ideas of Health and Illness?

What does it mean to be healthy? The World Health Organization proposes that **health** includes not merely the absence of disease and infirmity but complete physical, mental, and social well-being. This is a standard that few people in the world currently attain. Perhaps it is enough to be functionally healthy—not perfectly well, but healthy enough to do what you need to do: get up in the morning, go to school, go to work, reproduce the species. What level of health do you expect, hope for, and strive for? What level of health enables your culture to thrive?

Medical anthropologists have dedicated significant effort to document healing practices and health systems around the globe, from indigenous and tribal communities and urban metropolises to farming communities and groups of migrant workers. In the process, medical anthropologists have identified a vast array of healing practices and health systems created by people worldwide—ideas about the causes of health and disease, and varied cultural strategies to address pain, cure illness, and promote health. One key finding is that these beliefs and

health: The absence of disease and infirmity, as well as the presence of physical, mental, and social well-being.

practices are intricately intertwined with the way local cultures imagine the world works and the relationship of an individual's body to his or her surroundings.

In assessing how disease and health conditions affect specific populations and how specific cultural groups diagnose, manage, and treat health-related problems, medical anthropologists have found it useful to distinguish between disease and illness. A **disease** is a discrete, natural entity that can be clinically identified and treated by a health professional. A disease may be caused genetically or through infection by bacteria, a virus, or parasites. But the bacteria, virus, or parasite are the same regardless of location or cultural context. Illness, however, is more than the biological disease. **Illness** is the individual patient's experience of sickness—the culturally defined understanding of disease. It includes the way he or she feels about it, talks about it, thinks about it, and experiences it within a particular cultural context. Diseases can be observed, measured, and treated by sufferers and healers. But culture gives meaning to disease, shaping the human experience of illness, pain, suffering, dying, and death (Singer and Baer 2007).

People recognize widely different symptoms, illnesses, and causes for health challenges and have developed widely different strategies for achieving and maintaining health. Though the stereotypical Western images of health care often revolve around doctors in white coats, dentists' chairs, hospitals, strong medications, and advanced technology (such as X-rays, MRIs, and CT scans), medical anthropologists have found that these are not the primary points of access to health care for most people in the world. Nor are they even the first point of access for most people in Western countries. Rather, before seeking the assistance of a trained medical professional, people everywhere apply their personal medical knowledge, their own strategies—often handed down within families or communities—for dealing with disease, illness, pain, and discomfort.

The Anthropology of Childbirth

The anthropology of childbirth provides one clear example of the cross-cultural variation of health beliefs and practices. Childbirth is a universal biological event. Indeed, the physiology of childbirth—the biological process—is the same no matter where the birth occurs. But anthropological research shows that cultures around the world have developed unique practices and beliefs about pregnancy, delivery, and the treatment of newborns and their mothers that shape the way childbirth is understood and experienced.

A Comparative View of Four Cultures Different cultures conceptualize birth in different ways, and these shared understandings shape women's experiences. For example, a popular view of birth in the United States sees it as a

disease: A discrete natural entity that can be clinically identified and treated by a health professional.

illness: The individual patient's experience of sickness.

What Do You Do When You Get Sick?

Take a few minutes to consider your own strategies for getting healthy or staying healthy. The following questions may help you to assess your own understandings of health, disease, illness, and proper health care.

- *Whom do you call?* Do you call your mom, dad, doctor, pharmacy, health food store, pastor, friends, massage therapist, chiropractor, campus health center, hospital?
- *What strategies do you use to get well?* Do you sleep, drink orange juice, eat chicken soup, take vitamin C, get antibiotics? Do you starve a cold and feed a fever? Do you follow practices from a culture outside the United States?
- *What strategies do you use to relieve the pain?* Do you take medications for fever, headache, cough, and running nose, or do you let them run their course? Do you take over-the-counter pain relievers or get a doctor's prescription for something more powerful? Do you apply heat or ice? Do you ask for a massage?
- *How do you figure out what made you sick so you don't get sick again?* Do you wash your hands more often? Use hand sanitizer? Filter or boil your water? Consult an older adult, a doctor, or an online source such as WebMD?

- *When you are sick, how do you keep others from being infected?* Do you cover your mouth when you sneeze? Do you stop hugging and kissing your friends and loved ones? Do you take medications or other preparations more regularly?
- *How do you feel about getting sick?* What do you think getting sick says about you as a person? What does it say about you if you have certain symptoms: cold, fever, diarrhea, a sexually transmitted infection?
- *Is there a social cause of your illness or disease?* Is it from poor hygiene by others, lack of clean water, or improper food inspection or preparation? Does a stigma about the illness or disease keep you from seeking treatment? Is treatment too expensive for you? Is it too difficult for you to access health care (too far away)?

As you assess your replies, consider how your strategies have been shaped by your culture. How did you learn these things? What is the culture of information and communication about health, disease, and illness that shapes your attitudes and actions? Can you imagine that someone from another culture might have very different strategies and responses, yet ones that are just as effective?

---

medical procedure—what Robbie Davis-Floyd calls the "technocratic birth" (Davis-Floyd 1992). In this view, women become patients—sick and helpless, seeking the assistance of a medical professional to resolve a dangerous life crisis. In contrast, in Holland birth is perceived as an entirely natural process; in Sweden, as an intensely personal and fulfilling achievement; in Yucatán, Mexico, as a stressful but normal part of life. These differing conceptualizations

FIGURE 16.2 The physiological process of childbirth may be universal, but the experience of childbirth, including the approach toward pain, varies from culture to culture. *Left to right:* The Dutch view birth as an entirely natural process that often takes place at home with no pain medication. In Sweden, delivery rooms are quiet, comforting spaces where women decide on their own pain medication. In the Yucatán, Mexico, women labor in a hammock or on a stool at home, surrounded by family and supported by a midwife. In the U.S. delivery room, women become patients admitted for a procedure in a sterile environment with lots of equipment.

shape and justify the practices each culture puts into place to support, monitor, and control the birth process. Such practices include the location of the birth, the personnel who attend, the decision-making authority as the birth proceeds, and the expectations of pain and pain management. These differences underlie Brigitte Jordan and Robbie Davis-Floyd's (1993) study *Birth in Four Cultures*.

Birth experiences in Yucatán and the United States contrast sharply. Birth for many Mayan women surveyed in Jordan's study occurred in a small, dimly lit home with a dirt floor, attended by a local midwife using everyday materials, while family life continued around them. Mayan women rested in a hammock, considered the best position for labor, although in the final stages of pushing the women might sit astride a wooden chair turned on its side. The husband and the woman's mother were usually present throughout the entire process. Other women of the extended family, particularly those who had given birth before, might be present as well. During the final stages of labor, the husband and the woman's mother took turns sitting behind the woman, supporting her head and lifting her up toward the ceiling to relieve pressure from the contractions. In a difficult labor, other women would provide emotional and physical support, offering encouragement and participating in "birth talk" by urging, cajoling, and challenging the mother to finish pushing her baby out into the world. There were no drugs and no machines (Jordan and Davis-Floyd 1993).

In contrast, 98 percent of American births today occur in a sterile, brightly lit hospital with sophisticated equipment and the attention of highly trained medical professionals who enforce a strict separation of the laboring mother from family and daily life. The father may be present. Elaborate machinery monitors pregnancy and birth. Sonograms and amniocentesis assess the health of the fetus during pregnancy, and fetal heart monitors track the newborn's heartbeat and stress levels during delivery. Medications are sometimes administered

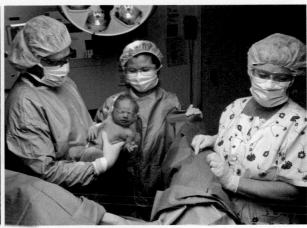

through epidural injections near the spinal cord to deaden the mother's pain. To advance childbirth during a difficult delivery, obstetricians may perform episiotomies, surgically widening the opening to the birth canal.

In 2010, one-third of all babies in the United States were delivered by cesarean section, a surgical procedure by which the baby is removed directly from the mother's abdomen rather than through the birth canal. This number was an increase from 20.7 percent in 1996 (U.S. Centers for Disease Control 2012). This rate of C-sections is among the highest in the world, a fact that raises questions about whether these procedures are performed out of necessity or are influenced by cultural understandings of birth and the institutional pressures that shape health care in hospitals. Rates also vary from region to region in the United States, a reflection of the regional cultural variations in the practice of Western medicine rather than an indication of regional variation in rates of complications.

Pain during Childbirth Can culture shape women's experience of pain during childbirth? Jordan notes that some women in every culture give birth without pain. But a certain amount of pain is expected in almost all cultures. What differs from one medical system to another is the way in which that pain is handled. Jordan's study explores the possibility that cultural expectations of pain during childbirth shape the actual experience and display of pain by laboring mothers.

The introduction of pain medication during childbirth is a recent phenomenon, emerging as part of twentieth-century medicine. Jordan's study found that the use of pain medication during labor was not consistent across cultures. In the United States, pain medication was administered at the discretion of the medical attendants and often delayed lest the drugs slow the course of labor. Jordan also found that to receive medication, a woman must convince her physician that her pain is severe. Jordan suggests that this dynamic shaped the woman's experience of childbirth, drawing attention away from the delivery and more toward pain—both the experience of pain and the performance of that pain. Obstetric wards in the United States, notes Jordan, as a result of this negotiation between patient and physician, have a relatively high level of noise, anxiety, and vocal despair bordering on panic during the birth process.

In contrast, obstetric wards in Sweden are characterized by quiet, intense concentration on the process of giving birth. Before labor begins, Swedish women are introduced to a variety of pain medicines, their benefits, and side effects. During labor the women themselves make decisions about how much, if any, medication to take and when. Women do not need to convince medical staff of the need for pain medication.

The Dutch view birth as an entirely natural process. They administer no pain medication during the normal course of labor, even in many of the same situations that would lead to the use of pain medication in the United States. The Dutch, like the Maya of Yucatán, are reluctant to interfere with the birth process, waiting for nature to take its course and trusting that women's bodies know best how to handle the process. Birth is not considered a crisis or a medical emergency.

In Yucatán, pain is seen as a natural and expected part of childbirth. It is not frightening. The work of labor is considered a normal part of life. In this view the suffering and pain will pass soon, especially if the mother works hard. Labor is considered a collective process—an experience shared by the woman's husband, mother, and female family members. The pain marks a significant yet normal part of the life experience.

Jordan reflects that the intense experience of childbirth reinforces key Mayan cultural values, particularly local understandings of the importance of hard work, endurance, and the tolerance of difficulty. The Maya view these values and personal qualities as desirable in childbirth as well as in life. During the stress of childbirth, women display these qualities in the public sphere.

As you reflect on the anthropology of birth described above, consider what you have heard about your own birth. Where did it take place? Who was present? What was your mother's experience like? Consider interviewing your mother or another woman in your extended family about her experience giving birth. How does her experience vary from what you might have expected? How does it compare to those described in this chapter? Can you identify culturally specific approaches to pregnancy and childbirth that emerge in their stories?

The variation of cultural approaches to labor and childbirth—a common human biological activity—suggest the extent to which cultural concepts of the body, health, illness, and pain may shape every aspect of a medical system.

Ethnomedicine

Over the years, medical anthropologists have focused extensive research on **ethnomedicine**. This field involves the comparative study of local systems of health and healing rooted in culturally specific norms and values; it includes the ways in which local cultures create unique strategies for identifying and treating disease and conceptualizing the experience of health, illness, and the physical world.

Early research on ethnomedicine focused primarily on non-Western health systems and emphasized natural healing remedies such as herbs, teas, and massage; reliance on religious ritual in health practices; and the role of locally trained healers such as shamans, spirit mediums, and priests as health care professionals. The subdiscipline of **ethnopharmacology** emerged from efforts to document and describe the local use of natural substances, such as herbs, powders, teas, and animal products in healing remedies and practices. But today, as we will see, even Western biomedicine, which emphasizes science and technology in healing but also reflects a particular system of cultural meanings, is considered through the lens of ethnomedicine. Today, medical anthropologists use the concept of ethnomedicine to refer to local health systems everywhere (Saillant and Genest 2007; Green 1999).

Healing Practices of Tibetan Buddhism Applied in Northern India

French anthropologist Laurent Pordié has documented one typical system of ethnomedicine—a variation of Tibetan medicine practiced in the sparsely populated Ladakh region of northern India. Roughly three times the size of Switzerland and straddling the northwestern Himalayas, Ladakh is home to 250,000 villagers, mostly Tibetans, living primarily in remote areas at altitudes up to 5,000 meters (16,400 feet). Their only health care is provided by approximately two hundred *amchis*, traditional healers whose healing practices are deeply rooted in Tibetan Buddhism.

Amchi medicine is based on achieving bodily and spiritual balance between the individual and the surrounding universe. *Amchis* diagnose ailments by asking questions of the patient, examining bodily wastes, and carefully taking the pulse. Recommended treatments include changes in diet and behavior—both social and religious—and the use of natural medicines made from local plants and minerals. Shaped into pills, these remedies are then boiled in water and taken by the patient as an infusion, or drink. Pordié reports that *amchi* treatments are effective for the vast majority of the Ladakhis' health problems, such as respiratory difficulty from the high altitude and smoke in dwellings, hypertension from high-salt diets, and psychological stress. *Amchis* do not perform surgery. Patients who need surgery are transported, if possible, to an urban area to be treated by a doctor trained in Western biological medicine.

ethnomedicine: Local systems of health and healing rooted in culturally specific norms and values.

ethnopharmacology: The documentation and description of the local use of natural substances in healing remedies and practices.

MAP 16.1
Ladakh

FIGURE 16.3 An *amchi*, a traditional healer, mixes medicines in his home pharmacy in Ladakh, India.

Amchi medicine plays a vital role in the survival of Ladakhis. But the *amchi* and their healing practices are under threat from Westernization, militarization, and economic liberalization. For example, the Indian government strongly favors Western biological medicine over traditional ethnomedicine, though it is still unable to provide care to its dispersed rural population. The pervasive presence of the Indian military in response to civil unrest in the bordering Kashmir region inhibits the movement of *amchi* as they gather plants and minerals for natural medicines. In addition, urbanization and modernization, particularly market-oriented economic activity, have increasingly fragmented community life. In the past, *amchi* healers bartered their services for help in plowing, harvesting, and raising livestock. The *amchi* then had time to forage for medicinal plants. But with the penetration of market-oriented economics even into the rural areas, the barter system has been undermined. *Amchis* must now run their therapeutic practices more like businesses, selling medicines and charging for services rather than bartering. Their time to gather medicines has become limited. And with increasing social mobility, the intergenerational transmission of *amchi* skills has been disrupted.

To address this challenge to the *amchi* system, Pordié and a French nongovernmental organization, Nomad RSI, have been working with local *amchis* to establish a coordinated system for growing medicinal plants and distributing them among far-flung villages. *Amchis* from across Ladakh now gather annually to share diagnosis and treatment strategies, and a school has been established to train new practitioners.

Although Tibetan medicine struggles in rural areas where it has been practiced for centuries, it is experiencing unprecedented prominence internationally. Pordié's study also considers how the local *amchi* system of healing is entering the global health arena. Over the last thirty years, as more Tibetans migrate abroad and carry their cultural and religious practices with them, Tibetan medicine has been embraced as an "alternative medicine." The international health market, particularly in Europe and North America, has welcomed Tibetan medicine as natural, spiritual, and holistic, drawing as it does from indigenous, traditional practices, Buddhist moral values, and Tibetan ecological worldviews. *Amchis* and their practices of Tibetan medicine have become quite popular.

Pordié recounts the story of meeting one *amchi* who was returning from an international speaking tour:

> Impeccably dressed in crimson flannel trousers and a mustard yellow shirt, a Buddhist rosary clasped between the fingers of one hand and a passport replete with visas clutched in the other, the *amchi* from the mountains of the western Himalayas returns to his country after another visit to the United States of America, where for two months he had delivered his teachings on his centuries-old medical art. I meet up with him again in the airport in Delhi. . . . [T]he *amchi* invites me to accompany him to the nearest cybercafé. He wants to check his email immediately. He announces proudly that he is expecting an official invitation abroad. This man, who a few years earlier had marveled at my laptop computer, is today a confirmed Internet user. He even amiably makes fun of me when he notices my astonishment at the speed at which his messages appear on the screen. "You stayed too long in the mountains," he says, and bursts out laughing. (2008, 6–7)

With this portrait, Pordié warns against representing these cultures and their medical practices as artifacts in a museum. Instead, practitioners of what medical anthropologists call ethnomedicine hail from vibrant communities and use their healing practices to cure those at home while reinventing their traditions to engage today's world. Because it is perceived as traditional, Tibetan medicine is highly sought by people in the West. But this tradition has also been reinvented and reinterpreted to meet the contemporary medical needs of the Tibetan community and the healing desires of others far beyond their local borders.

So, after all, why not the Internet for everyone? This mountain dweller with long hair tied in a chignon, a Tibetan physician by trade, a Tantric practitioner returning from the Americas with an ultra-bright smile and brand new spectacles . . . why shouldn't he communicate with I don't know which extremity of the planet thanks to a high-speed electronic connection? Why should this man remain trapped in the mountains, an image from a postcard or tourist's photo album, when his role is also to provide remedies for illnesses afflicting people elsewhere? (2008, 7)

In this era of globalization, this transnational *amchi* is just as authentic as the *amchi* prescribing healing remedies in a remote village in Ladakh.

From the perspective of medical anthropology, all medical systems constitute a form of ethnomedicine because they develop from and are embedded in a particular local cultural reality. Medical anthropologists have played a significant role in documenting the diverse forms of treatment and care as well as the complex medical epistemologies (ways of knowing) that have been developed by local cultures across the globe. As local systems have come into contact and adopted care and healing strategies from one another, these anthropological efforts have helped to legitimize and advance their status in the global conversation about health and illness. From the perspective of medical anthropology, we might call all healers ethno-healers, practicing local health knowledge about disease, illness, and health. We now turn to consider why this may be true, whether the healer is an *amchi* or a cardiovascular surgeon.

Biomedicine

Biomedicine is the approach to health that has risen to predominance in many Western cultures. **Biomedicine** seeks to apply the principles of biology and the natural sciences (such as physics and chemistry) to the practice of diagnosing diseases and promoting healing. Individual and institutional practitioners of biomedicine—whether doctors, pharmacies, hospitals, medical schools, or pharmaceutical companies—work to clinically identify discrete natural disease entities that can be diagnosed and treated by biomedically trained health professionals. The term *biomedicine* encompasses many local variations and a wide range of treatment practices. But the use of medication, surgery, and other invasive treatments is characteristic of biomedical healing practices (Saillant and Genest 2007; Baer, Singer, and Susser 2003).

Varieties of biomedicine occur across Western industrialized countries, as we considered in our earlier discussion of the anthropology of birth. For

biomedicine: A practice, often associated with Western medicine, that seeks to apply the principles of biology and the natural sciences to the practice of diagnosing disease and promoting healing.

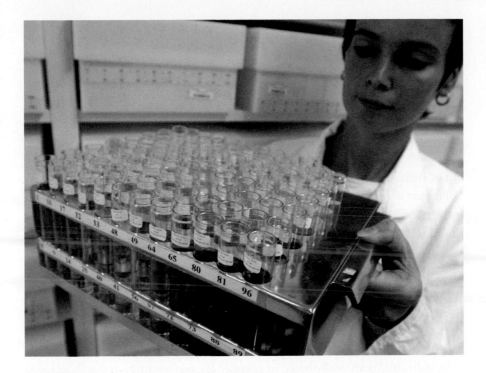

example, British doctors are far less concerned about elevated blood pressure and cholesterol counts than are their counterparts in the United States. The German health system, which uses far fewer antibiotics than other Western health systems, recognizes two complementary approaches: *schulmedizin* (school medicine), which focuses on typical biomedical treatments, and *naturheilkunde* (nature cure), which draws on natural remedies. Biomedicine in the United States emphasizes the most extreme treatments—psychotropic drugs, antibiotics, cholesterol and blood pressure medications, C-section births, hysterectomies, and breast cancer screenings (Payer 1996).

Because biomedicine is closely linked with Western economic and political expansion, it has taken hold well beyond its original local cultural boundaries and increasingly has gained an aura of universality, modernity, and progress. But medical anthropologists have been careful to point out the ways in which, like other ethnomedical systems, the epistemology (ways of knowing) and practice of Western biomedicine are rooted in a particular system of knowledge that draws heavily on European enlightenment values. This system includes ideas of rationality, individualism, and progress—values and ideas that are culturally specific and not universally held. The individual body is the focus of treatment. Diagnosis and treatment are based on rational scientific data. And there is a firm conviction that direct intervention through surgery and medications based on scientific facts will positively affect health.

Biomedical Conceptions of the Body Nancy Scheper-Hughes and Margaret Lock (1987) recount a now-famous story of a challenging case that illustrates the powerful influence of cultural values on biomedical healing practices. At a teaching hospital, the case of a woman suffering chronic, debilitating headaches was presented to a lecture hall of 250 medical students. When asked about her ailment, the woman recounted that her alcoholic husband beat her, that she had been virtually housebound for five years while caring for her ailing and incontinent mother-in-law, and that she worried about her teenage son, who was failing out of high school. Then one of the medical students raised her hand and asked, "But what is the *real* cause of her headaches?" By this the student meant, What is the real *biomedical* diagnosis; what neurochemical changes created the pain? In the mind of the medical student, the patient's statements were irrelevant to the task of identifying the cause of her pain or determining a treatment. The student's biomedical training, with its focus on the individual body, science, and technology, had not prepared her to recognize that social experiences might produce embodied responses.

The Human Microbiome Is a typical biomedical notion of the discrete, treatable, individual body really based in science? Recent scientific research suggests that our bodies are not as independent or as self-contained as we have thought. Researchers at the Human Microbiome Project have discovered that the human body, made up of ten trillion cells, is also host to one hundred trillion microbes—microscopic organisms such as bacteria, viruses, and fungi—that live on and within our bodies. Rather than being discrete biological entities, our bodies appear to be more like complex ecosystems (think tropical rainforests), habitats for trillions of different organisms living with us. Thus, we can define the **human microbiome** as the complete collection of microorganisms in the body's ecosystem.

human microbiome: The complete collection of micoorganisms in the human body's ecosystem.

These microbes are not random hitchhikers, opportunistic parasites, or dangerous outsider enemies of our bodies. They are deeply integrated into the ways our bodies work. Microbes help us digest food, synthesize vitamins, make natural antibiotics, produce natural moisturizer for the skin, guide the immune system, and spur the development of body parts (such as the intestines). Scientists suggest that we have evolved with these microbes as part of our personal ecosystem for promoting health and combating the pathogens that create disease in our bodies. We not only tolerate these microbes; we need them (Helmreich 2009).

Discoveries of the role of microbes in our bodies' experience of health and illness open the door to rethinking one of the central tenets of Western biomedicine—the notion of the discrete individual body—and offer new pathways for the innovative treatment of both common and rare diseases (Zimmer 2010, 2011).

Biomedical Rituals of Surgery Another central tenet of biomedicine has been its reliance on modern, rational science as the basis for diagnosis and treatment. But are all of its theories and practices truly rational and scientific? Or might some lie in the realm of local cultural belief and ritual? Let's consider the practice of surgery.

Surgery is perhaps the zenith of biomedical activity. A dangerous and delicate procedure, its practice utilizes high-tech equipment and requires intensive medical training. During surgery, which is a radically invasive practice, surgeons cut open their patients and alter what is inside them. But anthropological analysis suggests that biomedical practices and procedures have both scientific and ritual components. Pearl Katz's *The Scalpel's Edge* (1999), for example, examines the elaborate rituals of surgeons at a Canadian hospital, rituals that are common practice for all surgeons today.

Katz focuses on the surgeons' practice of scrubbing before surgery. Scrubbing involves elaborate actions and equipment, performed in a prescribed order, style, and duration. Because infecting a patient's internal organs is an ever-present danger in surgery, scrubbing limits the likelihood that the surgeon will introduce pathogens to the operating arena. Surgeons, however, know that scrubbing does not eliminate all pathogens. Yet they follow the scrubbing protocols without deviation. Based on interviews and observations, Katz suggests that the elaborate practices of scrubbing serve a purpose beyond a strictly biomedical one. Scrubbing and following the rules of a ritual-like practice serve an additional unarticulated, unscientific benefit of reducing anxiety in nurses and doctors, boosting their confidence, and limiting errors as they engage in delicate and dangerous operations.

Are There Other Global Health Systems?

Although Western biomedicine is intimately tied to Western culture and its values, anthropologists also acknowledge that with the spread of Western cultural influences, biomedicine has crossed beyond its cultural and regional boundaries to become a global health system now used in a wide array of countries as well as in international health agencies that engage in health promotion globally. But are there health systems other than biomedicine that function on a global level? Earlier in this chapter, we discussed the growing popularity of Tibetan medicine, especially in Europe and North America. Now let's consider Chinese medicine today as one health system with a long history, elaborate theories of health and illness, a global reach, and proven effectiveness (e.g., Zhan 2009; Farquhar 1986; Scheid 2002).

Chinese Medicine Today In very general terms, Chinese medicine conceptualizes health as a harmonious relationship between Heaven and Earth, which

MAP 16.2
Canada

FIGURE 16.5 Doctors perform elaborate scrubbing rituals before surgery. Are all the reasons for this practice scientific?

are considered the major forces of the universe. An individual's *qi*—translated as "breath" or "air" and referring to an energy found in all living things—must be balanced and flowing in equilibrium with the rest of the universe for a person to be healthy. Illness occurs when the *qi* is blocked and the flow and balance are disrupted. In traditional Chinese medicine, health care practices such as acupuncture, *tuina* (therapeutic massage), acupressure, moxibustion (the burning of herbs near the skin), and the consumption of healing herbs and teas promote health by restoring the free flow of *qi* along the body's meridians, or energy pathways (Farquhar 1986; Scheid 2002).

In her book *Other-Worldly: Making Chinese Medicine through Transnational Frames* (2009), medical anthropologist Mei Zhan challenges many of the stereotypes of Chinese medicine: that it is somehow emblematic of an ancient Chinese culture, regionally limited with fixed healing practices that are the antithesis of, or merely "alternative" to, Western biomedicine. Instead, Zhan argues that Chinese medical practices vary widely even within China. Rather than undergoing a regimented and fixed set of health care practices, patients participate in a dynamic health care environment. Patients and doctors carefully negotiate treatments. And no good physician ever writes the same prescription twice because the treatment must meet the needs of each specific patient (Scheid 2002).

Not only does Chinese medical practice vary within China today, but it has varied significantly over time. Zhan notes three key historical moments over the past century that have significantly reshaped modern Chinese medicine. First, the early-twentieth-century expansion of Western biomedicine into China influenced the practice of Chinese medicine. Western biomedicine's emphasis on institution building, laboratory research, clinical and teaching practices, and even insurance policies reshaped Chinese medical thinking and practice. Today, the everyday world of Chinese medicine includes interactions with biomedical professionals. Patients move back and forth between biomedicine and Chinese medicine.

Second, upon the founding of the People's Republic of China in 1949, the new Chinese government moved to institutionalize traditional Chinese medicine, subsidize research, formalize teaching, and establish a process for professional certification. The government widely promoted traditional Chinese medicine as a low-tech, low-cost approach to preventive care and trained and deployed "barefoot doctors" to promote health care in every rural Chinese community. The government also exported traditional Chinese medicine—including medicines, doctors, and health-promotion strategies—to the developing world, particularly Africa, to establish international ties of solidarity with other developing nations. This move marked a rapid expansion of Chinese medicine beyond China's national borders into the international arena.

Finally, Zhan documents the shift of Chinese medicine beginning in the 1980s from primarily a developing-world medical practice to one with established niches in developed countries. Traditional Chinese medicine has become popular with cosmopolitan consumers in China, North America, and Europe, both as a preventive medicine and as an alternative treatment for illness when biomedicine proves ineffective. Flows of Chinese medical practitioners and Chinese medical knowledge have increased encounters with Chinese medicine, particularly along routes between Asia and Europe and across the Pacific Ocean. Throughout much of California, for example, acupuncture and Chinese herbal medicine have grown increasingly popular. They have gained a foothold in mainstream medical practices ranging from biomedical hospitals to medical schools, and they are increasingly covered by U.S. health insurance policies—a sign of their growing acceptance even within the predominant Western biomedical framework.

Zhan carefully demonstrates how Chinese medicine—often viewed as an ancient, culturally specific, fixed ethnomedicine "alternative" to Western biomedicine—has been relocated in both time and space to represent a modern, effective, globally respected body of health care practices (Zhan 2009; Farquhar 1994; Scheid and MacPherson 2012).

FIGURE 16.6 Chinese medicine is a globalized health system with its own internal logic for diagnosing disease and promoting healing. *Left,* Chinese diagram of meridians, or energy pathways, indicates potential sites of blockage that can be restored through treatment with acupuncture (*right*), massage, herbs, and teas.

How Can Anthropologists Help Solve Health Care Problems?

Anthropologists can apply research strategies and key theoretical concepts of our field to solve pressing public health problems, understand the spread of disease, and improve the delivery of health care. In fact, the work of an anthropologist may be just as crucial to explaining and resolving health challenges as that of a physician, epidemiologist, pathologist, or virologist. The discussion below illustrates this point through the groundbreaking efforts of anthropologists working in Haiti and Papua New Guinea.

Creating a Public Health System in Rural Haiti

When the American Paul Farmer first visited Cange, Haiti, in 1983, the remote village of one hundred families was one of the poorest places in one of the world's poorest countries. Most people in Haiti lived on $1 a day, but residents of Cange lived on less. Along with intense poverty, Farmer found a village overwhelmed by high levels of infant mortality, childhood malnutrition, typhoid, dysentery, HIV/AIDS, and tuberculosis. Many residents were water refugees, having been pushed off their land by the construction of a hydroelectric dam that flooded their valley to provide power to Haiti's cities and irrigation for large landholders and agribusinesses downstream. With the best farmland taken out of production by the dam's reservoir, the surrounding area suffered from widespread deforestation, soil erosion, and terrible health statistics (Farmer 2006).

Farmer's work in Cange, popularized in the best-selling biography *Mountains beyond Mountains* (Kidder 2003), began with the encouragement of a Haitian Anglican priest, Fritz Lafontant, who had been working in the area for years. In 1984, the year after Farmer's first visit to Haiti, he enrolled in Harvard's medical school and doctoral program in anthropology. He believed that anthropology would be essential to addressing the health needs of poor Haitians. The delivery of medicines and medical procedures would not be enough, he felt. Deeper questions would need to be asked: What made the people sick? How could they stay healthy after being treated? The basic approaches of an anthropologist—understanding the local language, norms, values, classifications of reality, and religious beliefs—would help a trained physician to think about health in the broadest possible sense.

While at Harvard, Farmer immediately began to apply what he was learning, using the research strategies of anthropology and the professional knowledge of medicine to create a public health system for Cange. Living in the community and speaking the local language, Farmer engaged in a process of listening to the residents' needs and experiences and working with them to identify and

MAP 16.3
Cange

FIGURE 16.7 How do you create an effective public health system? *Left,* people seeking health care in rural Haiti sleep outside following long journeys from their villages. *Right,* patients receive direct treatment at a clinic.

treat their public health problems. First he recruited a few villagers to help him conduct a health census. Moving from hut to hut in Cange and two neighboring villages, the census takers identified the breadth of the residents' health problems and established a baseline by which to measure future success. To address the community's needs, Farmer launched Partners in Health, or Zanmi Lasante in the Cange language, with financial support from backers in the United States.

Zanmi Lasante began to create multiple lines of defense to protect the Cange villagers' health. Clean water came first. Because they lived on Haiti's central plateau, the villagers had been climbing down an eight-hundred-foot hillside to draw water from the stagnant reservoir created by the hydroelectric dam. Using old plastic jugs and calabash gourds, they had been carrying water back up the hill to their huts, where it sometimes sat uncovered for days. But now Father Lafontant recruited a construction crew from an Episcopal Church diocese in South Carolina to tap into an underground river to provide fresh water to the families at the top of the hill. Thereafter, Farmer and his associates noticed that the incidence of infant deaths began to drop almost immediately.

Sanitation and hygiene came next. Father LaFontant organized the construction of latrines (outdoor toilets) to improve human waste disposal and protect the water supply. He and Farmer raised money to replace the dirt floors and thatched roofs of the residents' crude lean-to homes with tin roofs and cement floors. An expanded village school provided a place to teach children to read and write and a place to teach the community about basic health practices. Malnourished schoolchildren received free meals with dignity. Childhood vaccinations dramatically improved health in the community.

Perhaps most significant, Zanmi Lasante trained local community members as community health workers. Being familiar with the local language, social structure, values, and religious beliefs, the community health workers were able to identify emerging health care problems, administer vaccinations, and assist

Paul Farmer

Upon receiving a copy of Paul Farmer's *Infections and Inequalities: The Modern Plagues* (1999), Farmer's biographer told him that he planned on reading his other two books, his "oeuvre" (his complete body of work). To which Farmer replied: "Ah, but that is not my oeuvre. To see my oeuvre you have to come to Haiti."[a]

Farmer, a medical anthropologist with both a medical degree and a doctorate in anthropology from Harvard University, examines the connections between poverty and disease, as well as the unequal distribution of medical technologies around the globe. "We have to think about health in the broadest sense," Farmer says.

Critical of the U.S. government's plan for fixing Haiti's economy, a plan that Farmer insisted would only aid business interests but do nothing to relieve the suffering of the Haitian people, Farmer co-founded Partners in Health (PIH) in 1987. This organization's work began in Cange, in the central plateau of Haiti, but has since spread to many other countries, developing into a worldwide health organization. Although PIH now regularly takes him around the world, Farmer still spends a significant amount of time working as the medical director at Zanmi Lasante, a PIH hospital in Cange.

Farmer's work is divided into research, medicine, and advocacy. Indeed, he effectively illustrates that exorbitant costs need not characterize health care. "Farmer and his staff of community health workers treated most tuberculosis patients in their huts and spent between $150 and $200 to cure an uncomplicated case. The same cure in the United States, where most TB patients were hospitalized, usually cost between $15,000 and $20,000. [A] local hospital in Massachusetts was treating about 175,000 patients a year and had an annual operating budget of $60 million. In 1999 Zanmi Lasante had treated roughly the same number of people, at the medical complex and out in the communities, and had spent about $1.5 million."

Farmer's work reveals the value of integrating anthropological research and medicine. Early on in his career, Farmer gathered a group of community health workers and professionals in Haiti to discuss what was wrong with their system for treating tuberculosis. The health care workers argued that malnutrition contributed to ineffective TB treatment: "Giving people medicine for TB and not giving them food is like washing your hands and drying them in the dirt." Yet most of the Haitian professionals countered that the problem was rooted more in the minds of the patients, that "once they felt better but long before they were cured, patients stopped taking their pills.... [T]hey did this in part because they didn't believe TB came from microbes but believed it was sent to them by enemies, via sorcery."

Torn between these two positions, Farmer created a study. He selected two groups of TB patients, most of whom believed that TB was caused by sorcery. Each group received free treatment, but one group got other services

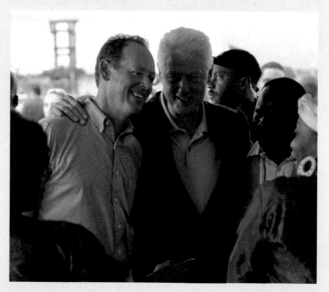

Anthropologist and medical doctor Paul Farmer worked with former U.S. president Bill Clinton to deliver U.S. aid to Haiti in 2009.

as well, "including regular visits from community health workers and small monthly cash stipends for food and child care and transportation to Cange." The results were dramatic: "Of the patients who had received only free medicine, a mere 48 percent were cured. By contrast, everyone in the group that received the cash stipends and other services made a full recovery. Whether a patient believed that TB came from germs or sorcery didn't seem to have made any difference at all." At the conclusion of the study, Farmer interviewed one of his patients, an elderly Haitian woman who had simultaneously claimed to know that TB comes from microbes and to believe in sorcery. When he asked her how she could maintain these two seemingly contradictory beliefs, she said, "Honey, are you incapable of complexity?" This study, then, was a sign for Farmer to worry not about a patient's beliefs, but about the material and structural conditions of disease. Significantly, the results of this study emerged from the careful implementation of standard anthropological methods—namely, interviews and statistical analysis.

Since the 1990s, PIH has expanded to conduct community health promotion and community-based research on the spread of infectious disease—including tuberculosis, malaria and HIV / AIDS—in Haiti, Peru, Mexico, Guatemala, Russia, Rwanda, Burundi, Lesotho, and Malawi. In each locale, Farmer and his team examine the various social, political, and economic issues that dispro-portionately contribute to infection. PIH's vision is both medical and moral, based on solidarity rather than charity alone. As such, PIH simultaneously strives to "care for . . . patients, alleviate the root causes of disease, and share lessons learned with other countries and NGOs."[b]

When reflecting on anthropology's role, Farmer recalls being taught that "an ethnographer should observe, not try to change what was being observed. But practiced in that way, anthropology seemed 'impotent' in the face of 'every-day problems of adequate nutrition, clean water, and illness prevention.'"[c] As such, anthropology interests him less as a discipline unto itself and more as a tool for intervention.

Farmer's particular approach is a significant one. But it is not easy. Nevertheless, his practice of medical anthropology has enhanced our understanding of the spread of disease and, as a result, has reduced rates of infection worldwide. First, you perform "the distal intervention," curing the family of a disease. But vitally, "then you start changing the conditions that made them especially vulnerable to [disease] in the first place."[d]

[a] All quotes, unless otherwise noted, are from Kidder, Tracy. 2003. *Mountains Beyond Mountains: The Quest of Dr. Paul Farmer, a Man Who Could Cure the World.* New York: Random House.

[b] Partners In Health. www.pih.org/pages/what-we-do/.

[c] Farmer, Paul. 1985. "The Anthropologist Within." *Harvard Medical Alumni Bulletin* 59(1): 23–28.

[d] Ibid., 23.

people in taking medications. The newly constructed health clinic and hospital of Zanmi Lasante served those who were too sick to be cared for at home. Over time, Zanmi Lasante became one of the largest nongovernmental health care providers in Haiti, serving an area of 1.2 million people with more than four thousand doctors, nurses, and community health workers. The success of Zanmi Lasante in addressing the health needs of the people of Cange grew directly from Paul Farmer's anthropological approach.

In an essay written during his fieldwork and medical practice in Cange, Farmer commented that anthropology must involve more than the careful observation of problems (Farmer 1985). If anthropologists stop there, they fail to use their full power. Anthropology must be a tool for intervention, he argued. Farmer's research and work in Cange explored how anthropology could tackle the day-to-day challenges of health on the ground—nutrition, clean water, prevention of illness, and promotion of health. Public health work could be guided and greatly improved by the strategies and theoretical concerns of anthropology. However, to truly make a difference, anthropology must be used not only to analyze and scrutinize a problem but also to turn research into action.

Connecting Kuru and Cannibalism in Papua New Guinea

One of the early pioneers in medical anthropology, Shirley Lindenbaum, investigated the origins and spread of a disease called kuru among the South Fore people of the Eastern Highlands of Papua New Guinea. By the 1960s, the incidence of kuru had reached epidemic proportions. Lindenbaum's work provided insights crucial to developing successful strategies for its control and eventual eradication.

MAP 16.4
Papua New Guinea

Kuru, translated as "tremble" or "fear" for the uncontrollable tremors that its victims experience, is an acute degenerative disease of the central nervous system. Lindenbaum and her partner, Robert Glasse, arrived among the South Fore in 1961 at the height of the kuru epidemic. Earlier researchers had hypothesized that kuru was a genetic disease, passed down among biological kin from generation to generation. But patterns of infection observed by Lindenbaum raised questions about its genetic origins. Men were rarely affected; the victims were primarily women and children of both sexes. Among this part of the population, kuru was common and fatal. To test the genetic hypothesis, Lindenbaum used her anthropological training to track potential genetic links to kuru.

Lindenbaum studied the kinship patterns of the South Fore, mapping kinship terms, creating kinship charts, and conducting participant observation within families. Like Janet Carsten's study (see Chapter 10), Lindenbaum's research found that South Fore kinship was not strictly biological. Instead, it was very flexible, constructed among those who shared "one blood"—a concept created not by genetic inheritance but by eating together and residing in the same household. Even immigrants from other parts of Papua New Guinea could be incorporated into the kin group if they showed loyalty and observed local expectations and obligations. Lindenbaum concluded that kinship was not a reliable guide to genetic relationships, so she began to explore other potential factors in the spread of kuru.

Intensive fieldwork in the South Fore and neighboring communities documented political systems, agricultural production, gender roles, and ritual practices. Oral histories gathered from villagers throughout the highlands revealed that kuru had emerged only recently, around 1900, and had spread along a specific, traceable route, arriving in South Fore between 1930 and 1940. Kuru's rapid spread further ruled out a genetic basis for the disease. Instead, transmission patterns suggested that kuru might be an infectious disease spreading from person to person. But how did this occur?

Disease Transmission via a Death Ritual Of particular interest in Lindenbaum's fieldwork, the South Fore and other groups in the Papua New Guinea highlands practiced cannibalism, ingesting cooked human tissue. Specifically, as part of the death ritual, members of the kin group ate the bodies of their deceased relatives. Hypothesizing that the spread of kuru might be related to this ritual practice, Lindenbaum and Glasse collected the names of all those who had died of kuru and of all those who had consumed the body parts of deceased ancestors.

Although the practice was suppressed in the 1960s by the government and by Christian missionaries, the ingestion of cooked human tissue previously had been quite common among the South Fore. Because of this history, Lindenbaum and Glasse were able to collect extensive ethnographic data on the rules for consuming human flesh. The South Fore ate deceased ancestors, not enemies. They ate all body parts except the gall bladder, which was considered too bitter. While they did not eat ancestors who died of leprosy, dysentery, or certain other diseases, kuru forebears were looked upon favorably for ritual consumption. Not all Fore were cannibals. Most adult women consumed cooked human tissue, as did children of both sexes who ate what their mothers gave them. Few adult men ate flesh. Those who did never ate the bodies of women.

By correlating this data, the researchers found that the ritual guidelines matched the patterns of the epidemic's spread. This led to the conclusion that the infectious agent causing kuru was transmitted through the mortuary ceremonies as kin ate the bodies of their deceased ancestors and ingested the infection. Although kuru likely emerged spontaneously in the brain of one individual, the infectious agent that caused kuru was recycled and transmitted through the eating of deceased relatives' bodies, particularly the brain matter, spreading and amplifying within the communities of the South Fore and their neighbors over a relatively short period.

Through the careful anthropological research of Lindenbaum and Glasse, public health practices were developed to contain the spread of the kuru infectious agent. Combined with the elimination of cannibalism, the epidemic of kuru was alleviated and the spread of kuru stopped. Kuru has an extremely long gestation period in the infected person, so the last case was diagnosed in 2009, nearly fifty years after the end of ritual ingestion of human tissue. That case is still being monitored (Lindenbaum 2009).

Why Does the Distribution of Health and Illness Mirror That of Wealth and Power?

Writing in the late 1800s, Rudolf Virchow, a renowned pathologist considered to be one of the ancestors of medical anthropology, asked why the distribution of health and illness appeared to mirror the distribution of wealth and power. Although anthropology from its inception has focused on concerns of health and illness, in recent years Virchow's question has become central to the critical medical anthropology approach to health and illness. If the distribution of health and illness cannot be explained solely on the basis of genetic vulnerabilities, individual behaviors, and the random spread of pathogens through a population, then what are the root causes of health disparities?

Health Transition and Critical Medical Anthropology

Over the twentieth century, much of the human population experienced dramatic improvements in health. Life expectancy rose significantly. Infectious diseases (with the exception of HIV) declined as the primary causes of death and were replaced by chronic diseases such as cancer and heart disease and by syndromes such as stroke. Unfortunately, despite improvements in global health statistics, local populations have not experienced the **health transition** equally. Inequalities of health—sometimes extreme—and unequal access to health care persist between local populations and within them.

Although overall human life expectancy increased from 31 years in 1900 to 65 in 2010 (from 49.2 in 1900 to 78.3 in 2010 in the United States), extreme differences exist among countries. As Figure 16.8 shows, in 2010 Japan ranked first in overall life expectancy at birth at 82.6 years. Swaziland ranked last of

health transition: The significant improvements in human health made over the course of the twentieth century that were not, however, distributed evenly across the world's population.

FIGURE 16.8 Global Life Expectancy by Country

Country (state/territory)	Rank	Life expectancy at birth (in years)
Japan	1	82.6
Hong Kong	2	82.2
Iceland	3	81.8
Switzerland	4	81.7
Australia	5	81.2
Spain	6	80.9
Sweden	7	80.9
Israel	8	80.7
Macau	9	80.7
France (metropolitan)	10	80.7
Singapore	15	80.0
United Kingdom	20	79.4
United States	36	78.3
India	139	64.7
Haiti	149	60.9
Afghanistan	188	43.8
Sierra Leone	190	42.6
Mozambique	193	42.1
Swaziland	194	39.6 (40% below world average)

SOURCE: *UN Department of Economic and Social Affairs, Population Division. 2012. "World Population Prospects, the 2010 Revision." http://esa.un.org/wpp/.*

194 countries, with an overall life expectancy at birth of 39.6 years, 40 percent below the world average. The United States ranked 36.

These statistics raise crucial questions about health disparities that are central to the concerns of critical medical anthropologists. If the United States is the richest and most technologically advanced country in the world, why is its population's average life expectancy shorter than that of people in thirty-five other countries? Why is the average life expectancy of the population of Swaziland 40 percent below the global average?

Critical medical anthropology examines health as a system of power. Specifically, it explores the impact of inequality on human health by examining (1) how economic and political systems, race, class, gender, and sexuality create and perpetuate unequal access to health care, and (2) how health systems themselves are systems of power that generate disparities in health by defining who is sick, who gets treated, and how. Critical medical anthropologists look beyond Western biomedicine's traditional focus on individual patients' problems; instead, they analyze patterns of health and illness among entire groups. Critical medical anthropologists search for the origins of these health disparities, the mechanisms that perpetuate them, and strategies for overcoming them (Baer, Singer, and Susser 2003; Budrys 2010).

Each of us develops our own individual way of thinking about health, including strategies for treating disease and illness and addressing other threats to our well-being. On an individual level, we may each choose from a set of home remedies and cures passed along from family and friends. But on a structural level, our universe of options is not of our own making. The available choices are far from equal for each of us. For example, consider the following questions: What kind of health insurance do you have? Do you have health insurance at all? Do you have access to clean water, childhood immunizations, nutritious food, clean air, and exceptional health care facilities? Do you have a choice of doctors? Do you have social networks to help identify the best doctors to treat your particular problems? Are your home and neighborhood safe from violence and war? After you answer these questions for yourself, think about how the president of the United States would answer them. Think about how a resident of Cange, Haiti, would answer them.

Patterns of inequality in a culture create patterns of inequality in health care. Health practices and policies in turn create and reinforce patterns of inequality. We might actually say that illness can have social origins in poverty, violence, fear of violence, and discrimination based on race, ethnicity, gender, sexuality, and age. Illness and disease can result from cultural patterns of inequality and the distribution of health care resources within a population (Schulz and Mullings 2006).

critical medical anthropology: An approach to the study of health and illness that analyzes the impact of inequality and stratification within systems of power on individual and group health outcomes.

Staff Attitudes Affect Health Care Delivery in a New York Women's Clinic

Various systems of power—including economics, politics, race, class, gender, and sexuality—shape the distribution and accessibility of health care resources (Chapman and Berggren 2005). In *Reproducing Race* (2011), legal scholar and anthropologist Khiara Bridges examines the ways in which race, class, and gender intersect to shape the delivery of health care in a women's health clinic at a famous trauma hospital on Manhattan's East Side. This facility provides prenatal, delivery, and postpartum checkups and services to pregnant women who are poor. The women's health clinic of Alpha Hospital (a pseudonym), which also serves as a top-tier teaching hospital, treats an incredibly diverse population of patients, including some whites but mostly people of color. Because of their economic status, all patients qualify for the U.S. federal government's Medicaid program.

In contrast to the patient population, physicians working in Alpha's women's health clinic are predominantly white. Most medical staffers are women of color but of immigrant backgrounds. Tensions exist between these groups. During a year and a half of fieldwork, Bridges documented the stereotypes and prejudices expressed by physicians and medical staff about their patients. In a Medicaid-supported women's health clinic, women of color are already treated in ways that non-Medicaid patients would not be. For example, because the government has categorized Medicaid patients as an "at risk" population whose exceptional health issues require special treatment, these women are subjected to

MAP 16.5
New York City

FIGURE 16.9 How might dynamics of race, gender, age, and class affect the medical care that patients receive in a hospital, clinic, or doctor's office?

interviews, counseling sessions, intrusive procedures, and invasive examinations that non–Medicaid pregnant women do not undergo. In addition to the exceptional institutional requirements, Bridges raises the possibility that physicians' racial attitudes may contribute to the health disparities experienced by patients who are women of color.

Bridges' research documents a racist oral tradition within the medical profession that features stories and folklore about black women's bodies. One common theme centers on the supposedly unique strength and hardiness of black women and other women of color, who, often referred to as more "primitive" by health workers, were assumed to be able to endure more intense pain and overcome more hardship in medical procedures than other women.

Bridges presents these troubling anecdotes in relationship to statistics that show significant racial disparities in infant and maternal mortality. In the United States, black babies are nearly two and a half times more likely to die as infants than white babies. Black women are three times more likely than white women to die from complications of pregnancy and childbirth. In New York City, they are five times more likely to do so!

Are these women and infants dying because they are poor or because they are black? Bridges suggests that the mortality rates reflect more than poverty. Studies consistently show that racial and ethnic minorities in the United States receive lower-quality health care. But even when ruling out variables such as insurance status, income, age, and severity of medical condition, black women and infants have higher mortality rates than whites with similar profiles.

Bridges notes a deep reluctance within Western medicine to invade physicians' privacy by interrogating their human frailties. Perhaps as a result, the existence of physicians' racism is never addressed in the larger medical literature. But based on the patterns of behavior she observed at Alpha Hospital's women's health clinic, Bridges argues for the need to explore the possibility that physicians' views regarding patients of color may lead to different treatment during pregnancy and childbirth, disparate health outcomes, and higher infant and maternal mortality rates (Bridges 2011; Chapman and Berggren 2005).

How Is Globalization Changing the Experience of Health and Illness and the Practice of Medicine?

Even though globalization is not an exclusively recent phenomenon, the current era of worldwide interconnectedness is bringing profound changes to individuals' experience of health and illness and to the practice of medicine. Various facets of medical migration, as well as encounters among multiple systems of healing, make today's era of globalization unique.

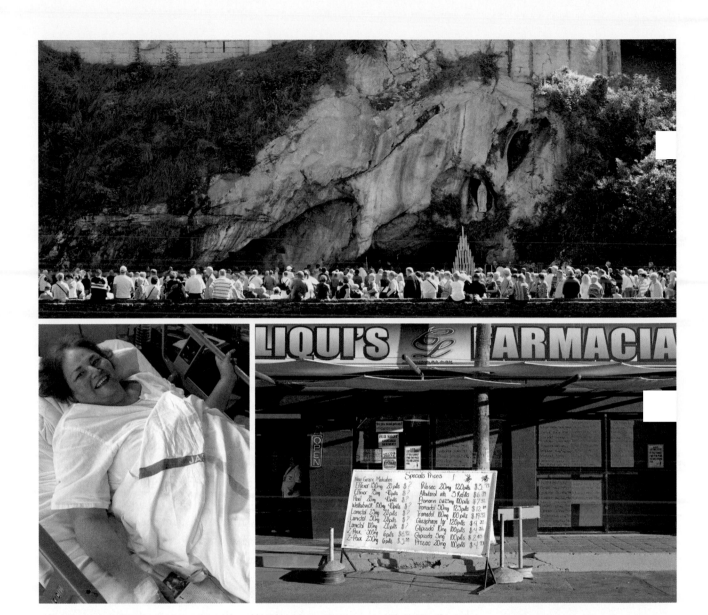

Medical Migration

The small town of De Leon Springs and its crystal clear lake on Florida's eastern coast bear the name of the Spanish explorer Juan Ponce de León. Legend tells that he entered Florida in 1513, at the beginning of an earlier period of globalization, looking for the fountain of youth. It was rumored to restore the vitality of anyone who drank from it. But while Ponce de León sought a fountain of youth, his transatlantic voyage, like those of other European explorers, merchants, and colonialists, introduced an array of foreign diseases to the population of the Americas—a medical migration with devastating effect.

FIGURE 16.10 Globalization has spurred many forms of medical migration. *Clockwise from top:* Crowds seek healing at the sacred grotto sanctuary of Our Lady of Lourdes in France. Thousands of Americans cross the border from Arizona to buy prescription drugs at Mexican pharmacies for a fraction of their U.S. cost. A school bus driver, Edna Harsha, from Minnesota, traveled to Bombay, India, for hip replacement surgery.

Globalization today has launched a new and intensified era of **medical migration** — not only of disease but also of health care systems, diagnoses, and treatments (Roberts and Scheper-Hughes 2011), with both positive and negative results. Medical treatments and technologies cross national borders as vaccines have been introduced worldwide to treat previously fatal or debilitating illnesses such as polio, tuberculosis, measles, mumps, rubella, tetanus, typhoid, and diphtheria. Antibiotics treat bacterial infections. Pesticides inhibit the spread of disease-carrying insects. At the same time, diseases migrate on a global scale. HIV/AIDS knows no national boundaries. Medical researchers travel with their scientific knowledge and technology in search of subjects for medical research and experimental clinical trials. Images of youth, health, and beauty (as well as consumer products that purport to provide and prolong them) infuse global media, even though their benefits are as fleeting as the promised restorative powers of the fountain of youth.

Medical travelers cross borders in search of cures and therapies for every condition possible, from heart disease to obesity, failed organs, infertility, and sexual dysfunction. Senior citizens travel from the United States to Canada and Mexico to buy lower-priced generic drugs that are unavailable or unaffordable at home. The wealthy travel on tourist visas to impoverished countries to receive organ transplants. The poor travel without documents to wealthy countries to receive basic health care. Surgeons and patients migrate. So do body parts (see Scheper-Hughes's work in Chapter 3) and medicines (both legally and illegally). Many medical travelers search for alternative cures outside the world of biomedicine, including Chinese or Indian treatments for chronic ailments such as cancer or diabetes. Muslims, Christians, Buddhists, Daoists, and Hindus make pilgrimages to sacred shrines, holy mountains, and healing waters. They bathe in the Ganges River in India, scale Mount Tai in China, and pray to the Virgin Mary at the Sanctuary of Our Lady of Lourdes in France.

Multiple Systems of Healing

This era of medical migration has spurred the encounter of multiple systems of healing, including ideas of health and illness that overlap and often conflict. The intersection of multiple cultural approaches to healing, called **medical pluralism**, often creates tensions, especially in the encounter between Western biomedicine and other cultural patterns of health and illness. But the engagement also provides opportunities for additional alternative and complementary choices and medical options to emerge (Lock 1993, 2002).

Colliding Cultures: Hmong Refugees and the U.S. Health Care System

Anne Fadiman's *The Spirit Catches You and You Fall Down* (1997) captures the intensity and danger of cross-cultural medical encounters through the story of the Lees, a Hmong refugee family from Laos in Southeast Asia. The Lees settled in the city of Merced in California's agricultural Central Valley in the 1980s. More than 150,000 Hmong refugees fled Laos in the 1970s and 1980s. Many had fought clandestinely with the United States on the losing side of wars in Vietnam and Laos. More than 12,000 Hmong eventually settled in Merced, a city of only 61,000 people.

The Lees' fourteenth child, Lia Lee, was born on July 9, 1982, apparently a healthy, happy baby. But at three months of age, her seizures began. At first, her family comforted her and cared for her at home. Her uncontrollable convulsions on October 24 led the family to Merced Community Medical Center (MCMC), a small county hospital but also a teaching hospital where first-year residents from the University of California–Davis train in family practice. The October 24 visit began a long and painful encounter—a collision—between the Lee family and the U.S. health care system.

MAP 16.6
Merced

Unbeknownst to the doctors at MCMC, the Lees had already diagnosed Lia's illness as *qaug dab peg,* which translates into English as epilepsy. Familiar with *qaug dab peg* in their own cultural context, the Lees were ambivalent about their daughter's illness. The seizures, they knew, could be dangerous. But among the Hmong, those suffering from *qaug dab peg* were held in high esteem. Many became powerful shamans—traditional healers and community visionaries. The Lees had come to the hospital for their daughter to be healed, but they also wondered about her potentially auspicious future.

Also unbeknownst to the MCMC doctors, the Lees knew what had caused Lia's illness and how to treat it. She suffered from soul loss. Her older sister had allowed the front door of their small home to slam, and the loud noise had scared Lia's soul away. An elaborate ritual of soul-calling conducted by a Hmong shaman could trap the lost soul and return it to Lia's body. But her seizures on that October night were overwhelming, and her parents feared that she would die without immediate care.

By the time the Lees arrived at the hospital, the seizures had stopped. With no clear symptoms to treat, the doctors were at a loss. The hospital had no translator, and the Lees spoke no English. The resident on call misdiagnosed the remaining symptoms as an infection, prescribed medication, and sent the family home. Unfortunately, the prescription and medication instructions were written in English, which the Lees could not understand. Lia Lee was misdiagnosed at the hospital again on November 11. Finally, on March 3, 1983, the family arrived with Lia still convulsing. A young family member who spoke some English translated. The resident on call diagnosed the cause as epilepsy. Then the child was subjected to a battery of invasive tests, including a spinal tap, a CT scan, a chest X-ray, and blood work—none of which the hospital staff could adequately explain to Lia's parents. The child had experienced five months of seizures small and large without proper diagnosis and medication, and now she endured a terrifying night at the hospital.

Between the ages of eight months and four and a half years, Lia Lee was admitted to MCMC seventeen times and made more than one hundred outpatient visits for treatment of her seizures. Over the same period, her doctors prescribed fourteen different medications in different combinations and dosages, changing her prescription twenty-three times — all with a family unfamiliar with English, Western medical practices, or the U.S. system of weights and measures needed to determine the proper dosage.

The collision of cultures escalated when doctors decided that Lia Lee's ongoing seizures were caused by her parents' failure to comply with the medication prescriptions. This, the lead doctor determined, qualified as child neglect and child abuse. Acting on the doctor's concerns, the county courts ordered Lia Lee removed from her parents' custody and placed in foster care so that her medicines could be properly administered. The doctors thought they were acting to protect the child. Her parents, however, unable to understand the medical, legal, or moral logic of removing a child from her family and convinced that they were doing everything in their power to care for their daughter, could only imagine that they were being punished for some unknown reason.

The courts eventually returned Lia Lee to her parents after nearly a year in foster care. Her condition had not improved. Her parents, in fact, felt that her cognitive abilities and social skills had deteriorated during the year away. Despite the parents' efforts to comply with Lia's drug regimen, another series of catastrophic epileptic seizures landed her in MCMC again and finally in a children's hospital in nearby Fresno. Treatment of the seizures was ultimately ineffective. Despite what hospital staff considered heroic measures, Lia was left with the dramatically reduced brain activity that doctors call a "persistent vegetative state." Doctors removed all life support and feeding tubes. She was returned to MCMC and finally to the Lees' home.

Considering her lingering fevers, the medical professionals expected her to die. But Lia's parents bathed her in soothing herbal baths, fed her, carried her with them, slept with her in their bed, and continued the elaborate Hmong rituals of soul-calling to return her to health. Though her brain activity never returned, Lia did not die. Her parents were convinced that all the medicines the doctors had forced on her had left her in this condition. (Indeed, Fadiman found some evidence suggesting that Lia's massive final seizure may have been caused by a hospital-acquired infection.) They hoped that their traditional healing methods might still return her lost soul to her body.

Bridging Cultural Divides via Illness Narratives Fadiman's interviews found that the parties in this cross-cultural health encounter held vastly

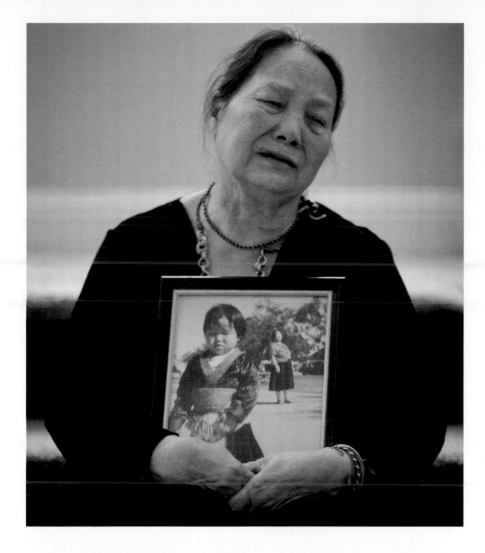

FIGURE 16.11 Foua Yang weeps as she talks about her daughter, Lia Lee, who died on August 31, 2012, at the age of 30 after a lifelong struggle for health. A collision of two cultural approaches to healing left her severely wounded in childhood.

different views of what had occurred. Most of the doctors criticized the parents as uncooperative. They debated whether this stemmed from cultural barriers, lack of intelligence, or character flaws that kept them from caring properly for their daughter. Many saw the parents as ungrateful for all the effort and resources that had been expended on their daughter's case. Few made any attempt to ask the Lees how they understood Lia's illness and how they would treat it. In contrast, the Lees considered most of the medical staff to be uncommunicative, arrogant, cold, and punitive; they also described the medical procedures Lia had undergone as invasive, culturally inappropriate, and ineffective. They never understood how the government could take their beloved daughter from them to be put in the care of strangers.

The conflict between the Lees and the MCMC staff reflected broader misunderstandings between the Hmong community and the hospital's medical staff. These misunderstandings were based on language barriers, cultural barriers, varied interpretations of what health and illness mean, and different strategies for taking care of ill family members. The Lees never understood the biomedical assessment of epilepsy as a misfiring of brain cells caused by an electromagnetic storm in their daughter's head. The doctors never understood the Lees' assessment of *qaug dab peg* as caused by soul loss, treatable through the healing traditions of their local community.

At the conclusion of her research, Fadiman contacted a preeminent medical anthropologist, Arthur Kleinman of Harvard University. Kleinman, a specialist in cross-cultural issues in health and illness, has been instrumental in formulating a concept of collecting illness narratives as a way to bridge cultural divides in treating illness and promoting health (Kleinman 1988). **Illness narratives** are the personal stories that people tell to explain their illness. The narratives reveal the psychological, social, and cultural aspects that give illness its context and meaning. These stories can provide healers with an essential framework for developing treatment strategies that will make sense to the patient and have the greatest chance of success. To elicit the illness narrative, Kleinman suggests asking the following questions:

1. What do you call the problem?
2. What do you think has caused the problem?
3. Why do you think it started when it did?
4. What do you think the sickness does? How does it work?
5. How severe is the sickness? Will it have a short or long course?
6. What kind of treatment do you think the patient should receive? What are the most important results you hope the patient will receive from this treatment?

Kleinman argues that in order to provide effective treatment, "you need to understand that as powerful an influence as the culture of the Hmong patient and her family is on this case, the culture of biomedicine is equally powerful. If you can't see that your own culture has its own set of interests, emotions, and biases, how can you expect to deal successfully with someone else's culture?" (Fadiman 1997, 261).

Fadiman concludes by asking Kleinman if Lia Lee's treatment would have been effective had the MCMC medical staff asked the family to provide this illness narrative—the cultural framework through which they viewed the cause and potential treatment of her illness. Doing so might have provided an avenue to engage the family in a cooperative treatment process. Through that process, multiple systems of healing and concepts of health and illness might have intersected to create a multifaceted approach to healing for Lia Lee.

illness narratives: The personal stories that people tell to explain their illnesses.

Encounters of distinct medical systems like that experienced by Lia Lee and her family in the California health care system will only increase as globalization continues to break down barriers to the flow of ideas, people, diseases, medical treatments, and health practitioners from one world region to another. These encounters will continue to challenge and expand our notions of disease, illness, and health care. As we have seen in this chapter, medical anthropologists are deeply engaged in the analysis and understanding of these transitions and in the articulation of strategies to develop and promote sophisticated, people-centered, and holistic approaches to the challenges of health and illness.

Thinking Like an Anthropologist: Health in the Individual and in the Global Population

The human body is a spectacularly sophisticated organism. Its ten trillion cells constitute complex cardiovascular, pulmonary, and digestive systems made up of muscles, ligaments, organs, veins, and arteries, all shaped and guided by approximately twenty thousand protein-coding genes that form our DNA sequence. The body, which has evolved over millions of years, enables us to interact with one another, reproduce our species, and adapt to the remarkable variety of environments found on Earth.

Healthy bodies are produced through a complex interaction between genetics and culture. As we saw in Chapter 5, the human genetic code provides a basic framework for the body's growth, but culture and the natural environment influence how our bodies actually develop. Nutrition, disease, and exercise, along with our collective human health care practices, impact what we look like, how we feel, how well we live, and how long we live. Even the human mind is not fully formed at birth. Nutrition, stimulation, affection, and trauma after birth continue to shape the contours of our brains.

When medical anthropologists consider issues of health, they think about both the individual body and the social body. As discussed in this chapter, we humans and our individual bodies do not live in isolation. Nor is our health created in isolation. We live in relation to one another as part of a social body—a collection of individuals whose health is tied to the success of the group as well (Scheper-Hughes and Lock 1987). The health of the hundred-year-old twins Ena and Lily and the residents of *colonias* on the Texas–Mexico border discussed in the chapter opener, like the health of Lia Lee, are directly related to the health of those around them and to the system of health care created and shared by the larger culture in which they live.

As you think more about health and illness—perhaps your own personal experiences or those of people around you—remember the big questions we have been exploring:

- How does culture shape our ideas of health and illness?
- How can anthropologists help solve health care problems?
- Why does the distribution of health and illness mirror that of wealth and power?
- How is globalization changing the experience of health and illness and the practice of medicine?

After reading this chapter, are you able to apply these questions to specific situations?

As we have seen, medical anthropologists examine the diverse strategies that cultures have developed to protect and promote the health of the body. And they work to apply the methodological and analytical tools of anthropology to enhance and expand health care in the face of increasing global health inequalities. Debates about health and illness are all around us: Will the U.S. government fully fund and implement the 2010 Affordable Care Act? Will the law address women's reproductive health needs? Will the Medicare eligibility age be raised, making it harder for seniors to find health coverage? Will your college or university adequately fund its student health center to provide for all of a student's health needs? Who sets the health center's policies and budget? Would you consider joining or supporting an organization like Paul Farmer's Partners in Health to help address the health care needs of people in another part of the world? How will you engage these debates? Thinking like an anthropologist can help you better understand and address these issues, whether they present themselves as your own personal issues of health and illness, those of your friends and family, or the health of the global human population.

Key Terms

health (p. 621)
disease (p. 622)
illness (p. 622)
ethnomedicine (p. 627)
ethnopharmacology (p. 627)
biomedicine (p. 630)
human microbiome (p. 632)
health transition (p. 642)
critical medical anthropology (p. 644)
medical migration (p. 648)
medical pluralism (p. 648)
illness narratives (p. 652)

For Further Exploration

Amchi Medicine. www.rolexawards.com/profiles /laureates/laurent_pordi. Short video about *amchi* medicine in India and the work of French anthropologist Laurent Pordié.

The Business of Being Born. 2008. Directed by Abby Epstein. Barranca Productions. www .thebusinessofbeingborn.com. Examines childbirth practices in the United States.

Fadiman, Anne. 1997. *The Spirit Catches You and You Fall Down: A Hmong Child, Her American Doctors, and the Collision of Two Cultures.* New York: Farrar, Straus, and Giroux.

Go Ask Alice. www.goaskalice.columbia.edu. Columbia University's health website designed specifically for college students.

Kidder, Tracy. 2003. *Mountains beyond Mountains: The Quest of Dr. Paul Farmer, a Man Who Would Cure the World.* New York: Random House.

Nomad RSI. www.nomadrsi.org. French nongovernmental organization founded by Laurent Pordié that supports *amchi* medical practices in Ladakh, India.

Pandemic: Facing AIDS. 2003. HBO. Five 30-minute films exposing the worldwide AIDS epidemic with stories from Thailand, Brazil, India, Uganda, and Russia.

Partners in Health. www.pih.org. Paul Farmer's global health organization.

Society for Medical Anthropology. www.medanthro.net. Lists films and resources for the study of medical anthropology.

WebMD. www.webmd.com. Online health information.

Youth in a Brazilian shantytown have constructed a miniature city where they reenact their complex urban world in an elaborate game started in 1997.

p. 660

p. 669

p. 679

p. 684

p. 685

p. 689

CHAPTER 17

Art and Media

In a favela, or shantytown, set on a steep hillside above Rio de Janeiro, Brazil, a remarkable four-thousand-square-foot miniature model of the city overlooks the sprawling metropolis below. Known as Morrinho ("Little Hill"), this virtual urban world began as a children's game in 1997 and today draws the attention of government officials, filmmakers, development agencies, and artists from around the world.

Working and playing together with other neighborhood kids, two brothers began to construct the miniature city out of discarded bricks, tiles, mortar, and borrowed masonry tools. As the game gradually grew in size and complexity, streets began to emerge, followed by homes, restaurants, stores, hospitals, and police stations. Each of the children began to inhabit the game, making avatars for themselves from bottle caps and batteries. The streets came alive with human interactions: friendships and fights, games and business. The constructed city took on a life of its own, yet it was a life that reflected and illuminated human relations and social conditions in the favela and the city of Rio.

Today thousands of avatars placed within the miniature city engage in an elaborate dramatization of community life. They live and die, work and play, break the law and make love. Battles rage between gangs and with police. Brazilian pennies have become currency, exchanged in the game for goods and services, motorcycle rides, and bags of drugs. Each youth controls his or her avatar and portion of the model.

Anthropologist Alessandro Angelini has conducted ethnographic fieldwork in this miniature world and the surrounding community since 2008. He notes the ways in which Morrinho has developed significance

657

FIGURE 17.1 Art? Play? Politics? All are expressed in the reconstruction of Morrinho, a virtual urban world in a Brazilian favela (*left*) begun as a children's game but now a national and international destination. Youth from Morrinho have even re-created their favela as art installations in cities abroad, including London (*right*), where they integrated miniatures of St. Paul's Cathedral, Big Ben, the London Eye, and the London "tube" subway.

beyond the interactive model city, particularly as the youths' manipulation of miniature urban life has cast a spotlight on the intersection of poverty, class, power, kinship, identity, the state, and politics. For instance, Morrinho has drawn the attention of Brazilian political authorities. The community—now well known in Rio and beyond—became one of the first favelas to receive state infrastructure improvements, including sewage systems, housing, road paving, lighting, pathways, and railings. The community was also one of the first to be targeted with increased police presence and paramilitary security forces as the government sought to pacify and eliminate any undesirable elements.

Morrinho has also drawn the attention of artists and activists, crossing a boundary between play, creative expression, politics, and art. Tourists visit from Rio and beyond. Filmmakers document the story of the miniature city and its surrounding community through artistic films shown at international festivals. A small group of Morrinho's originators have been invited on multiple occasions since 2004 to reproduce a model of Morrinho at art festivals in cities such as Barcelona, Paris, Vienna, Munich, Venice, and Innsbruck, as well as in places in Holland, Colombia, and East Timor. Collaborating with local underprivileged youth from South London in the summer of 2010, the group created an installation of Morrinho at a prominent Brazilian arts festival in England, while adding to their miniature city certain elements of London—Big Ben, prisons, and other features important to London youth. In these settings what began as a game is admired as art, not as play.

In this chapter we will explore the array of human creative expression and interaction that anthropologists consider when exploring the world of art. Humans express themselves creatively and interact meaningfully through the visual and written arts, movement, sound, and more. An anthropological approach to art may include attention to paintings, drawings, weavings, photographs, film, sculpture, architecture, dance, music, songs, games, sports, clothing, cuisine, and even virtual online design and creativity. In addition, we will consider the intersection of art and globalization, art and politics, and art and media as technologies such as television, radio, film, and Internet-based social media establish new venues for creative expression and new avenues for communicating and engaging those expressions. In particular, we will consider the following questions:

- What is art?
- What is unique about how anthropologists study art?
- What is the relationship between art and power?
- How do art and media intersect?

By the end of the chapter you will have gained an understanding of the unique approach that anthropologists take to the study of art, the many ways in which art reflects and transforms culture, and the ways in which globalization and new forms of media are transforming art and its dissemination.

What Is Art?

Anthropologists define **art** broadly as all the ideas, forms, techniques, and strategies that humans employ to express themselves creatively and to communicate their creativity and inspiration to others. Art may include a vast array of music, songs, stories, paintings, plays, sculpture, architecture, clothing, food, and games. But art is not limited to the artist.

art: All ideas, forms, techniques, and strategies that humans employ to express themselves creatively and to communicate their creativity and inspiration to others.

The Anthropology of Art

Art is both created and received. Cooking and building, fashion and oratory, decorating and dressing, sewing and play all represent media through which artists and audience communicate. Through these often dynamic encounters, art takes its shape not only in creation but also in perception. In the chapter-opening story, for example, the full impact of the game created by the young people of Morrinho emerges in the interaction of those who are creating it with those who are perceiving it, interpreting it, and making it come alive for the community—a community that stretches far beyond the boundaries of the local.

When thinking anthropologically about art in its global context, it is helpful to first consider some of the common but flawed assumptions that Western traditions have developed about how to evaluate what is and is not art. In particular, we will examine how the anthropology of art challenges commonplace notions of (1) a distinction between fine art and popular art, (2) the existence of a universal art aesthetic, and (3) the assumption of qualitative differences between Western art and so-called primitive art.

Fine Art versus Popular Art Art in Western traditions has often been associated with notions of "high culture" or "fine art," especially elite representations of visual and performance arts experienced in formal venues. Paintings and sculptures displayed in museums and art galleries; operas, symphonies, and ballets performed in recital halls; musicals and plays performed in theaters; fashion shows on runways; and fine cuisine prepared in expensive restaurants fit a view of **fine art** as the province of the elite. Such art is often evaluated and portrayed in contrast to **popular art**—less refined and less sophisticated creative expressions associated with the general population—in the same way that high culture might be simplistically compared to popular culture.

From an anthropological perspective, however, art is not the sole province of the elites or professional artists. Art is integral to all of human life. As such, it can be expressed through elaborate performances in specialized venues as well as though routine activities in mundane settings. Later in this chapter, for example, we will explore powerful expressions of art in such diverse media as Australian indigenous paintings, Haitian marching bands, and African American children's games. Seen from a broad anthropological perspective, any members of a group can create and experience art.

The significance of art cannot be underestimated as anthropologists consider the full expression of human life. All creativity expressed through cultural products such as songs, paintings, dance, architecture, clothing, games, and food carries rich deposits of information about culture as a system of meaning and

fine art: Creative expression and communication often associated with cultural elites.

popular art: Creative expression and communication often associated with the general population.

FIGURE 17.2 What is art? Art can be expressed in various venues and through an array of media (*left to right*): *Maman* by Louise Bourgeois at the Guggenheim Museum, Bilbao, Spain; Chinese artists performing Beijing Opera at the National Theater in Algeria; South Korean singer Psy performing his hit "Gangnam Style" on a morning TV show in Australia; and Stingray Mola, a fabric design of the Kuna Indians of Panama, Central America.

as a system of power. In fact, the very distinction between fine art and popular art may have more to do with political choices and hierarchies of power than with an intrinsic character of the art itself. Who decides, for instance, what will be performed in an opera house or displayed in a national museum? Who directs and who funds the selection, acquisition, and presentation? Can you identify other cultural dynamics of power and stratification—perhaps race, gender, class, religion, or sexuality—that might be reflected in these decisions and representations of what is fine art and what is popular art? (See Perkins and Morphy 2006; Marcus and Myers 1995; Schneider and Wright 2006.)

Considering Aesthetics across Cultures The human encounter with art entails an **aesthetic experience**—broadly speaking, the perception through one's senses in contrast with the perception through intellect and logic. Western art traditions have tended to focus primarily on the aesthetic value of art and on a particular concept of aesthetics associated with certain standards of beauty, creativity, and innovation that are presumed to represent the most refined expressions of a group's culture. But is there a universal art aesthetic found across cultures that informs what people consider to be art and not art? Is there a **universal gaze**—an intrinsic way of perceiving art—that guides the ways people respond to art? Anthropologists of art have been deeply involved in this debate.

The Western concept of a universal art aesthetic traces back to the German philosophers Immanuel Kant (1724–1804) and Georg W. F. Hegel (1770–1831). They suggested that nature creates a universal aesthetic in humans—particularly a sense of what is beautiful—and that it establishes the foundation of a universal gaze through which all art can be seen. Through this universal gaze, art can

aesthetic experience: Perception through one's senses.

universal gaze: An intrinsic way of perceiving art—thought by many in the Western art world to be found across cultures—that informs what people consider to be art or not art.

provide viewers with a "transcendental" aesthetic experience, lift them out of the day-to-day, and transform their vision of the world (Stoller 2003).

A presumption of a universal art aesthetic was prevalent in much of the Western art world throughout most of the twentieth century. Reflecting this, Western art institutions, particularly those focusing on fine art, strove to reinforce this aesthetic experience through their style of presentation. Curators displayed art in a minimalist manner, perhaps only accompanied by its title, date, and name of artist, in an attempt to allow the art to speak for itself. Neutral, objective presentation encouraged the contemplation of objects removed from their worldly context, including their social and economic conditions of production, marketing, and consumption. Similarly, architects designed the physical spaces of Western art galleries and museums to symbolize this universal aesthetic, constructing high ceilings, bare white walls, and open areas that offered unique spaces for experiencing objects' transcendental qualities. The intent was for people to experience art as art—the intrinsic aesthetic of art objects re-created through a universal gaze.

Anthropologists of art have actively challenged the widespread belief in and representation of a universal art aesthetic. Not all cultures have the same aesthetic. Perceptions of beauty, imagination, skill, and style vary widely across cultures as do approaches to artistic ideas, objects, and practices. In fact, what many people have considered to be a universal aesthetic has frequently proven to be a unique product of Western history and culture (Alexander 1996; Alpers 1991; Price 1989; Karp and Lavine 1991).

The expectations of art and the cultural frameworks for perceiving art may also vary from culture to culture. Art may be viewed as beautiful and inspirational: a painting, sculpture, dance, or song may bring pleasure and joy to those who experience it. But the perception and response to art is not limited to only those emotions. Art may also shock, terrify, horrify, or anger its audience. Like other key elements of culture, art is deeply embedded in the processes of enculturation that shape the observer's perceptions, expectations, and experience when evaluating art.

To further illustrate the vast range of possible aesthetic perspectives, consider the following simple contrasts. Whereas Western art traditions may emphasize innovation and originality—creating something entirely new—other traditions may celebrate improvisation on already-existing themes (Price 1989). In such traditions, artistic value is created as the artist explores variations on established themes (Vogel 1991, 30). Likewise, whereas many Western cultures may idealize the artist as an individual genius—as a cultural outsider separated from mundane daily life—other cultures may prioritize engagement with the audience and interaction with the community as the highest aspects of artistic expression. In such instances, the artist may be celebrated for playing a central role in the community's life rather than for his or her individual behavior (Perkins and Morphy 2006).

Beyond "Primitive" Art Western art traditions have often created a problematic distinction between Western art and so-called primitive art. Early anthropologists played key roles in the nineteenth and early twentieth centuries in building great ethnographic museum collections to store and display the art and life ways of "other" cultures for a Western audience, though these treasure troves were often acquired through the colonial encounter (that is, taken rather than purchased or borrowed).

The Western art world became interested in what came to be known as "primitive art" in the early twentieth century. At that time, modernist European artists such as Pablo Picasso began to incorporate African and Oceanic art features and themes into their own work, though largely without reference to the art's original cultural context. In the twentieth century, museums and galleries mounted prominent displays, dioramas, and collections of "primitive" art itself (typically, the art of Africa, Oceania, and Latin America).

In contrast to the anthropological approach to world art, which seeks to understand the development and meaning of local art forms within their unique and complex cultural contexts, the distinction between Western and "primitive" art drawn in Western traditions reinforced the perception of a hierarchy of world art and an evolutionary trajectory in its development from simple to complex, primitive to civilized. The tendency to display art from other cultures without reference to its original context or meaning reinforced the stereotypes about non-Western people and their relationship to Western civilization.

Anthropologists of art (as well as economic anthropologists and political anthropologists) reject an evolutionary framing and evaluation. As noted, through their research and writing, as well as through direct engagement with Western art institutions, anthropologists of art have been instrumental in challenging and transforming the ways museums and other institutions of art depict non-Western cultures and their creative expressions. These anthropologists have also been encouraging an ethnographic turn toward a thorough contextualization of the processes and meaning of art as it emerges in each local context; investigating art's "social life" as it moves beyond local borders; and even reconsidering Western art within its own indigenous, local cultural context (Price 1989; Karp and Lavine 1991; Alpers 1991; Alexander 1996).

Art in Human History

An examination of art in human history provides a crucial context to our deliberations as we consider the question "What is art?" Although common images of our human ancestors may not depict them as artists, the expanding archaeological record reveals a deep historical connection between humans and art that reaches back tens of thousands of years. Art appears to be a fundamental aspect of what it means to be human. Though the archaeological record of human artistic work expands dramatically around 40,000 years ago, clear evidence has emerged of human creative expression dating back at least 100,000 years.

MAP 17.1
South Africa

Blombos Cave, South Africa Archaeological discoveries over the past two decades in South Africa's Blombos Cave—set high in a cliff overlooking the Indian Ocean—reveal that as early as 75,000 years ago, anatomically modern humans were making finely crafted stone weapon points, carving tools out of animal bones, and engraving symbols on blocks of a red stone called ochre. The treasure trove of artifacts, initially discovered in 1993 by Norwegian archaeologist Christopher Henshilwood and colleagues, provides the earliest evidence of what could be considered artistic expression by our modern human ancestors.

In 2008 Henshilwood's team uncovered what amounts to a 100,000-year-old painters' workshop: bone tools for mixing paint, stones for pounding and grinding, yellow and red ochre for color. The ochre would have been blended with fat, charcoal, and mammal-bone marrow to form a paint mixture. The bone tools retained traces of red ocher. Samples of the reddish material were still attached to the interior of two large abalone shells used to mix the paint (Henshilwood et al. 2011; Larsen 2011).

FIGURE 17.4 The connection between humans and art reaches back tens of thousands of years. Here, archaeologists excavate a 100,000-year-old "artists' studio" in Blombos Cave, South Africa, with artifacts in the foreground.

Archaeologists are uncertain what the paint was used for, but they suggest that this isolated cave served as a kind of artists' studio to prepare material for use on the body, on clothing, or in ritual ceremonies. The extensive use of paint may, in turn, indicate an early capacity for symbolic thought. Unlike weapons and tools, which could be used to hunt or build or protect the group, the utilitarian value of paint is less clear. Though perhaps applied to the skin or clothing as camoflauge for hunting, paint might also have been used symbolically to convey a social message, perhaps in a group's social or ritual practices beyond the immediate group. Finds from this early date suggest that humans had already developed a rudimentary knowledge of chemistry and engaged in complex social practices, including the long-range planning required to find, store, and combine the materials found in Blombos Cave. And, perhaps most significant, the finds push back the date of the earliest indications of human capacity for symbolic thought.

A comprehensive study of artifacts gleaned from various African sites reveals the gradual emergence of human artistic expression that later spread to other world regions. Recent archaeological evidence suggests that our human ancestors in Africa may have become cognitively and behaviorally "modern" as early as 300,000 to 400,000 years ago. Later, the development of bone and stone tools—along with the processing and use of pigment, art, and decoration at sites across Africa and from various eras—suggests that our human ancestors in Africa gradually assembled the package of modern human behaviors associated with art, eventually carrying them to other regions of the world (McBrearty and Brooks 2000).

MAP 17.2
Spain / France

Paleolithic Cave Paintings in Europe Perhaps the best-known examples of early art outside Africa are the spectacular Paleolithic cave paintings that have been discovered in areas of southern France (Lascaux Cave and Chauvet-Pont-d'Arc Cave) and northern Spain (Altamira Cave). The artwork dates from 32,000 to 10,000 years ago. The early artists elaborately depicted reindeer, bison, mammoth, horses, lions, and other animals prevalent in that period. Carved human figurines, jewelry, ritual objects, and bone and ivory carvings accompany elaborate burial sites found in the caves.

The cave art reveals highly developed artistic skills, including the incorporation of the contours of partially sculpted cave walls to provide a sense of dynamism and movement in the paintings. Analysis of the paintings reveals that the cave art was not the work of a few individuals or small groups, but that it developed over a twenty-thousand-year period through the efforts of many different artists who reused, modified, and painted over the artwork of their predecessors (Larsen 2011; Herzog 2010).

The purpose of the cave paintings is not clear. Our ancestors may have utilized them in storytelling, record keeping, rituals, ceremonies, or perhaps all of

FIGURE 17.5 This elaborate wall painting in Lascaux Cave, France, depicting horses, bison, mammoth, and lions and dating between 32,000 to 12,000 B.C.E., reveals the highly developed artistic skills of our immediate ancestors.

these. Despite the uncertainty over their purpose, it is clear that the complexity of materials, subjects, and symbolism reveals an elaborate social life and an advanced level of cognitive development that does not fit contemporary stereotypes of "cavemen" living during the most recent ice age in Europe.

Whether through a 100,000-year-old painters' studio in southern Africa, Paleolithic cave art in southern France, or a fine art museum in a contemporary global city, we see that art is integral to all of human life. It can be expressed in elaborate displays or through simple craftwork. But through these events, objects, and expressions, anthropologists can gather crucial insights into people and their cultures. Anthropologists bring a unique perspective to the study of art. As we will explore in the following section, one of these unique contributions lies in careful ethnographic analysis and attention to the cultural production and transaction of art. This focus illuminates the complex social life of art as it is produced and exchanged between people and across geographic spaces and cultural boundaries.

What Is Unique about How Anthropologists Study Art?

Anthropologists' unique approach to art includes particular attention to how art is embedded in a community. Who makes it and why? What does it mean to the people who create it and to those who perceive it? What are its functional and inspirational roles? As ethnographers, anthropologists of art attend to context. We consider not only the creative production of a piece of art but also each work's unique and often complex history as it journeys through human culture. After all, as we will see, art is embedded in everyday exchanges, social networks, business negotiations, and other struggles over profit, power, and prestige.

The Ethnography of Art

Placing art in context has become more complicated and interesting in recent years. Today, in an era of intensifying globalization, local art is created in a global landscape. Local art practices, objects, and events intersect with global movements of people and ideas. Art is often a key juncture through which local communities engage the global economy (Kopytoff 1986). Within this global "artscape" (Appadurai 1986), the creation of local art may provide not only a means of economic activity but also a venue to demonstrate cultural skills and values and to assert local cultural identity in the face of rapid change (Perkins and Morphy 2006). As a result, contemporary anthropologists of art explore the journeys of objects across boundaries and the implications of the "traffic in culture" both for those who produce and for those who consume art (Marcus and Myers 1995; Venbrux, Rosi, and Welsch 2006; Schneider and Wright 2006).

Let's consider a few case studies that illuminate contemporary anthropological approaches to the study of art through ethnography.

MAP 17.3
Abidjan

The Trade in West African Art In *African Art in Transit* (1994), anthropologist Christopher Steiner explores the dynamic role of art in human culture through an ethnographic study of art traders in Abidjan, the main port city of Côte d'Ivoire in West Africa. Abidjan's art traders, mostly Muslims, serve as middlemen in the flow of African art between its creators (mostly rural villagers) and its consumers (Western tourists and international art collectors).

Within this flow, itinerant African traders circulate among upcountry villages, purchasing wooden carvings and clay figurines. The traders sometimes buy unique ritual items and family heirlooms directly from individuals, but generally they acquire mass-produced objects from artisan workshops that cater to the tourist and export art trade. The traders then sell to urban dealers, small and large, who resell the pieces to street hawkers, market stands, and upscale galleries. Within this milieu, Steiner investigates the intricate business practices and networks that link traders, suppliers, and consumers. And he details the elaborate production, presentation, description, alteration, authentication, and pricing of local art pieces within an increasingly globalized art market driven by tourists, Western and non-Western art dealers, and art connoisseurs.

As is true in all art markets, whether for carvings, paintings, fabrics, jewelry, or cuisine, an object's aesthetic value translates into a monetary value. Steiner examines the process by which West African art objects acquire value as they move through the art market. For example, how does a piece of carved wood

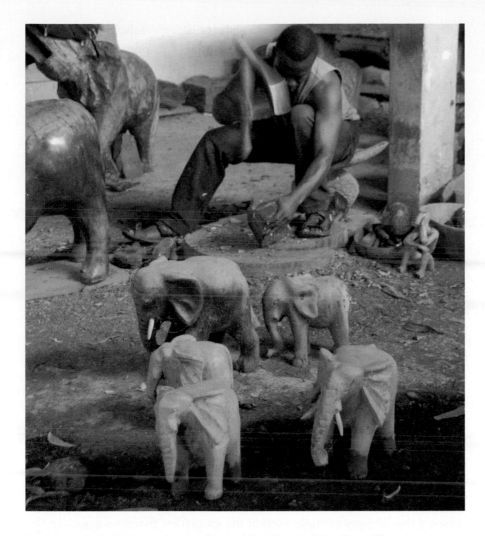

become a desired object for purchase and collection? In Côte d'Ivoire, it is primarily a few Western tourists and art dealers who determine these values. For the most highly valued objects, an influential and wealthy elite of dealers, scholars, collectors, and exhibitioners establishes their worth.

Key to the creation of value in the African art market is the perception of art objects as "authentic" or "genuine." Indeed, buyers and collectors are drawn to objects perceived to be of a certain origin and initial use. In turn, Côte d'Ivoire's local traders actively engage in the construction of **authenticity**—the perception of an object's antiquity, uniqueness, and originality within a local culture. Art objects are dirtied, artificially aged, stained, made to appear "primitive" to Western eyes, and altered to fit the buyers' ideals. Local traders tell stories about the objects' origin, meaning, and use to enhance the impression of authenticity. For tourists, traders create stories that appeal to the buyers' aesthetic tastes and desires to acquire a genuine, authentic object. For high-end

authenticity: The perception of an object's antiquity, uniqueness, and originality within a local culture.

collectors, traders provide an elaborate market history—a description of when, where, and how the object was collected, as well as its origins. Most of these stories, Steiner finds, are fabricated to meet the tastes of Western consumers and thereby raise the objects' value.

Many traders are highly skilled at constructing the illusion of discovery, uniqueness, and authenticity as they work to enhance their economic success in the art trade. Steiner recounts visits to local markets with Western collectors. At the front of a sprawling market, small booths and stands overflowed with local art objects. Of the first items encountered, none would hold interest for the tourist or collector. Later, a trader might lead the customer deeper into the market, down narrow, winding, dark alleys and into enclosed stalls and tents. Inside these dimly lit spaces, traders would hesitantly reveal objects tucked away in antique-looking wooden chests and cabinets. Here, customers would suddenly express keen interest, feeling they had discovered something more authentic than what the average tourist might find. Only then would they agree to pay higher prices. Steiner reveals that many art objects purchased in this way were identical to objects displayed in booths on the outskirts of the market. Only the traders' performance had changed, demonstrating their mastery in conveying the characteristics of discovery, uniqueness, and authenticity that are central to consumers' aesthetic expectations.

The aesthetic values of Western tourists and collectors, expressed in their consumption patterns, significantly influence the production, marketing, and display of West African art. In fact, West African art traders continually move between local and global art markets, communicating between image creators and image consumers, between artists and audiences. In this context, the production of art does not occur solely for art's sake but is part of an economic strategy that engages multiple levels of the art market. Steiner notes,

> West African traders leave each negotiation with a new sense of the aesthetic sense of the Western buyers, a sense that the traders and manufacturers must be closely in tune with as they go about their business of making a living in a rapidly globalizing world and in their niche in a rapidly globalizing art market. (Steiner 1995, 164)

In this way, West African art traders play a sophisticated role in a global art market. They serve as cultural brokers and mediators who communicate Western desires to the native artists and who promote a particular image of African art and culture to the West (Beidelman 1994; Gell 1995; Zilberg 1996).

Think about your own perception of art. What makes a piece of art "authentic" in your eyes?

Transforming West African "Wood" and "Mud" into Global Art In recent years, facilitated by increased migration and enhanced global transportation and communication systems, West African art traders have extended their business networks across the Atlantic Ocean to New York and throughout the United States. As a result, the long-distance trade of West African artwork, particularly "wood" (carved statues and masks) and "mud" (terra-cotta clay figurines), is leading to encounters between cultures and commerce at the intersection of two worlds (Stoller 2003).

The hub of the West African art trade in the United States is New York City—in particular, a multistory building on the west side of Midtown Manhattan called the Warehouse. The Warehouse is packed with stalls and shelves and display tables, each overflowing with "wood" and "mud." Every day, moving vans unload shipments newly arrived from West Africa while others onload pieces to be distributed by itinerant traders across the United States. West African traders cater to a wide array of clients: high-end art collectors, middle-class shoppers, and low-end street markets. High-end collectors search the New York galleries and art shows for what they consider fine art. At the same time, male and female West African art traders crisscross the country delivering mass-produced art objects for sale at boutiques, street markets, flea markets, and cultural festivals. They even deliver directly to some individual clients. The traders rely on networks of "cousins" and other fictive kin who provide housing, marketing advice, cultural interpretation, and shared transport in an extension of practices developed in West African long-distance trade networks.

The production of West African art for consumption in the United States leads to a mutual transformation of artistic meaning, aesthetics, and economic

FIGURE 17.7 How do wood and mud become art? West African traders have transformed a Manhattan warehouse into an African art market (*left*), full of stalls, shelves, and tables from which art is circulated to markets, vendors, galleries, and private collections across the United States, including this African art stall (*right*) at the San Diego County Fair, California.

practice. It also provides a context within which an ethnologist can address the following questions: What exactly is art? What is considered aesthetically pleasing in each culture? What communicates? What moves people? What inspires people? What sells?

Stoller reflects on the power of global flows of people, art, and ideas to shape worlds of work and worlds of meaning. The introduction of West African art pieces into Western art worlds expands Western cultural notions of art and beauty. Simultaneously, Western notions of art affect West African patterns of production and marketing. With each exchange, each negotiation, each sale or lost sale, attentive traders gain deeper insight into the aesthetic values and practical interests of Western collectors, connoisseurs, and mass-market consumers. In turn, these assessments shape what they will buy from artisans in the mud and wood workshops in towns and villages throughout West Africa.

Moreover, on a practical level, these encounters at the crossroads of immigration and trade enable West African traders to meet their own social and economic obligations. They can pay off debts acquired in the immigration process and in starting up their small businesses. They can send remittances home to West Africa to support close family and extended kin groups. They can contribute to the economic well-being and social status of relatives in their home country by providing small amounts of start-up capital for rural and urban enterprises. In the process of meeting these obligations, the traders themselves receive honor and respect from their home communities. Stoller expresses this insight candidly:

> As for the African art traders, many of them have a sophisticated comprehension of the aesthetic, economic, and political forces that drive the markets they attempt—often with great success—to exploit. In the end, the art that they sell has only a fleeting value. It is a material investment that enables many of them to meet their considerable economic and social obligations. (2003, 228)

The studies by Steiner and Stoller provide an insightful ethnographic analysis of the power of movement, encounter, and exchange to shape key aspects of human life, including categories such as art. By considering the production, marketing, and consumption of art within this framework, Steiner and Stoller challenge notions of ideal art types and universal standards of aesthetic beauty. They discuss how aesthetic perceptions, commonly viewed as timeless and universal, can be constructed and negotiated in the encounters among humans—person to person, group to group, locally and globally.

Native Australian Painters Invent Traditional Art Forms Do the words *invent* and *traditional* seem contradictory to you when used to describe artwork? The case study discussed here offers insights into the relationships between traditional and newly developed art forms, between local markets and global art worlds, and the effects of globalization on the production, distribution, and consumption of art today.

MAP 17.4
Australia

American anthropologist Fred Myers has been conducting fieldwork among the Pintupi-speaking people of the Australian Western Desert region since 1973. Until the 1960s the Pintupi were primarily nomadic hunter-gatherers, but by 1973 nearly all of them had been relocated by the national government to settlements in central Australia. The Pintupi were now residing in small towns administered by the Australian government where their social, political, and economic lives changed dramatically. While living in these towns, they were drawn into a complex web of interactions with the Australian state through educational systems, welfare payments, and other social services; international Christian evangelical mission work; and the global spectrum of images and sounds through film, music, and advertising.

Myers's first book, *Pintupi Country, Pintupi Self: Sentiment, Place, and Politics among Western Desert Aborigines* (1986), had focused on issues of kinship, religion, politics, and food foraging—typical concerns for anthropology at the time. However, a plane ride in 1988 to the Western Desert town of Alice Springs, Australia, radically reoriented Myers's research. On the plane he was surprised to see an elegant, well-dressed woman wearing golden Italian leather sandals, designer silk jacket and pants, and scarlet nail polish accompanied by a man in a long black coat, with long black hair worn in a ponytail and goatee and mustache. Over the years Myers had grown accustomed to the range of clothing seen in Australia's Western Desert towns: the tourists' sweat suits and sneakers, the locals' country and western clothes and boots, and the casual wear of the hippie travelers. This couple looked starkly out of place. They seemed dressed for an art gallery opening, not a landing in a frontier town.

Shortly after landing, Myers stopped to greet old friends at the Papunya Tula Artists Company shop, only to be formally introduced to the stylishly dressed woman and her companion. The couple, it seems, were not strangers in the area. Over the previous seventeen years, the Aboriginal people with whom Myers was working—the Pintupi—had developed a unique style of acrylic painting that captured the imaginations not only of tourists visiting Australian Western Desert towns but also of art collectors and gallery owners across Australia and worldwide. The well-dressed couple were art dealers from Melbourne, and they were the key distributors of Pintupi art.

As Myers noted, "My discomfort with *their* entry into a domain I had considered refreshingly remote from the pretensions of our own society's high culture led me to examine the world from which *they* came" (1991, 26). His subsequent book, *Painting Culture* (2002), traces the development of Aboriginal acrylic "dot" paintings and the transformation of paint, canvas, and wood from obscure ethnographic objects originating in the Australian Western Desert to what is today viewed as fine art that circulates widely and is collected and displayed in major galleries and museums worldwide.

Acrylic dot painting—a new art form—was created by the local population in the settlement of Papunya beginning in 1971. At that time a visiting Euro-Australian art teacher, concerned about high unemployment and poverty in the community, encouraged local people to paint traditional ritual designs on wood to make money from visiting tourists. The goal was to develop a local enterprise to generate income for an economically depressed population. Over time, local artisans drew upon designs and stories from indigenous religious traditions—including religious ceremonies, body painting, cave painting, and sand stories—to invent new dot painting designs. As the new art form emerged and as local artisans invented new objects for sale, Pintupi designs changed in both form and meaning. The new works drew on indigenous religious themes, mythical narratives, and ritual performances with deep religious significance and connection to the land.

Despite the art form's recent invention, the Pintupi proclaimed their designs to be "authentic," "traditional," and "true." In fact, they believe that the paintings have a power of their own. This power derives from the designs drawn from the indigenous mythology of the Dreaming, a sacred experience of creation among the Aboriginal people. The claims of authenticity are crucial to elevating the value of their artwork on the Australian and global art markets.

The Pintupi believe that their paintings have the power to transform the world. And in fact they have done exactly that. Acrylic dot paintings have acquired both economic and cultural importance for Australia's Aboriginal people. Pintupi art that before 1971 had no significant role in the local community or beyond has created a world of new economic possibilities—one that offers employment, wealth, land, and power. Moreover, the circulation of Aboriginal art across cultural and art worlds has materially transformed lives while mutually transforming the imaginations of the Aboriginal Australian community and the art world beyond. In just a few decades, the paintings have come to represent and produce Aboriginal culture in local, national, and international arenas.

The new art form, developed in desert towns by a people transitioning from a hunting and gathering lifestyle, has become a key element of Aboriginal self-representation. It has enabled indigenous people to establish an identity in the cultural milieu of the Australian people and state, and to paint their culture onto the global landscape (Bennett 2010; Brumm 2004).

What Is the Relationship between Art and Power?

Anthropologists do not approach art for art's sake. Instead, they inquire about the intersection of art with key systems of power such as race, ethnicity, class, gender, sexuality, politics, and economics (Marcus and Myers 1995; Perkins and Morphy 2006). Creative expressions, performances, and interactions through music, dance, song, and other art forms can produce venues for staging dynamic engagements with these systems of power, unmasking patterns of stratification, making the unconscious conscious, and opening space for alternative visions of reality (see Shannon 2006; Downey 2005; Dunham 1969). Artistic expressions enable people to explore and perform alternative identities to those that seem "normal" within the dominant culture.

In the following sections, including the Anthropologists Engage the World feature, we examine four cross-cultural examples of creative artistic performances that challenge dominant ways of thinking and the underlying systems of power that support them.

Political Critique and Self-Affirmation

As we have noted, creative expression and engagement can take many forms and serve many purposes. As part of its role in reflecting a culture's social dynamics, art can sometimes function within the political arena. The following discussion explores how music, dance, and song enable a marginalized group to protest unequal power relationships and to assert a strong sense of identity despite that inequality.

Rara Bands, Performance, and Politics in Haiti In the six weeks leading up to Easter, *rara* bands take center stage in Haiti's rural and urban poor communities. Small ensembles of twenty or so musical revelers, singers, musicians, and dancers, dressed in elaborate, colorful, sequined or striped costumes, parade through the night. As they wind through rural and urban poor communities, they gather audiences along the way.

MAP 17.5
Haiti

To the casual observer, the *rara* processions may appear to be unruly groups of revelers as band members march and sing, drum, and joke through the streets of urban centers and rural communities. Competition among bands is fierce, and heated battles frequently erupt when groups collide and "crash the *rara*" in the middle of the street, attempting to disrupt one another's performance. But, like small armies, *rara* bands are actually carefully organized and highly disciplined. For instance, members hold formal rank, wear prescribed costumes, and perform songs, dances, and rituals that are thoroughly orchestrated and choreographed. The distinctive performance of the *rara* band features a dynamic combination of bamboo wind instruments, drummers, singers, and dancers. Less complex *rara* bands may establish a rhythm through foot-stomping or hand-clapping. More elaborate bands might include a brass section.

In *Rara!: Vodou, Power, and Performance in Haiti and Its Diaspora* (2002), anthropologist Elizabeth McAlister documents the dynamic performances of *rara* bands that have become key features of Haitian culture. As an ethnographer, she situates them within the political and religious context of Haiti, revealing the complex layers of meaning and power that make *rara* music come alive for the poor and marginalized in Haiti's population. "*Rara* is about play, religion and politics and also about remembering a bloody history and persevering in its face. But at its most bare philosophical level, *Rara* is a ritual enactment of life itself and an affirmation of life's difficulties" (McAlister 2002, 23).

The vast majority of Haitians are poor peasants and urban dwellers who are excluded from political discourse and denied access to political and economic power. Every day they confront conditions of poverty, violence, and terror perpetrated by military and paramilitary forces intent on protecting the economic and political resources of the Haitian elites and their own political power. *Rara* bands and *rara* festivals open up a social space for popular religious and political expressions that might otherwise be silenced. This space enables Haiti's marginalized to contest the violence and political oppression of the present and the past through performances, processions, and song. McAlister reflects on the ways in which *rara* performances perform social critique, particularly

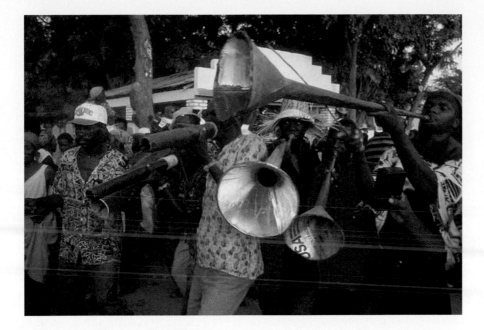

FIGURE 17.9 The raucous music, dances, and lyrics of Haitian *rara* bands open a space for political commentary and critique in a situation of intense poverty and oppression.

through an elaborate interweaving of musical genres: Vodou prayers, obscene *betiz* songs, and politically pointed *pwen* songs.

Rara bands perform a type of religious "work" amid the appearances of all-night play. *Rara* festivals, processionals, and ceremonies, although conducted during the Christian season of Lent, publicly celebrate Vodoun religious culture. The participants sing, drum, pray, and enact religious rituals for Vodoun spirits as the bands stop at crossroads, cemeteries, and shrines, serving the spirit world and in the process celebrating the whole community around which these religious practices are built. The bands' work may include complex negotiations with supernatural spirits. In fact, *rara* bands may call on Vodou spirits for protection and may, in return, be claimed by and drafted by *lwa*—Vodou spirits—to work on their behalf.

Outside the religious rituals, *rara* bands perform two unique genres of songs as they move in procession. *Betiz* songs feature vulgar lyrics laced with sexual innuendo, obscenity, and profanity, creating a raucous environment—a form of popular laughter in the face of daily conditions. The more political messages and metaphors of *pwen* songs playfully open up a public conversation that indirectly critiques the political conditions of Haitian life. These songs use metaphor and musical misdirection to elude the wrath of military authorities and paramilitary forces.

Creating space for social protests and critique runs the risk of reprisal, even when performed through the raucous *rara* bands. McAlister recalls accompanying one band through Port-au-Prince on what appeared to be a normal night of *rara* revelry. After starting the evening with a religious ritual to invoke the presence of protective spirits, the band, attracting a large crowd, danced into the streets, moving quickly through the capital to the sounds of bamboo instruments, drums, and songs. Abruptly and without warning, McAlister recalls, the band leader switched the tune from a *pwen* critiquing the military to a raunchy *betiz*—but too late. A Haitian military attaché, apparently incensed by the band's political commentary, stepped from behind a pillar and opened fire on the *rara* band and its audience with a semiautomatic rifle. Perhaps protected by their accompanying Vodoun spirits, the band members peeled themselves off the pavement—unhurt—and raced down a side street out of harm's way.

Clearly, in this case the open space for political critique created by the late-night *rara* procession had limits. A member of Haiti's security forces had chosen to send a message of displeasure. The band's performance had captivated the wrong audience. Its song had not changed genres from *pwen* to *betiz* quickly enough to avoid potentially deadly discipline by a representative of Haiti's powerful elite. Nevertheless, after a rest and a few drinks, the *rara* band regrouped and, with McAlister still in tow, set off down another street, boisterously singing another *betiz* song (Averill 2003; Miller 2003; Neely 2005; Walls 2005).

Renegotiation of Immigrant Identity and Ethnic Authenticity

In another example of art's multifaceted role in delineating power relationships, here we examine how music, dance, and fashion merge to address the tension that arises when immigrant culture meets that of the host nation.

Indian American Youth Model U.S. "Cool" vs. Indian "Authenticity" Indian Americans are the fourth-largest Asian American population in the United States (after Chinese, Japanese, and Koreans). Their immigration largely began in the late 1960s, when passage of the U.S. Immigration and Nationalities Act of 1965 opened the country's doors to a broader range of immigrants. As discussed in Chapter 13, anthropological studies of the children of immigrants—the second generation—offer insights into the processes of incorporation, identity construction, gender, and race faced by new arrivals and their families.

In *Desis in the House* (2002), anthropologist Sunaina Maira investigates the intersection of dance, music, fashion, immigration, ethnicity, and race through a study of the Indian dance party scene of 1990s New York City. Maira's study reveals the complex negotiation that children of recent immigrants undertake to establish their own identity within the Indian American community and the U.S. population in general.

Every weekend, Asian Indian party producers stage elaborate dance parties in rented clubs, restaurants, and college campus halls, attended by droves of young, second-generation South Asian Americans. Maira describes *desis* (meaning "people from South Asia") as caught between the social pressures of two cultural worlds—the need to be "cool" in mainstream U.S. youth culture, and the need to be ethnically authentic Indians in the eyes of parents and potential marriage partners. The Indian dance parties provide a dynamic environment through which *desis* collectively create a new space for themselves and experiment with new identities through dance, music, and fashion.

The distinctive beat of *desi* dance parties blends Punjabi *bhangra* music and dance, Hindi film tunes, and U.S. hip-hop, rap, reggae, and techno dance music. This creative remix of musical and dance styles is central to *desi* attempts to define their place in U.S. culture and in the rapidly evolving culture of the first- and second-generation Indian immigrant community. Maira's interviews and participant observation reveal that *desis* employ music, dance, and fashion on many fronts. Through them they not only rebel against their parents' expectations of proper Indian children but also challenge U.S. stereotypes that locate them in the nation's hierarchy of race and ethnicity. Neither exclusively Indian nor American, *desi* music, dance, and fashion provide an alternate place for renegotiating ethnicity, performing gender roles, and enacting class aspirations.

Maira notes that young *desis* struggle to balance "cool" with authentic. Cool is desirable for young Indian American women and men on the party scene because it builds social networks, gets attention, and attracts dates. The women perform cool through a hypersexualized expression of gender identity, wearing sexually provocative clothing, heavy makeup, and gaudy jewelry to attract Indian American men looking for girlfriends. In contrast, the young *desi* men perform "cool" masculinity by adopting hip-hop and rap musical styles and clothing, complete with baggy pants, hoodies, and designer shirts. Despite outward appearances, these performances are not a statement of solidarity with other U.S. youth of color or an expression of resistance to economic and racial

FIGURE 17.10 In the search for unique cultural identity, second-generation Indian immigrants struggle to balance the expectations of "cool," as expressed in the Indian dance party scene (*left*), with demands for "authenticity," including being part of an appropriate marriage match, like this couple (*right*), participating in a Hindu marriage ceremony in the United States.

stratification in the United States. Instead, they focus on the particular concern of *desi* men to appear cool while creating a unique identity within the multi-ethnic mix of the U.S. population.

These performances of "cool" coexist and often conflict with the need to perform the markers of South Asian "authenticity." The powerful expectations of parents, at least partially absorbed and replicated in the second generation, define an authentic Indian American along more traditional lines as someone who is familiar with Indian art, religion, language, film, cultural traditions, and even India itself. Notions of cool directly conflict with these powerful expectations of authenticity. Under these standards, the sexually provocative young women who are so attractive to young men at the dance parties do not reflect the ideal of the authentic Indian woman who ultimately—after the dance parties are over—must be seen as a potentially chaste, submissive, future Indian wife. Likewise, the authentically Indian marriageable man is defined not by his performance of cool and his stylish hoodie, but by his progress toward a professional career and the ability to support a wife and family.

Maira captures the strategic deployment of creative expression through music, dance, and fashion by *desi* youth to explore identities and life choices outside the mold of their Indian immigrant parents and the expectations of U.S. cultural thinking about race and ethnicity (Haritaworn 2003; Kurien 2004; Replogle 2003).

Construction of Gender Identity through "Kinetic Orality"

Just as music plays a role in the identity formation of second-generation Indian Americans, it can also influence the development of gender identity among young black girls. In the following discussion, we see how a musical form can both reflect a type of cultural continuity and also gain new meaning when adapted to a different context.

Black Girls' Playground Games and Musical Socialization When we think of kids jumping rope on the sidewalk or standing in a circle in the playground calling out rhymes and clapping to keep the beat, we may not automatically think of art. But in *The Games Black Girls Play* (2006), ethnomusicologist Kyra Gaunt explores the sophisticated musical forms that are taught and learned, particularly by young black girls, on the playground.

Gaunt, herself a gifted musician and an anthropologist trained in **ethnomusicology**—the study of music and culture (see Nettl 2005)—applies a unique combination of musical analysis and gender analysis in her study of games that black girls play. According to Gaunt, the girls' hand-clapping and rope-jumping games embody a unique musical genre that combines body movement and voice to produce what she calls a **kinetic orality**. Hand-clapping, foot-stomping, and highly percussive singing create a musical expression deeply

ethnomusicology: The study of music in cultural context.

kinetic orality: A musical genre combining body movement and voice.

FIGURE 17.11 Art? Play? Gender construction? These girls display their skills at a double-dutch competition in Harlem, New York City.

tied to the body—a performance that does not rely on musical instruments but only on body and voice.

These performances may appear to be improvised on the playground, street corner, or schoolyard. But Gaunt argues that they are learned in an elaborate process of enculturation. Through this process, complex rhythmic syncopations, chants, call-and-response vocal patterns, dances, and melodies are transferred from generation to generation as central lessons of socialization for young African American girls. Gaunt challenges the stereotypes that attribute musical patterns and bodily movement in black children's games to biology. Instead, she traces the enculturation processes of what she calls "learned musical blackness" that begins at an early age as part of African American identity construction.

Gaunt also explores how black girls' games and songs influence the development of commercially popular music associated with the African American community—namely, hip-hop, soul, and rhythm and blues. In particular, she details the ways in which the rhyming, syncopations, dance-like gestures, melodies, and lyrics from black girls' game songs have been adopted from and borrowed by the commercial music of black male artists from the 1950s to the present. Although others have suggested that black girls' games and songs imitate music from radio and television, borrowing from genres such as rhythm and blues and hip-hop, Gaunt documents a dynamic circular relationship. Commercial songs may indeed be adopted, modified, and played within the girls' games and songs, but their games, musical styles, and group play are also sampled, borrowed, and appropriated by the popular music industry. Moreover, this occurs with a particular gender twist, as they are incorporated into music predominately associated with men and masculinity.

WHAT IS THE RELATIONSHIP BETWEEN ART AND POWER?   681

Aimee Cox

"I'm a black woman who grew up in the Midwest. For me, that is the lens through which I learned to see the world. As a young girl I became fascinated with the women in my family. My grandmother was born in 1898, had eleven children. Ten of them were girls. And some of them had really interesting pasts. Through those stories I was starting to understand that there was more to life and more to history than what I was learning in school.

"When I was applying to college, it dawned on me that what really interested me were all those other stories that were never told to me. Not just in my family, but what was left out of my educational process. I was searching so desperately for a history and an understanding of social processes that would help me place myself in the world. I felt like I was always missing."

Cox first encountered anthropology in an undergraduate introductory course at Vassar College. "That really opened the world for me. It allowed me to begin to see connections globally that I had never thought about."

She had been dancing since she was three years old, including studying classical ballet in high school at the College Conservatory of Music at the University of Cincinnati. While at Vassar, Cox spent a semester studying with the Dance Theatre of Harlem—the world's first black ballet company—and then spent a semester at the Alvin Ailey School to pursue modern dance. Eventually Cox danced professionally with Ailey II in New York City. Reflecting on those years, Cox recalls, "Through dance, through moving my body and telling stories through my body, I felt like that was a space where I had a certain type of voice and I could express myself. But I still felt limited. I was marrying modern dance and classical ballet. But I felt like I was telling the story in somebody else's language—classical ballet, for example."

That feeling began to change in graduate school as she explored the connections between anthropology and the performing arts—particularly through directing a homeless shelter in Detroit for young women ages 16 to 21 while conducting her doctoral fieldwork.

"When I came to graduate school, I had this vague idea that I was interested in studying how young women, low-income young women, who are seen as the most marginal people in society, find ways to navigate social systems. How do they find ways to survive, and in some ways be successful in the ways that they define success, despite all of these odds? What are the creative ways that they do that?

"I came into graduate school in anthropology and decided consciously, I was no longer a dancer, I was no longer an artist. I left that all behind because I did not, at that time, understand this whole world of performing. I think that had a lot to do with being a black woman, too, in higher education and not wanting to be seen as a performing body. I figured: I need to be an intellectual. But the minute I came to the homeless shelter, those young women would not allow me to leave that behind. They were dancing on their own—not trained, they were not

Anthropologist Aimee Cox

taking classes—they were moving their bodies, choreographing for each other, making these connections across their individual stories through dance and through writing. When I saw that, I said to myself, 'I need to start dancing again. I can't act like this is not a part of me.'

"It started off for them as kind of a creative healing space. They were frustrated at the end of the day by their struggles to survive in Detroit, and they started moving and dancing. I helped turn it into an artistic medium and a community, an educative creative space where they used those art forms to connect their stories. Then they realized, 'Oh, yeah! I'm not the only one who feels this way at the end of the day.' Through dance and storytelling they began to move from feeling their frustration and anger, to in-house community building, to political commentary.

"These young women were the catalysts. They were the ones who created that space. I didn't come in and say, 'Okay, today we're going to learn ballet.' They were already doing these things. I was talking about dance, but the dance became less about techniques and more about 'How can we use our bodies to say something about life? How can we use our bodies to tell this story? How can we then choreograph a group scene that connects the stories we just talked about?' Here we can begin to understand the importance of using the performing arts as a vehicle for transforming communities and to transform self."

In what eventually became the BlackLight Project, these women developed community workshops, training sessions, and street theater. "They did a lot of this on the street, because if they stayed in the shelter, no one would come and see it. Let's say they were at a bus stop in Detroit. And they'd have a hat, like street performers in New York City have a hat, saying that we're trying to collect some money. They would have the hat, and it would already be full with slips of paper with facts and stories, comments about the city, about the mayor at the time. They would start performing, and as the audience grew

around them, they would stop; and in order for them to continue with the performance, one of those in the audience would have to take a piece of paper, read it, and start a discussion about it. So, in a small way, that was the way that these women used performance as more than just a spectacle, but also as a way to engage in a dialogue.

"Through this kind of embodiment, something else opens up—a different space, a different way of seeing the world, a different language, and even a different sort of courage around thinking about possibilities.

"Up until then, I didn't really understand anthropology. I was getting a very traditional understanding in graduate school. But what I wasn't getting, and what no graduate student really gets until they get to the field, I think, is that explosion of what all this really means in the world. These women exploded anthropology for me.

"Performance, in many ways, is the foundation for culture. We perform language. We perform in everything we do. The narrative construct of performing, communicating, telling a story is very tied to anthropology, to cultural anthropology. To making connections, making something clear. In the specificity, for example, of an individual performer—or an individual piece of art—there's a larger story that we can all step into.

"Anthropology is more than just a discipline that studies some abstract notion of culture or power. It's a way to break apart problems. And that takes a real understanding of culture, of how social processes work, of our interconnectedness, of possibilities that are latently embedded in society. And that's what anthropologists are able to do creatively. We see those things. And we bring those things that are not readily apparent to the surface through our ethnographic work. Not because we're wired differently than anybody else, but because we've worked to see outside and inside at the same time, to reveal people to themselves. We give people possibilities to see themselves."

FIGURE 17.12 How have the rhyming, syncopations, dancelike gestures, melodies, and lyrics from black girls' game songs (*left*) shaped commercial music, like that performed by rap artist Nelly (*right*)?

As an example of this borrowing, Gaunt documents how a common song in black girls' games, "Down, Down Baby," was appropriated into the chorus of the 2000 song "Country Grammar" by Grammy award–winning rap artist Nelly. Elements of "Down, Down Baby" appear not only in "Country Grammar" but in many other commercial music sources as well, including the 1988 Tom Hanks movie *Big*. In "Country Grammar," Nelly incorporates significant lyrical, rhythmic, melodic, and linguistic features of the game-song while revising the lyrics to fit commercial, masculine-centered rap expectations.

By examining musical performance through the lens of gender, Gaunt raises important questions about the performance of gender and the patterns of interaction between women and men that are reflected through music. This is occurring as women transfer embodied music across generations as a form of socialization while men appropriate women's music for commercial purposes, often without attribution. Nelly's rewritten lyrics, complete with macho references to being "cocked ready to let it go" and marijuana culture, stand in sharp contrast to the language and tone of girls' performances on the playground. Unlike many artists who have borrowed from girls' games, Nelly has publicly acknowledged the borrowing from a chant in a popular "children's game," although he fails to acknowledge girls as the primary performers of schoolyard songs.

Gaunt's examination of kinetic orality in the games black girls play opens a window on the dynamic process of identity construction, including the construction of racial and gender identities, that emerges at the intersection of play, performance, creative expression, and art (Jamison 2006).

Conducting an Ethnography of Art

Throughout this chapter you have been developing your skills as an ethnographer of art, developing a set of concepts and analytical frames for thinking about what art is, what it means to artist and audience, how it moves, how it is valued by markets. In this exercise, you will apply those skills to the study of a piece of art of your own choosing.

Select a piece of art. It can be any object, event, or other expressive form. In this chapter we consider reproductions of urban life, wood carvings, mud sculptures, acrylic paintings, fashion, dance, music, processions, kids' games, and online virtual lives. You might also choose a banquet, a parade, a festival, a concert, a religious ritual. Don't be constrained by your previously held notions of popular art or fine art.

Now get out your anthropological toolkit. Approach your piece of art as an ethnographer. Participate in it. Observe it. Interview the artist or the audience. Take notes, and be prepared to discuss your findings with a classmate. Consider the following to stimulate your thinking:

- As a form of communication, art is meant to evoke emotional responses (laughter, crying, melancholy, or joy) as well as intellectual responses to its shape, order, and form. The artistic message may be intended to communicate moral or cautionary messages, to teach or inspire, to engage in an exchange about values, goals, standards, and imagination of the artist and community. It may commemorate individuals, groups, events, or deities and attempt to create enduring messages or memories. Or it may seek to provoke action, influence events, or inspire social change, like the *rara* bands of Haiti.

Can you see art in the performance of a skateboarder at a graffiti-covered park?

- As you consider your object, event, or experience, consider the artist's original intent as well as the way your chosen art object communicates between artist and audience. Is the audience's perception the same as the artist's intention?
- Consider its history, its role in the local community, and its connections beyond the local community. Where did this piece of art come from? Has it moved across geographic space? Who paid for it, bought it, developed it? Can it be sold?
- See how it is embedded in relationships of power. Who told you it was "art"? Who controls it? If it is displayed, who designed the display and determined how it would be contextualized?

Compare notes with your classmates. With all the information you have gathered, see if you can collectively develop a universal definition of art. Try to limit yourself to one sentence. (Now you know how it feels to be a textbook author!)

How Do Art and Media Intersect?

Recently, anthropologists have turned their attention to the partnering of creative expression with new media technologies (Askew and Wilk 2007). Just as globalization has intensified the worldwide movement of people, money, data, goods, and services, so globalization has transformed the flow of images and sounds through new media technologies. The anthropologist Arjun Appadurai calls this new formation a **global mediascape**: global cultural flows of media and visual images enable linkages and communication across boundaries of culture, language, geography, economics, and politics in ways unimaginable one hundred years ago (Appadurai 1990).

Just as newspapers dominated the mediascape in the late nineteenth century, radio, audio-recording devices, film, television, and the Internet have shaped communication in the twentieth and twenty-first centuries. In contemporary culture the image, whether in photograph, film, or video, has replaced written texts as the primary educator. This phenomenon gives a new dimension to the role of visual art.

Today, media reaches every corner of the globe and permeates all aspects of daily life. Media is everywhere humans live and everywhere anthropologists work. In fact, it is fair to say that media is central to human life in the twenty-first century. The decentralized production and circulation of new media, facilitated by satellites, computers, and handheld communication devices, has undermined the old media empires and has challenged the state's ability to control media content and media flows. In turn, new media has facilitated opportunities for activism as marginalized groups use photographs, film, text, and video to mobilize movements for social change and to challenge existing power structures (Ginsburg, Abu-Lughod, and Larkin 2002; Askew and Wilk 2007; Juris 2013).

The Global Mediascape

New media technologies have transformed the communities that anthropologists study as well as the practice of anthropology itself. In today's interconnected global age, video is one form of visual art that has tremendous potential to unify immigrants far from home and to reinforce their solidarity with their native communities. My own experience bears out this observation.

Chinese Villagers Stay Connected through Festival Videos In early 2007 I attended a temple festival in a small village on China's southeast coast. I had visited previously, but the opportunity to participate in a full two weeks of festivities at the invitation of the temple master was a unique privilege. Vivid rituals, raucous processions, solemn prayers, and bountiful banquets filled the days.

global mediascape: Global cultural flows of media and visual images that enable linkages and communication across boundaries in ways unimaginable a century ago.

But the constant presence of a small film crew documenting every element of temple life surprised me. One afternoon the temple master asked if I would be willing to be interviewed on camera to say a few words about the festival. As a grateful guest—and an oddity as the only non-Chinese at the festival—I readily agreed, gave an interview at the foot of a beautiful new pagoda overlooking the harbor, and thought little more about the matter.

Back in New York a few weeks later, I placed a call to a young woman from the village now living in Flushing, Queens. Her mother, still living in China, had entrusted me to deliver some baby clothes for her new granddaughter. We agreed to meet the next day on a corner of Main Street in Flushing—a meeting that, despite her assurances, I doubted would go smoothly on one of the busiest intersections in New York City.

I patiently waited the next day on the appointed corner. Much to my surprise, at the agreed-upon time a car pulled up, a window rolled down, and a young woman said in Chinese, "Professor Guest, get in!" Over dumplings and tea she explained, "Everyone from the village knows you! You're in the video!" It turns out that in order to keep immigrant villagers connected to the home temple and engaged in its spiritual and financial life, the master regularly produces and circulates festival videos to his devotees now living in the New York metropolitan area. Video of the festival I attended had traversed the globe from a rural Chinese village to the streets of New York City, serving to build solidarity among immigrant villagers now in the United States and to strengthen connections with their kinfolk, fellow townspeople, and religious co-adherents in China.

The forces of globalization move people, money, things—and images. A Chinese village festival had now entered the global mediascape.

Visual Images and Cultural Identity

Visual anthropology explores the production, circulation, and consumption of visual images, including photographs, film, television, and new media, focusing on the power of visual representations in art, performance, museums, and the mass media to influence culture and cultural identity (Hockings 2003). As you read the following discussion, you may be surprised to discover the power that photographs have to wield such influence.

visual anthropology: A field of anthropology that explores the production, circulation, and consumption of visual images, focusing on the power of visual representation to influence culture and cultural identity.

National Geographic's **Photographic Gaze** In a classic work of visual anthropology, *Reading National Geographic* (1993), anthropologists Catherine Lutz and Jane Collins examine the photographs of the popular U.S. magazine *National Geographic* to reveal the power of visual images to shape cultural perspectives and behavior. Launched in 1888, *National Geographic* has successfully blended science, art, photojournalism, and entertainment to become one of the most popular and influential U.S. sources of information about other cultures. Indeed, it collects "the world between its covers" (Lutz and Collins 1993, 24). At its peak, the reasonably priced magazine attracted more than ten million monthly subscribers (97 percent white and middle class) and, with multiple reads in classrooms, lobbies, and doctor's offices, perhaps 40 million total viewers. *National Geographic's* beautiful photos of smiling people from around the globe have inspired world travel, scientific exploration, and even sexual fantasies for generations of U.S. readers.

National Geographic may at first glance appear to offer a straightforward presentation of evidence about human nature and the natural world. But Lutz and Collins, using the analytical frameworks of visual anthropology, ask how the particular "gaze" of *National Geographic* photographs may reflect the worldview of those behind the lens—that is, the magazine's owners, editors, photographers, and graphic designers. This gaze, the authors suggest, can shape

the understandings of the magazine's readers as they think about humanity, the natural world, and their own culture's position in the global arena.

To investigate this claim, Lutz and Collins interviewed editors and readers and analyzed photographs from the magazine's nearly six hundred articles published about non-Western topics between 1950 and 1986. The researchers asked: What messages did these images convey? What was their intent?

According to the magazine's mission statement, issued in 1915, "only what is of a kindly nature is printed about any country or people; everything unpleasant or unduly critical is to be avoided" (1993, 27). Indeed, underlying the exquisite photos of seemingly happy people, elaborate rituals, and exotic costumes, Lutz and Collins perceive a particular editorial perspective and philosophical worldview. They draw the following conclusion: "Clearly, photographic practice at *National Geographic* is geared to a classic form of humanism, drawing readers' attention through its portrayal of difference, and then showing that under the colorful dress and skin, as it were, we are all more or less the same" (1993, 61). Even though this editorial viewpoint—expressed in the **photographic gaze**—appeared neutral, it projected a particular perspective on human nature, the natural world, history, and difference.

In projecting an almost magical sense of unity, the magazine's photographic gaze tended to overlook key aspects of human history. Photographers and editors selected and framed images to limit political and economic contexts. Conflict, inequality, poverty, and hunger were downplayed or completely avoided. In keeping with this editorial approach, photos of the period under study rarely portrayed dramatic world events of the time. Struggles for decolonization, the Cold War, the Vietnam War, or movements for civil rights, women's rights, and gay rights in the United States were left out of the magazine's photographic gaze. Lutz and Collins note that the magazine's editorial choices consistently minimized diversity and difference, especially along the lines of race and gender.

photographic gaze: The presumed neutral viewpoint of the camera that in fact projects the perspective of the person behind the camera onto human nature, the natural world, and history.

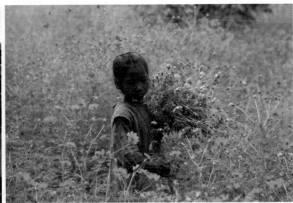

The authors suggest that during the period they studied, the gaze of *National Geographic*'s images created a cultural lens that mediated U.S. readers' experience of the world and its diverse people. The photographs avoided images that might disrupt readers' views of the world and the United States' place in it. Instead, as a primary source for U.S. middle-class information about the world, the magazine's gaze provided reassurance that (1) in essential ways the world that seems so diverse is actually quite familiar; (2) fundamentally, all is well with the world; and (3) the readers and their country play a benevolent role in world events. Here, Lutz and Collins suggest, the power of *National Geographic*'s photographs to shape the U.S. cultural worldview held deep implications for the way the magazine's primarily middle-class readers engaged debates about the nation's domestic and foreign policy (Fernea 1996; Goldstein 1998).

National Geographic's photographic gaze has continued to change over the years. But the concept of the gaze, central to visual anthropology, provides an important tool for thinking about how the form and content of media are

FIGURE 17.13 How might the visual images of *National Geographic*—its photographic gaze—shape readers' perspectives on the world? What messages emerge from these photos? *Left to right:* an Egyptian girl and man sit in front of the Sphinx, Giza, Egypt (Nov. 1955); a Mayan man reads to a crowd from his Bible during Holy Week, Guatemala (March 1960); an Imperial Bodyguard member rides in a war game, Ethiopia (March 1964); a Swazi princess accepts a new suitcase at her wedding ceremony, Swaziland (Jan. 1978); and a highland girl gathers wild cosmos flowers near Lake Itasy, Madagascar (Oct. 1967).

shaped by those "behind the camera." As you engage with media throughout your day—through television shows, news broadcasts, websites, tweets, YouTube channels, movies, Facebook pages—can you use the concept of the photographic gaze as a tool to analyze the intentionally and unintentionally expressed worldviews of the owners, editors, designers, videographers, and others behind the scenes?

The Anthropology of Virtual Environments

New forms of **social media**, including Facebook, YouTube, Twitter, and Tumblr, have transformed communication for many people in today's world. Now, computer- and Internet-based technologies serve as sources of pleasure and social engagement, not merely as tools for work. In *Coming of Age in Second Life* (2008), anthropologist Tom Boellstorff explores how computers and online virtual environments offer new opportunities for human community, intimacy, and social interaction.

Avatars Build Culture in a Virtual World Between 2004 and 2007, Tom Boellstorff conducted ethnographic fieldwork in an online, virtual world called Second Life. Created by Linden Labs in 2003, Second Life's "inhabitants" now number in the millions. In this alternate online world, the inhabitants' virtual characters, known as **avatars**, make friends, go to work, build homes, converse, walk around, exchange linden dollars in an elaborate economy, shop in malls, dance, get married, sail boats, and wrestle with the challenges of gender, race, and sexuality.

Through his avatar—named Tom Bukowski—Boellstorff used standard fieldwork research methods, including participant observation, interviews, and focus groups, to investigate the emergent human culture of a large-scale virtual social world. Second Life is accessible only through the computer screen, so Boellstorff conducted his research entirely inside the game. Like many participants in Second Life, he never communicated with fellow participants outside in the real world.

Like any anthropologist entering a new community, Boellstorff considered Second Life on its own terms, exploring its diverse cultural practices and beliefs in their own context. Although some observers consider Second Life an online game, Boellstorff resisted applying that label. A game, he argues, has a beginning and an end. A game has an ultimate goal. Second Life has none of these characteristics. People do play games in Second Life, but Second Life itself is not a game. Instead, Boellstorff suggests that Second Life is a real community of people who interact, create intimate relationships, and develop a unique culture and sets of beliefs. Second Life is, to use Benedict Anderson's concept, an imagined community (Anderson 1991). Its inhabitants experience

social media: New forms of communication based on computer- and Internet-based technologies that facilitate social engagement, work, and pleasure.

avatar: An object, real or virtual, that graphically represents a participant in a game or other activity.

a deep connection even when avatars have never been introduced. At the same time, in terms of the actual players, Second Life comprises real people who have significant connections with other members of the group, even if they have never met.

To illustrate the complexity and vitality of the Second Life virtual world, Boellstorff identifies the many cultures he encountered during his years of online fieldwork. He suggests that studying Second Life was remarkably similar to studying other human cultures. He previously conducted fieldwork in Indonesian communities holding unique notions of space, time, economics, politics, conflict, friendship, and sex—just like in Second Life. But Boellstorff goes one step further, comparing the virtual world of Second Life to real life. Human experience, he suggests, whether real or online, is always mediated by culture. Humans' uniqueness is rooted in our ability to continually reinvent social and physical realities through the creation of culture.

According to Boellstorff, "*It is in being virtual that we are human*" (2008, 29). Because human life is experienced and acquires meaning through the lens of culture, Boellstorff suggests that real life has been virtual all along. To use new media terminology, culture is our "app" for processing what we see, feel, think, and do. The process of creatively shaping a virtual world and virtual lives happens online in Second Life, but this is not dissimilar to the ways humans in the real world creatively express their visions of a different world and act individually and collectively to reshape reality. The processes of using online social media to create new opportunities for friendship, community, meaning making, and intimacy should not seem so unfamiliar, Boellstorff argues. Although his specific ethnographic project focused on human culture evolving in a virtual world, his broader goal was to unveil the ways in which culture mediates our everyday lives and aspects of our identity as we navigate through our constructed environment (King and Warren 2009; Heartfield 2008; Robson 2008).

Today media is reshaping human life in every part of the world as it increasingly permeates the routines of daily life. As you think about the expanding global

TOOLKIT

Thinking Like an Anthropologist: The Landscape of World Art

Art is everywhere in our lives. From the games we play and the songs we sing, to the way we dress and the food we eat, we humans express ourselves creatively and interact with one another through creative expression. As we have seen throughout this chapter, communication between artist and audience through art objects, performances, events, and experiences is not limited to elite actors or venues but is present throughout human cultures and deeply rooted in the activities of everyday life. This chapter's opening story described the creative ways in which young people in a Brazilian favela have built community, challenged the political and economic assumptions of the state, and projected their concerns into a national and international dialogue. When do games take on a life of their own? How do they become political action or efforts at community building? How do they become art? What is the relationship among creative expression, play, performance, and art?

Through Morrinho, imaginative young people engage in an evolving drama that performs, imitates, and examines life, constructing artificial scenarios and relationships through which the players explore their own emotional and social worlds. By telling an untold story or history, speaking the truth of a community back to its members and the surrounding culture and political structures, the

virtual world of Morrinho explores those boundaries among real life, play, and the creative expressions and engagements that anthropologists call art.

In this chapter we have begun to consider the vast landscape of world art. Where can you find these dynamics in your own life? In what ways are you an artist? How are you utilizing new forms of media technology to express your creativity and communicate with others through the global mediascape?

As you think more about the world of art, remember the opening questions that framed this chapter's inquiries:

- What is art?
- What is unique about how anthropologists study art?
- What is the relationship between art and power?
- How do art and media intersect?

After reading this chapter, you should be able to apply these questions to situations in which you encounter art and media and the intersections of real life, play, politics, and creative expression. Thinking like an anthropologist about the world of art can give you a more complete set of tools for comprehending this complex part of human culture, understanding your own creativity, and engaging the world around you.

mediascape, can you see how your everyday actions—friendships, education, love life, job, entertainment, religion, political engagements, communications, and more—are mediated by new technologies in ways unimaginable even two decades ago? The anthropology of media will continue to develop as this global mediascape expands and deepens. What will the next two decades bring? How will anthropologists utilize the tools of our discipline to understand the impact of these changes on people and their communities across the globe?

Key Terms

For Further Exploration

Cave of Forgotten Dreams. 2010. Directed by Werner Herzog. IFC Films. For this documentary, award-winning filmmaker Werner Hertzog gained exclusive access to the Chauvet caves in southern France.

The Double Dutch Divas! (or the original full-length version *I Was Made to Love Her*). 2001. Directed by Nicole Franklin. Filmmakers Library. The art and play of double dutch.

In and Out of Africa. 1993. Produced by Ilisa Barbash and Lucien Taylor, based on research by Christopher Steiner. Berkeley Media LLC. Documentary film that explores the transnational trade in African art by following the journey of a remarkable art dealer, Gabai Baaré, from Niger in rural West Africa to East Hampton, Long Island.

McAlister, Elizabeth. 2002. *Rara!: Vodou, Power, and Performance in Haiti and Its Diaspora*. Berkeley: University of California Press. Comes with a CD of *rara* band music developed to accompany the book.

Glossary

acclimatization: The process of the body temporarily adjusting to the environment.

Acheulian stone tools: Stone tools associated with *Homo erectus*, including specialized hand axes for cutting, pounding, and scraping.

achieved status: Social position established and changeable during a person's lifetime.

aesthetic experience: Perception through one's senses.

affinal relationship: A kinship relationship established through marriage and/or alliance, not through biology or common descent.

agency: The potential power of individuals and groups to contest cultural norms, values, symbols, mental maps of reality, institutions, and structures of power.

agriculture: An intensive farming strategy for food production involving permanently cultivated land.

anonymity: Protecting the identities of the people involved in a study by changing or omitting their names or other identifying characteristics.

anthropologist's toolkit: The tools needed to conduct fieldwork, including a notebook, pen, camera, voice recorder, and dictionary.

anthropology: The study of the full scope of human diversity, past and present, and the application of that knowledge to help people of different backgrounds better understand one another.

archaeology: The investigation of the human past by means of excavating and analyzing artifacts.

arranged marriage: Marriage orchestrated by the families of the involved parties.

art: All ideas, forms, techniques, and strategies that humans employ to express themselves creatively and to communicate their creativity and inspiration to others.

ascribed status: Social position inherited, assigned at birth, and passed down from generation to generation with enforced boundaries.

asexuality: A lack of erotic attraction to others.

assimilation: The process through which minorities accept the patterns and norms of the dominant culture and cease to exist as separate groups.

authenticity: The perception of an object's antiquity, uniqueness, and originality within a local culture.

authorizing process: The complex historical and social developments through which symbols are given power and meaning.

avatar: An object, real or virtual, that graphically represents a participant in a game or other activity.

band: A small kinship-based group of foragers who hunt and gather for a living over a particular territory.

barter: The exchange of goods and services one for the other.

biomedicine: A practice, often associated with Western medicine, that seeks to apply the principles of biology and the natural sciences to the practice of diagnosing disease and promoting healing.

bipedalism: The ability to habitually walk on two legs; one of the key distinguishing characteristics of humans and our immediate ancestors.

bisexuality: Attraction to and sexual relations with members of both sexes.

bourgeoisie: Marxist term for the capitalist class that owns the means of production.

brain drain: Migration of highly skilled professionals from developing/periphery countries to developed/core countries.

bridewealth: The gift of goods or money from the groom's family to the bride's family as part of the marriage process.

bridges and barriers: The factors that enable or inhibit migration.

built environment: The intentionally designed features of human settlement, including buildings, transportation and public service infrastructure, and public spaces.

carrying capacity: The number of people who can be supported by the resources of the surrounding region.

caste: A closed system of stratification in a society.

chain migration: The movement of people facilitated by the support of networks of family and friends who have already immigrated.

chiefdom: An autonomous political unit composed of a number of villages or communities under the permanent control of a paramount chief.

civil society organization: A local nongovernmental organization that challenges state policies and uneven development, and advocates for resources and opportunities for members of its local communities.

clan: A type of descent group based on a claim to a founding ancestor but lacking genealogical documentation.

class: A system of power based on wealth, income, and status that creates an unequal distribution of a society's resources.

climate change: Changes to Earth's climate, including global warming produced primarily by increasing concentrations of greenhouse gases created by human activity such as burning fossil fuels and deforestation.

code switching: Switching back and forth between one linguistic variant and another depending on the cultural context.

colonialism: The practice by which a nation-state extends political, economic, and military power beyond its own borders over an extended period of time to secure access to raw materials, cheap labor, and markets in other countries or regions.

commodity chain: The hands an item passes through between producer and consumer.

communitas: A sense of camaraderie, a common vision of what constitutes a good life, and a commitment to take social action to move toward achieving this vision that is shaped by the common experience of rites of passage.

companionate marriage: Marriage built on love, intimacy, and personal choice rather than social obligation.

contagious magic: Ritual words or performances that achieve efficacy as certain materials that come into contact with one person carry a magical connection that allows power to be transferred from person to person.

core countries: Industrialized former colonial states that dominate the world economic system.

cosmopolitanism: A global outlook emerging in response to increasing globalization.

creationism: A belief that God created Earth and all living creatures in their present form as recently as six thousand years ago.

critical medical anthropology: An approach to the study of health and illness that analyzes the impact of inequality and stratification within systems of power on individual and group health outcomes.

cultural adaptation: A complex innovation, such as fans, furnaces, and lights, that allows humans to cope with their environment.

cultural anthropology: The study of people's communities, behaviors, beliefs, and institutions, including how people make meaning as they live, work, and play together.

cultural capital: The knowledge, habits, and tastes learned from parents and family that individuals can use to gain access to scarce and valuable resources in society.

cultural construction of gender: The ways humans learn to behave as a man or woman and to recognize behaviors as masculine or feminine within their cultural context.

cultural materialism: A theory that argues that material conditions, including technology, determine patterns of social organization, including religious principles.

cultural relativism: Understanding a group's beliefs and practices within their own cultural context, without making judgments.

culture: A system of knowledge, beliefs, patterns of behavior, artifacts, and institutions that are created, learned, and shared by a group of people.

cumulative causation: An accumulation of factors that create a culture in which migration comes to be expected.

dalits: Members of India's "lowest" caste; literally, "broken people." Also called "Untouchables."

deep time: A framework for considering the span of human history within the much larger age of the universe and planet Earth.

dependency theory: A critique of modernization theory that argued that, despite the end of colonialism, the underlying economic relations of the modern world economic system had not changed.

descent group: A kinship group in which primary relationships are traced through consanguine ("blood") relatives.

descriptive linguistics: The study of the sounds, symbols, and gestures of a language, and their combination into forms that communicate meaning.

descriptive linguists: Those who analyze languages and their component parts.

development: Post–World War II strategy of wealthy nations to spur global economic growth, alleviate poverty, and raise living standards through strategic investment in national economies of former colonies.

developmental adaptation: The way in which human growth and development can be influenced by factors other than genetics, such as nutrition, disease, and stress.

dialect: A nonstandard variation of a language.

digital natives: A generation of people born after 1980 who have been raised in a digital age.

disease: A discrete natural entity that can be clinically identified and treated by a health professional.

displacement: The ability to use words to refer to objects not immediately present or events occurring in the past or future.

DNA: Deoxyribonucleic acid; the feature of a cell that provides the genetic code for the organism.

dowry: The gift of goods or money from the bride's family to the groom's family as part of the marriage process.

economy: A cultural adaptation to the environment that enables a group of humans to use the available resources to satisfy their needs and to thrive.

egalitarian society: A group based on the sharing of resources to ensure success with a relative absence of hierarchy and violence.

emic: An approach to gathering data that investigates how local people think and how they understand the world.

enculturation: The process of learning culture.

endogamy: Marriage to someone within the kinship group.

entrepreneurial immigrant: A person who moves to a new location to conduct trade and establish a business.

ethnic boundary marker: A practice or belief, such as food, clothing, language, shared name, or religion, used to signify who is in a group and who is not.

ethnic cleansing: Efforts by representatives of one ethnic or religious group to remove or destroy another group in a particular geographic area.

ethnicity: A sense of historical, cultural, and sometimes ancestral connection to a group of people who are imagined to be distinct from those outside the group.

ethnocentrism: The belief that one's own culture or way of life is normal and natural; using one's own culture to evaluate and judge the practices and ideals of others.

ethnographic fieldwork: A primary research strategy in cultural anthropology involving living with a community of people over an extended period to better understand their lives.

ethnology: The analysis and comparison of ethnographic data across cultures.

ethnomedicine: Local systems of health and healing rooted in culturally specific norms and values.

ethnomusicology: The study of music in cultural context.

ethnopharmacology: The documentation and description of the local use of natural substances in healing remedies and practices.

etic: Description of local behavior and beliefs from the anthropologist's perspective in ways that can be compared across cultures.

eugenics: A pseudoscience attempting to scientifically prove the existence of separate human races to improve the population's genetic composition by favoring some races over others.

exogamy: Marriage to someone outside the kinship group.

family of orientation: The family group in which one is born, grows up, and develops life skills.

family of procreation: The family group created when one reproduces and within which one rears children.

field notes: The anthropologist's written observations and reflections on places, practices, events, and interviews.

fine art: Creative expression and communication often associated with cultural elites.

first-generation immigrant: A person who left his or her home country as an adult.

flexible accumulation: The increasingly flexible strategies that corporations use to accumulate profits in an era of globalization, enabled by innovative communication and transportation technologies.

focal vocabulary: The words and terminology that develop with particular sophistication to describe the unique cultural realities experienced by a group of people.

food foragers: Humans who subsist by hunting, fishing, and gathering plants to eat.

Fordism: The dominant model of industrial production for much of the twentieth century, based on a social compact between labor, capital, and government.

fossils: The remains of an organism that have been preserved by a natural chemical process that turns them partially or wholly into rock.

four-field approach: The use of four interrelated disciplines to study humanity: physical anthropology, archaeology, linguistic anthropology, and cultural anthropology.

framing process: The creation of shared meanings and definitions that motivate and justify collective action by social movements.

gender: The expectations of thought and behavior that each culture assigns to people of different sexes.

gender ideology: A set of cultural ideas, usually stereotypical, about the essential character of different genders that functions to promote and justify gender stratification.

gender performance: The way gender identity is expressed through action.

gender stereotype: A preconceived notion about the attributes of, differences between, and proper roles for men and women in a culture.

gender stratification: An unequal distribution of power and access to a group's resources, opportunities, rights, and privileges based on gender.

gender studies: Research into the cultural construction of masculinity and femininity across cultures as flexible, complex, and historically and culturally constructed categories.

gender violence: Forms of violence shaped by the gender identities of the people involved.

gene migration: The movement of genetic material within a population and among diverse populations.

genetic adaptation: Changes in genetics that occur at a population level in response to certain features of the environment.

genetic drift: The process whereby one segment of a population is removed from the larger pool, thereby limiting the flow of genetic material between the two groups.

genocide: The deliberate and systematic destruction of an ethnic or religious group.

genotype: The inherited genetic factors that provide the framework for an organism's physical form.

global city: A former industrial center that has reinvented itself as a command center for global production.

globalization: The worldwide intensification of interactions and increased movement of money, people, goods, and ideas within and across national borders.

global mediascape: Global cultural flows of media and visual images that enable linkages and communication across boundaries in ways unimaginable a century ago.

grammar: The combined set of observations about the rules governing the formation of morphemes and syntax that guide language use.

guest worker program: A policy that allows labor immigrants to enter a country temporarily to work.

habitus: Bourdieu's term to describe the self-perceptions and beliefs that develop as part of one's social identity and shape one's conceptions of the world and where one fits in it.

health: The absence of disease and infirmity, as well as the presence of physical, mental, and social well-being.

health transition: The significant improvements in human health made over the course of the twentieth century that were not, however, distributed evenly across the world's population.

hegemony: The ability of a dominant group to create consent and agreement within a population without the use or threat of force.

heterosexuality: Attraction to and sexual relations between individuals of the opposite sex.

historic archaeology: The exploration of the more recent past through an examination of physical remains and artifacts as well as written or oral records.

historical linguistics: The study of the development of language over time, including its changes and variations.

historic linguists: Those who study how language changes over time within a culture and how languages travel across cultures.

historical particularism: The idea, attributed to Franz Boas, that cultures develop in specific ways because of their unique histories.

holism: The anthropological commitment to consider the full scope of human life, including culture, biology, history, and language, across space and time.

hometown association: An organization created for mutual support by immigrants from the same home town or region.

homosexuality: Attraction to and sexual relations between individuals of the same sex.

horticulture: The cultivation of plants for subsistence through non-intensive use of land and labor.

human microbiome: The complete collection of micoorganisms in the human body's ecosystem.

hypodescent: Sometimes called the "one drop of blood rule"; the assignment of children of racially "mixed" unions to the subordinate group.

illness: The individual patient's experience of sickness.

illness narratives: The personal stories that people tell to explain their illnesses.

imagined community: The invented sense of connection and shared traditions that underlies identification with a particular ethnic group or nation whose members likely will never meet.

imitative magic: A ritual performance that achieves efficacy by imitating the desired magical result.

incest taboo: Cultural rules that forbid sexual relations with certain close relatives.

income: What people earn from work, plus dividends and interest on investments, along with rents and royalties.

increasing migration: The accelerated movement of people within and between countries.

individual racism: Personal prejudiced beliefs and discriminatory actions based on race.

industrial agriculture: Intensive farming practices involving mechanization and mass production.

Industrial Revolution: The eighteenth- and nineteenth-century shift from agriculture and artisanal skill craft to machine-based manufacturing.

informed consent: A key strategy for protecting those being studied by ensuring that they are fully informed of the goals of the project and have clearly indicated their consent to participate.

institutional racism: Patterns by which racial inequality is structured through key cultural institutions, policies, and systems.

intelligent design: An updated version of creationism that claims to propose an evidence-based argument to contradict the theory of evolution.

internally displaced person: A person who has been forced to move within his or her country of origin because of persecution, armed conflict, or natural disasters.

internal migration: The movement of people within their own national borders.

interpretivist approach: A conceptual framework that sees culture primarily as a symbolic system of deep meaning.

intersectionality: An analytic framework for assessing how factors such as race, gender, and class interact to shape individual life chances and societal patterns of stratification.

intersexual: An individual who is born with a combination of male and female genitalia, gonads, and/or chromosomes.

interview: A research strategy of gathering data through formal or informal conversation with informants.

Jim Crow: Laws implemented after the U.S. Civil War to legally enforce segregation, particularly in the South, after the end of slavery.

key informant: A community member who advises the anthropologist on community issues, provides feedback, and warns against cultural miscues. Also called cultural consultant.

kinesics: The study of the relationship between body movements and communication.

kinetic orality: A musical genre combining body movement and voice.

kinship: The system of meaning and power that cultures create to determine who is related to whom and to define their mutual expectations, rights, and responsibilities.

kinship analysis: A traditional strategy of examining genealogies to uncover the relationships built upon structures such as marriage and family ties.

labor immigrant: A person who moves in search of a low-skill and low-wage job, often filling an economic niche that native-born workers will not fill.

language: A system of communication organized by rules that uses symbols such as words, sounds, and gestures to convey information.

language continuum: The idea that variation in languages appears gradually over distance so that groups of people who live near one another speak in a way that is mutually intelligible.

language loss: The extinction of languages that have very few speakers.

leveling mechanism: Practices and organizations that reallocate resources among a group to maximize collective good.

lexicon: All the words for names, ideas, and events that make up a language's dictionary.

life chances: An individual's opportunities to improve quality of life and achieve life goals.

life history: A form of interview that traces the biography of a person over time, examining changes and illuminating the interlocking network of relationships in the community.

liminality: One stage in a rite of passage during which a ritual participant experiences a period of outsiderhood, set apart from normal society, that is key to achieving a new perspective on the past, future, and current community.

lineage: A type of descent group that traces genealogical connection through generations by linking persons to a founding ancestor.

linguistic anthropology: The study of human language in the past and present.

literature review: The process of reading all the available published material about a research site and/or research issues, usually done before fieldwork begins.

magic: The use of spells, incantations, words, and actions in an attempt to compel supernatural forces to act in certain ways, whether for good or for evil.

mapping: The analysis of the physical and/or geographic space where fieldwork is being conducted.

marriage: A socially recognized relationship that may involve physical and emotional intimacy as well as legal rights to property and inheritance.

martyr: A person who sacrifices his or her life for the sake of religion.

means of production: The factories, machines, tools, raw materials, land, and financial capital needed to make things.

medical migration: The movement of diseases, medical treatments, and entire healthcare systems, as well as those seeking medical care, across national borders.

medical pluralism: The intersection of multiple cultural approaches to healing.

melanin: The pigment that gives human skin its color.

melting pot: A metaphor used to describe the process of immigrant assimilation into U.S. dominant culture.

mental maps of reality: Cultural classifications of what kinds of people and things exist, and the assignment of meaning to those classifications.

militarization: The contested social process through which a civil society organizes for the production of military violence.

miscegenation: A demeaning historical term for interracial marriage.

modernization theories: Post–World War II economic theories that predicted that with the end of colonialism, less-developed countries would follow the same trajectory toward modernization as the industrialized countries.

monogamy: A relationship between only two partners.

morphemes: The smallest units of sound that carry meaning on their own.

morphology: The study of patterns and rules of how sounds combine to make morphemes.

multiculturalism: A pattern of ethnic relations in which new immigrants and their children enculturate into the dominant national culture and yet retain an ethnic culture.

multiregional continuity thesis: The theory that modern *Homo sapiens* evolved directly from archaic *Homo sapiens* living in regions across the world.

mutagen: Any agent that increases the frequency or extent of mutations.

mutation: A deviation from the standard DNA code.

mutual transformation: The potential for both the anthropologist and the members of the community being studied to be transformed by the interactions of fieldwork.

nation: A term once used to describe a group of people who shared a place of origin; now used interchangeably with nation-state.

nation-state: A political entity, located within a geographic territory with enforced borders, where the population shares a sense of culture, ancestry, and destiny as a people.

nationalism: The desire of an ethnic community to create and/or maintain a nation-state.

nativism: Favoring certain long-term inhabitants over new immigrants.

natural selection: The evolutionary process by which some organisms, with features that enable them to adapt to the environment, preferentially survive and reproduce, thereby increasing the frequency of those features in the population.

Neandertal: A late variety of archaic *Homo sapien* prevalent in Europe.

neocolonialism: A continued pattern of unequal economic relations despite the formal end of colonial political and military control.

neoliberalism: An economic and political worldview that sees the free market as the main mechanism for ensuring economic growth, with a severely restricted role for government.

norms: Ideas or rules about how people should behave in particular situations or toward certain other people.

nuclear family: The kinship unit of mother, father, and children.

Oldowan tools: Stone tools shaped for chopping and cutting found in the Olduvai Gorge and associated with *Australopithecus garhi*.

1.5-generation immigrant: The child of immigrants who is born in the family's home country but at a young age moves with his or her parents to a new host country.

origin myth: A story told about the founding and history of a particular group to reinforce a sense of common identity.

"out of Africa" theory: The theory that modern *Homo sapiens* evolved first in Africa, migrated outward, and eventually replaced the archaic *Homo sapiens*. Also called *replacement theory*.

paleoanthropology: The study of the history of human evolution through the fossil record.

paleogeneticist: Scientist who studies the past through the examination of preserved genetic material.

paralanguage: An extensive set of noises (such as cries) and tones of voice that convey significant information about the speaker.

participant observation: A key anthropological research strategy involving both participation in and observation of the daily life of the people being studied.

pastoralism: A strategy for food production involving the domestication of animals.

periphery countries: The least developed and least powerful nations; often exploited by the core countries as sources of raw materials, cheap labor, and markets.

phenotype: The way genes are expressed in an organism's physical form as a result of genotype interaction with environmental factors.

phonemes: The smallest units of sound that can make a difference in meaning.

phonology: The study of what sounds exist and which ones are important for a particular language.

photographic gaze: The presumed neutral viewpoint of the camera that in fact projects the perspective of the person behind the camera onto human nature, the natural world, and history.

physical anthropology: The study of humans from a biological perspective, particularly focused on human evolution.

pilgrimage: A religious journey to a sacred place as a sign of devotion and in search of transformation and enlightenment.

polyandry: Marriage between one woman and two or more men.

polygyny: Marriage between one man and two or more women.

polyvocality: The practice of using many different voices in ethnographic writing and research question development, allowing the reader to hear more directly from the people in the study.

popular art: Creative expression and communication often associated with the general population.

potlach: Elaborate redistribution ceremony practiced among the Kwakiutl of the Pacific Northwest.

power: The ability or potential to bring about change through action or influence.

prehistoric archaeology: The reconstruction of human behavior in the distant past (before written records) through the examination of artifacts.

prestige: The reputation, influence, and deference bestowed on certain people because of their membership in certain groups.

prestige language: A particular way of speaking, or language variation, that is associated with wealth, success, education, and power.

primatology: The study of living nonhuman primates as well as primate fossils to better understand human evolution and early human behavior.

productivity: The linguistic ability to use known words to invent new word combinations.

profane: Anything that is considered not holy.

professional immigrant: A highly trained individual who moves to fill an economic niche in a middle-class profession often marked by shortages in the receiving country.

proletariat: Marxist term for the class of laborers who own only their labor.

pushes and pulls: The forces that spur migration from the country of origin and draw immigrants to a particular new destination country.

qualitative data: Descriptive data drawn from nonstatistical sources, including participant observation, personal stories, interviews, and life histories.

quantitative data: Statistical information about a community that can be measured and compared.

race: A flawed system of classification, with no biological basis, that uses certain physical characteristics to divide the human population into supposedly discrete groups.

racial ideology: A set of popular ideas about race that allows the discriminatory behaviors of individuals and institutions to seem reasonable, rational, and normal.

racialization: To categorize, differentiate, and attribute a particular racial character to a person or group of people.

racism: Individual thoughts and actions and institutional patterns and policies that create unequal access to power, resources, and opportunities based on imagined differences among groups.

ranked society: A group in which wealth is not stratified but prestige and status are.

rapid change: The dramatic transformations of economics, politics, and culture characteristic of contemporary globalization.

rapport: The relationships of trust and familiarity developed with members of the community being studied.

reciprocity: The exchange of resources, goods, and services among people of relatively equal status; meant to create and reinforce social ties.

redistribution: A form of exchange in which accumulated wealth is collected from the members of the group and reallocated in a different pattern.

reflexivity: A critical self-examination of the role the anthropologist plays and an awareness that one's identity affects one's fieldwork and theoretical analyses.

refugee: A person who has been forced to move beyond his or her national borders because of persecution, armed conflict, or natural disasters.

religion: A set of beliefs based on a unique vision of how the world ought to be, often revealed through insights into a supernatural power and lived out in community.

remittance: Resources transferred from migrants working abroad to individuals, families, and institutions in their country of origin.

rite of passage: A category of ritual that enacts a change of status from one life stage to another, either for an individual or a group.

ritual: An act or series of acts regularly repeated over years or generations that embody the beliefs of a group of people and create a sense of continuity and belonging.

sacred: Anything that is considered holy.

saint: An individual who is considered exceptionally close to God and is exalted after death.

salvage ethnography: Fieldwork strategy developed by Franz Boas to rapidly collect cultural, material, linguistic, and biological information about U.S. Native populations being devastated by Western expansion.

Sapir-Whorf hypothesis: The idea that different languages create different ways of thinking.

second-generation immigrant: The child of immigrants who is born and raised in the new host country.

semiperiphery countries: Nations ranking in between core and periphery countries, with some attributes of the core countries but with less of a central role in the global economy.

sex: The observable physical differences between male and female, especially biological expressions related to human reproduction.

sex tourism: Travel, usually organized through the tourism sector, to facilitate commercial sexual relations between tourists and local residents.

sexual dimorphism: The phenotypic differences between males and females of the same species.

sexuality: The complex range of desires, beliefs, and behaviors that are related to erotic physical contact and the cultural arena within which people debate about what kinds of physical desires and behaviors are right, appropriate, and natural.

sexual violence: Violence perpetuated through sexually related physical assaults such as rape.

sex work: Labor through which one provides sexual services for money.

shaman: A part-time religious practitioner with special abilities to connect individuals with supernatural powers or beings.

situational negotiation of identity: An individual's self-identification with a particular group that can shift according to social location.

slash and burn agriculture: A practice of clearing land for cultivation. Also called *swidden farming.*

social capital: Assets and skills such as language, education, and social networks that can be mobilized in lieu of or as complementary to financial capital.

social media: New forms of communication based on computer- and Internet-based technologies that facilitate social engagement, work, and pleasure.

social mobility: The movement of one's class position, upward or downward, in stratified societies.

social movement: Collective group actions in response to uneven development, inequality, and injustice that seek to build institutional networks to transform cultural patterns and government policies.

social network analysis: A method for examining relationships in a community, often conducted by identifying who people turn to in times of need.

social reproduction: The phenomenon whereby social and class relations of prestige or lack of prestige are passed from one generation to the next.

sociolinguistics: The study of the ways culture shapes language and language shapes culture, particularly the intersection of language and systems of power such as race, gender, class, and age.

sociolinguists: Those who study language in its social and cultural contexts.

species: A group of related organisms that can interbreed and produce fertile, viable offspring.

state: An autonomous regional structure of political, economic, and military rule with a central government authorized to make laws and use force to maintain order and defend its territory.

stratification: The uneven distribution of resources and privileges among participants in a group or culture.

structural functionalism: A conceptual framework positing that each element of society serves a particular function to keep the entire system in equilibrium.

structural gender violence: gendered societal patterns of unequal access to wealth, power, and basic resources such as food, shelter, and health care that differentially affect women in particular.

survey: An information-gathering tool for quantitative data analysis.

symbol: Anything that signifies something else.

syntax: The specific patterns and rules for constructing phrases and sentences.

theory of evolution: The theory that biological adaptations in organisms occur in response to changes in the natural environment and develop in populations over generations.

time-space compression: The rapid innovation of communication and transportation technologies associated with globalization that transforms the way people think about space and time.

transgender: A gender identity or performance that does not fit with cultural norms related to one's assigned sex at birth.

transnationalism: The practice of maintaining active participation in social, economic, religious, and political spheres across national borders.

triangle trade: The extensive exchange of slaves, sugar, cotton, and furs between Europe, Africa, and the Americas that transformed economic, political, and social life on both sides of the Atlantic.

tribe: Originally viewed as a culturally distinct, multiband population that imagined itself as one people descended from a common ancestor; currently used to describe an indigenous group with its own set of loyalties and leaders living to some extent outside the control of a centralized authoritative state.

underdevelopment: The term used to suggest that poor countries are poor as a result of their relationship to an unbalanced global economic system.

uneven development: The unequal distribution of the benefits of globalization.

unilineal cultural evolution: The theory proposed by nineteenth-century anthropologists that all cultures naturally evolve through the same sequence of stages from simple to complex.

universal gaze: An intrinsic way of perceiving art—thought by many in the Western art world to be found across cultures—that informs what people consider to be art or not art.

values: Fundamental beliefs about what is important, true, or beautiful, and what makes a good life.

visual anthropology: A field of anthropology that explores the production, circulation, and consumption of visual images, focusing on the power of visual representation to influence culture and cultural identity.

wealth: The total value of what someone owns, minus any debt.

whiteness: A culturally constructed concept originating in 1691 Virginia designed to establish clear boundaries of who is white & who is not, a process central to the formation of U.S. racial stratification.

white supremacy: The belief that whites are biologically different and superior to people of other races.

zeros: Elements of a story or a picture that are not told or seen and yet offer key insights into issues that might be too sensitive to discuss or display publicly.

References

Abu-Lughod, Janet L. 1989. *Before European Hegemony: The World System A.D. 1250–1350*. New York: Oxford University Press.

———. 2000. *Veiled Sentiments: Honor and Poetry in a Bedouin Society*. Berkeley: University of California Press.

———. 2005. *Dramas of Nationhood: The Politics of Television in Egypt*. Chicago: University of Chicago Press.

———. 2012. "Living the 'Revolution' in an Egyptian Village: Moral Action in a National Sphere." *American Ethnologist* 39(1): 21–25.

Agrama, Hussein Ali. 2010. "Ethics, Tradition, Authority: Toward an Anthropology of the Fatwa." *American Ethnologist* 37(1): 2–18.

———. 2012. *Questioning Secularism: Islam, Sovereignty and the Rule of Law in Modern Egypt*. Chicago: Chicago University Press.

Aiyer, Ananthakrishnan. 2007. "The Allure of the Transnational: Notes on Some Aspects of the Political Economy of Water in India." *Cultural Anthropology* 22(4): 640–58.

Alexander, Edward P. 1996. "What Is a Museum?" In *Museums in Motion: An Introduction to the History and Functions of Museums*, edited by Edward P. Alexander and Mary Alexander. Walnut Creek, CA: AltaMira. Published in cooperation with the American Association for State and Local History.

Alexander, J. 2001. "Islam, Archaeology, and Slavery in Africa." *World Archaeology*, 33(1): 44–60.

Allison, Anthony C. 2004. "Two Lessons from the Interface of Genetics and Medicine." *Genetics* 166: 1591–99.

Alpers, Svetlana. 1991. "Museums as a Way of Seeing." In *Exhibiting Cultures: The Poetics and Politics of Museum Display*, edited by Ivan Karp and Steven Lavine, 25–32. Washington, DC: Smithsonian Institution.

American Academy of Pediatrics. 2000. "Evaluation of the Newborn with Developmental Anomalies of the External Genitalia." *Pediatrics* 106(1): 138–42.

———. 2006. "Children, Adolescents, and Advertising." *Pediatrics* 118(6): 2563–69.

American Anthropological Association. 1999. "Declaration on Anthropology and Human Rights." www.aaanet.org/about /Policies/statements/Declaration-on-Anthropology-and -Human-Rights.cfm.

———. 2004. "Statement on Marriage and the Family." www .aaanet.org/issues/policy-advocacy/Statement-on-Marriage -and-the-family.cfm.

Anderson, Benedict. 1983. *Imagined Communities: Reflections on the Origin and Spread of Nationalism*. London: Verso.

Anglin, Mary K. 2002. *Women, Power, and Dissent in the Hills of Carolina*. Urbana: University of Illinois.

Anton, Susan C. 2003. "A Natural History of *Homo erectus*." In "Yearbook of Physical Anthropology," supplement, *American Journal of Physical Anthropology* 122(37): 126–70.

Anton, Susan C., and Carl C. Swisher III. 2004. "Early Dispersals of *Homo* from Africa." *Annual Review of Anthropology* 33: 271–96.

Aparicio, Ana. 2006. *Dominican-Americans and the Politics of Empowerment*. Gainesville: University of Florida.

Appadurai, Arjun, ed. 1986. *The Social Life of Things: Commodities in Cultural Perspective*. Cambridge, UK: Cambridge University Press.

———. 1990. "Disjuncture and Difference in the Global Cultural Economy." *Public Culture* 2(2): 1–24.

Appiah, Kwame Anthony. 2006. *Cosmopolitanism: Ethics in a World of Strangers*. New York: Norton.

Arango, Tim. 2010. "Biden Offers Diplomacy amid Impasse in Iraq." *New York Times*, July 3.

Archetti, Eduardo P. 1999. *Masculinities: Football, Polo and the Tango in Argentina*. Oxford, UK: Berg.

Arobba, Biagio, Robert E. McGrath, Joe Futrelle, and Alan B. Craig. 2010. *A Community-Based Social Media Approach for Preserving Endangered Languages and Culture*. www.ideals .illinois.edu/bitstream/handle/2142/17078/lat-comm-info-2 -sep-2010.pdf?sequence=2.

Asad, Talal, ed. 1992. *Anthropology & the Colonial Encounter*. Atlantic Highlands, NJ: Humanity Books.

———. 1993. *Genealogies of Religion: Discipline and Reasons of Power in Christianity and Islam*. Baltimore: Johns Hopkins University Press.

Askew, Kelly Michelle, and Richard R. Wilk, eds. 2007. *The Anthropology of Media: A Reader*. Malden, MA: Blackwell.

Averill, Gage. 2003. "Rara! Vodou, Power and Performance in Haiti and Its Diaspora [Review]." *Latin American Music Review* 24(1): 136–39.

Baer, Hans A., Merrill Singer, and Ida Susser. 2003. *Medical Anthropology and the World System*. Westport, CT: Praeger.

Baker, Lee D. 1995. "Racism in Professional Settings: Forms of Address as Clues to Power Relations." *Journal of Applied Behavioral Science* 31(2): 186–201.

———. 2004. "Franz Boas Out of the Ivory Tower." *Anthropological Theory* 4(1): 29–51.

Barboza, David, and Keith Bradsher. 2010. "In China, Labor Movement Enabled by Technology." *New York Times*, June 17.

Barker, D. J. P. 1998. *Mothers, Babies, and Health in Later Life*, 2nd ed. Edinburgh and New York: Churchill Livingstone.

Barker, Holly M. 2008. "The Inequities of Climate Change and the Small Island Experience." *Counterpunch*, November 4.

Barth, Fredrik. 1959. *Political Leadership among Swat Pathans*. London: Athlone Press.

———. 1969. "Introduction." In *Ethnic Groups and Boundaries*, edited by Fredrik Barth. Boston: Little, Brown.

Basso, Keith. 1996. *Wisdom Sits in Places: Landscape and Language among the Western Apache*. Albuquerque: University of New Mexico Press.

The Battle of Algiers. 1965. Directed by Gillo Pontecorvo. Allied Artists Corporation.

Baumann, Gerd. 1995. "Managing a Polyethnic Milieu: Kinship and Interaction in a London Suburb." *Journal of the Royal Anthropological Institute* 1(4): 725–41.

Beall, Cynthia. 2001. "Adaptations to Altitude: A Current Assessment." *Annual Review of Anthropology* 30: 423–56.

———. 2006. "Andean, Tibetan, and Ethiopian Patterns of Adaptation to High-Altitude Hypoxia." *Integrative and Comparative Biology* 46: 18–24.

Beidelman, T. O. 1994. "African Art in Transit [Review]." *Anthropos* 89(4/6): 653–54.

Bellah, Robert. 1980. *Varieties of Civil Religion*. San Francisco: Harper & Row.

Bellamy, Carla. 2011. *The Powerful Ephemeral: Everyday Healing in an Ambiguously Islamic Place*. Berkeley: University of California Press.

Benedict, Ruth. 1934. *Patterns of Culture*. Boston: Houghton Mifflin.

———. 1946. *The Chrysanthemum and the Sword: Patterns of Japanese Culture*. Boston: Houghton Mifflin.

Bennet, R. L., A. G. Motulsky, A. H. Bittles, S. A. Uhrich, D. L. Doyle, K. A. Silvey, E. Cheng, R. A. Steiner, and B. McGillivray. 2002. "Genetic Counseling and Screening of Consanguineous Couples and Their Offspring: Recommendations of the National Society of Genetic Counselors." *Journal of Genetic Counseling* 11(2): 97–119.

Bennett, Tony. 2010. "Painting Culture: The Making of an Aboriginal Art [Review]." *International Journal of Cultural Policy* 16(1): 11–12.

Berger, Peter, ed. 1999. *The Desecularization of the World: Resurgent Religion and World Politics*. Grand Rapids, MI: Wm. B. Eerdmans.

Bern, Sandra Lipsitz. 1981. "Gender Schema Theory: A Cognitive Account of Sex Typing." *Psychological Review* 88: 354–64.

———. 1983. "Gender Schema Theory and Its Implications for Child Development: Raising Gender-Aschematic Children in a Gender-Schematic Society." *Signs: Journal of Women in Culture and Society* 8: 598–616.

Besteman, Catherine L. ed. 2002. *Violence: A Reader*. New York: New York University Press.

Besteman, Catherine L., and Lee V. Cassanelli. 1996. *The Struggle for Land in Southern Somalia: The War Behind the War*. Boulder, CO: Westview Press.

Bestor, Theodore C. 2001. "Supply-Side Sushi: Commodity, Market, and the Global City." *American Anthropologist* 102(1): 76–95.

———. 2004. *Tsukiji: The Fish Market at the Center of the World*. Berkeley: University of California Press.

Bickford, Andrew. 2011. *Fallen Elites: The Military Other in Post-unification Germany*. Stanford, CA: Stanford University Press.

Binder, Frederick M., and David M. Reimers. 1995. *All Nations under Heaven: An Ethnic and Racial History of New York City*. New York: Columbia University Press.

Black Gold: Wake Up and Smell the Coffee. 2006. Directed by Marc Francis and Nick Francis. Speak It/Fulcrum.

Blackless, Melanie, Anthony Charuvastra, Amanda Derryck, Anne Fausto-Sterling, Karl Lauzanne, and Ellen Lee. 2000. "How Sexually Dimorphic Are We? Review and Synthesis." *American Journal of Human Biology* 12: 151–66.

Board of Governors of the Federal Reserve System. 2012a. "Consumer Credit-G.19." www.federalreserve.gov /releases/g19 /current/default.htm.

———. 2012b. "Mortgage Debt Outstanding." www.federalreserve .gov/econresdata/releases/mortoutstand/current.htm.

Boas, Franz. 1912. "Changes in the Bodily Form of Descendants of Immigrants." *American Anthropologist* 14(3).

———. 1966. *Kwakiutl Ethnography* (Classics of Anthropology). Helen F. Codere, ed. Chicago: University of Chicago Press.

Boehm, Christopher. 1999. *Hierarchy in the Forest: The Evolution of Egalitarian Behavior*. Cambridge, MA: Harvard University Press.

Boellstorff, Tom. 2008. *Coming of Age in Second Life: An Anthropologist Explores the Virtually Human*. Princeton, NJ: Princeton University Press.

Bohannan, Laura. 1966. "Shakespeare in the Bush: An American Anthropologist Set Out to Study the Tiv of West Africa and Was Taught the True Meaning of *Hamlet*." *Natural History* 75: 28–33.

Bolin, Anne. 1992. "Families We Choose: Lesbians, Gays, Kinship [Review]." *American Anthropologist* 94(4): 947–48.

Bonaccorso, Monica M. E. 2009. *Conceiving Kinship: Assisted Conception, Procreation and Family in Southern Europe*. New York: Berghahn.

Bonilla-Silva, Eduardo. 2010. *Racism without Racists: Color-Blind Racism and Racial Inequality in Contemporary America*, 3rd ed. New York: Rowan and Littlefield.

Bonvillain, Nancy. 2007. *Women and Men: Cultural Constructions of Gender*, 4th ed. Upper Saddle River, NJ: Prentice Hall.

Bourdieu, Pierre. 1982. *Ce que parler veut dire*. Paris: Fayard.

———. 1984. *Distinction: A Social Critique of the Judgment of Taste.* Translated by R. Nice. Cambridge, MA: Harvard University Press.

Bourdieu, Pierre, with Jean-Claude Passeron. (1970) 1990. *Reproduction in Education, Society and Culture,* 2nd ed. (Theory, Culture, and Society Series vol 4). Translated by Lois Wacquant. New York: Sage.

Bourgois, Philippe I. 2003. *In Search of Respect: Selling Crack in El Barrio,* 2nd ed. Cambridge, UK: Cambridge University Press.

Bowen, John R. 2006. *Why the French Don't Like Headscarves: Islam, the State, and Public Space.* Princeton, NJ: Princeton University Press.

Bowie, Fiona. 2006. *The Anthropology of Religion: An Introduction,* 2nd ed. Malden, MA: Blackwell.

Brash, Julian. 2011. *Bloomberg's New York: Class and Governance in the Luxury City.* Athens: University of Georgia

Braudel, Fernand. (1979) 1992. *Civilization and Capitalism, 15th to 18th Centuries,* vol. 3, *The Perspective of the World.* Translated by Siân Reynolds. Berkeley: University of California Press.

Brennan, Denise. 2004. *What's Love Got to Do with It? Transnational Desires and Sex Tourism in the Dominican Republic.* Durham, NC: Duke University Press.

Brettell, Caroline B., and C. F. Sargent, eds. 2009. *Gender in Cross-Cultural Perspective,* 5th ed. Upper Saddle River, NJ: Pearson/Prentice Hall.

Brewis, Alexandra A. 2000. "Sambia Sexual Culture [Review]." *American Anthropologist* 102(2): 392–93.

Bridges, Khiara M. 2011. *Reproducing Race: An Ethnography of Pregnancy as a Site of Racialization.* Berkeley: University of California Press.

Bridges, Tristan S. 2007. "Dude You're a Fag: Masculinity and Sexuality in High School [Review]." *Gender and Society* 21(5): 776–78.

Brimelow, Peter. 1995. *Alien Nation: Common Sense about America's Immigration Disaster.* New York: Random House.

Bringa, Tone. 1993. *Bosnia: We Are All Neighbors.* Granada Television.

———. 1995. *Being Muslim the Bosnian Way: Identity and Community in a Central Bosnian Village.* Princeton, NJ: Princeton University Press.

Bringa, Tone, and Peter Loizos. 2002. *Returning Home: Revival of a Bosnian Village.* Sage Film and Video (Sarajevo).

Brodkin, Karen. 1998. *How the Jews Became White Folks: And What That Says about Race in America.* New Brunswick, NJ: Rutgers University Press.

———. 2007. "Foreword." In *The Gender of Globalization: Women Navigating Cultural and Economic Marginalities,* edited by Nandini Gunewardena and Ann Kingsolver. Santa Fe, NM: School for Advanced Research Press.

Brown, Jacqueline Nassy. 2007. "Suriname, Sweet Suriname [Review]." *GLQ: A Journal of Lesbian and Gay Studies* 13(2–3): 406–8.

Brown, Lester R. 2011. "When the Nile Runs Dry." *New York Times,* June 1. www.nytimes.com/2011/06/02/opinion/02Brown.html.

———. 2011. *World on the Edge: How to Prevent Environmental and Economic Collapse.* New York: Norton.

Brown, P., T. Sutikna, M. J. Morwood, R. P. Seojono, Jatmiko, E. Wayhu Saptomo, and Rokus Awe Due. 2004. "A New Small-Bodied Hominin from the Late Pleistocene of Flores, Indonesia." *Nature* 431: 1055–61.

Brubaker, Rogers. 2004. *Ethnicity without Groups.* Cambridge, MA: Harvard University Press.

Brumm, Adam. 2004. "Painting Culture: The Making of an Aboriginal Art [Review]." *Australian Journal of Politics and History* 50(1): 123–24.

Brundage, W. Fitzhugh. 1993. *Lynching in the New South: Georgia and Virginia, 1880–1930.* Chicago: University of Illinois Press.

Brunet, M., F. Guy, D. Pilbeam, H. T. Mackaye, A. Likius, D. Ahounta, A. Beauvilain, C. Blondel, H. Bocherens, J. R. Boisserie, L. De Bonis, Y. Coppens, J. Dejax, C. Denys, P. Duringer, V. Eisenmann, G. Fanone, P. Fronty, D. Geraads, T. Lehmann, F. Lihoreeau, A. Louchart, A Mahamat, G. Merceron, G. Mouchelin, O. Otero, P. P. Campomanes, M. P. De Leon, J. C. Rage, M. Sapanet, M. Schuster, J. Sudre, P. Tassy, X. Valentin, P. Vignaud, L. Viriot, A. Zazzo, and C. Zollikofer. 2002. "A New Hominid from the Upper Miocene of Chad, Central Africa." *Nature* 418: 145–51.

Buck, Pem Davidson. 2001. *Worked to the Bone: Race, Class, Power, and Privilege in Kentucky.* New York: Monthly Review Press.

———. 2009. *In/equality: An Alternative Anthropology.* Redding, CA: CAT Publishing.

Budrys, Grace. 2010. *Unequal Health: How Inequality Contributes to Health or Illness.* Lanham, MD: Rowman & Littlefield.

Butler, Judith. 1990. *Gender Trouble: Feminism and the Subversion of Identity.* New York: Routledge.

Cahn, Naomi. 2004. "Beyond Retribution and Impunity: Responding to War Crimes of Sexual Violence." Public Law and Legal Theory Working Paper 104, George Washington University Law School, Washington D.C.

Calderwood, Brent. 2008. "Be Butch or Be Bashed." *Gay and Lesbian Review* 155(1): 38–39.

Cameron, Deborah. 1994. "Degrees of Consent: The Antioch College Sexual Offense Policy." In *The Language and Sexuality Reader,* edited by Deborah Cameron and Don Kulick. New York: Routledge, 2006.

———. 2007. *The Myth of Mars and Venus.* Oxford, UK: Oxford University Press.

Cameron, Deborah, and Don Kulick, eds. 2006. *The Language and Sexuality Reader*. New York: Routledge.

Cann, Rebecca L., Mark Stoneking, and Allan C. Wilson. 1987. "Mitochondrial DNA and Human Evolution." *Nature* 325: 31–36.

Cardoso, Fernando Henrique, and Enzo Faletto. 1969. *Dependencia y desarrollo en American Latina: ensayo de interpretación sociologica*. México: Siglo Veintiuno Editores.

Carneiro, Robert. 1981. "The Chiefdom: Precursor of the State." In *The Transition to Statehood in the New World*, edited by Grant Jones and Robert Kautz, 37–79. Cambridge, UK: Cambridge University Press.

Carney, Judith A. 2002. *Black Rice: The African Origins of Rice Cultivation in the Americas*. Cambridge, MA: Harvard University Press.

Carroll, John B., ed. 1956. *Language, Thought, and Reality: Selected Writings of Benjamin Lee Whorf*. Cambridge, MA: MIT Press.

Carsten, Janet. 1997. *The Heat of the Hearth: The Process of Kinship in a Malay Fishing Community*. Oxford, UK: Clarendon Press.

———. 2004. *After Kinship*. Cambridge, UK: Cambridge University Press.

Casanova, Jose. 1994. *Public Religions in the Modern World*. Chicago: University of Chicago Press.

Cavanagh, John, Daphne Wysham, and Marcos Aruda, eds. 2002. *Alternatives to Economic Globalization: A Better World Is Possible*. San Francisco: Berrett-Koehler.

Cawthon Lang, Kristina. 2005. "Primate Factsheets: Gorilla Taxonomy, Morphology, & Ecology." Primate Info Net. http://pin.primate.wisc.edu/factsheets/entry/gorilla/taxon.

Cazenave, Noel A. 2011. *The Urban Racial State: Managing Race Relations in American Cities*. Lanham, MD: Rowan and Littlefield.

Chagnon, Napoleon A. 1968. *Yąnomamö: The Fierce People*. New York: Holt, Rinehart and Winston.

Chang, Grace. 1998. "Undocumented Latinas: The New Employable Mothers." In *Race, Class and Gender*, 3rd ed., edited by Margaret L. Anderson and Patricia Hill Collins. Boulder, CO: Wadsworth.

Chang, Leslie T. 2008. *Factory Girls: From Village to City in a Changing China*. New York: Spiegel & Grau.

Chapman, Gary. 2010. *The 5 Love Languages: The Secret to Love That Lasts*. Chicago: Northfield Publishing.

Chapman, Rachel R., and Jean R. Berggren. 2005. "Radical Contextualization: Contributions to an Anthropology of Racial/Ethnic Health Disparities." *Health* 9(2): 145–67.

Chau, Adam Yuet. 2006. *Miraculous Response: Doing Popular Religion in Contemporary China*. Stanford, CA: Stanford University Press.

Checker, Melissa. 2005. *Polluted Promises: Environmental Racism and the Search for Justice in a Southern Town*. New York: New York University Press.

Chodorow, Nancy. 1974. "Strategies, Cooperation and Conflict among Women in Domestic Groups." In *Woman, Culture and Society*, edited by Michelle Z. Rosaldo and Louise Lamphere, 97–113. Stanford, CA: Stanford University Press.

Chomsky, Noam. 1957. *Syntactic Structures*. The Hague/Paris: Mouton.

Clifford, James, and George E. Marcus. 1986. "Introduction: Partial Truths." In *Writing Culture: The Poetics and Politics of Ethnography*, edited by James Clifford and George E. Marcus, 1–26. Berkeley: University of California Press.

Cochrane, J. 2006. "Religion, Public Health and a Church for the 21st Century." *International Review of Mission* 95(376/377): 59–72.

Cohen, Yehudi A. 1974. *Man in Adaptation: The Cultural Present*. Chicago: Aldine.

Collins, John F. 2007. "Recent Approaches in English to Brazilian Racial Ideologies: Ambiguity, Research Methods and Semiotic Ideologies. A Review Essay." *Comparative Studies in Society and History* 49(4): 997–1009.

Comaroff, Jean, and John L. Comaroff. 1991. *Of Revelation and Revolution*, vol. 1, *Christianity, Colonialism, and Consciousness in South Africa*. Chicago: University of Chicago Press.

Comaroff, John L., and Jean Comaroff. 2009. *Ethnicity, Inc.* Chicago: University of Chicago Press.

Constable, Nicole. 2007. *Maid to Order in Hong Kong: Stories of Migrant Workers*. Ithaca, NY: Cornell University Press.

Coontz, Stephanie. 1988. *The Social Origins of Private Life: A History of American Families 1600–1900*. New York: Verso.

———. 1992. *The Way We Never Were: American Families and the Nostalgia Trap*. New York: Basic Books.

———. 1997. *The Way We Really Are: Coming to Terms with America's Changing Families*. New York: Basic Books.

Copelon, Rhonda. 1995. "Gendered War Crimes: Reconceptualizing Rape in Time of War." In *Women's Rights, Human Rights: International Feminist Perspectives*, edited by Julie Peters and Andrea Wolper, 197–215. New York: Routledge.

Cowen, M. P., and R. W. Shenton. 1996. *Doctrines of Development*. London: Routledge.

Crapanzano, Vincent. 1980. *Tuhami: Portrait of a Moroccan*. Chicago: University of Chicago.

Currah, Paisley, Richard M. Juang, and Shannon Price Minter, eds. 2006. *Transgender Rights*. Minneapolis: University of Minnesota Press.

Curtis, Debra. 2009. *Pleasures and Perils: Girls' Sexuality in a Caribbean Consumer Culture*. New Brunswick, NJ: Rutgers University Press.

Dahlberg, Frances, ed. 1981. *Woman the Gatherer*. New Haven, CT: Yale University Press.

Daily Mail. 2010. "200 Not Out! Meet Welsh Wonders Lily and Ena, The World's Oldest Twins." *Daily Mail* [London], October 4.

"Dan Rather Reports: Kidney Pirates." Jan.12, 2010. http://blip.tv /hdnet-news-and-documentaries/dan-rather-reports-kidney -pirates-5455011.

Das, Veena. 1995. "National Honor and Practical Kinship: Unwanted Women and Children." In *Conceiving the New World Order: The Global Politics of Reproduction*, edited by Faye D. Ginsburg and Rayna Rapp. Berkeley: University of California Press.

Davies, G. 2005. *A History of Money from the Earliest Times to Present Day*, 3rd ed. Cardiff, UK: University of Wales Press.

Davies, James B., Susanna Sandstrom, Anthony Shorrocks, and Edward N. Wolff. 2007. *Estimating the Level and Distribution of Global Household Wealth*. Helsinki: UNU-WIDER. www .wider.unu.edu/publications/working-papers/research-papers /2007/en_GB/rp2007-77/.

Davis, Dána-Ain. 2006. *Battered Black Women and Welfare Reform: Between a Rock and a Hard Place*. Albany: State University of New York.

Davis-Floyd, Robbie. 1992. *Birth as an American Rite of Passage*. Berkeley: University of California Press.

Davis-Floyd, Robbie, and Joseph Dumit, eds. 1997. *Cyborg Babies: From Techno-Sex to Techno-Tots*. London: Routledge.

Deliege, Robert. 2011. "Caste, Class, and Untouchability." In *A Companion to the Anthropology of India*, edited by Isabelle Clark-Decès. Hoboken, NJ: Wiley-Blackwell.

D'Emilio, John, and Estelle B. Freedman. 1998. *Intimate Matters: A History of Sexuality in America*, 2nd ed. Chicago: University of Chicago Press.

De Vos, George. 1987. "Shamans, Housewives, and Other Restless Spirits: Women in Korean Ritual Life [Review]." *American Ethnologist* 14(2): 407–8.

de Waal, Frans. 2002. "Primate Behavior and Human Aggression." In *Must We Fight?: From the Battlefield to the Schoolyard, a New Perspective on Violent Conflict and Its Prevention*, edited by William L. Ury, 13–25. San Francisco: Jossey-Bass.

Diamond, Jared. 1997. "The Animal with the Weirdest Sex Life." In *Constructing Sexualities: Readings in Sexuality, Gender and Culture*, edited by Suzanne LaFont. Upper Saddle River, NJ: Prentice Hall, 2002.

Di Leonardo, Micaela. 1991. "Introduction: Gender, Culture, and Political Economy: Feminist Anthropology in Historical Perspective." In *Gender at the Crossroads of Knowledge: Feminist Anthropology in the Post-Modern Era*, edited by Micaela di Leonardo, 1–51. Berkeley: University of California Press.

Dill, Bonnie Thornton. 1983. "Race, Class and Gender: Prospects for an All-Inclusive Sisterhood." *Feminist Studies* 9: 131–50.

Domhoff, G. William. 2012. "Power in America: Wealth, Income, and Power." *Who Rules America?* http://sociology.ucsc.edu /whorulesamerica/power/wealth.html.

Dorow, Sara. 2006. *Transnational Adoption: A Cultural Economy of Race, Gender, and Kinship*. New York: New York University Press.

Douglas, Mary. 1966. *Purity and Danger: An Analysis of the Concepts of Pollution and Taboo*. London: Routledge & Kegan Paul.

Downey, Greg. 2005. *Learning Capoeira: Lessons in Cunning from an Afro-Brazilian Art*. New York: Oxford University Press.

Dudley, Kathryn Marie. 2000. *Debt and Dispossession: Farm Loss in America's Heartland*. Chicago: University of Chicago Press.

Dunham, Katherine. 1969. *Island Possessed*. Garden City, NY: Doubleday.

Durkheim, Émile. (1912) 1965. *The Elementary Forms of Religious Life*. New York: Free Press.

Durrenberger, E. Paul. 2001. "No Shame in My Game: The Working Poor in the Inner City [Review]." *American Anthropologist* 103(4): 1210–11.

Durrenberger, E. Paul, and Suzan Erem. 2010. *Anthropology Unbound: A Field Guide to the 21st Century*, 2nd ed. Boulder, CO: Paradigm.

Economic Policy Institute. 2011. "Wealth Holdings Remain Unequal in Good and Bad Times." *The State of Working America*. Washington, DC: Economic Policy Institute.

Edelman, Marc. 1999. *Peasants against Globalization: Rural Social Movements in Costa Rica*. Stanford, CA: Stanford University Press.

———. 2001. "Social Movements: Changing Paradigms and Forms of Politics." *Annual Review of Anthropology* 30: 285–317.

Edelman, Marc, and Angelique Haugerud. 2005. *The Anthropology of Development and Globalization: From Classical Political Economy to Contemporary Neoliberalism*. Malden, MA: Blackwell.

Ehrenreich, Barbara, and Arlie Russell Hochschild, eds. 2004. *Global Woman: Nannies, Maids, and Sex Workers in the New Economy*. New York: Holt Paperbacks.

Eller, Jack David. 1999. *From Culture to Ethnicity to Conflict: An Anthropological Perspective on Ethnic Conflict*. Ann Arbor: University of Michigan Press.

Elliot, Diana B. 2009. "Understanding Changes in Families and Households Pre- and Post-Katrina." Lecture. American Sociological Association Meeting, San Francisco, August 10. www .census.gov/hhes/families/files/katrina-asa.pdf.

England, Sarah. 2002. "The Production and Consumption of Pink-Collar Identities in the Caribbean." *Current Anthropology* 43(3): 522–23.

Englund, Harri. 1999. "A Different Kind of War Story [Review]." *Journal of the Royal Anthropological Institute* 5(1): 141–42.

Ericksen, Thomas Hylland. 2010. *Ethnicity and Nationalism*, 3rd ed. Boulder, CO: Pluto Press.

Escobar, Arturo. 1991. "Anthropology and the Development Encounter: The Making and Marketing of Development Anthropology." *American Ethnologist* 18(4): 658–82.

———. 1995. *Encountering Development: The Making and Unmaking of the Third World.* Princeton, NJ: Princeton University Press.

Evans-Pritchard, E. E. 1937. *Witchcraft, Oracles and Magic among the Azande.* Oxford, UK: Clarendon Press.

———. 1940. *The Nuer: A Description of the Modes of Livelihood and Political Institutions of a Nilotic People.* Oxford, UK: Clarendon Press.

———. 1951. *Kinship and Marriage among the Nuer.* Oxford, UK: Clarendon Press.

Fadiman, Anne. 1997. *The Spirit Catches You and You Fall Down: A Hmong Child, Her American Doctors, and the Collision of Two Cultures.* New York: Farrar, Straus, and Giroux.

Falk, R. 1993. "The Making of Global Citizenship." In *Global Visions: Beyond the New World Order,* edited by Jeremy Brecher, John B. Childs, and Jill Cutler, 39–50. Boston: South End.

Farmer, Paul. 1985. "The Anthropologist Within." *Harvard Medical Alumni Bulletin* 59(1): 23–28.

———. 1999. *Infections and Inequalities: The Modern Plagues.* Berkeley: University of California Press.

———. 2003. *Pathologies of Power: Health, Human Rights and the New War on the Poor.* Berkeley: University of California Press.

———. 2006. *AIDS and Accusation: Haiti and the Geography of Blame.* Berkeley: University of California Press.

Farquhar, Judith Brooke. 1986. "Knowledge and Practice in Chinese Medicine." PhD diss., University of Chicago, Department of Anthropology.

———. 1994. *Knowing Practice: The Clinical Encounter of Chinese Medicine.* Boulder, CO: Westview Press.

Fausto-Sterling, Anne. 1993. "The Five Sexes: Why Male and Female Are Not Enough." *The Sciences* May/April: 20–24.

Feagin, Joe R., and Clairece Booher Feagin. 2011. *Racial and Ethnic Relations,* 9th ed. New York: Pearson.

Feagin, Joe R., and Melvin P. Sikes. 1994. *Living with Racism: The Black Middle-Class Experience.* Boston: Beacon Press.

Fedigan, Linda. 1982. *Primate Paradigms: Sex Roles and Social Bonds.* Montreal: Eden Press.

———. 1986. "The Changing Role of Women in Models of Human Evolution." *Annual Reviews of Anthropology* 15: 25–66.

Feldman, Jeffrey D. 2001. "Reproducing Jews: A Cultural Account of Assisted Conception in Israel [Review]." *American Ethnologist* 28(4): 924–25.

Ferguson, Brian R. 2002. "The History of War: Fact vs. Fiction." In *Must We Fight?: From the Battlefield to the Schoolyard, a New Perspective on Violent Conflict and Its Prevention,* edited by William L. Ury, 26–37. San Francisco: Jossey-Bass.

———. 2011. "Tribal Warfare." In *Encyclopedia of War,* 1st ed., 1–13. Malden, MA: Blackwell.

Ferguson, James. 1997. "Anthropology and Its Evil Twin: 'Development' in the Constitution of A Discipline." In *International Development and the Social Sciences: Essays on the History and Politics of Knowledge,* edited by Frederick Cooper and Randall Packard, 150–75. Berkeley: University of California Press.

Ferguson, James, and Akhil Gupta. 2002. "Spatializing States: Toward an Ethnography of Neoliberal Governmentality." *American Ethnologist* 29(4): 981–1002.

Fernandez-Kelly, Maria Patricia. 1983. *For We Are Sold, I and My People: Women and Industry in Mexico's Frontier.* Albany: State University of New York Press.

Fernea, Robert. 1996. "Photographic Politics." *Current Anthropology* 37(1): 183–84.

Fields-Black, Edda L. 2008. *Deep Roots: Rice Farmers in West Africa and the African Diaspora.* Bloomington: Indiana University Press.

FinAid. 2013. "Student Loan Debt Clock." www.finaid.org/loans /studentloandebtclock.phtml.

Finkler, Kaja. 2002. "Reproducing Jews: A Cultural Account of Assisted Conception in Israel [Review]." *Journal of Anthropological Research* 58(2): 299–301.

Finnstrom, Sverker. 2005. "Shadows of War: Violence, Power and International Profiteering in the Twenty-First Century [Review]." *Anthropological Quarterly* 78(2): 491–96.

Fisher, Bonnie, Francis T. Cullen, and Michael G. Turner. 2000. *The Sexual Victimization of College Women.* Washington, DC: U.S. Department of Justice, Office of Justice Programs, National Institute of Justice.

Fisher, Bonnie, Leah E. Daigle, and Francis T. Cullen. 2010. *Unsafe in the Ivory Tower: The Sexual Victimization of College Women.* Los Angeles: Sage Publications.

Fisher, Helen. 2004. *Why We Love: The Nature and Chemistry of Romantic Love.* New York: Henry Holt.

Fisher, Roger, William Ury, and Bruce Patton. 2012. *Getting to Yes: Negotiating an Agreement without Giving In.* London: Random House Business.

Flanagan, James G. 1986. "Ritualized Homosexuality in Melanesia [Review]." *American Anthropologist* 88(2): 489–90.

Floyd, Charlene J. 1996. "A Theology of Insurrection? Religion and Politics in Mexico." *Journal of International Affairs* 50(1): 142–65.

Flueckiger, Joyce. 2006. *In Amma's Healing Room: Gender and Vernacular Islam in South India.* Bloomington: Indiana University Press.

Fluehr-Lobban, Carolyn. 2006. *Race and Racism: An Introduction.* Lanham, MD: Altamira Press.

Foner, Nancy. 2000. *From Ellis Island to JFK: New York's Two Great Waves of Immigration.* New Haven, CT: Yale University Press.

———. 2003. *American Arrivals: Anthropology Engages the New Immigration.* Santa Fe, NM: School of American Research.

Forster, P., R. Harding, A. Torroni, and H. J. Bandelt. 1996. "Origin and Evolution of Native American mtDNA Variation: A Reappraisal." *American Journal of Human Genetics* 59(4): 935–45.

Fortes, Meyer. 1949. "Time and Social Structure: An Ashanti Case Study." In *Social Structure: Studies Presented to A. R. Radcliffe-Brown*, edited by Meyer Fortes. Oxford, UK: Clarendon Press.

Fortes, Meyer, and E. E. Evans-Pritchard. 1940. *African Political Systems*. London: Published for the International Institute of African Languages & Cultures by the Oxford University Press.

Foucault, Michel. (1976) 1990. *The History of Sexuality*, vol. 1, *An Introduction*. New York: Vintage Books.

———. 1978. *The History of Sexuality*. New York: Pantheon.

———. 1977. *Discipline and Punish: The Birth of the Prison*. New York: Pantheon.

Fouts, Roger. 1997. *Next of Kin: What Chimpanzees Have Taught Me about Who We Are*. New York: William Morrow.

Frank, Andre Gunder. 1969. *Latin America: Underdevelopment or Revolution. Essays on the Development of Underdevelopment and the Immediate Enemy*. New York: Monthly Review Press.

———. 1998. *ReORIENT: Global Economy in the Asian Age*. Berkeley: University of California Press.

Franklin, Sarah. 1997. *Embodied Progress: A Cultural Account of Assisted Conception*. London: Routledge.

———. 2007. *Dolly Mixtures: The Remaking of Genealogy*. Durham, NC: Duke University Press.

Frazer, James George. 1890. *The Golden Bough: A Study in Magic and Religion*. Reprint, New York: Macmillan, 1951.

Freud, Sigmund. 1952. *Totem and Taboo: Some Points of Agreement between the Mental Lives of Savages and Neurotics*. New York: Norton.

Freyre, Gilberto. (1933) 1944. *The Masters and the Slaves: A Study in the Development of Brazilian Civilization*. New York: Knopf.

Friedman, Jaclyn, and Jessica Valenti. 2008. *Yes Means Yes! Visions of Female Sexual Power and a World without Rape*. Berkeley, CA: Seal Press.

Galvez, Alyshia. 2009. *Guadalupe in New York: Devotion and the Struggle for Citizenship Rights among Mexican Immigrants*. New York: New York University Press.

Gardner, Christine J. 2011. *Making Chastity Sexy: The Rhetoric of Evangelical Abstinence Campaigns*. Berkeley: University of California Press.

Gardner, R. Allen, Beatrix T. Gardner, and Thomas E. Van Cantfort, eds. 1989. *Teaching Sign Language to Chimpanzees*. Albany: State University of New York Press.

Gaudio, Rudolf. 2009. *Allah Made Us: Sexual Outlaws in an Islamic African City*. Malden, MA: Wiley-Blackwell.

Gaunt, Kyra Danielle. 2006. *The Games Black Girls Play: Learning the Ropes from Double-Dutch to Hip-Hop*. New York: New York University Press.

Geertz, Clifford. 1973. "Deep Play: Notes on a Balinese Cockfight." In *The Interpretation of Cultures*. New York: Basic Books.

———. 1973. "Religion as a Cultural System." In *The Interpretation of Cultures*. New York: Basic Books.

———. 1973. "Thick Description: Toward an Interpretive Theory of Culture." In *The Interpretation of Cultures*. New York: Basic Books.

Gell, A. F. 1995. "African Art in Transit [Review]." *Journal of the Royal Anthropological Institute* 1(4): 841–42.

Gellner, Ernest. 1983. *Nations and Nationalism*. Ithaca, NY: Cornell University Press.

Geromel, Ricardo. 2013. "Forbes' Billionaires World Map." *Forbes*, March 22. www.forbes.com/sites/ricardogeromel/2013/03/22/forbes-billionaires-map/.

Geyer, Michael. 1989. "The Militarization of Europe, 1914–1945." In *The Militarization of the Western World*, edited by John Gillis, 65–102. New Brunswick, NJ: Rutgers University Press.

Ghannam, Farha. 2012. "Meanings and Feelings: Local Interpretations of the Use of Violence in the Egyptian Revolution." *American Ethnologist* 39(1): 32–36.

Gibson, Jane. 1996. "The Social Construction of Whiteness in Shellcracker Haven, Florida." *Human Organization* 55(4): 379–89.

Giddens, Anthony. 1985. *The Nation-State and Violence*. Cambridge, UK: Polity.

Ginsburg, Faye D., Lila Abu-Lughod, and Brian Larkin, eds. 2002. *Media Worlds: Anthropology on New Terrain*. Berkeley: University of California Press.

Glazer, Nathan, and Daniel Patrick Moynihan. 1970. *Beyond the Melting Pot*, 2nd ed. Cambridge, MA: MIT Press.

Gledhill, John. 2000. *Power and Its Disguises: Anthropological Perspectives on Politics*. London: Pluto.

Global Footprint Network. 2013. http://footprintnetwork.org.

Global Witness. 2007. *Hot Chocolate: How Cocoa Fuelled the Conflict in Côte D'Ivoire*. www.globalwitness.org/sites/default/files/pdfs/cotedivoire.pdf.

Gluckman, Max. 1954. *Rituals of Rebellion in South-East Africa*. Manchester, UK: Manchester University Press.

Gmelch, George. 1992. "Superstition and Ritual in American Baseball." *Elysian Fields Quarterly* 11(3): 25–36.

Gold, Steven J. 1995. *From the Workers' State to the Golden State: Jews from the Former Soviet Union in California*. Boston: Allyn & Bacon.

Goldstein, Donna M. 2003. *Laughter Out of Place: Race, Class, Violence, and Sexuality in a Rio Shantytown*. Berkeley: University of California Press.

Goldstein, Judith L. 1998. "Reading National Geographic [Review]." *American Ethnologist* 25(1): 9–10.

Goode, Judith, and Jeff Maskovsky, eds. 2001. *The New Poverty Studies: The Ethnography of Power, Politics, and Impoverished People in the United States*. New York: New York University Press.

Goodman, Roger. 2004. "Brokered Homeland: Japanese Brazilian Migrants in Japan [Review]." *Journal of Japanese Studies* 30(2): 465–71.

Gough, Kathleen. 1971. "Nuer Kinship: A Reexamination." In *The Translation of Culture: Essays to E. E. Evans-Pritchard*, 79–121. Thomas O. Beidelman, editor. London: Tavistock Publications.

Gould, Stephen Jay. 1987. *Time's Arrow, Time's Cycle: Myth and Metaphor in the Discovery of Geological Time*. Cambridge, MA: Harvard University Press.

Graeber, David. 2002. "The New Anarchists." *New Left Review* 13(Jan–Feb).

———. 2011. *Debt: The First Five Thousand Years*. Brooklyn, NY: Melville House.

Gramsci, Antonio. 1971. *Selections from the Prison Notebooks*. Quintin Hoare and Geoffrey Nowell Smith, translators and editors. New York: International Publishers.

Gray, John. 2004. *Men Are from Mars, Women Are from Venus: The Classic Guide to Understanding the Opposite Sex*. New York: Harper.

Green, Edward C. 1999. *Indigenous Theories of Contagious Disease*. Walnut Creek, CA: AltaMira.

Gregory, Steven. 1998. *Black Corona: Race and the Politics of Place in an Urban Community*. Princeton, NJ: Princeton University Press.

———. 2006. *The Devil behind the Mirror: Globalization and Politics in the Dominican Republic*. Berkeley: University of California Press.

Gregory, Steven, and Roger Sanjek, eds. 1994. *Race*. New Brunswick, NJ: Rutgers University Press.

Gross, Ariela J. 2010. *What Blood Won't Tell: A History of Race on Trial in America*. Cambridge, MA: Harvard University Press.

Gudmundson, Lowell. 2001. "Peasants against Globalization: Rural Social Movement in Costa Rica [Review]." *Agricultural History* 75(4): 504–6.

Guest, Kenneth J. 2003. *God in Chinatown: Religion and Survival in New York's Evolving Immigrant Community*. New York: New York University Press.

———. 2011. "From Mott Street to East Broadway: Fuzhounese Immigrants and the Revitalization of New York's Chinatown." *Journal of Chinese Overseas* 2011(7): 24–44.

Guest, Kenneth J., and Peter Kwong. 2000. "Ethnic Enclaves and Cultural Diversity." In *Cultural Diversity in the United States: A Critical Reader*, edited by Ida Susser and Thomas C. Patterson, 39–50. Malden, MA: Blackwell.

Guilmoto, Christophe Z. 2011. "Demography for Anthropologists: Populations, Castes, and Classes." In *A Companion to the Anthropology of India*, edited by Isabelle Clark-Decès. Hoboken, NJ: Wiley-Blackwell.

Gupta, Akhil, and James Ferguson, eds. 1997. *Culture, Power, Place: Explorations in Critical Anthropology*. Durham, NC: Duke University Press.

Gusterson, Hugh. 1996. *Nuclear Rites: A Weapons Laboratory at the End of the Cold War*. Berkeley: University of California Press.

———. 2004. *People of the Bomb: Portraits of America's Nuclear Complex*. Minneapolis: University of Minnesota Press.

Gutmann, Matthew C. 2007. *The Meanings of Macho: Being a Man in Mexico City*. Berkeley: University of California Press. Originally published in 1996.

Hall, Edward T. 1966. *The Hidden Dimension*. New York: Anchor Books.

Hamdy, Sherine F. 2012. "Strength and Vulnerability after Egypt's Arab Spring Uprisings." *American Ethnologist* 39(1): 43–48.

Hannerz, Ulf. 1996. *Transnational Connections: Culture, People, Places*. London: Routledge.

Harding, Jennifer. 1998. "Investigating Sex: Essentialism and Constructionism." In *Sex Acts*, 8–22. London: Sage Publications.

Hargrove, Melissa D. 2009. "Mapping the 'Social Field of Whiteness': White Racism as Habitus in the City Where History Lives." *Transforming Anthropology* 17(2): 93–104.

Haritaworn, Jinthana. 2003. "Desis in the House [Review]." *Racial and Ethnic Studies* 26(3): 575–76.

Harries, Patrick. 2007. "The Battle of Algiers." In *Black and White in Colour: African History on Screen*, edited by Vivian Bickford-Smith and Richard Mendelsohn. Oxford, UK: James Currey.

Harris, Marvin. 1964. *Patterns of Race in the Americas*. New York: Walker.

———. 1970. "Referential Ambiguity in the Calculus of Brazilian Racial Identity." *Southwestern Journal of Anthropology* 21(1): 1–14.

———. 1974. *Cows, Pigs, Wars & Witches: The Riddles of Culture*. New York: Random House.

Harris, Reginald. 2009. "Allah Made Us [Review]." *Gay and Lesbian Review Worldwide* 16(6): 42.

Harrison, Faye V. 1998. "Introduction: Expanding the Discourse on 'Race.'" *American Anthropologist* 100(3): 609–31.

———. 2002a. "Subverting the Cultural Logics of Marked and Unmarked Racisms in the Global Era." In *Discrimination and Tolerations*, edited by K. Hastrup and G. Ulrich, 97–125. London: Kluwer Law International.

———. 2002b. "Unraveling 'Race' for the 21st Century." In *Exotic No More: Anthropology on the Front Lines*, edited by Jeremy MacClancy. Chicago: University of Chicago Press.

Harrison, K. David. 2007. *When Languages Die: The Extinction of the World's Languages and the Erosion of Human Knowledge*. New York: Oxford University Press.

Hartigan, John Jr. 1999. *Racial Situations: Class Predicaments of Whiteness in Detroit*. Princeton, NJ: Princeton University Press.

———. 2005. *Odd Tribes: Toward a Cultural Analysis of White People*. Durham, NC: Duke University Press.

Harvey, David. 1990. *The Condition of Postmodernity: An Enquiry into the Origins of Cultural Change*. Malden, MA: Blackwell.

Haugerud, Angelique, Margaret Priscilla Stone, and Peter D. Little. 2000. *Commodities and Globalization: Anthropological Perspectives*. Lanham, MD: Rowman & Littlefield.

Hayes, Catherine. 1951. *The Ape in Our House*. New York: Harper.

Hearn, Jonathan. 2006. *Rethinking Nationalism: A Critical Introduction*. New York: Palgrave Macmillan.

Heartfield, James. 2008. "Coming of Age in Second Life [Review]." *Art Review* 25: 160.

Helmreich, Stefan. 2009. *Alien Ocean: Anthropological Voyages in Microbial Seas*. Berkeley: University of California Press.

Helweg, Arthur W. 1998. "Contesting Culture: Discourses of Identity in Multi-Ethnic London [Review]." *International Migration Review* 32(1): 252.

Henshilwood, Christopher S., Francesco d'Errico, Karen K. van Niekerk, Yvan Coquinot, Zenobia Jacobs, Stein-Erik Lauritzen, Michel Menu, and Renata Garcia-Moreno. 2011. "A 100,000-Year-Old Ochre-Processing Workshop at Blombos Cave, South Africa." *Science* 334(6053): 219–22.

Herdt, Gilbert. 1981. *Guardians of the Flute: Idioms of Masculinity*. New York: McGraw-Hill.

———. 1987. *The Sambia: Ritual and Gender in New Guinea*. New York: Holt, Rinehart and Winston.

———, ed. 1993. *Ritualized Homosexuality in Melanesia*, rev. ed. Berkeley: University of California Press. First published 1984.

———. 1999. *Sambia Sexual Culture: Essays from the Field*. Chicago: University of Chicago Press.

Herzog, Werner (director). *Cave of Forgotten Dreams*. 2010. IFC Films.

Higgenbotham, Evelyn Brooks. 1992. "African-American Women's History and the Metalanguage of Race." *Signs: Journal of Women in Culture and Society* 17: 251–74.

Hill, Jane H. 2008. *The Everyday Language of White Racism*. Malden, MA: Wiley-Blackwell.

Hirsch, Jennifer. 2007. "'Love Makes a Family': Globalization, Companionate Marriage, and the Modernization of Gender Equality." In *Love and Globalization: Transformations of Intimacy in the Contemporary World*, edited by Mark Padilla, Jennifer Hirsch, Miguel Munoz-Laboy, Richard Sember, and Richard Parker, 93–106. Nashville, TN: Vanderbilt University Press.

Hirschkind, Charles. 2012. "Beyond Secular and Religious: An Intellectual Genealogy of Tahrir Square." *American Ethnologist* 39(1): 49–53.

Ho, Karen. 2008. *Liquidated: An Ethnography of Wall Street*. Durham, NC: Duke University Press.

Hobhouse, L. T. 1915. *Morals in Evolution; A Study in Comparative Ethics*. New York: Holt.

Hobsbawm, Eric, and Terence Ranger. 1983. *Invented Traditions*. Cambridge, UK: Cambridge University Press.

Hockings, Paul Edward, ed. 2003. *Principles of Visual Anthropology*, 3rd ed. Berlin: Mouton De Gruyter.

Hodgson, Dorothy L. 2001. *Once Intrepid Warriors: Gender, Ethnicity, and the Cultural Politics of Maasai Development*. Bloomington: Indiana University Press.

———. 2005. *The Church of Women: Gendered Encounters between Maasai and Missionaries*. Bloomington: Indiana University Press.

———. 2011. *Being Maasai, Becoming Indigenous: Postcolonial Politics in a Neoliberal World*. Bloomington: Indiana University Press.

Holmes, Janet. 1998. "Women's Talk: The Question of Sociolinguistic Universals." In *Language and Gender: A Reader*, edited by Jennifer Coates, 461–83. Oxford, UK: Blackwell.

Homewood, Katherine. 2012. "Being Maasai, Becoming Indigenous: Postcolonial Politics in a Neoliberal World [Review]." *African Affairs* 111(445): 682–84.

Hondagneu-Sotelo, Pierrette. 1994. *Gendered Transitions: Mexican Experiences of Immigration*. Berkeley: University of California.

———. 2001. *Domestica: Immigrant Workers Cleaning and Caring in the Shadows of Affluence*. Berkeley: University of California Press.

Honwana, Alcinda. 1999. "A Different Kind of War Story [Review]." *American Ethnologist* 26(2): 504–5.

Hopkins, Nancy. 1999. "A Study on the Status of Women Faculty in Science at MIT." *MIT Faculty Newsletter*, 11(4): 1–15. http://web.mit.edu/fnl/women/fnl114x.pdf.

Hostetler, John A. 1993. *Amish Society*, 4th ed. Baltimore: Johns Hopkins University Press.

———. 1997. *Hutterite Society*, 2nd ed. Baltimore: Johns Hopkins University Press.

Howard, David. 2001. "Dominican Republic Spurns Haitian Migrants: Rejection of African Heritage Fuels Anti-Haitian Views." *NACLA Report on the Americas* 35(2): 24–28.

Howell, David L. 2004. "Brokered Homeland: Japanese Brazilian Migrants in Japan [Review]." *Pacific Affairs* 77(1): 130–31.

Hubbard, Ruth. 1990. "The Social Construction of Sexuality." In *The Politics of Women's Biology*. New Brunswick, NJ: Rutgers University Press.

Human Rights Watch. 2004. "'Bad Dreams:' Exploitation and Abuse of Migrant Workers in Saudi Arabia," July 14, E1605. www.refworld.org/docid/412ef32a4.html.

———. 2012. "Democratic Republic of Congo." In *World Report 2012*, 104–9. www.hrw.org/world-report-2012.

Ignatiev, Noel. 1995. *How the Irish Became White*. New York: Routledge Press.

Illouz, Eva. 1997. *Consuming the Romantic Utopia: Love and Cultural Contradictions of Capitalism*. Berkeley: University of California Press.

Inda, Jonathan Xavier, and Renato Rosaldo. 2002. *The Anthropology of Globalization: A Reader*. Malden, MA: Blackwell.

Ingraham, Chrys. 2008. *White Weddings: Romancing Heterosexuality in Popular Culture*, rev. ed. New York: Routledge. First published in 1999.

Internal Displacement Monitoring Center. 2012. "Internal Displacement Global Overview 2011: People Internally Displaced by Conflict and Violence." www.internal-displacement.org /publications/global-overview.

International Organization for Migration. 2010. "A Study of Remittances and Investment Opportunities for Egyptian Migrants." Cairo, Egypt: International Organization for Migration.

———. 2012. "Global Trends." www.iom.int/cms/en/sites/iom /home/about-migration/facts—figures-1.html.

Ishi, Angelo. 2003. "Transnational Strategies by Japanese-Brazilian Migrants in the Age of IT." In *Global Japan: The Experience of Japan's New Immigrant and Overseas Communities*, edited by Roger Goodman, Ceri Peach, Ayumi Takenaka, and Paul White, 209–21. London: RoutledgeCurzon.

Jablonski, Nina G. 2006. *Skin: A Natural History*. Berkeley: University of California Press.

Jablonski, Nina G., and George Chaplin. 2000. "The Evolution of Skin Coloration." *Journal of Human Evolution* 39: 57–106.

Jacobs, A. J. 2005. "Tsukiji: The Fish Market at the Center of the World [Review]." *Contemporary Sociology* 34(4): 373–75.

Jacobs, Sue-Ellen, ed. 1997. *Two-Spirit People: Native American Gender Identity, Sexuality, and Spirituality*. Champaign: University of Illinois Press.

Jamison, Sandra L. 2006. "The Games Black Girls Play [Review]." *Black Issues Book Review*, 43–44.

Jankowiak, William, and Edward Fisher. 1992. "A Cross-Cultural Perspective on Romantic Love." *Ethnology* 31(2): 149–55.

Jaynes, Gregory. 1982. "A Louisiana Lawsuit Asks What It Means to Be Black, White, or 'Colored' in America." *Providence Sunday Journal*, October 14, A-19.

Jenkins, Richard. 1996. *Social Identity*. New York: Routledge.

———. 2008. *Rethinking Ethnicity*, 2nd ed. Thousand Oaks, CA: Sage.

Johanson, Donald C., Fidelis T. Masao, Gerald G. Eck, Tim D. White, Robert C. Walter, William H. Kimbel, Berhane Asfaw, Paul Manega, Prosper Ndessokia, and Gen Suwa. 1987. "New Partial Skeleton of *Homo habilis* from Olduvai Gorge, Tanzania." *Nature* 327: 205–9.

Jones, Camara Phyllis. 2000. "Levels of Racism: A Theoretic Framework and a Gardener's Tale." *American Journal of Public Health* 90(8): 1212–15.

Jordan, Brigitte. 1993. *Birth in Four Cultures: A Crosscultural Investigation of Childbirth in Yucatan, Holland, Sweden, and the United States*. Rev. and expanded by Robbie Davis-Floyd. Prospect Heights, IL: Waveland Press.

Jordan, Miriam. 2010. "Arizona Grades Teachers on Fluency: State Pushes School Districts to Reassign Instructors with Heavy Accents or Other Shortcomings in Their English." *Wall Street Journal*, April 30.

Juris, Jeffrey S. 2008. *Networking Futures: The Movements against Corporate Globalization*. Durham, NC: Duke University Press.

———. 2012. "Reflections on #Occupy Everywhere: Social Media, Public Space, and Emerging Logics of Aggregation." *American Ethnologist* 39(2): 259–79.

Juris, Jeffrey S., and Alex Khasnabish. 2013. *Insurgent Encounters: Transnational Activism, Ethnography, and the Political*. Durham, NC: Duke University Press.

Jurmain, Robert, and Harry Nelson. 1994. *Introduction to Physical Anthropology*, 6th ed. St. Paul, MN: West Publishing.

Kahn, Susan Martha. 2000. *Reproducing Jews: A Cultural Account of Assisted Conception in Israel*. Durham, NC: Duke University Press.

Karp, Ivan, and Steven Lavine. 1991. *Exhibiting Cultures: The Poetics and Politics of Museum Display*. Washington, DC: Smithsonian Institution.

Kasinitz, Philip, Mary C. Waters, John H. Mollenkopf, and Jennifer Holdaway. 2008. *Inheriting the City: The Children of Immigrants Come of Age*. New York: Russell Sage Foundation.

Katz, Jonathan Ned. 2007. *The Invention of Heterosexuality*, with a new preface. Chicago: University of Chicago Press. First published in 1995.

Katz, Pearl. 1999. *The Scalpel's Edge: The Culture of Surgeons*. Boston: Allyn & Bacon.

Kelly, Patty. 2008a. "Legalize Prostitution." *Los Angeles Times*, March 13. http://articles.latimes.com/2008/mar/13 /opinion/oe-kelly13.

———. 2008b. *Lydia's Open Door: Inside Mexico's Most Modern Brothel*. Berkeley: University of California Press.

Kendall, Laurel. 1985. *Shamans, Housewives, and Other Restless Spirits: Women in Korean Ritual Life*. Honolulu: University of Hawaii Press.

———. 1988. *The Life and Hard Times of a Korean Shaman: Of Tales and the Telling of Tales*. Honolulu: University of Hawaii Press.

Kennedy, Elizabeth Lapovsky. 1999. "Recognizing Ourselves [Review]." *American Ethnologist* 26(4): 1020–21.

Keynes, John Maynard. (1936) 2007. *The General Theory of Employment Interest and Money*. Houndmills, UK: Palgrave Macmillan.

Kidder, Tracy. 2003. *Mountains beyond Mountains: The Quest of Dr. Paul Farmer, A Man Who Would Cure the World*. New York: Random House.

Kim, Eleana. 2007. "Transnational Adoption: A Cultural Economy of Race, Gender, and Kinship [Review]." *Anthropological Quarterly* 80(2): 589.

———. 2010. *Adopted Territory: Transnational Korean Adoptees and the Politics of Belonging*. Durham, NC: Duke University Press.

King, Tanya, and Ian Warren. 2009. "Coming of Age in Second Life [Review]." *Australian Journal of Anthropology* 20(3): 404–5.

Kingfisher, Catherine. 2001. "Poverty and Downward Mobility in the Land of Opportunity." *American Anthropologist* 103(3): 824–27.

Kinsey, Alfred C. 1953. *Sexual Behavior in the Human Female.* Philadelphia: W. B. Saunders.

Kinsey, Alfred C., Wardell Baxter Pomeroy, and Clyde E. Martin. 1948. *Sexual Behavior in the Human Male.* Philadelphia: W. B. Saunders.

Klein, Naomi. 2002. "The New Apartheid." *The Nation,* November 26.

Kleinman, Arthur. 1988. *The Illness Narratives: Suffering, Healing, and the Human Condition.* New York: Basic Books.

Knauft, Bruce M. 1987. "Ritualized Homosexuality in Melanesia [Review]." *American Ethnologist* 14(2): 401–4.

———. 1991. "Violence and Sociality in Human Evolution." *Current Anthropology* 32(4): 391–408.

Kopytoff, Igor. 1986. "The Cultural Biography of Things: Commoditization as Process." In *The Social Life of Things: Commodities in Cultural Perspective*, edited by Arjun Appadurai, 64–91. Cambridge, UK: Cambridge University Press.

Korten, David C. 2001. *When Corporations Rule the World.* San Francisco: Berrett-Koehler.

Kottak, Conrad P. 2006. *Assault on Paradise: The Globalization of a Little Community in Brazil*, 4th ed. New York: McGraw-Hill.

Krause, Johannes, Qiaomei Fu, Jeffrey M. Good, Bence Viola, Michael V. Shunkov, Anatoli P. Derevianko, and Svante Pääbo. 2010. "The Complete Mitochondrial DNA Genome of an Unknown Hominin from Southern Siberia." *Nature* 464: 894–97.

Krause, Johannes, Ludovic Orlando, David Serre, Bence Viola, Kay Prüfer, Michael P. Richards, Jean-Jacques Hublin, Catherine Hänni, Anatoly P. Derevianko, and Svante Pääbo. 2007. "Neanderthals in Central Asia and Siberia." *Nature* 449: 902–4.

Kromidas, Maria. 2004. "Learning War/Learning Race: Fourth-Grade Students in the Aftermath of September 11th in New York City." *Critique of Anthropology* 24(1).

Krugman, Paul R. 2009. *The Return of Depression Economics and the Crisis of 2008.* New York: Norton.

Kulick, Don. 2003. "No." *Language and Communication* 1: 139–51.

Kuper, Adam. 1983. *Anthropology and Anthropologists: The Modern British School.* London: Routledge & Kegan Paul.

Kurien, Prema. 2004. "Desis in the House [Review]." *American Journal of Sociology* 109(6): 1516–17.

Kurtz, Donald V. 2001. *Political Anthropology: Power and Paradigms.* Boulder, CO: Westview Press.

Labov, William. 1972a. *Language in the Inner City: Studies in the Black English Vernacular.* Philadelphia: University of Pennsylvania Press.

———. 1972b. *Sociolinguistic Patterns.* Philadelphia: University of Pennsylvania Press.

Lakoff, Robin T. 2004. *Language and Woman's Place: Text and Commentaries.* Edited by Mary Bucholtz. New York: Oxford University Press.

Lan, David. 1985. *Guns and Rain: Guerillas and Spirit Mediums in Zimbabwe.* Berkeley: University of California Press.

Lancaster, Roger N. 1994. *Life Is Hard: Machismo, Danger, and the Intimacy of Power in Nicaragua.* Berkeley: University of California Press.

———. 2003. *The Trouble with Nature: Sex in Science and Popular Culture.* Berkeley: University of California Press.

Landers, Melissa A., and Gary Alan Fine. 1996. "Learning Life's Lessons in Tee Ball: The Reinforcement of Gender and Status in Kindergarten Sport." *Sociology of Sport Journal* 13(1).

Larrain, Jorge, 1989. *Theories of Development: Capitalism, Colonialism and Dependency.* London: Polity Press.

Larsen, Clark Spencer. 2008. *Our Origins: Discovering Physical Anthropology.* New York: Norton.

———. 2011. *Our Origins: Discovering Physical Anthropology*, 2nd ed. New York: Norton.

Leach, Edmund. 1954. *Political Systems of Highland Burma: A Study of Kachin Social Structure.* Cambridge, MA: Harvard University Press.

Leacock, Eleanor Burke. 1971. *The Culture of Poverty: A Critique.* New York: Simon & Schuster.

———. 1981. *Myths of Male Dominance: Collected Articles on Women Cross-Culturally.* New York: Monthly Review Press.

Leap, William L. 2010. "Allah Made Us [Review]." *Journal of the Royal Anthropological Institute* 16: 938–39.

Lee, Richard B. 1984. *The Dobe !Kung.* New York: Holt, Rinehart and Winston.

———. 2003. *The Dobe JuHoansi*, 3rd ed. (Case Studies in Cultural Anthropology). Belmont, CA: Wadsworth Publishing.

Lee, Richard B., and Irven Devore, eds. 1968. *Man the Hunter: The First Intensive Survey of a Single Crucial Stage of Human Development—Man's Once Universal Hunting Way of Life.* New York: The Wenner-Gren Foundation for Anthropological Research.

Lesorogol, Carolyn. 2012. "Being Maasai, Becoming Indigenous: Postcolonial Politics in a Neoliberal World [Review]." *International Journal of African Historical Studies* 45(2): 299–301.

Lessinger, Johanna. 1995. *From the Ganges to the Hudson: Indian Immigrants in New York City.* Boston: Allyn & Bacon.

Levitt, Peggy. 2001. *The Transnational Villagers.* Berkeley: University of California Press.

Lewellen, Ted C. 2002. *The Anthropology of Globalization: Cultural Anthropology Enters the 21st Century.* Westport, CT: Praeger.

———. 2003. *Political Anthropology: An Introduction.* Westport, CT: Praeger.

Lewin, Ellen. 1992. "Families We Choose: Lesbians, Gays, Kinship [Review]." *American Ethnologist* 19(4): 825–26.

———. 1995. "Life Is Hard [Review]." *American Ethnologist* 22(2): 441–42.

———. 1998. *Recognizing Ourselves: Ceremonies of Lesbian and Gay Commitment.* New York: Columbia University Press.

Lewis, M. Paul, ed. 2009. *Ethnologue: Languages of the World,* 16th ed. Dallas: SIL International. www.ethnologue.org.

Lewis, Oscar. 1959. *Five Families: Mexican Case Studies in the Culture of Poverty.* New York: Basic Books.

———. 1966. *La Vida: A Puerto Rican Family in the Culture of Poverty—San Juan and New York.* New York: Random House.

Leys, Colin. 1996. *The Rise and Fall of Development Theory.* Oxford, UK: James Currey.

Li, Jun Z., Devin M. Absher, Hua Tang, Audrey M. Southwick, Amanda M. Casto, Sohini Ramachandran, Howard M. Cann, Gregory S. Barsh, Marcus Feldman, Luigi L. Cavalli-Sforza, and Richard M. Myers. 2008. "Worldwide Human Relationships Inferred from Genome-Wide Patterns of Variation." *Science* 319: 1100–4.

Liang, Zai. 2012. "Recent Migration Trends in China: Geographic and Demographic Aspects of Development Implications." Presentation for UN Expert Group Meeting on New Trends in Migration: Demographic Aspects, New York, December 3. www.un.org/esa/population/meetings/EGM_MigrationTrends/UN_presentation_Dec_2012_FINAL_SH.pdf.

Lieberman, Leonard, and Rodney C. Kirk. 1996. "The Trial of Darwin Is Over: Religious Voices for Evolution and the 'Fairness' Doctrine." *Creation/Evolution* 16(2): 1–9.

Life and Debt. 2001. Directed by Stephanie Black. Tuff Gong Pictures.

Limon, Jose E. 1997. "The Meanings of Macho: Being a Man in Mexico City [Review]." *American Anthropologist* 99(1): 185.

Lindenbaum, Shirley. 2009. "Cannibalism, Kuru and Anthropology." *Folia Neuropathologica* 47(2): 138–44.

Livingstone, Frank B. 1958. "Anthropological Implications of Sickle Cell Gene Distribution in West Africa." *American Anthropologist* 60: 533–62.

Lock, Margaret M. 1993. *Encounters with Aging: Mythologies of Menopause in Japan and North America.* Berkeley: University of California Press.

———. 2002. *Twice Dead: Organ Transplants and the Reinvention of Death.* Berkeley: University of California Press.

Loe, Meika. 2004. *The Rise of Viagra: How the Little Blue Pill Changed Sex in America.* New York: New York University Press.

Loomis, William F. 1967. "Skin-Pigment Regulation of Vitamin-D Biosynthesis in Man." *Science* 157: 501–6.

Lopez, Ian Haney. 2006. *White by Law: The Legal Construction of Race,* 2nd ed. New York: New York University Press.

Lorber, Judith. 1994. *Paradoxes of Gender.* New Haven, CT: Yale University Press.

Low, Setha. 2004. *Behind the Gates: Life, Security, and the Pursuit of Happiness in Fortress America.* New York: Routledge.

Lowie, Robert Harry. (1920) 1961. *Primitive Society.* Reprint, New York: Harper & Brothers.

Lutz, Catherine. 2001. *Homefront: A Military City and the American Twentieth Century.* Boston: Beacon.

———. 2004. "Militarization." In *A Companion to the Anthropology of Politics,* edited by David Nugent and Joan Vincent, 318–31. Malden, MA: Blackwell.

Lutz, Catherine, and Jane L. Collins. 1993. *Reading National Geographic.* Chicago: University of Chicago Press.

Lydon, Ghislaine. 2009. *On Trans-Saharan Trails: Islamic Law, Trade Networks, and Cross-Cultural Exchange in Nineteenth-Century Western Africa.* Cambridge, UK: Cambridge University Press.

MacClancy, Jeremy, ed. 1996. *Sport, Identity and Ethnicity.* Oxford, UK: Berg.

MacKinnon, Catharine A. 1993. *Only Words.* Cambridge, MA: Harvard University Press.

Mahler, Sarah, and Patricia Pessar, eds. 2001. "Special Issue: Gendering Transnational Spaces." *Identities: Global Studies in Culture and Power* 7(4).

Maira, Sunaina. 2002. *Desis in the House: Indian American Youth Culture in New York City.* Philadelphia: Temple University Press.

Malinowski, Bronislaw. (1922) 2002. *Argonauts of the Western Pacific.* Reprint, London: Routledge.

———. 1927. *Sex and Repression in Savage Society.* London: Kegan Paul, Trench, Trübner & Co.

———. 1929. *The Sexual Life of Savages in North Western Melanesia: An Ethnographic Account of Courtship, Marriage and Family Life among the Natives of the Trobriand Islands, British New Guinea.* London: Kegan Paul, Trench, Trübner & Co.

———. 1930. "Parenthood—The Basis of Social Structure." In *The New Generation: The Intimate Problems of Modern Parents and Children,* edited by Victor F. Calverton and Samuel D. Schmalhausen. London: George Allen & Unwin.

Mallory, J. P., and D. Q. Adams. 2006. *The Oxford Introduction to Proto-Indo-European and the Proto-Indo-European World.* Oxford, UK: Oxford University Press.

Mamdani, Mahmood. 2002. *When Victims Become Killers: Colonialism, Nativism, and the Genocide in Rwanda.* Princeton, NJ: Princeton University Press.

Mantsios, Gregory. 2003. "Media Magic: Making Class Invisible." In *Race, Class, and Gender in the United States,* 6th ed., edited by Paula Rothenberg. New York: Worth Publishers.

Marable, Manning. 2000. *The Great Wells of Democracy: The Meaning of Race in American Life.* New York: Perseus.

———. 2002. "Whither Whiteness." *Souls: A Critical Journal of Black Politics, Culture and Society* 4(4): 45–73.

———. 2006. "Katrina's Unnatural Disaster: A Tragedy of Black Suffering and White Denial." *Souls: A Critical Journal of Black Politics, Culture and Society* 8(1): 1–8.

Marcus, George E., and Fred R. Myers. 1995. *The Traffic in Culture: Refiguring Art and Anthropology.* Berkeley: University of California Press.

Mardi Gras: Made in China. 2005. Directed by David Redmon. Carnivalesque Films.

Marks, Jonathan. 1995. *Human Biodiversity: Genes, Race, and History.* New York: Aldine de Gruyter.

Marlowe, Frank. 2010. *The Hadza: Hunter-Gatherers of Tanzania.* Berkeley: University of California Press.

Martin, Emily. 1991. "The Egg and the Sperm: How Science Has Constructed a Romance Based on Stereotypical Male-Female Roles." *Signs: Journal of Women in Culture and Society* 16(3): 485–501.

Martin, Joann. 1999. "Women and Social Movements in Latin America: Power from Below [Review]." *American Ethnologist* 26(2): 482–83.

Martinez, Samuel. 1996. *Peripheral Migrants: Haitians and Dominican Republic Sugar Plantations.* Knoxville: University of Tennessee Press.

———. 2003. "Not a Cockfight: Rethinking Haitian-Dominican Relations." *Latin American Perspectives* 3(3): 80–101.

Marx, Karl. 1867. *Capital.* Reprint, London: Penguin, 1986.

Marx, Karl, and Friedrich Engels. 1848. *The Communist Manifesto.* Reprint, London: Penguin, 1967.

———. 1957. *On Religion.* Moscow: Foreign Languages Publishing House.

Mascia-Lees, Frances E. 2009. *Gender and Difference in a Globalizing World: Twenty-First Century Anthropology.* Prospect Heights, IL: Waveland Press.

Mauss, Marcel. 1979. "Body Techniques." In *Sociology and Psychology: Essays by Marcel Mauss.* Translated by Ben Brewster. London: Routledge and Kegan Paul.

McAdam, Doug, John D. McCarthy, and Mayer N. Zald. 1996. *Comparative Perspectives on Social Movements: Political Opportunities, Mobilizing Structures, and Cultural Framings.* Cambridge, UK: Cambridge University Press.

McAdoo, Harriette Pipes. 2000. "All Our Kin: Strategies for Survival in a Black Community [Review]." *Journal of Marriage and Family* 62(3): 864–65.

McAlister, Elizabeth A. 2002. *Rara! Vodou, Power, and Performance in Haiti and Its Diaspora.* Berkeley: University of California Press.

McBrearty, Sally, and Alison S. Brooks. 2000. "The Revolution That Wasn't: A New Interpretation of the Origin of Modern Human Behaviour." *Journal of Human Evolution* 39(5): 453–563.

McCracken, Grant. 1991. *Culture and Consumption: New Approaches to the Symbolic Character of Consumer Goods and Activities.* Bloomington: Indiana University Press.

———. 2005. *Culture and Consumption II: Markets, Meaning, and Brand Management.* Bloomington: Indiana University Press.

McFate, Montgomery. 2005. "Anthropology and Counterinsurgency: The Strange Story of Their Curious Relationship." *Military Review* (March-April): 24–38.

McGrath, Charles. 2005. "In Fiction, a Long History of Fixation on the Social Gap." *New York Times,* June 8.

McHenry, Henry M., and Katherine Coffing. 2000. "*Australopithecus* to *Homo*: Transformations in Body and Mind." *Annual Review of Anthropology* 29: 125–46.

McIntosh, Peggy. 1989. "White Privilege: Unpacking the Invisible Knapsack." *Peace and Freedom* (July–August): 10–12.

McKay, Deirdre. 2006. "Friction: An Ethnography of Global Connection [Review]." *Women's Studies Quarterly* 34(1–2): 476–80.

McKibben, William. 2010. *Eaarth: Making a Life on a Tough New Planet.* New York: Henry Holt.

———. 2012. "Global Warming's Terrifying New Math." *Rolling Stone,* July 19. www.rollingstone.com/politics/news/global -warmings-terrifying -new-math-20120719.

McWhorter, John H. 2001. *The Power of Babel: A Natural History of Language.* New York: HarperCollins.

Mead, Margaret. 1928. *Coming of Age in Samoa: A Psychological Study of Primitive Youth for Western Civilization.* New York: William Morrow.

———. 1935. *Sex and Temperament in Three Primitive Societies.* New York: William Morrow.

Merry, Sally Engle. 2008. *Gender Violence: A Cultural Perspective.* New York: Wiley-Blackwell.

Miles, H. Lyn White. 1993. "Language and the Orangutan: The Old 'Person of the Forest.'" In *The Great Ape Project,* edited by Paola Cavalieri and Peter Singer, 45–50. New York: St. Martin's Press.

Milkie, Melissa A. 2000. "White Weddings [Review]." *Gender and Society* 14(6): 824–26.

Miller, Raegen, and Diana Epstein. 2011. "There Still Be Dragons: Racial Disparity in School Funding Is No Myth." Center for American Progress. www.americanprogress.org/issues /education/report/2011/07/05/9943/there-still-be-dragons/.

Miller, Rebecca. 2003. "Rara! Vodou, Power, and Performance in Haiti and Its Diaspora [Review]." *Notes,* 2nd ser., 59(3): 626–28.

Mills, C. Wright. 1956. *The Power Elite.* New York: Oxford University Press.

Mills, Mary Beth. 2003. "Gender and Inequality in the Global Labor Force." *Annual Review of Anthropology* 32: 41–62.

Miner, Horace. 1956. "Body Ritual among the Nacirema." *American Anthropologist* 58(3): 503–7.

Mintz, Sidney W. 1985. *Sweetness and Power: The Place of Sugar in Modern History.* New York: Viking Penguin.

Mintz, Sidney W. 1990. "Food, Gender, and Poverty in the Ecuadorian Andes [Review]." *American Anthropologist* 92(4): 1045–46.

Molyneux, Maxine. 1999. "Women and Social Movements in Latin America: Power from Below [Review]." *Journal of Latin American Studies* 31(2): 535–37.

Monnier, Oliver. 2013. "Agribusiness: Smoothing Out the Bumps in Côte d'Ivoire." *The Africa Report.* July 25. www.theafricareport.com/West-Africa/agribusiness-smoothing-out-the-bumps-in-Cote-divoire.html (accessed 7/26/13).

Moore, Mignon R. 2011. *Invisible Families: Gay Identities, Relationships, and Motherhood among Black Women.* Berkeley: University of California Press.

———. 2012. "Intersectionality and the Study of Black, Sexual Minority Women." *Gender and Society* 26: 33–39.

Moore, Sally Falk. 1993. *Moralizing States and the Ethnography of the Present.* Arlington, VA: American Anthropological Association.

Moran, Emilio F. 2006. *People and Nature: An Introduction to Human Ecological Relations.* Malden, MA: Blackwell.

Morgan, Lewis Henry. (1877) 1964. *Ancient Society.* Reprint, Cambridge, MA: Belknap Press.

Morrell, Virginia. 2008. "Inside Animal Minds: Birds, Apes, Dolphins and a Dog with a World-Class Vocabulary." *National Geographic,* March.

Moynihan, Daniel Patrick. 1965. *The Negro Family: The Case for National Action.* Washington, DC: U.S. Department of Labor.

Mukhopadhyay, Carol C., Rosemary Henze, and Yolanda T. Moses. 2007. *How Real Is Race? A Sourcebook on Race, Culture, and Biology.* Lanham, MD: Rowman & Littlefield.

Mullings, Leith. 2005. "Interrogating Racism: Toward an Anti-Racist Anthropology." *Annual Review of Anthropology* 34: 667–93.

———. 2005. "Resistance and Resilience: The Sojourner Syndrome and the Social Context of Reproduction in Central Harlem." *Transforming Anthropology* 13(2): 79–91.

Mullings, Leith, and Alaka Wali. 2001. *Stress and Resilience: The Social Context of Reproduction in Central Harlem.* New York: Kluwer Academic/Plenum Publishers.

Myerhoff, Barbara G. 1974. *Peyote Hunt: The Sacred Journey of the Huichol Indians.* Ithaca, NY: Cornell University Press.

———. 1978. *Number Our Days.* New York: Dutton.

Myers, Fred R. 1986. *Pintupi Country, Pintupi Self: Sentiment, Place, and Politics among Western Desert Aborigines.* Washington, DC: Smithsonian Institution.

———. 1991. "Representing Culture: The Production of Discourse(s) for Aboriginal Acrylic Paintings." *Cultural Anthropology* 6(1): 26–62.

———. 2002. *Painting Culture: The Making of an Aboriginal High Art.* Durham, NC: Duke University Press.

Nader, Laura. 1972. "Up the Anthropologist: Perspectives Gained from Studying Up." In *Reinventing Anthropology,* edited by Dell H. Hymes, 284–311. New York: Pantheon.

Nahman, Michal Rachel. 2002. "Reproducing Jews: A Cultural Account of Assisted Conception in Israel [Review]." *Canadian Review of Sociology and Anthropology* 39(3): 359–61.

Nanda, Serena. 1998. *Neither Man nor Woman: The Hijras of India,* 2nd ed. Florence, KY: Wadsworth.

———. 2000. "Hijra and Sadhim: Neither Man nor Woman in India." In *Gender Diversity: Cross-Cultural Variations.* Prospect Heights, IL: Waveland Press.

Nash, June C., ed. 2005. *Social Movements: An Anthropological Reader.* Malden, MA: Blackwell.

National Center for Women and Information Technology. 2012. "By the Numbers." www.ncwit.org/pdf/BytheNumbers09.pdf.

Neely, Daniel Tanehill. 2005. "Rara! Vodou, Power, and Performance in Haiti and Its Diaspora [Review]." *Ethnomusicology* 49(1): 126–28.

Nettl, Bruno. 2005. *The Study of Ethnomusicology: Thirty-One Issues and Concepts.* Urbana: University of Illinois Press.

Neubeck, Kenneth J., and Noel A. Cazenave. 2001. *Welfare Racism: Playing the Race Card against America's Poor.* New York: Routledge.

Newman, Katherine S. (1988) 1999. *Falling from Grace: Downward Mobility in the Age of Affluence.* Reprint, Berkeley: University of California Press.

———. 1993. *Declining Fortunes: The Withering of the American Dream.* New York: Basic Books.

———. 1999. *No Shame in My Game: The Working Poor in the Inner City.* New York: Vintage.

Nissenbaum, Stephen. 1996. *The Battle for Christmas.* New York: Knopf.

Nordstrom, Carolyn. 1997. *A Different Kind of War Story.* Philadelphia: University of Pennsylvania Press.

———. 2004. *Shadows of War: Violence, Power, and International Profiteering in the Twenty-First Century.* Berkeley: University of California Press.

North, James. 2011. "The Roots of the Côte d'Ivoire Crisis: How the Demand for Chocolate—Yes, Chocolate!—Helped Fuel the Country's Civil War." *The Nation,* April 25, 2011.

Norton, M. I., and D. Ariely. 2011. "Building a Better America—One Wealth Quintile at a Time." *Perspectives on Psychological Science* 6(1): 9–12.

Nugent, David, and Joan Vincent, eds. 2004. *A Companion to the Anthropology of Politics.* Malden, MA: Blackwell.

Number Our Days. 1976. Directed by Lynne Littman. Community Television of Southern California.

Ogden, Cynthia L., Cheryl D. Fryar, Margaret D. Carroll, and Katherine M. Flegal. 2004. "Mean Body Weight, Height, and Body Mass Index, United States 1960–2002." *Advance Data from Vital and Health Statistics* 347(October 27).

Omi, Michael, and Howard Winant. 1994. *Racial Formation in the United States from the 1960s to the 1990s*, 2nd ed. New York: Routledge.

Ong, Aihwa. 1987. *Spirits of Resistance and Capitalist Discipline*. Albany: State University of New York Press.

Ong, Aihwa, and Donald M. Nonini. 1997. *Ungrounded Empires: The Cultural Politics of Modern Chinese Transnationalism*. New York: Routledge.

Ore, Tracy. 2010. *The Social Construction of Difference and Inequality: Race, Class, Gender, and Sexuality*. New York: McGraw-Hill.

Orleck, Annelise. 1999. *The Soviet Jewish Americans*. Westport, CT: Greenwood.

Ortner, Sherri. 1974. "Is Female to Male as Nature Is to Culture?" In *Woman, Culture and Society*, edited by Michelle Z. Rosaldo and Louise Lamphere. Stanford, CA: Stanford University Press.

Pacini-Hernandez, Deborah. 1995. *Bachata: A Social History of a Dominican Popular Music*. Philadelphia: Temple University Press.

Palfrey, John, and Urs Gasser. 2008. *Born Digital: Understanding the First Generation of Digital Natives*. New York: Basic Books.

Parker, Richard. 1999. "The Meanings of Macho [Review]." *American Ethnologist* 26(2): 497–98.

Parsons, Talcott. 1964. *Theory of Social and Economic Organization*. New York: Simon & Schuster.

Pascoe, C. J. 2007. *Dude, You're a Fag: Masculinity and Sexuality in High School*. Berkeley: University of California Press.

Patel, Reena. 2010. *Working the Night Shift: Women in India's Call Center Industry*. Stanford, CA: Stanford University Press.

Patterson, Francine. 1978. "Conversations with a Gorilla." *National Geographic,* October, 438–65.

Payer, Lynn. 1996. *Medicine and Culture: Varieties of Treatment in the United States, England, West Germany, and France*. New York: Henry Holt.

PayScale. 2012. www.payscale.com.

Peletz, Michael G. 1999. "The Heat of the Hearth [Review]." *American Ethnologist* 26(1): 251–52.

Pérez-Alemán, Paola. 1994. "Life Is Hard [Review]." *American Journal of Sociology* 99(5): 1393–95.

Perkins, Morgan, and Howard Morphy, eds. 2006. *The Anthropology of Art: A Reader*. Malden, MA: Blackwell.

Perlroth, Nicole. 2012. "Venture Capital Partner Claims Sexual Harassment." *New York Times*, May 22. http://bits.blogs .nytimes.com/2012/05/22/kleiner-perkins-accused-of-sexual -harassment/.

Petersen, Glenn. 2009. *Traditional Micronesian Societies: Adaptation, Integration, and Political Organization*. Honolulu: University of Hawaii Press.

Pew Forum on Religion & Public Life. 2006. "Many Americans Uneasy with Mix of Religion and Politics." Poll, August 24. http://pewforum.org/docs/?DocID=153#3.

———. 2012. "'Nones' on the Rise." Poll, October 9. www .pewforum.org/Unaffiliated/nones-on-the-rise.aspx.

Pew Research Center. 2008. "Inside the Middle Class: Bad Times Hit the Good Life." Social & Demographic Trends. April 9. www.pewresearch.org/pubs/793/inside-the-middle-class.

Pierce, Ellie. 2008. "Driven by Faith or Customer Service? Muslim Taxi Drivers at the MSP Airport." The Pluralism Project at Harvard University. www.pluralism.org/casestudy/.

Pietsch, Theodore W. 1975. "Precocious Sexual Parasitism in the Deep Sea Ceratioid Anglerfish, *Cryptopsaras couesi* Gill" *Nature* 256(July 3): 38–40.

Pinker, Steven. 2002. *The Blank Slate: The Modern Denial of Human Nature*. New York: Viking.

Pollitt, Katha. 2005. "Summers of Our Discontent." *The Nation*, February 21.

Polanyi, Karl. (1944) 2001. *The Great Transformation*. Reprint, Boston: Beacon.

Pordié, Laurent. 2008. *Tibetan Medicine in the Contemporary World: Global Politics of Medical Knowledge and Practice*. London: Routledge.

Portes, Alejandro, Patricia Fernández-Kelly, and William Haller. 2009. "The Adaptation of the Immigrant Second Generation in America: Theoretical Overview and Recent Evidence." *Journal of Ethnic and Migration Studies* 35(7): 1077–1104.

Portes, Alejandro, and Rubén G. Rumbaut. 2001. *Legacies: The Story of the Immigrant Second Generation*. Berkeley: University of California Press.

———. 2006. *Immigrant America: A Portrait*. Berkeley: University of California Press.

Powell, Adam, Stephen Shennan, and Mark G. Thomas. 2009. "Late Pleistocene Demography and the Appearance of Modern Human Behavior." *Science* 324: 1298–1301.

Prashad, Vijay. 2001. *Cataracts of Silence: Race on the Edge of Indian Thought*. Geneva: United Nations Research Institute for Social Development.

Price, David H. 2011. *Weaponizing Anthropology: Social Science in Service of the Militarized State*. Oakland, CA: AK Distribution.

Price, Sally. 1989. *Primitive Art in Civilized Places*. Chicago: University of Chicago Press.

Quinn, Naomi. 1977. "Anthropological Studies on Women's Status." *Annual Review of Anthropology* 6: 181–222.

Radcliffe-Brown, A. R. 1950. "Introduction," In *African Systems of Kinship and Marriage*, edited by A. R. Radcliffe-Brown and Daryll Forde. London: Oxford University Press.

Ragoné, Helena. 1994. *Surrogate Motherhood: Conception in the Heart*. Boulder, CO: Westview Press.

Rajakumar, Kumaravel, and Stephen B. Thomas. 2005. "Reemerging Nutritional Rickets." *Archives of Pediatrics & Adolescent Medicine* 159(4): 335–41.

Ramshaw, Emily. 2011. "Major Health Problems Linked to Poverty." *New York Times*, July 9. www.nytimes.com/2011/07/10/us/10tthealth.html.

Rathje, William, and Cullen Murphy. 2001. *Rubbish!: The Archaeology of Garbage*. Tucson: University of Arizona Press.

Raymond, Janice G. 1993. *Women as Wombs: Reproductive Technologies and the Battle over Women's Freedom*. San Francisco: Harper San Francisco.

Redfield, Robert. 1941. *The Folk Culture of the Yucatan*. Chicago: University of Chicago Press.

Replogle, Elaine. 2003. "Desis in the House [Review]." *Contemporary Sociology* 32(2): 194–95.

Richards, Audrey. 1956. *Chisungu: A Girl's Initiation Ceremony among the Bemba of Northern Rhodesia*. London: Faber.

Richards, Paul. 1999. "A Different Kind of War Story [Review]." *American Anthropologist* 101(1): 214–15.

Richman, Karen. 2001. "High Tech and High Heels in the Global Economy [Review]." *American Ethnologist* 28(4): 954–55.

Richtel, Matt. 2006. "The Long-Distance Journey of a Fast Food Order." *New York Times*, April 11.

Rickford, John R., and Russell J. Rickford. 2000. *Spoken Soul: The Story of Black English*. New York: Wiley.

Robbins, Richard H. 2005. *Global Problems and the Culture of Capitalism*, 3rd ed. Boston: Pearson/Allyn & Bacon.

Roberts, Elizabeth F. S., and Nancy Scheper-Hughes. 2011. "Introduction: Medical Migrations." *Body and Society* 17(2&3): 1–30.

Robson, David. 2008. "Coming of Age in Second Life [Review]." *Nature* 455(4): 32–33.

Rodriquez, Clara. 2000. *Changing Race: Latinos, the Census, and the History of Ethnicity*. New York: New York University Press.

Rodseth, L., R. W. Wrangham, A. M. Harrigan, and B. Smuts. 1991. "The Human Community as a Primate Society." *Current Anthropology* 32: 221–54.

Roediger, David. 1992. *The Wages of Whiteness: Race and the Making of the American Working Class*. New York: Verso.

Root, Robin. 2006. "Mixing as an Ethnoetiology of HIV/AIDS in Malaysia's Multinational Factories." *Medical Anthropology Quarterly* 20(3): 321–44.

———. 2009. "Religious Participation and HIV-Disclosure Rationales among People Living with HIV/AIDS in Rural Swaziland." *African Journal of AIDS Research* 8(3): 295–309.

Rosaldo, Michelle Z. 1974. "Women, Culture and Society: A Theoretical Overview." In *Woman, Culture and Society*, edited by Michelle Z. Rosaldo and Louise Lamphere. Stanford, CA: Stanford University Press.

———. 1980. "The Use and Abuse of Anthropology: Reflections on Feminism and Cross-Cultural Understanding." *Signs: Journal of Women in Culture and Society* 5(3): 389–417.

Roscoe, Will. 1991. *The Zuni Man-Woman*. Albuquerque: University of New Mexico Press.

Rosenhouse, Jason. 2012. *Among the Creationists*. New York: Oxford University Press.

Roth, Joshua Hotaka. 2002. *Brokered Homeland: Japanese Brazilian Migrants in Japan*. Ithaca, NY: Cornell University Press.

Rouse, Roger. 1994. "Life Is Hard [Review]." *Contemporary Sociology* 23(1): 57–59.

Rubin, Gayle. 1975. "The Traffic in Women: Notes on the 'Political Economy' of Sex." In *Toward an Anthropology of Women*, edited by Rayna Reiter. New York: Monthly Review Press.

Rumbaut, Ruben G., and Alejandro Portes, eds. 2001. *Ethnicities: Children of Immigrants in America*. Berkeley: University of California Press.

Sachs, Jeffrey. 2005. *The End of Poverty: Economic Possibilities for Our Time*. New York: Penguin.

Sacks, Karen Brodkin. 1989. "Toward a Unified Theory of Class, Race, and Gender." *American Ethnologist* 16(3): 534–50.

Sacks, Peter. 2007. *Tearing Down the Gates: Confronting the Class Divide in American Education*. Berkeley: University of California Press.

Sadker, Myra, and David Sadker. 1985. "Sexism in the Schoolroom of the 80s." *Psychology Today* (March): 54–57.

Safa, Helen. 1995. *The Myth of the Male Breadwinner: Women and Industrialization in the Caribbean*. Boulder, CO: Westview Press.

Sahlins, Marshall D. 1971. *Social Stratification in Polynesia*. Seattle: University of Washington Press.

———. (1974) 2004. *Stone Age Economics*. New York: Routledge.

Saillant, Francine, and Serge Genest, eds. 2007. *Medical Anthropology: Regional Perspectives and Shared Concerns*. Malden, MA: Blackwell.

Sanday, Peggy. 1990. *Fraternity Gang Rape: Sex, Brotherhood, and Privilege on Campus*. New York: New York University Press.

Sanders, Stephanie A., and June Machover Reinisch. 2006. "Would You Say You 'Had Sex' If . . . ?" In *The Language and Sexuality Reader*, edited by Deborah Cameron and Don Kulick. New York: Routledge.

Sanjek, Roger. 1994. "The Enduring Inequalities of Race." In *Race*, edited by Steven Gregory and Roger Sanjek, 1–17. New Brunswick, NJ: Rutgers University Press.

Sapir, Edward, and Morris Swadesh. 1946. "Word 2." In *American Indian Grammatical Categories*, 103–12. Reedited for Dell Hymes in *Language in Culture and Society*, 100–7. New York: Harper and Row, 1964.

Sarroub, Loukia K. 2005. *All American Yemeni Girls: Being Muslim in a Public School*. Philadelphia: University of Pennsylvania Press.

Sassen, Saskia. 1998. *Globalization and Its Discontents*. New York: New Press.

———. 2001. *The Global City: New York, London, Tokyo*. Princeton, NJ: Princeton University Press.

Savage, Michael. 2003. *The Savage Nation: Saving America from the Liberal Assault on Our Borders, Language, and Culture.* Washington, DC: WND Books.

Savage, Michael, and Karel Williams, eds. 2008. *Remembering Elites.* Malden, MA: Blackwell.

Scheid, Volker. 2002. *Chinese Medicine in Contemporary China: Plurality and Synthesis.* Durham, NC: Duke University Press.

Scheid, Volker, and Hugh MacPherson. 2012. *Integrating East Asian Medicine into Contemporary Healthcare.* Edinburgh, UK: Churchill Livingstone Elsevier.

Scheper-Hughes, Nancy. 1989. "Death without Weeping: Has Poverty Ravaged Mother Love in the Shantytowns of Brazil?" *Natural History* 98(10): 8–16.

———. 1992. *Death without Weeping: The Violence of Everyday Life in Brazil.* Berkeley: University of California Press.

———. 2002. "Min(d)ing the Body: On the Trail of Organ Stealing Rumors." In *Exotic No More: Anthropology on the Front Lines,* edited by Jeremy MacClancy, 33–63. Chicago: University of Chicago Press.

———. 2013. "No More Angel Babies on the Alto do Cruzeiro: A Dispatch from Brazil's Revolution in Child Survival." *Natural History.* www.naturalhistorymag.com/features/282558/no-more-angel-babies-on-the-alto-do-cruzeiro.

Scheper-Hughes, Nancy, and Margaret M. Lock. 1987. "The Mindful Body: A Prolegomenon to Future Work in Medical Anthropology." *Medical Anthropology Quarterly* 1(1): 6–41.

Schneider, Arnd, and Christopher Wright. 2006. *Contemporary Art and Anthropology.* Oxford, UK: Berg.

Schneider, David M. 1980. *American Kinship: A Cultural Account,* 2nd ed. Chicago: University of Chicago Press.

Schneider, Jane. 1977. "Was There a Pre-Capitalist World System?" *Peasant Studies* 6(1): 20–29.

Schoendorf, Kenneth C., Carol J. R. Hogue, and Joel C. Kleinman. 1992. "Mortality among Infants of Blacks as Compared to White College-Educated Parents." *New England Journal of Medicine* 326(23): 1522–26.

Schulz, Amy J., and Leith Mullings. 2006. *Gender, Race, Class, and Health: Intersectional Approaches.* San Francisco: Jossey-Bass.

Scott, Eugenie C. 2009. *Evolution vs. Creationism: An Introduction,* 2nd ed. Berkeley: University of California Press.

Scott, James C. 1985. *Weapons of the Weak: Everyday Forms of Peasant Resistance.* New Haven, CT: Yale University Press.

Sebeok, Thomas A., and Donna J. Umiker-Sebeok, eds. 1980. *Speaking of Apes: A Critical Anthology of Two-Way Communication with Man,* 407–27. New York: Plenum Press.

Service, Elman R. 1962. *Primitive Social Organization: An Evolutionary Perspective.* New York: Random House.

———. 1966. *The Hunters.* Englewood Cliffs, NJ: Prentice Hall.

Severson, Kim. 2011. "Race-Based Names Dot the Landscape." *New York Times,* October 6.

Shanklin, Eugenia. 1998. "The Profession of the Color Blind: Sociocultural Anthropology and Racism in the 21st Century." *American Anthropologist* 100(3): 669–79.

Shannon, Jonathan Holt. 2006. *Among the Jasmine Trees: Music and Modernity in Contemporary Syria.* Middletown, CT: Wesleyan University Press.

Shapiro, Harry L. 1974. *Peking Man: The Discovery, Disappearance, and Mystery of a Priceless Scientific Treasure.* New York: Simon & Schuster.

Sharma, Aradhana, and Akhil Gupta, eds. 2006. *The Anthropology of the State: A Reader.* Malden, MA: Blackwell.

Sharp, Gene. 1993. *From Dictatorship to Democracy: A Conceptual Framework for Liberation.* East Boston, MA: Albert Einstein Institution.

Shaw, Alison. 1998. "Contesting Culture: Discourses of Identity in Multi-Ethnic London [Review]." *Journal of the Royal Anthropological Institute* 4(1): 174–75.

Shaw, Stephanie. 1996. *What a Woman Ought to Be and to Do: Black Professional Women Workers during the Jim Crow Era.* Chicago: University of Chicago Press.

Shiva, Vandana. 2006. "Building Water Democracy: People's Victory against Coca-Cola in Plachimada." In *Beyond Borders: Thinking Critically about Global Issues,* edited by Paula S. Rothenberg, 580–83. New York: Worth Publishers.

Shweder, Richard A. 2003. "The Moral Challenge in Cultural Migration." In *American Arrivals: Anthropology Engages the New Immigration,* edited by Nancy Foner. Santa Fe, NM: School of American Research.

Siebel, Catherine. 2000. "White Weddings [Review]." *Teaching Sociology* 28(2): 175–76.

Singer, Merrill, and Hans A. Baer. 2007. *Introducing Medical Anthropology: A Discipline in Action.* Lanham, MD: AltaMira.

Small, Cathy. 1997. *Voyages: From Tongan Villages to American Suburbs.* Ithaca, NY: Cornell University Press.

Smedley, Audrey. 1993. *Race in North America: Origins and Evolution of a Worldview.* Boulder, CO: Westview Press.

Smith, Adam. 1776. *Wealth of Nations.* Reprint, New York: Simon & Brown, 2010.

Smith, Neil. 2006. "There's No Such Thing as a Natural Disaster." In *Understanding Katrina: Perspectives from the Social Sciences.* Social Science Research Council. http://understandingkatrina.ssrc.org/Smith.

Smith, Robert C. 2006. *Mexican New York: Transnational Lives of New Immigrants.* Berkeley: University of California Press.

Snow, Dean R. 1994. *The Iroquois.* Cambridge, MA: Blackwell.

Solinger, Dorothy J. 1999. *Contesting Citizenship in Urban China: Peasant Migrants, the State, and the Logic of the Market.* Berkeley: University of California Press.

Spence, Jonathan D. 2013. *The Search for Modern China,* 3rd ed. New York: Norton.

Spencer, Robert F. 1987. "Shamans, Housewives, and Other Restless Spirits: Women in Korean Ritual Life [Review]." *Man*, new ser., 22(3): 583–84.

Stack, Carol B. 1974. *All Our Kin: Strategies for Survival in a Black Community*. New York: Harper & Row.

Stange, Mary Zeiss. 1997. *Woman the Hunter*. Boston: Beacon Press.

Stark, Rodney, and William Sims Bainbridge. 1985. *The Future of Religion: Secularization, Revival, and Cult Formation*. Berkeley: University of California Press.

Steele, D. G., and J. F. Powell. 1993. "Paleobiology of the First Americans." *Evolutionary Anthropology* 2: 138–46.

Steiner, Christopher Burghard. 1994. *African Art in Transit*. Cambridge, UK: Cambridge University Press.

———. 1995. "The Art of the Trade: On the Creation of Authenticity in the African Art Market." In *The Traffic in Culture*, edited by George E. Marcus and Fred R. Myers, 151–66. Berkeley: University of California Press.

Stephen, Lynn. 1995. "Women's Rights Are Human Rights: The Merging of Feminine and Feminist Interests among El Salvador's Mothers of the Disappeared (CO-MADRES)." *American Ethnologist* 22(4): 807–27.

Sterk, Claire E. 2000. *Tricking and Tripping: Prostitution in the Era of AIDS*. Putnam Valley, NY: Social Change.

Stevens, Carolyn S. 2005. "Tsukiji: The Fish Market at the Center of the World [Review]." *Journal of Asian Studies*, 64(4): 1022–23.

Steward, Julian H. 1956. *The People of Puerto Rico: A Study in Social Anthropology*. Urbana: University of Illinois Press.

Stiglitz, Joseph E. 2010. *Freefall: America, Free Markets, and the Sinking of the World Economy*. New York: Norton.

———. 2012. *The Price of Inequality: How Today's Divided Society Endangers Our Future*. New York: Norton.

Stocking, George W. 1983. *Observers Observed: Essays on Ethnographic Fieldwork*. Madison: University of Wisconsin Press.

———, ed. 1989. *A Franz Boas Reader: The Shaping of American Anthropology, 1883–1911*. Chicago: University of Chicago Press.

Stoler, Ann Laura. 2010. *Carnal Knowledge and Imperial Power: Race and the Intimate in Colonial Rule*, rev. ed. Berkeley: University of California Press.

Stoller, Paul. 2002. *Money Has No Smell: The Africanization of New York City*. Chicago: University of Chicago Press.

———. 2003. "Circuits of African Art/Paths of Wood: Exploring an Anthropological Trail." *Anthropological Quarterly* 76(2): 207–34.

Stoller, Paul, and Cheryl Olkes. 1987. *In Sorcery's Shadow: A Memoir of Apprenticeship among the Songhay of Niger*. Chicago: University of Chicago Press.

Stone, Amy L. 2007. "Sexuality and Social Change: Sexual Relations in a Capitalist System." *American Anthropologist* 109(4): 753–55.

Stone, Linda. 2009. *Kinship and Gender: An Introduction*, 4th ed. Boulder, CO: Westview Press.

Straus, Murray, and Richard Gelles. 1990. *Physical Violence in American Families: Risk Factors and Adaptations to Violence in 8,145 Families*. Piscataway, NJ: Transaction Publishers.

Stringer, Chris, and Robin McKie. 1998. *African Exodus: The Origins of Modern Humanity*. New York: Henry Holt.

Suarez-Orosco, Marcelo. 2003. "Right Moves? Immigration, Globalization, Utopia, and Dystopia." In *American Arrivals: Anthropology Engages the New Immigration*, edited by Nancy Foner, 45–74. Santa Fe, NM: School of American Research.

Sullivan, Daniel Monroe. 2006. "Behind the Gates: Life, Security, and the Pursuit of Happiness in Fortress America [Review]." *Contemporary Sociology* 35(2): 163–64.

Susser, Ida. (1982) 2012. *Norman Street: Poverty and Politics in an Urban Neighborhood*. New York: Oxford University Press.

Swann, Joan. 2007. "Talk Control: An Illustration from the Classroom of Problems in Analysing Male Dominance of Conversation." In *Language and Gender: A Reader*, edited by Jennifer Coates, 185–96. London: Blackwell.

Tannen, Deborah. 2001. *You Just Don't Understand: Women and Men in Conversation*, 2nd ed. New York: Ballantine.

Tattersall, Ian. 2012. *Masters of the Planet: The Search for Our Human Origins*. New York: Palgrave Macmillan.

Tax Policy Center. 2012. Tax Facts. www.taxpolicycenter.org/taxfacts/displayafact.cfm?Docid=213.

Taylor, Robert Joseph. 2000. "All Our Kin: Strategies for Survival in a Black Community [Review]." *Journal of Marriage and Family* 62(3): 865–67.

Teman, Elly. 2010. *Birthing a Mother: The Surrogate Body and the Pregnant Self*. Berkeley: University of California Press.

Terrace, Herbert S., L. A. Petitto, R. J. Sanders, and T. G. Bever. 1979. "Can an Ape Create a Sentence?" *Science* 206(4421): 891–902.

Tett, Gillian. 2010. *Fool's Gold: The Inside Story of J.P. Morgan and How Wall Street Greed Corrupted Its Bold Dream and Created a Financial Catastrophe*. New York: Free Press.

Tierney, Patrick. 2000. *Darkness in El Dorado: How Scientists and Journalists Devastated the Amazon*. New York: Norton.

Trinkaus, Erik, and Pat Shipman. 1994. *The Neandertals: Of Skeletons, Scientists, and Scandal*. New York: Vintage.

Trivedi, Bijal P. 2001. "Scientists Identify a Language Gene." *National Geographic News*, October 4. http://news.nationalgeographic.com/news/2001/10/1004_TVlanguagegene.html.

Trouillot, Michel-Rolph. 1994. "Culture, Color, and Politics in Haiti." In *Race*, edited by Steven Gregory and Roger Sanjek, 146–74. New Brunswick, NJ: Rutgers University Press.

———. 2003. *Global Transformations: Anthropology and the Modern World*. New York: Palgrave Macmillan.

Tsing, Anna Lowenhaupt. 2005. *Friction: An Ethnography of Global Connection*. Princeton, NJ: Princeton University Press.

Turnbull, Colin M. (1961) 2010. *The Forest People*. New York: Simon & Schuster.

Turner, Victor. 1957. *Schism and Continuity in an African Society: A Study of Ndembu Village Life*. Manchester, UK: Manchester University Press.

———. 1969. *The Ritual Process: Structure and Anti-Structure*. Chicago: Aldine.

Tylor, Edward Burnett. 1871. *Primitive Culture*. London: Murray.

United Nations. 2012. "Millennium Development Goals: End Poverty 2015." www.un.org/millenniumgoals/poverty .shtml.

United Nations Department of Economic and Social Affairs, Population Division. 2009. International Migrant Stock. http: //esa.un.org/migration/index.asp?panel=1.

United Nations Department of Economic and Social Affairs, Population Division. 2012. "Trends in International Migrant Stock: Migrants by Destination and Origin." http://esa.un.org /MigOrigin (accessed 7/28/13).

United Nations Development Programme. 2013. "The Millennium Development Goals: Eight Goals for 2015." www.undp.org /mdg/.

United Nations High Commissioner for Refugees. 2012. "Total Population of Concern to UNHCR: Refugees, Asylum-Seekers, IDPs, Returnees, Stateless Persons, and Others of Concern to UNHCR by Country/Territory of Asylum, End-2010." www.unhcr.org/pages/4a0174156.html.

Urciuoli, Bonnie. 1996. *Exposing Prejudice: Puerto Rican Experiences of Language, Race, and Class*. Boulder, CO: Westview Press.

Ury, William, ed. 2002. *Must We Fight? From the Battlefield to the Schoolyard—A New Perspective on Violent Conflict and Its Prevention*. San Francisco: Jossey-Bass.

———. 2007. *The Power of a Positive No: How to Say No and Still Get to Yes*. New York: Bantam.

Useem, Elizabeth. 1992. "Middle Schools and Math Groups: Parents' Involvement in Children's Math Placement." *Sociology of Education* 65: 263–79.

U.S. Census Bureau. 2010. "America's Families and Living Arrangements: 2010," Table FG3. www.census.gov/hhes/families/files /cps2010/tabFG4-all.xls.

———. 2011. "Income, Poverty, and Health Insurance Coverage in the United States: 2011." www.census.gov/prod/2012pubs /p60-243.pdf.

———. 2012. "The Foreign-Born Population in the United States: 2010." www.census.gov/prod/2012pubs/acs-19.pdf.

———. 2013. "New Orleans (city), Louisiana." State & County QuickFacts. http://quickfacts.census.gov/qfd/states /22/2255000.html.

U.S. Centers for Disease Control. 2012. "Births: Final Data for 2010." *National Vital Statistics Reports*, August 28. www.cdc .gov/nchs/data/nvsr/nvsr61/nvsr61_01.pdf#table02.

U.S. Department of Health & Human Services, Administration for Children & Families. 2012. Child Welfare Information Gateway. www.childwelfare.gov.

U.S. Internal Revenue Service. 2009. "The 400 Individual Income Tax Returns Reporting the Largest Adjusted Gross Incomes Each Year, 1992–2009." www.irs.gov/pub/irs-soi/09intop400 .pdf.

Valentine, David. 2007. *Imagining Transgender: An Ethnography of a Category*. Durham, NC: Duke University Press.

Van Gennep, Arnold. (1908) 1960. *The Rites of Passage*. Reprint, Chicago: University of Chicago Press.

Venbrux, Eric, Pamela Sheffield Rosi, and Robert L. Welsch. 2006. *Exploring World Art*. Long Grove, IL: Waveland Press.

Vogel, Susan Mullin. 1991. *Africa Explores: 20th Century African Art*. New York: Center for African Art.

Volkman, Toby Alice. 2005. *Cultures of Transnational Adoption*. Durham, NC: Duke University Press.

Wacquant, Loic. 2002. "Scrutinizing the Street: Poverty, Morality, and the Pitfalls of Urban Ethnography." *American Journal of Sociology* 107(6): 1468–1532.

Wakin, Eric. 1992. *Anthropology Goes to War: Professional Ethics & Counterinsurgency in Thailand*. Madison: University of Wisconsin, Center for Southeast Asian Studies.

Walker, Sheila S. 2002. "Africanity vs Blackness: Race, Class and Culture in Brazil." *NACLA Report on the Americas* 35(6): 16–20.

Walklate, Sandra. 2005. "Behind the Gates: Life, Security, and the Pursuit of Happiness in Fortress America [Review]." *Urban Studies* 42(10): 1882–83.

Wallace, Anthony F. C. 1957. "Political Organization and Land Tenure among the Northwestern Indians, 1600–1830." *Southwest Journal of Anthropology* 13: 301–21.

Wallerstein, Immanuel Maurice. 1974. *World-Systems Analysis: An Introduction*. Durham, NC: Duke University Press.

Walls, Bryan. 2005. "Rara! Vodou, Power and Performance in Haiti and Its Diaspora [Review]." *Latin American Music Review* 26(2): 356–65.

Wardhaugh, Ronald. 2009. *An Introduction to Sociolinguistics*, 6th ed. London: Blackwell.

Waterston, Alisse. 2009. *An Anthropology of War: Views from War Zones*. New York: Berghahn.

Watson, James L., ed. 1998. *Golden Arches East: McDonald's in East Asia*. Stanford, CA: Stanford University Press.

Weber, Eugen. 1976. *Peasants into Frenchmen: The Modernization of Rural France, 1870–1914*. Stanford, CA: Stanford University Press.

Weber, Max. 1905. *The Protestant Ethic and the Spirit of Capitalism*. Reprint, London: Routledge, 2002.

———. 1919. *Politics as a Vocation*. Reprint, Philadelphia: Fortress, 1965.

Weber, Max. (1920) 1946. "Class, Status and Party." In *From Max Weber: Essays in Sociology*, edited and translated by Hans Gerth and C. Wright Mills. Reprint, New York: Free Press.

———. 1920. *Sociology of Religion*. Reprint, Boston: Beacon Press, 1993.

Weiner, Annette. 1976. *Women of Value, Men of Renown: New Perspectives in Trobriand Exchange*. Austin: University of Texas Press.

———. 1988. *The Trobrianders of Papua New Guinea*. New York: Holt, Rinehart and Winston.

Wekker, Gloria. 1999. "What's Identity Got to Do with It? Rethinking Identity in Light of the Mati Work in Suriname." In *Female Desires: Same-Sex and Transgender Practices across Cultures*, edited by Evelyn Blackwood and Saskia E. Wieringa, 119–38. New York: Columbia University Press.

———. 2006. *The Politics of Passion: Women's Sexual Culture in Afro-Surinamese Diaspora*. New York: Columbia University Press.

Welch, Cliff. 2001. "Peasants against Globalization: Rural Social Movement in Costa Rica [Review]." *Latin American Politics and Society* 43(4): 166–68.

Wesch, Michael. 2007. *A Vision of Students Today*. www.youtube.com/watch?v=dGCJ46vyR90&feature=channel.

———. 2008. *An Anthropological Introduction to YouTube*. www.youtube.com/watch?v=TPAO-1Z4_hU&feature=channel.

West, Candace. 1998. "When the Doctor Is a 'Lady': Power, Status and Gender in Physician-Patient Encounters." In *Language and Gender: A Reader*, edited by Jennifer Coates, 396–412. London: Blackwell.

Weston, Kath. 1991. *Families We Choose: Lesbians, Gays, Kinship*. New York: Columbia University Press.

———. 1993. "Lesbian/Gay Studies in the House of Anthropology." *Annual Review of Anthropology* 22: 339–67.

White, Tim D., Berhane Asfaw, Yonas Beyene, Yohannes Haile-Selassie, C. Owen Lovejoy, Gen Suwa, and Giday WoldeGabriel. 2009. "*Ardipithecus ramidus* and the Paleobiology of Early Hominids." *Science* 326: 64, 75–86.

Whitehouse, Bruce. 2012. *Migrants and Strangers in an African City: Exile, Dignity, Belonging*. Bloomington: Indiana University Press.

Whiteside, Alan, Catarina Andrade, Lisa Arrehag, Solomon Dlamini, Themba Ginindza, and Anokhi Parikh. 2006. *The Socio-Economic Impact of HIV/AIDS in Swaziland*. Mbabane, Swaziland: National Emergency Response Council on HIV/AIDS (NERCHA) and Health Economics & HIV/AIDS Research Division (HEARD).

Wilkins, Amy C. 2008. "Dude You're a Fag: Masculinity and Sexuality in High School [Review]." *Contemporary Sociology* 37(3): 242–43.

Williams, Brackette F. 1995. "The Public I/Eye: Conducting Fieldwork to Do Homework on Homelessness and Begging in Two U.S. Cities." *Current Anthropology* 36(1): 25–51.

Williams, Brett. 2004. *Debt for Sale: A Social History of the Credit Trap*. Philadelphia: University of Pennsylvania Press.

Williams, Walter. 1992. *The Spirit and the Flesh: Sexual Diversity in American Indian Cultures*, 2nd ed. Boston: Beacon Press.

Wilson, William Julius. 1987. *The Truly Disadvantaged: The Inner City, the Underclass, and Public Policy*. Chicago: University of Chicago Press.

Wolcott, Victoria W. 2001. *Remaking Respectability: African American Women in Interwar Detroit*. Chapel Hill: University of North Carolina Press.

Wolf, Eric R. 1966. *Peasants*. Englewood Cliffs, NJ: Prentice-Hall.

———. 1982. *Europe and the People without History*. Berkeley: University of California Press.

———. 1990. "Distinguished Lecture: Facing Power—Old Insights, New Questions." *American Anthropologist* 92: 586–96.

———. 1999. *Envisioning Power: Ideologies of Dominance and Crisis*. Berkeley: University of California Press.

———. 2001. "Ethnicity and Nationhood." In *Pathways of Power: Building an Anthropology of the Modern World*. Berkeley: University of California Press.

Wolf, Margery. 1992. *A Thrice-Told Tale: Feminism, Postmodernism, and Ethnographic Responsibility*. Stanford, CA: Stanford University Press.

Wolf-Meyer, Matthew J. 2012. *The Slumbering Masses: Sleep, Medicine, and Modern American Life*. Minneapolis: University of Minnesota Press.

World Food Programme. 2013. www.wfp.org.

Wray, Matt, and Annalee Newitz, eds. 1996. *White Trash: Class, Race and the Construction of American Identity*. London: Routledge.

Yamanaka, Keiko. 2003. "Brokered Homeland: Japanese Brazilian Migrants in Japan [Review]." *International Migration Review* 37(4): 1319–20.

Yang, Guobin. 2009. *The Power of the Internet in China: Citizen Activism Online*. New York: Columbia University Press.

Yngvesson, Barbara. 2003. "Going 'Home': Adoption, Loss of Bearings, and the Mythology of Roots." *Social Text* 74: 7–27.

Younge, Gary. 2010. "What Soccer Says about Us." *The Nation*, July 19.

Zhan, Mei. 2009. *Other-Worldly: Making Chinese Medicine through Transnational Frames*. Durham, NC: Duke University Press.

Zhang, Li. 2001. *Strangers in the City: Reconfigurations of Space, Power, and Social Networks within China's Floating Population*. Stanford, CA: Stanford University Press.

Zhou, Min, and Carl L. Bankston. 1998. *Growing up American: How Vietnamese Children Adapt to Life in the United States*. New York: Russell Sage Foundation.

Zilberg, Jonathan. 1996. "African Art in Transit [Review]." *International Journal of African Historical Studies* 29(1): 147–49.

Zillow. 2012. "The U.S. Housing Crisis: Where Are Home Loans Underwater?" The Zillow Negative Equity Report. www.zillow.com/visuals/negative-equity/.

Zimmer, Carl. 2010. "How Microbes Defend and Define Us." *New York Times,* July 13.

———. 2011. "Bacterial Ecosystems Divide People into 3 Groups, Scientists Say." *New York Times,* April 20.

Zinn, Howard. 2005. *A People's History of the United States: 1492–Present,* rev. ed. New York: HarperPerennial.

Zirin, David, and Sherry Wolf. 2010. "Let Caster Run!" *The Nation,* April 2.

Credits

Opening photograph for Part 1

2–3 Reuters/Mohammad Ismail

Chapter 1

Photographs: 4 Raveendran/AFP/Getty Images; 5a Giacomo Pirozzi/Panos; 5b Dennis MacDonald/agefotostock; 5c Mark Henley/Panos; 5d HIP/Art Resource, NY; 5e Michael Nichols/National Geographic Image Collection; 5f Courtesy of Kenneth Guest; 7 AP Photo/Pavel Rahman; 9 **bottom left** Dennis MacDonald/agefotostock; 9 **right** Elena Givone/Contrasto/Redux; 9 **top left** Giacomo Pirozzi/Panos; 10 Mark Henley/Panos; 12 HIP/Art Resource, NY; 13 Tarmizy Harva/Reuters/Landov; 14 Michael Nichols/NationalGeographic Image Collection; 16 Jeff Smith/Alamy; 19 AP Photo/Italian Coast Guard, Francesco Malavolta, HO; 23 © Chris Jordan, courtesy of Kopeikin Gallery, Los Angeles; 24 © Meryl Schenker; 27 Alamy; 29 Courtesy of Kenneth Guest; 31a Raveendran/AFP/Getty Images; 31b Elena Givone/Contrasto/Redux; 31c Tarmizy Harva/Reuters/Landov; 31d Jeff Smith/Alamy; 31e AP Photo/Italian Coast Guard, Francesco Malavolta, HO; 31f Alamy

Chapter 2

Photographs: 32 Stringer India/Reuters/Landov; 33a Mario Weigt/Anzenberger/Redux; 33b Ozier Muhammad/The New York Times/Redux; 33d Hamilton/REA/Redux; 33e CHARLES PLATIAU/Reuters/Landov; 33f Chris Stowers/Panos; 35 **bottom left** Yellow Dog Productions/Getty Images; 35 **bottom right** Mario Weigt/Anzenberger/Redux; 35 **top** Vittorio Sciosia/Alamy; 37 OZIER MUHAMMAD/The New York Times/Redux; 39 Karl Mondon/MCT/Landov; 41 Feng Zi/ColorChinaPhoto/AP Images; 44 The Granger Collection, New York; 46 © Pitt Rivers Museum, University of Oxford; 47 The Granger Collection, New York; 49 Hamilton/REA/Redux; 51 Charles Platiau/Reuters/Landov; 52 Cory Library/Rhodes University/Africa Media Online; 55 **bottom** Chris Stowers/Panos; 55 **top** EPA/KHALED ELFIQI/LANDOV; 56 Matthew HINTON/AFP/Getty Images; 59 © 2004 HarperCollins Publishers; 60 © Carl Studna; 65 ERIK S. LESSER/EPA/LANDOV; 67 Chris Stowers/Panos; 69 Mark Henley/Panos; 71a Stringer India/Reuters/Landov; 71b Vittorio Sciosia/Alamy; 71c Feng Zi/ColorChinaPhoto/AP Images; 71d The Granger Collection, New York; 71e Matthew HINTON/AFP/Getty Images; 71f The Granger Collection, New York

Chapter 3

Text: 73–77 Excerpts from "Death without Weeping," from *Natural History*, October 1989. © 1989 by Nancy Scheper-Hughes. Reprinted with permission. 103–05, 108 "Min(d)ing the Body: On the Trail of Organ-Stealing Rumors," from *Exotic No More: Anthropology on the Front Lines*, ed. Jeremy McClancy, pp. 33–36. Copyright © 2002 by The University of Chicago. Reprinted by permission of the University of Chicago Press.

Photographs: 72 Eneraldo Carneiro/BrazilPhoto; 73a Nancy Scheper-Hughes; 73b Bettmann/Corbis; 73c University Archives, University of Southern California East Library Building; 73d Courtesy of Kenneth Guest; 73e Nancy Scheper-Hughes; 73f Pat Rogue/AP; 75 Nancy Scheper-Hughes; 79 Jeff Greenberg/Alamy; 82 Biblioteca Estense, Modena, Italy/Scala/Art Resource, NY; 83 American Philosophical Society; 84 London School of Economics and Political Science; 85 © Pitt Rivers Museum, University of Oxford; 86 Bettmann/Corbis; 88 University Archives, University of Southern California East Library Building; 94a–d Courtesy of Kenneth Guest (mapmakers, top to bottom: Yuliya Feldman, Michelle Sigalov and Sunny Xu, Michelle Sigalov and Sunny Xu, Vanessa F. Castanier); 96a Courtesy of Kenneth Guest ; 96b Capucine Bailly/Redux; 99 © 1992 Stanford University Press; 100a Philip Jones Griffiths/Magnum Photos; 100b AP Photo/The Virginian-Pilot, Hyunsoo Leo Kim; 106 Nancy Scheper-Hughes; 108 Pat Rogue/AP; 111a Eneraldo Carneiro/BrazilPhotos; 111b American Philosophical Society; 111c © Pitt Rivers Museum, University of Oxford; 111d London School of Economics and Political Science; 111e Philip Jones Griffiths/Magnum Photos; 111f AP Photo/The Virginian-Pilot, Hyunsoo Leo Kim

Chapter 4

Drawn art: 143 David Constantine, "How Many Do You Speak" From *The New York Times*, July 19, 2005. © 2005 The New York Times. All rights reserved. Used by permission and protected by the Copyright Laws of the United States. The printing, copying, redistribution, or retransmission of the Content without express written permission is prohibited.

Photographs: 112 Jack Kurtz/ZUMApress.com; 113a Vincent J. Musi; 113c GUILLAUME BAPTISTE/AFP/GettyImages 113d AP Photo/Eric Gay; 113e Lynn Johnson/National Geographic Stock; 113f Jeremy Fahringer/Living Tongues Instituter; 115 Vincent J. Musi; 117 Gorilla Foundation/AP; 119a The Print Collector/Alamy; 119b Jason Lindsey/Alamy; 120 Wikimedia Commons; 123 Tom Beam/Alamy; 125 GUILLAUME BAPTISTE/AFP/GettyImages, 127a

Brian Summers/First Light/Getty Images; **127b** Kevin Dodge/Corbis; **129** Digital Vision/Getty Images; **131a** Joe Raedle/Getty Images; **131b** Suzanne DeChillo/The New York Times/Redux; **134** AP Photo/Ben Margo; **136** AP Photo/Eric Gay; **137** Travel Ink/Getty Images; **141a** LYNN JOHNSON/National Geographic Stock; **141b** Lynn Johnson/National Geographic Stock; **144** Jeremy Fahringer/Living Tongues Instituter; **148** Ariana Lindquist/The New York Times/Redux; **151a** Jack Kurtz/ZUMApress.com; **151b** The Print Collector/Alamy; **151c** Wikimedia Commons; **151d** Kevin Dodge/Corbis; **151e** Digital Vision/Getty Images; **151f** Travel Ink/Getty Images

Chapter 5

Drawn art: 187 Map by George Chaplin. Originally published in *Skin: A Natural History* by Nina C. Jablonski (University of California Press, 2006). Reprinted by permission of George Chaplin.

Photographs: 152 John Reader/Photo Researchers Inc.; **153a** The Natural History Museum/Alamy; **153b** Emmanuel Laurent/Photo Researchers, Inc.; **153c** AP Photo; **153d** AMNH/Denis Finnin; **153e** Ulrike Welsch/Photo Researchers Inc.; **153f** Tom Grill/Corbis; **154a** The Natural History Museum/Alamy; **154b** Denis Farrell/AP; **154c** Philippe Wojazer/AFP/Getty Images; **155a** © David L. Brill; **155b** Emmanuel Laurent/Photo Researchers, Inc.; **161** Staff photo Kris Snibbe/Harvard News Office; **162** Volker Steger/Photo Researchers Inc.; **163** Classic Image/Alamy; **165a** AP/Wide World Photos; **165b** AP Photo; **169** David Fox/Oxford Scientific/Getty Images; **172a** © Institute of Human Origins/Nanci Kahn; **172b** © David Brill; **173** Javier Trueba/MSF/Photo Researchers Inc.; **176** Alan Walker; **179** DEA/A. DAGLI ORTI/De Agostini/Getty Images; **180** AMNH/Denis Finnin; **182** Peter Brown; **184** Ulrike Welsch/Photo Researchers Inc.; **185** Tom Hauck/Getty Images; **189a** Tom Grill/Corbis; **189b** Clark Spencer Larsen; **191a** John Reader/Photo Researchers Inc.; **191b** Denis Farrell/AP; **191c** Classic Image/Alamy; **191d** AP/Wide World Photos; **191e** © Institute of Human Origins/Nanci Kahn; **191f** Tom Hauck/Getty Images

Opening photograph for Part 2

192–93 Travel Ink/Getty Images

Chapter 6

Text: 221–22 From Maria Kromidas, "Learning War/Learning Race: Fourth-Grade Students in the Aftermath of September 11 in New York City," *Critique of Anthropology*, Vol. 2, No. 1, March 2004, pp. 15–33. Copyright © 2004, SAGE Publications. Reprinted by permission of SAGE.

Photographs:194 MICHAEL AINSWORTH/KRT/Newscom; **195a** Corbis/SuperStock; **195b** Jorge Royan/Alamy; **195c** Scott Portelli/Getty Images; **195d** Reinhard Dirscherl/Alamy; **195e** Carl Iwasaki/Time & Life Pictures/Getty Images; **195f** Brenda Ann Kenneally; **198a** Image Source/SuperStock; **198b** Corbis/SuperStock; **198c** Jon Feingersh Photography/SuperStock; **199a** Jon Feingersh Photography/SuperStock; **199b** RubberBall/SuperStock; **199c** Jorge Royan/Alamy; **202a** Scott Portelli/Getty Images; **202b** Caterina Bernardi/Getty Images; **203** Wikimedia Commons; **204a** The Granger Collection, New York; **204b** The Art Gallery Collection/Alamy; **205** Reinhard Dirscherl/Alamy; **207** Benjamin de Menil, iASO Records; **211a** Goh Seng Chong/Bloomberg/Getty Images; **211b** Andrew Watson/Getty Images; **211c** John Brown/Alamy; **213a-b** United States Census Bureau; **215a** The Granger Collection, New York; **215b** Bettman/Corbis; **216** Everett Collection Inc/Alamy; **218** Fotosearch/Getty Images; **220** Library of Congress; **225** Carl Iwasaki/Time & Life Pictures/Getty Images; **227** Jim West/Alamy; **228** Courtesy of Raymond Codrington; **233a-c** Brenda Ann Kenneally; **235a** Jon Feingersh Photography/SuperStock; **235b** Caterina Bernardi/Getty Images; **235c** John Brown/Alamy; **235d** Fotosearch/Getty Images; **235e** Jim West/Alamy; **235f** Brenda Ann Kenneally

Chapter 7

Photographs: 236 Reuters/Kai Pfaffenbach; **237a** AP Photo/Desmond Scholtz; **237b** AP Photo/Jeff Christensen; **237c** HRC/WENN.com/Newscom; **237d** A. Demotes/Photononstop/Alamy; **237e** Shiho Fukada/The New York Times/Redux; **237f 261** Rodrigo Arangua/AFP/Getty Images; **239** AP Photo/Desmond Scholtz; **241a** The Granger Collection, New York; **241b** AP Photo/Jeff Christensen; **243** AP Photo/Michael Dwyer; **244** HRC/WENN.com/Newscom; **247** A. Demotes/Photononstop/Alamy; **249** AP Photo/Amel Emric; **250a** Yankee Photography/Alamy; **250b** Mark Peterson/Redux; **253a-d** Shiho Fukada/The New York Times/Redux; **256** Keystone-France/Gamma-Keystone via Getty Images; **259** Courtesy of David Lan; **261** Rodrigo Arangua/AFP/Getty Images; **262** Courtesy Haley Duschinsky; **267a** Reuters/Kai Pfaffenbach; **267b** AP Photo/Michael Dwyer; **267c** AP Photo/Amel Emric; **267d** Yankee Photography/Alamy; **267e** Shiho Fukada/The New York Times/Redux; **267f** Courtesy Haley Duschinsky

Chapter 8

Photographs: 268 Nicole Bengiveno/The New York Times/Redux; **269a** Adek Berry/AFP/Getty Images; **269b** Stetson Freeman/The Christian Science Monitor via Getty Images; **269c** Tanya Constantine/Blend Images/Alamy; **269d** Anne Medley Missoula Independent; **269e** Caroline Penn/Alamy; **269f** John Costello/KRT/Newscom; **272** Adek Berry/AFP/Getty Images; **274** Tanya Constantine/Blend Images/Alamy; **275** Toni L. Sandys/The Washington Post/Getty Images; **277** Chris Ryan/OJO Images Ltd/Alamy; **279** Melanie Stetson Freeman/The Christian Science Monitor via Getty Images; **280** The Advertising Archives; **281** AP Photo/Anja Niedringhaus; **285** Louise Batalla Duran/Alamy; **287** Anne Medley Missoula Independent; **289** Don Pollard, CUNY Graduate Center; **292a** Images & Stories/Alamy; **292b** Caroline Penn/Alamy; **294** Clouds Hill Imaging Ltd./Science Source; **295** Hassan Ammar/AFP/Getty Images; **298** BOYS DON'T CRY, 1999, TM and Copy-

Index

AAA, *See* American Anthropological Association

Abidjan, 668

absolute dating, 160, 161

Abu-Lughod, Lila, 68–70

acclimatization, 184–85

Aceh province, Indonesia, 13

Acheulian stone tools, 176

achieved status, 430

adaptation(s)
  acclimatization, 184–85
  biological, 162
  cultural, 23, 185, 187–89, 191
  developmental, 183–84
  general, 22
  genetic, 183, 189
  historic, 183–85
  physiological, 187–89
  at the present time, 188–91
  in skin color, 201

Admiralty Islands, South Pacific, 86

adoptions, transnational, 385–89

advertising
  as bridge for immigration, 496
  and consumerism, 64, 66

aesthetic experience, cultural differences in, 661–63

affinal relationships
  defined, 360
  kinship through, 360–66

Afghanistan
  anthropologists as cross-cultural experts in, 101
  generalized reciprocity in, 451
  Kabul women-only Internet café, 2
  life expectancy in, 643
  Marjah, 100

Africa
  arranged marriages in, 360
  artifacts from, 666
  art of, 663
  creation of states in, 257
  DNA variation in, 162
  European colonization and racial framework in, 196, 203
  fossils in, 158, 160
  Homo erectus in, 176
  Homo habilis in, 175
  Homo sapiens in, 14, 177, 178, 181–82
  homosexuality in, 344–45
  incest taboos in, 363
  migrants from, 513
  and migration, 490
  mitochondrial DNA variation in, 162
  national independence movements in, 258
  professional immigrants from, 501
  religious rituals of, 585–86
  trade with China, 438, 447
  See also individual regions and countries

African Americans
  assimilation of, 254
  Black English, 132–34
  black networks around Chicago, 371
  class status of, 232
  and culture of poverty, 422–23
  and environmental injustices, 564–65
  gender identity through kinetic orality, 680–84
  Harlem Birth Right Project, 406–10
  historically black churches in the U.S., 575
  and Hurricane Katrina in New Orleans, 195
  infant mortality rates for, 406–10
  and Jena High School nooses, 56–57
  lack of vitamin D in, 188
  "N-word" for, 124–26
  poverty rates for, 422
  race and sexuality for black gay women, 332–34
  racial discrimination in New York City, 226, 230
  and slavery in colonies, 214–16
  wealth of, 415

African Art in Transit (Steiner), 668–70

Africa Watch, 546

age
  mental maps of, 43
  and ritual life and community, 87–88

agency
  defined, 54, 559
  and power, 54–55

Agrama, Hussein Ali, 567–69

agriculture, 445–49
  defined, 446
  industrial, 447–49

Alabama
  segregation in, 216
  Selma, 106

Algeria, 460

Algiers, Battle of, 461

alienation, 582

Aliyah Senior Center, California, 88

Allah Made Us (Gaudio), 340, 344

All American Yemeni Girls (Sarroub), 523, 524

Allison, Anthony, 168

All Our Kin (Stack), 371

al-Salam Boccaccio 98 disaster, 488–90, 500

Alto do Cruzeiro, Brazil, 73–77, 89–90, 94, 97, 98, 102

ambilineal descent groups, 352

amchi medicine, 627–30

American Anthropological Association (AAA)
  Declaration on Anthropology and Human Rights, 45
  ethical guidelines of, 100
  on same-sex marriage, 384
  and Vietnam War research, 100–101

American dream, 418

American Museum of Natural History, 178, 180

Americas
  early Asian migration to, 170
  early migration from Africa to, 162
  gene migration from Europe to, 169
  See also Central America; North America; South America

Amish (North America), 397

Amma (healer), 580–81

Amnesty International, 546

Anderson, Benedict, 255, 374

Angelini, Alessandro, 657–58

Angelos, Peter, 394

Angola, war and violence in, 558

animals
  communication by, 115–17
  enculturation in, 36, 37
  See also specific entries, e.g.: primates

capitalism (*continued*)
  and manufactured desire to consume,
    63–66
  and neoliberalism, 471–74
  and new poverty in the U.S., 424
  and Protestant ethic, 62
  religious beliefs hindering, 589–90
capitalists
  contemporary competition among, 401
  in Marx's class theory, 400
Caribbean
  migrants from, 513
  national independence movements in,
    258
Carnal Knowledge and Imperial Power
  (Stoler), 330–32
carrying capacity, 448, 480–85
Carsten, Janet, 366, 374
caste, 430–33
Catalan Atlas, 82
Catholic Church
  and antimiscegenation laws, 39
  in China, 93
  on evolution, 165
  revitalization of, in the U.S., 610–13
  and revolution in Mexico, 604–6
Catholicism
  in China, 602
  in the U.S., 575
CCA (Concerned Community Adults), 226
Central Africa, confederacies of tribes in, 537
Central America, 507; *See also individual*
  countries
Central Asia, creation of states in, 257
Central Council of American Rabbis, 165
Chad, fossils in, 160
Chagnon, Napolean, 101
chain migration, 496
Chantek (orangutan), 116
Chaplin, George, 185
Checker, Melissa, 564–65
Chen Dawei, 495–96
Chiapas, Mexico, 604–6
Chicago, Illinois, 371
chiefdoms, 538–39
  defined, 538
  influences on, 542
chiefs, in ranked societies, 398
childbirth, anthropology of, 622–26
child labor, 44
chimpanzees
  communication by, 116
  emergence of, 157

enculturation in, 36
language capacity of, 116
China
  calendars in, 43
  capitalism in, 590
  Catholic churches in, 93
  Chinese medicine, 633–35
  companionate marriage in, 362
  consumerism in, 63
  cultural patterns in, 58
  descent groups in, 357–59
  digital activism in, 147–48
  digital divide in, 149
  economic growth in, 22
  entrepreneurial immigrants from, 502
  ethno-parks in, 251
  forms of the state in, 542
  Fuzhou, 28–31, 357–59, 494–96,
    686–87
  Honda factory in, 148
  incest taboos in, 363
  internal migration in, 492, 516–17
  kinship terminology in, 373
  kinship through choice in, 380
  language continuum in, 138
  Malaysian immigrants from, 210, 211
  Mardi Gras beads made in, 96
  migrants in, 21
  and migration, 490
  and multi-sited ethnography, 28–31
  personal space in, 41
  religious revival in, 602–4
  religious rituals relocated from, 613–15
  Shaanbei, 602–3
  Shenzhen, 517
  time zones in, 43
  top occupations by prestige, 403
  trade with Africa, 438, 447
  U.S. adoptions from, 385–88
  U.S. immigrants from, 218–20,
    522, 524
  Zhoukoudian, 153, 176
Chinatown, New York, 28–31, 357–60,
  494–96, 613–15, 686–87
Chinese Exclusion Acts, 522
Chinese medicine, 633–35
Chinese popular religion, 602–4, 613–15
Chisungu (Richards), 8
Chomsky, Noam, 120–21
Christianity
  in China, 602
  and creationism, 164
  rationalization in, 590

  rituals of, 586
  in South Africa, 52–53
  Swaziland's religious health assets,
    606–10
  symbols of, 598, 599
  in the U.S., 575
  Western, 600, 601
  in the world, 577
  See also Catholic Church; Protestantism
Christian pilgrimages, 585
Chrysanthemum and the Sword, The
  (Benedict), 47
Church of the Lukumi Babulu Ayea,
  Hialeah, Florida, 525
Church of the Lukumi Babulu Ayea v. City of
  Hialeah, 525–26
citizenship
  alternative, 612–13
  of children adopted abroad, 387–88
  paths to, 374
civil rights
  Arizona undocumented immigrant
    law, 113
  Brown v. Board of Education, 224, 225,
    229
  invasion of privacy protests, 40
  Loving v. Virginia, 38, 39, 364
civil rights movement, in the U.S., 204,
  230
civil society organizations, 547
  defined, 546
  global reach of, 546–47
  in Tanzania, 547–49
clans, 352
  defined, 352
  Micronesian, 540
class (in general)
  as achieved status, 430
  in Brazil, 207–9
  at Camden Yards, 393–94
  and caste, 430–33
  defined, 395
  in Dominican Republic, 204–7
  intersections of race, gender and,
    405
  intersections of race and, 232–34
  theories of, 399–407, 410
  and women's health care, 645–46
class and inequality, 393–435
  and caste, 430–33
  and egalitarian societies, 396–97
  global, 433–35
  invisibility of, in the U.S., 426–30

and international financial institutions, 546

and new poverty in the U.S., 424

economic strategies, 444–59

  agriculture, 445–49

  food foraging, 444–45

  horticulture, 445, 446

  industrialism, 447–49

  pastoralism, 445, 446

economy(-ies)

  defined, 443

  distribution and exchange in, 449–52

  of India, social mobility and, 432, 433

  of Kentucky, 417–18

  modern world economic system, 462–66; *See also* global economy

  purpose of, 443–44

  of Trobriand Islands, 291–92

Edelman, Marc, 560–62

education

  cultural capital in, 404–5

  meritocracy of, 402, 404

  and poverty, 434

educational system (U.S.), racism in, 223–24

egalitarian societies, 396–97

  bands as, 536

  defined, 396

"egg and sperm," 293–94

Egypt, 68

  al-Salam Boccaccio 98 disaster, 488–90

  Benghazi, 501

  Cairo, 55, 530, 567, 568, 569

  companionate marriage in, 362

  guest workers from, 490, 497

  Islamic Fatwa Councils in, 567–69

  revolution in, 530–33

  television in, 69

Egyptian royalty, incest taboos for, 363

Ehrenreich, Barbara, 305

Elementary Forms of Religion (Durkheim), 582

elites, studies of, 10

El Salvador, 299–301

Emancipation Proclamation, 216

emic (term), 96

emic perspective, in ethnography, 96

emoticons, 120

enculturation, 36–37

  advertising as tool of, 64, 66

  defined, 36

  as group process, 36–37

  Mead's study of, 47

and mental maps, 42

for 1.5 generation immigrants, 507, 508

endangered languages, 141–42, 144–45

endogamy, 39, 364

energy consumption, 484

Engels, Friedrich, 401

England

  Hertfordshire, 184

  immigrants in Southall, 370

  London, 10, 370

  as part of United Kingdom, 238

  and soccer, 238

entrepreneurial immigrants, 502–4

environment

  human adaptation to, 23, 162–63, 166–70, 183–90

  human impact on, 23–26, 479–85

environmental justice movement, 564–65

Episcopal Church, 383

Eskimo kinship naming system, 354, 356

ethical concerns

  about cloning, 383

  about surrogacy, 382

  in fieldwork, 100–102

Ethiopia

  Awash River Valley, 171–72

  Hadar, 154–55

  U.S. adoptions from, 385

ethnic boundary markers, 242

  for Indian Americans, 244

ethnic cleansing, 248; *see* genocide

ethnic groups, 245

ethnic identity, 240

  creating, 241–44

  of England, 238

ethnicity, 237–65

  activating, 244–45

  authentic, 678–80

  defined, 240

  as identity, 240–44

  and nationalism, 237–39, 254–65

  and nations, 254–61, 264

  as source of conflict, 245–49

  as source of opportunity, 250–52

  as term, 240

  in the U.S., 253–54

Ethnicity without Groups (Brubaker), 245

ethnocentrism, 44

  counteracting, 45

  and cultural relativism, 44–45

  defined, 9

  and project of anthropology, 9

ethno-corporations

  Pequot Foxwoods Resort, 250–51

  Royal Bafokeng Nation, 252–53

ethnogenesis, 242

ethnographic authority, 99

ethnographic fieldwork, 10, 97–100

  in Alto do Cruzeiro, 73–77

  defined, 10, 74

  and ethnology, 18

  multi-sited, 28–31

  participant observation in, 18

  as unique strategy, 78–81

ethnography

  of art, 668–75

  multi-sited, 28–31

  salvage, 83

  skills and perspectives for, 92–94

  writing, 97–100

Ethnologue (SIL), 141

ethnology, 18, 96

ethnomedicine, 627–30

ethnomusicology, 680

ethnopharmacology, 627

etic (term), 96

etic perspective, in ethnography, 96

eugenics, 218

Europe

  Argentinian immigrants from, 261

  colonialism by, 203

  conceptualizations of sexuality in, 317–18

  cultural patterns in, 58

  descent groups in, 352

  early migration from Africa to, 162

  fossils in, 160

  gene migration to Americas from, 169

  high-tech consumption in, 22

  Homo erectus in, 176

  Homo sapiens in, 177

  imagined communities in, 255

  kissing in, 34

  migrants from, 513

  paleolithic cave paintings in, 666–67

  professional immigrants to, 501

  restriction of women immigrating to Asia from, 331–32

  social movements in, 560

  U.S. immigrants from, 218–19, 522

  worker-to-CEO pay in, 412

  World War II and destruction of economies in, 257–58

  See also individual regions and countries

Hong Kong
    immigrants to, 512
    life expectancy in, 643
Hopi language, 121
horticulture, 445, 446
How the Jews Became White Folks
        (Brodkin), 219
Huichol Indians, 87
human agency, *See* agency
human fossil record, 158, 160
human microbiome, 632
human organ harvesting, 103–5, 108–9
human origins, 153–91
    adaptations, 183–85, 188–91
    Australopithecus, 173–75
    in Awash River Valley, 171
    and dating of fossils, 160–62
    discoveries relating to, 153–56
    evolution process, 166–70, 188–91
    fossil evidence for, 158–60
    and history of Earth/universe,
        156–57
    Homo erectus, 176–77
    Homo habilis, 175–76
    Homo sapiens, 177–79, 182–83
    learning about, 157–58
    pre-*Australopithecus*, 172–73
    and skin color variations, 185–88
    and theory of evolution, 162–66
Human Relations Area Files, Yale
        University, 96
human rights, 45
    and cultural relativism, 45
    organ theft, 103–5, 107–9
Human Rights Watch, 546
Human Terrain System, 101
hunger, global, 434
hunting and gathering, 294–95, 536
Hurricane Katrina, 194–96, 435
Husain Tekri shrine, India, 579–80
Hutterites (North America), 397
Hutu (Rwanda), 245–47
hypodescent
    defined, 216
    and race in Brazil, 208
    rule of, 216–17
    and Susie Phipps, 217

Ibn Battutah, 491
Iceland
    excavations in, 16
    life expectancy in, 643
    same-sex marriage in, 364

identity
    ethnicity as, 240–44
    fluidity of, 242
    gender, 680–84
    immigrant, art and, 678–80
    national, 261, 264
    and sports, 261
Ilaria, Giuseppe, 327
illness
    cultural ideas about, 621–22
    defined, 622
    globalization's effect on experience of,
        646–53
    See also health
illness narratives, 652
Illouz, Eva, 429
Imagined Communities (Anderson),
        374
imagined community, 255, 261
imitative magic, 592
immigrants
    in Argentina, 261
    art and identity of, 678–80
    "cousins" among, 371
    digital, 147
    entrepreneurial, 502–4
    generations of, 507–8
    labor, 500
    languages spoken by, 114
    professional, 500–502
    refugees, 504–5
    in Southall, England, 370
    transnational, 517–18
    types of, 498–505
    in the U.S., 523, 524
    "whitening" process of, 219
    women, work of, 304–5
immigration
    and assimilation vs. multiculturalism,
        253–54
    Boas' studies of, 8
    of Chinese to New York, 359
    policies, as barrier to migration, 496
    and race, 213–14
    and race construct in the U.S., 217–22
    and religions in the U.S., 574
    restriction of European women immi-
        grating to Asia, 331–32
    to the U.S., 520–27
    women and, 506–7
    See also migration
Immorality Act (South Africa), 38
Inca (Peru), incest taboos in, 363

incest taboos, 363–64
income
    and class, 395; *See also* class and
        inequality
    and consumer culture, 428–29
    defined, 411
    living wage, 394
    and voluntary isolation, 427
    world distribution of, 434
income inequality, in the U.S., 411–13
India, 243, 432, 588
    abducted women from Western Punjab,
        374–76
    Bangalore, 21, 432, 576
    capitalism in, 590
    caste in, 430–33
    consumerism in, 63
    cultural patterns in, 58
    dowries in, 365–66
    endangered languages in, 144
    immigrants to U.S. from, 242–44,
        501–2
    incest taboos in, 363
    and Kashmiri ethnic community, 262,
        263
    life expectancy in, 643
    Malaysian immigrants from, 209–11
    and migration, 490
    Mumbai, 33
    partition of Pakistan and, 374
    pilgrimage in, 584, 585
    Plachimada, 4–5, 27
    polyandry in, 362
    popular expressions of Islam in, 579–81
    Prasanna Ganapathy Temple, Banga-
        lore, 576
    sacred cows in, 588–89
    Tibetan medicine in, 627–30
    U.S. immigrants from, 524
Indian Americans, 242–44, 678–80
indigenous people, 11
    endangered languages of, 144–45
    European racial framework and
        eradication of, 203
    See also specific peoples
individual racism, 223
Indonesia
    Aceh province, 13
    Dutch colonists in, 331
    Homo floresiensis, "Hobbits," in Flores,
        182
    Java, 331, 332
industrial agriculture, 447–49

Industrial Revolution, 400, 458–59
  defined, 458
  pollution during, 167–68
inequality, 396–99
  in Brazilian life, 208
  and class, *See* class and inequality
  and egalitarian societies, 396–97
  global, 433–35
  in health care, 642–46
  race and patterns of, 197; *See also*
    racism[s]
  and ranked societies, 397–98
  in school funding, 224
  in the U.S., 411–21
  and wedding industry, 324–25
infant mortality (Harlem Birth Right
    Project), 406–10
informed consent, 102
Ingraham, Chrys, 323–27
In Sorcery's Shadow (Stoller), 595–96
institutional racism, 223–24
intelligent design
  defined, 164
  evolution vs., 164–66
  See also creationism
interdependence, increasing levels of, 6
internally displaced person, 505
internal migration
  in China, 492, 516–17
  defined, 516
International Covenant on Civil and
    Political Rights, 45
International Covenant on Social,
    Economic, and Cultural Rights, 45
international migration, 509, 512–16
International Monetary Fund, 546,
    561
international nonstate actors, 545–46
Internet
  and the digital age, 142–43, 146–49
  language related to, 17
  and time-space compression, 20
interpretivist approach, 48–49, 620
interracial marriage, 364
  antimiscegenation laws, 38, 39,
    53, 364
  in Brazil, 208
  Loving v. Virginia, 38, 39, 364
  Lowe, Jeanne, 39
  in the U.S., 38, 54
intersectionality
  defined, 406
  Mullings work on, 405–10

intersexual, 282
interviews
  defined, 90
  in fieldwork, 90
intimate zone (personal space), 42
Inuit, 73, 535
invented traditions, 255–56, 261
Invisible Families (Moore), 333–34
in vitro fertilization, 381
Iowa, same-sex marriage in, 364
iPhone, 465
Iraq, 259
  anthropologists as cross-cultural experts
    in, 101
  sense of nationhood in, 259–61
Ireland
  immigrants to, 512
  U.S. immigrants from, 218, 521, 524
Iroquois Confederacy, 537, 538
Iroquois kinship naming system, 354, 357
Islam
  in China, 602
  Five Pillars of, 578
  local expressions of, 578–81
  pilgrimage, 585
  political power and beliefs of, 601–2
  symbols of, 598
  in the U.S., 575
  in the world, 577
  See also Muslims
Islamic Fatwa Councils, 567–69
Israel, 376, 377
  artificial insemination in, 376–77
  immigrants to, 512
  life expectancy in, 643
Istanbul, Turkey, 555
Italy
  Homo erectus in, 176
  U.S. immigrants from, 218, 522, 524

Jablonski, Nina G., 185
Jainism, nonviolence and respect in, 588
Jamaica, 472
Jankowiak, William, 361
Japan
  life expectancy in, 642–44
  return migration to, 518–19
  Tokyo, 475
Japanese American Citizens League, 39
Java, Indonesia, 331, 332
Jena, Louisiana, 56
Jena High School (Jena, Louisiana), 56–57
Jewish Family Services, 505

Jewish refugees, 505
Jews
  and beliefs about Jewish descent, 376–77
  Jerusalem prayer site of, 599
  pilgrimages of, 585
  Soviet refugees to the U.S., 505
  in the U.S., 575
  See also Judaism
Jim Crow laws, 216
Johanson, Donald, 154–55
Johnson, Virginia, 322
John XXIII, pope, 605
Jordan, Brigitte, 624–26
Judaism
  dietary laws in, 586
  rituals of, 586
  symbols of, 598, 599
  in the world, 577
Juris, Jeffrey, 563, 566

Kahn, Susan, 376
Kant, Immanuel, 661
Karaim community (Lithuania), 144
Kasanaj, Trobriand Islands, 84
Kash, MC, 262
Kashmiris (Himalayas), 262–63
Katz, Jonathan, 321
Katz, Pearl, 633
Kealing Junior High School, Austin, Texas,
    315
Kelly, Patty, 342–43
Kendall, Laurel, 591–92
Kennedy, John F., 353
Kennedy, Joseph, Sr., 353
Kennedy, Robert, 353
Kennewick Man, 155–56
Kentucky, 416
  economy of, 417–18
  poor whites in, 416–18
Kenya
  female marriage among Nandi,
    364
  Nariokotome (Turkana) Boy in, 176
  sickle-cell anemia in, 168
key informant, 90
kindred exogamy, 364
kinesics, 119–20
kinetic orality, 680–84
Kinsey, Alfred C., 322, 323
kinship, 349–89
  in China, 357–60, 380
  defined, 350
  by descent, 351–60

Maasai (Tanzania), 547–49
Macau, life expectancy in, 643
machismo, 318–19
Madoff, Bernard, 451
Madrid, Spain, demonstration, 473
magic
    defined, 592
    in Niger, 595–96
    religion and, 592–98
    in Sudan, 593–95
    in U.S. baseball, 596–97
Maine, same-sex marriage in, 364
Maira, Sunaina, 678–80
Makah Nation (U.S. Pacific Northwest),
    399; see also potlach
Malaysia, 209
    companionate marriage in, 362
    export-processing zones, 210
    export-processing zones in, 302, 303
    farmers' slowdown protest in, 55
    Langkawi, 366–67
    Minah Karan, 210–12
    race, gender, and globalization in,
        209–12
    racial framework in, 211
    Scott's agency studies in, 54–55
male dominance, early research on,
    290–92
Mali, West Africa, 12, 513–16
Malinowski, Bronislaw, 46, 48, 83–84, 89,
    291, 310, 363
Maman (Bourgeois), 661
"Man the Hunter, Woman the Gatherer,
    myth," 294–95
Manila, the Philippines, 21, 67
Mantsios, Gregory, 426–27
mapping, 91–92
    defined, 91
    exercise in, 95
    in fieldwork, 91–92
    of kinship, 372–73
Mardi Gras, 95–96
Mardi Gras (film), 95
Marjah, Afghanistan, 100
Markakis, Nick, 393
markets, in global economy, 474–77
Marks, Jonathan, 201
marriage
    antimiscegenation laws, 53
    bridewealth in, 365
    cultural norms for, 38, 39
    defined, 360
    dowries, 365–66

exogamy and endogamy, 364
and gene migration, 169
and incest taboos, 363–64
interracial, *See* interracial marriage
kinship through, 360–66
and lesbian/gay commitment
    ceremonies, 327–29
monogamy, polygyny, and polyandry,
    362
weddings, 323–27
Marshall Islands, 24–25
Martin, Emily, 293, 294
Martin, T. T., 164
Martinez, Samuel, 206
martyr, 579
Marx, Karl, 399–402, 581, 586–87
Maryland
    Camden Yards Stadium, 392–95, 410
    same-sex marriage in, 364
Masculinities (Archetti), 261
Maskovsky, Jeff, 424
Massachusetts
    Boston, 68, 131, 563
    same-sex marriage in, 364
Masters, William, 322
Masters of the Planet, The (Tattersall), 181
material power, 52–53
mathematics, as cultural capital, 405
matrilineal descent groups, 352
Mayaki, Issifi, 503
McAlister, Elizabeth, 676–78
McDonald's, 67, 401
McIntosh, Peggy, 231–32
MCMC (Merced Community Medical
    Center), 649–52
Mead, Margaret, 47, 86, 310
meaning
    and culture, 48–49
    of illness, 622
    interpretivist approach to, 48–49
    from mental maps, 43, 44
    and power, 56–57
    and religion, 602–7, 610
    religion as system of, 598–600
    and warfare, 558
means of production, 400, 401
media
    as bridge for immigration, 496
    intersection of art and, 686–92
    and invisibility of class stratification,
        426–27
    See also social media
mediation, 60

medical anthropology, 618–55; *see also*
    health; illness
medical anthropology (term), 620
medical ecology, 620
medical migration, 647–48
medical pluralism, 648–50
medicine
    amchi, 627–30
    biomedicine, 630–33
    Chinese, 633–35
    ethnomedicine, 627–30
    globalization and the practice of,
        646–53
melanin, 186
melanocytes, 186, 187
melting pot
    defined, 253
    U.S. as, 253, 254
Men Are from Mars, Women Are from Venus
    (Gray), 59
mental maps of reality
    cultural differences in, 37, 42–44
    defined, 42
Merced, California, 649
Merced Community Medical Center
    (MCMC), 649–52
meritocracy, 225, 402, 404
Mexican New York (Smith), 68
Mexico
    childbirth in, 623, 624, 626
    factory workers in, 302, 303
    and migration, 490
    Procession of Absent Sons, 361, 362
    religion and revolution in, 604–6
    Seri people, 141
    sex work in, 342–43
    transnational immigrants from, 518
    U.S. immigrants from, 507, 524
    Zona Galactica, 342–43
Mexico City, Mexico, 278, 279
Miami, Florida, sea-level rise and, 26
Micronesia, 539
    adapting to ecological challenges in,
        539–40
    violence and conflict resolution in,
        540–41
Middle Awash River Valley, 171–72, 173,
    177
middle class
    African Americans in, 232
    Americans' perception of, 411
    in Brazil, 209
    in Harlem, New York, 406–7

radiopotassium dating, 161
Ragoné, Helena, 382
Ranger, Terence, 255
ranked societies, 397–98
rape
    of college women, 298, 335
    in El Salvador, 300
    in Western Punjab, 374–76
rapid change, 22
rapport
    defined, 90
    and informed consent, 102
Rara! (McAlister), 676–78
rara bands (Haiti), 676–78
RateMyProfessor.com, 148
Rathje, William, 16–17
Reading National Geographic (Lutz and
    Collins), 687–90
reciprocity
    in Amish and Hutterite communities,
        397
    contemporary patterns of, 398
    defined, 396, 449
    in egalitarian societies, 396
Recognizing Ourselves (Lewin), 327–29
recruitment agencies, for migrant workers,
    496
redistribution, 398, 450
Redmon, David, 96
Red Sea, 490
reflexivity
    defined, 87
    feminism and, 87
    in fieldwork, 87
    in writing ethnography, 98
refugees, 492, 504–5
    defined, 504
    internally displaced, 505
    Muslims Indians in Pakistan, 375
    Uganda refugee camps, 506
relationships, power in, 50
relative dating, 160, 161
religion, 573–615
    as bridge for immigration, 496
    Church of the Lukumi Babulu Ayea v.
        City of Hialeah, 525–26
    constructing a universal definition of,
        575–81
    defined, 577
    Durkheim and study of, 581–82
    fundamentalist movements in, 591
    global distribution of, 577
    globalization's effect on, 610–15

Harris' work on, 587–89
    and interrelation of meaning and power,
        602–7, 610
    local expressions vs. universal
        definitions in, 578–81
    and magic, 592–98
    Marx's view of, 586–87
    as power system, 587
    and ritual, 582–86
    shamanism, 591–92
    as system of meaning, 598–600
    as system of power, 600–602
    in the U.S., 575
    Weber's view of, 589–91
    See also specific religions
religious beliefs
    about Jewish descent, 376–77
    about sexuality, 345
    and evolution, 164–66
    and Indian caste system, 430–31
    of Muslim taxi drivers in Minnesota,
        526
remittances, 497–98
replacement theory, 178
Reproducing Jews, 376–77
Reproducing Race (Bridges), 645–46
reproductive technologies, 350; *see also*
    assisted reproductive technologies
Republic of the Congo
    Brazzaville, 514–16
    Homo sapiens in, 178
    internally displaced persons in,
        505–6
research strategies, 90–91
    in anthropology, 28–31
    of cultural relativism, 45
    globalization and change in, 28–31
Returning Home (documentary film),
    248
return migration, 518–19
Rhode Island, same-sex marriage in, 364
Rhodesia, Pondal's imprisonment by, 259
Richards, Audrey, 8, 583
Rickford, John R., 133
Rickford, Russell J., 133
Riff Raff Immigration (cartoon), 220
rites of passage, 583–84
ritual(s)
    defined, 581
    in religion, 582–86
    relocated from immigrants' home
        countries, 613–15
Robinson, Eugene, 383

Rockefeller, John D., 352
Romania, wedding industry in, 325
romantic love, 361–62, 429
Root, Robin, 212, 587, 608–9
Roth, Joshua Hotaka, 519
Roundtable on Community Change, 228
Rowling, J. K., 593
Royal Bafokeng Nation (RBN), 252–53
Ruiz García, Bishop Samuel, 605–6
Rune stone, 119
Russia
    consumerism in, 64
    time zones in, 43
    U.S. adoptions from, 385, 386
    U.S. immigrants from, 524
Rwanda, 246
    mobilizing ethnic differences in, 245–47
    refugees from, 505

Sabin, Ashley, 96
sacred
    defined, 581
    in Durkheim's work, 581–82
Sadker, David, 129
Sadker, Myra, 129
Safa, Helen, 302
Sahelanthropus, 172
Sahelanthropus tchadensis, 159, 160
Said, Edward, 263
saint, 579
Sajad, Malik, 262
SALGA (South Asian Lesbian and Gay
    Alliance), 244
salvage ethnography, 73, 83
same-sex families
    in China, 380
    in the U.S., 383–85
same-sex marriage, 364, 383–85
Samoa, 47, 86
San Diego County Fair, 671
Santería, 525–26
Sapir, Edward, 121
Sapir-Whorf hypothesis, 121
Sarroub, Loukia K., 523, 524
Saudi Arabia
    guest workers in, 490, 496, 500, 512
    Hael petroglyphs, 295
Saussure, Ferdinand de, 120
Savage, Michael, 113
Scalpel's Edge, The (Katz), 633
Scheper-Hughes, Nancy, 106–7, 632
    Alto do Cruzeiro study, 73–77, 89–90,
        94, 97, 98, 102

Tarazona, Elas, 507
Task Force on the Education of African American Students (Oakland, California), 134
Tattersall, Ian, 180–81
Taung, South Africa, 153
Taung child, 153–54
taxes, U.S., 414
technologies
    in the digital age, 142–43, 146–49
    for DNA dating, 162
    in eighteenth and nineteenth centuries, 8
    and flexible accumulation, 21
    and globalization, 6
    for mapping, 92
    and time-space compression, 20
    and uneven high-tech consumption, 22
    See also Internet
Teena, Brandon, 298
teeth, adaptation of, 188–89
television
    and cosmopolitanism, 68–70
    invisibility of class in, 426–27
    reality shows, 427
Tembuland, South Africa, 53
Tennessee, Scopes Trial in, 165
terrorism
    cultural institutions' responses to, 51
    USA PATRIOT Acts, 40
    and voluntary isolation, 428
"terror warfare," in Mozambique, 556, 558
Texas
    colonias in, 619–20
    Kealing Junior High School, Austin, 315
Thind, Bhagat Singh, 219
thought
    race as system of, 197
    shaped by language, 120–22
Thrice-Told Tale, A (Wolf), 99–100
Tibetan medicine, 627–30
Tierney, Patrick, 101
time
    categories of, 42–44
    deep, 157
    language shaping idea of, 145
time-space compression
    defined, 20
    and globalization, 20–21
    and migration experience, 491, 517–18
    and social movements, 560
    and transnational network formation, 546

time zones, 43
Tiv language, 121
Tokyo, Japan, 475
Tolkien, J. R. R., 593
Tonga, 509, 512
tools
    Acheulian stone, 176
    Oldowan, 173, 175
trade routes, 453
Traditional Micronesian Societies (Petersen), 539–41
traditions, invented, 255–56
transgender, 284, 320
transgendered individuals, violence against, 298
Transnational Adoption (Dorow), 386
transnational adoptions, 385–89
transnational immigrants, 517–18
transnationalism, 518
transportation
    as bridge to migration, 496
    and transnational network formation, 546
triangle trade, 455–58
tribes, 537–38
    defined, 538
    influences on, 542
Trinity United Methodist Church, Sacramento, California, 512
Trobriand Islands, 48, 291
    economic system of, 291
    Kula Ring, 291, 450
    Malinowski's studies in, 48, 84
    Weiner's study of, 87
    women's economic activity in, 292
Truth, Sojourner, 410
Tsukiji Fish Market, Tokyo, 475
Tswana-speaking people (South Africa), 52–53
Tucson, Arizona, homelessness and begging in, 81
Turkana Boy, 176
Turkic languages, 144
Turner, Victor, 48, 88, 583–85
Tutsi (Rwanda), 245–47
Tuva language, 144, 145
Tylor, Edward Burnett, 46, 82

Uganda, refugee camps in, 506
UN, *see* United Nations
underdevelopment, 463
uneven development
    defined, 22

    and global inequality, 433–35
    and globalization, 22
    and global migration, 493
    and social movements, 560
unilineal cultural evolution, 46, 48
unilineal descent groups, 352
United Kingdom
    England in, 238
    kissing and greetings in, 34
    life expectancy in, 643
    same-sex marriage in, 364
United Nations (UN), 546
    on global poverty, 433, 434
    human rights documents of, 45
    on migration, 492
    World Food Programme, 434
United States
    adoptions in, 385
    antimiscegenation laws in, 38, 53
    arranged marriages in, 360
    assimilation vs. multiculturalism in, 253–54
    balance of security and privacy in, 40
    baseball rituals in, 596–97
    biomedicine in, 631
    Black English in, 132–34
    black gay women in, 332–34
    changing kinship in, 377–89
    childbirth in, 622–26
    class and inequality in, 410–21
    colonias in, 619–20
    construction of race in, 212–22
    consumerism in, 63
    and effects on Costa Rican food market, 561
    credit card debt in, 66
    cultural patterns in, 58
    Dominican immigrants in, 509–11
    ethnic interaction in, 253–54
    fortified milk in, 188
    Garbage Project in, 17
    gender role norms in, 86
    household income in, 412–13
    households by type, 378
    immigration to, 512, 520–27
    incest taboos in, 363
    interracial marriage in, 53, 54
    invisibility of class and inequality in, 426–30
    kinship in, 377–89
    language variation in, 114, 130–36
    life expectancy in, 643, 644
    marriage in, 360, 363, 364